DÆMONOLOGIA SACRA;

OR,

A TREATISE OF SATAN'S TEMPTATIONS.

IN THREE PARTS.

BY

RICHARD GILPIN, M.D.,

VICAR OF GREYSTOKE, CUMBERLAND; LATER OF NEWCASTLE-ON-TYNE.

Foreword by
Dr. Cyril J. Barber

EDITED, WITH MEMOIR,

BY THE REV. ALEXANDER BALLOCH GROSART,

LIVERPOOL.

WIPF & STOCK · Eugene, Oregon

Wipf and Stock Publishers
199 W 8th Ave, Suite 3
Eugene, OR 97401

Daemonologia Sacra
A Treatise of Satan's Temptations, In Three Parts
By Gilpin, Richard
ISBN 13: 978-1-55635-743-5
ISBN 10: 1-55635-743-5
Publication date 12/3/2007
Previously published by James Nisbet & Co., 1867

FOREWORD

Books on demonology have come tumbling from the presses in this and other lands at such a rate that it is hard even for the most ardent advocates and devotees of the occult to keep pace with them.

At one time occultism was confined to travelling gypsies and a few old ladies who read the future in tea leaves. Today the practice of clairvoyance and the use of tarot cards is widespread. Children are being indoctrinated as they watch people in trances on television, and are given seance games at Christmas time by their parents. Ouija boards are found in college dormitories, and women join in witches' covens to put hexes on those whom they dislike. The church of Satan is growing, and all kinds of trinkets and apparel bear the signs of the zodiac.

According to the *New York Times* "heads of state" bow before the winds of the occult. During her years in office Prime Minister Sirimavo Bandaranaike of Sri Lanka (former Ceylon), after a landslide victory, refused to take office until she had consulted her astrologers as to the most auspicious day to form her new government.

Indira Gandhi of India delayed calling a new election until the planet Saturn was in the right position for such a risky undertaking.

In the United Kingdom witches and warlocks outnumber preachers of the gospel, and publishing houses formerly known for their secondhand collection of theological books now are given over to stocking books on occultism.

And in the United States, Jeane Dixon is ranked as America's leading prophetess, boasting annually of the large numbers of high government officials who seek her counsel.

Without doubt the influence of those who pretend to be able to fortell the future is increasing. Daily horoscopes in all of our major newspapers are designed to help the man in the street and the woman "on her way to the top" plan their day in the most opportune way.

Paul could write those in Corinth that "we are not ignorant of Satan's devices" (II Corinthians 2:11), yet most of us are afraid of what we see going on around us and quite unable to engage in any form of spiritual warfare.

Of course, there have not been wanting those who have written on the subject of demonology. Most books on the subject may confidently be placed in one of two catagories. They either deal with the theology of demonism and its practice in pagan religions, or they are devoted to a discussion of contemporary manifestations of the occult. The former has little to say to us for the content deals with cultures far removed from our Western civilization. The latter frequently are esoteric in nature and lack a sound theological foundation. As a result, books have appeared on both ends of the continuum, but have failed to meet the needs of Christian laypeople.

The work presently before the reader falls into neither of these catagories. Originally published in 1677 under the title *Demonologia Sacra*, this book treats the biblical evidence relating to Satan, his position in the world and his method of tempting believers and unbelievers. As such, it is a masterful treatise on demonology as well as hamartiology!

The author, Richard Gilpin (1625-1700), was a nonconformist theologian and physician. He was graduated from the University of Edinburgh (M.A., 1646) and the University of Leyden (M.D., 1676), and ministered for many years near Durham in Northern England.

Dr. Gilpin was keenly sensitive to the needs of those in his congregation and frequently dispensed medical service while carefully watching over the spiritual needs of each member of his "flock."

In *Biblical Demonology*, this kindly "physician of the soul," described more fully than any other writer the devious and deceitful ways which Satan employs to ensnare unweary "sons of Adam." Each discussion is clear and direct, and once these truths have been mastered, believers will never again be "ignorant of Satan's devices."

Dr. Gilpin designed this book for the edification of God's people wherever they may be found. His work will not fail to bless laypeople as well as those in the ministry, for it retains its original vitality and thereby commends itself to us for our careful attention.

Cyril J. Barber
Author, *The Minister's Library*.

CONTENTS.

	PAGE
I. PREFATORY NOTE,	xiii
II. MEMOIR OF DR GILPIN,	xv
III. DÆMONOLOGIA SACRA.	
To the Reader,	3–6

CHAPTER I.—The introduction to the text, from a consideration of the desperate ruin of the souls of men—The text opened, expressing Satan's malice, power, cruelty, and diligence, . . 8–10

CHAPTER II.—Of the malice of Satan in particular—The grounds and causes of that malice—The greatness of it proved; and instances of that greatness given, ... 10–14

CHAPTER III.—Of Satan's power—His power as an angel considered—That he lost not that power by his fall—His power as a devil—Of his commission—The extent of his authority—The efficacy of his power—The advantages which he hath for the management of it, from the number, order, place, and knowledge of devils, ... 14–20

CHAPTER IV.—That Satan hath a great measure of knowledge, proved, by comparing him with the knowledge of Adam in innocency, and by his titles—Of his knowledge, natural, experimental, and accessory—Of his knowledge of our thoughts—How far he doth not know them, and how far he doth, and by what means—Of his knowledge of things future, and by what ways he doth conjecture them—The advantages in point of temptation that he hath by his knowledge, . . 21–26

CHAPTER V.—Instances of Satan's power—Of witchcraft, what it is—Satan's power argued from thence—Of wonders—Whether Satan can do miracles—An account of what he can do that way—His power argued from apparitions and possessions, . 27–35

CHAPTER VI.—Of Satan's cruelty—Instances thereof in his dealing with wounded spirits in ordinary temptations of the wicked and godly, in persecutions, cruelties in worship—His cruel handling of his slaves, ... 35–44

CHAPTER VII.—Of Satan's diligence in several instances—The question about the being of spirits and devils handled—The Sadducees' opinion discovered—The reality of spirits proved, 45–52

CHAPTER VIII.—Of Satan's cunning and craft in the general—Several demonstrations proving Satan to be deceitful; and of the reasons why he makes use of his cunning,	52–58
CHAPTER IX.—Of Satan's deceits in particular—What temptation is—Of tempting to sin—His first general rule—The consideration of our condition—His second rule—Of providing suitable temptations—In what cases he tempts us to things unsuitable to our inclinations—His third rule—The cautious proposal of the temptation, and the several ways thereof—His fourth rule is to entice—The way thereof in the general, by bringing a darkness upon the mind through lust,	58–63
CHAPTER X.—That Satan enticeth by our lust—The several ways by which he doth it—Of the power and danger of the violence of affections,	63–68
CHAPTER XI.—That lust darkens the mind—Evidences thereof—The five ways by which it doth blind men: (1.) By preventing the exercise of reason—The ways of that prevention: (1.) Secrecy in tempting; Satan's subtlety therein; (2.) Surprisal; (3.) Gradual entanglements,	68–72
CHAPTER XII.—Of Satan's perverting our reason—His second way of blinding—The possibility of this, and the manner of accomplishing it directly, several ways; and indirectly, by the delights of sin, and by sophistical arguments; with an account of them,	72–76
CHAPTER XIII.—Of Satan's diverting our reason, being the third way of blinding men—His policies for diverting our thoughts—His attempts to that purpose in a more direct manner; with the degrees of that procedure—Of disturbing or distracting our reason, which is Satan's fourth way of blinding men—His deceits therein—Of precipitancy, Satan's fifth way of blinding men—Several deceits to bring men to that,	77–83
CHAPTER XIV.—Of Satan's maintaining his possession—His first engine for that purpose is his finishing of sin, in its reiteration and aggravation—His policies herein,	83–86
CHAPTER XV.—Of Satan's keeping all in quiet, which is his second engine for keeping his possession, and for that purpose his keeping us from going to the light by several subtleties; also of making us rise up against the light, and by what ways he doth that,	86–91
CHAPTER XVI.—Of Satan's third grand policy for maintaining his possession; which is his feigned departure: (1.) By ceasing the prosecution of his design; and the cases in which he doth it—(2.) By abating the eagerness of pursuit; and how he doth that—(3.) By exchanging temptations; and his policy therein—The advantage he seeks by seeming to fly—Of his fourth stratagem for keeping his possession, which is his stopping all ways of retreat; and how he doth that,	91–100

CHAPTER XVII.—Satan's deceits against religious services and duties—The grounds of his displeasure against religious duties—His first design against duties is to prevent them—His several subtleties for that end, by external hindrances, by indispositions bodily and spiritual, by discouragements; the ways thereof, by dislike; the grounds thereof, by sophistical arguings—His various pleas therein, . . . 100–118

CHAPTER XVIII.—Satan's second grand design against duties is to spoil them—(1.) In the manner of undertaking, and how he effects this—(2.) In the act or performance, by distracting outwardly and inwardly—His various ways therein, by vitiating the duty itself—How he doth that—(3.) After performance, the manner thereof, ... 118–125

PART II.

CHAPTER I.—That it is Satan's grand design to corrupt the minds of men with error—The evidences that it is so—and the reasons of his endeavours that way, . . . 127–140

CHAPTER II.—Of the advantages which Satan hath, and useth, for the introduction of error—(1.) From his own power of spiritual fascination—That there is such a power, proved from Scripture, and from the effects of it—(2.) From our imperfection of knowledge; the particulars thereof explained—(3.) From the bias of the mind—What things do bias it, and the power of them to sway the understanding—(4.) From curiosity—(5.) From atheistical debauchery of conscience, . . 140–158

CHAPTER III.—Of Satan's improving these advantages for error—1. By deluding the understanding directly: which he doth, (1.) By countenancing error from Scripture—Of his cunning therein—(2.) By specious pretences of mysteries; and what these are—Of personal flatteries—(3.) By affected expressions—Reason of their prevalency—(4.) By bold assertions—The reasons of that policy—(5.) By the excellency of the persons appearing for it, either for gifts or holiness—His method of managing that design—(6.) By pretended inspiration—(7.) By pretended miracles—His cunning herein—(8.) By peace and prosperity in ways of error—(9.) By lies against truth, and the professors of it, ... 158–189

CHAPTER IV.—Of Satan's second way of improving his advantages, which is by working upon the understanding indirectly by the affections—This he doth, (1.) By a silent, insensible introduction of error—His method herein—(2.) By entangling the affections with the external garb of error, a gorgeous dress, or affected plainness—(3.) By fabulous imitations of truth—The design thereof—(4.) By accomodating truth to a compliance with parties that differ from it—Various instances hereof—(5.) By driving to a contrary extreme—(6.) By bribing the affections with rewards, or forcing them by fears—(7.) By engaging pride and anger—(8.) By adorning error with the ornaments of truth, ... 190–208

CHAPTER V.—Satan's attempts against the peace of God's children evidenced—(1.) From his malice—(2.) From the concernment of peace to God's children—What these concerns are, explained—(3.) From the advantages which he hath against them by disquieting their minds—1. Confusion of mind—2. Unfitness for duty, and how—3. Rejection of duty—4. A stumbling-block to others—5. Preparation of the mind to entertain venomous impressions, and what they are—6. Bodily weakness—7. Our miseries Satan's contentment, ... 209–218

CHAPTER VI.—Of the various ways by which he hinders peace—First way, By discomposures of spirit—These discomposures explained : by shewing, (1.) What advantage he takes from our natural temper, and what tempers give him this advantage—(2.) By what occasions he works upon our natural tempers—(3.) With what success—[1.] These occasions suited to natural inclinations, raise great disturbance—[2.] They have a tendency to spiritual trouble—The thing proved, and the manner how discovered—[3.] These disturbances much in his power—General and particular considerations about that power, ... 219–237

CHAPTER VII.—Of the second way to hinder peace—Affrightments, the general nature and burden of them, in several particulars—What are the ways by which he affrights—1. Atheistical injections—Observations of his proceeding in them—2. Blasphemous thoughts—3. Affrightful suggestions of reprobation—Observations of his proceedings in that course—4. Frightful motions to sin—5. Strong immediate impressions of fear—6. Affrightful scrupulosity of conscience, 238–254

CHAPTER VIII.—Of his third way to hinder peace, by spiritual sadness—Wherein, 1. Of the degrees of spiritual sadness—2. Of the frequency of this trouble, evidenced several ways—Of the difference betwixt God and Satan in wounding the conscience—3. Of the solemn occasions of this trouble—4. The engines by which Satan works spiritual sadness :—(1.) His sophistry—His topics enumerated and explained—[1.] Scriptures perverted—[2.] False notions—[3.] Misrepresentations of God—[4.] Sins : how he aggravates them—[5.] Lessening their graces : how he doth that—(2.) His second engine, fear : how he forwards his design that way, 254–286

CHAPTER IX.—Of his fourth way to hinder peace, by spiritual distresses—1. The nature of these distresses—The ingredients and degrees of them—Whether all distresses of soul arise from melancholy—2. Satan's method in working them ; the occasions he makes use of ; the arguments he urgeth, the strengthening of them by fears—3. Their weight and burden explained in several particulars—Some concluding cautions, ... 287–311

PART III.

CHAPTER I.—The first circumstance of the combat, the time when it happened—The two solemn seasons of temptation—The reasons thereof, ... 313–316

CHAPTER II.—The second circumstance, Christ's being led by the Spirit—What hand the Spirit of God hath in temptations—and of running into temptations when not led into it, 316–321

CHAPTER III.—The third circumstance, the place of the combat—The advantage given to temptations by solitude, . 321–322

CHAPTER IV.—The fourth circumstance, the end wherefore Christ was led to the wilderness—Holiness, employment, privileges, exempt not from temptation—Of temptations that leave not impressions of sin behind them—How Satan's temptations are distinguished from the lusts of our own heart, ... 322–328

CHAPTER V.—Of Christ's fast, with the design thereof—Of Satan's tempting in an invisible way—Of his incessant importunities, and how he flies when resisted—Of inward temptations, with outward afflictions—Several advantages Satan hath by tempting in affliction, . . . 328–336

CHAPTER VI.—That Christ's temptations were real, and not in vision—That temptation is Satan's employment, with the evidences and instances thereof—Of Satan's tempting visibly, with the reasons thereof, ... 337–341

CHAPTER VII.—The general view of these temptations—Of Satan's gradual proceeding in temptations—Of reserving a great temptation last—What a great temptation is; in what cases to be expected—Of Satan's using a common road, in comparing these temptations with the ordinary temptations of men—Of the advantage Satan takes of natural appetite, sense, and affections, ... 341–346

CHAPTER VIII.—The rise of Christ's first temptation—Of Satan's suiting his temptations to the conditions of men—Of tempting men upon the plea of necessity—The reasons and cheats of that plea—His pretences of friendship in tempting, with the danger thereof, ... 346–350

CHAPTER IX.—A particular consideration of the matter of the first temptation, what Satan aimed at in bidding him turn stones into bread—Of Satan's moving us to things good or lawful—The end of such a motion—How to know whether such motions are from Satan or the Spirit—What to do in case they be from Satan—Of his various aims in one temptation—What they are, and of his policy therein—Of his artificial contrivement of motions to make one thing infer another, ... 350–355

CHAPTER X.—Of Satan's chief end in this temptation—His skill in making the means to sin plausible—The reasons of that policy, with his art therein—Men's ignorance his advantage—Of the differences of things propounded to our use, . 355–359

CHAPTER XI.—Of the temptation to distrust upon the failure of ordinary means—Of the power of that temptation, and the reasons of its prevalency—Of unwarrantable attempts for relief, with the causes thereof—Of waiting on God, and keeping his way—In what cases a particular mercy is to be expected, ... 360–367

CHAPTER XII.—Of Satan's proceeding to infer distrust of sonship from distrust of providences—Instances of the probability of such a design—The reasons of this undertaking—Of Satan's endeavour to weaken the assurance and hopes of God's children—His general method to that purpose, . 367–376

CHAPTER XIII.—The preparation to the second temptation—Of his nimbleness to catch advantages from our answers to temptation—That Satan carried Christ in the air—Of his power to molest the bodies of God's children—How little the supposed holiness of places privilegeth us from Satan—Of Satan's policy in seeming to countenance imaginary defences—Of his pretended flight in such cases, with the reasons of that policy—Of his improving a temptation to serve several ends, ... 376–382

CHAPTER XIV.—That presumption was the chief design of this temptation—Of tempting to extremes—What presumption is—The several ways of presuming—The frequency of this temptation, in the generality of professors, in hypocrites, in despairing persons, and in the children of God—The reasons of Satan's industry in this design—His deceitful contrivance in bringing about this sin—Preservatives against it, . 382–390

CHAPTER XV.—Self-murder, another of his designs in this temptation—How he tempts to self-murder directly, and upon what advantage he urgeth it—How he tempts to it indirectly, and the ways thereof—Of necessary preservatives against this temptation, ... 390–396

CHAPTER XVI.—Of pride, Satan's chief engine to bring on presumption—What pride is, and how it prepares men for sinning presumptuously—Considerations against pride—The remedies for its cure—Pride kindled by a confidence of privileges and popular applause, ... 397–401

CHAPTER XVII.—Of Satan's subtlety in urging that of Psalm xci. 11, 12, to Christ—Of his imitating the Spirit of God in various ways of teaching—Of his pretending Scripture to further temptation—The reasons of such pretendings, and the ends to which he doth abuse it—Of Satan's unfaithfulness in managing of Scripture—Cautions against that deceit—The ways by which it may be discovered, . . 402–415

CHAPTER XVIII.—The manner of Satan's shewing the kingdoms of the world—Of Satan's preparations before the motion of sin—Of his confronting the Almighty by presumptuous imitation, and in what cases he doth so—Of his beautifying the objects of a temptation, and how he doth it—His way of engaging the affections by the senses—Of his seeming shyness, . 415–423

CHAPTER XIX.—Satan's end in tempting Christ to fall down and worship him—Of blasphemous injections—What blasphemy is—The ways of Satan in that temptation, with the advantages he takes therein, and the reason of urging blasphemies upon men—Consolations to such as are concerned in such temptations—Advice to such as are so afflicted, . . 424–430

CHAPTER XX.—The nature of idolatry—Satan's design to corrupt the worship of God—The evidences thereof, with the reasons of such endeavours—His general design of withdrawing the hearts of men from God to his service—The proof that this is his design—Upon whom he prevails—That professions and confidences are no evidences to the contrary—His deceit of propounding sin as a small matter—The evidences of that method, and the reason thereof, ... 430–437

CHAPTER XXI.—Of worldly pleasure—Proofs that this is Satan's great engine—What there is in worldly delights that make them so—Counsels and cautions against that snare, . 438–444

CHAPTER XXII.—Of Christ's answer in the general—That these temptations were upon design for our instruction—Of the agreement betwixt Eph. vi. and Mat. iv.—The first direction, of courageous resolves in resisting temptations—Its consistency with some kind of fear—The necessity of this courage—Wherein it consists; and that there is a courage in mourning spirits, ... 445–450

CHAPTER XXIII.—The second direction, that temptations are not to be disputed—The several ways of disputing a temptation—In what cases it is convenient and necessary to dispute with Satan—In what cases inconvenient, and the reasons of it, ... 451–458

CHAPTER XXIV.—The third direction, of repelling a temptation without delay—The necessity of so doing—What a speedy denial doth contain, ... 459–462

CHAPTER XXV.—The fourth direction, of repelling a temptation by Scripture arguments—Of several things implied in the direction—The necessity of answering by Scripture arguments—The excellency of the remedy—How Scripture arguments are to be managed, ... 462–469

CHAPTER XXVI.—The fifth direction, of prayer, and of the seriousness required of those that expect the advantage of prayer—Of God's hearing prayer while the temptation is continued—Of some that are troubled more, while they pray more, . 470–471

INDICES, &c., ... 472–480

PREFATORY NOTE.

FEW who know the fine old quarto '*Dæmonologia Sacra*' of Dr Gilpin will dispute its right to a place of honour in the Series of later Puritan Divines. To those who have not hitherto heard,—or only heard of it,—we commend it with all confidence and urgency as in various respects a remarkable book by a remarkable man. It will be found—as an early writer says of another—'*matter-full*,' and nevertheless suggestive rather than exhaustive—that is, you have many rich lodes of the ore of thought opened, but many others indicated, not worked; clear and keen of insight into the deepest places of the deepest things discussed; wide in its out-look, yet concentrated in its in-look; sagacious and wise in its general conclusions, and passionate as compassionate in its warnings, remonstrances, and counsels; full of faith in all 'written' in The Word, and pathetically credulous in accepting testimony when a given fact (alleged) is fitted to barb an appeal; curious and quaint in its lore; intense and anxious in its trackings of sin without and within; pre-Raphaelite in the vivid fidelity of its portrayals of satanic guiles, and guises that are always disguises; and above all, tenderly *experimental* in its consolation to the tried and troubled. The third part is an exposition of the Temptation of our Lord, which may bear comparison for thoroughness and power with any extant.

For our Memoir of Dr Gilpin we have had literally to do everything, inasmuch as next to nothing has thus far been published concerning him—not even his birthplace, or birth or death dates known. If still we feel the result of our 'labour of love' in prosecuting the necessary researches, to be very inadequate, it is gratifying that we have secured so much as we have done.

As in the preparation of former Memoirs, our visits and investigations have brought us much pleasant intercourse and correspondence with descendants, representatives, and reverers of the old Worthy. Family papers of the most private nature have been unreservedly confided to us—as duly acknowledged in each place where referred to or used; and altogether the most ungrudging help has been rendered. The various friends mentioned in the foot-notes of the Memoir will be so good as accept this further general acknowledgment.

It only remains to state that the present volume has been edited on the same principle with Sibbes and Brooks. The text is given with scrupulous integrity; references and quotations are traced, and less known names and dates annotated; every reference or quotation of Scripture verified and filled in; and copious indices are subjoined; the two last the more important, that Dr Gilpin himself seems to have quoted Scripture from memory, and furnished no 'table' or index beyond the heading of the several chapters as 'contents.'

May this revised treatise be used at this later day as in the past, to help in the great warfare against the Adversary.

ALEXANDER B. GROSART.

* It has not been deemed needful to give a list of such slight *errata* as have come under our eye in preparing the indices; but mark, with reference to the 'Note,' page 2, that for 'Dr' there is a misprint of 'Mr,' and that 'deficiency' is spelled with an 'i' for an 'e.'—G.

MEMOIR OF THE REV. RICHARD GILPIN, M.D.

IN pursuing our investigations for our Memoir of RICHARD SIBBES, we found and noted, that his name—in every one of its odd variations of spelling, numerous as those of Shakespeare and Raleigh—had quite died out at once of his native county and country, being traceable nowhere for fully a century of years—the stream which rose at Cony-Weston, Norfolk, in 1524, lapsing in a 'Richard Sibbes, clerk, rector of Gedding, aged 93, February 2, 1737;' and the blood thenceforward flowing in the female line.[1]

Very different is it with the name of GILPIN, now before us. From family-muniments and genealogies intrusted to us by various representatives, of nearer and remoter kin, it were easy to go back many generations before the earliest-noticed SIBBES; while at the present day, in nearly all gradations of circumstance, at home and abroad—from the original Cumberland and Westmoreland, to 'the gray metropolis of the North;' from the Castle of Scaleby, to 'huts, where poor men lie;' and from Wyoming of Pennsylvania to Acadie of Evangeline and 'distant Ind'—GILPINS, descending from our Worthy, and proud of the descent—sustain the ancient renown of goodness and brain-power. As I sit down to put my collections into shape, I am called to place therein the statesman-like Speech on a great public question of our age, of CHARLES GILPIN, in the House of Commons—words destined to re-echo again and again, and determine legislation—so grave, wise, patriotic, Christian are they; and now the Libraries are being besieged for the 'New America' of William Hepworth Dixon, wherein I was gladdened with a splendid, yet penetrative and measured, eulogy of the Founder of Colorado, WILLIAM GILPIN;[2] both, as I am informed, as do nearly all of the name—in this re-

[1] Works of Sibbes, vol. i. pp. 25, 142.
[2] New America. By W. H. Dixon. With Illustrations from Original Photographs. 2 vols 8vo. 1867. (Hurst and Blackett.) Vol. i., pp. 134-137.

sembling the Rogerses of the United States, who all claim descent from John Rogers, proto-martyr of England—counting from Bernard Gilpin, the apostle of the North, the venerable and holy St Bernard of Protestantism; and so, as we shall see, from our Richard.

I place in an Appendix[1] such genealogical-antiquarian details as some readers may look for in a Memoir of a Gilpin; and summarise here that the author of '*Dæmonologia Sacra*' was sprung of a race such as old Dan Chaucer would have cited in teaching '*who is worthy to be called gentill*' as we may judge by a few of his golden lines:—

> 'The first stocke was full of rightwisnes,
> Trewe of his worde, sober, pitous, and free.
> Clene of his goste; and loved besinesse,
> Against the vice of slouth, in honeste:
> And but his heire love vertue as did he,
> He is not gentill, though he rich seme,
> All weare he miter, crowne, or diademe.'[2]

Turning now to DR RICHARD GILPIN—whose remarkable book is in the present volume faithfully reprinted; he was grandson of Richard, a younger brother of the illustrious Bernard, his father being an Isaac Gilpin. We get a glimpse of both grandfather and father in the county History as follows:—' In a small manuscript by one Isaac Gilpin,—whose father [Richard Gilpin, *as before*] had been steward of several manors within the barony of Kendal, and died about the year 1630, at the age of 92 years,—he says he had heard of his father, and observed the same himself, that by general custom within the said barony, if a woman hath an estate, and married, hereby the estate is so far vested in the husband, that he may sell it in his life-time; but if in his life-time he doth not alter the property, then it shall continue to her and her heirs.'[3] This little record takes us to 'the barony of Kendal,' the 'Land' of Bernard Gilpin; and thither accordingly, we turned our search. There was a vague traditionary understanding that our Richard Gilpin was born, as of the same family, so in the same region of 'Kentmere;' but nothing definite had hitherto been known. The Kentmere 'Registers' do not commence until A.D. 1700; and thus we were baffled there. But Kentmere being a chapelry in the old Parish of Kendal, a hope was indulged that in the parent-parish the wished-for facts should be discovered; nor were we disappointed, for in the Baptism-Register, under date 'October 23, 1625,' there is this entry:—

'Richard, son of Isaac Gilpin, of Strickland Kettle,'

[1] See Appendix A., lii-lv.

[2] From above, and other parallels, it will be seen that Burns only put more tersely and memorably an old sentiment in his—
> 'The rank is but the guinea stamp,
> The man's the gowd for a' that.'

[3] Nicolson and Burns's Cumberland and Westmoreland, vol. i., p. 26.

which is our Worthy, as after-dates will shew.[1] He might be born a week more or less previously, according to the then 'use and wont' of infant baptism. The same Register furnishes another earlier entry, which—if we are correct in surmising that the Isaac Gilpin of Strickland Kettle in 1625, was the same with the Isaac of it—informs us Richard was a younger son :—

'1623, May 3, Henry, ye soun of Mr Isaacke Gilpin of Helsington.'

Elsewhere he is named 'of Gilthroton, co. Westmoreland;' and seems to have been the same who was clerk to the Standing Committee of county Durham in 1645.[2] That Isaac Gilpin was 'steward of *several* manors' probably covers the different local designations. There are so many Gilpins, and so many of the same Christian name, that it is hard to decide on given personalities; but, after considerable comparison and sifting, such appears to us to be the parentage paternally of Dr Gilpin. Maternally I have come on nothing; for an Elizabeth Gilpin, widow of Isaac Gilpin, merchant, Newcastle, though of the same stock, was not his mother. This 'widow' was buried in All Saints, 7th November, 1694.[3] Archdeacon Cooper, of Kendal, in transmitting these data, remarks: 'The mode of writing, and the insertion of *Mr*, indicates a person of some importance.' But with reference to 'Mr,' I suspect it is rather accidental, as it is inserted in the one, and left out in the other; and moreover, is frequently omitted when, from other sources, we know the family was of importance. Little Richard must have been just beginning to toddle about when his venerable grandfather's snow-white head ['aged 92'] was laid in the old Church-yard. One delights to picture the aged Simeon, before his serene departure, 'blessing' by prayer his dear little grandchild, after the manner of such ancient Puritans as were the Gilpins in every branch.

Strickland-Ketel, not Kettle, as in the Register and vulgarly,[4]—now settled to have been the birth-place of Dr Gilpin,—was a most fitting

---

[1] I owe hearty thanks to the Rev. Thomas Lees, M.A., Wreay, Carlisle, formerly Curate of Greystoke, for much help in tracing out birth-place, &c., and throughout; also to Archdeacon Cooper, Kendal, for his prompt and full answers to my queries.

[2] See Memoirs of Alderman Barnes, edited for Surtees Society by W. H. D. Longstaffe, Esq., of Gateshead, p. 143. As I write this, these Memoirs are passing through the press; and I am indebted to Mr Longstaffe for early proof-sheets of the notices of Gilpin contained in the Manuscript. No common service is being rendered by Mr L. and the Surtees Society, to Ecclesiastical History, in so lovingly and competently preparing these important memoirs, which shed light on innumerable events and names, from sixteenth to eighteenth centuries. An abstract of the more interesting passages was published in 1828 by Sir Charles Sharpe, 8vo, pp. vii. and 35. I have to thank J. Hodgson Hinde, Esq., of Stelling Hall, Stocksfield, for this scarce pamphlet.

[3] See Longstaffe's Barnes, as before. The Manuscript now belongs to the Literary and Philosophical Society, Newcastle-on-Tyne.

[4] So called after Ketel, son of Eldred, son of Ivo de Tailbois, first Baron of Kendal, who came over with William the Conqueror.

nest for one destined to serve the master-Shepherd so well. It is an English Bethlehem—a rich, kine-fragrant, pleasant, breezy tract of pasture-land, sloping from the west down to the river Kent, its eastern boundary, which river, issuing out of a fair 'mere,' or lake, gives its name to Kent*mere* Hall, the seat of the elder house of the Gilpins. The hamlet of Ketel itself is on the road from Kendal to the Ferry on Windermere; and thus partakes of the glory of Wordsworth's poetry, as of Scott's, who in Rokeby celebrates a local incident of the Cromwellian time.[1] It is somewhat noticeable that within the space of an ordinarily-sized farm should have been born BERNARD GILPIN and HENRY AIRAY,[2] and later, Richard Gilpin.

Of the childhood of our Richard, we can tell nothing directly. But with the famous 'School' founded by his honoured ancestor available, we are safe in assuming that he entered it. It is of this School that the later biographer of Bernard Gilpin,—himself a Gilpin,—thus writes: 'The effects of his endowment were very quickly seen. His school was no sooner opened than it began to flourish, and to afford the agreeable prospect of a succeeding generation rising above the ignorance and errors of their forefathers.' . . . ' That such might be its effects, no care on his part was wanting. He not only placed able masters in his school, whom he procured from Oxford, but he likewise constantly inspected it himself.'[3] The saintly Apostle was long gone to his rest before the advent of Master Richard; but as bearing the name, and being of the blood of the Founder, he could not fail to be welcomed to all its privileges. The more's the pity that no memorial seems to have been kept of the scholars of this celebrated Institution. Before proceeding to Houghton, he was probably initiated into learning at the nearer Kendal, then all astir with the enterprise of the Flemings. So I gather from family communications made to me; and thus we have to think of the 'little lad' trotting down the quiet rural roads among the sunny hills, much as another Richard earlier, from Packenham to Thurston,[4]

. . . 'with his satchel
And shining morning face,'

---

[1] Canto vi., stanza 33, 'Robin the Devil' and Col. Briggs. See also 'Annals of Kendal,' (1861,) pp. 55, 56.

[2] The Commentator on Philippians; cf. my Memoir of him, prefixed to the reprint of his masterly book, p. vii. Since this Memoir was published, I have discovered that Dr Airay was son of Bernard Gilpin's sister Helen. See the Apostle's 'Will,' in the Surtees' volume of 'Wills and Inventories, from the Registry at Durham,' (1860,) Part II., pp. 83-94. So that the Gilpins and Airays were related. I have to thank William Jackson, Esq., Fleatham House, St Bees, for calling my attention to this. It explains obscurities in the life of Airay, and gives a key to Bernard Gilpin's special interest in him.

[3] The Life of Bernard Gilpin. By William Gilpin, M.A., Prebendary of Salisbury. With an Introductory Essay by Edward Irving. 1824. Page 123.

[4] That is, Richard Sibbes; Memoir, as before; Works, Vol. I. p. xxxi.

not, we may be sure,

>   . . . 'creeping like snail
>   Unwillingly to school.'[1]

There is a tradition,—reported by various descendants,—that our Gilpin went from 'School' to Queen's College, Oxford. This, it will be remembered, was Bernard Gilpin's own College, and whither he sent his favourite scholars, as Airay, Carleton, Ironside, and others. So that if Richard went to Oxford at all, Queen's would most naturally be selected. No mention of him, however, occurs in any of the College Registers. Therefore he cannot at any rate have graduated.[2] I place in Appendix incidental valuable *data* concerning other related Gilpins gleaned in Oxford.[3]

In lack of the facts of the case, it is impossible to explain why one so well-born and well-introduced did not, apparently, follow out a full University career. That the circumstances of his own Family and kindred were adequate thereto—apart from the Gilpin 'endowments,' which were open to him specially—and that they were of the right stamp to appreciate a sound, liberal education, is certain from numerous notices of the house that occur in old records.[4]

Another floating tradition,—also brought before me by descendants, is, that our Gilpin studied at the University of Glasgow; which so far receives confirmation from the statement of his bosom-friend Alderman Barnes of Newcastle—of whose MS. 'Memoirs' I have already spoken —that 'he was educated in Scotland;' but neither there does his name occur.[5]

Equally uncertain is it,—advancing further,—when or by whom Dr Gilpin was 'licensed' or 'ordained' as a Preacher of the Gospel or Clergyman. Barnes again says that he 'administered the Lord's Supper to a small congregation in Durham;'[6] and Calamy, that 'he had been [*i.e.*, before Greystoke] a Preacher in Lambeth, at the Savoy —where he was assistant to Dr Wilkins—and at Durham.'[7] Of all of these, the memorial has perished. Neither under 'Lambeth,' nor

---

[1] Shakespeare, *As you Like it*, ii. 7.

[2] In a large quarto manuscript volume of 'Memoirs' of the Gilpins, drawn up by the Prebendary of Salisbury, (*supra*,) now before me by the kindness of its possessor, Charles Bernard Gilpin, Esq., Juniper Green, Edinburgh, I find the following concerning the above points: 'He was the son of a younger brother, and being born to no estate, applied the first years of his life to the study of physic. But feeling a stronger inclination to divinity, he laid aside all thoughts of practising as a physician, and changing entirely the course of his studies, *he took his degrees in divinity;* but at what university, I *find no account*,' (page 1.)

[3] See Appendix B. I have here gratefully to acknowledge the painstaking of Mr T. A. Eaglesim, M.A., of Worcester College, Oxford, by himself and the Bursar of Queen's, in examining every likely source of information.

[4] See Appendix C, for some of these.

[5] Barnes' Memoirs, page 141, as before. The Maitland Club 'Munimenta' of the University of Glasgow, (4 vols. 4to,) gives a 'Richardus Gilpin, Anglus, entered 11th January,' 1717,—none other.   [6] As before, pp. 141 142.   [7] Account, vol. ii. 157.

'Savoy, nor 'Wilkins'—afterwards Bishop of Chester[1]—nor 'Gilpin,' does Newcourt's *Repertorium*[2] mention him; nor, after considerable investigation in each place, has any trace of him been found beyond the above statements. So that his presentation to the Living of Greystoke in Cumberland is really the first definite fact we have, after his now ascertained birth-place, baptism-date, and family connexion. The Rector of Greystoke had been 'sequestered'[3] by Sir Arthur Haselrigge and the Parliamentary Commissioners for the Propagation of the Gospel in the four northern counties; which sentence having been appealed against, was confirmed by the Committee for (as they were called) Plundered Ministers. The Rector was William Moreland, M.A., 'bred,' according to Walker of the 'Sufferings,' folio, 'at Jesus College, Cambridge.'[4] This 'ejection' took place in 1649-50. He was succeeded by 'one West, who died in about two years' time.'[5] Such is all Walker says of West; but from another overlooked authority, we learn a little more of him. In the 'Postscript' concerning 'Mr John Noble,' added to Audland's funeral sermon on that notable man, it is said, after mentioning the 'laying aside' of Mr Moreland, 'certain Commissioners appointed others, in his room, to supply the Parish, when John Noble was little turned of twenty years of age;' and then, 'In the year 1650, Mr West was sent, a zealous Preacher, and one mighty in prayer, but sickly; and he soon died of a consumption. His doctrine being exemplified in his own life, was very effectual on many in that Parish, and particularly on John Noble, who received lively convictions of Divine truth and the world to come, and so began earnestly to inquire about the life and power of godliness.'[6] Gilpin immediately succeeded Mr West, and thus must have entered on his duties in 1652 or 1653, when he was in his twenty-eighth or twenty-ninth year.

What influence procured our Worthy the 'presentation' to this (comparatively) rich benefice,—for it was then worth £300 per annum, now nearly trebled, being from £700 to £800, we do not know; but among the neighbouring gentry there were intermarriages with the Gilpins, *e.g.*, the Laytons and Whartons—the former the ancient owners of Dalemain in Dacre, the next parish to Greystoke. The Living was

---

[1] The 'Life' of this singularly original and inventive Prelate is so scanty and unworthy of his fame, that we do not wonder at no notice of his Savoy ministry, or of Gilpin as his assistant. Calamy is rarely wrong in his facts. [2] 2 Vols. folio, 1708.

[3] Walker, 'Sufferings,' page 306. [4] *Ibid.*

[5] *Ibid.* In various authorities the ground of Moreland's ejection is given as 'ignorance and insufficiency'—whatever the latter may mean; but as Walker, who is usually referred to for it, makes no such statement, I have not adduced it. It is sufficient that the Commissioners were picked men for intellect and character; and that wherever *data* remain, their decisions are almost invariably warranted by the premises.

[6] 'A Sermon preached at the Funeral of Mr John Noble of Penruddock, near Penrith, in Cumberland, March 14, 1707-8. By Samuel Audland. To which is added a Postscript concerning the Deceased, by another hand.' London (reprinted) 1818, pp. 37, 38.

held by the family of Arundel—with a branch of whom it remains—but was subject no doubt to the Commissioners of Parliament during the Commonwealth.

We have Richard Gilpin, then in 1652-53 installed as the 'parish priest' of Greystoke; and save him of Bemerton, none ever brought a finer spirit, or a more entire consecration, or a more 'ingenuous' activity, to the service of the one great Master.

Visiting Greystoke recently, I found it a quaint-visaged, gray, long, low-roofed church, venerable and time-stained still, though 'restored'—tenderly—in 1848. It is dedicated to St Andrew. It nestles in a 'bit' of woodland such as—flushed with autumnal tints of green and gold equal to the glories of a New England Indian summer among the maples and elms—would have burdened and kindled the eyes of a Ruysdael or Gainsborough, aye and until the 'studies' were transferred to imperishable canvas; and the whole surrounding district, sweet, soft, and tranquil enough for the Valley of Rip Van Winkle's long dreamless sleep—much more so indeed than Irving's own, behind the shaggy bluffs of the Hudson. It is a genuinely English 'parish.' When Gilpin came to it, the '*common people*' were intelligent and godly after the antique type of the mid-Reformation period, having a spice of sturdy originality of character and speech that is not altogether gone even now. For 'leisure hours,' if the cultured Rector wished it, there were in the country Seats—embracing ducal Castle and historic family mansion—men and 'faire ladyes' of rare force and worth. There are 'Sunny Memories' still—treasured in dim old manuscripts —of the full 'gatherings' from far and near, from hall and hut, from plain and fell, of the 'gentle and simple' over a wide area—to hang on the lips of the 'good Parson,'—as everywhere he came to be named. We have a fine 'testimony' to the integrity and devotedness of the Rector in the 'Postscript' of John Noble's Funeral Sermon, previously quoted: 'Graistock parish was large, had a fair glebe and liberal revenue. It had four chapels: the nearest three miles distant from the Church. Mr Gilpin provided worthy, preaching ministers for those, and allowed generously for their support; himself residing at

The little 'Chapel' wherein this Sermon was preached still remains, and has now as its minister the Rev. David Y. Storrar, who occupies it as a mission-charge of the United Presbyterian Church (of Scotland). This congregation originated, it is believed, from those who could not remain in the Parish Church of Greystoke after Gilpin left and Moreland returned; and thus is of the oldest of the Presbyterian congregations in England. See above tractate, whence we learn that on Dr Gilpin's 'motion,' the Nonconformists of Greystoke 'called' another to fill his place for them. Then the Narrative continues : ' Mr Anthony Sleigh, a native of the same parish, and bred in the College of Durham, was obtained to become their minister, and so continued about forty years, though he had only slender [pecuniary] encouragements there. Their meeting was held mostly in the house of John Noble, and sometimes under covert of the night, as Christ's disciples sometimes did,' (page 44.)

Graistock, where he had a society of communicants prepared by the foregoing efficacy of the word on their minds and hearts, and manifested in a new life,' (page 41.)

Altogether Greystoke could not be other than a most congenial portion of the great 'Vineyard' for one like RICHARD GILPIN, who breathed the very spirit of saintly GEORGE HERBERT, and had little taste for the controversies in which some of his contemporaries were engaged.

Not very long after his settlement at Greystoke, viz., in 1654-5, a sad disaster befell the parent or 'Kentmere' house of the Gilpins, springing out of the 'confusions' of the Commonwealth. I shall let the good Prebendary tell it,—preliminary remarks and all, from the manuscript already quoted,—reserving comment: 'In the year 1655, says he, 'Cromwell dissolved his refractory parliament, and the members of the House retiring to their several counties, spread everywhere such new matter of discontent that measures were no longer observed. Men were levied in many places against the usurper, and a general rising was expected. But Cromwell, who had his eyes in all places, soon dispersed every insurrection as it made its appearance. It was at that time he sent his major-generals throughout the kingdom to punish with fines and proscriptions all delinquents. Among the families ruined by the severity of these military magistrates was Mr Gilpin of Kentmere Hall, near Kendal, in Westmoreland. He was the head of the family, and lived respectably on an estate which had been in the hands of his ancestors from the days of King John. *It seems probable he had taken an active part against Cromwell in the king's life-time;* but his affairs being composed, *he lived quietly* till these new disturbances broke out on Cromwell's violent measures with the parliament. *Having joined an unsuccessful insurrection*, he became a marked man, and was obliged to provide for his safety as he could. To avoid a sequestration he gave up his estate in a kind of trust-mortgage to a friend, and went abroad. There he died; but in a time of quiet, his heir not being able to get hold of the proper deeds to recover the estate, it was totally lost to the family. *In the meantime Dr Gilpin lived quietly at Greystoke*, concerning himself only with his own parish, and lamenting those public evils, which he could not remove.'[1] One can smile at this time of day at the name 'Usurper' applied to England's mighty Protector; can understand the inevitable royalism of a dignitary of the Church, that holds for 'the king' as against 'the kingdom,' can leave the admissions of former freedom to 'live quietly,' and of an active part 'against Cromwell,' to justify any enforced flight, without either refuting allegations or exposing prejudices. But as matter of fact, while Dr Gilpin, in common with many

[1] As before, pp. 3, 4.

of his Presbyterian brethren, condemned the execution of Charles, and while the shadow that fell on Kentmere doubtless darkened the rectory of Greystoke, he yet unreservedly accepted the government of Cromwell, and in every way sought to carry out the measures devised by the Parliament. Moreover, far from '*living quietly at Greystoke*,' and '*concerning himself only with his own parish*,' it is the very opposite of the facts. Instead of retiring in the timid, nerveless fashion suggested, he took a foremost part in organising that modification of Church government which the abolition of Episcopacy demanded. The evidence of this, spite of the wreck and loss of contemporary 'records,' is abundant; and it is the next landmark in the Life we are telling.

It needeth not that in a necessarily brief Memoir such as this we should enter on the *merits* of the national change of Church 'Polity' which gave supremacy for the time to Presbytery over Prelacy. The materials for judgment lie in fulness in every worthy Ecclesiastical History of England; and the whole story has just been re-written with fine candour and attractiveness by Mr Stoughton.[1] Presbyterianism in England during the Commonwealth can hold its own,—lustrous as it is with the names of Edmund Calamy and Bates and Manton, Richard Baxter and William Jenkyn and Thomas Watson, Samuel Clark and Thomas Wilson of Maidstone, and Thomas Hall of King's Norton,—selecting a few, urban and rural, almost at random.

Suffice it to recall that, outside of the more ambitious organisation of London,—whose unpublished 'Memorial' lies all but unknown in Sion College Library,[2]—there were various voluntary Asssociations which took a semi-Presbyterian mould, in the counties of Chester, Cumberland, Westmoreland, Dorset, Wilts, Worcestershire, and others. These Associations embraced the 'clergymen,' and 'ministers' or 'pastors,' and laymen belonging to the Episcopalians, the Presbyterians, and the Independents, and sought to combine the presidency of the first with the union and co-operation of the second, and the freedom of the third; in short, a federated rather than organic oneness. Subordinating everything else, was an intense yearning after nearness to all who loved the one Lord Jesus, and heroic as devout endeavours for 'discipline,' so as to vitalise and Christianise 'the *masses*.' It is pathetic to read of the days and nights of these good men's Fasting and Prayer 'unto the breaking of the light,' for one another's Parishes and Charges. Their ideal was lofty, their own practice beautiful, their success marked in changing the face of erewhile godless and heathen-dark communities. What RICHARD BAX-

---

[1] Ecclesiastical History of England, from the Opening of the Long Parliament to the Death of Oliver Cromwell. 2 vols. 8vo. 1867. (Jackson, Walford, and Co.) See vol. II., c. viii., *et alibi*.

[2] Mr Stoughton justly speaks of the strange neglect of these important MSS.

TER was in Worcestershire, RICHARD GILPIN was in Cumberland and Westmoreland; and as the author of 'The Saint's Everlasting Rest' was chosen to draw up the 'Agreement' for his county, so the author of '*Dæmonologia Sacra*' was selected to execute the same office for Cumberland and Westmoreland. The 'Agreement,'—of which the title-page will be found in the list at the close of our Memoir, must be studied by all who would master the problems of the period. It is comprehensive, without being general or vague; decisive in dogma, but not uncharitable; high in aim, but most practical; earnest, but not fanatic; stern to offences, but hopeful and tender toward offenders; richly scriptural, but also, and because of it, most human, all a-glow with wide sympathies, and unutterably wistful in its appeals for oblivion on all lesser matters, so as to set a firm front to the evils and passions, the divisions and heart-burnings, the rivalries and recriminations, of the time. The whole is perfumed, so to speak, with prayer. If it was a Utopia, it was a grander and more celestial one than ever More or Bacon imagined; nor while it lasted was it a mere paper Agreement. For years through all the Counties enumerated the 'good men and true' made their 'gatherings' so many centres of light and love; and their Parishes were as spiritual Goshens amid the national formalism and barrenness.

Seeing that the extent to which '*Dæmonologia Sacra*' has gone prevents our reprinting the minor writings of Gilpin, as we had desired, we shall here give a few brief extracts from the 'Agreement,' to illustrate its aims, tone, and style. Thus he struck the key-note: ' When we compare the present miseries and distempers with our former confident expectations of unity and reformation, our hearts bleed and melt within us. We are become a byword to our adversaries; they clap their hands at us, saying, " Is this the city that men call the perfection of beauty ?" Piety is generally decayed, most men placing their religion in " doting about questions" which they understand not; profaneness thrives through want of discipline; error, blasphemy domineers; jealousies, divisions, unmerciful revilings and censurings, are fomented among brethren of the same household of faith; the weak ones are discouraged and distracted by the multitude of opinions and fierce opposition of each party, and that which is worst of all, God's honour suffers deeply, and the credit of religion is brought very low. "Is this nothing to you, all ye that pass by ?"' But having lamented, as with Jeremiah, he assumes a more hopeful and encouraging attitude, thus: ' Though these things can never be sufficiently lamented, yet seeing it is not sufficient barely to lament them, without endeavouring to heal them, and considering that it is a duty incumbent upon all Christians, according to their several places and abilities, to promote the welfare of Zion, especially when we have tasted so much of the bitterness of our divisions, and because a brotherly Union hath so much of God in it, and consequently gives so much hope that God will take that course in establishing his Church when he shall arise to build Jerusalem, and seeing it is an unjustifiable pettishness and peevishness of spirit to be averse from joining together in anything because we cannot join in all things, therefore we resolve, ["the associated ministers,"] setting aside all carnal interests, and casting ourselves, with all our concernments, at the Lord's feet, to walk together as far as we can for the present, not resting here, nor tying ourselves from further progress in union, as the Lord shall give light and satisfaction, much less binding ourselves from a submission to and compliance with a more general accommodation, if any such thing should hereafter be agreed on, which might be more suitable and fitted for the composure of the different principles of brethren throughout the nation.'—(Pp. 1–3.) Hereupon follows the 'Basis' of the 'Agreement,' which was very much the same with Baxter's in Worcestershire, and that of Essex, &c., &c. 'In order,' he proceeds, 'to the carrying on of this great work, we lay down and assent unto these general rules as the Basis and Foundation which must support and bear up our following Agreement:—

'1. That in the exercise of discipline it is not only the most safe course, but also the most conducing to brotherly union and satisfaction, that particular churches carry on as much of their work with joint and mutual assistance as they can with conveniency and edification, and as little as may be, in their actings, to stand distinctly by themselves and apart from each other.

'2. That in matters of church discipline those things which belong only *ad melius esse*, ought to be laid aside, both in respect of publication and practice, rather than that the Church's peace should be hindered.

'3. That where different principles lead to the same practice, we may join together in that practice, reserving to each of us our own principles.

'4. That where we can neither agree in principle nor in practice, we are to bear with one another's differences that are of a less and disputable nature, without making them a ground of division amongst us. Yet notwithstanding we do not hereby bind up ourselves from endeavouring to inform one another in those things wherein we differ, so that it be done with a spirit of love and meekness, and with resolutions to continue our brotherly amity and association, though in those particulars our differences should remain uncomposed,' (pp. 3, 4.)

Further, all pledge themselves to be true and faithful ambassadors, stewards, workmen, and overseers, and 'to this end we resolve in the course of our ministry to observe the temper, disposition, and capacity of the generality of the people, and to suit ourselves not only in our matter to the people's condition, but also in our expressions to the people's apprehension, that so our sermons may be plain, piercing, seasonable, and profitable,' (p. 4.) Speaking next of 'catechising' from the Assembly's 'Larger and Shorter' Catechisms, and of 'inspection,' there are these wise counsels, that there be tender dealing in consideration of 'first, unacquaintedness with the terms and words of the question; or, secondly, from bashfulness or shamefacedness,' (p. 11.) And in regard to 'supervision,' to be cautious 'lest brotherly inspection degenerate into an unbrotherly prying,' (p. 15.) And there is this pronouncement on a *questio vexata* of the period: 'We agree not to press a declaration of the time and manner of the work of grace upon the people as a necessary proof of their actual present right to the Lord's Supper, nor to exclude persons merely for want of that; yet will we accept it if any will be pleased to offer it freely,' (p. 16); and onwards there is encouraged a 'holy modesty and bashfulness' in speaking of the 'passage and transaction 'twixt God and our soul,' (p. 39.) Finally, the Confession of Faith consists of the Creed paraphrased, and confirmed by texts, (pp. 23-25.)

Another incident proved with equal unmistakableness that RICHARD GILPIN regarded Oliver as no 'usurper,' but the rightful governor of the nation. I must leave the reader to consult the authorities on the history of the establishment of the University of Durham. Every one who knows anything of 'the times' knows that the efforts to found a University there—which the death of Cromwell delayed, and the Restoration quashed—is one of the 'boasts' of the Protector's reign.[1] In honoured association with Sir Thomas Widdrington, Lords Fairfax, Grey, Wharton, and Falconbridge, Sir Henry Vane, and Sir Arthur Haselrigge, and other well-known names, Gilpin was appointed one of the 'Visitors.'[2] He had entered into the scheme with enthusiasm and hope. It is difficult to estimate what was lost herein by the death of Cromwell. If we may conjecture from the 'Model' of the learned and pious Matthew Pool—issued in 1657-58, while the grand jury were addressing Richard to complete what his father had begun—it is all but certain that a more strictly theological training would have been inaugurated than any of the great Universities even to this day supplies.[3]

To shew that Dr Gilpin still adhered to his former action in Church matters, it must here be stated that in 1658 he preached a 'Sermon'

---

[1] Stoughton, as before, *sub nominibus*.

[2] Burton's 'Cromwellian Diary,' ii. 531, where the 'Ordinance' is given *in extenso*, with notes by the editor, [Rutt.]

[3] I suspect few know this rare and very valuable tractate. Its title-page runs, 'A Model for the maintaining of Students of choice abilities at the University, and principally in order to the Ministry. Together with a Preface before it, and after it a Recom-

before the 'associated ministers of Cumberland' at Keswick. By the request of the 'General Meeting' he published it. The title-page will be found in our list of his writings at close of this Memoir. It was with reluctance the good man consented to give his sermon 'to print,' as he intimated in the 'Epistle Dedicatory.' 'What your commands,' says he, 'have wrested from me—for of that force and prevalency with me are your desires—I now lay at your feet. If I could have prevailed with you to have altered your vote, or after you had passed it, durst have resisted—this had gone no further than your own hearing. But when you would not be persuaded, I endeavoured to conform myself to those Christians in Acts xxi. 14, and took up with that which put a stop to their entreaties. "The will of the Lord be done,"' (pp. 1, 2.) The Text of this sermon—which is no common one—is Zech. vi. 13, 'Even He shall build the Temple of the Lord,' &c., and hence its title, 'The Temple Rebuilt.' I select a few of the more easily detached sentences. First of all, concerning 'Controversy,' he says admirably: 'Disputings, though they have their fruits, yet are they like trees growing upon a rocky precipice, where the fruit cannot be gathered by all, and not by any without difficulty and hazard,' (p. 3.) Again, on the office of the ministry, he exclaims: 'Dream not of ease in an employment of this nature. God, angels, and men have their eyes upon you to see how you will bestir yourselves: it is your duty, and not a matter of unnecessary courtesy which you may give or hold back at your pleasure. He that hath commanded you ἐν τούτοις εἶναι, (1 Tim. iv. 15,) to "give yourselves up wholly to these things," will not take himself to be beholden to you when you have done your best: neither is it any disparagement to you to become even servants to any: so that you may but gain them and forward Christ's work. They that think it below them to trouble themselves so much with catechising, reproof, admonition, and are of Ptolemæus his mind, who changed the title of Heraclides his book, from πονου ἐγκωμιον to ὄνου ἐγκωμιον: as if laboriousness were nothing but an ass-like dulness, making a man crouch under every burden; but God having made the ox which treadeth out the corn to be the hieroglyphic of your employment, he doth thereby teach you that labour and patience are so far from being a disgrace to you, that they are necessary qualifications for the calling of the ministry,' (pp. 3, 4.) Lastly—for we may not linger—take a burning and fearless reproof of the lukewarm: 'How cowardly and sinfully shamefaced,' he observes, kindling as he advances, 'are many when they should plead for God

mendation from the University, [this bears the signatures of Worthington, Arrowsmith, Tuckney, Whichcot, Ralph Cudworth, and William Dillingham;] and two serious Exhortations, recommended unto all the unfeigned lovers of Piety and Learning, and more particularly to those rich men who desire to honour the Lord with their substance.' [1658-60.] There is a characteristic letter in it from Baxter.

and truth, as if their own hearts did secretly question the reality of religion! How strangely do many of the gentry spend their time! What irreligious, prayerless families do some of them keep, when they should shew better example to the meaner sort; and yet how confidently can they censure others for hypocrites—sometime unjustly concluding against the strictness of God's ways from the liberty of some professors—not considering what their own carriage and vanity do testify against themselves! How do we needlessly multiply our controversies and disputes! and with what bitterness do we manage them, even when the strife is merely about words and method! and, generally, how is the name of God and religion abused to serve the designs of men! What strange religious people have we! Some must needs be religious by taking up a singular conceit and opinion, though a man may easily see their hearts through their lives: others have all their religion on their tongue's-end: they can have good discourses, and yet be unconscionable in their callings, shops, and trading,' (pp. 33, 34.)

Thus taking a conspicuous part in all that belonged to the interests of the Church of Christ, our Worthy behind these went out and in before his flock a 'master-builder,' from Sabbath to Sabbath preaching the very gospel of Jesus Christ, with unequalled power, pungency, and pathos combined, while he drew all hearts to himself; for he acted on the maxim—

'All worldly joys go less
To the one joy of doing kindnesses.'[1]

He was a large-hearted and open-handed man, as well as a faithful 'preacher'—his life an exemplification of his teaching. He was, says the 'Noble' memorial, 'a gentleman and a Christian indeed; one of singular gravity, temper, learning, and all valuable qualifications for a minister; of a good family too, and an eligible estate; a witness and an honour to the good cause of a further Reformation,' (p. 38.) And so he pursued the 'even tenor of his way' in his tranquil sphere. He had married shortly after coming to Greystoke; but, curiously enough, the lady's name has not been preserved in any of the numerous family papers put into my hands. The Greystoke 'Registers' record the baptism of two of his children, William and Susannah. The 'entries' may be given here:—

'1657. September. Borne the 5th Day in ye afternoune, and ye 23d day Baptized, William, the Soune of Mr Richard Gilpin, p'son, [=parson], of Graistock.

'1659. Susanna, ye Daughter of Mr Gilpin, p'son, of Graistocke, was borne ye 17th day of October, And Baptized ye 7th of December, 1659.'[2]

[1] Herbert: The Temple; Church-Porch.
[2] Here again I owe thanks to Mr Lees of Wreay, as before; also to Rev. David Y.

I have described the parish of Greystoke as tranquil; but even into it there swept—as the sea-swell sweeps into the smallest nook of shore—the ruffle of that agitation which pervaded the nation in religious matters; and, inasmuch as it gives colour and tone to not a few passages of the '*Dæmonologia Sacra*,'—his difficulty with the Quakers—to which I have made reference—falls now to be chronicled. We shall have an after-occasion to notice subsequent interviews with the pre-eminently good, though provoking, Quaker missionary-preacher, Thomas Story. Here I glean my information from the 'Memoir' of a 'Greystoke' celebrity, HENRY WINDER, D.D.[1] The following, then, is the narrative, omitting irrelevant portions:—

'The Reverend Richard Gilpin, M.D., was the parish minister of Graystock before the Restoration. . . . . . Some time before the Restoration Quakerism began to spread in Cumberland and Westmoreland. Among other things remarkable in their behaviour, the Quakers would go into the parish church of Graystock, and disturb Dr Gilpin in the pulpit during divine worship. And such were their novel phrases and cross questions and answers, that the Doctor seemed sometimes at a loss what to say to them. Upon that, some of his parishioners were stumbled, withdrew from their former communion, and defended the cause of the Quakers. Among others Henry Winder was seduced, to the no small grief of good Dr Gilpin and his friends. A day of humiliation and prayer was appointed, in which Dr Gilpin, and some of the neighbouring ministers, as well as some of the laity of that parish, took such proper methods as to recover some that had fallen, and to confirm and establish those that were wavering, though, before that, the infection had spread far and wide. Then was Henry Winder secretly resolved to comply with the desire of Dr Gilpin and his church, and make some public recantation. But these convictions did not last long. For notwithstanding several conferences with him, Henry Winder openly joined with the Quakers, and continued among them some years. . . . . . Henry Winder and his [second] wife [finally] left the Quakers, returning to Dr Gilpin's church, in which they afterwards continued.'[2]

All this goes far to explain the unusual severity of the '*Dæmonologia Sacra*' against Quakers and Quakerism—as also the 'Agreement'—and the grave classification of 'double meanings,' and 'light

Storrar, Penruddock, and the present curate of Greystoke, (Mr Raby), for result of searching through the 'Registers,' which have some curious entries.

[1] 'A Critical and Chronological History of the Rise, Progress, Declension and Revival of Knowledge, chiefly Religious. In two Periods. 1. The Period of Tradition, from Adam to Moses. 2. The Period of Letters, from Moses to Christ. Second edition. By Henry Winder, D.D. To which are prefixed Memoirs of Dr Winder's Life. By George Benson, D.D.' London: 1756. 2 vols. 4to.

[2] I have left unquoted the process by which Winder was (1.) seduced to, and (2.) recovered from Quakerism, though the reader will do well to consult it.

within,' &c., &c., among evident 'devices' of the Devil. At this later day we willingly forget the eccentricities and vulgarities and blunders of the early followers of GEORGE FOX, and in the spirit of the 'Quakers' Meeting' of winsome Elia, reverence the service of this once powerful and still honoured and altogether inoffensive section of God's people.

With these minor 'troubles' now and again annoying him,—for they ended in the setting up of Quaker 'tabernacles' in the district, remains of which survive until now,—the Rector of Greystoke fulfilled his 'labour of love,' as a good servant of Jesus Christ, until the Restoration. That event found him with a mind made up and 'ready' for all loss and sacrifice. Unable to accept the notorious 'Act' of Uniformity, he anticipated the memorable 'Ejection' of 1662 by withdrawing from Greystoke; whereupon the former 'sequestered Rector Morland re-entered on possession.'

We turn to the Family-Manuscript,[1] formerly quoted, for the circumstances of the resignation. 'After the Restoration,' observes Prebendary Gilpin, 'when Episcopacy again took the lead, the Presbyterian party made what stand they were able. But the Act of Uniformity passed, and was executed with rigour. Dr Gilpin, notwithstanding his moderation, could not subscribe it in all its parts, and therefore resigned his benefice, trusting God for the maintenance of himself and family, which consisted of a wife and five children.'[2]

The good Rector was not without a home when he thus left his beloved Greystoke—which was turned into a Bochim when his 'parishioners' looked their last upon him. During his incumbency he had invested what 'monies' he had at his disposal in the purchase from the Musgraves, of the Castle and small estate of Scaleby near Carlisle—filling up the amount of the purchase-money by a mortgage. Thither accordingly he retired into privacy; but holding with the old Nonconformists the indefeasibility of his office as a preacher of the gospel by an ordination more sure than that from quasi-apostolic hands, he was wont to assemble his employés and neighbours in a 'great room' of the old Castle—originally a Border-fortalice erected against the Scots—and there 'preach' to them on the Sabbaths.[3]

---

[1] The 'Noble' Postscript says, 'Somewhat remarkable happened at his resuming the pulpit, which some living (1708) can tell, but I omit it.' Moreover, Morland's return was against the wishes of the parishioners: for the narrative continues, 'After this some offered to put up one Mr Jackson in the pulpit: which the contrary party did so violently oppose with threats to crush them into the earth, that Mr Jackson went with them to the parsonage-house, and preached there,' (p. 43.) M. died in about a year.

[2] As before, p. 6.

[3] 'A good old aunt of mine—mother of the present Mr Fawcett of Scaleby Castle—took particular pride in shewing a certain very large room in her Castle. Her theory was that this was one of the great attractions of the place in Dr Gilpin's view: for here he would have room enough to preach to as many people as were likely to attend, and

Moreover, he resumed his previous medical studies and practice, to the great advantage more especially of the poor. 'How acceptable,' says our Manuscript, ' his services were among the poor people of those parts, and how much they revered him for wisdom and sanctity, appears from the superstitious respect they paid him. During many years after his death, it was believed among them that he had " laid the devil," as they phrased it, in a morass not far from his house.'[1] Besides these semi-professional duties, he set about improving the somewhat dilapidated castle, and the lands, more particularly planted trees extensively; the result of which was an entire change of the appearance of the estate, and now the fine woodland within which venerable Scaleby lifts its gray towers, still worthily held by a descendant through the female line.[2]

liberty also : Scaleby, as she observed, being at just such a distance from Carlisle as to place him beyond the operation of the Conventicle Act.'—*Charles Bernard Gilpin, Esq., Juniper Green, Edinburgh.*   [1] *Ibid.*, p. 9.

[2] That is James Fawcett, Esq. I do not know how sufficiently to acknowledge the courtesy and kindness of Mr and Mrs Fawcett in furthering my Gilpin inquiries. Besides early drawings and recent photographs of the Castle and grounds, I have had an ancient unpublished family-volume of rare interest confided to me. It is entitled 'An Accompt of the most Considerable Estates and Families in the County of Cumberland, from the Conquest unto the beginning of the Reign of K. James the First.' The original MS., an inscription informs us, is supposed to have been ' writ by an ancestor of Mr Denton's of Cardow during ye time of his imprisont. (as 'tis said) in ye Tower upon a Contest yt happ'ned to be betwixt him and Dr Robinson, then Bp. of Carliell.' This ' copy' seems to have been taken about 1687. I cull the following *memoranda* concerning Scaleby from this precious little volume : ' Ye Castle . . . took name first of ye buyldings there wch they call Scheales or Scales, more properly of ye Latin word Scalinga, a caban or cottage.   When King Henry 1st had established Carliell [Carlisle] he gave yt lordship unto one Richard the Ryder, whose surname was Tylliolf, who first planted there habitations. From him it descended by one or two degrees unto Symon Tylliolf in ye later end of King Henry 2d's tyme. His son, Piers Tylliolf or Peter, was ward to Geoffrey de Lucy by the king's grant about ye tyme of K. John. This Geoffrey de Lucy did bear ye cap of maintenance before K. Richard 1st at his coronation. Sr. Peter de Tilliol, kt., son of Sr. Robt., dyed, A.D. 1434 : 13 Henr. 6, having enjoyed his estate 67 years. He had issue one son who dyed without issue in 1435, when the estates were divided between two sisters and co-heirs, Isabella and Margaret. Isabella had married one John Colville, and his son Wm. succeeded and died 1479, leaving two daughters, Phillis and Margaret. The eldest was married to Wm. Musgrave. Margaret, the 2d daughter, married to Nicholas Musgrave, and transferred Scaleby, Haydon, and other Lands to his posterity. Sr. Edwd. Musgrave, Kt., son of Wm., married Katherine Penruddock : he built or repaired part of ye Castle at Scaleby A.D. 1606. . . . Sir Wm. Edwd. Musgrave, Bart., of Nova Scotia, who afterwards suffering great losses on ye account of his faithful service to K. Charles 1 and K. Charles ye 2d, he was forced to dismember a great part of his estate. He sold Kirklevington to Edmund Appelby, Houghton to Arthur Forster, Richardby to Cuthbert Studholm, and *Scaleby* to Richard Gilpin, who now [1687] enjoys ye same together wth Richardby, wch he also purchased of Michael Studholm, *fil* Cuthberti,' [p. 432.] [On Scaleby, cf. pp. 429–435.] There are similar interesting notices of Greystoke, or Graystock, or Graistock, which is explained to mean 'a badger,' [cf. pp. 311–315,] going back with old lore to Syolf, and Phorne, and Ranulph in the days of the 1st Henry, on to the Dacres, and Norfolks, and Arundel. Scaleby Castle has been much enlarged, together with the Estates, and the visitor of the

RICHARD GILPIN was too eminent and potential a man to be allowed to withdraw thus from the stage of public events. He had not been long in his retreat when a 'tempting' offer was made him of a Bishopric, as Bernard Gilpin had been 'tempted' before him. I recur here again to our Manuscript. Following on the passage already given we read, 'The king and council however seemed to have been apprehensive lest this rigorous step against the Presbyterians ['Act of Uniformity'] might have ill consequences. They were much inclined therefore to compound the matter, at least, with some of the leaders of the party; and, in this view, three or four bishoprics and many superior dignities in the Church were offered to them. Among others, Dr Gilpin was represented to the king as a person highly esteemed in the Northern parts of England, and as a man of great moderation. Accordingly, in filling up the vacant bishoprics, his name was inserted for the see of Carlisle: and it was not doubted by his friends but he would get over the few scruples he had to the Act of Uniformity, and accept the preferment: for he had always spoken favourably of the Church of England, and considered the line between the two parties with regard to their religious sentiments as almost an invisible one. But, to the surprise of his nearest friends, he declined the offer.'[1] The 'friends,' who so lightly estimated the 'scruples' of the 'retired' Rector, little knew the stamp of man he was. Everything before and subsequent goes to shew that DR GILPIN remained a Nonconformist, with, no doubt, the same reluctance as Baxter and Calamy and the rest,—to whom bishoprics had similarly been offered, and by whom they had similarly been promptly declined,—but also from the same deep conviction of necessity so long as that 'Act' outraged the truth, and ignored conscience. And so, as his ancestor, Bernard Gilpin to Elizabeth,[2] did Richard Gilpin to Charles II.

district will find it a delightful pilgrimage. The older trees are all the more venerable that one knows Dr Gilpin himself 'planted' them.

To shew the way Royalists suffered themselves to speak of even so 'moderate' and so inestimable a man as our Worthy, simply because he continued conscientiously a Nonconformist at enormous sacrifices, I add here a quotation from the 'County' History: N. and B.'s Westmoreland and Cumberland, as before, vol. ii. p. 459: 'Scaleby: Mr Sandford—in the true spirit of those times—speaking of Scaleby, says, "It was sometime the estate of Sir Edward Musgrave of Hayton, baronet; but now sold to Mr Gilpin, a quondam preacher of the fanatical parliament, and his wife, Mr Brisco's daughter, of Crofton, brethren of confusion in their brains; knew what they would not have, but knew not what they would have, if they might chuse."' This 'reviling' is High Church charity; and it is wondered at that Nonconformists retort sharply when occasion offers.   [1] As before, pp. 6, 7.

[2] 'Life' of BERNARD GILPIN, as before, p. 128, *seq*. The coincidence is certainly striking of the double offer, at the distance of fully a century, of a bishopric, and the same bishopric, to two Gilpins, and a double declinature and actualisation of the '*nolo episcopari*.' This and even more remarkable, because more intricate and manifold, repetitions, in the Lives of the elder and younger Edwards of America, [Cf. Memoir of the latter, prefixed to his Works, Vol. i. pp. xxxiii., xxxiv. Andover, U.S. 1842.] have

refuse that mitre which he could not have worn unless at the sacrifice of principles which were dearer to him then all civil or ecclesiastical dignities, and life itself.[1] We have an incidental allusion—as I read it—in 'Dæmonologia Sacra' to the 'temptation,' and the casuistic pleas of the 'friends' alluded to. Speaking of the 'wiles' of the Tempter, and his many snares to induce to sin, he specially notices this, that 'he extenuates the offence by propounding some smaller good or convenience that may follow that evil,' and he continues, evidently speaking from his own experience of the 'fiery dart :' ' This, though it be a way of arguing directly contrary to that rule, " Do not evil that good may come," yet it oft proves too successful ; and it is like that common stratagem of war when, by the proposal of a small booty in view, the enemies are drawn out of their hold into a fore-contrived danger. Thus Satan pleads, This one act of sin may put you into a capacity of honouring God the more. *Some have admitted advancements and dignities against conscience, upon no better ground but they might keep out knaves, and that they might be in a condition to be helpful to good men.* . . . . . Thus a pretended good to come becomes a pander to a present certain iniquity.' There are other like intimations in the book, which give new significance and a strange passion to the words ; but this one must suffice.

Recurring to our Family-Manuscript—which though somewhat stilted in its style, is generally accurate in its facts—we reach the next point in our Worthy's ' Life.' ' The Dissenters,' remarks the Prebendary, 'having now found they could get nothing from government beyond a Toleration, began to separate everywhere into assemblies, and choose pastors of their own ;' and so eyes and hearts turned toward the Doctor, secluded at Scaleby. ' Among other places,' the Narrative proceeds, ' a large congregation united at Newcastle-upon-Tyne, where they built a handsome meeting-house, and sent an invitation to Dr Gilpin to be their minister ; and though he had now taken his measures, and laid his plan for a life of quiet and repose, he accepted their invitation, and as soon as he could settle his affairs at Scaleby, removed with his family to Newcastle.' ' Here,' continues the Manuscript, ' a new scene of life opened before him. Hitherto he had lived in a country retirement, both at Greystock and at Scaleby, where party prevailed little. But here he was in the midst of a large town, divided by various opinions, where his candour and moderation had an ample field for exercise. In fact, I have heard it said that his meeting-house was a kind of centre of unity among them all. It was frequented

been turned to excellent account in refuting the so-called objections of scepticism and rationalism to the repetition of the incidents and miracles and sayings of the Lord in the Gospels.

[1] Further on, and in his epitaph, we shall find allusions to the declined bishopric, as having greatly added to the influence of Dr Gilpin, as the acceptance of one by Reynolds neutralised even his worth, and stains his memory indelibly.

as much by Churchmen as Dissenters, and they all found here, what was seldom found in the pulpits of those times, their common Christianity preached, unsullied by the religious contests which everywhere prevailed. His preaching was extremely pleasing and popular. His subject-matter, his language, his voice, his manner, were all engaging, and made such an impression on the people as was never worn out, but with the lives of his contemporaries.'[1]

Gilpin arrived in Newcastle, as the successor of the admirable SAMUEL HAMMOND, one of the ejected,[2] and the spiritual father of Oliver Heywood,—about 1668–69, that is, in the crisis of the 'troubles' to all who bore the 'mark' of Nonconformity. High-Churchmen were 'building-up,' as they deemed it, the Church, by persecuting relentlessly those who dared not acquiesce in the 'Act of Uniformity;' and accordingly 'Dissenters' had to preach furtively, even as 'of old,'— and all was clamour and confusion. One of themselves, who, if not of kin, was, in wit and wiseness, of kind, in more than name to Thomas Fuller,—thus vividly describes the period during which the recluse of Scaleby went to his new charge in Newcastle : ' I am ashamed,' says Ignatius Fuller, 'that whilst the Jews' temple was building, there was neither hammer, nor axe, nor any tool of iron heard in the house,— now when we are raising an house to Him that dwells not in temples made with hands, we should make so much use of iron and steel, and should reckon guns and swords, flames and fagots amongst our means of grace. I am sorry we should seem to have more of Nimrod than Solomon in our building; that we should partake of the curse poured upon the workmen at Babel—

> " Let's make the brother,
> The sire and son, not understand each other."[3]

Thus plunged into the midst of all manner of ' oppositions' and intolerance, RICHARD GILPIN, for a goodly number of years—as William Durant before him—confined his ' preaching' to his own private house in Newcastle. Very sad is it to come on 'records' such as these from the 'Depositions from the Castle of York, relating to offences committed in the northern counties in the seventeenth century.'[4] They may be well left to speak for themselves, without a word of comment :—

' clxxvi. Richard Gilpin, Clerk, and others. For holding a *Conventicle.*

' Aug. 4, 1669.—Before Ralph Jenison, Mayor of Newcastle, Cuth-

---

[1] As before, pp. 9–11.

[2] For information on Hammond, consult Calamy, Palmer, Longstaffes' Barnes, as before, and the different Newcastle ' Histories,' &c.

[3] 'Peace and Holiness : in Three Sermons upon Several Occasions.' By Ignatius Fuller, [of Sherrington, Bucks,] 1672, 12mo, pp. 3, 4, 6, 8.

[4] Surtees Society : edited by Raine, 1861, pp. 172–174.

bert Nicholson, cordyner, [= cordwainer,] saith, that upon Sunday last, about five or six of the clock in the morneng, he did see a great nomber of people goe inn to the house of Mr Richard Gilpyn, minister, in the White Freers, and afterward, he went to parson Jo^n. Shaw, and acquainted him with the premisses. Whereupon the said Mr Shaw togeither with the church-wardens, constables, and serjeants-at-mace, by the comaund of Mr Maor, did repaire to the said Richard Gilpin's howse. And when they came there all the dores were shutt and made fast. And after the dores were broken open, he did see these severall persons come out, viz., Robert Johnson, merchant, Dr Tunstall, Wm. Cutter, James Hargraves, merchant, Wm. Hutchinson, George Headlyn, fitter, Charles Newton, gent, Humphrey Gill, gent, Jno. Bittleston, tanner, Matthew Soulsbey, roper, Michaell Jobling, pullymaker, Robert Finley, chapman, and diverse other persons to the nomber of fortie.'

Again:—
'The information of Cuthbert Nicholas, cordwainer, against the persons hereinafter named, for being att meetings and conventicles:—Mr Richard Gilping, Mr William Deurant, Mr John Pringle, Mr Henry Lever, preachers,' &c. &c. &c. &c.

So early as 1663—which would intimate that Gilpin had previously resided and 'preached' in Newcastle — Bishop Cosin wrote to the Mayor of Newcastle, telling him to look sharply after '*the caterpillars,*' naming as the ringleaders, 'William Durant, Henry Leaver, *Richard Gilpin*, and John Pringle.'[1] When we consider who these men were—every one a 'pattern' of godliness and consuming consecration to the Master, and more especially that one of them, viz., Gilpin, had lately refused to elevate himself to a level with Cosin, it is hard to repress indignation; while the word of scorn, '*caterpillars,*' reminds one of the Popish parallel of Pope Alexander, wondering how the Signory of Florence could so far have forgotten what was due to him and to themselves as to aid and abet that 'contemptible *reptile,*' [vermicciattolo] in offending the majesty of the Holy See— the 'reptile' being SAVONAROLA; or the '*heretici et imperiti homines*' of SALMERON, as applied to Augustine and Chrysostom, Jerome, *et hoc genus omne.*[2] Very different was the 'letter' of Cosin, Bishop of Durham to the Mayor, from that of another 'in authority,' who had also addressed to his Worship of Newcastle 'a letter,' wherein he had counselled amity and forbearance; so much so, that Mr Durant and others of the preachers in Newcastle, returned him an answer of thanks for his 'inculcated exhortations to love the whole flock of

---

[1] Bourne's 'Newcastle,' *s.n.*

[2] Quoted by Villari, Vita di Savonarola, vol. ii., lib. iv. cap. 6: cf. Trollope's Florence,' iv. 178, 179.

Christ, *though not walking in the same order of the gospel.*' The writer was OLIVER CROMWELL.[1]

Until the 'Indulgence' of 1672, Gilpin carried on his 'ministry' in the half-public, half-hidden, manner which these deplorable acts indicate. At one time he had to leave his own house; for in the Barnes' 'Memoirs,' we read, ' When the Five Mile Act came out, Dr Gilpin lodged at Mr Barnes his house, for more security. When his goods were destrained upon, Mr Barnes—to prevent their being squandered away—replevyed them.' . . . . 'And when there was a design to banish the Doctor from Newcastle, Mr Barnes, by persuading the magistrates of his great usefulness in the town, by his skill in physic, procured him quietness to the end of King Charles his reign.'[2] Not however until 1672 was there anything approaching 'religious liberty' in England, and that only by connivance. Until that year, practically, Nonconformity and Dissent from the Church of England was politically treason, and ecclesiastically 'illegal.'

The Reader will have noticed that by Barnes and others, our Worthy is designated 'Doctor,' and that this stood him in stead on one occasion. But the title was not due technically until 1676. In that year he proceeded to Leyden—like Sir Thomas Browne earlier—and there 'took' the 'degree' of M.D. By the kindness of Professor J. Van Hoeden of Leyden, I am enabled—for the first time—to give the 'record' of it from the 'Inscriptions of the Students.'[3] It is as follows:—' Richard Gilpin, [misspelled " Gulpin,"] Cumbridus,' obtained his degrees July 6, 1676—*post disputationem privatam de Historia Hystericæ Passionis medicinæ doctor renunciatus est a clarissimo Kraame*—and again, Richard Gilpin—*Med. Candid.*, anno 50, *apud Prof. Spinæus, die* xxix. *Junii* 1676. This second inscription is only a week before ' the promotion, *die* vi. *Julii* 1676.' Gilpin 'lodged' with Professor Spinæus during his brief visit. In the list at close of the Memoir, along with his other Writings, is given the title-page of the medical Dissertation or 'Disputation,' which he read on the occasion and published. In passing, I may remark that the 'Disputation' is entirely technical, so that there is nothing to interest an unscientific reader.[4]

---

[1] Carlyle's Cromwell, vol. iv. 151–153.

[2] Barnes, as before, p. 142. Besides authorities already named, I am under obligation to Dr Bruce (author of 'The Roman Wall') for Turner's 'Sketch' of his Church in Newcastle; also to Mr James Clephan, Newcastle, for his valuable Paper, ' Nonconformity in Newcastle Two Hundred Years Ago.' A new edition of the latter will doubtless correct certain inadvertencies and misprints in an otherwise well-timed and vigorous tractate.

[3] I must cordially acknowledge my obligation to Sir James Y. Simpson, Bart., M.D., for putting me in communication with the Leyden Professor.

[4] Copies of this ' Disputatio,' which Gilpin must have neglected to deposit in Leyden, will be found in the Bodleian and in the British Museum ' Libraries.'

Returned from Holland as Dr RICHARD GILPIN,—and by this time married to his second wife, a daughter of a Cumberland squire, Brisco or Briscoe of Crofton Hall,—he gave himself to his work with unflagging zeal, with ever-deepening power and influence, and with most gratifying tokens that he was not labouring in vain, nor spending his strength for nought. He was now in 'easy' circumstances. 'The purchase,' says Barnes, ' of the Lordship of Scaleby had put him into debt, but he now cleared it off,' and Mr Barnes went with him to Sir Richard Musgrave, and got the conveyances finished, and this because ' by the encouragement his ministry met with from the liberality of the people, and his emoluments by the practice of physic, he [had] raised a considerable estate.'[1] He was vigilant as a ' watchman ' on the walls of Zion ; and as he mellowed into a beautiful old age, surrounded by a gifted and affectionate family, and having ' troops of friends,' he came to be *the* representative man of Nonconformity, so that the ' care ' of all their churches, in large measure, came upon him. Very pleasant must have been those holiday ' escapes ' from smoky Newcastle to the sylvan solitudes and brightness of Scaleby, which he interposed between his toils.

His Congregation enormously increased—at a bound probably, for, on the death of William Durant in 1681, his 'flock' was received by Gilpin.[2] Accordingly, in the course of years, he received several ' helpers.' One was the excellent William Pell, M.A., who, 'ejected' from Great Stainton in 1662, after being 'seven years minister of a congregation at Boston,' removed to Newcastle, where, says Calamy, ' he became assistant to Dr Gilpin, and died there, aged 63.' This was in 1698.[3] Another was Timothy Manlove, M.D., who settled at Pontefract in 1688, removed to Leeds in 1694, and became assistant to Dr Gilpin in 1698. He died August 3, 1699, and Gilpin preached two 'Sermons' before his funeral, informed by a fine spirit. They were published ; and the title-page will be found in our list of his Writings at close.

As before with the 'Temple Rebuilt,' it was only by constraint that Gilpin issued these Sermons—two in one. 'The following Discourse,' he says, ' was preached without the least thought of offering it to public view ; and yet I was persuaded to yield to the publication of it to prevent the printing of more imperfect notes.' The

---

[1] As before, p. 142.

[2] Raine's ' Depositions ' as before : foot-note by Mr Longstaffe, pp. 172,173. Theologically, *William Durant* was unquestionably evangelically orthodox, and in no sense, save that the Church-property is held by the Unitarians, can he be called the 'founder' of their Church in Newcastle. By the same plea Matthew Henry of Chester, and scores of others, might be claimed as 'Founders' of Unitarian congregations. I state this simply as matter-of-fact, and not controversially. I may observe that Gilpin's 'Letter' to Stratton (onwards) more probably indicates the commencement of the Unitarian ' separation.' [3] See Calamy, and authorities, as before.

melancholy duty interrupted a series of Sermons on 'Striving to enter in at the strait gate,' and from Galatians v. 16, 'This I say then, Walk in the Spirit, and ye shall not fulfil the lust of the flesh;' but, he continues, 'having received an intimation that my dear brother and fellow-labourer, now deceased, had found such comfort in his meditations of this scripture in his prospect of death, that he expressed his desires that his funeral sermon might be upon this text,' [Romans viii. 35–39,] he had chosen it. I have space for only a very few sentences from these 'Sermons' as follow:—"In all these things we are more than conquerors." It is a glorious victory to stand in an evil day when Satan hath drawn up all his forces against us. It is a glorious victory not only to escape without loss, but to gain by his opposition. Thus we outshoot him in his own bow; and all this, *sine labore et sudore*, easily through Divine assistance,' (page 17.) Again : " We are led by the Spirit" ver. 14. Whether we read the sense backward or forward it holds true, " as many as are led by the Spirit are the sons of God," and 'as many as are the sons of God have been and shall be led by the Spirit," (page 30.) He pays affectionate tribute to his departed 'assistants.' 'It hath pleased God Almighty and the all-wise Disposer of all things to make another breach upon us. It is not long since he took Mr Pell from us, and now he hath called home Mr Manlove, both of them excellent men, worthy ministers of the Gospel, singularly both of them fitted with abilities for their work. They were successively my dear brethren and fellow-labourers in this part of God's vineyard. It must be acknowledged that it is a stroke to be lamented : and if we look upon the present Providence we may have some cause to fear that when God is discharging His servants from His work, and paying them their wages, that He may shortly break up His house with us,' (page 21.)

From what must have been a large correspondence, only two letters of Dr GILPIN have come down to us, in so far as known. The one is an unimportant 'note' given in Horsley's 'Life of Dr Harle,' (8vo, 1730,)—not worth reprinting; the other hitherto unpublished, and of much interest and value, as shewing how staunch and true he was to the last in his Nonconformity, and how his one fear in his 'old age' was lest the Church of England should absorb his large congregation on his death.

This Letter is among the Ayscough MSS. 4275 in the British Museum (Birchiana.) We have transcribed it *verbatim*.

'NEWCASTLE, *Decemb*. 13 '98.

'DEARE SR,—Since I writ last to you concerning ye proposed correspondence, I received a lr from you, wherein you give answer to yr two objections wch I had mentioned to you. Your lr I communicated to ye brethren; but then there arose new mutterings about ye designe of yr late reflections on the circular lre, [and they] have taken hold of ye same advantages against it: so yt at present little is to be expected of any procedure in yt matter till men see what will become of ye publick outcry against it.

'It hath pleased God to take from me my deare assistant, Mr Pell, by a feaver; we buryed him last weeke. It is a sad stroke upon us all, but it falls at present most heavy upon me. Ever since his sickness, it became necessary for me (such are our circumstances) to preach twice every Lord's day, and I must continue to do so at least every other Lord's day for some time, because there are a small party (and but a very small one) who have formed a designe, and are now encouraged upon this sad occasion to open it. This party were ye few remainders of Mr Durant's congregation, who have kept communion wth ours in all ordinances, wthout making any exceptions, about 15 years; but when old Mr Barnes (their politick engineer) brought home his young son Thomas, from London, they presently shewed their intentions to choose him for their pastor; but as introductory to that they (in my absence) thrust him into ye pulpit, without so much as asking leave. I was silent, and suffered him to preach in ye evenings; but they being weary of that—few people staying to heare him—they thought it more conduceable to their designe to separate from us, and set up at ye Anabaptists' meeting-house; but no great party would follow them, and now they have chosen him to be their pastor, though before this he had in our pulpit vented some unsound Crispian notions, and at last had ye confidence to contradict what I had preached about preparation to conversion. For this, I thought it necessary to give him a publick rebuke, and to answer his exceptions. That theire designe is to worme us out of or meeting-house, and to breake or congregation, is visible to all: they now openly claime ye meeting-house for their pastor's use, (when he pleaseth,) and pretend old Mr Hutchinson (upon whose ground ye house is built) promised them so much when they contributed towards ye charge of building; but Mr Jonathan Hutchinson, his son, denyes any such promise, and stands firmly to us, though Mr Barnes (his father-in-law) surprised him wth solicitations; but we offer to repay them all ye money they contributed towards ye building.

'You see, Sr, how much I need your prayers, and (if it could be) ye nomination of a man of parts, prudence, piety, and authority to assist me at present, and to succeed me when I am gone. *Much of ye dissenters' interest in ye North depends upon ye welfare of or congregation. The Episcopall party have long since made their prognostik, yt when I die, ye congregation will be broken, and then there will be an end of ye dissenters' interest in Newcastle.* I pray give my deare love and respects to all ye brethren wth you, and pardon the trouble given by, Revd. sr, your affectionate brother and servant,

RICH. GILPIN.'

On the 4th page, folio—For the Reverend Mr Richard Stratton, minister of ye gospel, at the house, Hatton Garden, in London.

We have little more to tell of the author of *Dæmonologia Sacra*. He survived his estimable 'assistant' Manlove but a short time. But to the last he was 'in harness.' Looking over old Papers he came upon a Sermon which he had preached so far back as '1660,' at the 'Assize' in Carlisle, revised and published it; and it bears the same date of '1700' as his own death: so that, like Sibbes, he must have had proof-sheets passing through his hands very near 'the end.' The 'Epistle' or 'Preface' prefixed is as terse and effective as ever; and the 'Sermon' itself manly, outspoken, faithful, and truly characteristic of the man. The title-page will be found in our list.[1] This 'Sermon' having been preached before Judge Twisselton and Serjeant Bernard and the 'gentry' present at the Assize, is specially searching on 'sins' in 'high places,' for Gilpin acted on the sentiment of Edward Boteler, who, in his own quaint way, says of Earl Mulgrave, 'He knew what great evils evil great ones are; that they have many followers, go they whither they will, and seldom go to hell alone.' [As after, p. 48.] I detach a single 'particular' from this weighty Sermon :—' If magistrates advance not the throne of Christ, they commonly prove furious against it, and plagues of God's people. If this proceed from a careless blockish temper, then judgment of itself will degenerate into gall, and the "fruit of righteousness into hemlock." Justice, like water, purifies itself by motion, when it " runs down like a stream :" if it be a standing water, it corrupts, and *corruptio optimorum pessima*. If this neglect proceed from enmity to Christ, then, seeing they have the greatest advantages in their hands to do evil, they may " establish wickedness by a law :" they can " push with the horn, and tread down the pasture with their feet." [Ezek. xxxiv. 18.] " When the wicked beareth rule, the people mourn." [Prov. xxix. 2.] Or if it proceed from apostasy, then " the revolters are profound to make slaughter." [Hosea v. 27.] And this happens not so much from the churlish and cruel dispositions of men, as from God's giving them up judicially to rage against His ways, either as a scourge to his people, or in order to their own ruin. Hence it is noted that the cruellest persecutions were set on foot by emperors, sometimes of the best parts, and most civil dispositions, as Antoninus Philosophus, Trajan, Severus, Decius, &c. Magistrates are for the most part like the prophet's figs, either very good or very bad : they are the heads of the people, and all

---

[1] This Sermon, from some unexplained cause, is extremely rare and high-priced. I was indebted to Mr Wilson, Tunbridge Wells, for a copy.

diseases in the head are dangerous; so when the leprosy appeared in the head deeper than the skin, the party was pronounced utterly unclean,' (pp. 13, 14.)

Calamy and Mr Thompson of Stockton thus record the 'good man's end:'—' He went,' says the former, ' into the pulpit the last time he was in it under a feverish indisposition, and preached from 2 Cor. v. 2, " For in this we groan, earnestly," &c.; and to the surprise of all, he rather 'groaned' than spake this sermon. The lungs being at that time too tender for work, his disease seized that part, and he was brought home in a *peripneumonia*, which in ten days put a period to his life.'[1] Mr Thompson, in his ' Diary,'[2] thus writes:—' Dr Gilpin, y^t eminent servant of God, died much lamented by all, on (Tuesday) Feb. 13, $\frac{1699}{1700,}$ about eight o'clock in y^e morning.'[3] He was interred in the churchyard of All Saints, Newcastle. And the following is the 'entry' in its Register of Burials:—'1699 [=1699–1700] Feb. 16. Rich. Gilpin, doctor of physick.'[4] The 'scutcheon of the ' Kentmere' Gilpins was placed on his coffin. He left a widow, who retired, as her husband had asked, with her family, to Scaleby Castle.

From point to point of our Memoir, it has been our endeavour to bring out the character of Dr Gilpin under his varying circumstances; so that, unless I have failed more than I can suppose, my Readers must by this time—even out of the scanty material which has been left to us —have formed an idea of him, such as will bear me out, I anticipate, in characterising him summarily as a man of no ordinary type, large of soul,—with the spaciousness of genius that has been hallowed,—strong and inevitable in his convictions, quick and sensitive in conscience, intense and full of *momentum* in whatever he undertook; and, as his ' *Dæmonologia Sacra*' proves, profound, sagacious, keen in his scrutiny of human and celestial-demoniac problems, and one who must have carried sunshine with him wherever he went. His portrait—preserved in Nova Scotia by a descendant, Dr Gilpin of Halifax—as engraved in the earlier edition of Palmer, shews the liquid eye of genius, the mobile lip, the brow compact and packed of brain, a nose somewhat audacious, and a touch of sauciness in the chin, while the long cavalier-like curled ' locks' of his wig seem to proclaim the lord of the manor of Scaleby as much as the Preacher; for as Edward Boteler puts

---

[1] Account, p. 57.

[2] Given in ' A Brief History of Protestant Nonconformists, and of the Society assembling in the Old Meeting-house, High Street, Stockton, 1856,' [by Rev. J. Richmond,] p. 16. Mr Clephan of Stockton was good enough to send me this careful little volume.

[3] Turner, in giving the above extract, misled by 1699, imagines it must refer to some other Dr Gilpin. He forgot that the year did not begin then until March 25; so that, while under our reckoning it was 1700, under the old it was 1699; and hence the marking until the change of the going and coming year, *e.g.*, 1699-1700.

[4] I have to thank Mr Clephan, as before, for getting me this.

it of another, with Fullerian alliteration, 'Though he was very humble, yet he knew how to be a man and no worm, as well as when to be "a worm and no man." He knew when to lay his honour in the dust, and when to let no dust be upon his honour.'[1]

I would now bring together several 'estimates' of our Worthy by those who knew him well, and thus could form an accurate judgment concerning him. First of all, I am fortunate enough to be able to give, from an old, worn, and weather-stained holograph preserved by Prebendary Gilpin, a quaint 'Poem,' which probably represents in portions of it the inscription placed on his 'monument'—long since mouldered away. Here it is, rude and halting in rhyme and rhythm, but biographically interesting:—

TO THE MEMORY OF YE EXCELLENT DR GILPIN.

In mournfull numbers I did weep of late,
Criton the wise,[2] and sweet Philander's fate,[3]
And Calvus,[4] to ye learned world well known.
Oppress'd and wth repeated grief borne down,
Palæmon's[5] death succeeding struck me dumb,
My tears were all I offer'd at his tomb.
   Thus th' Eastern sage[6] wth wondrous patience bore
Thrice dismal news, but he could bear no more,
Did weep, fall down, and silently adore.
My trouble now swells o'er, and artless strays,
Where nature yields, and passion leads ye ways.
   Thou man of peace! born in our publick rage,
Designed to correct ye giddy age:
Thy solid judgment did resist ye flame,
In midst of civil fury still ye same.
When the grave world run madly uniform,
Serene within thou weather'd out ye storm.
The miter thou refused with a brow
Wch calmness shew'd, and resolution too.
Esteemed by ye good, by ill men fear'd,
By ye wise admired, and followed by ye herd.
Ev'n Satan did trembling on thy lectures wait,
When thou display'd his mysteries of state.
Begg'd leave to plague thee, but he begg'd in vain,
Vowing revenge upon ye list'ning train.
   Great prophet! who could'st prudently dispense,
With a becoming warmth, substantial sense;
In such a manner thou thy God addrest
As both thy rev'rence and thy wants exprest.
Thy zeal was not confined to th' sacred chair,
But bright through all thy actions did appear.
Thy spotless life thy doctrine best apply'd,
Truth recommending wch thou first had try'd.

---

[1] The Worthy of Ephratah,' 1659, 12mo, pp. 46, 47.
[2] Mr Pell, [as before.]   [3] Mr Manlove, [as before.]   [4] Mr Calvert.
[5] Dr Gilpin.   [6] Job.

Our honour and defence¹ with thee depart,
The gift of preaching and ye healing art.
J. H.

Artes infernas Divinâ Gilpinus arte
Detexit, vicit, jam requiescit ovans.
Id.

Presbyterûm præses, præco optimus, et medicinæ
Doctor Gilpinus, conditur hoc tumulo.
T. P.

Fitly accompanying this 'elegy' and—as verse little superior but—similarly valuable as a 'testimony,' come the lines of Dr Harle, which Horsley thus prefaces:—'I have oft heard him mention the severe shock the death of Dr Gilpin gave him.' His tribute to Gilpin occurs in a 'copy of verses upon the death of the Rev. John Turnbull of North Shields.' It is as follows:—

' How oft have we with admiration hung
On the angelic Gilpin's pow'rful tongue,
Who in perfection had the mighty art,
To form the soul and captivate the heart;
Pour Gospel balm into the wounded soul,
And vengeance on the harden'd conscience rowl.
When he hell's gloomy stratagems did clear ²
Man ceased, and Satan then began to fear
His empire's utter ruin drawing near.
Great man! whom goodness did to greatness raise,
Nor forced applause, nor warmly courted praise.
The tempting dignity he did despise
Made him more glorious still in good men's eyes.'³
(As before, pp. 20, 21.)

I have next to set forth the famous 'story' of THOMAS STORY the Quaker missionary-preacher—of his interviews with Dr Gilpin; wherein it will be seen he shews the deepest respect for him, albeit in his self-opinionativeness unconvinced of the erroneous tendency of his 'views' and practice. These 'notes' are found in a folio that has now gone out of sight, and become among the rarest of rare Quaker books.⁴ The narrative is too tedious for reproduction in full; but a specimen will interest. Having told of his conversion to the prin-

---

¹ Præsidium et decus meum.
² 'Satan's Temptations.' ³ The Bishoprick of C——le.
⁴ A Journal of the Life of Thomas Story: containing an Account of his remarkable Convincement of and Embracing of the Principles of Truth as held by the people called Quakers: and also of his Travels and Labours in the Service of the Gospel: with many other Occurrences and Observations. Newcastle-upon-Tyne, printed by Isaac Thompson and Company, at the New Printing Office on the Side. MDCCXLVII. Apart from the light under which everything is seen, this book is a perfect repertory of facts on the moral and religious condition of our country at the period. There are innumerable sketches of persons and places of mark all over North and South, given with a transparent *naiveté* and occasional raciness of wording that is very taking. Story continued to be received on the most friendly terms by the Gilpins, and by sons and daughters after Dr Gilpin himself was dead. Cf. pp. 470-473.

ciples of Quakerism, and more especially of the result of the reading of 'three small books,' he goes on: 'Some time after this, [1691,] Dr Gilpin, before mentioned, sent his son, a counsellor-[at-law], under whom I had been initiated into the study of the law, and who was one of those at the tavern aforesaid, and still retained a great affection for me—to invite me to his house at Scaleby Castle, and desired to see some of the Quakers' books, supposing I had been imposed upon by reading them; and I sent him, as I remember, all that I had. Soon after I had parted with these books, I observed a cloud come over my mind and an unusual concern; and therein the two sacraments—commonly so termed—came afresh into my remembrance, and divers scriptures and arguments *pro* and *con:* and then I was apprehensive the Doctor was preparing something of that sort to discourse me upon; and I began to search out some scriptures in defence of my own sentiments on those subjects: but as I proceeded a little in that work I became more uneasy and clouded: upon which I laid aside the Scripture and sat still, looking towards the Lord for counsel. For I considered the Doctor as a man of great learning, religious in his way, an ancient preacher and writer too, famous in Oliver's time, and a "throne" among his brethren: and that he might advance such subtilties as I could not readily confute nor would concede to, as knowing them erroneous, though I might not be suddenly furnished with arguments to demonstrate their fallacy; and so might receive hurt. And then it was clear in my understanding that as he was in his own will and strength, though with a good intent, in his own sense, searching the letter [of the Scripture,] and depending upon that and his own wisdom, acquirements, and subtilty, leaning to his own spirit and understanding, I must decline that way and trust in the Spirit of Christ, the divine Author of the Holy Scriptures. And as this caution was presented in the life and virtue of truth, I rested satisfied therein, and searched no further on that occasion. When I went to his house, he entered into a discourse on those subjects; and had such passages of Scripture folded down as he purposed to use. And when I observed it, I was confirmed that my sight of him in my own chamber at Carlisle, and of his work some days before, was right, [as if, to intercalate a remark, it needed prescience to foretell that the Doctor's appeal would be 'to the Law and to the Testimony'!!] and my mind was strengthened thereby. But before he began to move upon the subject, he dismissed every other person out of the room, so that himself and I remained alone. The first thing he said was, in a calm manner, to admonish me to be very cautious how I espoused the errors of the Quakers; for he had heard of late and with concern that I had been among them, or seemed to incline that way. I answered that I had not been much among them, nor seen any of their books but those I had sent him, and knew not of any errors they held. Yes, said he, they deny the ordinances of Christ, the two sacraments —Baptism and the Lord's Supper; and then opened his book [his!] at one of his down-folded leaves, where he read thus, 1 Cor. i. 2, xi. 23, 26. . . . .' Now follows the usual delusive appeals beyond the 'letter,' as 'carnal,' and all the unconsciously-blaspheming, '*setting-aside*,' of plain words that reveal 'the mind of the Spirit,' commingled with a simple-minded self-superiority which need not be illustrated. Very patient and wonderingly-silent must have been the Doctor with his undoubtedly pious and acute, but most perverse, visitor. He thus closes, 'The Doctor did not oppose this, [about prayer,] but only said I had given him better satisfaction on that point than he had found in the book; and afterwards he was much more free and familiar with me than before, or than I expected: and so we parted in friendship, and I returned in peace and gladness,'[1] (pp. 41–45.)

But by far the most important, as it is the most elaborate, 'estimate' of our Worthy, is that of Calamy, who, usually marked by judicial calm, and chary of praise, glows and burns in the fulness of his admiration. The fervour of his eulogy of Gilpin contrasts with his usual matter-of-fact statements, and surprises by its suddenness and passion. With this I shall close those personal tributes by contemporaries. Thus the 'Account' under 'Grastoke' runs:—

'Richard Gilpin, M.D. He was designed by God for great work in his church, and was singularly qualified for it. He had a large share of natural abilities, which he had wonderfully improved by an unwearied industry and long and hard study, so that there was scarce anything that accomplished a man, a scholar, a physician, or divine, but he possessed it in great perfection.

'His stature was of the middle sort, rather inclining to the lesser size; but his presence was far from being mean. There was a pleasing mixture of majesty and sweetness, affableness and gravity in his aspect. He could readily set his countenance to a severity or

---

[1] It may be well to give in a foot-note Story's account of another and later visit to Dr Gilpin:—'The same evening I visited Dr Richard Gilpin, formerly mentioned, having still a great respect for him and all his family. He was an eminent physician and preacher among the Presbyterians at Newcastle; to which place he had removed from Cumberland after the Revolution. And with him also I had some discourse about matters of religion; in which he discovered more passion and prejudice than became his high profession or years, and could not bear any contradiction. But I advised him to beware of that spirit, for it wanted mortification: and this I did in a calm and respectful mind, which reached the better part in him, and brought it over the evil; and then I left him in a loving temper. For though he was naturally high, and the most eminent and celebrated preacher of that profession in the North, and from his very early days deeply prejudiced, and almost envious, against Friends, yet he heard me with more patience—though that was little—than he ever did any other.'—P. 100.

mildness as the business or persons he had to do with required; and he did it not by any artificial affectation, but naturally and with ease, in such a way as kept up the dignity of his profession, and to such an end as made religion both more awful and more alluring.

'He had a delicate, fine, and polite fancy, expressing itself in a plenty of words, which gave clear and lively images of things, and kept up the life, strength, and elegancy of the English tongue.

'His memory was strong and faithful, and gave back with great exactness what he committed to it, though it was a treasury of very great reading, and filled with variety of matter in several sciences.

'To these was added a most penetrating, discerning judgment. This enabled him in reading to choose well, and to form a just opinion of the sentiments of others, which was always with that candour as made another considerable addition to his many excellences.

'He had so well digested all necessary parts of learning that he had them in readiness when he needed them. He used such things in their proper place, and adorned his discourses with them as there was occasion; and was able to make that which was little else but pageantry appear with a due gracefulness and beautiful in its season.

'As he had a rich fund of sense, learning, experience, and reading to fit him for a divine, so he had all the qualifications necessary for a preacher in the highest degree that can well be thought attainable. The several endowments that make a man a true, divine, orator did jointly meet in him.

'He had a voice strong enough to command the most usual public places of divine worship. It was piercing and sweet, and naturally well modelled. He had the true skill of fixing an accent upon particular words where the matter needed it. There was a force attended his way of speaking without an undue transport. He was vigorous and vehement, but under great conduct. His expressions were conceived and his sermons delivered without the use of notes: and he was qualified for that way of preaching. His pregnant memory, his ready invention, his great presence of mind, his natural fluency, that made him able to speak well and gracefully, with ease and assurance, entitled him to it. He could clothe any matter in apt words, with all the ornaments of a regular elocution. He fell neither into too swift an utterance, nor was forced upon any unbecoming, unguarded expressions. There was no restraint upon his delivery by being thus managed. It made him only capable of speaking what he did with much greater warmth and life and decency of gesture. It had all the smoothness of style and propriety of words to make it acceptable. It had all the graces of natural oratory, all the decencies of behaviour to recommend it. And that which completed all, it came from a serious mind, the concern of which was visibly to be read both in his countenance and expressions. He spoke from his very heart, as appeared sometimes in the force of his words, sometimes in his tears, and usually in both. He spake with solemnity and seriousness, with gravity and majesty, and yet with so much meekness mixed with all, as declared him to be a man of God and ambassador of Christ. There was a lively air of delivery, a sacred vehemence of affection in what he spake, that were very much his peculiar talent. He knew how to temper his discourses with due motion. His gestures were admirably taking and graceful, and further expressive of what he was delivering. In prayer he was likewise most solemn and fervent, and usually expressed himself much in Scripture language, and with a flood of affection. The very fountains of it seemed in the performance of that duty to be broken up and the great deep of it opened. It often forced him to silence for a little till it had flowed out at his eyes. In his pulpit discourses he was a very great example, both as to the design and method of them. His design was vast and noble in the ordinary course of his preachings. He usually proposed some subject, and pursued it on various texts. Every head with its enlargements was closely studied, and his particulars under each general were admirably chosen. If he had ever so many, none could be wanting; if never so few, there seemed to need no more. In the handling of any subject, after he had explained and proved what he had undertaken, with a great deal of clearness and affection, he was most plain, familiar, and moving in his applications. His way in these was another particular talent that he had. In all his uses he was excellent, but mostly so in his exhortations. He made them as so many set discourses of persuasion. They were delivered with most address and greatest warmth and vigour. He entered upon them usually with some rousing, lively preface to gain attention, and then offered his motives, which were prosecuted with the most pungent expressions. Here his earnestness increased, together with his voice, and the vehemency of it. He had a feeling apprehension of the importance of what he was then urging upon his hearers, and every word was big with concern of mind. He affected an elaborate eloquence at no time, but least of all then. In easy but moving expressions, and with a distinguishing πάθος, he would plead with sinners sometimes for a whole sermon together, without flagging in his affections or suffering his attentive hearers to do it in theirs. He was a man of a distinguishing knowledge and experience in the mysteries of Christianity; and of a discerning spirit in understanding a work of grace upon the hearts of others. With a clear head and searching skill in divine things, he had a sincere and warm heart. The fire of zeal and the light of knowledge accompanied one another. He kept up a serious temper at all times and in all places and company, without much discernible alteration or abatement; but this did not in the least sour his disposition, which was cheerful, though thinking and solid. His skill in government appeared in the managing a numerous congregation of very different opinions and tempers. His integrity, modesty, and contempt of the world, in refusing the bishopric of Carlisle, as another of the family (Mr Bernard Gilpin) had done before him, consonant to their motto, *dictis factisque simplex*. The care of the churches lay upon him. His unblamable character had obtained amongst all but those whose ill-nature would suffer them to speak well of none who differed from them. He was much respected by many for the good he had done them as a physician. Among persons of rank and quality in the parts where he lived, all necessary means were scarce thought to have been used if he had not been consulted. He went about doing good to the souls and bodies of men. This world was not in his eye, none could charge him with anything like covetousness.'

Be it remembered that these are the ' words ' in every case, of men who knew not to flatter, and spake out of ' perfect knowledge.' Above all, be it specially remembered that I have been quoting from no ' Funeral Sermon,' with its almost inevitable exaggerations.

It only remains that I give a complete annotated list of the extant writings of Dr Gilpin, arranged chronologically as published, also an account of the manuscript of *Dæmonologia Sacra*, and the destruction of other MSS.

I. The Agreement of the Associated Ministers and Churches of the Counties of Cumberland and Westmerland [*sic.*]. With something for Explication and Exhortation annexed. London : Printed by T. L., for Simon Waterson, and are sold at the sign of the Globe, in Paul's Churchyard, and by Richard Scot, Bookseller in Carlisle. 1656. Pp. 59. 4to.

    ⁂ In the copy of above in St Patrick's (Cathedral) Library, (Marsh's,) at p. 52, there is a careful correction in Gilpin's autograph of Carolostadius for Oecolompadius, which itself confirms the authorship. There is no name on title-page or elsewhere; but Calamy gives it in his enumeration. Account, vol. ii. p. 157.

II. The Temple Rebuilt : a Discourse on Zachery vi. 13. Preached at a Generall Meeting of the Associated Ministers of the County of Cumberland, at Keswick, May 19. By Richard Gilpin, Pastor of the Church at Graistock, in Cumberland. London : Printed by E. T., for Luke Fawne, at the Parrot, in Paul's Churchyard, and are to be sold by Richard Scott, Bookseller in Carlisle. 1658. 4to. Ep. Dedy., pp. 6, and 40. On reverse of title-page is this note : ' We, the Associate Ministers of the County of Cumberland, do earnestly desire our reverend brother, Mr Richard Gilpin, to print his acceptable Sermon preached this day at our Generall Meeting. Timothy Tullie, *Modr. pro Temp.* John Jackson, *Scribe.*'

⁎ My own copy has inscribed in Gilpin's autograph, '*Ex dono Authoris*,' and again misprints are carefully corrected.

III. Disputatio Medica Inauguralis de Hysterica Passione, quam Præside Deo Opt. Max. ex autoritate magnifici D. Rectoris D. Johannis Coccii, in Inclytâ Lugd. Batav. Academia Eloquentiæ et Historiarum Professoris celeberrimi nec non amplissimi Senatûs Academici, Consensu et Almæ Facultatis Medicæ Decreto, Pro Gradu Doctoratus, Summisque in Medicina Honoribus ac Privilegiis legitime obtinendis, Eruditorum examini subjicit Richardus Gilpin, Anglus Cumbriens. Die 6 Julii, loco horisque solitis, ante merid. Lugduni Batavorum, Apud Viduam et Haeredes Johannis Elsevirii Academiæ Typograph. 1676. 4to. Pp. 8.

⁎ The following is the dedication to his (second) father-in-law : ' Celeberrimo et virtute maxime conspicuo viro Gulielmo Brisco de Crofton, in Comitatu Cumbriæ Armigero, Socero suo venerando. Hanc Disputationem Inauguralem observantiæ signum offert et inscribit Richardus Gilpin.'

IV. *Dæmonologia Sacra.* 1677. 4to. See our reprint, pp. 2, 7, 126, 312, for general and special title-pages.

⁎ In our ' Prefatory Note,' I have characterised this the most important of Gilpin's works, and add here a little from the Barnes' ' Memoirs,' (as before,) and from one well capable of pronouncing an opinion. 1. Barnes: ' What had greatly raised Dr Gilpin's fame was his treatise of " Satan's Temptations,' which, in imitation of a book of King James I., he entitled " Dæmonologia Sacra," the largest and completest of any extant upon that subject. Being out of print, both it and an account of its author, and others of his writings, may be given the world when his posterity think it convenient," (pp. 145, 146.) 2. John Ryland, M.A. : ' If ever there was a man that was clearly acquainted with the cabinet-councils of hell, this author is the man,' [in his ' Cotton Mather.']

V. The Comforts of Divine Love : Preached upon the Occasion of the much Lamented Death of the Reverend Mr Timothy Manlove.

With his Character, done by another Hand. London. 1700. 12mo. Epistle, pp. 2. Character, pp. 4. Sermons, pp. 46.

⁎ The Williams' copy is marked contemporaneously '16th January 1699.' Prefixed is a portrait of Dr Manlove—for, like Gilpin and Pringle, he too was an M.D.—by Vander Gucht.

VI. An Assize Sermon, Preached before Judge Twisselton and Serg. Bernard at Carlisle, September the 10th, Anno 1660. And Now Publish'd and Recommended to the Magistrates of the Nation, as a Means, by God's Blessing, to quicken them to a serious Pursuit of the Honourable and truly Religious Design, for the Reformation of Manners, which is now on foot, and Countenanced by the Nobility, Bishops, and Judges, in the late Account of the Societies for the Reformation of Manners, and applauded by the Serious and Religious Men of all Persuasions. By R. Gilpin, now Minister of the Gospel in Newcastle-upon-Tyne. London: Printed for Tho. Parkhurst, at the Bible and Three Crowns, near Mercers Chapple; and Sarah Burton, Bookseller at Newcastle. 1700. 4to.

I have now to notice the MANUSCRIPTS of Gilpin. By the courtesy of the Rev. Bernard Gilpin, Bengeo, Hertford, I have had confided to me the original holograph of 'Dæmonologia Sacra,' and in our reprint I have found it clearing up occasional misprints and mis-pointings. The MS. is not complete; the collation is as follows: General title and three special titles, pp. 3. To the Reader, pp. 6, signed 'Rich. Gilpin.' Treatise on to Part II., page 255, (in our edition,) ending in line 21st from top, 'disqui[eting].' The penmanship is clear and legible, with few erasures, and having a margin on either side. On the top of the page whereon Part I. begins, there is the date, 'Newcastle, July 9, 1671.'[1] Further: Calamy, in his 'Account,' thus mentions a *manuscript* treatise of which he had heard: 'Among other things he hath left behind him in manuscript, a valuable Treatise concerning The Pleasantness of the Ways of Religion; and in whatsoever hands it lies, it is pity but it should see the light,' (vol. ii. p. 157.) It is to be lamented that this appeal was not responded to, as Prebendary Gilpin records sorrowfully its loss as follows: 'Among his other papers was found a treatise of considerable length, prepared, as it seemed, for the press, "On the Pleasures of Religion." This MS., and several other MSS. of Dr Gilpin's, consisting chiefly of heads and divisions of sermons, from which he used commonly to preach, fell into the hands of the author of this memoir; and

[1] By the favour of Mr Nichol I have had one hundred large-paper copies of this edition of 'Dæmonologia Sacra' thrown off—quarto: and prefixed is the portrait of Gilpin, and a fac-simile of a portion of this manuscript.

being deposited in a box with other papers, and placed in the corner of a closet, were attacked by what is commonly called dry damp, and were almost entirely spoiled. If anything had been interposed between the bottom of the box and the floor so as to have suffered the air to circulate, the mischief had been prevented;' and what levity in the custodier of so precious a legacy that this little care was neglected. Mr Gilpin of Juniper Green writes me concerning these spoiled MSS. : ' Nevertheless [*i.e.*, notwithstanding their utter destruction by the dry-rot] my mother kept the fragments all the days of her life with great veneration. But now these relics—they were little better than ashes—of our ancestor have perished.'

I have thus done my best to revivify the story of RICHARD GILPIN, His highest 'record' is 'on high;' but those who love the memory of our Worthy, will, it is hoped, accept kindly our endeavours to keep his grave green, and to import, so to speak, personality to the name in an old title-page—of one who did valiant service for The Master :

> ' Sword and spear he might not wield,
> But with faith his heart to shield,
> Marched he to the battle-field.'—[' *Paradisus Animæ*.']

And so I close with like verses by leal-hearted Sir Egerton Brydges :

> ' His tongue, the Spirit's two-edged sword,
>   Had magic in its blade ;
> For while it smote with every word,
>   It healed the wounds it made.
> Yet, who so humbly walked as he,
>   A conqueror in the field ;
> Wreathing the rose of victory
>   Around his radiant shield ! '

ALEXANDER B. GROSART.

LIVERPOOL.

APPENDIX TO MEMOIR.

A.—Page xvi.—ANCESTRY AND DESCENDANTS OF THE GILPINS.

THE different 'County' Historians, and Works on the old families of England, give more or less full details concerning the Gilpins in all their many branches. The 'Arms' are *Or*, a boar passant sable, armed and tusked Gules. A fine book-plate of this adorns Prebendary Gilpin's Family Manuscript. These 'Arms' are hereditarily understood to have been derived from the fact that a Richard de Gylpyn or Gilpin—who is regarded as the founder of the house—killed a wild boar which had infested the neighbourhood of Kentmere, in the reign of King John. [See Nicholson and Burns' 'Antiquities of Westmoreland and Cumberland,' (as before,) vol. i. pp. 135-137.] This is confirmed by Sir Daniel Fleming's Collection of Pedigrees, in the possession of Sir W. Fleming of Rydal, Co. Westm. Bart. A.D. 1713; and is given by Bishop Carleton in his Life of Bernard Gilpin. From these authorities, and various other Family documents, I construct this genealogy of the elder House:—

1. Richard . . . . founder. He a son, 2. William, who married a daughter of Thomas Ayray, bailiff of Kentmere. He a son, 3. Richard, who married daughter of Fleming of Coningston, from whom many descendants are found in and around Kendal. He a son, 4. William. He a son, 5. Richard. He a son, 6. William, a captain at Bosworth field, and there killed. He a brother, 7. Edwin, two of whose sons were distinguished—viz., (1.) The ambassador of Queen Elizabeth to the States of Holland. (2.) Bernard, the 'Apostle of the North,' was the fourth son. He, [*i.e.*, Edwin,] a son, 8. William. He a son, 9. George. He a son, 10. William. He a son, 11. George. He succeeded by, 12. Christopher Gilpin, a half brother of George, in whom the direct *male* line ended. The 'Kentmere' estate sold to Sir Charles Philipson.—[*N.* and *B.*—*as before.*]—William, son of Richard, [=the 4th of our list,] married a daughter of Thomas Lancaster of Sockbred, who descended of the baron of Kendal. His son Richard, again [= 5th in our list,] married a daughter of Sir Rowland Thornborroux, knight of Rampsell. This Richard married as his second wife Margaret Layton = Enwine, second daughter of Thomas Layton of Dalemaine, who had several sons—Anthony, Thomas, Sir William, Sir Bryan, Sir Cuthbert, Sir Richard, all famous men, mostly soldiers, and some knights of Rhodes. His daughters also intermarried with Redman,

Carelton, Clyborne, and Vaux. We may now tabulate the descent. From Richard, and his second wife, Margaret Layton, comes—

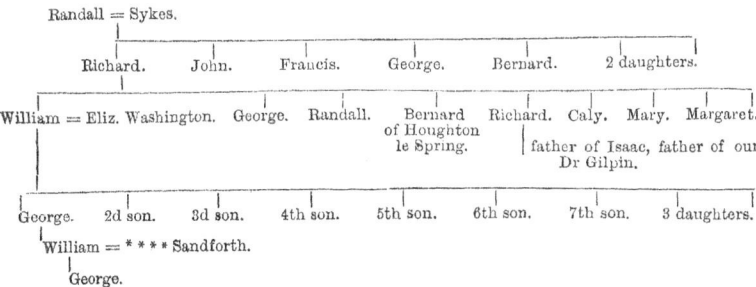

[See Hutchinson's 'History of Durham,' vol. ii. 703, account of the Gilpins, from a paper in the hands of Mr Rob. Sober of Sherburn, near Durham, without date.—Randall MSS. The last George, at the time of making out Sober's pedigree, is said to be living, and owner of the ancient house of the Gilpins, Kentmere Hall.]

Turning to *Dr Richard Gilpin*, I have had two elaborate pedigrees (of descent) entrusted to me, by the former of which, it appears our Worthy had a very large family by, (as I understand,) his two wives. By this also I find that his second wife was born 'Oct. 15th, 1625,' eldest daughter of William Brisco of Crofton—her name Susannah. I have a suspicion that the first Mrs Gilpin died at Greystoke, and that the Doctor re-married before leaving it; but owing to the time-worn state of the Greystoke 'Registers,' all the entries that remain concerning Dr Gilpin's family are the two children given in our Memoir. Following William and Susannah were, 1. Isaac, born July 12, 1658; married Elizabeth, daughter of Thomas Clagget. Then, 2. Susanna, born Nov. 27th, 1659; married Matthew Parlis, minister. [The former Susannah must have died as a child.] Then, 3. Anne, who married Sawrey of Broughton Tower, Esq. [On this marriage, see Barnes' 'Memoir,' as before, pp. 142, 143.] She was born December 5th, 1660. Then, 4. Elizabeth, born Aug. 3, 1662; died unmarried. Then, 5. Richard: died of a blow of his schoolmaster. Then, 6. Mary, born Dec. 28th, 1666; died unmarried. Then, 7. Dorothy, born Aug. 13, 1668; married, (1.) Jabez Cay, M.D.; (2.) Eli Fenton. Then, 8. John, born Feb. 13, 1669. [More of him immediately.] Then, 9. Francis, born July 27, 1671; ob. infant. Then, 10. Bernard, born Oct. 6, 1672, died in his youth at Jamaica, unmarried. Then, 11. Francis, born Jan. 27, 1675, died in infancy. Then, 12. Thomas, born July 27, 1677, died unmarried, June 20, 1700. Returning upon John, [eighth of this list,] he married Hannah, daughter of Robert Cay, Esq. of Newcastle, and left large issue, as follows: 1. Richard, born April 9, 1700, (soon after his grandfather died,) died unmarried, 1723. 2. Robert, born 17th Aug. 1702, married Ruth, daughter of Reynold Hall of Newbiggen, Esq. [More of this pair immediately.] 3. William, born Jan. 1, 1700 (?), married Mary, daughter of Thomas Dickenson, clerk. 4. John, born 1st Sept. 1705. 5. Thomas, born Jan. 8, 1711, ob. 12 March 1713. 6. Susanna. 7. A daughter. 8.

Barbara, born 16th May 1710, wife of Braithwaite of Stockton. 9. Susanna, born 28th April 1712, wife of Isaac Cookson of Newcastle. 10. Hannah, born 22d May 1715, wife of . . . . Goldsmith. Returning again upon Robert, [second of the list from John,] he had issue—1. John, who married daughter of John Cookson of London. He took the name of Sawrey on succeeding to the Broughton Tower estate. 2. Richard, died in East Indies. 3. Ruth. 4. 5. Jer. (?). William, [third of list from John,] had issue—1. Thomas, ob. an infant. 2. John, dead 1809. 3. Robert, *ib.* 4. Hannah, married. 5. William, died 18th September, æt. 67. So much for the first paper. Now for the second, which gives the descendants of the eldest son of Dr Gilpin, viz., William, born, as stated in Memoir, at Greystoke, 5th Sept. 1657. He became a barrister-at-law, justice of the peace, and deputy vice-admiral for county Cumberland, and recorder of the city of Carlisle; bought Highfield Moor and the tithes of Crosby; died at Scaleby Castle, Aug. 14, 1724, æt. 67. He married Mary, eldest daughter and one of the co-heiresses of Henry Fletcher of Talantyre. The issue were—1. Susan Maria, born at Scaleby Castle, 10th Nov. 1689, wife of Joshua Dacre Appleby of Kirklevington, by whom she had issue—[will be enumerated immediately]. 2. Anne, born April 14, 1691. 3. Richard, born 6th Feb. 1692, married Mary, daughter of Enoch Hudson. 4. Dorothy, ob. an infant. 5. Henry, *ibid.* 6. William, born at Whitehaven, married Margaret, daughter of G. Langstaff. 7. Henry, born Oct. 1692, ob. at Jamaica. 8. John Bernard, born at Scaleby, Jan. 24, 1701, ob. circa 1776, buried at Carlisle Cathedral. He married Matilda, eldest daugther of George Langstaff, ob. circa 1773, buried at Carlisle. 9. Dorothy, born at Scaleby, wife of Eaglivfield Griffith, born 4th Nov. 1703. 10. George, born at Scaleby, 29th Aug. 1706, married Elizabeth, third daughter of George Langstaff. Returning on Susan Maria, [eldest daughter,] she had a daughter, Elizabeth, born at Whitehaven, Feb. 12, 1708, ob. an infant, and a son, William, born June 1724, ob. at Whitehaven, 4th Dec. 1779. He married Elizabeth Hodgson, daughter of Robert Hodgson of Whitehaven, died at Denbigh Castle, 25th April 1792, æt. 60. They had issue—1. William Gilpin, born at Whitehaven, 12th Nov. 1758, ob. 15th Oct. 1822, at East Sheen, Surrey, having married Sarah, daughter of George Holland, Esq. of London, in 1793. Finally returning on John Bernard, [eighth, *supra,*] he was father of the Rev. William Gilpin, vicar of Boldre, prebendary of Salisbury, died April 5, 1804 at Boldre, æt 80. He will not soon be forgotten, as his delightful books, with their carefully finished ' Illustrations' on ' Picturesque Beauty,' are gathering increasing value as they become older. He had issue by his first cousin. John Bernard Gilpin, Esq., who went to Philadelphia, and afterwards became British Consul at Rhode Island. His descendants are now partly in Nova Scotia, [J. Bernard Gilpin, Esq., M.D., Halifax,] and in England and Scotland; and Rev. William Gilpin, born April 8, 1757, rector—an excellent and venerable man, and clergyman—in county Salop; and Sawrey Gilpin, born Oct. 30, 1733, ob. 1808. For the two Papers whence most of the preceding details have been collected, I owe thanks to my friend Joshua Wilson, Esq., Nevil Park, Tunbridge

Wells. I may add that in Prebendary Gilpin's Family-Manuscript there are 'Memoirs' of William Gilpin, Esq., the recorder of Carlisle, containing valuable and interesting letters to and from the Lowther family. The 'Recorder' was a man of mark. His portrait is at Scaleby Castle. Next, severally William 'merchant at Whitehaven.' [See Story, as before.] Henry, of 'the Navy,' Thomas, John Bernard, Anne, Dorothy, Susannah Maria, the eldest daughter, who must have been a lady of uncommon originality and force of character, and largeness of heart. [As *above*. She was married to Dacre Appleby, Esq. of Kirklinton, contiguous to Scaleby Castle. Curiously enough, their eldest son married a daughter of the Bishop of Carlisle. Mrs Appleby 'was followed by all the country, in tears, to her grave.'] John Bernard,—a very capital 'Memoir' of a gallant soldier. Somerville, in 'The Chase,' refers to the Windsor 'roads' constructed under his military supervision. He was a familiar friend of the good Colonel Gardiner. There are glimpses of the Rebellion of 1745 in this Memoir, throwing light on events at Carlisle. At 'leisure hours' he cultivated painting, and when he lived at Carlisle, he had sometimes half a dozen young people, or more, who used occasionally to attend him for instruction.' Of these some became famous, *e.g.*, John Smith, whom Lord Warwick sent to Rome, Robert Smirke, Esq., R.A., Mrs Head, &c. The Prebendary, in his MS., here gives also an account of literary society of the period, including Warburton, Dr Brown, and others. There are Letters of this many-gifted man, revealing a very beautiful and tender veneration for his departed wife, whose loss he 'mourned unto the grave.' The correspondence between Mr and Mrs Bernard Gilpin is striking and brilliant. Sawrey Gilpin, R.A., of Knightsbridge, their son, became celebrated as an animal painter. Sir J. D. A. Gilpin, another son, was knighted for his long services in America, West Indies, and Gibraltar. He was a friend of Washington's. Catherine, sister of the two last, born at Scaleby Castle, 1738, was a woman of rare intellect, and a friend of Miss Blamire, the sweet Poetess of Cumberland. In a new edition of Miss Blamire's 'Poems and Songs,' recently published, there are given some by Miss Gilpin, equal to the others. She died at Carlisle in 1811. Even these bare names and dates will suffice to reveal a Family distinguished in well-nigh every department of human achievement, to be placed in their hereditary talent with the Hunters, Gregorys, and Browns, and equally remarkable in their hereditary piety and worth, as well where they belonged to the Church of England as where they held true to Nonconformity, and their descent from the great and good Dr RICHARD GILPIN.

B.—Page xix.—GILPINS AT OXFORD.

The following memoranda are taken from the three Lists of Queen's College, as detailed:—

I. From the List of Fellows:

1555. Gilpin. [In another and later hand this note is appended:

'Bernardus (*ni fallor*) R^r de Houghton le Spring in Com. Dunelm. V. Batesii Vitas clar. virorum, p. 284.' The apostle.]
    1569. Richard Gilpin.
    1572. Joshua Gilpin.
  II. From the List of Entries:
    1594. Term. Mic. Gilpin.
    1602. ,,   Pasch. ,,
    1610. ,,   ,,   ,,
    1614. ,,   ,,   ,, *b*, [='bateller,' or exhibitioner.]
    1631. ,,   ,, Samuel Gilpin, *b*, [*ibid.*]
  III. From the List of Matriculations:
    1602. } Franciscus Gilpin, Lancastrensis filius ministri verbi Dei.
  Oct. 15. } Nat. An. 17.

C.—Page xix.—NOTICES OF GILPINS.

The following extract from N. and B. 'History,' (as before,) vol. i. p. 130, shews the Gilpins were freeholders in Strickland as early as the days of Queen Bess: 'And in the 14 Eliz. William Parr, marquis of Northampton, died seised thereof [*i.e.*, of the manor of Strykeland Rogers] and the same was assigned to his widow for dower, and the particulars in the rental made thereof was as follows: manor of Strickland Roger: freeholders there, Edward Lancaster, Esquire, 26s. 8d.: John Master, Esquire, 11s. 9d.: *William Gilpin*, 9s. 9d. Total of the (customary) rent of this manor £15, 14s. 5d.: ten shillings paid yearly by Mr Lancaster's tenants, to be free of their gift from the lord's will, being part of the said sum.' Further, this notice occurs under Chapel of Crosthwaite in parish of Heversham, 'The chancel and steeple of this chapel were built by one William Gilpin, who also contributed largely towards the three bells, in 1626: on which bells are the following inscriptions: on the first bell: "Jesus, be our speed:" on the second bell: "*Soli Deo gloria:*" on the third bell:

> "A young man grave in godliness
> William Gilpin by name
> Gave forty pounds to make these sounds
> To God's eternal fame."'

[Vol. I. p. 215.]

TO THE READER.

The accurate searches into the secrets of nature which this age hath produced, though they are in themselves sufficient evidences of a commendable industry, yet, seeing they fall so exceedingly short of that discovery which men aim at—giving us at best but probable conjectures and uncertain guesses—they are become as little satisfactory to men that look after the true causes of things, as those 'ships of desire' whose great undertaking for gold had raised high expectations in their attempts, but in the return brought nothing home for their ventures but 'apes and peacocks,'[1] [1 Kings x. 22, and 2 Chron. ix. 21.] While men reflect upon themselves under such disappointments, they cannot but check themselves, for over-promising themselves in their adventures, with that of Zophar, 'Vain man would be wise,' [Job xi. 12.]

But how happy would it be for men if such failures of expectation might better inform them! If our attainments in these pursuits will not bear our charges, nor recompense our pains and loss of time with an answerable profit, though we may see cause sometimes, as a divertisement or recreation, to use them, yet how shall we satisfy ourselves to make them our chief and sole business?

If we knew of nothing of higher concern to us than these, our neglect of greater matters were more excusable; but seeing we are sufficiently instructed that we have more weighty things to look after, such as relate to a certain future estate of happiness or misery, the very discovery of this to a rational being must needs entitle such things to the first and greatest part of his care. He that knows that there is 'one thing necessary,' and yet suffers himself to be diverted from the pursuit of that, by 'troubling himself about many things,' [Luke x. 41,] is more justly chargeable with folly, than he that neglects his estate, and finds himself no other employment but to pursue feathers in the wind.

Among those things that religion offers to our study, God and our own hearts are the chief. God is the first and last and whole of our happiness; the beginning, progress, and completement of it is from him and in him—for in that centre do all the lines meet; but our heart is the stage upon which this felicity, as to the application of it, is transacted: upon this little spot of earth doth God and Satan draw up their several armies; here doth each of them shew their power and wisdom; this is treated by both; each of them challenge an interest in it; it is attacked on the one side and defended on the other. So that here are skirmishes, battles, and stratagems managed. That man, then, that will not concern himself in his inquiries, how the matter goes in his own heart, what ground is got or lost, what forts are taken or defended, what mines are sprung, what ambuscados laid, or how the battle proceeds, must needs lie under a just imputation of the greatest folly; neither can he be excused in his neglect by the most pressing solicitations of other things that seem to require his attendance upon the highest imaginable pretences of necessity: 'For what is he profited, that gains the whole world, if he loses his soul?' [Mark viii. 36.]

But the exact and faithful management of such spiritual inquiries, with their necessary improvement to diligent watchfulness and careful endeavours of resistance, is another manner of work than most men dream of. To discover the intrigues of Satan's policy, to espy his haunts and lurking-places in our hearts, to note his subtle contrivances in taking advantages against us, and to observe how the pulse of the soul beats under his provocations and deceitful allurements, how far we comply or dissent, requires so much attendance and laborious skilfulness, that it cannot be expected that such men who design no more than to be Christians at the easiest rate, and content themselves with a formal superficiality of religion; or such who, having given up themselves to the deceitful sweets of worldly carnal delights, are not at leisure to engage themselves in so serious a work; or such whose secret guilt of rebellious combination with the devil against God, makes them fearful to consider fully the hazards of that wickedness, which they had rather practise with forgetfulness, lest the review of their ways and sight of their danger should awaken their consciences to give them an unwelcome disquiet; it cannot, I say, be expected that any of these sorts of men, whilst they are thus set, should give themselves the trouble of so much pains and toil as this business doth require.

Upon this consideration I might rationally fix my prognostic of the entertainment of the following treatise. What acceptance soever it may find with such as are cordially concerned for their souls and the realities of religion—and of such I may say as the apostle Paul concerning brotherly love, 1 Thes. iv. 9, as touching this matter, 'They need not that I write unto them, for they themselves are taught of God' to be suspicious of Satan's devices; and by experience they find his deceits so secret, and withal so dangerous, that any help for further discovery and caution must needs be welcome to them; yet—to be sure the prince of darkness, who is always jealous of the least attempts that may be made against his empire, will arm his forementioned subjects against it, and whomsoever else he can prevail upon, by the power of prejudice, to reject it, as urging us to a study more severe or harsh than is consistent either with the lower degrees of knowledge of many, or with that ease which most men desire to indulge to themselves; or as offering such things which they, to save themselves from further trouble, will be willing to call chimeras or idle speculations: and this last I may rather expect, because in this latter age Satan hath advanced so far in his general design against all Christianity, and for the introduction of paganism and atheism, that none now can express a serious conscientious care for holiness and the avoidance of sin, but upon pain of the imputation of silliness or whining preciseness; and none can speak or write of conversion, faith, or grace, but he shall be hazarded by the scoffs of those that are unwilling to judge the private workings of the heart to God-ward, or spiritual exercises of grace, to be any better than conceited whims and unintelligible nonsense: but seeing such men make bold to jeer, not only that language and those forms of speech which the Holy Ghost thought fit to make use of in the Scriptures, but also the very things of 'Faith,' 'Grace,' and 'Spirit,' which are everywhere in the sacred oracles recommended to us with the most weighty seriousness—which with them pass for no better than cheats and fancies—we can easily sit under their contempt; and shall, as we hope, be so far from being jeered out of our religion, that their scorns shall have no more impression upon us than the ravings of a frenzical person that knows not what he speaks.

Notwithstanding these, who are no way considerable for weight, there are, I hope, a great many who seriously employ themselves in the inwards as well as the outwards of religion—and who will not suffer themselves to be persuaded that the apostle obtruded an empty notion upon believers, when he recommended that observable truth to them, Rom. ii. 28, 'He is not a Jew which is one outwardly,' &c.; for their sakes have I undertaken this labour of collecting and methodising the grand stratagems and chief ways of delusion of the great deceiver. To these I must particularly account for some few things relating to this discourse. As,

1. That I have satisfied myself in the reasons of the publication of these papers, and do not judge it requisite to trouble any so far as to tell what these reasons are. They who desire to resist such an enemy, and whose experience doth convince them that all helps are necessary, will not need them; and those that are men of scorn or of avowed carelessness will not regard them, though I should declare them.

2. To prevent the misapprehensions, which possibly some may otherwise labour withal, of a monstrous product from one text, because they may observe one text in the front, and no other mentioned throughout the first and second parts; they may know that I made use of several in the preaching of these discourses, as suitable foundations for the several particulars herein mentioned; but in the moulding up of the whole into the method of a treatise, for the ease of the reader, I thought fit to lay aside those introductions—as also many other occasional applications which were proper for sermons, and a great many things which were necessary to be spoken for explication and illustration of these points to a popular auditory—and have only presented the substance in a more close connexion; because if there be any little obscurity that may at first appear to any for want of variety of words, the treatise being under their eye, will be at leisure to attend their review in a second or third reading; which, however, I would recom-

mend earnestly to those that in these concerns do really design to be 'wise for themselves.'

3. Neither should it seem strange that I have frequently made use of instances from history or other later relations. Whosoever shall consider the nature of the matter treated on will not complain of this as a needless trouble put upon them; yet withal I have been so careful of doing any persons an unkindness, by making too bold with them, that I mentioned no names but such as upon such occasions have been made public by others before. The rest I have only mentioned in the general, discovering their case where it was useful, but concealing the persons.

4. It may perhaps seem a defect, that the several directions, remedies, or counsels which are requisite to be observed in making resistance against Satan are not added, except some few hints in the latter end of the third part, and some other things in that part, in the applications of the several doctrines therein, which I thought fit, upon good grounds, to leave in the order of a preaching method; but such may be pleased to consider that several have performed that part very fully, to whose labours I had rather refer the reader than trouble him with a repetition. It was only my design to endeavour a more full discovery, though every way short of the thing itself, of Satan's craft, because the knowledge of this is so necessary, and withal others have done it more sparingly. Such as it is, accept and improve for thy spiritual advantage; for that was the end of this undertaking, by him who desires that thy soul may prosper,

RICH. GILPIN.

DÆMONOLOGIA SACRA:

OR, A

TREATISE

OF

𝕾atan𝖘 𝕮emptation𝖘

The First Part.

CONTAINING

A Discourse of the Malice, Power, Cruelty and Diligence of Satan. Of his cunning in Temptation in the general. Of his Method of tempting to Sin. Of his Policies for maintaining his Possession. Of his Deceits for the preventing and spoiling Religious Services and Duties.

By *R. G.*

2 Cor. 2. 11. *We are not ignorant of his Devices.*

London, Printed by *J. D.* for *Richard Randel,* and *Peter Maplisden,* Booksellers in *New-Castle* upon *Tine,* 1677.

A TREATISE OF SATAN'S TEMPTATIONS.

PART I.

Be sober, be vigilant; because your adversary the devil, as a roaring lion, walketh about, seeking whom he may devour.—1 PETER V. 8.

CHAPTER I.

The introduction to the text, from a consideration of the desperate ruin of the souls of men.—The text opened, expressing Satan's malice, power, cruelty, and diligence.

THE souls of men are 'precious.' The whole world cannot repair their loss. Hence by God are all men in particular charged with care and watchfulness about them. He hath also set up watchmen and overseers, whose business it is to watch over souls, and in the most strict and careful manner, as those that must 'give an account,' [Heb. xiii. 17.]

What can more stir up men to the discharge of this duty than the frequent alarms which we have of the assaults of such an adversary, whose business it is to destroy the soul? 'The Philistines are upon thee, Samson!' [Judges xvi. 9;] he fights continually, and useth all the policy and skill he hath for the management of his strength.

Besides, it is a consideration very affecting, when we view the 'desolations that are made in the earth,' [Ps. xlvi. 8,] what wounds, what overthrows, what cruelties, slaveries, and captivities these conquered vassals are put to. It was, as some think, an inexcusable cruelty in David against the Ammonites, when he 'put them under saws, and harrows of iron, and made them pass through the brick-kiln,' 2 Sam. xii. 31; but this spiritual Pharaoh hath a more grievous 'house of bondage,' and iron furnace. Neither is this miserable destruction ended, but will keep pace with time, and shall not cease till Christ shall at his appearance finally conquer him and tread him down. If Xerxes wept to look upon his army through the prospective of devouring time, which, upon an easy foresight, shewed him the death of so great a company of gallant men, we may well weep, as David at Ziklag, till we can weep no more; or as Rachel for her children, 'refusing to be comforted,' [Jer. xxxi. 15;] while we consider what a great number of succeeding generations, 'heaps upon heaps,' [Judges xv. 16,] will be drawn with him to a consuming Tophet. And could we follow him thither, to hear the cries of his prisoners, the roarings of his wounded, where they 'curse the day' that brought them forth, and themselves for their folly and madness in hearkening to his delusions, the dreadful outcries of eternity, and then their 'rage against heaven' in cursings and blasphemings, while they have no mitigations or ease, nor the refreshment of 'a drop of water to cool their tongues,' [Luke xvi. 24,] we would surely think we could never spend our time better than in opposing such an enemy, and warning men to 'flee from the wrath to come,' [Mat. iii. 7,] to take heed they come not into his snare. With what earnestness would we endeavour to persuade men! What diligence would we use to cast water upon these devouring flames, and to pluck men as brands out of the fire! It is true, if Satan had dealt plainly with men, and told them what wages they were to expect, and set a visible mark upon his slaves, or had managed a visibly destructive hostility, men have such natural principles of self-preservation, and of hatred of what appears to be evil, that we might expect they would have fled from him, and still have been upon their guard; but he useth such artifices, such sleights and cozenage, that men are cast into a sleep or a golden dream; while he binds them in chains of darkness they see not their end, the snare, nor the pit; nay, he intoxicates them with a love of their misery, and a delight in helping forward their ruin, so that they are volunteers in his service, and possessed with a madness and rage against all that will not be as willing as themselves to go to hell; but especially if they put forth a compassionate hand to help any out of that gulf of misery, they hate them, they 'gnash upon them with their teeth,' and run upon them with utmost violence, as if they had no enemies but these compassionate Samaritans, [Luke x. 33.]

How great is this mystery of darkness! Who shall be able to open the depths of it? Who shall declare it fully to the sons of men, to bring these 'hidden things to light'? Especially seeing these hellish secrets which are yet undiscovered, are double to those that have been observed, by any that have escaped from his power. He only whose prerogative it is 'to search the hearts of men' [Rev. ii. 23] can know, and make known, what is in the heart of Satan; he views all his goings, even those paths which the 'vulture's eye hath not seen,' [Job xxviii. 7,] and can trace those footsteps of his, which leave no more print or track behind them than 'a ship in the sea, or a bird in the air, or a serpent on a stone,' [Prov. xxx. 19.]

Yet notwithstanding, we may observe much of his policies; and more would God discover if we did but humbly and faithfully improve what we know already. It is my design to make some discovery of those haunts I have observed, if by that means I may be useful to you, to quicken and awaken you. And first I shall set before you the strength and power of your enemy, before I open his cunning and craft.

There are found in him whatsoever may render an adversary dreadful.

1. As, first, *Malice and enmity*. ὁ Ἀντίδικος is a law term, and signifies an adversary ' at law,' one that is against our cause ; and the text, as some think, heightens this malice, (1.) By the article ὁ, which denotes an arch enemy.[1] (2.) The name Διάβολος, which signifies a slanderer or calumniator—for the word is twice in the New Testament used for a slanderer—shewing his hatred to be so great that it will not stick at lying and falsehood, either in accusing God to us or us to God. Nay, it particularly hints that when he hath in malice tempted a poor wretch to sin, he spares not to accuse him for it, and to load him with all things that may aggravate his guilt or misery, accusing him for more than he hath really done, and for a worse estate than he is really in.[2]

2. Secondly, *His power*. Under the metaphor of a ' lion,' a beast of prey, whose innate property is to destroy, and is accordingly fitted with strength, with tearing paws, and a devouring mouth ; that as a lion would rend a kid with ease and without resistance, so are men swallowed up by him as with open mouth, so the word καταπιή signifies, he can sup them up at a draught, ἀ καταπίνω.

3. Thirdly, *His cruelty:* a 'roaring lion' implying not only his innate property to destroy, which must be a strange fierceness, but also that this innate principle is heightened and whetted on, as hunger in a lion sharpens and enrages that disposition till he get his prey, so that he becomes raving and roaring, putting an awful majesty upon cruelty, and frighting them out of endeavours or hopes of resistance, and increasing their misery with affrightments and tremblings. Thus Satan shews a fierce and truculent temper, whose power being put forth from such an implacable malice, must needs become rage and fierceness.

4. Fourthly, *His diligence:* which, together with his cruelty, are consequences of his malice and power ; he ' goes about and seeks.' He is restless in his pursuit, and diligent, as one that promiseth himself a satisfaction or joyful contentment in his conquests.

CHAPTER II.

Of the malice of Satan in particular.—The grounds and causes of that malice.—The greatness of it proved, and instances of that greatness given.

I shall first give some account of his malice, by which it shall appear we do not wrong the devil in calling him malicious, the truth of which charge will evidence itself in the following particulars :—

1. First, *The devil, though a ' spirit,' yet is a proper subject of sin.* We need no other evidence for this than what doth by daily experience result from ourselves. We have sins which our spirits and hearts do act, that relate not to the body, called ' a filthiness of the spirit,' in con-

---

[1] *Vide* Leigh Crit[ica] Sac[ra]. [Quarto, 1650, &c.—G.]
[2] The accuser of the brethren : Rev. xii. 10 ; Gen. iii. 3 ; Job i.

tradistinction to the 'filthiness of the flesh,' [2 Cor. vii. 1.] It is true, it cannot be denied but that those iniquities which have a necessary dependence upon the organs of the body, as drunkenness, fornication, &c., cannot properly, as to the formality of the act, be laid at Satan's door, though as a tempter and provoker of these men he may be called the father of these sins; yet the fore-mentioned iniquities, which are of a spiritual nature, are properly and formally committed by him, as lying, pride, hatred, and malice. And this distinction Christ himself doth hint: John viii. 44, 'When he speaketh a lie, he speaketh of his own,' where he asserts such spiritual sins to be properly and formally acted by himself. The certainty of all appears in the epithets given him—'the wicked one,' 'the unclean spirit;' as also those places that speak his fall, 'They kept not their first estate,' Jude 6; 'The angels that sinned,' 2 Peter ii. 4. If sins spiritual are in a true and proper sense attributed to the devil, then also may malice be attributed to him.

2. Secondly, *The wickedness of Satan is capable of increase*, a *magis et minus*. Though he be a wicked spirit, and as to inclination full of wickedness, though so strongly inclined that he cannot but sin, and therefore as God is set forth to us as the fountain of holiness, so is Satan called the author and father of sin, yet seeing we cannot ascribe an infiniteness to him, we must admit that, as to acts of sin at least, he may be more or less sinful, and that the wickedness of his heart may be drawn more out by occasions, motives, and provocations; besides, we are expressly taught thus much, Rev. xii. 12, 'The devil is come down, having great wrath, because his time is short.' Where we note (1.) That his wrath is called 'great,' implying greater than at other times; (2.) That external motives and incentives, as the shortness of his time, prevail with him to draw forth greater acts of fury.

3. Thirdly, *Whatsoever occasions do draw out or kindle malice to a rage, Satan hath met with them in an eminent degree, in his own fall and man's happiness.*[1] Nothing is more proper to beget malice than hurts or punishments, degradations from happiness. Satan's curse, though just, fills him with rage and fretting against God, when he considers that from the state and dignity of a blessed angel he is cast down to darkness and to the basest condition imaginable. For the part of his curse, which concerned Satan as well as the serpent, 'Upon thy belly shalt thou go, and dust shall be thy meat,' implies a state most base, as the use of the phrase proves: 'They shall lick the dust of thy feet,' Isa. xlix. 23; 'Thine enemies shall lick the dust,' Ps. lxxii. 9; 'They shall lick the dust as a serpent,' Micah vii. 17. Where the spirit is so wicked that it cannot accept the punishment of its iniquity, all punishment is as a poison, and envenoms the heart with a rage against the hand that afflicted it. Thus doth Satan's fall enrage him, and the more when he sees man enstated into a possibility of enjoying what he hath lost. The envy and pride of his heart boils up to a madness—for that is the only use that the wretchedly miserable can make of the sight of that happiness which they enjoy not,

---

[1] Quia inordinatam excellentiam affectando, ordinatam amiserunt, ideo de aliorum excellentia dolebant, et ad eam oppugnandam maliciose ferebantur.—*Am. Med.* lib. i. cap. 11. [Amesius 'Medulla Theologica,' 1627. 8vo.—G.]

especially if, having once enjoyed it, they are now deprived. This begot the rage and wrath in Cain against Abel, and afterward his murder. The eye of the wicked is evil where God is good. Hence may it be concluded that Satan, being a wicked spirit, and this wickedness being capable of acting higher or lower according to occasions, and with a suitableness thereto, cannot but shew an inconceivable malice against us, our happiness and his misery being such proper occasions for the wickedness of his heart to work upon.

4. Fourthly, *This malice in Satan must be great,*

(1.) First, *If we consider the greatness of his wickedness in so great and total an apostasy.* He is so filled with iniquity, that we can expect no small matters from him as to the workings of such cursed principles; not only is he wicked, but the spirit and extract of wickedness, as the phrase signifies, Eph. vi. 12, [πνευματικὰ τῆς πονηρίας.]

(2.) Secondly, *The Scripture lays to his charge all degrees, acts, and branches of malice;* as [1.] Anger, *in the impetuous haste and violence of it.* Rev. xii. 12, 'Great wrath,' θυμός, there signifies *excandescentia,* the inflammation of the heart and whole man, which is violent in its motion, as when the blood with a violent stream rusheth through the heart and sets all spirits on fire; and therefore this wrath is not only called great, but is also signified to be so, in its threatening 'a woe to the inhabitants of the earth.' [2.] *Indignation* is more than anger, as having more of a fixed fury; and this is applied to him, Eph. iv. 27, in that those that have this παροργισμὸς, are said 'to give place to the devil,' which is true not only in point of temptation, but also in respect of the resemblance they carry to the frame and temper of Satan's furious heart. [3.] *Hatred* is yet higher than wrath or indignation, as having deeper roots, a more confirmed and implacable resolution. Anger and indignation are but short furies, *ira brevis furor,* which, like a land-flood, are soon down, though they are apt to fill the banks on a sudden; but hatred is lasting, and this is so properly the devil's disposition, that Cain, in hating his brother, is [in] 1 John iii. 12 said to be the proper offspring and lively picture of that 'wicked one,' who is there so called rather than by the name of the devil, because the apostle would also insinuate that hatred is the masterpiece of Satan's wickedness, and that which gives the fullest character of him. [4.] All effects of his cruelty arise from this root; this makes him accuse and calumniate, this puts him upon breathing after those murders and destructions which damned spirits are now groaning under.

(3.) Thirdly, *This malice is the result of that curse laid upon Satan:* Gen. iii. 15, 'I will put enmity betwixt thee and the woman, betwixt her seed and thy seed.' Which implies, [1.] A *great enmity;* and some render it *inimicitias implacabiles,* implacable enmities. [2.] A *lasting enmity,* such as should continue as long as the curse should last. [3.] That this should be *his work and exercise,* to prosecute and be prosecuted with this enmity; so that it shews the devil's whole mind and desire is in this work, and that he is whetted on by the opposing enmity which he meets withal. It is the work of his curse, of his place, of his revenge, and that wherein all the delight he is capable of is placed. In that part of the curse, 'Dust shall be thy meat,' it is implied, if some interpret right,[1] that if Satan can be said to have any delight or ease in his condition, it is in the eating of this dust, the exercise of this enmity. No wonder, then, if Christ speak of his desires and solicitations with God to have a liberty and commission for this work: 'Satan hath desired to have thee, that he may winnow thee,' [Luke xxii. 31.]

That this curse relates not only to the serpent, who was the instrument, but also to Satan, who was the agent, is agreed by all almost. That it was not the serpent alone, but the devil speaking by it, is evinced from its speaking and reasoning. And that the curse reached further than a natural enmity betwixt a serpent and a man, is as evident, in that Christ is expressly held forth as giving the full accomplishment of this curse against Satan: 1 John iii. 8, 'The devil sinneth from the beginning; for this purpose was the Son of God manifested, that he might destroy the works of the devil,' which is a clear exposition and paraphrasis of the 'woman's seed bruising the serpent's head.'

(4.) Fourthly, *I shall add to this some few instances of Satan's malice, by which it will appear to be great.*

[1.] First, That malice must needs be great *which shews itself where there is such a load of anguish and horror that lies upon him.* He is now 'reserved in chains of darkness in hell,' 2 Peter ii. 4. He is in hell, a place of torment; or, which is all one, hell is in him. He carries it about him in his conscience, which, by God's decree, binds him to his horror like a chain. It is scarce imaginable that he should have a thought free from the contemplation of his own misery, to spend in a malicious pursuit of man. What can we think less of it than a desperate madness and revenge against God, wherein he shews his rage against heaven, and hunts after our blood as for a little water to cool his tongue; and when he finds his hand too short to pull the Almighty out of his throne, he endeavours, panther-like, to tear his image in man, and to put man, created after his image, upon blaspheming and dishonouring his Maker.

[2.] Secondly, That malice must needs be great that *seeks its own fuel, and provides or begs its own occasions, and those such as give no proper provocation to his anger.* Of this temper is his malice. He did thus with Job: he begs the commission, calumniates Job upon unjust surmises, presseth still for a further power to hurt him, insomuch that God expressly stints and bounds him—which shews how boundless he would have been if left to his own will—and gives him at last an open check, Job ii. 3, wherein he lays open the malice of his heart in three things: [1.] His own pressing urgency: 'Thou movedst me;' [2.] His destructive fury: no less would serve than Job's utter destruction; [3.] Job's innocency: all this without cause: 'Thou movedst me to destroy him without cause.'

[3.] Thirdly, That malice must needs be great that *will pursue a small matter.* What small game will the devil play rather than altogether sit out! If he can but trouble, or puzzle, or affright, yet that he will do, rather than nothing; if he can, like an adder in the

---

[1] Vide Pool 'Synop.' in loc.

path, but bite the heel, [Gen. xlix. 17,] though his head be bruised for it, he will notwithstanding busy himself in it.

[4.] Fourthly, That malice must be great which will *put itself forth where it knows it can prevail nothing, but is certain of a disappointment.* Thus did Satan tempt Christ. Those speeches, 'if thou be the Son of God,' do not imply any doubt in Satan; he knew what was prophesied of Christ, and what had been declared from heaven in testification of him, so that he could not but be certain he was God and man; and yet what base unworthy temptations doth he lay before him, as 'to fall down and worship him'! Was it that Satan thought to prevail against him? No surely; but such was his malice, that he would put an affront upon him, though he knew he could not prevail against him.

[5.] Fifthly, *The malice of wicked men is an argument of Satan's great malice.* They have an antipathy against the righteous, as the wolf against the sheep, and upon that very ground, that they are 'called out of the world.' How great this fury is, all ages have testified. This hath brought forth discord, revilings, slanders, imprisonments, spoiling of goods, banishments, persecutions, tortures, cruel deaths, as burning, racking, tearing, sawing asunder, and whatever the wit of man could devise for a satisfaction to those implacable, furious, murderous minds; and yet all this is done to men of the same image and lineage with themselves, of the same religion with themselves, as to the main; nay, sometime to men of their own kindred, their own flesh and blood, and all to those that would live peaceably in the land. What shall we say to these things? How come men to put on a savage nature, to act the part of lions, leopards, tigers, if not much worse? The reason of all we have, John viii. 54, 'Ye are of your father the devil; he was a murderer from the beginning:' as also Gen. iii. 15, 'I will put enmity between her seed and thy seed;' so that all this shews what malice is in Satan's heart, who urgeth and provokes his instruments to such bloody hatreds. Hence whoever were the agents [Rev. ii. 10] in imprisoning the saints, the malice of Satan in stirring them up to it, makes him become the author of it; 'Satan shall cast some of you into prison.'

CHAPTER III.

Of Satan's power.—His power as an angel considered.—That he lost not that power by his fall.—His power as a devil.—Of his commission.—The extent of his authority.—The efficacy of his power.—The advantages which he hath for the management of it, from the number, order, place, and knowledge of devils.

That Satan's power is great, is our next inquiry; where,

1. First, We will consider his power *as an angel.* In Ps. ciii. 20 angels are said 'to excel in strength;' and in ver. 21, as also Ps. cxlviii. 2, they are called 'God's host;' which is more fully expressed, 1 Kings xxii. 19, 'I saw the Lord sitting upon his throne, and all the host of

heaven standing by him on his right hand and on his left;' which phrase, though it import their order and observance, yet undoubtedly the main of its intendment is to set forth their power, as hosts are the strength of kings and nations. God himself, in putting on that title, 'The Lord of hosts,' makes it an evidence of his incomprehensible power, that such armies of strong and mighty creatures are at his command. But this only in the general. That which comes nearer to a particular account of their strength, is that notion of a spirit, by which they are frequently described, 'He maketh his angels spirits; his ministers flaming fire,' Ps. civ. 4. The being of a spirit is the highest our understanding is able to reach, and that it shews a being very excellent, is manifest in this, that God is pleased to represent himself to us under the notion of a spirit; not that he is truly and properly such, but that this is the most excellent being that falls under our apprehension. Besides that the term 'spirit' raiseth our understanding to conceive a being of a high and extraordinary power, it doth further tend to form our conceptions to some apprehensions of their nature. [1.] From the knowledge that we have of our own spirits. That our spirit is of a vast comprehension and activity, our thoughts, desires, reasonings, and the particular undertakings of some men of a raised spirit, do abundantly evidence. [2.] In that it represents a spiritual being, freed from the clog and hindrance of corporeity. Our own spirits are limited and restrained by our bodies, as fire, an active element, is retarded and made sluggish by matter unapt to serve its proper force, as when it is in a heap of earth; which is also sufficiently pointed at in that opposition betwixt flesh and blood, and principalities and powers, Eph. vi.; shewing that flesh and blood are a disadvantage and hindrance to the activity of a spirit. A spirit then, as incorporeal, may be conceived to move easily without molestation, quickly, imperceptibly, and irresistibly. [3.] This is yet further illustrated by the similitude of wind and fire, which are, to the common experience of all, of very great force. And it is yet further observable that the Scripture sometime speaks of the power of angels in the abstract, choosing rather to call them 'powers' than powerful, ἐξουσίαι, Col. i. 16; clearly shewing that angels are beings of vast strength, as indeed the actions done by them do abundantly testify. Such was the destroying Sennacherib's hosts in a night, the opening the prison doors for Peter, the carrying Philip in the air, and such other acts, which tend to the protection of the faithful, or punishing of the wicked.

Though this may fully satisfy us that angels excel in strength, yet the Scripture suggests another consideration relating to the office and employment of angels, where their commission shews not only a liberty for the exercise of this power, but also doth imply such a power as is fit to be commissionated to such acts. These invisible beings are called thrones, dominions, principalities, powers, Col. i. 16. It is indeed a task beyond a sober undertaking to distinguish these words, and to set their true bounds and marks of difference. This Augustine acknowledged;[1] yet may we hence conclude, [1.] That these words

[1] Quid inter se distant quatuor ista vocabula, dicant qui possunt, si tamen possunt probare quæ dicunt; ego me ista ignorare confiteor.—*Enchirid. ad Laurent.*, cap. 58.

imply a very great authority in angels; [2.] A power and strength suitable to their employment, and that God furnished them with power answerable to the work which he intended for them, in his moving the heavens, and governing the world, &c. However, in some cases, God works by instruments every way disproportionable to the service, 'that the excellency of the power might be of God,' [2 Cor. iv. 7;] yet, in the ordinary way of his working, he puts an innate, suitable force in creatures, for the acts to be done by them; as there is an innate power in the wind to blow, in the fire to burn, in herbs and plants for medicinal uses. Thus may we conceive of angels, that God using them as his host, his 'ministers to do his pleasure,' he hath endowed them with an innate natural power for those great things which he doth by them, which must not be supposed in the least derogatory to the power of God, in his ways of mercies or judgments, seeing all the strength of angels is originally from God. Hence is it that all the names of angels which we read of in Scripture carry this acknowledgment in their signification; Michael thus unfolds itself, 'Who is like God;' Gabriel thus, 'The glory of God;' and therefore may we suppose them not so much the proper names of angels, but, as Calvin noteth, *Nomina ad captum nostrum indita*, Names implying God's great power in them.[1]

Such a powerful spirit is Satan by creation. But because it will be doubted lest his fall hath bereaved him of his excellency, and cast him down from his strength, I shall evidence that he still retains the same natural power. To which purpose it is not unfit to be observed, [1.] That the same terms and names which were given to good angels, to signify their strength and commission, Col. i. 16, and ii. 10, are also given to Satan, Eph. vi. 12. Devils are called 'principalities,' 'powers,' 'rulers;' and Col. ii. 15, they have the same names which in ver. 10 were given to good angels, 'he spoiled principalities and powers.' [2.] The Scripture gives particular instances of Satan's power and working: as his raising tempests in the air, commanding fire from heaven—both which he did in prosecution of his malice against Job; his carrying the bodies of men in the air—as he did with Christ, hurrying him from the wilderness to the mountain, from thence to the pinnacle of the temple; his breaking chains and fetters of iron, Mark v. 4; his bringing diseases—instances whereof were that crooked woman whom Satan had bowed together, Luke xiii. 16, and the lunatic person, Luke ix. 31, with a great many more. [3.] It is also observable that, notwithstanding, Satan's fall hath made an alteration as to the ends, uses, and office of his power; yet, nevertheless, God makes use of this strength in him, not only as an executioner of wrath against his enemies—as when he vexed Saul by this evil spirit; and through this lying spirit, gave up Ahab to be deluded into his ruin, and inflicted plagues upon Egypt, by sending evil angels among them, 1 Sam. xvi. 14; 1 Kings xxii. 21; Ps. lxxviii. 49—but also for the trial of his own servants. Thus was Job afflicted by Satan, and Paul buffeted by his messenger.

2. Secondly, This power of his, as *a devil*, falls next under our consideration, wherein are divers particulars to be noted: as,

[1] Instit., lib. i. cap. 14, sec. 8.

(1.) First, *His commission and authority*. If any put that question to him which the Jews did to Christ, 'By what authority dost thou these things?' or, 'Who gave thee this authority?' we have the answer in John xii. 24, and xvi. 11, where he is called, 'the prince of this world;' and accordingly the Scripture speaks of a twofold kingdom, of light and of darkness; and in this we hear of Satan's seat or throne, of his servants and subjects. Yea, that which is more, the Scripture speaks of a kind of deity in Satan; he is called 'the god of this world,' 2 Cor. iv. 4; which doth not only set forth the intolerable pride and usurpation of Satan in propounding himself as such, so drawing on poor blind creatures to worship him, but also discovers his power, which by commission he hath obtained over the children of disobedience, [Zanchius.] Hence doth he challenge it as a kind of right and due from the poor Americans, and others, that they should fall down and worship him; and upon this supposition was he so intolerably presumptuous in offering the kingdoms of the world to Christ for such a service and worship.

If it be questioned what Satan's authority is, I shall answer it thus:—

[1.] First, His authority is not *absolute or unlimited*. He cannot do what he pleaseth, and therefore we do find him begging leave of God for the exerting of his power in particular cases, as when he was 'a lying spirit' in the mouth of Ahab's prophets, and in every assault he made upon Job; nay, he could not enter into the swine of the Gadarenes till he had Christ's commission for it.

[2.] Secondly, *Yet hath he a commission in general*—a standing commission, as petty kings and governors had under the Roman emperor, where they were authorised to exercise an authority and power, according to the rules and directions given them. This is clearly signified by those expressions, 'they are captives at his will,' [2 Tim. ii. 16,] and 'given up to Satan,' [1 Tim. i. 20,] as persons excommunicated; and when men are converted, they are said to be 'translated from his power,' and put under another jurisdiction, in the 'kingdom of Christ,' [Col. i. 13.] All which would have been highly improper, if a commission for Satan, and an authority for those works of darkness, had not been signified by them.

Next, let us view the *extent of this authority, both as to persons and things*. In relation to persons, the boundary of his kingdom reacheth as far as darkness. He rules in 'the dark places of the earth,' or the darkness of this world; and therefore his kingdom is hence denominated 'a kingdom of darkness.' This extends, we may well imagine, as far as heathenism reacheth, where he is worshipped as God, as far as any darkness of Mohammedanism stretcheth itself, as far as the darkness of infidelity and blindness upon the hearts of unconverted men; which, if summed up together, must needs take up the greatest part of the world by far; which is acknowledged, not only by that large expression *world*, 'prince of the world,' &c., but also by that prophetic speech of Rev. xi. 15, 'The kingdoms of this world are become the kingdoms of our Lord and his Christ,' which acknowledgeth they had not been so before, in the sense wherein we now speak.

Neither is his kingdom so bounded but that he also can, when allowed, make excursions and inroads into the kingdom of Christ, so far as to molest, disturb, and annoy his subjects; as the kings of any nation, besides the power which they exercise in their proper jurisdiction, may molest their neighbours. And Christ so far permits this as is useful to his own designs, yet still with straiter reserves and limitations to Satan, and a resolved rescue and conquest for his own people.

If we inquire the extent of his power in relation to things, we find the air in a peculiar manner permitted to him; so that he is named by it, as by one of his chief royalties, 'the prince of the power of the air.' We find also death, with the powers of it, given up to him; so that this is a *periphrasis* of him, 'He that hath the power of death,' Heb. ii. 14. And if we take notice of his large proffer to Christ of the kingdoms of the world, 'All this will I give thee,' we may imagine that his commission reacheth far this way, as rewards and encouragements to his service; which we will the readilier entertain when we find that, by God's allowance, wicked men have their 'portion in this life,' and that these are called 'their good things.'[2]

3. Thirdly, Let us proceed a step further, to *the efficacy of this authority;* which also,

(1.) First, *Upon wicked men is no less remarkable than is his commission.* He is called 'the strong man,' [Luke xi. 21,] in reference to their hearts, which he fortifies, as so many castles and garrisons, against God. He also 'rules in them' without control; his suggestions and temptations are as laws to them; he 'fills their hearts,' Acts v. 3, with his designs, and raiseth their affections to a high and greedy pursuit of them; he works in them, and by an inward force doth hurry them on to achieve his enterprises, in all this ensnaring and captivating them 'at his pleasure,' Eph. ii. 2; 2 Tim. ii. 26.

(2.) Secondly, *The saints, which are subjects of another kingdom, are still fearing, complaining, watching, praying, and spreading out their hands, with lifting up their eyes to heaven for help against him.* They complain of violence and restless assaults from him; they are sensible that he can suggest evil thoughts, and follow them with incessant importunities; that he can draw a darkness upon their understanding by bribing their wills and affections against them; that he can disturb their duties, and that because of him they cannot do the good they would. Many a fear doth he beget in their hearts; many a disquiet hour have they from him; their flesh hath no rest, and happy are they if they escape from him without broken bones; many excellent ones have been cast down by him, and for a time have been like dead men. It is sad to see so just a person as Lot under his feet; so choice a saint as David wounded almost to the death; so high an apostle as Peter, by force and fear from him, to open his mouth with curses and imprecations in the denial of his Saviour; to say nothing of the buffetings of others, which was sufficiently wearisome to Paul, and described by 'a thorn in the flesh,' 2 Cor. xii. 7; which, if a learned man think right, is compared, by a metaphor, to

---

[1] Ps. xvii. 14; Luke xv. 12, and xvi. 25.—G.

those sharp stakes upon which Christians were cruelly spitted and burnt.[1]

(3.) Thirdly, *His quick and ready accomplishment* is a further proof of the efficacy of his power. No sooner had God given him a commission in reference to Job, but he quickly raiseth the tempest, brings down the house, slays his children, brings fire from heaven; and, which would seem strange, hath the troops of the Sabeans and Chaldeans at his beck, as if they had been listed under his known command; so that in a little time he puts his malice into act.

(4.) Fourthly, If any would slight all this, as being the force of principalities and powers against flesh and blood, we may see he hath so much strength and confidence *as to grapple with an angel of light, as he did in the contesting for Moses his body*, Jude 9. This was a created angel, else he durst not sure have brought a 'railing accusation;' but in that he strove, and railingly accused, it shews he wanted not a daring boldness to second his commission and power.

4. Fourthly, It will be also requisite to lay open the *advantages he hath in the management of all this power*, which are great; as,

(1.) First, *The multitude of devils.* That there are many is not denied, upon the evidence of seven cast out of Mary Magdalene, and the legion which were settled in one poor man at once. It may be we may not credit the devil's own account of his strength so much as to believe that their number was exactly answerable to a Roman legion, which, if some speak right, was 6666; yet there being so plain an allusion to a Roman legion, and the Scripture in the recital favouring it so far as to consent to a truth in that part of the story, we can do no less than conclude that the number of devils in that person was a very great number, and so great, that the similitude of legion was proper to express it by. Besides, if the Scripture had been silent in this particular, our reason would have clearly drawn that conclusion from such premises as these, that he is the 'god' of the world, and rules in the 'children of disobedience;' for whatsoever we conceive of his power, we cannot think him omnipotent or omnipresent, these being the incommunicable attributes of the great Creator of all things, in which no creature can share with God. Being then assured that he is the tempter of all men, and that he cannot be in all places at once, we must needs apprehend the devils to be many, as is signified by that expression, 'the devil and his angels.'

(2.) Secondly, He hath also an advantage for the executing of his designs, from *that order, which from the fore-mentioned grounds we must be forced to conceive to be among devils.* I know the bold determination of the order of angels by Dionysius is justly rejected, not only by Irenæus and Augustine,[2] but also by the generality of protestants, who upon that and other grounds of like presumption do reject that author as not being the true Dionysius the Areopagite. Neither do some of our protestant authors, as Chamier and others, admit the government of angels to be monarchical, which supposition the papists would gladly make use of, as a foundation whereon to establish the universal headship of the pope, being a thing which

---

[1] σκόλοψ, Arrows[mith], Tract. Sacr., lib. ii. cap. 8, sec. 3.
[2] Lib. ii., Enchir., cap. 58.

Dionysius himself, as Chamier affirms, never dreamt of.[1] Yet do none of these authors deny an order among the angels, but willingly grant it, as clearly implied from the term *archangel* used by Paul, 1 Thes. iv. 16,[2] and from their being called God's host or army, where order is necessary for the right management of their strength, and confusion the way to the ruin of their designs. The thing they dislike is, the bold and peremptory determination of the particular orders among them, and the assignment of the several charges, employments, and stations to each; which whosoever shall do, must needs be guilty of 'intruding into things which he hath not seen.'[3] It would upon the same score be a presumptuous folly to make such a determination of the several ranks and particular employments of devils. Yet this hindereth not, but with a warrantable sobriety we may believe in the general that there is an order among the devils. Not only do these expressions, 'Beelzebub the prince of devils,' 'the devil and his angels,' and in that they are called 'principalities and powers,' warrant us so to think, but the fore-mentioned considerations about the multitude of devils will force our reason to an assent: for if they must be many, because all mankind is sensible of their assaults, they must have also an order in the management of their temptations—without which their designs of cruelty and malice must, at least in great part, fall to the ground.[4] Neither do I know well how those authors may be justly blamed, who proceed a little further in their suppositions, to tell us, as most probable,[5] that these infernal spirits do share the world among them, and are allotted to several countries and places, as their own proper charge and jurisdiction; for what other interpretation those passages in Dan. x. 13 can receive I cannot see: the prince of the kingdom of Persia withstanding the angel one and twenty days; and his help in that opposition from Michael, cannot, if things be well weighed, be properly understood of Cambyses the son of Cyrus, or a contest with any man. However, if we let this go as a thing uncertain, because this interpretation is denied by some,[6] yet that which is spoken of their order in the general, and the advantage these spirits have against us upon that consideration, seems to be past denial.

(3.) Thirdly, The advantage *of place among armies is reckoned much.* Satan seems to have something this way as an advantage of ground, in that he is styled spiritual wickedness in high places.[7] What advantage high places may be to devils and spirits we cannot further imagine, than that they, being thus above us and about us in the air, see and know our ways and actions, and so receive information from thence for their malicious proceedings against us.

(4.) Fourthly, But his greatest advantage is from *his knowledge,* which I shall a little explain in the following chapter.

[1] Panst., vol. ii. lib. ix. cap. 11. [Daniel Chamier, author of De Œcumenico Pontificio. Died 1621.—G.]   [2] Sclater, *in loc.*
[3] Cal[vin] Instit., lib. i. cap. 14, sec. 8.—[As before, see sec. 5-9.—G.]
[4] *Vide* Bayne on Eph. vi. 12.   [5] Bayne, *Ibid.*
[6] Calvin, *in loc.*   [7] Ἐν τοῖς ἐπουρανίοις, Eph. vi. 12.

CHAPTER IV.

That Satan hath a great measure of knowledge, proved by comparing him with the knowledge of Adam in innocency, and by his titles.—Of his knowledge, natural, experimental, and accessory.—Of his knowledge of our thoughts.—How far he doth not know them, and how far he doth, and by what means.—Of his knowledge of things future, and by what ways he doth conjecture them.—The advantages in point of temptation that he hath by his knowledge.

In the discovery of Satan's knowledge, I shall first give evidence and demonstration thereof. To which purpose—

1. Let us consider *the knowledge of Adam in innocency;* which being found to be great, it will thence be easily concluded that Satan's knowledge is far greater. Two notable discoveries we have of Adam's knowledge, the one was his giving of names to all creatures, Gen. ii. 29, which was not only a sign of his dominion, but also a notable instance of his understanding, seeing the names were given according to the natures of creatures; whereof Bochartus gives a large account, as the camel is called גמל, because it is apt to repay injuries; the kite, ראה, from its sharpness of sight; the pelican is named קאת, from its usual vomiting, &c.[1] The consideration of the aptness of names imposed on creatures made Plato acknowledge that it was a work above ordinary capacity. The other discovery of Adam's knowledge was his knowledge of the original of Eve at first sight, Gen ii. 23; he said, 'This is now bone of my bones, and flesh of my flesh,' &c. This instance Luther made use of to prove the knowledge that we shall have of one another in heaven; which shews that Adam's understanding was then incomparably more sublime than ours, and of a nearer approach to the knowledge which a state of glory shall furnish us withal. To this might be added a further proof from the rare inventions and excellent discoveries that some raised wits have made, of things that have laid deep and far out of the view of common capacities. As also those views, sights, and more than ordinary comprehensions which the souls of men have had, when they were a little freed from the clog and hindrance of the body, either in ecstasies or by approaching death; all which put together will go far to prove a very great measure of knowledge in Satan, if we take along with us this foundation, that in all the works of God we find the highest knowledge in the noblest being. Living creatures are more excellent than stones or trees, and therefore hath God furnished them with senses, and hath also distinguished them by higher degrees of sagacity, according to their excellency above others. Thus the ape, fox, elephant, &c., have such abilities above the worm and fly, &c., that some have questioned whether they had not some lower degrees of reason: yet as these are below man, so doth his reason far excel their greatest quickness of sense. Angels are a higher being than man—for he made him 'lower than the angels'—and consequently their knowledge is proportionably greater. So that if Adam in innocency

[1] Hierozoicon, part 1.

understood the nature of things, how much more exactly and fully must we imagine Satan to know them!

2. Secondly, But the proof is more full and direct, from those *appellations and titles which the Scripture and the experience of men have put upon him;* his usual name, Δαίμων, *quasi* Δαήμων, which—in Mat. viii. 31; Mark v. 12; Rev. xvi. 14—we translate *devil,* properly signifieth one that is wise, knowing, or skilful. And however the wickedness of that spirit hath so far dishonoured this word, that it is always, as some think, used to signify 'unclean spirits;' yet still it carries an evidence of their nature in reference to knowledge, that though they are wicked creatures, yet are they wise and knowing. It is said, Gen. iii. 1, 'The serpent was more subtle than any beast of the field;' which, though it be true literally of the serpent, whose wisdom and subtlety naturalists have abundantly noted, yet that expression hath an eye upon Satan, who was the principal agent; and the serpent there is called subtle, as influenced by Satan, whose instrument he was:[1] which we may believe, not only upon the credit of Austin and Lyra, but more securely upon the testimony of other scriptures, which name him 'the old serpent,' Rev. xvii. 9, and impute all that craft in the management of that temptation to a particular remarkable skill and subtlety of Satan. 'The serpent beguiled Eve through subtlety,' 2 Cor. xi. 3; and, if Beza conjecture right, the appellation Δαίμων do so fitly suit this history of the tree of knowledge, that the title of knowledge seems to be given him for this singular masterpiece of craft.

3. Thirdly, That Satan hath great knowledge is by these arguments discovered; but if further inquiry be made into the *nature of his knowledge,* we shall be nearer to a satisfaction in this particular; and here we may observe a threefold knowledge in Satan.

(1.) First, *A natural knowledge;* which the schoolmen have distinguished into these two: [1.] *An evening knowledge,* which he received from things created, whereby the *species* of things were impressed upon his mind, and so received, being a knowledge *à posteriori,* from the effects of things; which, because it is more dark and obscure than that which ariseth from the causes of things, they termed evening knowledge. [2.] The other is *morning knowledge,* which is a knowledge of things in the power and wisdom of God, in which he saw the ideas and images of all things. This knowledge they prefer before the other, as lines and figures are better known from mathematical instruction than by their bare tract as written in dust.[2]

(2.) Secondly, Besides this he hath an *experimental knowledge;* which is the improvement of that natural stock, by further acquisitions and attainments. And indeed Satan had very high advantages for an increase of knowledge. He had a great stock to begin withal; he hath had fit and suitable objects to work upon in his contemplations, so that by comparing things with things in so large a field of variety, and that for so many years together, it cannot be but that he

---

[1] Principaliter ad Diabolum referenda est calliditas.
[2] Cognitio Vespertina et Matutina. Barth. Sybillæ otium Theol. p. 361. Aug. in 3 Gen. et Civitat. Dei., lib. xi. cap. 29. Dr Jenison's 'Height of Israel's Idolatry,' p. 31. Ipsam creaturam melius ibi, hoc est, in sapientia Dei, tanquam in arte qua facta est, quam in ea ipsa sciunt.—*Aug.,* Civit. Dei., *ibid.*

SATAN'S TEMPTATIONS.

should be grown more experienced and subtle than he was at first; and the Scripture doth fairly countenance this supposition, by telling us of his devices, 2 Cor. ii. 11 ; of his wiles, Eph. vi. 11 ; and of his depths, Rev. ii. 24.[1] All which phrases imply that Satan hath so studied the point of temptation, that he hath now, from long experience and observation, digested it into an art and method, and that with such exactness that it is become a mystery and a depth, much covered and concealed from the notice and observation of men.

(3.) Thirdly, To both the former may be added another knowledge, which because it is from another spring, I may call it an *accessory knowledge*, consisting in occasional discoveries made to him, either when God is pleased to make known so much of his mind and purpose, as he employs him, as an instrument or servant, to execute, as he did in the case of Job and Ahab; or when he informs himself from the Scriptures, or catcheth hints of knowledge from the church and the ordinances thereof. If good angels have an increase of knowledge this way, as is evident they have, ' for to principalities and powers in heavenly places is made known by the church the manifold wisdom of God,' Eph. iii. 10, we cannot but imagine that Satan hath some addition of knowledge from such discoveries. While we are upon this point, it will be necessary to offer some satisfaction to two questions.

Quest. 1. First, Whether Satan knows our thoughts?

Ans. 1. It is undoubtedly God's prerogative to know the thoughts. He knows them intuitively, which is beyond the power of any creature: Jer. xvii. 9, ' Who can know it?' This is a challenge to all, implying the utter impossibility of it to any but to God alone ; ' I the Lord search the heart;' he knows the most inward thoughts : Rev. ii. 23, ' I am he which searcheth the reins, and the heart;' he knows them evidently and certainly: Heb. iv. 13, 'All things are naked and open[2] before him with whom we have to do.' Those secret thinkings and intendments which are hid from others, and which we ourselves cannot distinctly read, because of their secret intricacy or confusedness, yet the very inside and outside of them are uncased, cut up and anatomised by his eye; in all which expressions God is careful to reserve this to himself, ' I the Lord do it,' or ' I am he, &c., that searcheth ;' and signifies that none else is able to do the like.

Ans. 2. Yet Satan can do much this way; for if we consider how he can come so near to our spirits, as to communicate his injections to us, and that he often entertains a dispute with us in this secret way of access that he hath to our thoughts ; if we observe his arguings, his answers and replies to our refusals, so direct, so pertinent, so continued, we shall be constrained to grant that he can do more this way than is commonly imagined. That I may explain this with a due respect to God's prerogative of knowing the heart, I shall,

1. First, *Shew that there are two things which are clearly out of Satan's reach.* [1.] Our future thoughts; he cannot tell what shall be our thoughts for time to come. He may possibly adventure to tell what suggestions he resolves to put into our hearts, but what shall be our resolves and determinations thereupon he knows not. This is singled out as one part of God's prerogative, that he knoweth the

[1] Νοήματα, μεθοδείας, βάθη. [2] Γυμνά, τετραχηλισμένα.

determinate purposes and resolves of the heart aforehand, because he turneth the heart as he pleaseth, Prov. xxi. 1. [2.] Our present formed thoughts, the immediate and imminent[1] acts of the mind he cannot directly see into. He may tell what floating thinkings he hath put into our heart, but our own proper thoughts, or formed resolves, he cannot directly view. This is also particularly insisted on as proper to God alone: John ii. 24, 25, 'Christ knew all men,' so directly, that 'he needed not that any should testify of man.' This Satan stands in need of; he sometimes knows men and their thoughts, but he needs a sign or notification of these thoughts, and cannot immediately look into them. The reason why Christ needed not this, is rendered thus: 'For he knew what was in man,' Mat. xii. 25, that is, intuitively he knew his thoughts, and could immediately read them.

2. Secondly, *I shall endeavour to explain how much, or how far he can pry into our thoughts.* Several things are granted which argue Satan can go a great way toward a discovery. As,

(1.) First, *That he knows the objects in our fancy or phantasms*, and this as clearly as we do behold things with our eyes. And the proof given hereof is this: that there are diabolical dreams, in which the devil cannot create new species, and such as our senses were never acquainted withal, as to make a blind man dream of colours, but that he can only call forth and set in order those objects, of which our imagination doth retain the shadows or impressions; and this he could not do if he did not visibly behold them in our fancy.[2]

(2.) Secondly, It is certain he knows *his own suggestions and temptations darted into our minds*, upon which he can at present know what our thoughts are busied upon.

(3.) Thirdly, He knows *the secret workings of our passions, as love, desire, fear*, &c., because these depend upon, or are in a concomitancy of the motions of the blood and spirits, which he can easily discern, though their motions and workings may be kept secret from the observation of all bystanders.

(4.) Fourthly, Some go further, as Scotus, *(referente Barthol. Sybilla,)*[3] supposing that he knows what is in our thoughts at any time, only he knows not to what these thoughts incline; but I leave this to those that can determine it certainly. In the meantime I proceed,

3. Thirdly, *To shew what a guessing faculty he hath of what he doth not directly know.* He hath such grounds and advantages for conjecture, that he seldom fails of finding our mind. As,

(1.) First, *His long experience hath taught him what usually men do think*, in such cases as are commonly before them. By a cunning observation of their actions and ways he knows this.

(2.) Secondly, *He by study and observation knows our temper and inclination*, and consequently what temptations do most suit them, and how we do ordinarily entertain them.

[1] Query, 'immanent'?—ED.
[2] Dr Jenison's 'Height of Israel's Idolatry,' p. 35. *Vide* Godwin's 'Child of Light,' p. 65.
[3] Quest. Peregrinarum p. 392. Dæmones cognoscunt cogitationes nostras, quantum ad subjectum, objectum et affectum, non autem quantum ad finem. Sciunt quid cogitamus, sed ignorant ad quem finem.

(3.) Thirdly, He knows this the more, *by taking notice of our prayers, our complainings and mournings over our defects and miscarriages.*

(4.) Fourthly, *He is quick and ready to take notice of any exterior sign, by which the mind is signified,* as the pulse, the motion of the body, the change of the countenance, all which do usually shew the assent or dissent of the mind, and at least tell him what entertainment his offers have in our thoughts.

(5.) Fifthly, Being so quick-sighted, he can understand *those particular signs which would escape the observation of the wisest men.*[1] There are some things small in themselves, and therefore unobserved, which yet to wise men are very great *indicia* of things. The like may be said of us, in reference to our inclinations, our acceptance or resistance of temptations, which yet he hath curiously marked out.

(6.) Sixthly, No doubt but he hath ways to *put us upon a discovery of our thoughts, while we conceal them,* as by continuing and prosecuting temptations or suggestions, till our trouble or passions do some way discover how it is with us. By all which it appears that his guessings and conjectures do seldom fail him. It is now time to speak to the other question, which is,

Quest. 2. Whether and how far Satan knows things to come?

Ans. To this I shall return answer in these two conclusions:

Conclusion 1. First, There is a way of knowing future things, *which is beyond the knowledge of devils, and proper only to God,* Isa. xli. 23; there God puts the competition betwixt himself and idols, about the truth of a deity, upon this issue, that ' he that can shew the things that are to come hereafter, he is God;' which because they cannot do, he doth hereby evince them to be no gods. If Satan could truly and properly have done this, he had had a plea for a godhead. In divine predictions two things are to be considered. [1.] The matter foretold; when the events of things contingent, and as to second causes casual, depending upon indeterminate causes, are foretold. [2.] The manner; when these things are not uncertainly, or conjecturally, or darkly, but clearly, certainly, infallibly, and fully predicted. Of this nature are divine predictions, which Satan cannot perform, nor yet the angels in heaven.

Conclusion 2. Secondly, *Yet Satan hath such advantages for the knowledge of future things, and such means and helps for a discovery of them, that his conjectures have often come to pass.*

[1.] First, He knows *the causes of things, which are secret to us.* Upon which he seems to foretell many things strange to us; as a physician may foretell the effects, workings, and issues of a disease, as seeing them in the causes, which would pass for little less than prophecy among the vulgar. Thus an astrologer foretells eclipses, which would be taken for a divine excellency, where the knowledge of the ground of these foretellings had not taken away the wonder.

[2.] Secondly, Many things are made known to him *by immediate divine revelation.* We know not the intercourse betwixt God and Satan in the matter of Job. Satan having obtained his commission to

---

[1] Deprehendas animi tormenta latentia ex ægrotorum facie. Sæpe tacens vocem verbaque vultus habet.

afflict him, might have made a long prophecy of what should come to pass in reference to Job, his children and substance. How many such predictions he might make, we little know.

[3.] Thirdly, He hath *a deep insight in affairs of kingdoms and states*, and so might, from his experience and observation, easily conjecture mutations and alterations. A politician may do much this way. For aught we know, Satan's prophecy, in the likeness of Samuel, to Saul, of his ruin, and the translation of his kingdom to David, might be no more than a conjectural conclusion, from his comparing the order of the present providence with former threatenings and promises.

[4.] Fourthly, He hath *a greater understanding of Scripture prophecies, than ordinarily the wisest men have*, so that at second hand he might be able to foretell what shall come to pass; whilst we that do not so clearly see into Scripture predictions, may not be able to find out the matter. Hence by oracle he foretold Alexander of his success, which he knew from the prophecy of Daniel, chap. xi., long before.[1]

[5.] Fifthly, He hath advantage from his nature *as a spirit, by which he overhears and sees the private actings, complottings, and preparations of men in reference to certain undertakings*, and can easily, by his agents, communicate such counsels or resolves in remote countries and kingdoms, which must pass for real predictions, if the event answer accordingly.

[6.] Sixthly, *He can foretell, and with probability of success, such things as he by temptation is about to put men upon*, especially seeing he can choose such instruments as he, from experience, knows are not likely to fail his enterprise.

[7.] Seventhly, To this may be added, *the way and manner by which he expresseth himself, either in doubtful or enigmatical terms, or in general expressions*, which may be applied to the event, what way soever it should happen. Of these, authors have observed many instances, which were superfluous to enumerate.[2]

Satan's knowledge being thus explained, it is easy to imagine what an advantage it is to him in the management of his temptations. For,

First, He by this means knows our tempers and dispositions.

Secondly, And what is most likely to prevail with us.

Thirdly, How inclinable we are upon any motion made to us, and what hope to gain upon us.

Fourthly, He knows fit times, seasons, and advantages against us.

Fifthly, He knows how to pursue suggestions, and can choose strong reasons to urge us withal.

Sixthly, He knows how to delude our senses, to disturb our passions.

Seventhly, He knows all the ways and arts of affrightments, vexations, disquietments, hindrances, and disturbances of duty.

[8.] Eighthly, He by this means is furnished *with skill for his public cheats and delusions in the world;* how to amuse, astonish, and amaze men into errors and mistakes, which he hath always endeavoured with very great success in the world, as we shall see hereafter.

---

[1] Invictus eris Alexander.—*Plutarch in vit Alexandri.*

[2] Non non superabit Gallus Apulum. Ibis redibis nunquam per bella peribis.

CHAPTER V.

Instances of Satan's power.—Of witchcraft, what it is.—Satan's power argued from thence.—Of wonders.—Whether Satan can do miracles?—An account of what he can do that way.—His power argued from apparitions and possessions.

I shall add, in the fifth place, some particular instances of his power, in which I shall insist upon these four—witchcraft, wonders, apparitions, and possessions.

1. First, *Witchcraft* affords a very great discovery of Satan's power. But because some give such interpretations of witchcraft, as, if true, would wholly take away the force of this instance, I shall first endeavour to establish a true notion of witchcraft; and secondly, from thence argue Satan's power.

(1.) First, Though the being of witches is not directly denied, because the authority of Scripture—Exod. xxii. 18; Deut. xviii. 10, &c.—hath determined beyond controversy that such there are; yet some will allow no other interpretation of the word,[1] than a skill and practice in the art of poisoning, because the Septuagint doth interpret the Hebrew word, מכשפה, by φάρμακον, *veneficam;* which apprehension they strengthen by the authority of Josephus,[2] who giveth this account of the law, 'Let none of the children of Israel use any deadly poison, or any drug wherewith he may do hurt,' &c. It is easy to observe that this conceit ariseth from a great inobservancy of the reason of the application of these words, φάρμακος and *veneficus*, to witchcraft, in Greek and Latin authors.

Witchcrafts were supposed to be helped forward by the strength of several herbs, and these, by incantations and other ceremonies at their gathering, imagined to attain a poisonous and evil quality or efficacy for such effects as were intended to be produced by them, as appears by Ovid, Virgil, and other authors.[3] Hence was it that the word φάρμακος became applicable to any sort of witchcraft. To this may be added, that such persons were resorted to for help against diseases, [*vide* Leigh. Crit. Sac. in Voc.] As also that they used unguents

---

[1] Scot, 'Discovery of Witchcraft,' lib. vi. cap. 1.   [2] Antiq. lib. iv. cap. 8.
[3] Here quotations are given somewhat imperfectly and inaccurately from Ovid and Virgil. The following are correct:—

'Non facient ut vivat amor Medeides herbæ
Mistaque cum magicis venena Marsa Sonis.'
Ovid, Art. Amand., ii. 98, 99.

'Has herbas atque hæc Ponto mihi lecta venena.
Ipse dedit Mœris: nascuntur plurima Ponto.
His ego sæpe lupum fieri et se condere silvis
Mærim, sæpe animas imis excire sepulchris.'
Virgil, Bucol. Ecl. viii.

Φαρμακία, philtrum, et magicas actiones quæ in imaginibus, et characteribus, certis verbis, ac similibus consistunt, significat. Unde pharmaceutria appellatur, Idyllium ii. Theocriti et Eclog. viii. Virgilii. Et Antiquis etiam vocabulum φαρμακίας, pro omni veneficii genere, quo vel hominibus, vel jumentis, vel frugibus, seu carminibus, seu aliis modis nocetur, accipere, manifeste patet ex Platone, lib. x. de Legibus. Et apud Aristot. Hist. Animal., cap. 25, φαρμακίδες nominantur. Et Apocal., cap. 18, φαρμακία pro præstigiis et imposturis sumitur.—*Dan Sennert.*, tom. iii. lib. vi. part 9. cap 2.

for transportations. Hence Godwin [Jew. Antiq., lib. iv. cap. 10] renders φαρμάκους by *unguentarios.* Diascorides [Cap. de Rhamno] hath an expression to this purpose, 'that the branch of that tree, being placed before the doors, doth drive away τῶν φαρμάκων κακουργίας, witchcrafts.' It were ridiculous to say it drives away poisonings; which is a sufficient evidence that the Grecians used that word to signify another kind of witchcraft than that which this mistake would establish. Besides this, the Scripture doth afford two strong arguments against this interpretation of witchcraft.

[1.] That this word is ranked with others, as being of the same alliance, which will carry the apprehensions of any considerate man to effects done by the help of Satan, in an unusual way, as Deut. xviii. 10, 'There shall not be found among you any that maketh his son or his daughter to pass through the fire'—this is not the consuming of their children to Moloch, but by way of lustration, a mock baptism, a piece of witchcraft, to preserve from violent death—'or that useth divination, an observer of times, or an enchanter, or a witch,' &c.[1] The very neighbourhood of the witch will tell us that this witch must be a diviner, divination being the general term, comprehending the seven particulars following.[2] It would be a harsh straining to put in the poisoner, in the sense of our opposites, among the diviners. Yet the second argument is more cogent, which is this: That among those whom Pharaoh called together to encounter with Moses, Exod. vii. 11, we find witches or sorcerers expressed by the same word, מכשפים, which is used in Exod. xxii. and Deut. xviii. What can more certainly fix the interpretation of the word than this place, where the end of Pharaoh's calling them together was, not to poison Moses and Aaron, but by enchantment to outvie them in point of miracles? which will shew that witchcraft is not poisoning, but the doing of strange acts by the aid of Satan. Neither was this the act of one man—who might possibly, together with that present age, be under a mistake concerning witches, though it be a thing not to be supposed—but long after him, Nebuchadnezzar, in Dan. ii. 4, being astonished with his dreams, calls for the sorcerers or witches, and magicians, to give him the interpretation; which had been a matter very improper for them, if their skill had lain only in mixing poisons.[3]

When we have thus silenced this imagination, we have yet another to encounter with, and that is, Of those that think these witches, of which the fore-cited texts do speak, are but mere cheats, and by some tricks of delusion and legerdemain pretend they can do things which indeed they cannot do at all; and yet finding death threatened to such, which, in a business of mere juggling, would seem too great a severity, they have framed this answer to it,[4] that the death is threatened, not for juggling, but for their presumptuous and blasphemous undertaking to do things that belong to a divine power, and for taking

---

[1] Fuller, Pisg. Sight., lib. iv. cap. 7, p. 128. Maimon[ides.] *Vide* Pool, *in loc.*
[2] Godwin's Jewish Antiq., lib. iv. cap. 40, Pool, *in loc.*
[3] Witchcraft is reckoned as distinct from murder in Gal. v. 20, 21.
[4] Scot Witchcraft, lib. vi. cap. 2.

his name in vain. Or, as others are pleased to say,[1] though they have no real power, they are justly punished for the belief they have, that they can do such mischief, joined with their purpose to do it, if they can.

In answer to this apprehension, I shall not much insist upon these reasons, which yet are sufficiently weak—the latter accusing God's laws of unreasonable severity, and the former accusing them of unnecessary redundancy, seeing enough in other places is provided against blasphemers[2]—but shall offer a consideration or two, which I judge will be of force to rectify the mistake.

[1.] First, Though it cannot be denied but that a great many cheats there have been in all ages, by which men have endeavoured to raise the repute and esteem of their own skill and excellencies, or for other base ends; yet, from hence to conclude that all these things that have been done under the name of witchcraft were such, must be an unsufferable piece of insolence; not only denying that credit which all sober men owe to history, to the constant belief of all ages, to the faithfulness and wisdom of judges, jurors, witnesses, laws, and sanctions, but also dangerously overthrowing all our senses; so that at this rate we may well question whether we really eat, drink, move, sleep, and anything else that we do. This reason is urged by grave and serious men.[3]

[2.] Secondly, It cannot be imagined that such things are merely delusory, where the voluntary confessions of so many have accused themselves and others, not of thinking or juggling, but of really acting and doing such things—with such circumstances as have particularised time, place, thing, and manner.

[3.] Thirdly, The real effects done by the power of witchcraft shew it not to be delusion. Such are the transportation of persons many miles from their habitations, and leaving them there; their telling things done in remote places; raising of storms and tempests; vomiting of pins, needles, stones, cloth, leather, and such like; and these, some of them, attested by sober and intelligent persons who were eye-witnesses. Large accounts you have of these in Bodinus, Sprengerius, and several others that have borrowed these relations from them.[4]

The notion of poisonings, or delusory jugglings, being below what the Scripture intends to set forth as witchcraft, it is evident that witchcraft is a power of doing great things by the aid of the devil; by which our way is open to improve this instance, to demonstrate—

[1] Hobbes' Leviath., cap. ii. p. 7.
[2] Tenison, Hobbes' Creed Exam. Art. 4, p. 63. [Tenison, Archbishop of Canterbury: 'The Creed of Mr (Thomas) Hobbes Examined.' London, 1670, 8vo.—G.]
[3] Baxter: 'Sin against the Holy Ghost,' p. 83. J. Glanvil: 'Considerations of Witchcraft,' p. 6. Tenison against Hobbes, Art. 4, p. 59.
[4] Vide Epist. D. Balthasaris Han. M.D. *in calce,* tom. iii. Oper. Dan. Sennerti *de fœmina fascinatâ in cujis cute, literæ* N.B. notæ Crucis † à capite ad calcem, cum astronomicorum et chymicorum characteribus, rosæ figura in dextra et trifolii in sinistrâ artificiosè picta cum Anno Christi 1635, cor servatoris telis transfixum, et imago stulti, cum verbo Germanico *Narr,* procumbebant. [Dr More.] Mr Baxter *ut supra.* Dan. Sennertus, tom. iii. lib. vi. par. 9; varias historias enumerat de morbis incantatione inductis. Ex. Jo. Langio, Alex. Benedicto, Cornel. Gemmæ, Foresto, et aliis.

which was the second thing promised—that Satan's power must be great. For,

[1.] First, It is acknowledged that a great part of those things that are done in this matter, as concurrent with, or helpful toward the promoting of such acts, are Satan's proper works—as the troubling of the air, raising storms, apparitions, various shapes and appearances, transportations from place to place, and a great many more things of wonder and amazement, all which exceed human power.[1]

[2.] Secondly, Many things of wonder done by such persons, to which some suppose the secret powers of herbs or things contribute their natural aids or concurrence, are evidences of Satan's deep knowledge of and insight into natural causes. Of this nature is that ointment with which witches are said to besmear themselves in order to their transportation; the power and efficacy whereof is by some imagined to consist in this, that it keeps the body tenantable and in a fit condition to receive the soul by re-entry after such separations, as, by all circumstances are concluded, have been really made in pursuit of those visionary perambulations and transactions; which things, if they be so—as they are not improbable—witches have them from Satan's discovery, and they are to be ascribed to his power.[2]

[3.] Thirdly, Those actions that are most properly the witch's own actions, and in which the power of hurting doth, as some suppose, reside, are notwithstanding either awakened or influenced by Satan; so though we grant, what some would have, that the power of hurting is a natural power, and a venomous magnetism of the witch, and that her imagination, by her eye darts those malignant beams which produce real hurts upon men—after the manner of the imagination's force upon a child in the womb, which hath, as by daily experience and history is confirmed, produced marks, impressions, deformities, and wounds—and that Satan doth but cheat the witch into a belief of his aid in that matter; that with a greater advantage he may make use of her power, without which he could do nothing; yet even this speaks his ability, in that at least he doth awaken and raise up that magical force which otherwise would be asleep, and so puts the sword into their hand. Yet some attribute far more to him—to wit, the infusion of a poisonous ferment—by that action of sucking the witch in some part of the body—by which not only her imagination might be heightened by poisonous streams breathed in, which might infect blood and spirits with a noxious tincture.[3]

2. The second grand instance of his power I shall produce from those actions of *wonder and astonishment which he sometime performs, which indeed have been so great that they have occasioned that question—*

---

[1] Helmont. Magnet. Vuln. Cura., sec. 87.

[2] Dr More:—Death consists not so much in an actual separation of soul and body as in the indisposition and unfitness of the body for vital union. What is the meaning else of that expression, 'Whether in the body or out of the body I cannot tell,' except the soul may be separated from the body without death ?—*J. Glanvil*, 'Witchcraft,' pp. 15, 18.

[3] Helmont, *ubi supra.* Avicenna; *vide* Barthol. Sybilla.; Perig. Quæst, p. 401. Nescio quis teneros oculos, &c. Glanvil, 'Witchcraft,' p. 24; Helmont, *ut supra*, sec. 102. Satan itaque vim magicam hanc excitat (secus dormientem et scientia exterioris hominis impeditam) in suis mancipiis.—*Glanvil*, 'Witchcraft,' p. 18.

Whether Satan can do miracles?

To this we answer—

(1.) *That God alone can work miracles*, a miracle being a real act, done visibly, and above the power of nature. Such works some have ranked into three heads:[1] [1.] Such as created power cannot produce; as to make the sun stand still or go backward. [2.] Such as are in themselves produceable by nature,[2] but not in such an order; as to make the dead to live, and those that were born blind to see, which is strongly argued, John ix. 32, to be above human power; and, John x. 21, to be above the power of devils. [3.] Such as are the usual works of nature, yet produced, above the principles and helps of nature, as to cure a disease by a word or touch.

Things that are thus truly and properly miraculous are peculiarly works of God; neither can it be imagined, that since he hath been pleased to justify his commands, ways, and messages, by such mighty acts—2 Cor. xii. 12; Heb. ii. 4; John x. 38—and also hath been put to it, to justify himself and his sole supreme being and godhead from false competitors—Ps. lxxxvi. 10, and lxxii. 18—by his miraculous works, it cannot be imagined, I say, that he would permit any created being, much less Satan, to do such things.

(2.) Secondly, *Though Satan cannot do things miraculous, yet he can do things wonderful and amazing—mira non miracula*. And in this point lies the danger of delusion, as Christ foretells: Mat. xxiv. 24, 'False Christs shall arise, and shew great signs and wonders.' In 2 Thes. ii. 4, the apostle tells us, 'The coming of antichrist shall be with all power, and signs, and wonders'—that is, as some interpret,[3] with the power of signs and wonders; which, however they be lying, both in reference to the design they drive at—which is to propagate errors—and also in their own nature, being truly such, in respect of their form, false as miracles, being indeed no such matter, but juggling cheats; yet, notwithstanding, there is no small cunning and working of Satan in them, insomuch that the uncautious and injudicious are 'deceived by those wonders that he hath power to do,' Rev. xiii. 13. In this matter, though we are not able to give a particular account of these underground actions, yet thus much we may say—

[1.] First, That in many cases his great acts, that pass for miracles, are no more *but deceptions of sense*. Naturalists have shewn several feats and knacks of this kind. Jo. Bap. Porta[4] hath a great many ways of such deceptions, by lamps and the several compositions of oils, by which not only the colours of things are changed, but men appear without heads, or with the heads of horses, &c. The like deceptions are wrought by glasses of various figures and shapes. If art can do such things, much more can Satan.

[2.] Secondly, He can mightily work upon *the fancy and imagination;* by which means men are abused into a belief of things that are not; as in dreams, the fancy presents things which are really imagined to be done and said, whenas they are visions of the night, which vanish

---

[1] Polanus, 1632.
[2] Tho[mas Aquinas] Cont. Gent., lib. iii. cap. 101, cited by Sclater on 2 Thes. ii. 9. [4to, 1627, pp. 148, 149.—G.]
[3] Sclater, *in loc.*
[4] Magia Naturalis, lib. ii. cap. 17.

when the man is awake; or as in melancholy persons, the fancy of men doth so strongly impose upon them, that they believe strange absurd things of themselves—that they have horns on their head, that they are made of glass, that they are dead, and what not. If fancy, both asleep and awake, may thus abuse men into an apprehension of impossible things, and that with confidence, no wonder if Satan, whose power reacheth thus far, as was before proved, doth take this advantage for the amusing of men with strange things. Nebuchadnezzar his judgment, Dan. iv. 25, whereby he was 'driven from men, and ate grass as oxen,' was not a metamorphosis, or real change into an ox. This all expositors reject as too hard. Neither seems it to be only his extreme necessity and low estate, whereby he seemed to be little better than a beast, though Calvin favour this interpretation;[1] but but by that expression, ver. 25, 'then my understanding came to me,' it seems evident, as most commentators think, that his understanding was so changed in that punishment that he imagined himself to be a beast, and behaved himself accordingly, by eating grass, and lying in the open fields. There are several stories to this purpose of strange transformations, as the bodies of men into asses, and other beasts, which Augustine thinks to be nothing else but the devil's power upon the fancy.[2]

[3.] Thirdly, There are wonderful *secrets in nature, which if cunningly used and applied to fit things and times, must needs amaze vulgar heads;* and though some of these are known to philosophers and scholars, yet are there many secret things locked from the wisest men, whose powers and natures because they know not, they may also be deluded by them. Augustine[3] reckons up many instances, as the loadstone, the stone pyrites, selenites, the fountain of Epirus, that can kindle a torch, and many more; and determines that many strange things are done by the application of these natural powers, either by the wit of man or diabolical art. To this purpose he gives an account of an unextinguishable lamp, $Λύχνος$ $ἄσβεστος$, in a temple of Venus, which allured men to worship there, as to an unquestionable deity, when in truth the thing was but an ingenious composition from the stone asbeston, of which Pliny makes mention, that being kindled, it will not be quenched with water.[4] Of this nature were those lamps found in several vaults accompanying the ashes of the dead, reserved there in urns, both in England and elsewhere.[5] If men by such helps find such easy ways to delude men, what exactness of workmanship and seeming wonders may be expected from Satan upon such advantages!

[4.] Fourthly, Many of his wonders may challenge *a higher rise.* Satan knows the secret ways of nature's operations, and the ways of accelerating or retarding those works; so that he cannot only do what nature can do, by a due application of active to passive principles,[6] and the help of those seminal powers that are in things, but he may be supposed to perform them in a quicker and more expeditious man-

---

[1] Calvin, *in loc.*   [2] Civit. Dei, lib. xviii. cap. 18.
[3] De Civit. Dei, lib. xxi. cap. 5, 6.   [4] Plin., lib. xxviii.
[5] *Vide* L. Vives Comment. in lib. xxi. cap. 6. De Civit. Dei.
[6] Determinata activa ad determinata passiva applicando.

ner. Thus worms, flies, and serpents, that are bred of putrefaction, Satan may speedily produce; and who can tell how far this help may reach in his works of wonders?

[5.] Fifthly, *The secret way of Satan's movings and actings is no small matter in these affairs.* How many things do common jugglers by the swift motions of their hands, that seem incredible! Thus they make the bystanders believe they change the substances, natures, and forms of things, when they only, by a speedy conveyance, take these things away, and put others in their room. They that shall consider Satan as a spirit, subtle, imperceptible, quick of motion, &c., will easily believe him to be more accomplished for such conveyances than all the men in the world.

Having now seen the way of his wonders, let us next consider the advantage he hath by such actions. If we look upon Simon Magus, Acts viii. 10, 11, we find that he by these ways had a general influence upon the people, ' To him they all gave heed, from the least to the greatest;' and that his actions were reckoned no less than miraculous, as done by 'the mighty power of God.' If we go from hence to the magicians of Pharaoh, Exod. vii. 11, it is said, ' They did so with their enchantments,' which, howsoever the matter was, prevailed so with Pharaoh and the court, that they saw no difference betwixt the wonders done by Moses and them, save that, it may be, they thought Moses the more skilful magician. But besides this, if we consider what they did, it will argue much for his power, if we can imagine, as some do,[1] that they turned their rods into real serpents; the power is evident: and there is this that favours that opinion; it is said they could not make lice, which seems to imply they really did the other things, and it had been as easy to delude the senses in the matter of lice as in the rods, if it had been no more than a delusion. Neither are some awanting to give a reason of such a power—viz., serpents, lice, &c., being the offspring of putrefaction; by his dexterous application of the seminal principles of things, he might quickly produce them. If we go lower, and take up with the opinion of those that think that they were neither mere delusions, nor yet true serpents; but real bodies like serpents, though without life, this will argue a very great power.[2] Or if we suppose, as some do,[3] that Satan took away the rods, and secretly conveyed serpents in their stead, or—which is the lowest apprehension we can have—that Pharaoh's sight was deceived, the matter is still far from being contemptible, forasmuch as we see the spectators were not able to discern the cheat.

3. Thirdly, The next instance produceable for evidencing his power is that *of apparitions.* It cannot be denied but that the fancy of melancholic or timorous persons is fruitful enough to create a thousand bugbears; and also that the villainy of some persons hath been designedly employed to deceive people with mock apparitions—of which abundance of instances might be given from the knavery of the papists, discovered to the world beyond contradiction; but all this will not conclude that there are no real appearances of spirit or devils. Such sad effects in all ages there have been of these things, that most men will take it for an undeniable truth.

---

[1] Tho., Cajetan, Delrio.   [2] Barth. Sybilla Pereg. Quæst., p. 372.   [3] Rivetus.

Instead of others, let the apparition at Endor to Saul come to examination. Some indeed[1] will have us believe that all that was but a subtle cheat managed by that old woman; and that neither Samuel nor the devil did appear, but that the woman, in another room by herself, or with a confederate, gave the answer to Saul. But whosoever shall read that story, and shall consider Saul's bowing and discourse, and the answers given, must acknowledge that Saul thought at least he saw and spake with Samuel; and indeed the whole transaction is such, that such a cheat cannot be supposed.

Satisfying ourselves, then, that there was an apparition, we must next inquire whether it was true Samuel or Satan. It cannot be denied but that many judge it was true Samuel, but their reasons are weak.[2]

[1.] That proof from Ecclesiasticus xlvi. 23, is not canonical with us.

[2.] That he was called Samuel, is of no force. Scripture often gives names of things according to their appearances.

[3.] That things future were foretold, was but from conjecture; in which Satan yet, all things considered, had good ground for his guessing.

[4.] That the name Jehovah is oft repeated, signifies nothing. The devil is not so scarce of words. 'Jesus I know,' saith that spirit in the Acts.

[5.] That he reproved sin in Saul, is no more than what the devil doth daily to afflicted consciences in order to despair.

I must go then with those that believe this was Satan in Samuel's likeness.

[1.] Because God refused to answer Saul by prophets or Urim; and it is too harsh to think he would send Samuel from the dead, and so answer him in an extraordinary way.

[2.] This, if it had been Samuel, would have given too much countenance to witchcraft, contrary to that check to Ahaziah, 2 Kings i. 3, 'Is it not because there is not a God in Israel, that ye go to inquire of Baal-zebub?'

[3.] The prediction of Saul's death, though true for substance, yet failed as to the exactness of time, for the battle was not fought the next day.

[4.] The acknowledgment of the witch's power, 'Why hast thou disquieted me?' shews it could not be true Samuel, the power of witchcraft not being able to reach souls at rest with God.

[5.] That expression of 'gods ascending out of the earth,' is evidently suspicious.

The reality of apparitions being thus established, Satan's power will be easily evinced from it. To say nothing of the bodies in which spirits appear, the haunting of places and persons, and the other effects done by such appearances, speak abundantly for it.

4. Fourthly, The last instance is *of possessions*, the reality of which can no way be questioned, because the New Testament affords so much for it. I shall only note some things as concerning this head. As,

(1.) First, The multitudes of men possessed. Scarce was there

---

[1] Scot. 'Witchcraft,' lib. vii. cap. 12. [2] *Vide* Pool Synops. *in loc.*

anything in which Christ had more opportunities to shew his authority than in casting out of Satan. Such objects of compassion he met with in every place.

(2.) Secondly, The multitudes of spirits in one person is a consideration not to be passed by.

(3.) Thirdly, These persons were often strongly acted, sometime with fierceness and rage, Mat. viii. 28; some living without clothes and without house, Luke viii. 27; some by an incredible strength breaking chains and fetters, Mark v. 3.

(4.) Fourthly, Sometime the possessed were sadly vexed and afflicted, cast into the fire and water, &c.

(5.) Fifthly, Some were strangely influenced. We read of one, Acts xvi. 16, that had a spirit of divination, and told many things to come, which we may suppose frequently came to pass, else she could have brought 'no gain to her master by soothsaying.' Another we hear of whose possession was with a lunacy, and had fits at certain times and seasons. The possessed person with whom Mr Rothwell discoursed, within the memory of some living, could play the critic in the Hebrew language.[1]

(6.) Sixthly, In some the possession was so strong, and so firmly seated, that ordinary means and ways could not dispossess them: 'This kind comes not out but by prayer and fasting,' Mat. xvii. 21; which shews that all possession was not of one kind and manner, nor alike liable to ejection.

(7.) Seventhly, To all these may be added *obsessions:* where the devil afflicts the bodies of men, disquiets them, haunts them, or strikes in with their melancholy temper, and so annoys by hideous and black representations. Thus was Saul vexed by 'an evil spirit from the Lord,' which as most conceive was the devil working in his melancholy humour. That the devil should take possession of the bodies of men, and thus act, drive, trouble, and distress them, so distort, distend, and rack their members; so seat himself in their tongues and minds that a man cannot command his own faculties and powers, but seems to be rather changed into the nature of a devil than to retain anything of a man, this shews a power in him to be trembled at.

Satan's power being thus explained and proved, I shall next speak something of his cruelty.

CHAPTER VI.

Of Satan's cruelty.—Instances thereof in his dealing with wounded spirits, in ordinary temptations of the wicked and godly, in persecutions, cruelties in worship.—His cruel handling of his slaves.

He that shall consider his malice and power, must unavoidably conclude him to be cruel. Malice is always so where it hath the advantage of a proportionable strength and opportunity for the effecting of its hateful contrivances. It banisheth all pity and commiseration,

[1] *Vide* Clark's Lives. ['The Lives of Thirty-two English Divines.' Folio. 1677. 3d ed. p. 671, *seq.*—G.]

and follows only the dictate of its own rage, with such fierceness, that it is only limited by wanting power to execute. We may then say of Satan, that according to his malice and power such is his cruelty. The truth of this will be abundantly manifested by instances: as,

1. First, *From his desperate pursuits of advantage upon those whose spirits are wounded.* The anguish of a distressed conscience is unspeakably great, insomuch that many are, as Heman, Ps. lxxxviii. 15, 'even distracted, while they suffer the terrors of the Almighty.' These, though they look round about them for help, and invite all that pass by to pity them, 'because the hand of the Lord hath touched them,' [Job xix. 21,] yet Satan laughs at their calamity, and mocks at them under their fears, and doth all he can to augment the flame. He suggests dreadful thoughts of an incensed majesty, begets terrible apprehensions of infinite wrath and damnation, he aggravates all their sins to make them seem unpardonable. Every action he calls a sin, and every sin he represents as a wilful forsaking of God, and every deliberate transgression he tells them is 'the sin against the Holy Ghost.' He baffles them in their prayers and services, and then accuseth their duties for intolerable profanations of God's name; and if they be at last affrighted from them, he then clamours that they are 'forsaken of God' because they have forsaken him. He, as a right Baal-zebub,[1] rakes in their wounds, as flies are ever sucking where there is a sore. Their outcries and lamentations are such music to him, that he gives them no rest; and with such triumph doth he tread upon those that thus lie in the dust, that he makes them sometimes accuse themselves for that which they never did, and in derision he insults over them in their greatest perplexities, with this, 'Where is now thy God?' [Ps. xlii. 3,] and 'Who shall deliver thee out of my hand?' This were enough to evidence him altogether void of compassion. But,

2. Secondly, He shews no less cruelty *in his usage of those that are his slaves.* The service that he exacts of those that are his most willing servants, is no less than the highest cruelty; and not only [1.] in regard of the misery and destruction which he makes them work out for themselves, which is far greater than where men are forced by the most brutish tyrants to buy their own poison or to cut their own throats, because this is unspeakably less than the endless miseries of eternal torments; but [2.] also in regard of the very slavery and drudging toil of the service which he exacts from them. He is not pleased that they sin, but the vilest iniquities most contrary to God and most abominable to man, as the highest violations of the laws of nature and reason, are the things which he will put them upon, where there are no restraints in his way. He drave the heathens, as Paul testifies, Rom. i., to affections so vile and loathsome, that in their way of sinning they seemed to act rather like brutes than men, their minds becoming so injudicious that they lost all sense of what was fit and comely. Neither [3.] doth this satisfy his cruelty, that the worst of abominations be practised, but he urgeth them to the highest desperateness in the manner of performance, and so draws them out to the front of the battle, that they might contemn and outdare God to

[1] God of a fly, or fly-god.—G.

his face. He will have them sin with a high hand, and in the highest bravado of madness to rush into sin as 'the horse into the battle.' This cruelty of Satan were yet the less if he only brought them forth presumptuously in some one or two set battles upon special occasions; but [4.] he would have this to be their constant work, the task of every day, upon the same score that Ahithophel advised Absalom to an open and avouched defilement of his father's concubines, that so the breach betwixt them and God might be fixed by a resolute determination, and consequently that their hands might be strong and their hearts hardened in rebellion against God. And [5.] that Satan might not come short of the utmost of what cruelty could do, we may yet further observe, that though sinners offer themselves willingly enough to conflict against God in the high places of the field, yet, as not satisfied with their forwardness, he lasheth and whips them on to their work, and sometime overdrives them in their own earnestness. Haman was so hurried and overborne with violent hatred against Mordecai and the Jews, that his own advancement and the marks of singular favour from the king availed him not, as to any satisfaction and present contentment, Esther v. 13. Ahab, though king of Israel, is so vehemently urged in his desires for Naboth's vineyard, that he covered his face and grew sick upon it, [1 Kings xxi. 1, *seq.*] Thus as galley-slaves were they chained to their oar, and forced to their work beyond their own strength.

3. Thirdly, There is also a cruelty seen in *his incessant provokings and force upon the children of God*, while he urgeth his loathed temptations upon them against their will. When I consider Paul's outcry in this case, Rom. vii. 15, 19, 'That which I do, I allow not; the evil which I would not, that do I,' &c., my thoughts represent him to me, like those Christians that were tortured in the trough, where water was poured by a continued stream upon their mouths, till the cloth that lay upon their lips was forced down their throats; or like those that had stinking puddle-water by a tunnel poured into their stomachs, till they were ready to burst; and surely he apprehended himself to be under very cruel dealing by Satan when he cried out, 'O wretched man that I am! who shall deliver me?' If we seriously consider the mind and endeavours of those children of God that are striving against sin, and have cast it off as the most loathsome abominable thing, when Satan urgeth them to evil with his incessant importunities, it is as if they were forced to eat their own excrements, or to swallow down again their own vomit; for the devil doth but as it were cram these temptations down their throats against their will.

4. Fourthly, If we cast our eye upon *the persecutions of all ages*, we shall have thence enough to charge Satan withal in point of cruelty, for he who is styled ' a murderer from the beginning,' [John viii. 44,] set them all on foot. It is he that hath filled the world with blood and fury, and hath in all ages, in one place or other, made it a very shambles and slaughter-house of men. [1.] Can we reckon how often Satan hath been at this work? That is impossible. His most public and general attempts of this kind are noted by histories of all ages. The persecutions of Pharaoh against Israel, and of the prevailing adversaries of Israel and Judah against both or either of them,

are recorded for the most part in Scripture. The persecutions of the Roman emperors against Christianity are sufficiently known, and what is yet to come who can tell? A great persecution by Antichrist was the general belief and expectation of those that lived in Austin's time, and long before; but whether this be one more to the ten former persecutions, that so the parallel betwixt these and Pharaoh's ruin in the Red Sea after his ten plagues might run even, be only to be looked for, or that others are also to be expected, he thinks it would be presumption and rashness to determine.¹ But, however, his particular assaults of this nature cannot be numbered: how busy is he still at this work in all times and places! insomuch that 'He that will live godly in this world must suffer persecution,' 2 Tim. iii. 12. But [2.] If we withal consider what inventions and devices of cruelty and torture he hath found out, and what endless variety of pains and miseries he hath prepared, a catalogue whereof would fill a great deal of paper, we can do no less than wonder at the merciless fury and implacable rage of him that contrived them. Satan, the great engineer, doth but give us the picture of his mind in all those instruments of destruction. And when we see amongst tyrants ways of torturing every member of the body, and arts of multiplying deaths, that so those that perish by their hands might not have so much as the mercy of a speedy despatch, but that they might feel themselves to die, we may reflect it upon Satan, in Jacob's words to Simeon and Levi, 'Cursed be his anger, for it is fierce; and his wrath, for it is cruel,' [Gen. xlix. 7.] [3.] But if we consider what instruments he useth, and against whom, we shall see cruelty in a higher exaltation. Had he used some of the beasts of the earth, or some of his apostate associates, to persecute and afflict the innocent lambs of Christ, it might have been much excused from the natural instinct or cursed antipathy of such agents; or had he used only the vilest of the children of men to act his tragical fury, the matter had been less; but as not content with common revenge, he persecutes men by men, though all of one blood and offspring, and so perverts the ends of nature, making those that should be the comforts and support of men to be the greatest terror and curse to them—a thing which nature itself abhors, and in regard of which, that the impressions of pity might be more permanent and efficacious, God forbade Israel to 'seethe a kid in the mother's milk,' [Exod. xxiii. 19;] nay, he hath prevailed with some of good inclinations and rare accomplishments—for such were some of the persecuting emperors—to be his deputies for authorising the rack, for providing fire and faggot, and, which is strange, hath prevailed so far with them, that they have been willing to open their ears to the most palpable lies, the grossest forgeries, the most unreasonable suggestions that known malice could invent; and then after all, when they were drawn out to butchery and slaughter by multitudes, they have made such spectacles—which might make impressions upon an iron breast or an adamant heart—only advancements of their jollity; and as Nero upon the sight of flaming Rome took his harp and made melody, so have these tormenting furies fired, by the help of combustible matter, multitudes of such harmless creatures, and then taken the opportunity of their light for their night

¹ De Civit. Dei, lib. xviii. cap. 52.

sports. And yet, methinks, the devil hath discovered a keener fury when he hath made them rage against the dead, and dig their graves, and revenge themselves upon their senseless ashes, and when they could do no more, seek to please themselves by executing their rage against their pictures or statues; which actions, though they might be condemned for follies, yet are they evidences of highest fury, which commonly destroys the judgment, and sacrificeth wit, reason, and honour upon the altar of revenge. That the devil should so poison man's nature that he should thus rise up against his fellow, that carries the same specific being with himself, shews enough of his temper against man, but never more than when he prevails against the engagements of kindness, blood, affinity, and relation, to raise a man's enemies out of his own house, 'the father against the son, and the son against the father, the daughter against the mother, and the mother against the daughter,' [Mat. x. 35;] for this is little less than an unnatural mutiny of the members against the body.

5. Fifthly, We have yet a more visible instance of his cruelty in *his bloody and tyrannical superstitions.* Look but into the rites and ways of his worship among the heathen in all ages and places, and you will find nothing but vile and ridiculous fooleries, or insolent and despiteful usages. In the former he hath driven men to villainous debaucheries, in the latter to execrable cruelties. Of the latter I shall only speak; though in the former, by debasing man to be his laughing-stock, he is cruel in his scorn and mockery. Here I might mention his tyrannical ceremonies of the lower order, such as touch not life; such were their tedious pilgrimages, as in Zeilan; their painful whippings, as of the youth of Lacedæmon at the altar of Diana; of their priests, and that with knotted cords upon their shoulders, as at Mexico and New Spain; their harsh usages in tedious fastings, stinking drenches, hard lyings upon stones, eating earth, strict forbearances of wine and commerce, their torturings and manglings of their bodies by terrible lancings and cuttings for the effusion of blood, 1 Kings xviii.; their dismembering themselves, plucking out their eyes, mangling their flesh, to cast in the idol's face, sacrificing their own blood, as did the priests of Bellona and Dea Syria.[1] So did the kings of New Spain at their election, as Montezuma the Second, who sacrificed by drawing blood from his ears and the calves of his legs.[2] In Narsinga and Bisnagar they go their pilgrimages with knives sticking on their arms and legs till the wounded flesh festered. Some cast themselves under the wheels of the waggon on which their idol is drawn in procession.[3] Yet are all these but small matters in comparison of the bloody outrages committed upon mankind in the abominable custom of sacrificing men to him. Of this many authors give us a large account.[4] The Lacedæmonians to avert the plague sacrifice a virgin; the Athenians, by the advice of Apollo's oracle, sent yearly to King Minos seven males and so many females to be sacrificed to appease the wrath of the god for their killing of Androgeus. The Carthaginians, being vanquished by

---

[1] Tertul. Apolog., cap. 9. [2] Purchas, Pilgrim., part i. lib. viii. cap. 10.
[3] *Idem*, part i. lib. v. cap. 11.
[4] Iphigenia Sacrificata, de qua. . . . Sanguine placastis ventos et virgine cæsa.—*Virg.* Plut. Paral., cap. 66.

Agathocles, king of Sicily, sacrificed two hundred noblemen's children at once. The Romans had every year such sacrifices of men and women, of each sex two, for a long time; and this was so common among the wiser pagan nations, that whensoever they fell into danger, either of war, sicknesses, or of any other calamity, they presently, to expiate their offences against their supposed incensed gods, and to clear themselves of their present miseries or dangers, sacrificed some mean persons, who for this reason were called $\kappa\alpha\theta\acute{\alpha}\rho\mu\alpha\tau\alpha$, expiations,[1] and to this doth the apostle allude in 1 Cor. iv. 13, as Budæus, Stephanus, Grotius, and many others think; as if he should say, we are as much despised and loaded with cursings as those that are sacrificed for public expiation. But what cruel usage may we expect for the poor barbarous nations of the world, where he had all possible advantages for the exercise of his bloody tyranny! Many sad instances of this kind are collected by Purchas in his Pilgrimage, in his discourses of Virginia, Peru, Brasilia, Mexico, Florida, and other places, whose stories of this subject are so terrible, and occur so frequently, that they are almost beyond all belief,[2] all which for brevity's sake I omit, contenting myself to note one instance or two out of the Scripture: 2 Kings iii. 27, the king of Moab 'took his eldest son that should have reigned in his stead, and offered him for a burnt-offering upon the wall.' This he did, according to the customs of the Phœnicians and others, being reduced to great straits, as supposing by this means, as his last refuge, to turn away the wrath of his God. Of Ahaz it is recorded, 2 Chron. xxviii. 3, that 'he burnt his children in the fire, after the abominations of the heathen.' That this was not a lustration or consecration of their children, though that also was used, but a real sacrificing, is without doubt to Josephus, who expresseth it thus: 'He offered his son as an holocaust,' [$\dot{o}\lambda o\kappa\acute{a}\upsilon\sigma\tau\omega\sigma\epsilon$.] But whatever Ahaz did, it is certain the children of Israel did so; 'They offered their sons and daughters to devils,' Ps. cvi. 37. And if the 'sacrifices of the dead' which they ate in the wilderness, mentioned ver. 28, be understood of the feasts which were made at 'the burning of their children,' as some think [3]—though many understand it of their senseless dead gods or their deceased heroes, or for their deceased friends—then this cruelty had soon possessed them. However, possess them it did, as appears also by the description of their devouring Moloch, which the Jewish Rabbins say was a hollow brazen image in the form of a man, saving that it had the head of a calf, the arms stretched in a posture of receiving; the image was heated with fire, and the priest put the child in his arms, where it was burnt to death; in the meantime a noise was made with drums, that the cries of the child might not be heard, and hence was it called Tophet, from *toph*, which signifies a drum; so that the name and shape of the image shews that it was used to these execrable cruelties.[4]

These Scripture evidences, if we were backward to credit what histories say of this matter, may assure us of the temper and disposition

---

[1] Godwyn, 'Moses and Aaron,' lib. iii. cap. 8.
[2] His 'Pilgrimage; or, Relations of the World and the Religions observed in all Ages,' 1614, folio; and his 'Pilgrimes,' 5 vols. folio, 1625-26.—G.
[3] Lightfoot on Acts vii. 43.   [4] Godwyn, 'Moses and Aaron,' lib. iv. cap. 2.

of Satan, and may enable us to believe what bloody work he hath made in the world, which I shall briefly sum up in these particulars:—

[1.] First, These inhuman, or rather, as Purchas calls them, overhuman sacrifices, were practised in most nations. Not only the Indians, Parthians, Mexicans, &c., but Æthiopians, Syrians, Carthaginians, Grecians, Romans, Germans, French, and Britons used them.

[2.] Secondly, These cruelties were acted not only upon slaves and captives, but upon children, whose age and innocency might have commanded the compassions of their parents for better usage.

[3.] Thirdly, These sacrificings were used upon several occasions, as at the sprouting of their corn, at the inauguration, coronation, and deaths of their kings and noblemen, in time of war, dearth, pestilence, or any danger; in a word, as the priests in Florida and Mexico used to say, whenever the devil is hungry or thirsty, that is, as oft as he hath a mind.

[4.] Fourthly, In some places the devil brought them to set times for those offerings; some were monthly, some annual. The Latins sacrificed the tenth child; the annual drowning of a boy and a girl in the lake of Mexico; the casting of two yearly from the *Pons Milvius* [1] at Rome into Tiber, are but petty instances in comparison of the rest.

[5.] Fifthly, We cannot pass by the vast number of men offered up at one time. So thirsty is Satan of human blood, that from one or two, he hath raised the number incredibly high. In some sacrifices five, in some ten, in some a hundred, in some a thousand have been offered up. It was the argument which Montezuma, the last Emperor of Mexico, used to Cortez to prove his strength and greatness by, that he sacrificed yearly twenty thousand men, and some years fifty thousand. Some have reserved their captives for that end, others have made war only to furnish themselves with men for such occasions.

[6.] Sixthly, There are also several circumstances of these diabolical outrages that may give a further discovery of his cruelty, as that these miserable creatures thus led to be butchered have been loaden with all the cursings, revilings, and contumacious reproaches as a necessary concomitant of their violent deaths. Thus were those used who were forced to be the public καθάρματα, or expiation, for the removal of common calamities. Death also was not enough, except it had been most tormenting in the manner of it, as of those that suffered by the embracements of Moloch. The joy and feastings of such sacrificings, which were in themselves spectacles of mourning and sorrow, were cruelties to the dead, and a barbarous enforcement against the laws of nature in the living. But the dashing of the smoking heart in the idol's face, and the pulling off the skins from the massacred bodies, that men and women might dance in them, were yet more cruel ceremonies. And lastly, In those that have been prepared for those solemnities, by delicious fare, gorgeous ornaments, and the highest reverence or honours, as was the manner of several countries; yet was this no other than Satan's insulting over their miseries, of which we can say no otherwise, than that his tenderest mercies are cruelties.

[7.] Seventhly, I may cast into the account, that in some places

---

[1] On the Via Flaminia: Aur. Vict. de Viris Illustr. cap. 27, sec. 8: Tacitus, *Ann.* xiii. 47.—G.

Satan, by a strange madness of devotion, hath persuaded some to be volunteers in suffering these tortures and deaths. Some have cast themselves under the chariot-wheels of their idols, and so have been crushed to pieces.[1] Some sacrifice themselves to their gods: first they cut off several pieces of their flesh, crying every time, 'For the worship of my god, I cut this my flesh;' and at last say, 'Now do I yield myself to death in the behalf of my god,' and so kills himself outright.

[8.] Eighthly, It is wonderful to think that the devil should, by strange pretexts of reason, have smoothed over these barbarous inhumanities, so that they have become plausible things in the judgments of those miserable wretches. In piacular sacrifices they believed that except the life of a man were given for the life of men, that the gods could not be pacified.[2] In other sacrifices, both eucharistical and for atonement, they retained this principle, 'that those things are to be offered to the gods that are most pleasing and acceptable to us; and that the offering of a calf or a pigeon was not suitable to such an end.' This maxim they further improved by the addition of another of the same kind, 'that if it were fit to offer a human sacrifice, it must also be innocent, and consequently little children are the fittest for such a purpose.' And some have also conjectured that the devil hath not been awanting to improve the example of Abraham sacrificing his son, or the law in Lev. xxvii. 28, or the prophecies concerning the death of Christ, as the great sacrifice of atonement, to justify and warrant his hellish cruelty.[3] In some cases cruelty hath arisen from the very principles of reverence and love which children have to parents, and friends to friends: as in Dragoian, when any are sick, they send to their oracle to know whether the parties shall live or die; if it be answered they shall die, then their friends strangle them and eat them; and all this from a kind of religious respect to their kindred, to preserve, as they imagine, their flesh from putrefaction, and their souls from torment.[4] The like they do at Javamajor, when their friends grow old and cannot work, only they eat not their own friends, but carry them to the market and sell them to those that do eat them.[5]

[9.] Lastly, Let us call to mind how long the devil domineered in the world at this rate of cruelty. When the world grew to a freer use of reason and greater exercise of civility, they found out ways of mitigation, and changed these barbarous rites into more tolerable sacrifices; as in Laodicea, they substituted a hart to be sacrificed instead of a virgin; in Cyprus, an ox was put instead of a man; in Egypt, waxen images instead of men. Images of straw at Rome were cast into Tiber in the place of living men; and the terrible burnings of Moloch, which was not peculiar only to the nations near to Canaan, but was in use also at Carthage, and found in the American islands by the Spaniards; the like brazen images were also found in Lodovicus Vives his time, by the French, in an island called by them Carolina.[6]

[1] Purchas, Pilgr., part i. lib. v. cap. 11, [*e.g.*, Juggernath in India.—G.]
[2] Pro vita hominum nisi vita hominis reddatur, non posse deorum numen placari, arbitrantur.—*Jean d'Espan.*, [*i.e.*, John Despagne.] 'Popular Errors' [in the Knowledge of Religion. London, 1648, 8vo.—G.] cap. 18.
[3] *Vide* Lud. Capel. de voto Jephtæ, [*ac corban.*—G.] sec. 9. *Vide* Pool Synops. Crit. on 2 Kings iii. 27. [4] Purchas, Pilgr., part i. lib. v. cap. 16. [5] Purchas, *ibid.*
[6] Diod. Siculus, Biblioth., lib. xx. Lod. Vives on Aug. De Civ. Dei, lib. vii. cap. 19.

These were at last changed into a *februation*,[1] and instead of burning their children, they only passed them betwixt two fires; but it was long before it came to this. In the time of Socrates, human sacrifices were in use at Carthage, and they continued in the Roman provinces till the time of Tertullian, Eusebius, and Lactantius; though they had been severely forbidden by Augustus Cæsar, and afterward by Tiberius, who was forced to crucify some of the priests that dared to offer such sacrifices, to affright them from those barbarous customs. In other places of the world, how long such things continued, who can tell, especially seeing they were found at Carolina not so very long since?

How impossible is it to cast up the total sum of so many large items! When these terrible customs have had so general a practice in most nations, upon so many occasions, upon such seeming plausible principles; when such great numbers have been destroyed at once, and these usages have been so long practised in the world, and with such difficulty restrained, what vast multitudes of men must, we imagine, have been consumed by Satan's execrable cruelty!

6. Sixthly, There remains one instance more of the devil's cruelty, which is yet different from the former, which I may call his *personal cruelties;* because they are acted by his own immediate hand upon certain of his vassals, without the help or interposure of men, who, in most of the fore-mentioned cases, have been as instruments acted by him. Here I might take notice of his fury to those that are possessed. Some have been as it were racked and tortured in their bodies, and their limbs and members so distorted, that it hath been not only matter of pity to the beholders to see them so abused, but also of admiration[2] to consider how such abuses should be consistent with their lives, and that such rendings and tearings have not quite separated the soul from the body. In the Gospels we read of some such 'cast into the fire, and into the water,' [Mat. xvii. 15;] others, conversing 'with tombs and sepulchres,' in the cold nights 'without clothes;' and all of them spoken of as creatures sadly tormented, and 'miserably vexed.' The histories of later days tell us of some that vomited crooked pins, pieces of leather, coals, cloth, and such like; of others snatched out of their houses, and tired even to fainting, and waste of their spirits, as Domina Rossa, mentioned by Bodin, with a great many more to this same purpose. We may take a view of his dealing with witches, who, though he seem to gratify them in their transportations from place to place, and in their feastings with music and dancings, are but cruelly handled by him very often. The very work they are put upon—which is the destruction of children, men, women, cattle, and the fruits of the earth —is but a base employment; but the account he takes of them, of the full performance of their enterprizes, and the cruel beatings they have of him, when they cannot accomplish any of their revenges, is no less than a severe cruelty. He gives them no rest unless they be doing hurt; and when they cannot do it to the persons designed, they are forced to do the same mischief to their own children or relations, that they may gratify their tyrannical master. Bodin relates the story of

---

[1] Purifying sacrifices for the *manes* of the dead, offered in *February*.—G.
[2] 'Astonishment.'—G.

a French baron, [p. 180,] who was afterward put to death for witchcraft, that after he had killed eight children, was at last upon a design of sacrificing his own child to the devil. And if at any time they grew weary of so execrable a slavery, or confess their wickedness, they are so miserably tormented that they choose rather to die than live. And what else but cruelty can these slaves expect from him, when the ceremonies of their entrance into that cursed service betokens nothing else; for their bonds and obligations are usually writ or subscribed with their own blood; and some magical books have been writ with the blood of many children; besides, the farewell that they have of him at their usual meetings, is commonly this thundering threatening, 'Avenge yourselves, or you shall die.' All these particulars are collected from the confessions of witches by Bodin, Wierus, and others.

But leaving these, let us further inquire into Satan's carriage toward those that in America and other dark and barbarous places know no other god, and give their devoutest worship to him. To those he is not so kind as might be expected; but his constant way is to terrify and torment them, insomuch that some know no other reason of their worship but that he may not hurt them. And since the English colonies went into these parts, these Americans have learned to make this distinction between the Englishman's God and theirs, that theirs is an evil god, and the other a good God; though that distinction in other places is in the general far more ancient, where they acknowledge two gods, one good, the other bad; and the worse the god is, the saddest, most mournful rites of sacrificing were used, as in caves, and in the night—the manner of the worship fitly expressing the nature of the god they served.[1] Our countrymen have noted of the natives of New England, that the devil appeared to them in ugly shapes, and in hideous places, as in swamps and woods. But these are only the prologue to the tragedy itself, for they only serve to impress upon the minds of his worshippers what cruelties and severities they are to expect from him; and accordingly he often lets them feel his hand, and makes them know that those dark and dismal *preludiums* are not for nothing. For sometimes he appears to the worshippers, tormenting and afflicting their bodies, tearing the flesh from the bones, and carrying them away quick[2] with him; sometimes six have been carried away at once, none ever knowing what became of them.[3] By such bloody acts as these he kept the poor Americans in fear and slavery; so that as bad a master as he is, they durst not but pay their homage and service to him. All these particulars being put together, will shew we do the devil no wrong when we call him cruel.

---

[1] Porphyrius, lib. ii. De Abstinent. Plutarch. Lod. Vives in Aug. De Civ. Dei, lib. viii. cap. 13.   [2] 'Alive.'—G.
[3] Wonder-working Prov[idences] for N[ew] E[ngland], lib. i. cap. 10.

CHAPTER VII.

Of Satan's diligence in several instances.—The question about the being of spirits and devils handled.—The Sadducees' opinion discovered.—The reality of spirits proved.

The last particular observed in the text is his *diligence*. This adds force and strength to his malice, power, and cruelty, and shews they are not idle, dead, or inactive principles in him, which, if they could be so supposed, would render him less hurtful and formidable. This I shall despatch in a few instances, noting to this purpose,

1. First, *His pains he takes in hunting his prey, and pursuing his designs.* It is nothing for him to 'compass sea and land,' to labour to the utmost in his employment; it is all his business to tempt and destroy, and his whole heart is in it. Hence intermission or cessation cannot be expected. He faints not by his labour; and his labour, with the success of it, is all the delight we can suppose him to have. So that, being pushed and hurried by the hellish satisfactions of deadly revenge, and having a strength answerable to those violent impulses, we must suppose him to undergo, with a kind of pleasing willingness, all imaginable toil and labour. If we look into ourselves, we find it true, to our no small trouble and hazard. Doth he at any time easily desist when we give him a repulse? Doth he not come again and again, with often and impudently-repeated importunities? Doth he not carry a design in his mind for months and years against us? And when the motion is not feasible, yet he forgets it not, but after a long interruption begins again where he left; which shews that he is big with his projects, and his mind hath no rest. He stretcheth out his nets all the day long. We may say of him, that he riseth up early, and sitteth up late at his work, and is content to labour in the very fire, so that he might but either disturb a child of God or gain a proselyte.

2. Secondly, Diligence is not only discovered in laboriousness, but also in *a peculiar readiness to espy and to close in with fit occasions, which may in probability answer the end we drive at.* In this is Satan admirably diligent; no occasion shall slip, or through inadvertency escape him. No sooner are opportunities before us, but we may perceive him suggesting to us, 'Do this, satisfy that lust, take that gain, please yourselves with that revenge.' No sooner obtains he a commission against a child of God, but presently he is upon his back, as he dealt with Job; he lost no time, but goes out immediately from the presence of the Lord and falls upon him. Besides what he doth upon solemn and extraordinary occasions, these that are common and ordinary are so carefully improved by him, that everything we hear or see is ready to become our snare, and Satan will assay to tempt us by them, though they lie something out of the way of our inclination, and be not so likely to prevail with us.

3. Thirdly, It is also a discovery of his diligence, that he never *fails to pursue every advantage which he gets against us to the utmost.* If the occasion and motion thereupon incline us, so that if we are per-

suaded by them, he follows it on, and is not satisfied with either a lower degree of acting sinfully, or with one or two acts; but then he presseth upon us to sin to the height, with the greater contempt of God and grievance of his Spirit, the greater scandal and offence to our brethren; and having once caused us to begin, he would never have us to make an end. His temptations roll themselves upon us like the breaking in of waters, which, by the fierceness of their current, make a large way for more to follow. He knows how to improve his victories, and will not, through slothfulness or pity, neglect to complete them. Hence it is that sometimes he reaps a large harvest where he had sown little, and from one temptation not only wounds the soul of him that committed it, but endeavours to diffuse the venom and poisonous steam of it to the infection of others, to the disgrace of religion, the hardening the hearts of wicked men, and the turning the ignorant out of the way of truth. In like manner, if he perceive the spirits of men grow distempered and wounded, he then plies them with threatenings, fills them with all manner of discouragements, dresseth every truth with the worst appearance, that it may be apprehended otherwise than it is, and puts such interpretations on all providences, that everything may augment the smart of the wound, till they be overwhelmed with terrors.

4. Fourthly, *The various ways which he takes*, shews also his diligence. If one plot take not, he is immediately upon another. He confines not himself to one design nor to one method; but if he find one temptation doth not relish, he prepares another more suitable. If covetousness doth not please us, then he urgeth to profuseness; if terrors do not affright us to despair, then he abuseth mercies to make us careless and presuming. If we are not content to be openly wicked, then he endeavours to make us secretly hypocritical or formal. Sometime he urgeth men to be profane; if that hit not, then to be erroneous. If he cannot work by one tool, then he takes another; and if anything in his way disgust, he will not urge it over-hard, but straight takes another course. Such is his diligence, that we may say of him, as it was said of Paul upon a better ground, he will 'become all things to all men, that he may gain some,' [1 Cor. ix. 19.]

5. Fifthly, Diligence will most shew itself *when things are at the greatest hazard, or when the hopes of success are ready to bring forth.* In this point of diligence our adversary is not wanting. If men are upon the point of error or sin, how industriously doth he labour to bring them wholly over, and to settle them in evil! One would think at such times he laid aside all other business, and only attended this. How frequent, incessant, and earnest are his persuasions and arguings with such! The like diligence he sheweth in obstructing, disturbing, and discouraging us when we are upon our greatest services or near our greatest mercies. What part of the day are we more wandering and vain in our thoughts, if we take not great care, than when we set about prayer? At other times we find some more ease and freedom in our imaginations, as if we could better rule or command them; but then, as if our thoughts were only confusion and disorder, we are not able to master them, and to keep the door of the heart so close but

that these troublesome, unwelcome guests will be crowding in, is impossible. Let us observe it seriously, and we shall find that our thoughts are not the same, and after the same manner impetuous at other times as they are when we set about holy things; which ariseth not only from the quickness of our spiritual sense in our readier observation of them at that time, but also from the devil's busy molestation and special diligence against us on such occasions. Besides, when he foresees our advantages or mercies, he bestirs himself to prevent or hinder us of them. If ministers set themselves to study and preach truths that are more piercing, weighty, or necessary, they may observe more molestations, interruptions, or discouragements of all sorts, than when they less concern themselves with the business of the souls of men. He foresees what sermons are provided, and often doth he upon such foresight endeavour to turn off those from hearing that have most need and are most likely to receive benefit by them. Many have noted it, that those sermons and occasions that have done them most good, when they came to them, they have been some way or other most dissuaded from and resolved against before they came; and then when they have broken through their strongest hindrances, they have found that all their obstruction was Satan's diligent foresight to hinder them of such a blessing as they have, beyond hope, met withal. The like might be observed of the constant returns of the Lord's day. If men watch not against it, they may meet with more than ordinary, either avocations to prevent and hinder them, or disturbances to annoy and trouble, or bodily indispositions to incapacitate and unfit them. And it is not to be contemned, that some have observed themselves more apt to be drowsy, dull, or sleepy on that day. Others have noted greater bodily indispositions than ordinarily, than at other times; all which make no unlikely conjecture of the devil's special diligence against us on such occasions.

Let us cast in another instance to these, and that is, of those that are upon the point of conversion, ready to forsake sin for Christ. Oh, what pains then doth the devil take to keep them back! He visits them every moment with one hindrance or other. Sometimes they are tempted to former pleasures, sometime affrighted with present fears and future disappointments; sometime discouraged with reproaches, scorns, and afflictions that may attend their alteration; otherwhile obstructed by the persuasion or threatening of friends and old acquaintances; but this they are sure of, that they have never more temptations, and those more sensibly troubling, than at that time—a clear evidence that Satan is as diligent as malicious.

I should now go on to display the subtlety of this powerful, malicious, cruel, and diligent adversary. There is but one thing in the way, which hitherto I have taken for granted, and that is, Whether indeed there be any such things as devils and wicked spirits, or that these are but theological engines contrived by persons that carry a goodwill to morality and the public peace, to keep men under an awful fear of such miscarriages as may render them otherwise a shame to themselves and a trouble to others. It must be acknowledged a transgression of the rules of method to offer a proof of that now, which, if at all, ought to have been proved in the beginning of the discourse: and indeed the question at this length, whether there be a devil, hath such affinity with that other, though for the matter they are as different as heaven and hell, whether there be a God, that as it well deserves a confirmation,—for the use that may be made of it to evidence that there is a God, because we feel there is a devil,—so would it require a serious endeavour to perform it substantially. But it would be not only a needless labour to levy an army against professed atheists, who with high scorn and derision roundly deny both God and devils—seeing others have frequently done that—but also it would occasion too large a digression from our present design. I shall therefore only speak a few things to those that own a God, and yet deny such a devil as we have described: and yet not to all of these neither, for there were many heathens who were confident assertors of a deity, that nevertheless denied the being of spirits as severed from corporeity; and others were so far from the acknowledgment of devils, that they confounded them in the number of their gods. Others there were who gave such credit to the frequent relations of apparitions and disturbances of that kind, that many had attested and complained of, that they expressed more ingenuity[1] than Lucian, who pertinaciously refused to believe, because he never saw them; and yet though they believed something of reality in that that was the affrightment and trouble of others, they nevertheless ascribed such extraordinary things to natural causes, some to the powers of the heavens and stars in their influences upon natural bodies, or by the mediation of certain herbs, stones, minerals, creatures, voices, and characters, under a special observation of the motion of the planets.[2] Some refer such things to the subtlety and quickness of the senses of hearing and seeing, which might create forms and images of things, or discover I know not what reflections from the sun and moon. Some [Pomponatius, Epicureans] fancy the shapes and visions to be *exuviæ*, thin scales or skins of natural things, giving representations of the bodies that cast them off, or exhalations from sepulchres, representing the shape of the body. Others [Cardan, Academics] make them the effects of our untrusty and deceitful senses, the debility and corruption whereof they conclude to be such, and so general, that most men are in hazard to be imposed upon by delusive appearances. But with far greater show of likelihood do some [Averrhoes] make all such things to be nothing else but the issues of melancholy and corrupt humours, which makes men believe they hear, see, and suffer strange things, when there is nothing near them; or really to undergo strange fits, as in lunacy and epilepsy.[3] Leaving these men as not capable of information from Scripture evidence, because disowning it, let us inquire what mistaken apprehensions there have been in this matter among those that have pretended a reverence to and belief of Scripture. The Sadducees deserve the first place, because they are by name noted in Scripture to have 'denied the resurrection,' and to have 'affirmed that there is neither angel nor spirit,' Acts xxiii. 8, and Mat. xxii. 23.

[1] 'Ingenuousness.'—G.
[2] The Peripatetics. Porphyrius. Aug[ustine], De Civ. Dei, lib. x. cap. 11. Galen.
[3] Cassius ad Brutum ex Plutarch. in vita Bruti.

This opinion of theirs, could we certainly find it out, would make much for the confirmation of the truth in question, seeing, whatever it was, it is positively condemned in Scripture, and the contrary asserted to be true. Many, and that upon considerable grounds, do think that they do not deny absolutely that there were any angels at all, but that, acknowledging that something there was which was called an angel, yet they imagining it to be far otherwise than what it is indeed, were accused justly for denying such a kind of angels as the Scripture had everywhere asserted and described. For considering that they owned a God, and, at least, the five books of Moses, if not all the other books of the Old Testament—as Scaliger and others judge, not without great probability, for neither doth the Scripture nor Josephus mention any such thing of the prophets—it is unimaginable that they would altogether deny that there was angel or spirit at all.[1] They read of angels appearing to Lot, to Abraham, and met with it so frequently, that, believing Scriptures to be true, they could not believe angels to be an absolute fiction; for one fable or falsity in Scripture, which so highly asserts itself to be an unerring oracle of the true God, must of necessity have destroyed the credit of all, and rendered them as justly suspected to be true in nothing, when apparently false or fabulous in anything.

Again, If we call to mind what apprehensions they had of God, which all consent they did acknowledge, we might more easily imagine what apprehensions they had of angels, for in regard that Moses made mention of God's face and back-parts, Exod. xxxiii., and that frequently hands and other parts of man's body were attributed to him, they concluded God to be corporeal; and seeing the best of creatures which God created cannot be supposed to have a more noble being than was that of their Creator, and, at the utmost, to be made according to the pattern of his own image and likeness, they might upon this bottom easily fix a denial of incorporeal spirits, and by consequence that the soul of man was mortal, and therefore that there could be no resurrection; so that the nature of angels being described under the notion of spiritual substances, they are judged to deny any such thing, supposing that to be incorporeal was as much as not to be at all; and yet it were unreasonable to deny that they had not some interpretation for those passages of Scripture that mentioned angels, which in their apprehensions might be some salvo to the truth of those historical writings, which they acknowledged; but what that was we are next to conjecture. And indeed Josephus, by a little hint of their opinion, seems to tell us that they did not so much deny the being of the soul, as the permanency of it; and so, by consequence, they might not so much deny absolutely the existence of spirits, as their natural being and continuance.[2] Something there was that was called by the name of angel—that they could not but own—and that this must be a real and not an imaginary thing, is evident from the real effect, and things done by them; yet observing their appearances to have been upon some special occasion, and their

---

[1] *Vide* Spanheim, Dub. Evang. part iii. dub. 29.
[2] Lib. ii. de Bello Jud. c. 7, Ψυχῆς τε τὴν διαμονὴν, καὶ τὰς καθ' ᾅδου τιμωρίας καὶ τιμὰς ἀναιροῦσι.

disappearing to have been on a sudden, they might conjecture them to be created by God for the present service, and then reduced to nothing when that service was done.

Their opinion, then, of angels seems to be one of these two: either that they were corporeal substances created upon a special emergency, but not permanent beings; or that they were but images and impressions supernaturally formed in the fancy by the special operation of God, to signify his mind and commands to men, upon which they might fitly be called God's messengers and ministers. I put in this last into the conjecture, because I find it mentioned by Calvin,[1] as the opinion of the Sadducees; but both are noted by Diodate,[2] on Acts xxiii. 8, as with equal probability belonging to them. His words are, 'They did not believe they were subsisting and immortal creatures, but transitory apparitions, or some divine actions and motions to produce some special and notable effect.'

Others also have been lately hammering out the same apprehension concerning angels, and profess themselves delivered from it with great difficulty, differing only in this from some of the heathens before mentioned, that what those ascribed to the puissance of the stars, natural powers, or to weakness of senses and corrupt humours, they, by the advantage of the general notions of Scripture, have ascribed to God, putting forth his power upon the minds and fancies of men, or working by the humours of the body.[3] Upon this foundation they will easilier make bold with devils, to deny, if not their being, yet their temptations, imagining that we may possibly do him wrong in fathering upon him these solicitations and provocations to sin, which we by experience find to be working and acting upon our minds, thinking that our own fancies or imaginations may be the only devils that vex us; and this they more readily hearken to, from the nature of dreams and visions which happen to men in an ordinary natural way, where our fancies play with us as if they were distinct from us; as also from this consideration, that the lunatic, epileptic, and frenzical persons are in Scripture called demoniacs, as Mat. xvii. 15, with Luke ix., where the person is called lunatic, and yet said to be taken and vexed by a spirit. So also John x. 20, he hath a devil, and is mad. But these reasonings can do little with an intelligent, considering man, to make him deny what he so really feels, and is so often forewarned of in Scripture; for suppose these were called demoniacs by the vulgar, it doth not compel us to believe they were so. Men are apt to ascribe natural diseases to Satan, and Christ did not concern himself to cure their misapprehensions, while he cured their diseases.[4] This some suggest as a reason that may answer many cases, though indeed it cannot answer that of Mat. xvii., because, ver. 18, it is said expressly that 'Jesus rebuked the devil, and he departed out of him,' which would not have been proper to have been spoken on the account of Christ by the evangelist, to express the cure

---

[1] Fuit illa quidem olim Sadducæorum opinio, per angelos nihil designari quam vel motus quos Deus hominibus aspirat, vel ea quæ edit virtutis suæ specimina.—Instit., lib. i. cap. 14, sec. 9.

[2] Diodati: his 'Notes' were published in English, 1664, folio, and in various lesser forms.—G.   [3] Hobbes Lev., cap. 34, pp. 212, 214.

[4] Dr More's 'Mystery of Godliness,' lib. iv. cap. 6, sec. 10.

of a natural disease, for so would he unavoidably have been rendered guilty of the same mistake with the vulgar. But if we should grant that divers mentioned under the name of demoniacs were men disturbed with melancholy, or the falling-sickness, all were not so; for those in Mat. viii. 31, 'besought Christ, after their ejection,' to have liberty 'to go into the herd of swine:' so that if Mr Mede intended to assert that all demoniacs were no other than madmen and lunatics, I question not but he was mistaken, and by his reason, not only must madmen and lunatic persons pass for demoniacs, but all diseases whatsoever; for the blind and dumb were called also demoniacs, Mat. ix. 32, and xii. 22.[1] But the matter seems to be this, that where men were afflicted with such distempers, Satan took the advantage of them, and acted the possessed accordingly; as he frequently takes the advantage of a melancholy indisposition, and works great terrors and affrightments by it, as in Saul; or at least that, where he possessed, he counterfeited the fits and furies of those natural distempers, and acted some like madmen, and others he made dumb and deaf—which seems to have been the case of those in Mat. ix. and xii., where the deafness and dumbness did depend upon the possession, and was cured with it—others were made to 'fall on a sudden into fire or water,' as those that are epileptic, and therefore might such be called both lunatic or epileptic, and also possessed with a devil.

As to that reason which some fetch from dreams, it is rather a dream than a reason against the being of devils, seeing the effects of these infernal spirits are far otherwise than the utmost of what can be imagined to be acted upon the stage of imaginations; so that the real and permanent being of devils may be easily proved:—

[1.] First, *From those real acts noted to be done by angels and devils.* The angels that appeared to Lot were seen and entertained in the family—seen and observed by the Sodomites. Those that appeared to Abraham were more than fancied appearances, in that they 'ate and drank' with him. The devil conveyed Christ from place to place. This could not be a fancy or imagination. Their begging leave to go 'into the swine' shews them real existences.

[2.] Secondly, *From the real effects done by them.* We have undoubted testimonies of men really hurt and tormented by Satan. Of some really snatched away, and carried a great distance from their dwellings. Of others possessed, in whom the devil really speaks audible voices and strange languages, gives notice of things past, and sometime of things to come. The oracles of the heathen, which however they were for the most part false or delusory, yet, in that they were responses from images and idols, were more than phantasms.

[3.] Thirdly, *From what the Scripture speaks everywhere of them.* Of their malice and cruelty; that devils are murderers from the beginning; their daily waiting how they may devour; their arts, wiles, and stratagems; their names and appellations, when styled principalities, powers, spiritual wickednesses, the prince of the power of the air, and a great many more to that purpose, shew that, without

[1] Lib. i. p. 85, on John x. 20.

apparent folly and dotage, we cannot interpret these of motions only upon the minds and fancies of men. Besides, the Scripture speaks of the offices of good angels, as their standing continually before the throne, their beholding the face of God, their accompanying Christ at his second coming, their gathering the elect from the four winds, &c., Dan. vii. 10, which cannot be understood of anything else but real and permanent beings; and this is also an evidence that devils are, seeing the Scripture mentions their fall and their punishment.

[4.] Fourthly, *Seeing also the Scripture condemned the opinion of the Sadducees, the contrary of that opinion must be true.* And expressly in Acts xii. 9, that which was done by an angel is opposed to what might be visional or imaginary.

[5.] Fifthly, The reality of devils and their malignity hath been the opinion of heathens. For there is nothing more common among them than the belief of inferior deities, which they called δαίμονες or δαιμόνια, that is, devils; and notwithstanding that they supposed these to be mediators to the supreme gods, yet they learned to distinguish them into good and evil.[1] The Platonists thought that the souls of tyrants after death became *lemures* and *larvæ*, that is, hurtful devils; and at last the name *devil* became of so bad a signification, that to say, 'thou hast a devil,' was reproach and not praise; but what these groped at in the dark, the Scripture doth fully determine, using the word *devil* only for a malignant spirit.

CHAPTER VIII.

Of Satan's cunning and craft in the general.—Several demonstrations proving Satan to be deceitful; and of the reasons why he makes use of his cunning.

We have taken a survey of our adversary's strength, and this will open the way to a clearer discovery of his subtlety and craft, which is his great engine by which he works all his tyranny and cruelty in the world, to the ruin or prejudice of the souls of men; of which the apostle in 2 Cor. ii. 11 speaks, as a thing known by the common experience of all discerning persons. His way is to overreach and take advantages, and for this end he useth devices and stratagems, which is a thing so ordinary with him, that none can be ignorant of the truth of it: 'We are not ignorant of his devices.'

This, before I come to the particulars, I shall prove and illustrate in the general, by the gradual procedure of these few following considerations:—

First, *All the malice, power, cruelty, and diligence of which we have spoken, with all the advantages of multitude, order, and knowledge, by which these cruel qualifications are heightened—these are but his furniture and acomplishment which fit him for his subtle contrivances of delusion, and make him able to deceive; neither hath he any use of his power and knowledge but in reference to deceit.* In

---

[1] Mede, 'Apost. Latter Times,' p. 19. August. De Civ. Dei, lib. ix. cap. 11, 19.

Eph. vi. 11, 12, which is a place wherein the apostle doth of purpose present Satan in his way of dealing with men, his whole practice is set forth under the term and notion of arts and wiles : ' that you may be able to stand against the wiles of the devil.' This is the whole work of Satan, against which the furniture of that spiritual armour is requisite; and lest any should think that his power or wickedness are other distinct things in him, which are to be provided against by other means of help, he presently adds, that these are no otherwise used by him but in order to his wiles and cunning, and therefore not to be looked upon as distinct, though indeed to be considered in conjunction with his subtlety and cunning, as things that make his wiles the more dangerous and hazardous: ' For we wrestle not against flesh and blood, but against principalities, against powers, against the rulers of the darkness of this world, against spiritual wickedness in high places;' which words do but strengthen the apostle's warning and caution about the forementioned wiles, which are therefore the more carefully to be observed and watched against, because his power is so great that he can contrive snares with the greatest skill and art imaginable ; and his wickedness is so great, that we cannot expect either honesty or modesty should restrain him from making the vilest and most disingenuous proposals, nor from attesting a conveniency or goodness in his motions, with the highest confidence of most notorious lying.

2. Secondly, *The subtlety that the Scriptures do attribute to sin, or to the heart, is mostly and chiefly intended to reflect upon Satan, as the author and contriver of these deceits.* In Heb. iii. 13 there is mention of the ' deceitfulness of sin,' but it is evident that something else besides sin is intended, to which deceitfulness must be properly ascribed ; for sin being, as most conclude, formally a privation, or if we should grant it a positive being, as some contend, yet seeing the highest notion we can arrive at this way, excluding but the figment of Flacius Illyricus, who seems to make original sin indistinct from the very essence of the soul, is but to call it an act.[1] Deceitfulness cannot be properly attributed to it, but with reference to him who orders that act in a way of deceitfulness and delusion ; which ultimately will bring it to Satan's door. If here the deceitfulness of sin be devolved upon the subject, then it runs into the same sense with Jer. xvii. 9, ' The heart is deceitful above all things.' But why is the deceitfulness fixed upon the heart ? The ground of that we have in the next words ; it is deceitful, because it is wicked, ' desperately wicked.' But who then inflames and stirs up the heart to this wickedness ? Is it not Satan ? Who then is the proper author of deceit but he ? It is true, indeed, that our hearts are proper fountains of sin, and so may be accused possibly in some cases where Satan cannot be justly blamed ; yet if we consider deceitfulness as a companion of every sin, though our hearts be to be blamed for the sin, Satan will be found guilty of the deceitfulness. It may be said a man complies with those things which are intended for his delusion, and so improperly by his negligence may fall under blame of self-deception ; but it is unimaginable that he can properly and formally intend to deceive himself. Deceit then, not

[1] *Vide* Barlow, Exer. Metaph., Exer. 2. Flac. Script. Tract. 6, p. 479.

being from sin nor ourselves properly, can find out no other parent for itself than Satan. Besides this, that these texts upon a rational inquiry do charge Satan with the deceitfulness of sin; they do over and above point at the known and constant way of Satan, working so commonly by delusion, that deceitfulness is a close companion of every sin. The deceitfulness of one sin is as much as the deceitfulness of every sin. Nay, further, that text of Jer. xvii. 9, shews this deceitfulness not to be an ordinary sleight, but the greatest of all deceits above measure, and of an unsearchable depth or mystery; 'who can know it?'

3. Thirdly, *All acts of sin, some way or other, come through Satan's fingers.* I do not say that all sin is Satan's proper offspring, for we have a cursed stock of our own; and it may be said of us, as elsewhere of Satan, sometime we sin out of our own inclination and disposition; yet in every sin, whether it arise from us or the world, Satan blows the sparks and manageth all. As David said to the woman of Tekoah, 'Is not the hand of Joab with thee in all this?' [2 Sam. xiv. 19;] so may we say, Is not the hand of Satan with thee in every sin thou committest? This is so eminently true, that the Scripture indifferently ascribes the sin sometimes to us, sometimes to the devil. It was Peter's sin to tempt Christ to decline suffering, yet Christ repelling it with this rebuke, 'Get thee behind me, Satan,' Mat. xvi. 23, doth plainly accuse both Peter and Satan. It is the personal sin of a man to be angry, yet in such acts he 'gives place to the devil;' both man and Satan concur in it, Eph. iv. 26. Paul's 'thorn in the flesh,' 2 Cor. xii. 7, whatever sin it was, he calls 'Satan's messenger.' He that submits not to God, doth in that comply with Satan; as, on the contrary, he that doth submit himself to God, doth resist the devil, James iv. 7.

Neither doth that expression of the apostle, James i. 14, 'Every man is tempted when he is drawn away of his own lust,' &c., give any contradiction to this. It is not the apostle's design to exclude Satan, but to include man as justly culpable, notwithstanding Satan's temptations; and that which he asserts is this, that there is sin and a temptation truly prevalent when there is the least consent of our lust or desire, and that it is that brings the blame upon us; so that his purpose is not to excuse Satan, or to deny him to have a hand in drawing or tempting us on to sin, but to shew that it is our own act that makes the sin to become ours.

4. Fourthly, *Such is the constitution of the soul of man, that its sinning cannot be conceived without some deception or delusion;*[1] for, granting that the soul of man is made up of desires, and that the soul were nothing else but, as it were, one willing or lusting power diversified by several objects; and that this power or these faculties are depraved by the fall, and corrupted; and that man in every action doth consult with his desires; and that they have so great an influence upon him, that they are the law of the members, and give out their commands accordingly for obedience; yet still these three things are firm and unshaken principles:—

[1.] First, That desires cannot be set upon any object but as it is

[1] Manton on James i. 14.

apprehended truly or apparently good. It is incompatible to a rational soul to desire evil as evil: *Omne appetit bonum.*

[2.] Secondly, The will doth not resolvedly embrace any object till the light of the understanding hath made out, some way or other, the goodness or conveniency of the object.[1]

[3.] Thirdly, There is no man that hath not a competent light for discovery of the goodness or evil of an object presented. Unregenerate men have, (1.) The light of nature. (2.) Some have an additional light from Scripture discovery. (3.) Some have yet more from common convictions, which beget sensible stirrings and awful impressions upon them. (4.) To those God sometime adds corrections and punishments, which are of force to make that light burn more clear, and to stir up care and caution in men for the due entertainment of these notices that God affords them. Regenerate men have all this light, and besides that, they have, (1.) The light of their own experience, of the vileness and odiousness of sin; they know what an evil and bitter thing it is. (2.) They have a more full discovery of God, which will make them abhor themselves in dust and ashes, Job xlii. 6; Isa. vi. 5. (3.) They have the advantage of a new heart, the law of the spirit of life, making them free from the law of sin and death. (4.) They have also the help and assistance of the Spirit, in its motions, suggestions, and teachings. (5.) They fortify themselves with the strongest resolutions not to give way to sin.

Notwithstanding all these, it is too true that both regenerate and unregenerate men do sin; the reason whereof cannot be given from any other account than what we have asserted—to wit, they are some way or other deluded or deceived; some curtain is drawn betwixt them and the light; some fallacy or other is put upon the understanding some way or other; the will is bribed or biassed; there is treachery in the case, for it is unimaginable that a man in any act of sin should offer a plain, open, and direct violence to his own nature and faculties; so that the whole business is here, evil is presented under the notion of good; and to make this out, some considerations of pleasure or profit do bribe the will, and give false light to the understanding. Hence is it, that in every act of sin, men, by compliance with Satan, are said to deceive, or to put tricks and fallacies upon themselves.[2]

5. Fifthly, *All kinds of subtlety are in Scripture directly charged upon Satan, and in the highest degrees.* Sometime under the notion of logical fallacies; those sleights which disputants, in arguing, put upon their antagonists. Of this import is that expression, 2 Cor. ii. 11, 'We are not ignorant of his devices,' where the word in the original is borrowed from the sophistical reasonings of disputants.[3] Sometime it is expressed in the similitude of political deceits; as the Scripture gives him the title of a prince, so doth it mark out his policies in the management of his kingdom, Rev. xii. 7, expressly calling them deceits, and comparing him to a dragon or serpent for his subtlety. Sometime he is represented as a warrior: Rev. xii. 17,

---

[1] Voluntas sequitur ultimum dictamen intellectus practici.
[2] James i. 22, 29, παραλογιζόμενοι ἑαυτούς.
[3] νοήματα. Thus Satan, Jude 9, disputed, urged sophisms about the body of Moses— διελέγετο.

'The dragon was wroth, and went to make war,' &c.; and here are his warlike stratagems pointed at. Mention is made, 2 Tim. ii. 26, of his snares, and the taking of men alive, or captive, directly alluding to warlike proceedings, [ἐζωγρήμενοι.] The subtle proceedings of arts and craft are charged on him and his instruments. Men are said to be enticed, James i., as fish or fowl, by a bait; others deluded, as by cheaters in false gaming: Eph. iv. 14, 'By the sleight of men, and the cunning craft of those that lie in wait to deceive.'[1] The overreaching of merchants or crafty tradesmen is alluded to in 2 Cor. ii. 11. All these sleights are in Satan, in their highest perfection and accomplishment. He can 'transform himself into an angel of light,' 2 Cor. xi. 14, where he hath an occasion for it; in a word, all 'deceiveableness of unrighteousness is in him,' 2 Thes. ii. 10. So that a general πανουργία, a dexterity and ability for all kind of subtle contrivances, is ascribed to him, 2 Cor. xi. 3, and that in his very first essay upon Eve, when the serpent deceived her ' through subtlety;' so that whatsoever malice can suggest, or wit and art contrive for delusion, or whatsoever diligence can practise, or cruelty execute, all that must be imagined to be in Satan.

6. Sixthly, All this might be further proved *by instances*. What temptation can be named wherein Satan hath not acted as a serpent? Who can imagine the cunning that Satan used with David in the matter of Uriah? How easily he got him to the roof of the house in order to the object to be presented to him! How he directs his eye, wrought upon his passions, suggested the thought, contrived the conveniences! What art must there be to bring a darkness into David's mind, a forgetfulness of God's law, a fearlessness of his displeasure, and a neglect of his own danger! Surely it was no small matter that could blind David's eye, or besot his heart to so great a wickedness. But, above all instances, let us take into consideration that of Eve, in the first transgression, wherein many things may be observed; as (1.) That he chose the serpent for his instrument, wherein, though we are ignorant of the depth of his design, yet that he had a design in it of subtlety, in reference to what he was about to suggest, is plain from the text, 'Now the serpent was more subtle than any beast of the field.' It had been needless and impertinent to have noted the serpent's subtlety as Satan's agent, if he had not chosen it upon that score, as advantageous for his purpose. (2.) He set upon the weaker vessel, the woman; and yet such, as once gained, he knew was likely enough to prevail with the man, which fell out accordingly. (3.) Some think he took the advantage of her husband's absence, which is probable, if we consider that it is unlikely that Adam should not interpose in the discourse if he had been present. (4.) He took the advantage of the object. It appears she was within sight of the tree, 'She saw that it was good for food, and pleasant to the eyes;' thus he made the object plead for him. (5.) He falls not directly upon what he intended, lest that should have scared her off, but fetcheth a compass and enters upon the business by an inquiry of the affair, as if he intended not hurt. (6.) He so inquires of the matter—

---

[1] ἐν τῇ κυβείᾳ. . . . πρὸς τὴν μεθοδείαν τῆς πλάνης. πλεονεκτεῖν dicit qui avaritia vel aliis malis artibus lucra comparat.—*Beza*.

'Hath God said, Ye shall not eat of every tree of the garden?'—as if he made a question of the reality of the command; and his words were so ordered that they might cast some doubt hereof into her mind. (7.) He, under a pretence of asserting God's liberality, secretly undermines the threatening, as if he had said, 'Is it possible that so bountiful a creator should deny the liberty of eating of any tree? To what purpose was it made, if it might not be tasted?' (8.) When he finds that by these arts he had gained a little ground, and brought her to some kind of questioning of the reality of the threatening, for she seems to extenuate it in saying, 'lest we die,' he grows more bold to speak out his mind, and plainly to annihilate the threatening, 'Ye shall not die.' This he durst not do, till he had gained in her mind a wavering suspicion, that possibly God was not in good earnest in that prohibition. (9.) Then he begins to urge the conveniency and excellency of the fruit, by equivocating upon the name of the tree, which he tells her could make them knowing as gods. (10.) He reflects upon God as prohibiting this out of envy and ill-will to them. (11.) In all this there is not a word of the danger, but impunity and advantage promised. (12.) This deadly advice he covers with a pretence of greater kindness and care than God had for them. See in this, as in a clear glass, Satan's way of policy; after this rate he proceeds in all his temptations.

If any inquire why so mighty and potent a prince useth rather the fox's skin than the lion's paw, these reasons may satisfy:—

[1.] First, *There is a necessity upon him so to do*.[1] He must use his craft, because he cannot compel; he must have God's leave before he can overcome; he cannot winnow Peter before he sue out a commission, nor deceive Ahab till he get a licence; neither can he prevail against us without our own consent. The Scripture indeed useth some words that signify a force in tempting, as that he 'put it into the heart of Judas,' 'filled the heart of Ananias,' 'provoked David,' 'rules in the hearts of the children of disobedience,' and 'leads them captive at his will,' &c.; yet all these and the like expressions intend no more than this, that he useth forcible importunities, frames strong delusions, and joins sometime his power to his temptations; as sometime fowlers shew themselves to the birds they intend to ensnare, that so they may be affrighted into an awe and amazement, to give a better opportunity to spread their nets over them.

[2.] Secondly, *If he could compel, yet his way of craft and subtlety is generally the most prevalent and successful.* Force stirs up an opposition; it usually alarms to caution and avoidance, and frights to an utter averseness in any design; so that where force should gain its thousands, subtlety will gain its ten thousands.

[3.] Thirdly, *His strength is not useless to him.* For besides that it enables him to deceive with higher advantage than otherwise he could do, as hath been said, he hath times and occasions to shew his strength and cruelty, when his cunning hath prevailed so far as to give him possession. What was said of Pope Boniface, that he

[1] *Vide* Capel. Temp., p. 27; Will. Paris in Ames Cas. Consc., lib. ii. cap. 19; Goodwin, Child of Light, p. 47; Caryl on Job i. 14. All are volunteers; he never constrains any, neither can he; the will is never forced by him, neither can it be.

entered like a fox, and ruled like a lion, may be applied to him; he insinuates himself by subtlety as a fox or serpent, and then rules with rigour as a lion.

CHAPTER IX.

Of Satan's deceits in particular.—What temptation is.—Of tempting to sin.—His first general rule.—The consideration of our condition.—His second rule.—Of providing suitable temptations.—In what cases he tempts us to things unsuitable to our inclinations.—His third rule.—The cautious proposal of the temptation, and the several ways thereof.—His fourth rule is to entice.—The way thereof in the general, by bringing a darkness upon the mind through lust.

Our next business is to inquire after these ways of deceit in particular; in which I shall first speak of such as are of more general and universal concernment—such are his temptations to sin, his deceits against duty, his cunning in promoting error, his attempts against the peace and comfort of the saints, &c.—and then I shall come to some ways of deceits that relate to cases more special.

As an introduction to the first, I shall speak a word *of temptation in the general.* This in its general notion is a trial or experiment made of a thing. The word that signifies to tempt, comes from a word that signifies to pierce, or bore through,[1] implying such a trial as goes to the very heart and inwards of a thing. In this sense it is attributed to God, who is said to have tempted Abraham, and to put our faith upon trial; and sometime to Satan, who is said to have tempted Christ, though he could not expect to prevail. But though God and Satan do make these trials, yet is there a vast difference betwixt them, and that not only in their intentions—the one designing only a discovery to men of what is in them, and that for most holy ends; the other intending ruin and destruction—but also in the way of their proceedings.[2] God by providence presents objects and occasions; Satan doth not only do that, but further inclineth and positively persuadeth to evil. Hence is it that temptations are distinguished into trials merely, and seducements; suitable to that of Tertullian, [De Orat.] *Diabolus tentat, Deus probat,* The devil tempts, God only tries. We speak of temptation as it is from Satan, and so it is described to be a drawing or moving men to sin under colour of some reason.[3] By which we may observe that, in every such temptation, there is the object to which the temptation tends, the endeavour of Satan to incline our hearts and draw on our consent, and the instrument by which is some pretence of reason; not that a real and solid reason can be given for sin, but that Satan offers some considerations to us to prevail with us, which, if they do, we take them to be reasons. This may a little help us to understand Satan's method in tempting to sin, &c., of which I am first to speak.

[1] πειράζω a πειρω.   [2] Calv. Instit., lib. iii. cap. 20, sec. 46.
[3] Capel. Tempt[ations,] p. 26. [1635, 12mo.—G.]

In temptations to sin, we may observe, Satan walks by four general rules:—

1. First, *He considers and acquaints himself with the condition of every man, and for that end he studies man.* God's question concerning Job, 'Hast thou considered my servant Job?' Job i. 8, doth imply, not only his diligent inquiry into Job's state—for the original expresseth it by Satan's 'putting his heart upon Job, or laying him to his heart'[1]—but that this is usual with Satan so to do; as if God had said, It is thy way to pry narrowly into every man: hast thou done this to Job? Hast thou considered him as thou usest to do? And indeed Satan owns this as his business and employment in his answer to God, 'I come from going to and fro in the earth, from walking up and down in it.' This cannot be properly said of him who is a spirit. Bodies go up and down, but not spirits; so that his meaning is, he had been at his work of inquiring and searching. And so Broughton translates it,[2] from searching to and fro in the earth; as it is said of the eyes of God, that they 'run to and fro,' which intends his intelligence, search, and knowledge of things. It is such a going to and fro as that in Dan. xii. 4, which is plainly there expressed to be for the increase of knowledge.

The matter of his inquiry or particulars of his study are such as these: (1.) Man's state; he considers and guesseth whether a man be regenerate or unregenerate. (2.) The degree of his state: if unregenerate, how near or far off he is the kingdom of God; if regenerate, he takes the compass of his knowledge, of his gifts, of his graces. (3.) He inquires into his constitution and temper; he observes what disposition he is of. (4.) His place, calling, and relation; his trade, employment, enjoyments, riches, or wants. (5.) His sex. (6.) His age, &c.

The way by which he knows these things is plain and easy. Most of these things are open to common observation; and what is intricate or dark, that he beats out, either by comparing us with ourselves, and considering a long tract of actions and carriage; or by comparing us with others, whose ways he had formerly noted and observed.

The end of this search is to give him light and instruction in point of advantage; hence he knows where to raise his batteries, and how to level his shot against us. This Christ plainly discovers to be the design of all his study, John xiv. 30, where he tells his disciples he expected yet another onset from Satan, and that near at hand; 'for the prince of the world' was then upon his motion, he was a-coming; but withal, he tells them of his security against his assaults, in that there was 'nothing in Christ' of advantage in any of these forementioned ways to foot a temptation upon. It appears, then, that he looks for such advantages, and that without these he hath little expectancy of prevailing.

2. Secondly, Satan having acquainted himself with our condition, makes it his next care to provide *suitable temptations, and to strike in the right vein;* for he loves to have his work easy and feasible, he loves not [to] go against the stream. Thus he considered Judas as a covetous person, and accordingly provided a temptation of gain for

[1] Caryl. *in loc.*   [2] שׁוּט, circumspexit, lustravit.—Metaph.

him. He did the like with Achan; and hence was it that he had the Sabeans so ready for the plunder of Job; he had observed them a people given to rapine and spoil; and accordingly, Job's goods being propounded to them as a good and easy booty, he straightway prevailed with them. It was easy for him to draw Absalom into an open rebellion against his father; he had taken notice of his ambitious and aspiring humour, and of the grudges and dissatisfactions under which he laboured; so that, providing him a fit opportunity, he engaged him immediately. According to this rule, where he observes men of shallow heads and low parts, he the more freely imposeth upon them in things palpably absurd; where he takes notice of a fearful temper, there he tempts them with terrors and affrightful suggestions. He hath temptations proper for the sanguine complexion and for the melancholy; he hath his methods of dealing with the lustful and wanton, with the passionate and revengeful; he hath novelties at hand for the itching ear, and suggestions proper for those that are atheistically inclined.

Obj. To this may be objected, That experience tells us Satan doth not always walk in this road, nor confine himself to this rule: sometime he tempts to things which are cross to our tempers and inclinations, &c.

Ans. It is true he doth so; but yet the general rule is not prejudiced by this exception, especially if we consider,

[1.] First, *That Satan being still under the commands and restraint of the Almighty, he cannot always tempt what he would, but according to a superior order and command.* Of this nature I suppose was that temptation of which Paul complained so much; 'he kept down his body,' 1 Cor. ix. 27, upon this very design, that he might have it in subjection, and yet is he buffeted with a temptation which expected an advantage usually from the temper and frames of our bodies—for so much, I suppose, that phrase, 'a thorn in the flesh,' will unavoidably imply—though it still leave us at uncertainties what the temptation was in particular. Here Satan tempts at a disadvantage, and contrary to this rule; but then we must know that he was not the master of his own game—God expressly ordering such a temptation as was disagreeing with the apostle's disposition, that it might the less prevail or hazard him, and yet be more available to keep him low, 'lest he should be exalted above measure,' which was God's design in the matter.

[2.] Secondly, *Sometime our temper alters;* as the tempers of our bodies in a sickness may in a fit be so changed that they may desire at that time what they could not endure at another. A special occasion or concurrence of circumstances may alter for the time our constitution, and so an unusual temptation may at that time agree with this design.

[3.] Thirdly, *Sometime by one temptation Satan intends but to lay the foundation of another;* and then of purpose he begins with a strange suggestion, either to keep us at the gaze while he covertly doth something else against us, or to move us to a contrary extreme by an over-hasty rashness.

[4.] Fourthly, *Sometime he tempts when his main design is only to trouble and disquiet us;* and in such cases the most unnatural temptations, backed with a violent impetuousness, do his work the best.

3. Thirdly, Satan's next work is *the proposal of the temptation.* In the two former he provided materials and laid the trains; in this he gives fire, by propounding his design; and this also he doth with caution these several ways:—

[1.] First, He makes *the object speak for him, and in many he is scarce put to any further trouble:* the object before them speaks Satan's mind, and gains their consent immediately; yet is there no small cunning used in fitting the object and occasion, and bringing things about to answer the very nick of time which he takes to be advantageous for him.

[2.] Secondly, Sometime he appoints *a proxy to speak for him;* not that he is shamefaced in temptation, and not always at leisure for his own work, but this way he insinuates himself the more dangerously into our affections, and with less suspicion, using our friends, relations, or intimate acquaintance to intercede for a wicked design. He did not speak himself to Eve, but chose a serpent: he thought Eve would sooner prevail upon Adam than the serpent could. He tempted Job by the tongue of his wife, as if he had hoped that what so near a relation had counselled would easily be hearkened to. He tempted Christ to avoid suffering by Peter, under a pretence of highest love and care, 'Master, spare thyself,' [Mat. xvi. 23;] yet our Saviour forbears not to note Satan's temptation closely twisted with Peter's kindness. At this rate are we often tempted where we little suspect danger.

[3.] Thirdly, If he finds the two first ways unhopeful or unsuitable, then he *injects the motion, and so plainly speaks to us inwardly himself,* 'Do this act, take this advantage for pleasure or profit,' &c. He thought it not enough to tempt Judas by the object of gain, but he brake his mind in direct terms, and 'put it into his heart,' John xiii. 2. He did the like to Ananias, whose heart he filled with a large motion for that lie, and backed it with many considerations of the necessity and expediency of it, Acts v. 3. There is no question to be made of this. Dr Goodwin gives clear proofs of it, and so do several others.[1] When we consider that thoughts are sometime cast upon the minds of men which are above their knowledge, and that they say and do things sometime which are far beyond any of their accomplishments and parts, and yet in the nature of it wicked, we must be forced to run so high as to charge it upon Satan. Saul's prophesying, 1 Sam. xviii. 10, was by the influence of the evil spirit; and this—as Junius, Tirinus, and others interpret[2]—must of necessity be understood of such a kind of action and speaking as the true prophets of the Lord usually expressed under the influences of the blessed Spirit; for from the likeness of the action in both must the name be borrowed. The experience that we have of inward disputings, the bandying of arguments and answers in several cases, is a proof of this beyond exception. Wounded consciences express an admirable dexterity in breaking all arguments urged for their peace and establishment; as also in framing

---

[1] Child of Light, p. 45. [As before.—G.]   [2] *Vide* Pool: Synops. *in loc.*

objections against themselves, so far above the usual measure of common capacities, that we cannot ascribe it to any other than Satan's private aid this way.

[4.] Fourthly, The motion being made, if there be need, he doth *irritate and stir up the mind to the embracement of it;* and this he doth two ways:—

First, By an earnestness of solicitation; when he urgeth the thing over and over, and gives no rest; when he joins with this an importunity of begging and entreating with the repeated motion; when he draws together and advantageously doth order a multitude of considerations to that end; and when in all this he doth hold down the mind and thoughts, and keep them upon a contemplation of the object, motions, and reasons. Thus he provoked David, 1 Chron. xxi. 1; and this kind of dealing occasioned the apostle to name his temptations and our resistance by the name of 'wrestlings,' in which usually there appears many endeavours and often repeated, to throw down the antagonist.

Secondly, He doth irritate *by a secret power and force that he hath upon our fancies and passions.* When men are said to be carried and led by Satan, it implies, in the judgment of some,[1] more than importunity; and that though he cannot force the spring of the will, yet he may considerably act upon it by pulling at the weights and plummets—that is, by moving and acting our imaginations and affections.

4. Fourthly, The motion being made, notwithstanding all his importunity, often finds resistance; in which case he comes to the practice of a fourth rule, which is *to draw away and entice the heart to consent*—as it is expressed, James i. 14, 'Every man is tempted, when he is drawn away and enticed.'[2] I shall avoid here the variety of the apprehensions which some declare at large about the meaning of the words, satisfying myself with this, that the apostle points at those artifices of Satan by which he draws and allures the will of man to a compliance with his motions, which when he effects in any degree, then may a man be said to be prevailed upon by the temptation. But then here is the wonder, how he should so far prevail against that reason and knowledge which God hath placed in man to fence and guard him against a thing so absurd and unreasonable as every sin is. The solution of this knot we have in 2 Cor. iv. 4, 'The god of this world blinds the eyes of men,' draws a curtain over this knowledge, and raiseth a darkness upon them: which darkness, though we cannot fully apprehend, yet that it is a very great and strange darkness may be discovered, (1.) Partly by considering the subject of it—man, a rational creature, in whom God hath placed a conscience, which is both a law, and witness, and judge. It cannot be supposed an easy matter to cloud or obliterate that law, to silence or pervert that witness, or to corrupt that judge; but it will rise higher in the wonder of it if we consider this in a godly man, one that sets God before him, and is wont to have his fear in his heart—such a man as David was, that in so plain a case, in so high a manner, so long a time, with so little sense and apprehension of the evil and danger, Satan should so quickly prevail, it is an astonishment: neither will it be less strange if

[1] Dr Goodwin, 'Child of Light.' [As before.—G.]   [2] Manton, *in loc.*

we consider, (2.) The issue and effect of this blindness. Some rise up against this law of conscience, arguing it false and erroneous, and making conclusions directly contrary, as Deut. xxix. 19, 'I shall have peace, though I walk on in the imaginations of my heart;' 'I have fellowship with him, though I walk in darkness,' 1 John i. 6; 'We will not hearken unto thee, but will certainly do whatsoever thing goeth out of our own mouth,' Jer. xlv. 16, 17; in which cases the συντήρησις, or principles of conscience, are quite overthrown. Some are hardened, and as to any application of their acts to this rule, quite dead and senseless. Though they rise not up against the light, yet are they willingly ignorant, without any consideration of what they are doing. Here the συνείδησις, or witnessing and excusing power of conscience, is idle and asleep. Some, though they know the law, and in some measure see their actions are sinful, yet they pass no judgment, apprehend no danger: 'No man smites upon his thigh, saying, What have I done?' Jer. viii. 6. Nay, some are so far from this, that they presumptuously justify themselves, though they see their own blame and ruin before them: 'I do well to be angry, and that to the death,' saith Jonah, when Satan had spread a darkness upon him.

What shall we say of these things? Here is darkness to be felt, Egyptian darkness. To explain the way of it fully is impossible for us; to do it in any tolerable way is difficult. To make some discovery herein I shall, (1.) Shew that the devil doth entice to sin by 'stirring up our lust;' (2.) That by the power and prevalency of our lust he brings on the blindness spoken of.

CHAPTER X.

That Satan enticeth by our lust.—The several ways by which he doth it.—Of the power and danger of the violence of affections.

The way, then, by which he doth entice is by 'stirring up our lust.' By 'lust' I mean those general desirings of our minds after any unlawful object which are forbidden in the tenth commandment. Thus we read of 'worldly lusts,' of the 'lusts of the flesh,' of 'lustings to envy,' and, in a word, we read of 'divers lusts,' the whole attempt and striving of corrupt nature against the Spirit being set forth by this expression 'of lusting against the Spirit,' Titus ii. 12; 1 Peter ii. 18; James iv. 5; Titus iii. 3; Gal. v. 17.

That Satan takes advantage of our own lusts, and so ploughs with our heifer, turning our own weapons against ourselves, is evident by the general vote of Scripture. The apostle James, chap. i. 14, tells us that every temptation prevails only by the power and working of our own lusts. Satan is the tempter, but our lusts are the advantages by which he draws and enticeth. The corrupt principle within us is called 'flesh,' but the way whereby it works, either in its own proper motion or as stirred up by the devil, is that of lust and affection; and therefore he that would stop that issue must look to mortify it in its affections and lusts, Gal. v. 24. We are further told by John, 1 Epist. ii. 16, that all those snares that are in the world are only hazardous and prevailing by our lusts. More generally the apostle Peter speaks, 2 Peter i. 4; the whole bundle of actual sins that have ever been in the world came in at this door, 'The corruption that is in the world is through lust.' In the stirring up our lusts Satan useth no small art and subtlety, and ordinarily he worketh by some of these following ways:—

1. First, He useth his skill *to dress up an object of lust that it may be taking and alluring.* He doth not content himself with a simple proposal of the object, but doth as it were paint and varnish it, to make it seem beautiful and lovely. Besides all that wooing and importunity which he useth to the soul by private and unseen suggestions, he hath no doubt a care to gather together all possible concurring circumstances, by which the seeming goodness or conveniency of the object is much heightened and enlarged. We see those that have skill to work upon the humours of men place a great part of it in the right circumstantiating a motion, and in taking the tempers and inclinations of men at a right time. And they observe that the missing of the right season is the hazard of the design, even there where the object and inclination ordinarily are suitable. There is much in placing a picture in a right position, to give it its proper grace and lustre in the eyes of the beholders. When a man is out of humour he nauseates his usual delights, and grows sullen to things of frequent practice. It is likely Eve was not a stranger to the tree of knowledge before the temptation, but when the serpent suggests the goodness of the fruit, the fruit itself seems more beautiful and desirable, 'good for food, and pleasant to the eyes,' [Gen. ii. 9.] Though we are not able to find out the way of Satan's beautifying an object that it may affect with more piercing and powerful delights, yet he that shall consider that not only prudence, in an advantageous management of things, adds an additional beauty to objects proposed, but also that art, by placing things in a right posture, may derive a radiancy and beam of beauty and light upon them, as an ordinary piece of glass may be so posited to the sunbeams that it may reflect a sparkling light as if it were a diamond,— he that shall consider this, I say, will not think it strange for the devil to use some arts of this kind for the adorning and setting off an object to the eye of our lusts.

2. Secondly, We have reason to suspect that he may have *ways of deceit and imposture upon our senses.* The deceits of the senses are so much noted, that some philosophers will scarce allow any credit to be given them; not that they are always deceitful, but that they are often so, and therefore always suspicious.[1] The soul hath no intelligence but by the senses. It is then a business of easy belief, that Satan may not altogether slight this advantage, but that when he sees it fit for his purpose, he may impose upon us by the deception of our eyes and ears. We little know how oft our senses have disguised things to us. In a pleasing object, our eyes may be as a magnifying or multiplying glass. In the first temptation Satan seems to have wrought both upon the object and also upon the senses; she 'saw it was good for food and pleasant.' Who can question but that she saw the fruit before? But this was another kind of sight, of more power

---

[1] Descartes, Ant. le grand, Philosoph. Vet., &c.

and attraction. An instance of Satan's cunning in both the forementioned particulars we have from Austin, relating the story of his friend Alypius, who by the importunity of his acquaintance consented to go to the theatre, yet with a resolve not to open his eyes, lest the sight of these spectacles should entice his heart; but being there, the noise and sudden shouting of the multitude prevailed so far with him that he forgot his resolution; takes the liberty to see what occasioned the shouting, and once seeing, is now so inflamed with delight that he shouts as the rest do, and becomes a frequenter of the theatre as others.[1] What was there to be seen and heard he knew before by the relation of others; but now being present, his eyes and ears were by Satan so heightened in their offices, that those bloody objects seemed pleasant beyond all that had been reported of them, and the lust of his heart drawn out by Satan's cunning disposal of the object and senses.

3. Thirdly, There is no small enticement arising from *the fitness and suitableness of occasion.* An occasion exactly fitted is more than half a temptation. This often makes a thief, an adulterer, &c., where the acts of these sins have their rise from a sudden fit of humour, which occasion puts them in, rather than from design or premeditation. Cunningly contrived occasions are like the danger of a precipice. If a man be so foolish as to take up a stand there, a small push will throw him over, though a far greater might not harm him if he were upon a level. It is Satan's cunning to draw a man within the reach of an occasion. All the resolves of Alypius were not safeguard to him, when once he was brought within hearing and sight of the temptation. If he had stayed at home, the hazard of Satan's suggestions, though earnest, had not been so much as the hearing of his ears and sight of his eyes. In 2 Cor. ii. 11, Paul's fears of Satan's taking advantage against the Corinthians, did manifestly arise from the present posture of their church affairs: for if the excommunicated person should not be received again into the church, an ordinary push of temptation might either have renewed or confirmed their contentions, or precipitated[2] them into an opinion of too much severity against an offending brother; and that their present frame made them more than ordinarily obnoxious to these snares, is evident from the apostle's caution inserted here in this discourse, so abruptly, that any man may observe the necessity of the matter, and the earnestness of his affections did lead his pen.[3] The souls of men have their general *discrasias* and disaffections, as our bodies have, from a lingering distemperature of the blood and humours; in which case, a small occasion, like a particular error of diet, &c., in a declining body, will easily form that inclination into particular acts of sin.

4. Fourthly, Satan hath yet a further reach in his enticements, by *the power which he hath upon our fancies and imaginations.* That he hath such a power was discovered before. This being then supposed, how serviceable it is for his end it is now to be considered. Our fancy is as a glass, which, with admirable celerity and quickness of

---

[1] Spectavit, clamavit, exarsit, abstulit inde secum insaniam qua stimularetur redire, &c.
[2] Spelled 'precipated,' which is noted as a transition-form found elsewhere.—G.
[3] *Vide* Calvin, *in loc.*

motion, can present before us all kinds of objects; it can in a moment run from one end of the earth to the other; and besides this, it hath a power of creating objects, and casting them into what forms and shapes it pleaseth, all which our understanding cannot avoid the sight of. Now the power of imagination is acknowledged by all to be very great, not only as working upon a melancholy and distempered spirit, of which authors give us large accounts,[1] but also upon minds more remote from such peremptory delusions; as may be daily observed in the prejudices and prepossessions of men, who by reason of the impressions of imagination, are not without difficulty drawn over to the acknowledgment of the truth of things, and the true understanding of matters; neither is the understanding only liable to a more than ordinary heat and rapture by it, but the will is also quickened and sharpened in its desires by this means. Hence is it, as one of the fore-cited authors observes,[2] that fancy doth often more toward a persuasion by its insinuations than a cogent argument or rational demonstration.

This is no less a powerful instrument in Satan's hand, than commonly and frequently made use of. Who amongst us doth not find and feel him dealing with us at this weapon? When he propounds an object to our lust, he doth not usually expose it naked under the hazard of dying out for want of prosecution, but presently calls in our fancy to his aid, and there raiseth a theatre, on which he acts before our minds the sin in all its ways and postures. If he put us upon revenge, or upon lusts of uncleanness, or covetousness, or ambition, we are sure, if we prevent it not, to have our imagination presenting these things to us as in lively pictures and resemblances, by which our desires may be inflamed and prepared for consent.

5. Fifthly, Sometime he shews his art *in preparing and fitting our bodies to his designs, or in fitting temptations to our bodies and the inclinations thereof.* The soul, though it be a noble being, yet is it limited by the body, and incommodated by the craziness and indispositions thereof, so that it can no more act strenuously or evenly to its principles in a disordered body, than it can rightly manage any member of it, in its natural motions, where the bones are disjointed. Hence sickness or other bodily weaknesses do alter the scene, and add another kind of bias to the soul than what it had before. This Satan takes notice of, and either follows his advantage of the present indisposition, or, if he hath some special design, endeavours to cast our body into such a disorder as may best suit his intention. Asa was more easily drawn to be overseen in peevishness and rash anger in his latter days, when his body grew diseased. Satan had his advantage against Solomon to draw him to idolatry when old age and uxoriousness had made him more ductile to the solicitations of his wives; 'When Solomon was old, his wives turned away his heart,' 1 Kings xi. 4. The devil, when he took upon him to foretell Job's blaspheming God to his face, yet he attempted not the main design till he thought he had thoroughly prepared him for it, by the anguish and smart of a distempered body and mind; and though he failed in the great business of his boast, yet he left us an experiment in Job, that the likeliest

---

[1] Burton's Melanch., part i. sec. 2, p. 93. Reynold's Treat. of Passions, cap. 4.
[2] Reynolds, *Ibid.*

way to prevail upon the mind in hideous and desperate temptations, is to mould the body to a suitable frame. He prevailed not against Job to cause him curse God, yet he prevailed far, 'he cursed the day of his birth,' and spake many things by the force of that distress, which he professeth himself ashamed of afterwards. The body then will be in danger, when it is disordered, to give a tincture to every action, as a distempered palate communicates a bitterness to everything it takes down.

6. Sixthly, *Evil company is a general preparatory to all kinds of temptation.* He enticeth strongly that way. For, (1.) Evil society doth insensibly dead the heart, and quench the heat of the affections to the things of God. It hath a kind of bewitching power to eat out the fear of the Lord in our hearts, and to take off the weight and power of religious duty. It not only stops our tongues, and retards them in speaking of good things, but influenceth the very heart, and poisons it into a kind of deadness and lethargy, so that our thoughts run low, and we begin to think that severe watchfulness of thoughts and the guard of our minds to be a needless and melancholy self-imposition. (2.) Example hath a strange insinuating force to enstamp a resemblance, and to beget imitation. Joseph, living where his ears were frequently beaten with oaths, finds it an easy thing, upon a feigned occasion, to swear by the life of Pharaoh, [Gen. xlii. 15.] Evil company is sin's nursery and Satan's academy, by which he trains up those whose knowledge and hopeful beginnings had made them shy of his temptations; and if he can prevail with men to take such companions, he will with a little labour presently bring them to any iniquity.

7. Seventhly, But his highest project in order to the enticing of men, is to *engage their affections to a height and passionateness.* The Scripture doth distinguish betwixt the ἐπιθυμίας and παθήματα, the affections and lusts, Gal. v. 24; clearly implying that the way to procure fixed desires and actual lustings, is to procure those passionate workings of the mind.

How powerful a part of his design this is, will appear from the nature of these passions: which are,

[1.] First, *Violent motions of the heart;* the very wings and sails of the soul, and every passion, in its own working, doth express a violence.[1] Choler is an earnest rage; voluptuousness is nothing less; fear is a desperate hurry of the soul; 'love strong as death; jealousy cruel as the grave;' each of them striving which should excel in violence, so that it is a question yet undetermined which passion may challenge the superiority.

[2.] Secondly, *Their fury is dangerous and unbridled;* like so many wild horses let loose, hurrying their rider which way they please. They move not upon the command of reason, but oft prevent it in their sudden rise; neither do they take reason's advice for their course proportionable to the occasion, for often their humour, rather than the matter of the provocation, gives them spurs; and when they have evaporated their heat, they cease, not as following the command of reason, but as weakened by their own violence.

[3.] Thirdly, *They are not easily conquered;* not only because

[1] *Vide* Fenner, 'Treat[ise] of Affections.' J. F. Senault of Passions, p. 30

they renew their strength and onset after a defeat, and, like so many hydra's heads, spring up as fast as cut off; but they are ourselves—we can neither run from them, nor from the love of them.

[4.] Fourthly, And consequently *highly advantageous in Satan's design and enticement when they are driven up to a fury and passionateness;* for besides their inward rage, which the Scripture calls burning, 1 Cor. vii. 9; Rom. i. 27, by which men are pricked and goaded on without rest or ease, to 'make provisions for the flesh,' and to enjoy or act what their unbridled violence will lead to in the execution of their desires, they carry all on before them, and engage the whole man with the highest eagerness 'to fulfil every lust,' Eph. ii. 3, to go up to the highest degrees, and with an unsatiable greediness to yield themselves 'servants of iniquity unto iniquity,' Rom. vi. 19.

CHAPTER XI.

That lust darkens the mind.—Evidences thereof.—The five ways by which it doth blind men: First, By preventing the exercise of reason.—The ways of that prevention: (1.) *Secrecy in tempting; Satan's subtlety therein;* (2.) *Surprisal;* (3.) *Gradual entanglements.*

That Satan doth entice us by stirring up our lust, hath been discovered; it remains that I next speak to the second thing propounded, which was,

That by this power of lust he *blinds and darkens our mind.* That the lusts of men are the great principle upon which Satan proceeds in drawing on so great a blindness as we have spoken of, I shall briefly evince from these few observations:—

1. First, *From the unreasonableness and absurdity of some actions in men otherwise sufficiently rational.* He that considers the acts of Alexander, in murdering Calisthenes, for no other crime than defending the cause of the gods, and affirming that temples could not be built to a king without provoking a deity; and yet this so smoothed, if Quintus Curtius represent him right, that he seemed to flatter Alexander with an opinion of deification after his death;[1] whosoever, I say, shall consider this cruelty, will condemn Alexander as blind and irrational in this matter; and yet no other cause can be assigned hereof, but that his lust after glory and honour darkened his reason. The like may be said of his killing Hephæstion's physician, because *he* died. The brutal fury of that consul, that made a slave to be eaten up with lampreys, for no other fault than the breaking of a glass, can be ascribed to nothing else but the boiling over of his passion. A sadder instance of this we have in Theodosius senior, who, for an affront given to some of his officers in Thessalonica, commanded the destruction of the city, and the slaughter of the citizens to the number of seven thousand, without any distinction of nocent

---

[1] Ego autem seram immortalitatem precor regi. . . . . Hominem consequitur aliquando, nunquam comitatur divinitas.—*Curt.*, lib. viii.

and innocent.[1] This blind rage the historian notes as the fruit of violent and unbridled lust in a man otherwise just and gracious. Thousands of instances of this nature might be added. But,

2. Secondly, If we consider *the known and visible hazards to life and estate, and, that which is more, to that part of them which is immortal;* upon all which men do desperately adventure, upon no other ground or motive than the gratifications of their lusts,—we may easily conclude that there is a strange force and power in their passions to blind and besot them; and this, notwithstanding, is the common practice of all men, where grace, as the only eye-salve, doth not restore the sight. The heathens in all these practices of filthiness and folly, recorded Rom. i. 29, they had so far a discovery of the danger, if they had not imprisoned that truth and light in unrighteousness, ver. 18, that they knew the 'judgment of God, that they which commit such things are worthy of death,' ver. 32. Yet, notwithstanding, the vanity of their imaginations, influenced by lust, darkened their heart so much that they did 'not only do these things,' of so great vileness and unspeakable hazard, 'but had pleasure in those that did them.'

3. Thirdly, The blinding power of lust is yet more remarkable, *when we see men glorying in their shame, and mounting their triumphal chariots to expose themselves a spectacle to all, in that garb of deformity which their lusts have put them in.* It is a blindness to do any act against the rules of reason, but it is a far greater blindness for men to pride themselves in them. What have the issues of most wars been, but burning of cities, devastations of flourishing kingdoms, spilling the blood of millions, besides all the famine and other miseries that follow; yet these actions, that better beseem tigers, lions, and savage brutes, than men of reason, are honoured with the great, triumphant names of virtue, manhood, courage, magnanimity, conquest, &c. If the power and humour of their lusts of vainglory and revenge had not quite muffled their understandings, these things would have been called by their proper names of murder, cruelty, robbery, &c.; and the actors of such tragedies, instead of triumphal arches and acclamations of praise, would have been buried under heaps of ignominy and perpetual disgraces, as prodigies of nature, monsters of men, and haters of mankind.

4. Fourthly, But there is yet one evidence more plain and convincing; *when our lusts are up, though reason offer its aids to allay the storm, yet the wisest of men, otherwise composed and calm, are so far from taking the advantage of its guidance, that oftentimes they trample upon it and despise it;* and as if lusts, by some secret incantation, had made them impenetrable, they are not capable of its light and conduct, and can make no more use of it than a blind man can do of a candle. To this purpose, let us observe the carriage of disputants. If men do any way publicly engage themselves in a contest of this nature, though truth can be but on the one side, yet both

---

[1] Immoderata animi concitatione impulsus . . . . facinus crudele et nefarium commisit. . . . . Iracundia . . . . velut tyrannus, omnia suo metu gubernans, ruptis habenis, et jugo rationis excusso, gladios inique contra omnes distrinxit.—*Theod. Hist. Eccles.*, lib. v. p. 587.

parties give arguments and answer objections with equal confidence of victory, and a contempt of the reasons and strength of each other's discourses; and this proves so fatal to him that maintains the mistake or untruth, that not one of a thousand hath the benefit and advantage for the finding of truth, which free and unprejudiced bystanders may have; so true is that, *Omne perit judicium cum res transit in affectum,* When affections are engaged, judgment is darkened. It is a thing of common observation, that when men are discoursed into anger and heat, they presently grow absurd; are disabled for speaking or understanding reason, and are oft hurried to such inconveniences and miscarriages, that they are ashamed of themselves; when they cool, and the fit is over, *Impedit ira animum,* &c. To all this might be added the power of lust in persons voluptuous, who dedicate themselves to the pleasures of the flesh. Those that 'serve divers lusts and pleasures,' their slavish estate, their base drudgery, do clearly evince that lust unmans them, and puts out their eyes. Mark Antony by this means became a slave to Cleopatra; never did a poor captive strive more to obtain the good-will of his lord than he to please this woman, insomuch that, besotted with his lust, he seemed to want that common foresight of his danger, which the smallest measure of reason might have afforded to any, and so dallied himself into his ruin. From all these considerations and instances, it appears our lusts afford such vapours and mists that our reason is darkened by them, or rather they are like a dose of opium, that strongly stupifies and binds up the senses. But yet it remains that the various ways by which our lusts do blind us be particularly opened, and they are five. (1.) Our lusts blind us by preventing the use and exercise of reason. (2.) By perverting it. (3.) By withdrawing the mind from it. (4.) By disturbing it in its operation. And (5.) By a desperate precipitancy; all which I shall more fully explain.

I. First, Our lusts blind us *by preventing and intercepting the exercise of light and reason;* and Satan in this case useth these deceits:—

1. First, He endeavours so to *stir up our lust as yet to conceal his design.* Secrecy is one of his main engines. He doth not in this case shew his weapon before he strikes; and indeed his policy herein is great. For, [1.] By this means he takes us at unawares, secure, and unprepared for resistance. [2.] We are often ensnared without noise, and before our consideration of things can come in to rescue us. [3.] If he get not his whole design upon us this way, yet he oft makes a half victory. By this means he procures a half content or inclination to sin, before we discover that we are under a temptation; for when the foundation of a temptation is laid unespied, then we awaken with the sin in our hand, as sleeping men awake sometime with the word in their mouths. If any question, How can these things be? How can he steal a temptation upon us with such secrecy? I answer, he can do it these three ways:—

(1.) First, He sometimes after *a careless manner, and as it were by the by, drops in a suggestion into our hearts, and that without noise or importunity, giving it as it were this charge, 'Stir not up nor awaken him;'* and then he sits by to observe the issue, and to see if the tinder will take fire of itself. Thus many a motion thrown into our hearts, as it were accidentally, ere ever we are aware, begets a sudden flame.

(2.) Secondly, He sometimes *fetcheth a compass, and makes a thing far different to be a preamble or introduction to his intended design.* Thus by objects, employments, discourse, or company, that shew not any direct tendency to evil, doth he insensibly occasion pride, passion, or lust. How slyly and secretly doth he put us upon what he intends as a further snare! How unawares, while we think of no such thing, are we carried sometime upon the borders of sin, and into the enemy's quarters! Satan in this acts like a fowler, who useth a stalking-horse, as if he were upon some other employment, when yet his design is the destruction of the bird.

(3.) Thirdly, Another way of secrecy is his raising *a crowd of other thoughts in the mind, and while these are mixed and confusedly floating in the understanding or fancy, then doth he thrust in among them the intended suggestion;* and then suffering the rest to vanish, he by little and little singles this out as a more special object of consideration, so that we cast a sudden glance upon this, and we are often taken with it before we consider the danger. In this Satan doth as soldiers, who take the advantage of a mist to make a nearer approach to their enemies, and to surprise them before discovery of the danger. This he doth with us while we are in a musing fit or a melancholy dream.

2. A second deceit for the preventing of a serious consideration is *sudden surprisal.* In the former he endeavoured to conceal the temptation while he is at work with us, but in this he shews the temptation plainly, only he sets upon us without giving of us warning of the onset; but then he backs it with all the violent importunity he can, and by this he hinders the recollecting of ourselves and the aid of reason. This course Satan only takes with those whose passions are apt to be very stirring and boisterous, or such as, being his slaves and vassals, are more subject to his commands. Thus a sudden provocation to an angry man gives him not time to consider, but carries him headlong. A surprise of occasion and opportunity is frequently a conquest to those that have any earnestness of hope, desire, or revenge. Surely David was taken at this advantage in the matter of Bathsheba. And here we may note that good men upon such a sudden motion do yield, without any blow or struggling, to that which at other times they could not be drawn to by many reasons.

3. Thirdly, Consideration is prevented by *gradual entanglements.* Satan so orders the matter that sin creeps on upon us as sleep, by insensible degrees. For this end sometimes he dissembles his strength, and sets upon us with lower temptations, and with less force than otherwise he could. He knows we are not moved to extremes, but by steps and habits; are not confirmed, but by gradual proceedings. To take too great strides may sometime prevail at present; but the suddenness and greatness of the alteration begetting a strangeness on the soul, may occasion after-thoughts and recoiling. Therefore he tempts first to thoughts, then to a delight in these thoughts, then to the continuation of them, then to resolve, and so on to practice. And in like manner, he tempts some to make bold with a small matter, which shall scarce

come under the notion of wrong; then to a greater, and so gradually to higher things, and thus he insensibly brings on a thievish inclination and practice. For the same end sometimes he shews his skill in the management of occasions; he imperceptibly hooks men into sin by drawing them first to be bold with occasions; he tells them they may sit at the ale-house, and yet not be drunk; that they may keep familiarity, and yet not be lewd; that they may look upon a commodity, and yet not steal; and when the occasions are by this means made familiar to them, then he puts them on a step further, but by such slow motions that the progress is scarce discerned till they be in the snare.

CHAPTER XII.

Of Satan's perverting our reason.—His second way of blinding.—The possibility of this, and the manner of accomplishing it directly, several ways; and indirectly, by the delights of sin, and by sophistical arguments; with an account of them.

II. Secondly, The second way by which Satan blinds us through the power of lust is by *perverting and corrupting our reason, drawing it to approve of that which it first disapproved.* That our lusts have such a power upon the understanding to make such an alteration, need not seem strange to those that shall consider that the Scripture, propounding the knowledge of the highest mysteries, doth positively require, as a necessary pre-requisite to these things, that we 'lay aside all filthiness and superfluity of naughtiness,' James i. 20,—in these terms, noting the loathsome defilement of our lusts,—that so we may 'receive the engrafted word;' strongly implying that our lusts have a power to elude and evade the strongest reasons, and to hinder their entertainment: which our Saviour notes to have been also the cause of the Jews' blindness, 'How can ye believe, which receive honour one of another?' John v. 44. Their lusts of honour stood in their light, and perverted their reason.

But because this may seem to some almost impossible, that lusts should turn our sun into darkness, I shall a little explain it.

The understanding doth usually, if practice of sin have not put out its light, at the first faithfully represent to our mind the nature of good and evil in matters of temptation and duty; yet its power in this case is only directive and suasive to the will, not absolutely imperative. The will must follow the understanding's dictate, but is not under any necessity of following its first advice; it is the *ultimum dictamen*, the last dictate, that it is engaged to follow. However the will, in the case last mentioned, be dependent upon the understanding, yet the understanding doth also, *quoad exercitium*, depend upon the will, and as to the act of consideration, is under its command; so that after the understanding hath faithfully represented the evil of a sin, the will can command it to another consideration, and force it to new thoughts and consultations about it; in which case the will doth prompt the understanding, tells it what verdict it would have it to bring in, and so doth really solicit and beg for a compliance.

The understanding is ductile and capable of being bribed, and therefore suffers its right eye to be put out by the will, and as a false witness or a partial judge gives sentence as the will would have it; and thus, as one observes,[1] the understanding and will are like Simeon and Levi, brethren in evil, mutually complying with and gratifying each other.

The possibility of lusts perverting our understanding being discovered, the way and manner how lust doth thus corrupt it, is needful to be opened.

Lust exerciseth this power under the management of Satan, directly and indirectly.

1. First, *Our reason is directly perverted when it is so far wrought upon as to call that good, which is indeed plainly and apparently evil.* So great a corruption is not common and ordinary, neither can the heart of man be easily drawn to go so palpably against clear light and evidence. It is therefore only in some cases and in some persons, either of weaker faculties or of extraordinary debauched principles, that Satan can work up lust to give so great a darkness. However, it is evident that Satan useth these deceits in this thing.

(1.) First, He strives, where the matter will bear it, *to put the name of virtue or good upon actions and things that are not so.* This temptation doth most appear in those things that are of a doubtful and disputable nature, or in those actions which in their appearance or pretensions may seem to be virtuous. Whatever sin is capable of any paint or varnish, that he takes the advantage of. Saul's sacrificing was a great iniquity, and yet the pretence of the general goodness of the action, being in itself commanded, and the supposed necessity of Saul's doing it, because Samuel came not, were considerations upon which his understanding warranted to him that undertaking. Paul's persecution, though a real gratification of his envious lustings, by his blinded understanding was judged duty. What more common than for worldly-mindedness and covetousness to be called a faithful and dutiful care for the provision of our families! Lukewarmness is often justified under the notion of moderation and prudence; and anything that can but pretend any kindred to or resemblance of good, our lusts presently prevail for an approbation and vindication of it.

(2.) Secondly, Satan useth *the advantage of extremes for the corrupting of our understandings.* To this purpose he doth all he can to make such an extreme odious and displeasing, that so we may run upon the contrary as matter of duty. Many there are whose heads are so weak, that if they see the danger of one extreme, they never think themselves in safety till they fly to a contrary excess, and then they think the extreme they embrace needs no other justification than the apparent evil of what they have avoided. Satan knowing this, like the lapwing, makes the greatest noise when he is furthest from his nest, and in much seeming earnestness tempts us to something that is most cross to our temper or present inclination; or endeavours to render something so to us, not with any hopes to prevail with us there, but to make us run as far from it as we can into another snare, and

---

[1] Fenner, Epistle Dedicatory to 'Mystery of Saving Grace.'

also to make us believe that we have done well and avoided a temptation, when indeed we have but exchanged it.

(3.) Thirdly, He directly binds our understandings in sinful practices, by engaging us *to corrupt opinions which lead to wicked or careless courses.* Satan with great ease can put men upon sin, when once he hath prevailed with them to receive an error which directly leads to it. Corrupt principles do naturally corrupt practices, and both these may be observed to meet in those deluded ones whom the Scripture mentions, 'that denied the only Lord God, and Jesus Christ, turning also the grace of God into lasciviousness,' Jude 4 ; false teachers that brought in 'damnable heresies,' counted it 'pleasure to riot,' had 'eyes full of adultery, and could not cease from sin,' 2 Pet. ii. 1, 13, 14. With what confidence and security will sin be practised, when an opinion signs a warrant and pleads a justification for it!

(4.) Fourthly, In actions whose goodness or badness is principally discoverable *by the ends upon which they are undertaken, it is no great difficulty for Satan to impose upon men a belief that they act by ends and respects which do not indeed move them at all;* and in this case men are so blinded that they do not, or will not know or acknowledge they do evil. The matter of the action being warrantable, and the end being out of the reach of common discovery, they readily believe the best of themselves ; and looking more at the warrantableness of the nature of the act in the general than at their grounds and intentions, they think not that they do evil. This was a fault which Christ observed in the disciples when they called for 'fire from heaven upon the Samaritans,' Luke ix. 55. The thing itself Elias had done before, and Christ might have done it then, but they wanted the spirit of Elias, and therefore Christ rejects their motion as unlawful in them, who considered not that a spirit of passion and revenge did altogether influence them ; and instead of shewing a just displeasure against the Samaritans, he shews that Satan had blinded them by their lust, and that the thing they urged was so far from being good, that it was apparently evil, in that they were acted by 'another spirit' than they imagined. This way of deceit is very common. How often may we observe Christians pretending conscientious dissatisfactions about the actions of others, when the private spring that animates them is some secret grudge that lies at the bottom ; and yet because the thing wherein they are dissatisfied may truly deserve blame, they are not apt to condemn themselves, but think they do well.

2. Secondly, *Lusts also pervert our reason and knowledge indirectly;* and this is, when we are not so far blinded as to believe the thing unto which we are tempted, to be good absolutely ; yet notwithstanding, we are persuaded of some considerable goodness in it, and such as may for the present be embraced. For this purpose Satan hath ready these two engines :—

(1.) First, He sets before us *the pleasures, profits, and other delights of sin.* These he heightens with all his art and skill, that he may fix in our minds this conclusion, that however it be forbidden, yet it would conduce much to our satisfaction or advantage if it were practised ; and here he promiseth such golden ends and fruits of sin as indeed it can never lead unto, inviting us in the words of the harlot, 'I have decked my bed with coverings of tapestry, with carved works, with fine linen of Egypt. I have perfumed it with myrrh, aloes, and cinnamon. Come, let us take our fill of these delights,' Prov. vii. 16. Thus he set upon Eve, 'Take this fruit, and ye shall be as gods.' Thus he attempted Christ himself, 'All these will I give thee,' [Mat. iv. 9,] proffering the kingdoms of the world, and the glory of them. The pleasures of sin are Satan's great bait, and these strongly invite and stir up our lusts; yet because the fear of the danger may stick in the heart, 'It is pleasant, but oh I dare not,' saith the sinner, 'I fear the hazard or the evil that may follow:' therefore Satan hath his other engine at hand to blind us, and to carry our minds from such considerations; and that is,

(2.) Secondly, *His sophistical arguments*, by which the danger may be lessened. Of these his quiver is full: as,

[1.] First, He urgeth that the sin tempted to *is little*. 'But a little one;' it is not, saith he, so great a matter as you make it; there are other sins far greater, and these also practised by men that profess as much as you. Thus he would shame us, as it were, out of our fear, by calling it severity, niceness, or an unnecessary preciseness. If this prevail not,

[2.] Secondly, He hath then another argument: Oh, saith he, be it so, that it is a little more than ordinary, yet it is but once; taste or try it; you need not engage yourselves to frequent practice, you may retreat at pleasure. But if the fear of the danger prevail against this, then,

[3.] Thirdly, He labours to put us under *a kind of necessity of sinning, and this he pleads as a justification of the evil*. It is not altogether right, but you cannot well avoid it. This plea of necessity is large; occasion, example, command of others, strength of inclination, custom, and what not, are pleaded by him in this case. Some particularly reckon them up;[1] and rather than some men will acknowledge the evil, they will blame God's decree, as if they were necessitated by it, or his providence, as Adam, 'The woman that thou gavest me, she gave me of the tree.' David's bloody resolve against the house of Nabal seems to be justified by him, from Nabal's great ingratitude, 'In vain have I kept all that this fellow hath in the wilderness,' &c., 1 Sam. xxv. 21; and as one engaged by a necessity of repaying such wrongs and affronts, doth he determine to cut them off. Aaron, when he was taxed by Moses about the golden calf, excuseth the matter by a pretended necessity of doing what he did upon the violent importunity of such a heady people, Exod. xxxii. 22; and that when Moses was not to be found, 'Thou knewest the people, that they are set on mischief.' This that he urged to Moses Satan no doubt had urged to him, and he had acquiesced in it as something that he thought would excuse, or at least mitigate the offence. Yet if the sinner break through this snare,

[4.] Fourthly, He comes on with *a softer plea of infirmity*, and endeavours to persuade men that they may yield under pretence of being forced, and that their strivings and reluctances will lessen the evil to an apparent sin of infirmity; and thus he bespeaks them, Have

[1] *Vide* Dyke, 'Deceitfulness of the Heart,' p. 139, &c.

not God's children infirmities? They sin, though with reluctancy, and dost not thou resist?—doth not the fear that is in thy heart shew an unwillingness? Mayest thou not plead, the evil that I would not do, that do I? If thou yield, will not God account it a rape upon thine integrity? If this arrow stick not,

[5.] Fifthly, Then he *extenuates the offence by propounding some smaller good or conveniency that may follow that evil.* And this, though it be a way of arguing directly contrary to that rule, 'Do not evil that good may come,' yet it oft proves too successful; and it is like that common stratagem of war, when, by the proposal of a small booty in view, the enemies are drawn out of their hold into a fore-contrived danger. Thus Satan pleads, This one act of sin may put you into a capacity of honouring God the more. Some have admitted advancements and dignities against conscience, upon no better ground but that they might keep out knaves, and that they might be in a condition to be helpful to good men. Surely the devil prevailed with Lot by this weapon, when he offered the prostitution of his daughters to the lusts of the Sodomites, that the strangers, as he thought them, might be preserved; by this evil, thinks he, a greater may be avoided. Herod's conscience could not at first consent to the cutting off the head of John Baptist, but when Satan suggests the obligation of his oath, he concludes that in the killing of John he should escape the violation of the oath. Thus a pretended good to come becomes a pander to a present certain iniquity. Now if after all these arguings the conscience carrieth an apprehension of danger, then,

[6.] Sixthly, He plainly disputeth *the possibility of the escape of danger, though the sin be committed.* All the insinuations of pleasure and advantage by which Eve was tempted could not at first blot out her fears of the consequence of that transgression; it did stick in her mind still, 'lest we die;' then Satan plainly denieth the danger she feared: 'Ye shall not surely die.' 'The threatening,' saith he, 'it may be, was but for trial, or without a strict and positive purpose in God to execute it; there is no certainty that God was in good earnest when he spake so.' The devil usually urgeth the mercy of God, the merits of Christ, his promises of pardon, the infirmities of the saints, their sins and repentances, &c.; from all these drawing this conclusion, that we may venture upon the temptation without any apparent hazard. It is but repenting, saith he, and that is an easy work to a gracious soul. God is ready to be reconciled, even to a prodigal son; he is not so cruel as to cast away any for a small matter; he that waits to be gracious will not lie at catch for opportunities and occasions to destroy us; he that delights not in the death of a sinner will not delight to take strict exceptions against every failing.

If Satan can prevail with us to extenuate the sin, to slight the hazard, or any way to lessen it upon any of the forementioned accounts; then having possessed us before with high apprehensions of delights and satisfactions in the sin, he quickly persuades to accept the motion, as having a conveniency and advantage in it not to be despised: and thus doth he indirectly pervert our reason; which is the second way by which he blinds us through the working of our lust.

CHAPTER XIII.

Of Satan's diverting our reason, being the third way of blinding men.—His policies for diverting our thoughts.—His attempts to that purpose in a more direct manner; with the degrees of that procedure.—Of disturbing or distracting our reason, which is Satan's fourth way of blinding men.—His deceits therein.—Of precipitancy, Satan's fifth way of blinding men.—Several deceits to bring men to that.

III. Thirdly, Satan blinds the sons of men by *diverting and withdrawing their reason*, and taking it off from the pursuit of its discovery or apprehensions. For sometimes it cannot be induced to go so contrary to its light as to call evil good, either directly or indirectly. Then is Satan put to a new piece of policy, and if the frame of the heart and the matter of the temptation suit his design, he endeavours to turn the stream of our thoughts either wholly another way, or to still them by turning them into a dead sea, or by some trick to beguile the understanding with some new dress of the temptation. So that we may observe in Satan a threefold policy in a subserviency to this design. For,

1. First, *Satan sometimes ceaseth his pursuit and lets the matter fall, and thinks it better to change the temptation than to continue a solicitation at so great a disadvantage.* When he tempted Christ and could not prevail, he 'departed for a season,' Luke iv. 13, with a purpose to return at some fitter time, which Christ himself was in expectation of, knowing it to be his manner to lie in wait for advantages; and accordingly when his suffering drew nigh, which, as he speaks to the Jews, was 'their hour and power of darkness,' Luke xxii. 53, he foretold his return upon him, 'Now the prince of this world cometh.' However this attempt of his against the Lord Jesus prevailed not, yet he shewed his art and skill in the suspending of his temptation to a more suitable time. And the success of this against us is sadly remarkable, for however we resist and at present stand out, yet his solicitations are often like leaven, which while it is hid in our thoughts, doth not a little ferment and change them, so that at his return he often finds our lusts prepared to raise greater clouds upon our mind. Many there are that resist strongly at present that which they easily slide into when Satan hath given them time to breathe; that say, 'I will not,' and yet 'do it afterwards,' [Mat. xxi. 29.]

2. Secondly, He sometimes withdraws their considerations, by *huffing them up with a confidence that they are above the temptation;* as a conquest in a small skirmish, begetting an opinion of victory, makes way for a total overthrow over a careless and secure army. We are too apt to triumph over temptations because we give the first onset with courage and resolution. Christ forewarned Peter of his denial; he stoutly defies it, and not improving this advertisement to fear and watchfulness, Satan, who then was upon a design to sift him, took him at that advantage of security, and by a contemptible instrument overthrew him. Thus while we grow strong in our apprehensions by

a denial of a sin, and undervalue it as below us, our confidence makes us careless, and this lets in our ruin.

3. Thirdly, If these ways of policy fail him, he *seemingly complies with us, and is content we judge the matter sinful, but then he proffers his service to bring us off by distinctions;* and here the sophister useth his skill to further our understanding in framing excuses, coining evasions, and so doth out-shoot us in our own bow. The Corinthians had learnt to distinguish betwixt eating of meat in an idol's temple in honour to the idol, and as a common feast in civility and respect to their friends that invited them. This presently withdrew their consideration, and so quieted them in that course, that the apostle was forced to discover the fallacy of it. The Israelites cursed him that gave a wife to any of the tribe of Benjamin; but when they turned to them in compassion, they satisfied themselves with this poor distinction, that they would not give them wives, but were willing to suffer them to take them, Judges xxi. 18, 20. It is a common snare in matters of promise or oath, where conscience is startled at a direct violation thereof, by some pitiful salvo or silly evasion to blind the eyes, and when they dare not break the hedge, to leap over it by the help of a broken reed.

But I must here further observe, that Satan doth sometimes set aside these deceits aforementioned, and tries his strength for the withdrawing of our consideration from the danger of sin in a more plain and direct manner—that is, by continuing the prospect of the sweets and pleasures of sin under our eye, and withal urging us by repeated solicitations to cast the thoughts of the danger behind our back: in which he so far prevails sometimes, that men are charged with a deep forgetfulness of God, his law, and of themselves; yet usually it ariseth to this by degrees. As,

(1.) First, When a temptation is before us, and our conscience *relucts it*. If there be any inclination to recede from a conviction, the motion is resisted with a secret regret and sorrow. As the young man was said to 'go away sorrowful,' [Mat. xix. 22,] when Christ propounded such terms for eternal life as he was not willing to hear of: so do we; our heart is divided betwixt judgment and affection, and we begin to wish that it might be lawful to commit such a sin, or that there were no danger in it; nay, often our wishes contradict our prayers, and while we desire to be delivered from the temptation, our private wishes beg a denial to those supplications.

(2.) Secondly, If we come thus far, we usually proceed to the next step, which is, to *give a dismission to those thoughts that oppose the sin*. We say to them, as Felix to Paul, 'Go thy way for this time, and when I have a convenient opportunity I will send for thee,' [Acts xxiv. 25.]

(3.) Thirdly, If a plain dismission serve not to repel these thoughts, we begin to *imprison the truth in unrighteousness*, Rom. i. 18; 2 Peter iii. 5, and by a more peremptory refusal to stifle it and to keep it under, and become at last willingly ignorant.

(4.) Fourthly, By this means at last the heart grows *sottish and forgetful*. The heart is 'taken away,' as the prophet speaks, and then do these thoughts of conviction and warning at present perish together.

This withdrawing of our consideration is Satan's third way of blinding us. Follows next,

IV. The fourth way by which our lust prevails in Satan's hand to blind knowledge, and that is by *distracting and disturbing it in its work*. This piece of subtlety Satan the rather useth, because it is attended with a double advantage, and, like a two-edged sword, will cut either way. For (1.) A confusion and distraction in the understanding will hinder the even and clear apprehensions of things, so that those principles of knowledge cannot reach so deep nor be so firm and full in their application. For as the senses, if any way distracted or hindered, though never so intent, must needs suffer prejudice in their operations, a thick air or mist not only hinders the sight of the eye, but also conduceth to a misrepresentation of objects. Thus is the understanding hindered by confusion. But (2.) If this succeed not, yet by this he hinders the peace and comfort of God's children. It is a trouble to be haunted with evil thoughts. To work this distraction,

1. First, Satan useth a *clamorous importunity*, and doth so follow us with suggestions, that what way soever we turn they follow us. We can think nothing else, or hear nothing else, they are ever before us.

2. Secondly, He worketh this disturbance in our thoughts by *levying a legion of temptations against us*—many at once, and of several kinds, from within, from without, on every side. He gathers all, from the Dan to the Beersheba of his empire, to oppress us with a multitude; so that while our thoughts are divided about many things, they are less fixed and observant in any particular.

3. Thirdly, He sometimes endeavours *to weary us out with long solicitations*: as those that besiege a city, when they cannot storm, endeavour to waste their strength and provisions by a long siege. His design in this is to come upon us, as Ahithophel counselled Absalom, when we are 'weary and weak-handed' by watching and long resistance.

4. Fourthly, But his chief design is *to take the advantage of any trouble, inward or outward*, and by the help of this he dangerously discomposeth and distracts our counsels and resolves. If any have a spirit distempered, or lie under the apprehensions of wrath, it is easy for him to confound and amaze such, that they shall scarce know what they do or what they think. The like advantage he hath from outward afflictions, and these opportunities he the rather takes, for these reasons :—

(1.) First, Usually inward or outward troubles leaves some *stamp of murmuring and sullenness upon our hearts*, and of themselves distemper our spirits with a sad inclination to speak 'in our haste,' or to act unadvisedly. Job's affliction imbittered his spirit, and Satan misseth not the advantage. Then he comes upon him with temptations, and prevailed so far that he spake many things in his anguish of which he was ashamed afterward, and hides his face for it. 'Once have I spoken, but I will not answer: yea, twice, but I will proceed no further,' Job xl. 5.

(2.) Secondly, By reason of our burden we are *less wieldy and more unapt to make any resistance.* God himself expresseth the condition of such, under the similitude of those that are 'great with young,' who, because they cannot be driven fast, he 'gently leads' them. But Satan knows a small matter will discompose them, and herein he deals with us, as Simeon and Levi dealt with the Shechemites, who set upon them when they were sore by circumcision.

(3.) Thirdly, *Troubles of themselves occasion confusion, multitudes of thought, distractions, and inadvertencies.* If men see a hazard before them they are presently at their wits' end, they are puzzled, they know not what to do—thoughts are divided, now resolving this, then presently changing to a contrary purpose. It is seldom but 'as in a multitude of words there is much folly,' Prov. x. 19, so in a distraction of thoughts there are many miscarriages, and Satan with a little labour can improve them to more. Here he works unseen; in these troubled waters he loves to angle, because his baits are not discerned.

V. Fifthly, Our considerations and reasonings against sin are hindered by *a bold forward precipitancy.* When men are hasted and pressed to the committing of sin, and like the 'deaf adder stop their ears against the voice of the charmer,' [Ps. lviii. 4;] in this case, the rebellious will is like a furious horse, that takes the bridle in his teeth, and instead of submitting to the government of his rider, he carries him violently whither he would not. Thus do men rush into sin, as the horse into the battle. The devices by which Satan doth forward this, we may observe to be these, among others :—

1. First, He endeavours *to affright men into a hopelessness of prevailing against him,* and so intimidates men that they throw down their weapons, and yield up themselves to the temptation; they conclude there is no hope by all their resistance to stand it out against him, and then they are easily persuaded to comply with him. To help this forward, Satan useth the policy of soldiers, who usually boast high of their strength and resolutions, that, the hearts and courage of their adversaries failing, the victory may fall to them without stroke. The devil expresseth a disdain and scorn of our weak opposition, as Goliath did of David, 'Am I a dog, that thou comest to me with staves? Dost thou think to stand it out against me? It is in vain to buckle on thine armour, and therefore better were it to save the trouble of striving than to fight to no purpose.' With such like arguings as these are men sometimes prevailed with to throw down their weapons, and to overrun their reason through fear and hopelessness.

2. Secondly, Sometimes he is more subtle, and *by threaping*[1] *men down, that they have consented already, he puts them upon desperate adventures of going forward.* This is usually where Satan hath used many solicitations before, after our hearts have been urged strongly with a temptation. When he sees he cannot win us over to him, then he triumphs and boasts we are conquered already, and that our thoughts could not have dwelt so long upon such a subject but that we had a liking to it, and thence would persuade us to go on and enjoy the fulness of that delight which we have already stolen privately: over shoes, over boots. Now though his arguings here be very weak —for though it be granted that by the stay of the temptation on our

[1] 'Arguing'=to maintain a thing against contradiction.—G.

thoughts he hath a little entangled us, it cannot hence be inferred that it is our wisdom to entangle ourselves further—yet are many overcome herewith, and give up themselves as already conquered, and so give a stop to any further consideration.

3. Thirdly, When men will not be trepanned into the snare by the former delusions, he attempts to work them up *to a sudden and hasty resolve of sinning;* he prepares all the materials of the sin, puts everything in order, and then carries us, as he did Christ, into the mountain, to give us a prospect of their beauty and glory: 'All these,' saith he, ' will I give thee,' [Mat. iv. 9;] do but consent, and all are thine. Now albeit there are arguments at hand, and serious considerations to deter us from practice, yet how are all laid aside by a quick resolve! Satan urgeth us by violent hurry, as Christ said to Judas, ' What thou hast to do, do it quickly,' [John xiii. 27.] The soul, persuaded with this, puts on a sudden boldness and resolution, and when reason doth offer to interpose, it holds fast the door, because the 'sound of its master's feet is behind it,' [2 Kings vi. 32.] Doth it not say to itself, ' Come, we will not consider, let us do it quickly, before these lively considerations come in to hinder us'? It is loath to be restrained, and conceiteth that if it can be done before conscience awaken and make a noise, all is well; as if sin ceased to be sinful because we by a violent haste endeavoured to prevent the admonition of conscience. Thus they enjoy their sin, as the Israelites ate their passover, ' in haste, and with their staves in their hands,' [Exod. xii. 11.]

4. Fourthly, *When opportunities and occasions will well suit it.* He takes the advantage of a passionate and sullen humour, and by this means he turns us clearly out of our bias; reason is trampled under foot, and passion quite overruns it. At this disadvantage the devil takes Jonah, and hardens him to a strange resolve of quarrelling God, and justifying himself in that insolency. The humour that Satan wrought upon was his fretful sullenness, raised up to a great height by the disappointment of his expectation; and this makes him break out into a choleric resolution, ' I do well to be angry,' [Jonah iv. 9.] Had he been composed in his spirit, had his mind been calm and sedate, the devil surely could not by any arguments have drawn him up to it; but when the spirit is in a rage, a little matter will bind reason in chains, and push a man upon a desperate carelessness of any danger that may follow; suitable to that expression of Job, chap xiii. 13, ' Let me alone, that I may speak, and let come on me what will.'

5. Fifthly, All these are but small in comparison of those *deliberate determinations which are to be found with most sinners*, who are therefore said to sin with a high hand, presumptuously, wilfully, against conscience, against knowledge; and this ordinarily to be found only among those whom a custom of sin hath hardened and confirmed into a boldness of a wicked way and course. When the spirits of men are thus harnessed and prepared, Satan can, at pleasure almost, form them into a deliberate resolve to cast the commandment behind their back, and to refuse to hearken. When any temptation is offered them, if God say, ' Ask for the old paths, and walk therein,' as Jer. vi. 16, they will readily answer, ' We will not walk therein.' If God say, ' Hearken to the sound of the trumpet,' they will reply, ' We will not

hearken.' When the people by a course of sinning had made themselves like the wild ass used to the wilderness, then did they peremptorily set up their will against all the reason and consideration that could come in to deter them, though they were told the inconveniences, Jer. ii. 25; that this did unshoe their foot, and afflicted them with thirst and want, yet was the advice slighted. 'There is no hope,' said they; there is no expectation that we will take any notice of these pleadings, for we have fixed our resolve, 'We have loved strangers, and after them will we go.' So Jer. xliv. 16, 'As for the word that thou hast spoken unto us in the name of the Lord, we will not hearken unto thee, but we will certainly do whatsoever thing goeth out of our own mouth.' A plain and full resolve of will dischargeth all the powers of reason, and commands it silence. And that this is most ordinary among men, may appear by these frequent expressions of Scripture, wherein God lays the blame of all that madness which their lives bring forth upon their will, 'Ye would not obey,' 'ye will not come to me'; 'their heart is set to do evil,' &c. It may indeed seem strange that Satan should proceed so far with the generality of men, and that they should do that should seem so inconsistent with those principles which they retain, and the light which must result from thence; but we must remember that these *wills* and *shalls* of wicked men are for the most part God's interpretation of their acts and carriage, which speaks as much, though it may be their minds and hearts do not so formally mould up their thoughts into such open and brazen-faced assertions. And yet we ought also further to consider, that when the Spirit of God chargeth man with wilfulness, there is surely more of a formal wilfulness in the heart of man than lieth open to our view. And this will be less strange to us when we call to mind,

6. Sixthly, That through the working of Satan *the minds of men are darkened, and the light thereof put out by the prevalency of atheistical principles.*[1] Something of atheism is by most divines concluded to be in every sin, and according to the height of it in its various degrees, is reason and consideration overturned. There are, it may be, few that are professed atheists in opinion, and dogmatically so, but all wicked men are so in practice. Though they profess God, yet 'the fool saith in his heart, There is no God,' [Ps. liii. 1,] and in 'their works they deny him,' [Titus i. 16.] This is a principle that directly strikes at the root: for if there be no God, no hell or punishment, who will be scared from taking his delight in sin by any such consideration? The devil, therefore, strives to instil this poison with his temptation. When he enticed Eve by secret insinuations, he first questions the truth of the threatening, and then proceeds to an open denial of it, 'ye shall not surely die;' and it is plain she was induced to the sin upon a secret disbelief of the danger. She reckons up the advantages, 'good for food, pleasant to the eye, to be desired to make one wise;' wherein it is evident she believed what Satan had affirmed, 'that they should be as God,' and then it was not to be feared that they should die. This kind of atheism is common. Men may not disbelieve a Godhead; nay, they may believe there is a God, and yet question the truth of his threatenings. Those conceits that men have

[1] Capel, 'Temptations,' [as before.—G.]

of God, whereby they mould and frame him in their fancies, suitable to their humours—which is a 'thinking that he is such a one as ourselves,' Ps. l.—are streams[1] and vapours from this pit, and 'the hearts of the sons of men are desperately set within them to do evil,' upon these grounds; much more when they arise so high as in some who say, 'Doth God know? Is there knowledge in the Most High?' [Ps. lxxiii. 11.] If men give way to this, what reason can be imagined to stand before them? All the comminations of Scripture are derided as so many theological scarecrows, and undervalued as so many pitiful contrivances to keep men in awe.

CHAPTER XIV.

Of Satan's maintaining his possession.—His first engine for that purpose is his finishing of sin, in its reiteration and aggravation.—His policies herein.

Having explained the five ways by which Satan through the power of lust causeth blindness of mind in tempting to sin, I shall next lay open Satan's devices for the *keeping and maintaining his possession*, which are these:—

1. First, He endeavours, after he hath prevailed with any man to commit an iniquity, *to finish sin:* James i. 15, 'After it is conceived and brought forth, then it is finished;' which notes its growth and increase. This compriseth these two things, its reiteration and its aggravation.

(1.) First, Its *reiteration* is, when by frequent acts it is strengthened and confirmed into a habit. There are various steps, by which men ascend into the seat of the scornful. *Nemo repentè turpissimus*, It is not one act that doth denominate men 'wise to do evil.' In Ps. i. 1 *seq.*, David shews there are gradations and degrees of sin: some walk in the counsel of the ungodly; some by progress and continuance of sin 'stand in the way of sinners;' some, by a hardness of heart and fixedness in wicked purposes, 'sit in the seat of the scornful.' To this height doth he labour to bring his proselytes; yet he further designs,

(2.) Secondly, That sin may have its utmost accomplishments in *all the aggravations whereof it may be capable*. He strives to put men upon such a course of sinning as may be most scandalous to the gospel, most ensnaring and offensive to others, most hardening and desperate to ourselves, most offensive and provoking to God. In this he imitates the counsel of Ahithophel to Absalom, when he advised him to go in unto his father's concubines in the sight of all Israel, that so the breach betwixt him and his father might be widened to an impossibility of reconciliation. Thus he labours that sinners should act at such a rate of open defiance against heaven, as if they resolved to lie down in their iniquity, and were purposed never to think of returning and making up their peace with God. That sin may be finished in both these respects, he useth these policies:—

[1] Query, 'steams'?—ED.

[1.] First, *After sin is once committed, he renews his motions and solicitations to act it again, and then again, and so onward till they be perfect and habituated to it.* In this case he acts over again the former method by which he first ensnared them, only with such alterations as the present case doth necessitate him unto. Before, he urged for the committing of it but once. How little is he to be trusted in these promises! Now, he urgeth them by the very act they have already done, Is it not a pleasant or profitable sin, to thy very experience? hast thou not tasted and seen? hast thou not already consented? Taste and try again, and yet further; withdraw not thy hand. A little temptation served before, but a less serves now; for by yielding to the first temptation our hearts are secretly inclined to the sin, and we carry a greater affection to it than before; for this is the stain and defilement of sin, that when once committed it leaves impressions of delight and love behind, which are still the more augmented by a further progress and frequent commission, till at last by a strong power of fascination it bewitches men that they cannot forbear; all the entreaties of friends, all their own promises, all their resolves and purposes, though never so strong and serious, except God strike in to rescue by an omnipotent hand, can no more restrain them than fetters of straw can hold a giant. God himself owns it as a natural impossibility, 'Can the Ethiopian change his skin? no more can ye do good,' [Jer. xiii. 23;] and the reason of that impossibility is from hence, that they are 'accustomed to do evil.' Such strong and powerful inclinations to the same sin again are begot in us by a sin already committed, that sometime one act of sin fills some men with as vehement and passionate desires for a further enjoyment, as custom and continuance doth others. Austin reports that Alypius, when once he gave way to the temptation of beholding the gladiators, was bewitched with such a delight, that he not only desired to come again with others, but also before others. Neither is it any great wonder it should be so, when, besides the inclinations that are begot in us by any act of sin to recommit it, sin puts us out of God's protection, debilitates and weakens our graces, strengthens Satan's arm, and often procures him further power and commission against us.

[2.] Secondly, Satan endeavours *to make one sin an engagement to another, and to force men to draw iniquity with cords of vanity.* Agur notes a concatenation in sins, 'Lest I steal, and take the name of God in vain,' Prov. xxx. 9. Adam sinning in the forbidden fruit, and proclaimed guilty by his conscience, runs into another sin for the excuse of the former, 'the woman that thou gavest me,' &c. David affords a sad instance of this, the sin with Bathsheba being committed, and she with child upon it, David to hide the shame of his offence, (1.) Hypocritically pretends great kindness to Uriah. (2.) When that served not, next he makes him drunk, and, it may be, he involved many others in that sin as accessories. (3.) When this course failed, his heart conceives a purpose and resolution to murder him. (4.) He cruelly makes him the messenger of his own destruction. (5.) He engageth Joab in it. (6.) And the death of many of his soldiers. (7.) By this puts the whole army upon a hazard. (8.) Excuseth the bloody contrivance by providence. (9.) In all using still the height of dissimulation. Satan knows how natural it is for men to hide the shame of their iniquity, and accordingly provides occasions and provocations to drive them on to a kind of necessity.

[3.] Thirdly, *By a perverse representation of the state of godly and wicked men*, he draws on sin to a higher completement. How often doth he set before us the misery, affliction, contempt, crosses, and sadnesses of the one, and the jollity, delights, plenty, peace, honours, and power of the other! It was a temptation that had almost brought David to an atheistical resolve against all religious duty, and that which he observed had prevailed altogether with many professors, Ps. lxxiii. When they observed 'they were not in trouble like other men,' and that their mouth and tongue had been insolent against God, without any rebuke or check from him; when in the meantime the godly were 'plagued all the day, and chastened every morning:' some that were, in profession or estimation at least, God's people, returned to take up these thoughts, and to resolve upon such practices, ver. 10; as if God, who sees all these with so much silence, must be supposed knowingly to give some countenance to such actions. This, indeed, when it is prosecuted upon our hearts in its full strength with those ugly surmises, jealousies, and misapprehensions that are wont to accompany it, is a sad step to a desperate neglect of duty and a carelessness in sinning, in that it insensibly introduceth atheistical impressions upon the hearts of men, and such are apt to catch hold even upon good men, who are but too ready to say as David, 'I have cleansed my hands in vain,' [ver. 13.]

[4.] Fourthly, Satan hath yet another piece of policy for the multiplication and aggravation of sin, which is *the enmity and opposition of the law*. Of this the apostle Paul sadly complains from his own experience: Rom. vii. 8, 'Sin taking occasion by the commandment, wrought in me all manner of concupiscence.' What he laments is this, that such is the perverseness of our natures, that the law, instead of restraining us, doth the more enrage us, so that accidentally the law doth multiply sin; for when the restraint of the law is before us, lust burns not only more inwardly, but when it cannot be kept in and smothered, then it breaks out with greater violence, 'Let us break their bonds asunder,' &c., [Ps. ii. 3.] When the law condemns our lusts, they grow surly and desperate: 'Let us eat and drink, for to-morrow we die,' &c., [Isa. xxii. 13.] If any wonder that the law, which was given of purpose to repress sin, and which is of so great use in its authority to kill it in us, and to hinder temptations, should thus be used by Satan to increase and enrage it, they may consider that it is but still an accidental occasion, and not a cause, and sin takes this occasion without any fault of the law. Satan to this end watcheth the time[1] when our hearts are most earnestly set upon our lusts, when our desires are most highly engaged, and then by a subtle art so opposeth the law, letting in its contradictions in way and measure suitable, that our hearts conceive a grudge at restraint, which together with its earnestness to satisfy the flesh, ariseth up to a furious madness, and violent striving to maintain a liberty and freedom to do according to the desires of their heart; whereas this same law, if it

[1] As Absalom his servants watched when Amnon's heart was merry with wine.

be applied to the heart when it is more cooled and not so highly engaged upon a design of lust, will break, terrify, and restrain the heart, and put such a damp upon temptations that they shall not be able to stand before it. So great a difference is there in the various seasons of the application of this law; in which art for the enflaming of the heart to iniquity, Satan shews a wonderful dexterity.

CHAPTER XV.

Of Satan's keeping all in quiet, which is his second engine for keeping his possession, and for that purpose his keeping us from going to the light by several subtleties; also of making us rise up against the light, and by what ways he doth that.

Satan's next engine for the maintaining his possession, is to *keep all in quiet;* which our Saviour notes: Luke xi. 21, ' When a strong man armed keepeth his palace, his goods are in peace.' He urgeth this against those that objected to him, that he cast out devils by Beelzebub, which calumny he confuteth, by shewing the inconsistency of that with Satan's principles and design—it being a thing sufficiently known and universally practised, that no man will disturb or dispute against his own peaceable possession; neither can it be supposed Satan will do it, because he acts by this common rule of keeping down and hindering anything that may disquiet. Breach of peace is hazardous to a possession. An uneasy government occasions mutinies and revolts of subjects; yet we might think that, the wages of sin, the light and power of conscience considered, it were no easy task for the devil to rule his slaves with so much quiet as it is observed he doth. His skill in this particular, and the way of managing his interest for such an end, we may clearly see in John iii. 20, ' Every one that doth evil, hateth the light, neither cometh to the light, lest his deeds should be reproved.' From which place we may observe—(1.) The great thing that doth disquiet Satan's possession is light. (2.) The reason of that disquietment is the discovery that light makes, and the shame that follows that discovery. (3.) The way to prevent that light, and the reproof of it, is to avoid coming to it; and where it cannot be avoided, to hate it. It is Satan's business then for keeping all in peace—(1.) To keep us from the light; or if that cannot be, then (2.) To make us rise up against it. I shall make inquiry after both these projects of the devil.

To keep us from coming to the light, he useth a great many subtleties. As,

1. First, *For his own part he forbears to do anything that might discompose or affright entangled souls.* At other times, and in other cases, he loves to torment and affright them, to cause their wounds to stink and corrupt; but in this case he takes a contrary course, he keeps off, as much as may be, all reflections of conscience; he conceals the evil and danger of sin, he sings them asleep in their folly, ' till a dart strike through their liver,' and hastens them to the snare, ' as a bird that knoweth not that it is for his life,' Prov. vii. 23. They that

shall consider that the heart of a sinner is hardened through the deceitfulness of sin, and that the greatest part of the affrightment that molests the consciences of such is from Satan's fury and malice, they will easily conceive how much his single forbearance to molest may contribute to the peace and ease of those that are 'settled upon their lees;' but besides his forbearance, we may expect that whatever clouds or darkness he can raise to exclude the light, or to muffle the eyes, he will not be negligent in the use of that power. Whatever he can positively do, in the raising up the confidence of presumption or security in the minds of men, whatever he can do to make them sottish or careless, that shall not be wanting.

2. Secondly, He shews no less skill and diligence *by secret contrivances to hinder occasions of reproof and discovery*. How much he can practise upon others, that out of pity and compassion to the souls of men, are ready to draw a sinner ' from the error of his way, and to save a soul from death!' [James v. 20.] We can scarce imagine what ways he hath to divert and hinder them. By what private discouragements he doth defer them, who can tell? He that could dispute with the angel about the body of Moses to prevent the secret interment of it, Jude 9; he that could give a stop of one and twenty days to the angel that was to bring the comfortable message to Daniel, chap. x. 13, of the hearing of his prayers, may more easily obstruct and oppose the designs of a faithful reprover. Sometime he doth this by visible means and instruments, stirring up the spirits of wicked men to give opposition to such as seek to deliver their souls from the blood of men, by faithful warnings or exhortations. The devil was so careful to keep Jeroboam quiet in his sinful course of idolatry, that he stirs up Amaziah to banish Amos from the court, lest his plain dealing should startle or awaken the conscience of the king: Amos vii. 12, 13, ' Go, flee thee away into the land of Judah, &c.; but prophesy not any more at Bethel, for it is the king's chapel, it is the king's court.'

3. Thirdly, In order to the keeping out the light from the consciences of men, he insinuates himself *as a lying spirit into the mouths of some of his mercenaries;* and they speak 'smooth things' and deceit to Satan's captives, telling them that they are in a good condition, Christians good enough, and may go to heaven as well as the precisest. It is a fault in unfaithful ministers, they do the devil this service. God highly complains of it: Jer. vi. 14, ' They have healed also the hurt of the daughter of my people slightly, saying, Peace, peace; when there is no peace;' Ezek. xiii. 10, ' They have seduced my people, saying, Peace; and there was no peace; and one built up a wall, and others daubed it with untempered mortar.' Besides, this stratagem is the more likely to prevail, because it takes the advantage of the humours and inclinations of men, who naturally think the best of themselves, and delight that others should speak what they would have them; so that when men by the devil's instigation prophesy deceit to sinful men, it is most likely they should be heard, seeing they desire such prophets, ' and love to have it so.'

4. Fourthly, Satan keeps off the light, by *catching away the word after it is sown*. This policy of his, Christ expressly discovers: Mat. xiii. 19, ' When any one heareth the word of the kingdom, and under-

standeth it not, then cometh the wicked one, and catcheth away that which was sown in his heart.' Such opportunities the devil doth narrowly watch. To be sure, he will be present at a sermon or good discourse, and if he perceive anything spoken that may endanger his peaceable possession, how busy is he to withdraw the heart, sometime by the sight of the eyes, sometimes by vain thoughts of business, occasions, delights, and what not; and if this come not up to his end, then he endeavours, after men have heard, to justle all out by impertinent discourses, urgencies of employment, and a thousand such divertisements, that so men may not lay the warning to heart, nor by serious meditation to apply it to their consciences.

5. Fifthly, He sometimes *snuffs out the light by persecution.* Those hearers, Mat. xiii. 20, 21, that had received the word with some workings of affections and joy, are 'presently offended when persecution, because of the word, ariseth.' By this he threatens men into an acquiescency in their present condition, that if they 'depart from iniquity, they shall make themselves a prey,' [Isa. lix. 15.] Bonds, imprisonments, and hatreds, he suggests, shall abide them, and by this means he scares men from the light.

6. Sixthly, He sometimes *smothers and chokes it with the cares of the world,* as those that received seed among thorns. By earnest engagements in business, all that time, strength, and affection which should have been laid out in the prosecution of heavenly things, are wholly taken up and spent on outward things. By this means that light that shines into the hearts of men is neglected and put by.

7. Seventhly, He staves off men from coming to the light, by putting them upon *misapprehensions of their estate in judging themselves by the common opinion.* Satan hath so far prevailed with men, that they are become confident of this conceit, that men may take a moderate liberty in sinning, and yet nevertheless be in a good condition; that sin is not so great a matter in God's esteem, as in the judgment of some rigorous precisian; that he will not be so extreme to mark what we do amiss, as some strict professors are. What can be of greater hindrance to that ingenuous search, strict examination, and impartial judging or shaming ourselves for our iniquities, which the light of Scripture would engage us unto, than such a conceit as this! And yet that this opinion is not only common, but ancient, is manifest by those warnings and cautions given by the apostle to the contrary: Gal. vi. 7, 'Be not deceived; God is not mocked: whatsoever a man soweth, that shall he also reap;' Eph. v. 6, 'Let no man deceive you with vain words: for because of these things cometh the wrath of God upon the children of disobedience.' If it had not been usual for men to live in uncleanness, covetousness, and such like offences, which he calls 'sowing to the flesh,' and yet in the midst of these to think they were not under the hazard of wrath, or if men had not professedly and avowedly maintained such an opinion, it had been superfluous for the apostle to have warned us with so much earnestness, 'Be not deceived; let no man deceive you with such vain words,' [1 Cor. vi. 9.]

8. Eighthly, It is usual for Satan to still and quiet the stirring thoughts of sinners *with hopes and assurances of secrecy.* As children are quieted and pleased with toys and rattles, so are sinners put off

and diverted from prosecuting the discoveries that the light would make in them, by this confidence, that though they have done amiss, yet their miscarriages shall not be laid open or manifested before men. It is incredible how much the hopes of concealment doth satisfy and delight those that have some sense of guilt. Sometime men are impudent, that 'they declare their sin as Sodom, they hide it not,' Isa. iii. 9. But before they arrive at so great an impudency, they usually 'seek deep to hide their counsel from the Lord, and their works are in the dark; and they say, Who seeth us? and who knoweth us?' Isa. xxix. 15. Like those foolish creatures that think themselves sufficiently concealed by hiding their heads in a bush, though all their bodies be exposed to open view, Isa. xxviii. 15, those that made 'lies their refuge, and under falsehood hid themselves,' became as confident of their security as if they had 'made a covenant with death, and were at an agreement with hell;' and when they have continued in this course for some time with impunity, the light is so banished that they carry it so as if God observed their actions done in the dark as little as men do. 'How doth God know?' say they; 'can he judge through the dark clouds? thick clouds are a covering to him, that he seeth not,' Job xxii. 13. And hence proceed they to promise themselves a safety from judgments: 'When the overflowing scourge shall pass through, it shall not come nigh unto us, for we have made lies our refuge,' &c.

9. Ninthly, Satan keeps them from going to the light by *demurs and delays*. If the light begin to break in upon their consciences, then he tells them that there is time enough afterward. Oh, saith he, thou art young, and hast many days before thee; it is time enough to repent when you begin to be old. Or thou art a servant, an apprentice under command, thou wantest fit opportunities and conveniences for serious consideration, defer till thou becomest free, and at thine own disposal. That this is one of Satan's deceits to hinder us from making use of the light, besides what common experience may teach every man, may be clearly gathered from the exhortations of Scripture, which do not only shew us 'the way wherein we ought to walk,' but also press us to a present embracement of that counsel: 'To-day, to-day, while it is called to-day, harden not your hearts;' 'Now is the accepted time, now is the day of salvation;' 'Remember thy Creator in the days of thy youth, before the evil day comes;' 'If ye will enquire, enquire: yea, return, come,' Heb. iii. 7; 2 Cor. vi. 2; Eccles. xii. 1; Isa. xxi. 12. This hasty urgency to close with the offered occasions, plainly accuse us of delays, and that it is usual with us to adjourn those thoughts to a fitter opportunity, which we are not willing to comply with for the present.

By these nine devices he keeps the light from ensnared sinners, or them from coming to the light. But if all this cannot draw a curtain before the sun, if its bright beams breaks through all, so that it cannot be avoided, but there will be a manifestation and discovery of 'the hidden things of darkness,' then Satan useth all his art and cunning to stir up in the hearts of men their hatred against the light.

This is his second grand piece of policy to keep all in quiet under his command, to which purpose,

1. First, He endeavours to draw on a hatred against the light, by raising in the minds of men *a prejudice against the person that brings or offers it.* If he that warns or reproves express himself anything warmly or cuttingly against his brother's sins, this the devil presently makes use of; and those that are concerned think they have a just cause to 'stop their ears and harden their necks,' because they conceive that anger, or ill-will, or some such base thing did dictate those, though just, rebukes. The devil turned the heart of Ahab against the faithful warnings of Micaiah upon a deep prejudice that he had taken up against him; for so he expresseth himself to Jehoshaphat, 'I hate him, for he never prophesieth good unto me,' 1 Kings xxii. 8. In this case men consider not how justly, how truly, how profitably anything is spoken; but, as some insects that feed upon sores, they pass by what is sound and good, and fix upon that which is corrupt and putrid, either through the weakness and inobservancy of the reprover, or pretended to be such, by the prejudice of the party which doth altogether disable him to put a right construction upon anything.

2. Secondly, If this help not, then he seeks to get the advantage *of a provoked, passionate, or otherwise distempered fit;* and then hatred is easily procured against anything that comes in its way.

3. Thirdly, Satan endeavours to engage our hatred against the light, by presenting our *interest as shaken or endangered by it.* If interest can be drawn in and made a party, it is not difficult to put all the passions of a man in arms, to give open defiance to any discovery it can make. That great rage and tumult of kings and people mentioned in Psalm ii., combining and taking counsel against the Lord and his laws, is upon the quarrel of interest. Their suspicions and jealousies that the setting up of Christ upon his throne would eclipse their power and greatness, makes them, out of a desperate hatred against the light, fall into resolves of open rebellion against his laws: 'Let us break his bands asunder, and cast away his cords from us.' This pretence of interest strengthened the accusation of Amaziah against Amos: chap. vii. 10, 'Amos hath conspired against thee in the midst of the house of Israel: the land is not able to bear all his words.' No wonder, then, if Jeroboam, instead of hearkening to the threatening, banish him out of the land. We find the like in Asa, a good man; the devil stirs up his hatred against the seer: 'He was wroth with him, and put him in the prison-house; for he was in a rage against him,' 2 Chron. xvi. 10. The ground of that rage was this: the king's interest, in his apprehension, was wrapped up in that league with the king of Syria, ver. 2, 3, so that he could not bear so plain a reproof, which directly laid the axe to the root of so great an interest as the safety of the king and kingdom, which seemed to depend so much upon that league.

4. Fourthly, Satan stirs up hatred against the light from the *unavoidable effects of light, which are discovery and manifestation:* Eph. v. 13, 'All things that are reproved are made manifest; for whatsoever doth make manifest is light.' Now the issue of this manifestation is shame, which however it be the daughter of sin and light, yet would it naturally destroy the sin that bred it; and therefore repentance is usually expressed by being 'ashamed and confounded:' but that Satan might avoid this, he turns the edge of shame against

the light, which should have been employed against sin. When men therefore have sinned, and are as 'a thief when he is taken,' Jer. ii. 26, ready to fall into the hands of shame; for the avoiding of that, they 'rebel against the light,' Job xxiv. 13. The ground of this hatred, Christ, in John iii. 20, tells us, is 'lest their deeds should be reproved,' and they forced to bear their shame. To this end they are put upon it to hide themselves from shame by lies, pretences, excuses, extenuations, or by any fig-leaf that comes first to hand. And as those that live in hotter regions curse the sun because it scorcheth them, so do these curse the light: and instead of taking its help, raise up an irreconcilable enmity against it; and so run from it.

CHAPTER XVI.

Of Satan's third grand policy for maintaining his possession; which is his feigned departure: (1.) By ceasing the prosecution of his design; and the cases in which he doth it. (2.) By abating the eagerness of pursuit; and how he doth that. (3.) By exchanging temptations; and his policy therein.—The advantage he seeks by seeming to fly.—Of his fourth stratagem for keeping his possession, which is his stopping all ways of retreat; and how he doth that.

Besides the two former designs, of finishing sin, and keeping all in quiet, by which the devil endeavours to maintain his possession, he hath a third grand subtlety, which is this: he keeps his hold by feigning himself dispossessed and cast out. Of this we have a full account: Luke xi. 24, 'When the unclean spirit is gone out of a man, he walketh through dry places, seeking rest; and finding none, he saith, I will return unto my house whence I came out.' Christ had there noted that it is Satan's great principle to do nothing by which his kingdom may be divided or undermined. Satan will not be divided against himself, and yet very seasonably he tells us, that for an advantage he will seem to quit his interest, and upon design he will sometimes so carry himself that he may be deemed and supposed to be ' gone out of a man;' as those that besiege forts or walled towns do sometimes raise the siege and feign a departure, intending thereby to take a sudden advantage of the carelessness of the besieged. In the explanation of this policy, I shall, (1.) Shew how many ways he feigns a departure. (2.) Upon what designs he doth it.

There are three ways whereby Satan seems to forsake his interest:—

1. First, He frequently *ceaseth the prosecution of a design, which yet he hath in his eye and desire, when he perceives that there are some things in his way that render it not feasible;* nay, he forbears to urge men to their darling sins, upon the same score: and who would not think Satan cast out in such a case? When a man spits out the sweet morsel which heretofore he kept under his tongue, and sucked a sweetness from it; when men of noted iniquities abstain

from them, and become smooth and civil, who would not think but that the unclean spirit were gone? This way and course he puts in practice in several cases.

[1.] First, When he perceives some *extraordinary occasion puts any of his subjects into a good mood or humour of religion.* Wicked men are not ordinarily so highly bent upon evil ways, but that they may be at some times softened and relaxed. Pharaoh, who is most eminently noted for a heart judicially hardened, at the appearance of the plagues upon himself and Egypt, usually relented somewhat, and would confess he had sinned, and that fit would continue upon him for some little time. But very frequently it is thus with others; an extraordinary occasion melts and thaws down the natural affections of men, as a warm day melts the snow upon the mountains, and then the stream will for a time run high and strong, at which time Satan sees it is in vain to urge them. Thus men that receive an eminent kindness and deliverance from God, what is more common than for such men to say, Oh, we will never be so wicked as we have been, we will never be drunk more, the world shall see us reformed and new men! These are indeed good words, and yet though Satan knows that such expressions are not from a good heart,—as that of Deut. v. 29 implies, 'They have well said, Oh that there were such an heart in them!'—he nevertheless thinks it not fit then to press them to their usual wickedness at that time; for natural affections raised high in a profession of religion will withstand temptations for a fit, and therefore he forbears till the stream run lower. What a fit of affection had the Israelites when their eyes had seen that miraculous deliverance at the Red Sea! What songs of rejoicing had they! what resolves never to distrust him again! Ps. cvi. 12, 'Then believed they his words, they sang his praise.' Satan doth not presently urge them to murmuring and unbelief, though that was his design, but he stays till the fit was over, and then he could soon tempt them to 'forget his works.' How like a convert did Saul look, after David had convinced him of his integrity, and had spared his life in the cave! 1 Sam. xxiv. 16, and xxvi. 21. He weeps, and acknowledgeth his iniquity, justifies David, owns his kindness, and seems to acquiesce in his succession to the kingdom. The devil had, no question, a great spite at David, and it was his great design to stir up Saul against him, and yet at that time he could not prevail with him to destroy David, though he might easily have done it; he was then in a good mood, and Satan was forced to give way to necessity, and to seem to go out of Saul for the present.

[2.] Secondly, He also ceaseth from his design when he sees he cannot fit his temptation with a *suitable opportunity.* What could be more the devil's design, and Esau's satisfaction, than to have had Jacob slain? Esau professeth it was the design of his heart, and yet he resolves to forbear so long as his father Isaac lived: Gen. xxvii. 41, 'The days of my father's mourning are at hand; then, but not till then, will I slay my brother Jacob.' The devil often sows his seed, and yet waiteth and hath long patience, not only in watering and fitting the hearts of men for it, but also in expectancy of fit opportunities; and in the meantime, he forbears to put men upon that which time and occasion cannot fitly bring forth to practice. The prophet, Hosea vii. 4, speaks of that people as notoriously wicked, 'they are all adulterers;' but withal, he observes that they forbare these enormous abominations for want of fit seasons, 'their heart was as an oven heated by the baker,' sufficiently enflamed after their wickedness, and yet the baker, after he had kneaded the dough, prepared all the groundwork of the temptation, ceased from raising, sleeping all the night till all was leavened; that is, though their hearts were enraged for sin, yet the devil doth wait till occasions present themselves, and becomes in the meantime like one asleep. Now while the devil thus sleeps, the fire that is secretly in the heart, being not seen, men gain the good opinion of converts with others, and often with themselves, not knowing what spirit they are of, because Satan ceaseth, upon the want of occasions, to tempt and provoke them.

[3.] Thirdly, Our adversary is content to forbear, when he perceives that *a restraining grace doth lock up the hearts and hands of men.* When 'a stronger than he cometh,' who can expect less but that he should be more quiet? That God doth restrain men sometime when he doth not change them, needs no proof; that Satan knows of these restraints, cannot be denied. Who can give an account of these communings and discourses that are betwixt God and Satan concerning us? His pleadings in reference to Job were as unknown to Job, till God discovered them, as his pleadings concerning ourselves are to us. Besides, who can tell how much of God's restraining grace may lie in this, of God's limiting and straitening Satan's commission? Now the devil hath not so badly improved his observations, but that he knows it is in vain to tempt where God doth stop his way and tie up men's hands. Abimelech was certainly resolved upon wickedness when he took Sarah from Abraham, Gen. xx. 2, and yet the matter is so carried for some time, how long we know not, as if the devil had been asleep, or forgot to hasten Abimelech to his intended wickedness; for when God cautions him, 'he had not come near her,' ver. 4. The ground of all this was neither in the devil's backwardness nor Abimelech's modesty, but Satan lets the matter rest, because he knew that 'God withheld him, and suffered him not to touch her.'

[4.] Fourthly, When men are under *the awe and fear of such as carry an authority in their countenances and employments for the discouraging of sin,* Satan, as hopeless to prevail, doth not solicit to scandalous iniquities. Much of external sanctity and saintlike behaviour ariseth from hence. The faces and presence of some men have such a shining splendour, that iniquity blusheth and hideth its head before them. Sin dare not do what it would; so great a reverence and esteem of such persons is kept up in the consciences of some, and so great an awe and fear is thence derived to others, that they will not or dare not give way to an insolency in evil. The Israelites were generally a wicked people, yet such an awe they had of 'Joshua, and the elders that outlived Joshua, who had seen all the great works of the Lord,' Josh. ii. 7, that Satan seemed to be cast out all their days. Who could have thought Joash had been so much under Satan's power, that had observed his ways all the time of Jehoiada the priest? 2 Chron. xxiv. 2, 'Then he did that which was right in the sight of the Lord.' Satan was content to let him alone, because Jehoiada's life and authority did overawe him; but after his death Satan returned to his possession, 'and the king hearkened to the princes of Judah, and served groves and idols,' ver. 17. The like is observed of Uzziah, 2 Chron. xxvi. 5. The reverence that he had for Zechariah, who had understanding in the visions of God, discouraged the tempter from soliciting him to those evils which afterward he engaged him in, ver. 16. Satan is willing, when he perceives the awe and authority of good men stands in his way, rather to suspend the prosecution of his design, than, by forcing it against so strong a current, to hazard the shipwreck of it.

[5.] Fifthly, He also makes as if he were cast out when he perceives *the consciences of men are scared by threatened or felt judgments.* He forbears to urge them against the pricks when God draws his sword and brings forth the glittering spear. Balaam's ass would not run against the angel that appeared terribly against him in his way. The devil knows the power of an awakened conscience, and sees it in vain to strive against such a stream; and when it will be no better he withdraws. As great a power as the devil had in Ahab, when he was affrighted and humbled he gave way, and for that season drave him not on to his wonted practice of wickedness. He also carried thus to the Ninevites, when they were awakened by the preaching of Jonah. Then we see them a reforming people, the devil surceased to carry them into their former provocations. How frequently is this seen among professors, where the word hath a searching power and force upon them! Sin is so curbed and kept under, that it is like a root of bitterness in winter, lying hid under ground, Satan forbearing to act upon it or to improve it, till the storms and noise of judgments cease, and then usually it will 'spring up and trouble them,' Heb. xii. 15. If Satan hath really lost his hold, he ceaseth not to molest and vex even awakened consciences with urgent solicitations to sin; but if he perceive that his interest in the hearts of men remains sure to him and unshaken, then, in case of affrightment and fear of wrath, it is his policy to conceal himself, and to dissemble a departure.

[6.] Sixthly, Satan is also forced to this by the *prevailing power of knowledge and principles of light.* Where the gospel in profession and preaching displays abroad his bright beams, then whatever shift men make to be wicked in secret, yet 'the light is as the shadow of death to them,' and it is even 'a shame to speak of these things in public,' Eph. v. 12. Here Satan cannot rage so freely, but is put to his shifts, and is forced to be silent, whilst the power of the gospel cuts off half his garments. Men begin to reform; some are clean escaped from error, 2 Pet. ii. 18; others abandon their filthy lusts and scandalous sins, and so 'escape the pollutions of the world, through the knowledge of our Lord and Saviour Jesus Christ,' ver. 20. Yet under all these great alterations and appearances of amendment, the devil is but seemingly ejected; for in the place mentioned, when the light declines, those that were escaped from error, and those that had fled from sinful pollutions, were both entangled again and carried to the same pitch, and a great deal further, of that sin and error in which they had been formerly engaged.

These are the six cases in which Satan ceaseth the prosecution of his design, which was his first policy in feigning himself to be cast out; but he further dissembles a flight when he thinks it not fit to cease wholly,

By abating his pursuit, by slacking his course; and this he doth,

[1.] First, When he tempts still, but yet *less than formerly*. So great is his cunning and patience, that when he cannot get what he would have, he contents himself with what he can get, rather than lose all. He desires that men would give up themselves fully and freely to his service; but if they like not this, he is willing to take them, as one speaks, as retainers, and to suffer them to take a liberty to come and go at pleasure.[1] He hath two main ends in tempting men to sin: one is to avenge himself upon God, in open defiance and dishonour of his name; the other is the ruin and perdition of souls. If he could, he would have these two ends meet in every temptation; yet he pleaseth himself with the latter when he cannot help it, and in that too he satisfies himself sometimes with as small an interest as may be, so that his possession and interest be but preserved. He knows that one sin loved and embraced brings death for its wages. A leak unstopped and neglected may sink the ship as well as a great storm; and therefore when he perceives the consciences of men shy and nice, he is willing they come to him, as Nicodemus came to Christ, by night in private, and that by stealth they do him service.

[2.] Secondly, He sometimes offers men *a composition, and so keeps his hold privately, by giving them an indulgence and toleration to comply with religious duties and observations.* Pharaoh condescended that Israel should go and serve the Lord in the wilderness, upon condition that their wives, children, and substance were left behind. So Satan saith to some, 'Go and serve the Lord,' only let your heart be with me; leave your affections behind upon the world. That serious warning of Christ, 'Ye cannot serve two masters; ye cannot serve God and mammon,' evidently shews that the devil useth to conceal his interest in the hearts of sinners by offering such terms; and that men are so apt to think that Satan is gone out when they have shared the heart betwixt God and him, that they stand in need of a full discovery of that cheat, and earnest caution against it. The devil was forced to yield, that Herod should do many things at the preaching of John; yet he maintained his possession of his heart, by fixing him in his resolved lust in the matter of Herodias: and this gives just ground of complaint against the generality of sinners, 'Ye return, but not to me, not with your whole hearts: have ye fasted to me? have ye mourned to me? they come and sit as my people, but their hearts are after their covetousness,' [Ezek. xxxiii. 31.]

[3.] Thirdly, Satan hath yet another wile by which he would cheat men into a belief that he is cast out of the heart; and this is a subtle way that he hath *to exchange temptations.* How weak and childish are sinners that suffer themselves thus to be abused! When they grow sick and weary of a sin, if the devil take that from them, and lay

[1] Greenham's Works, p. 793.

in the room of it another as bad, or the same again, only a little changed and altered, they please themselves that they have vomited up the first, but consider not that they have received into their embracement another as bad or worse. Concerning this exchange, we may note two things:—

First, That sometimes he attains his end by exchanging *one heinous sin for another as heinous, only not so much out of fashion:* as the customs and times and places give laws and rules for fashions, according to which the decencies or indecencies of garbs and garments are determined, so is it sometimes with sin. Men and countries have their darling sins; times and ages also have their peculiar iniquities, which, in the judgment of sinners, do clothe them with a fitness and suitableness. Sometimes men grow weary of sins, because they are everywhere spoken against; because men point at them with the finger. The devil in this case is ready to change with them. Drunkenness hath in some ages and places carried a brand of infamy in its forehead; so hath uncleanness and other sins. When sinners cannot practise these with credit and reputation, then they please themselves with an alteration. He that was a drunkard is now, it may be, grown ambitious and boasting; he that was covetous is become a prodigal or profuse waster; the heart is as vain and sottish as before, only their lusts are let out another way, and run in another channel. Sometimes lusts are changed also with the change of men's condition in the world. Poverty and plenty, a private and a public station, have their peculiar sins. He that of poor is made rich leaves his sins of distrust, envy, or deceitful dealing, and follows the bias of his present state to other wickednesses equally remarkable, and yet may be so blinded as to apprehend that Satan is departed from him.

Secondly, We may observe that Satan exchangeth sins with men in such *a secret private manner, that the change is not easily discovered;* and by this shift he casts a greater mist before the eyes of men. Thus he exchangeth open profaneness into secret sins: filthiness of the flesh into filthiness of the spirit. Men seem to reform their gross impieties, abstaining from drunkenness, swearing, adulteries; and then, it may be, they are taken up with spiritual pride, and their hearts are puffed up with high conceits of themselves, their gifts and attainments; or they are entangled with error, and spend their time in 'doting about questions that engender strife rather than edifying,' [1 Tim. vi. 4;] or they are taken up with hypocrisies. Thus the Pharisees left their open iniquities, washing the outside of the cup and platter, Mat. xxiii. 26; and instead of these, endeavoured to varnish and paint themselves over, so that in all this change they were but as graves that appeared not, Luke xi. 44. Or they acquiesce in formality and the outwards of religion; like that proud boaster, 'Lord, I thank thee I am not as other men are,' &c., [Luke xviii. 11.] In all these things the devil seems cast out and men reformed, when indeed he may continue his possession; only he lurks and hides himself under 'the stuff,' [1 Sam. x. 22.] These ways of sinning are but finer poisons, which, though not so nauseous to the stomach, nor so quick in their despatch, yet may be as surely and certainly deadly; such fly from the iron weapon, and a bow of steel strikes them through.

Having thus explained the three ways by which Satan pretends to depart from men, I must next shew his design in making such a pretence of forsaking his habitation.

[1.] First, That all this is done by him only *upon design*, may be easily concluded from several things hinted to us in the fore-cited place of Luke xi. As (1.) He doth not say that the devil is 'cast out,' as if there were a force upon him, but that he 'goeth out;' it is of choice, a voluntary departure. (2.) That his going out in this sense is notwithstanding irksome and troublesome to him. The heart of man, as one observes,[1] is a palace in his estimation, and dispossession, though upon design, is as a 'desert' to him, that affords him little ease or rest. (3.) That his going out is not a quitting of his interest; he calls it '*his* house' still : 'I will return to *my* house,' saith he. (4.) He takes care in going out to lock the door, that it may not be taken up with better guests; he keeps it 'empty' and tenantable for himself: he tempts still, though not so visibly, and strives to suppress such good thoughts and motions as he fears may quite out him of his possession. (5.) He goes out, *cum animo revertendi*, with a purpose of returning. (6.) His secession is so dexterously and advantageously managed, that he finds an easy admittance at his return, and his possession confirmed and enlarged : 'they enter in and dwell there.'

[2.] Secondly, *The advantages that he designs by this policy are these chiefly :* (1.) By this means men are dangerously confirmed *in their securities.* Thus the Pharisee blessed himself, 'Lord, I thank thee,' &c. They please themselves with this supposition, that the devil is cast out; and upon this they cease their war and watchfulness. As Saul, when he heard that David had escaped, 'went not out to seek after him;' so these trouble not themselves any further to inquire Satan's haunts in their hearts. Thus he sits securely within, whilst they think he is fled from them. (2.) By this means also he fits men as instruments *to serve his turn in other works of his.* He must have, in some cases, handsome tools to work withal. All men are not fit agents in persecution, either to credit it, or to carry it through with vigour and zeal; for this end he seems to go out of some, that under a smoother and profession-like behaviour, when they are stirred up to persecute, the rigour might seem just. Thus 'devout and honourable women' were stirred up to persecute Paul and Barnabas, Acts xiii. 50. The devil had gone out so far, that they had gained the reputation of devout, and then their zeal would easily take fire for persecution, and withal put a respect and credit upon it; for who would readily suspect that to be evil or Satan's design, which is carried on by such instruments? Besides, if he at any time intends to blemish the good ways of God by the miscarriages of professors, he fetcheth his arrow out of this quiver usually; if he brings a refined hypocrite to a scandalous sin, then doth the mouth of wickedness open itself to blaspheme 'the generation of the just,' as if none were better. Such agents could not be so commonly at hand for such a service, if Satan did not in the ways aforementioned seem to go out of men. (3.) It is another part of his design, after a pretended departure, to take the advantage of their

---

[1] Greenham, p. 796, [as before.—G.]

security, to return with greater strength and force. This Christ particularly notes, 'Then taketh he seven spirits worse than himself,' &c. Such, as Peter tells us, being 'again entangled, are totally overcome, and their latter end is worse with them than their beginning,' 2 Pet. ii. 20. How many might I name, if it were convenient, that I have known and observed, exactly answering this description of the apostle, that have for some years left off their wicked ways, and engaged for a profession of religion; and yet at last 'have returned like the dog to his own vomit again'! The devil, when he fights after the Parthian manner—*Terga vertentes metuendi Parthi*—is most to be feared; when he turns his back, he shoots most envenomed arrows, and whom he so wounds, he commonly wounds them to the death.

The fourth and last stratagem of Satan for the keeping his possession, is *to stop the way, to barricade up all passages, that there may be no possibility of escape or retreat.* When he perceives that his former ways of policy are not sufficient, but that his slaves and servants are so far enlightened in the discovery of the danger that they are ready to turn back from him, then he bestirs himself to oppose their revolt; and as God sometimes 'hedgeth up the way' of sinners with 'thorns,' that they should not follow their old lovers, so doth Satan, Hosea ii. 6; to which purpose,

[1.] First, He endeavours to turn them off such resolutions, by threatening *to reduce them with a strong hand.* Here he boasts and vaunts of his power and sinners' weakness; as Rabshakeh did against Hezekiah, 'What is that confidence wherein thou trustest? have the gods of Hamath and Arpad,' &c., 'delivered their land out of my hand?' [2 Kings xviii. 33, 34.] Have those that have gone before you been able to deliver themselves from me? Have they been able to rescue themselves? Did I not force those that were stronger than you? Did I not make David number the people? Did I not overcome him in the matter of Uriah? Did I not compel Peter to deny his Lord, notwithstanding his solemn profession to the contrary? And can you think to break away from me so easily? By this means he would weaken their heart, and enfeeble their resolutions, that they might sit down under their bondage, as hopeless ever to recover themselves from his snare: but if these affrightments hinder not, if, notwithstanding these brags, sinners prepare themselves to turn from sin to God; then,

[2.] Secondly, He *improves all he can that distance which sin hath made betwixt God and them.* Sins of ordinary infirmity and common incursion do not so break the peace of God's children, as sins of a higher nature do. Even in the saints themselves, we may observe, after notorious transgression, (1.) That the acquaintance and familiarity betwixt God and them is immediately broken. What a speedy alteration is made! How suddenly are all things changed! God hides himself. The sun that shined but now, and did afford a very comfortable and cherishing heat, before we are aware, is now hid in a cloud. Our warmth and refreshments are turned into cold and chillness. There is also a change on our part, and that suddenly. As in the resurrection, we shall be changed 'in the twinkling of an eye;' so here, in a moment, our joys flag and decay, our delights grow dull, our activity is impaired, we are bound and frozen up, and it is altogether winter with the soul. (2.) It may be noted, that this begets an enstrangement in us, and we so carry it as if we had resolved not to renew our league with God; for though we are not altogether so desperate as to make formal resolutions of continuing in sin, of casting off God, and bidding an everlasting farewell to our former acquaintance; though we do not say, We will now undo ourselves quite, and harden ourselves in our rebellion; yet sin hath left us in such a maze, and filled us with so many damps and misgiving thoughts, that we do not think of returning; we are at a stand, and like a mighty man astonished that cannot find his hands. We perceive we have lost so much, and have run into such great unkindnesses, that, like broken merchants, nothing is more irksome and tedious than to review our ways, or look into our debt-books. Instead of this, we endeavour to divert our thoughts, to cast off care, as if we conceived that time would eat it out, and that then of course we might fall into the old channel of freedom and comfort. (3.) When we return at last, oh, with what bashfulness and amazedness do we appear at our next supplications! what blushing, what damps, what apology! Nay, sometimes as the man without the wedding garment, 'we are speechless!' [Mat. xxii. 12.] How rightly doth such a man resemble the publican confessing, and the prodigal supplicating. While consulting what to say for himself, he now begins to feel with what sense and feeling the prophets and holy men of old used to express themselves in their confessions, 'We blush, we are ashamed, astonished, and confounded.' This distance sin makes betwixt saints and God sometimes; but betwixt God and the unconverted it is far greater. Now, when either an unconverted sinner or a fallen saint puts himself to look to God for reconciliation, then doth the devil labour to improve this for their hindrance. That he accuseth us to God, is evident by Satan's standing at Joshua's right hand, Zech.'iii. 1. How he accuseth God to us we know. He tells us it is in vain to seek to make up our peace after so great provocations; urging that he is 'a jealous God,' 'of pure eyes,' highly resenting the affronts we have given him, &c. Nay, he goes so high this way, that God is put to it in Scripture, of purpose to furnish us with an answer to these objections, to proclaim that he is 'slow to anger,' 'not easily provoked;' that if men return from the evil of their ways, he will 'return to them,' 'accept,' and 'pity' them, &c.

[3.] Thirdly, If this divert them not, but that they still persist in their resolves, then he *follows after them with a high hand;* sometimes, as Pharaoh did with Israel, he grows severe and imperious with them, and redoubles the tale of their bricks. He forceth them to higher and more frequent iniquities. Sometimes, as the same Pharaoh, he musters up all his chariots and horsemen to pursue after them, and in the highest diligence imaginable he brings forth his greatest power, besetting them on all sides with temptations and allurements of pleasures and delight. Where he perceives his time to be short, and his power shaken, he comes down in resolves to try his utmost strength. And hence it is that converts complain, that when they begin in earnest to look after God, they are most troubled with temptations. Besides this, whatever he can do to make them 'drive heavily,' [Exod. xiv. 25,] shall not be wanting. Sometimes he makes attempts upon their thoughts and affections, which are as their chariot wheels; and if these can be knocked off any way, it retards them. Sometimes he casts stumbling-blocks in their way. If any prejudice may divert them, if threatenings or penalties can hinder; if the frownings of friends or anything else can put a stop to their proceedings, he will have them ready. Sometimes he endeavours to retard them by solicitations of acquaintance, offers of former occasions and opportunities of sinning, or whatever else may be as a *remora* to their intentions.

[4.] Fourthly, But if none of these serve, then, as his last shift, he *proclaims open war against them, pursues them as enemies and rebels.* Now he begins to accuse them for that which they did by his advice and temptation. Now sins that were called little are aggravated. Now that day of repentance, which he was wont to say was long, he tells them it is quite spent, that the sun of their hope is set. Nothing now doth he suggest but hell, damnation, and wrath; he makes them, as it were, see it, hear it, and feel it in everything. That interest in their hearts which he dissembled before, now he stands upon and asserts, and will not be beat off; designing in all this either to make them weary of these new resolves by this unusual disquietment and hostility, or to precipitate them upon some desperate undertaking, or at least to avenge himself upon them, in venting his malice and rage against them; but of this more afterward.

CHAPTER XVII.

Satan's deceits against religious services and duties.—The grounds of his displeasure against religious duties.—His first design against duties is to prevent them.—His several subtleties for that end, by external hindrances, by indispositions bodily and spiritual, by discouragements; the ways thereof, by dislike; the grounds thereof, by sophistical arguings.—His various pleas therein.

Our next work is to take notice of the spite and methods of the serpent against the ways of worship and service. That these are things against which his heart carries a high fury, and for the overthrow of them employs no small part of his power and subtlety, needs no proof, seeing the experience of all the children of God is an irresistible evidence in this matter. I shall therefore first only set forth the grounds of his displeasure and earnest undertakings against them, before I come to his particular ways of deceit, which are these:—

1. First, By this means, if he prevail, *he deprives us of our weapons.* This is a stratagem of war which we find the Philistines practised against Israel: they took away all their smiths, lest the Hebrews should make them swords or spears; hence was it that in the battle there was 'neither sword nor spear found in the hand of any of the people that were with Saul and Jonathan,' 1 Sam. xiii. 19,

22. The word of God is expressly called 'the sword of the Spirit,' [Eph. vi. 17.] Prayer is as a spear, or rather a general piece of armour. If the devil deprive us of these, he robs us of our ammunition; for by reason of these the church is compared to 'a tower built for an armoury, wherein hang a thousand bucklers, all shields of mighty men,' Cant. iv. 4; and the apostle expressly calls them 'weapons of our warfare,' 2 Cor. x. 4, of purpose given us for 'the pulling down of strongholds,' and the demolishing of those forts and batteries of 'high imaginations' that Satan rears up in the hearts of men against their happiness. If these be taken away, our locks are cut, as Samson's were, our strength is departed, and we become weak as other men, [Judges xvi. 17,]—we are open to every incursion and inroad that he pleaseth to make against us.

2. Secondly, If he hinders these, *he intercepts our food and cuts off our provisions.* The word is called 'milk, sincere milk of the word.' It is that by which we are born, nourished, and increase; it is our cordial and comfort. Christ indeed is 'the bread of life,' and the fountain of all our consolations, but the word and prayer are the conduit pipes that convey all to us. If these be cut, we 'fade as a leaf,' we languish, we consume and waste, we become as a 'skin-bottle in the smoke,' 'our moisture as the drought in summer,' our 'soul fainteth,' 'our heart faileth, and we become as those that go down to the pit'; so that if the devil gain his design in this, he hath all. Give him this, and give him the kingdom also. This is the most compendious way of doing his work, and that which saves him a labour in his temptations. The strongest holds, that cannot otherwise be taken, are easily subdued by famine; and, like fig-trees with their ripe figs when they are shaken, 'even fall into the mouth of the eater,' Nahum iii. 12. If our spiritual food fail us, of our own accord we yield up ourselves to any lust that requires our compliance.

3. Thirdly, Besides these, there is no design whereby Satan can shew *more malice and spite against God.* He doth all he can to maintain a competition with the Almighty. His titles of 'the god of the world,' 'the prince of the power of the air,' shew what in the pride of his heart he aspires to, as well as what by commission God is pleased to grant him. These duties of worship and service are the homage of God's children, by which they testify the acknowledgments of his deity. By wresting these out of our hands, Satan robs God of that honour, and makes the allegiance of his servants to cease. If he could do more against God, doubtless he would; but seeing he hath not 'an arm like God,' and so cannot pull him out of heaven, by this means he sets up himself as the god of the world, and enlargeth his territories, and staves off the subjects of the God of heaven from giving him 'the honour due to his name;' and that the devil in these endeavours is carried on by a spite against God, as well as by an earnest desire of the ruin of souls, may be abundantly evidenced by his way of management of that opposition that he gives to the duties of service and worship. I shall only, to make out this, instance in three things:—(1.) That where the devil prevails to set up himself as an object of worship, there he doth it in a bold, insolent, presumptu-

ous imitation of God's appointments in the ways of his service. He enjoins covenants, seals, sacrifices, prayers, and services to his miserable slaves, as may appear by undoubted histories, of which more in due place. (2.) He never acknowledgeth the truth of God's ways, but with an evil mind and upon design to bring them under contempt. His confessions have so much of deceit in them that Christ would not accept them; and therefore we read that when the devil was sometime forward to give his testimony to Christ, as Mark i. 25, 'I know thee who thou art, the Holy One of God,' Jesus rebuked him, and commanded him to hold his peace. He clearly saw that he confessed him not to honour him, but by such a particular acknowledgment to stir up the rage and fury of the people against him. To this end Satan, in Acts xvi. 17, many days together publicly owns Paul and Silas, 'These men are the servants of the most high God, which shew unto us the way of salvation.' Though he spake truth, yet had he a malicious aim in it, which he accordingly brought about by this means; and that was to raise up persecution against them, and to give ground to that accusation which they afterwards met withal; ver. 21, 'That they taught customs which were not lawful to be received.' But (3.) his particular spite against God in seeking to undermine his service is further manifested in this, that the devil is not content to root out the service due to God, but when he hath done that, he delights to abuse those places where the name of God was most celebrated, with greatest profanations. I shall not in this insist upon the conjecture of Tilenus,[1] that *Sylva Dodonœa*, a place highly abused by the devil, and respected for an oracle, was the seat or a religious place of Dodanim, mentioned in Gen. x. 4; nor upon that supposal, mentioned also by the same author, that the oracle of Jupiter Hammon was the place where Cham [Ham] practised that religious worship which he learned in his father's house. We have at hand more certain evidences of the devil's spite. Such was his abuse of the tabernacle by the profane sons of Eli, who profaned that place with their uncleanness and filthy adulteries. Such was his carriage to the ark while it was captivated by the Philistines. Of like nature were his attempts against the temple itself. Solomon in his latter days was tempted to give an affront to it: he built a high place for Chemosh, the abomination of Moab, in the hill that is before Jerusalem, 1 Kings xi. 7, in the very sight and face of the temple; but afterward he prepared to defile the temple itself. Gilgal and Beth-aven are places of such high profanation, that the prophet Hosea, chap. ix. 15, tells them 'all their wickedness was in Gilgal,' none of their abominations were like to those; and in chap. iv. 15, they are dehorted from going to Gilgal or Beth-aven; and yet both these places had been famous for religion before.[2] Gilgal was the place of the general circumcision of the Israelites that were born in the wilderness; there was their first solemn passover kept after their entering into the land. Bethel was a place where God as it were kept house, 'the house of God.' Here Jacob had his vision. But the more famous they had been for duties of worship, the devil sought to put higher abuses upon

---

[1] Syntag., part. i. disput. 2. Thes. 20-22.
[2] Arrowsmith, Tact. Sacr., lib. i. cap. 5, sec. 9.

them, so that Gilgal became 'an hatred,' and Bethel became a Beth-aven, 'an house of vanity.'

4. Fourthly, Satan is the more animated to undertake a design against the ways of religious service, because *he seldom or never misseth at least something of success.* This attempt is like Saul and Jonathan's bow, that 'returned not empty,' [2 Sam. i. 22.] In other temptations sometimes Satan comes off baffled altogether, but in this work, as it was said of some Israelites, 'he can throw a stone at an hair's breadth, and not miss,' Judges xx. 16. He is sure in one thing or other to have the better of us. His advantage in this case is from our unsuitableness to our service. What we do in the duties of worship, requires a choice frame of spirit. Our hearts should be awed with the most serious apprehensions of divine majesty, filled with reverence, animated with love and delight, quickened by faith, clothed with humility and self-abhorrency, and in all the procedure of duties there must be a steady and firm prosecution under the strictest watchfulness. Of this nature is our work, which at the first view would put a man to a stand, and out of amazement force him to say, 'Who is sufficient for these things? who can stand before such an holy Lord God?' But when we come to an impartial consideration of our manifold weaknesses and insufficiencies in reference to these services, what shall we say? we find such a narrowness of spirit, such ignorances, sottishness, carelessness of mind, thoughts so confused, tumultuous, fickle, slippery, and unconstant, and our hearts generally so deceitful and desperately wicked, that it is not possible that Satan should altogether labour in vain or catch nothing. This being then a sure gain, we may expect it to be under a most constant practice.

5. Fifthly, If he so prevails against us that the services of worship become *grossly abused or neglected, then doth he put us under the greatest hazards and disadvantages.* Nothing so poisonous as duties of worship corrupted; for this is to abuse God to his face. By this, not only are his commands and injunctions slighted, as in other sins, but we carry it so as if we thought him no better than the idols of the heathens, that have 'eyes and see not, that have ears and hear not.' To come without a heart, or with our idols in our heart, is it anything of less scorn than to say, 'Tush, doth the Most High see?' Besides, he hath given such severe cautions and commands in these matters as will easily signify the aggravation of the offence. You see how sharply God speaks of those that came to inquire of the Lord with 'the stumbling-block of their iniquity before their face,' Ezek. xiv. 4, 7, 'I will answer them according to the multitude of their idols; I will answer them by myself.' Saul's miscarriage in offering sacrifice, 1 Sam. xiii. 13, was that great offence for which God determined to take the kingdom from him. God's severity against Nadab and Abihu, his stroke upon Uzziah, do all shew the hazard of such profanations. But, above all, that danger which both Old and New Testament speak of—the hardening of the heart, blinding the eyes, dulling the ears, that men should not hear nor see nor be converted and saved, but that the word should, instead of those cordial refreshing smells which beget and promote spiritual life in the obedient, breathe forth such envenomed, poisonous exhalations when it is thus abused

and profaned, that it becomes 'the savour of death unto death'—is most dreadful. No wonder, then, if Satan be very busy against these holy things, when, if he catch us at an advantage of this nature, it proves so deadly and dangerous to us; for what can more please him that makes it his delight and employment to destroy?

All these reasons evince that Satan hath an aching tooth against religious services, and that to weaken, prevent, or overthrow them is his great endeavour. Here then especially may we expect an assault, according to the advice of Sirach: Ecclus. ii. 1, 2, 'My son, when thou enterest God's service, stand fast in righteousness and fear, and prepare thy soul for temptation.'

What are the subtleties of Satan against the holy things of God, I am next to discover. Duties and services are opposed two ways: (1.) *By prevention*, when they are hindered. (2.) *By corruption*, when they are spoiled. He hath his arts and cunning, which he exerciseth in both these regards:—

1. First, then, Of Satan's policy for the preventing of religious services. He endeavours by various means to hinder them. As,

(1.) First, *By external hindrances.* In this he hath a very great foresight, and accordingly he foresees occasions and opportunities at a distance, and by a long reach of contrivance he studies to lay blocks and hindrances in the way. Much he doth in the dark for this end that we know not. As God hath 'secrets of wisdom that are double to that which is known,' Job xi. 6, so also hath Satan many ways and actings that are not discerned by us. His contrivances of businesses and avocations long aforehand are not so observed by us as they might be. Where he misseth of his end it comes not to light, and often where he is successful in his preventions we are ready to ascribe it to contingencies and the accidental hits of affairs, when indeed the hand and policy of Satan is in it. Paul, that was highly studied and skilful in Satan's devices, observing how his purposes of coming to the Thessalonians were often broken and obstructed, he knew where the blame lay, and therefore instead of laying the fault upon sickness, or imprisonments, or the oppositions of false brethren—which often made him trouble beyond expectation—he directly chargeth all upon Satan: 1 Thes. ii. 18, 'We would have come unto you, even I Paul, once and again, but Satan hindered us.' At the same rate, understanding the purposes of faithful men for the promoting the good of men's souls, he often useth means to stop or hinder them. Some have observed, having a watchful and jealous eye over Satan, that their resolves and endeavours of this nature have usually been put to struggle sore in their birth when their purposes for worldly affairs and matters go smoothly on without considerable opposition.

(2.) Secondly, He makes use of indispositions to hinder service; and here he works sometimes upon the body, sometimes upon the soul, for both may be indisposed.

[1.] First, Sometimes he takes the advantage of *bodily indispositions.* He doth all he can to create and frame these upon us, and then pleads them as a discharge to duty. If he can put the body into a fit of drowsiness or distemper, he will do it: and surely he can do more this way than every one will believe—he may agitate and stir the humours. Hence some have observed more frequent and stronger fits of sleepiness and illness to come upon them on the days and times that require their attendance upon God, than on other days; when they shall be lively, active, and free of dulness upon common occasions—at sports, songs, interludes—when they shall not have the like command of themselves in the exercises of worship. Surely it was more than an ordinary drowsiness that befell the apostles, Mat. xxvi. 41. He had told them the seriousness of the occasion, that he was 'betrayed,' that his 'soul was exceeding sorrowful even to the death:' these were considerations that might have kept their eyes from slumber. When they sleep, he awakens them with a piercing rebuke, 'Could ye not watch with me one hour?' and adds to this an admonition of their own danger, and the temptation that was upon them, and yet presently they are asleep again, and after that again. Strange drowsiness! But he gives an excuse for them, which also tells us the cause of it: the 'spirit is willing'—their hearts were not altogether unconcerned—'but the flesh,' that is, the body, that was 'weak'—that is, subject to be abused by Satan, who brought them into a more than ordinary indisposition, as is noted ver. 43, 'their eyes were heavy.'

[2.] Secondly, *The soul hath also its indispositions,* which he readily improves against duty to hinder it. As,

First, It is capable of *a spiritual sluggishness and dulness,* wherein the spiritual senses are so bound up, that it considers not, minds not, hath no list nor inclination to acts of service. What a stupefaction are our spirits capable of! as David in his adultery seems not to mind nor care what he had done. In like manner are some in a lethargy; as the prophet speaks, they 'care not to seek after God.' Bernard hath a description of it: *Contrahitur animus, subtrahitur gratia, defervescit novitius fervor, ingravescit torpor fastidiosus,* The spirit is contracted, grace withdrawn, fervour abates, sluggishness draws on, and then duties are neglected.

Secondly, The spirit is indisposed by *a throng of worldly affairs, and these oft jostle out duty.* Christ tells us they have the same influence upon men that gluttony and drunkenness have, and these unfit men for action. 'Take heed,' saith Luke xxi. 34, 'to yourselves, lest at any time your heart be overcharged with surfeiting and drunkenness, and the cares of this life.' These then may at so high a rate overcharge the souls of men so as to make them frame excuses: 'I have bought a farm or oxen,' and therefore 'I cannot attend;' and by this means may they grow so neglective that the 'day of the Lord may come upon them at unawares.'

Thirdly, Sometimes the soul is *discomposed through passion,* and then it is indisposed, which opportunity the devil espying, he closeth in with it. Sometime he 'blows the fire,' that the heat of anger may put them upon a carelessness. Sometimes he pleads their present frame as an unfitness for service, and so upon a pretence of reverence to the service, and 'leaving the gift at the altar' till they be in a better humour, many times the gift is not offered at all, 1 Pet. iii. 7. The apostle directs husbands to manage their authority over their wives with prudence, for the avoiding of brawls and contentions: 'Ye husbands, dwell with them according to knowledge, giving honour to the wife as the weaker vessel;' the reason of which advice he gives in these words, 'that your prayers be not hindered.' Prayers are hindered partly in their success when they prevail not, partly they are hindered when the duty of prayer is put by and suspended; and this doubtless the apostle aims at, to teach us that contentious quarrellings in a family hinder the exercise of the duty of prayer. Elisha, 2 Kings iii., discomposed himself in his earnest reproof of Jehoram, for with great vehemency he had spoken to him: ver. 13, 14, 'What have I to do with thee? get thee to the prophets of thy father. Were it not that I regard the presence of Jehoshaphat, I would not look toward thee, nor see thee.' But when he set himself to receive the visions of God, he calls for a minstrel, ver. 15, the reason whereof, as P[eter] Martyr and others suppose,[1] was this, that however what he spake to Jehoram proceeded from zeal, yet being but a man, and subject to the like infirmities of other men, it had distracted and discomposed his spirit, which made him unfit and uncapable to entertain the visions of God. Music then being a natural means for the composure and quiet of the mind, he takes that course to calm and fit himself for that work.

Fourthly, Ignorance and prejudice are spiritual indispositions, which are not neglected by the devil. Knowledge is the eye and guide of the soul. If there be darkness there, all acts which depend upon better instruction must cease. The disciples' ignorance of Scriptures brought in their unbelief. Christ notes that as the fountain-head of all their backwardness: Luke xxiv. 25, 'O fools, and slow of heart to believe all that the prophets have spoken.' In like manner, if men are not clear or knowing in the ways and necessities of duty and service, the devil can easily prevail with them to forbear and neglect. Prejudice riseth up to justify the disregard of duty, and offers reasons which it thinks cannot be answered.

(3.) Thirdly, Satan endeavours to prevent duty *by discouragements.* If he can make the 'knees feeble,' and the 'hands hang down,' he will quickly cause activity and motion to cease. The ways by which he endeavours to discourage men from the duties of service are these:—

[1.] First, He sets before them *the toil and burden of duty.* If a man sets his face toward heaven, thus he endeavours to scare him off: Is not, saith he, the way of religion a dull, melancholy way? Is it not a toil—a tedious task? Are not these unreasonable injunctions: 'Pray continually,' 'Pray without ceasing,' 'Preach in season and out of season'? This suggestion, though it be expressly contrary to command, yet being so suitable to the idle and sluggish tempers of men, they are the more apt to take notice of it, and accordingly they seek ways and shifts of accommodating the command to their inclinations. In Amos viii. 5, the toil of sabbaths and festival services, as they thought it, makes them weary of the duty, 'When will the new moon be gone, that we may sell corn? and the sabbath, that we may set forth wheat?' These men thought their services tedious and entrenching upon their callings and occupations: Mal. i. 13, 'They said, Behold, what a weariness is it!' looking upon it as

---

[1] Rutherford, 'Divine Influences.'

an insufferable burden, nay they proceeded so far as to snuff at it. Now when the devil had so far prevailed with them, it was easy to put them upon neglect; which, as the place cited speaks, presently followed upon it, they 'brought the torn, and the lame, and the sick for a sacrifice.' Satan first presented these services as a wearisome burden, then they snuffed at them; next they thought any service good enough, how mean soever, though to an open violation of the law of worship; and lastly, from a pollution of the table of the Lord they proceeded to a plain contempt of duty, 'the table of the Lord is polluted, and the fruit thereof, even his meat is contemptible,' ver. 12. In the management of this discouragement, the devil hath most success upon those that have not yet tasted the sweetness and easiness of the ways of the Lord, ' his yoke is indeed easy, his burden is light;' his service is a true freedom to those that are acquainted with God, and exercised in his service. But when men are first beginning to look after God and duty, and are not yet filled and 'satisfied with the fatness of his house,' this temptation hath the greater force upon them, and they are apt to be discouraged thereby.

[2.] Secondly, He endeavours to discourage them, from *the want of success in the duties of worship.* When they have waited long and sought the Lord, then he puts them upon resolves of declining any further prosecution, as he did with Joram at the siege of Samaria; 'Why wait I upon the Lord any longer?' 2 Kings vi. 33, said he, after he had expected deliverance a long time without any appearance of help. When Saul saw that God 'answered him not, neither by dreams, nor by Urim, nor by prophets,' 1 Sam. xxviii. 6, 7, the devil easily persuaded him to leave off the ordinary ways of attendance upon God, and to consult with the witch of Endor. The profane persons mentioned in Mal. iii. 14, that had cast off all regard to his laws, all respect to his ordinances, were brought to this pitch of iniquity by the suggestions of want of success; they said, 'It is vain to serve God: and what profit is it that we have kept his ordinances, and that we have walked mournfully before the Lord of hosts?' It seems they were like the people spoken of in Isa. lviii. 2, 3: they had fasted and prayed, and God delayed to answer them, which they looked upon as a disobligement from duty, and that which they could peremptorily insist upon as a reason which might justify their neglect. 'Wherefore have we fasted, say they, and thou seest not? wherefore have we afflicted our soul, and thou takest no knowledge?' Neither doth this discouragement fall heavy only upon those whose hearts are departed already from God, who might be supposed to be forward to embrace any excuse from his service; but we shall find it bears hard upon the children of God. David was ready to give over all, as a man forsaken of God: Ps. xxii. 1, 2, 'Why hast thou forsaken me? O my God, I cry in the daytime, but thou hearest not; and in the night season, and am not silent.' We may clearly gather from his expressions that this temptation had sorely bruised him, and that upon God's delay of answer, he was ready to charge an unrighteousness upon God's carriage toward him; for in that he adds that he kept his ground, and did not consent to it—as the words following, 'But thou continuest holy,' do imply—it shewed what the devil was objecting to him. And elsewhere, in Ps. lxix. 3, when he had cried and was not answered, he began to be 'weary, and his eyes failed; nay, his flesh and heart failed;' his spirit sunk, as a man almost vanquished and overcome with the temptation.

[3.] Thirdly, This our adversary raiseth up discouragements to us from *the unsuitableness of our hearts to our services*. Herein he endeavours to deaden our hearts, to clog our spirits, to hinder and molest us, and then he improves these indispositions and discomposures against the duty, in which he hath a double advantage; for (1.) He deprives us of that delight in duty which should whet on our desires to undertake it, so that we come to the Lord's table as old Barzillai, without a taste or relish of what we eat or drink. When we come to hear, ' the ear that trieth words,' as the palate tasteth meat, finds no savour in what is spoken; and this Satan can easily do by the inward deadness or disquiet of the heart, even as the anguish of diseases takes away all pleasures which the choicest dainties afford; as Job observes, ' When a man is chastened with pain upon his bed, his life abhors bread, and his soul dainty meat,' chap. xxxiii. 20. And when a man is brought to loathe his duties, as having nothing of that sweetness and satisfaction in them which is everywhere spoken of, a small temptation may put him upon neglect of them. (2.) He hath plausible and colourable arguments by which he formeth an opinion in the minds of men, that in cases of indisposition they may do better to forbear than to proceed. He tells them they ought not to pray or present any service while they are so indisposed, that no prayer is acceptable where the Spirit doth not enliven the heart and raise the affections; that they do but take his name in vain, and increase their sin, and that they should wait till the Spirit fill their sails: and to say the truth, it is a great difficulty for a child of God to hold his feet in such slippery places. How many have I known complaining of this, and persuading themselves verily that they might do far better to leave off all service than to perform them thus ! And scarcely have I restrained them from a compliance with Satan, by telling them that indispositions are no bar to duty, but that duty is the way to get our indispositions cured; that duty is absolutely required, and dispositions to be endeavoured; and that it is a less offence to keep to duty under indispositions, than wholly upon that pretence to neglect it; and indeed, where these indispositions are bemoaned and striven with, the services are often more acceptable to God than pleasing to ourselves. The principle is truly spiritual and excellent, a foundation of sapphires and precious stones, upon which, if we patiently wait, he will build a palace of silver; for that service is more spiritual that is bottomed and carried on by a conscientious regard to a command, when there are no moral motives from sense and comfort concurring, than that which hath more of delight to encourage it, while the power of the command is less swaying and influential.

[4.] Fourthly, Men are oft discouraged from *a sense of unworthiness of the privilege of duty, a kind of excess of humility*, which principally relates to the sacrament of the Lord's Supper, and prayer. The accuser of the brethren tells them that they have nothing to do to take the name of God in their mouths; that it is an insufferable presumption.

Hence some, like the woman with the bloody issue, dare not come to Christ to ask a cure, while yet they earnestly desire it, and would rather, if they could, privately steal it than openly beg it. The publican [Luke xviii. 10, *seq.*] is presented to us in the parable as one that could scarce get over that objection. He is set forth standing at a 'distance, not daring to lift up his eyes to heaven;' scarce attempting to speak, rather expressing his unworthiness to pray, than setting upon the duty; his 'smiting upon his breast,' and saying, 'God be merciful to me a sinner,' argued that much of these discouragements lay upon him. The like we may see in the prodigal, who it seems had it long in dispute whether he should go to his father, whose kindness he had so abused; and so long as he could make any other shift he yielded to the temptation: at last he came to that resolve, 'I will arise and go to my father, and say, I have sinned against heaven, and thee, and am not worthy to be called thy son.' Which shew that the sense of this kept him off till necessity forced him over it. And this is a discouragement the more likely to prevail for a neglect of service, because part of it is necessary, as the beginning of those convictions of our folly: to have such low thoughts of ourselves that we are not worthy to come into his presence, nor to look toward him, is very becoming; but to think that we should not come to him because our conscience accuseth of unworthiness, is a conclusion of Satan's making, and such as God never intended from the premises, but the direct contrary. Come, saith God, though unworthy. The like course doth the devil take to keep men off from the Lord's table. Oh, saith he, it is a very solemn ordinance; he that partaketh of it unworthily, eateth and drinketh damnation to himself. How darest thou make such bold approaches? While the hearts of men are tender, their consciences quick and accusing, the threatening begets a fear, and they are driven off long, and debar themselves unnecessarily from their mercies.

(4.) Fourthly, Satan endeavours to hinder duty by bringing them into *a dislike and loathing of duty.* This is a course most effectual. Dislike easily bringeth forth aversation, and withal doth strongly fix the mind in purposes of neglect and refusal. The devil bringeth this about many ways; as,

[1.] First, *By reproaches and ignominious terms.* It was an old trick of the wicked one to raise up nicknames and scoffs against the ways of God's service, thereby to beget an odium in the hearts of men against them. 'The seat of the scornful' is a chair that Satan had reared up from the beginning. By this art—when 'God was known in Jewry, and his name was great in Israel'—were the heathens kept off from laying hold on the covenant of God. He rendered them and the ordinances of worship ridiculous to the nations. The opprobium of circumcision, and their unreasonable faith, as the heathens thought it, upon things not seen, was a proverb in every man's mouth, *Credat Judæus Apella— non ego.*[1] The Jews were slandered with the yearly sacrifice of a Grecian. And Apion affirms that Antiochus found such a one in a bed in the temple; and that they worshipped an ass's head in the temple. Apion slandered the Jews with ulcers in their

---

[1] Horace: Ser. i. 5, 100.—G.

privy parts every seventh day; hence he derives *sabbath*, of *sabatosis*, which with the Egyptians signifies an ulcer.¹

Lysimachus slandered the Jews in Egypt as leprous church-robbers; and that their city was hence called *Hierosola*.² When the Gentiles were called into the fellowship of the gospel, it was aspersed with the like scoffs and flouts. It was frequently called a sect, a babbling and strange and uncouth doctrine, Acts xxviii. 22; besides a great many lies and forgeries that were invented to make it seem odious; and by this means it was 'everywhere spoken against,' Acts xvii. 18, 20. Machiavel, that propounded the policy of full and violent calumniations to render an adversary odious, knowing that how unjust soever they were, yet some impression of jealousy and suspicion would remain, had learned it of this old accuser, who had often and long experienced it to be a prevalent course, to bring the services of God under dislike, *Calumniare fortiter; aliquid adhærebit*. David, speaking of what befell himself in this kind, Ps. lxix. 9–12, that his zeal lay under reproach; his weeping and fasting became a proverb; and that in all these he was 'the song of the drunkard,' he expresseth such apprehensions of the power of this temptation upon the weak, that he doth earnestly beg that Satan might not make it a snare to them: ver. 6, 'Let not them that wait on thee, O Lord God of hosts, be ashamed for my sake: let not those that seek thee be confounded for my sake.' And further declares it, as a wonderful preservation and escape of this danger, that notwithstanding these reproaches, he had not declined his duty: ver. 13, 'But as for me, my prayer is unto thee, Lord.' Paul seems to speak his sense of this piece of policy; his imprisonment administered matter of reproach to his profession. Though his cause were good, yet he suffered trouble as 'an evil-doer,' 2 Tim. ii. 9. This he knew the devil would improve to a shame and disgrace unto the service of God, and therefore he chargeth Timothy to be aware of that temptation: 2 Tim. i. 8, 'Be not thou therefore ashamed of the testimony of our Lord, nor of me his prisoner.' And ver. 16, he takes notice of Onesiphorus, that had escaped that snare, and was not 'ashamed of his chain.' And we have the greater reason to fear the danger of this art, when we find that the tempter made use of it to turn away the affections of the Capernaumites from Christ himself: Mat. xiii. 57, when he had preached in their synagogues to the applause and astonishment of all his hearers, the devil, fearing the prevalency of his doctrine, finds out this shift to bring them to a dislike of him and his preaching: 'Is not this the carpenter's son? And they were offended in him.'

[2.] Secondly, Duties are brought under dislike *by the hazards that attend them*. The devil leaves it not untold what men shall meet with from the world if they 'run not with them into excess of vanity' and neglect. If bonds, imprisonments, banishments, hatreds, oppositions, spoiling of goods, sufferings of all kinds will divert them, he is sure to set all these affrightments before them; which though they do not

---

¹ Jos[ephus] cont. Apion, lib. vi. cap. 2. [More accurately: for the former about the Grecians, lib. ii. cap. 8; about the ass-head, lib. ii. cap. 7; and about *sabatosis* = buboes, lib. ii. cap. 2. The writings of Apion against the Jews, except in the fragments preserved by Josephus, have perished.—G.] ² Jos. cont. Apion, lib. i. [sec. 34.—G.]

move some from their steadfastness—such as Daniel, whose constancy in duty was not pierced by the fear of lions; and the three children, who would not decline the ways of the Lord for the terror of a fiery furnace—yet these considerations prevail with most; as Christ notes, in those that received seed in stony places, whose joy in the word was soon blasted, and they offended at the ways of duty, 'when tribulation and persecution because of the word arose,' Mat. xiii. 21. Christ pronouncing him blessed that should 'not be offended in him,' because of the dangers of his service, shews that the escape of such a temptation is not a common mercy, Mat. xi. 6. And if we shall observe Paul's practice upon his first undertaking of the ministry, when 'it pleased God to call him to preach his Son Christ among the heathen,' Gal. i. 16, we shall see, (1.) That he was aware of such objections as these; (2.) That flesh and blood are apt to comply with them, and to take notice of them; (3.) And that the best way to avoid them is to stop the ears against them, and not to hearken to them or consult with them; (4.) And that he that must do it to purpose, must, without delay, immediately resolve against such hindrances; it being most difficult for men that will be inclining to such motions, and hearkening to what the devil offers, under pretence of self-preservation, to disengage themselves after they have suffered their souls to take the impression.

[3.] Thirdly, *The meanness of religious appointments, as to the outward view, is also made use of to beget a loathing of them.* In this the devil hath this advantage, that however they are all 'glorious within,' and 'as the curtains of Solomon,' yet are they, as to their outward appearance, like 'the tents of Kedar,' without any of that pomp and splendour which the sons of men affect and admire. Christ himself, when he had veiled his glory by our flesh, was of no exterior 'form or beauty.' The ministration of his word, which is 'the sceptre of his kingdom,' seems contemptible, and a very 'foolishness to men;' insomuch that Paul was forced to make an apology for it, in that it wanted those outward braveries of 'excellency of speech and wisdom,' by shewing it was 'glorious in its power,' and was indeed a 'hidden wisdom'—though not like that 'wisdom which the princes of wisdom' and philosophy affected—'among such as were perfect,' 1 Cor. ii. 1, 4, 6. The sacraments, both of the Old and New Testament, seemed very low and contemptible things to a common eye; neither need we any other evidence to shew that men are apt to disrelish them, and to entertain strange thoughts of them upon this very account, than this, that some raise up batteries against these ordinances upon this ground, that because they seem low and mean to them, therefore they think it improbable that God should have indeed appointed them to be used in the literal sense, or that at best they are to be used as the first rudiments of Christianity, and not enjoined upon the more grown Christians. Neither may I altogether pass over that remarkable humour that is in some, to give additional ornaments of outward garb and form for the greater honour and lustre of these injunctions of Christ; so that while they endeavour to shew their greatest respects to them, they betray their inward thoughts to have carried some suspicion of their reality because of their plainness; and by this means, whilst they endeavour to put an honour upon Christ's institutions, they really despise them, and shew their respects to their own inventions. But that we may be further satisfied that Satan works by this engine, let us consider that of 1 Cor. i. 23. The Jews were for signs from heaven to give a credit and testimony to that doctrine which they would receive. The Greeks, who were then the only people for learning, were for philosophical speculations and disputes. Now, saith the apostle, the doctrine of the gospel, which is the preaching of Christ crucified, because it came not within the compass of what both these expected, therefore the devil so wrought upon this advantage, that both contemned it; 'It was to the Jews a stumbling-block, and to the Greeks foolishness.' Of this also he speaks more fully, 2 Cor. xi. 3, where he shews that the minds of the Corinthians were ready to be corrupted with error against the plain import of the gospel; and that which they took offence at was its simplicity. They looked upon it as contemptible, because not containing such gorgeous things as might suit a soaring and wanton fancy. Now he resolves all this into a cheat of Satan, taking the advantage of this, as he did upon Eve from the seeming inconsiderableness of the prohibition of eating a little fruit, to persuade them that so mean a thing as the gospel could not be of God. 'I fear,' saith he, 'lest by any means, as the serpent beguiled Eve through his subtlety, so your minds should be corrupted from the simplicity that is in Christ.'

[4.] Fourthly, *The sins of professors, through the craft of Satan, beget a loathing of these holy things.* If God loathe his own appointments, and 'cannot bear them,' because of the iniquities of those that offer them, no wonder if men be tempted to disgraceful apprehensions of them, when they observe some that pretend a high care and deep respect for them live profanely. The sins of Eli's sons wrought this sad effect upon the people, that men, for their sakes, abhorred the offerings of the Lord, 1 Sam. ii. 17. Those that fell off to error, and thence to abominable practices, 'caused the way of truth to be evil spoken of,' 2 Pet. ii. 2. The priests that departed out of the way, 'caused many to stumble at the law,' Mal. ii. 8. Nay, so high doth Satan pursue this sometimes, that it becomes an inlet to direct atheism.

[5.] Fifthly, Satan also works mightily *in the profane dispositions of men, and acts that principle to a disregard and weariness of the services of God.* A flagitious wicked life naturally leads to it. Those that 'eat up God's people as bread,' Ps. xiv. 4, 'called not upon God.' This eats out at last the very exterior and formal observation of religious duties. In this Satan bends his force against them, (1.) By heightening the spirits of men to an insolent defiance of God by a continued prosperity. He draws out the pride and vanity of their spirits to a bold contempt: 'Who is the Lord that we should serve him? We are lords; we will come no more at thee; our tongues are our own,' &c., Jer. ii. 31. Thus they 'set their mouths against heaven.' Eliphaz tells us this, as the usual carriage of those that lived in peace and jollity: Job xxi. 15, 'Therefore say they unto God, Depart from us; for we desire not the knowledge of thy ways:

who is the Almighty that we should serve him?' (2.) By hiding from them the necessities of duty. Job speaking of the hypocrite, chap. xxvii. 10, describes him by these neglects of duty, 'Will he delight himself in the Almighty? will he always call upon God?' Of this he gives the reason, ver. 9, 'He will call and cry when trouble comes upon him.' When distresses make duties necessary, then he will use them; in his 'affliction he will seek him early,' Hosea v. 15; as the Israelites did, Ps. lxxviii. 34, 'When he slew them, then they sought him, and enquired early after God.' But when he is not thus pinched—and Satan will endeavour in this case, that he be as far from the rod of God as he can make him—he gives over seeking God and loathes it, nay, accounts it as ridiculous so to do; they 'mock at his counsel,' and contemn his advice of waiting upon him.

[6.] Sixthly, Satan picks quarrels in men *at the manner of performance of duty*. When duty cannot be spoken against, then he endeavours to destroy it by the modes, circumstances, and way of performance: as (1.) If those that act in them discover any weakness —as who doth not, when he hath done his best?—this he endeavours to blemish the duty withal. The bodily presence of Paul was objected against him, as being 'contemptible,' and his 'speech as weak,' [2 Cor. x. 10;] but the design of that objection lay higher, the devil thereby endeavouring to render the duties of his ministry as contemptible, and not to be regarded. (2.) If the circumstances please not, he teacheth them to take pet with the substance, and, like children, to reject all, because everything is not suitable to their wills. (3.) If it be managed in any way not grateful to their expectations, if too cuttingly and plain, then they think they be justified to say they hate it, as Ahab did Micaiah; if any way too high or abstrusely, then likewise they fling off. On this point the devil persuaded many of Christ's followers to desert him, John vi. 66, because he had spoken of himself in comparisons that they judged too high. When he said he was that 'bread that came down from heaven,' ver. 58, they said 'that was a saying not to be borne;' and on that occasion 'they went back, and walked no more with him.'

[7.] Seventhly, The devil brings a nauseating of the duties of worship, by *a wrong representation of them, in the carriage and gestures of those that engage in them*. It seems strange to some that are but as idle spectators to observe the postures of saints, seriously lifting up their eyes to heaven, or humbly mourning and smiting on their breasts. These the devil would render ridiculous, and as the suspicious managements of an histrionical or hypocritical devotion; as men at a distance beholding the strange variety of actions and postures of such as dance, being out of the sound of their music, shall think them a company of madmen and frantic people. Such perverse prospects doth he sometimes afford to those that come rather to observe what others do, than to concern themselves in such duties, that, not seeing their private influences, nor the secret spring that moves them, they judge them foolish, and from thence they contract an inward loathing of the duties themselves.

(5.) Fifthly, In order to the hindering or preventing of duty, Satan useth to impose upon men *by fallacious arguings:* and by a piece of his sophistry he endeavours to cheat them out of their services. I shall note some of his remarkable dealings in this kind: as,

[1.] First, *He heightens the dignity of God's children, upon a design to spoil their duty.* He tells them they are 'partakers of the divine nature,' [2 Pet. i. 4;] that they are 'in God and Christ,' and have the communications of his Spirit, and therefore they need not now drink of the cistern, seeing they enjoy the fountain; and that these services, in their attainments, are as useless as scaffolds are when once the house is built. To prosecute this he takes advantage, (1.) of the natural pride of their hearts. He puffs them up with conceits of the excellency of their condition—a thing which all men are apt to catch at with greediness upon the least imaginary grounds, 1 Cor. viii. 7; Col. ii. 18. If a man have but a little knowledge, or have attained to any vain speculations, he is presently apt to be vainly 'puffed up by his fleshly mind.' The same hazard attends any conceited excellency which a man apprehends he hath reached unto. Those monsters of religion, mentioned by Peter and Jude, that made no other use of the 'grace of God' but to 'turn it into wantonness,' Jude 4; yet were they so tumefied with the apprehensions of their privileges, that whilst they designed no other thing than plain licentiousness and a wantonness in the lusts of the flesh, yet it seems they encouraged themselves and allured others from a supposed liberty which their privileges gave them; and to this purpose had frequently in their mouths 'great swelling words of vanity,' 2 Pet. ii. 18, even whilst they 'walked after their own lusts,' Jude 16. (2.) To strengthen their proud conceits, the devil improves what the Scriptures speak of the differences of God's children—that some are spiritual, some are carnal; some weak, others strong; some perfect, some less perfect; some little children, some young men, some fathers, 1 Cor. ii. 1; Phil. iii. 15; 1 John ii. 12, 13. The end of all this is to make them apprehend themselves Christians of a higher rank and order, which also makes way consequently for a further inference, viz., that there must needs be immunities and privileges suitable to these heights and attainments. To this purpose (3.) he produceth those scriptures that are designed by God to raise up the minds of men to look after the internal work and power of his ordinances, and not to centre their minds and hopes in the bare formal use of them, without applying their thoughts to God and Christ, unto whom they are appointed to lead us. Such as these scriptures: Rom. ii. 28, 'He is not a Jew which is one outwardly; neither is that circumcision, which is outward in the flesh: but he is a Jew which is one inwardly; and circumcision is that of the heart, in the spirit, and not in the letter.' And Rom. vi. 7, we should 'serve in newness of spirit, and not in the oldness of the letter.' 2 Cor. v. 16, 'Wherefore henceforth know we no man after the flesh: yea, though we have known Christ after the flesh, yet now henceforth know we him no more.' Eph. iv. 13, 'He gave some apostles, and some prophets,' &c., 'for the perfecting of the saints, . . . till we all come in the unity of the faith, and of the knowledge of the Son of God, unto a perfect man.' By a perverse interpretation of these, and some other scriptures of like import, he would persuade them that the great thing that Christ designed by his ordinances was but to 'train up the weaker Christians by these rudiments,' as the A B C to children, to a more spiritual and immediate way of living upon God; and that these become altogether useless when Christians have gotten up to any of these imaginary degrees of a supposed perfection. Enough of this may be seen in the writings of Saltmarsh, Winstanly, and others, in the late times. How great a trade Satan drove by such misapprehensions not long since cannot easily be forgotten; so that God's worship did almost lie waste, and in many places 'the way to Zion did mourn.'

[2.] Secondly, He will sometimes confess an *equality of privilege among the children of God, and yet plead an inequality of duty.* That God is as good and strong to us, and that we have all an equal advantage by Christ, he will readily acknowledge; but then, when we should propound the diligence of the saints in their services for our pattern, as of David's 'praying seven times a-day,' Daniel's three times, Anna's serving God with fastings and prayers night and day, &c.,[1] he tells us these were extraordinary services, and as it were works of supererogation, more than the command of God laid upon them. So that we are not tied to such strictness; and we, being naturally apt to indulge ourselves in our own ease, are too ready to comply with such delusions. And by degrees men are thus brought to a confident belief that they may be good enough, and do as much as is required, though they slacken their pace, and do not fast, pray, or hear so often as others have done.

[3.] Thirdly, Another sophism of his *is to heighten one duty, to the ruin of another.* He strives to make an intestine war among the several parts of the services we owe to God; and from the excellency of one, to raise up an enmity and undervaluing disregard of another. Thus would he sever as inconsistent those things that God hath joined together. As among false teachers, some say, 'Lo, here is Christ,' and others, 'Lo, he is there;' so we find Satan dealing with duties. He puts some upon such high respects to preaching, that, say they, Christ is to be found here most frequently, rather than in prayer or other ordinances; others are made to have the like esteem for prayer: and they affirm in this is Christ especially to be met withal; others say the like of sacraments or meditation. In all these Satan labours to beget a dislike and neglect of other services. Thus, in what relates to the constitution of churches, he endeavours to set up purity of churches, to the destruction of unity, or unity to the ruin of purity. A notable example hereof we have in the *Euchytæ*, a sect of praying heretics, which arose in the time of Valentinian and Valens, who, upon the pretence of the commands of Christ and Paul for praying continually, or without ceasing and fainting, owned no other duty as necessary; vilifying preaching and sacraments as things at best useless and unprofitable.[2] The like attempts he makes daily upon men, where though he prevail not so far as to bring some necessary duties of service into open contempt, yet he carries them into too much secret neglect and disregard, Luke xviii. 1; 1 Thes. xv. 17.

[4.] Fourthly, He improves the grace of the gospel to infer **an** *unnecessariness of duty;* and this he doth not only from the advantage of a profane and careless spirit in such as presumptuously expect

[1] Greenham, p. 35, [as before.—G.]   [2] Theod. Eccles. Historia.

heaven, though they mind not the way that leads to it; for with such it is usual, as one observes,[1] for Satan to sever the means from the end in things that are good; to make them believe they shall have peace, though they walk in the imaginations of their heart; to make them lean upon the Lord for heaven, in the apparent neglect of holiness and duty; as in evil things he severs the end from the means, making them confident they shall escape hell and condemnation, though they walk in the path that leads thither. But besides this, he abuseth the understandings and affections of men by strange and uncouth inferences; as that God hath received a satisfaction, and Christ hath done all, so that nothing is left for us to do. The apostle Paul was so much aware of this kind of arguing, that when he was to 'magnify the grace of God,' he always took care to fence against such perverse reasonings, severely rebuking and refelling such objections: as in Rom. iii. 7, 8, where speaking that our 'unrighteousness did commend the righteousness of God,' he falls upon that reply, 'Why then am I judged as a sinner?' which he sharply refells, as an inference of slanderous imputation to the gospel, which hath nothing in it to give the least countenance to that conclusion, 'Let us do evil, that good may come;' and adds, that damnation shall justly overtake such as practise accordingly. The like we have, Rom. vi. 1, 'Shall we continue in sin, that grace may abound?' which he rejected with the greatest abhorrency, 'God forbid!' From both which places we may plainly gather, that as unsound as such arguings are, yet men, through Satan's subtlety, are too prone, upon such pretences, to dispute themselves to a careless neglect of duty. This might be enlarged in many other instances, as that of Maximus Tyrius, who disputed all duties unnecessary upon this ground, 'That what God will give, cannot be hindered; and what he will not give, cannot be obtained; and therefore it were needless to seek after anything.' Much to the same purpose do many argue, if they be predestinated to salvation, they shall be saved, though they do never so little; if they be not predestinated, they shall not be saved, though they do never so much. In all which inferences the devil proceeds upon a false foundation of severing the means and the end, which the decree of God hath joined together; but the main of the design is to hide the necessity of duty from them.

[5.] Fifthly, By urging a necessity or conveniency for *suspending or remitting duties*. In temptations to sin, he doth from a little draw on the sinner to more; but in omissions of duty he would entice us from much to little, and from little to nothing. Very busy he is with us to break or interrupt our constant course of duty. Duties in order and practice, are like so many pearls upon one string; if the thread be broken, it may hazard the scattering of all. If we be once put out of our way, we are in danger to rove far before we be set in our rank again. To effect this, (1.) he will be sure to straiten or hinder us in our opportunities if he can, and then to plead necessity for a dispensation. It is true indeed, necessities, when unavoidable—as the issue of providence rather than our negligence—may excuse an omission of duty, because in such cases, God accepting the will for the

---

[1] Greenham, p. 35, [as before.—G.]

deed, will have mercy and not sacrifice. But necessity is most-what[1] a prefence or cover to the slothfulness of professors, and the devil will do all he can to gratify them in that humour, and to prepare excuses for them from such hindrances or interruptions as business or disturbances can make; yet if these be not in readiness, he will (2.) endeavour to take off our earnestness by suggesting to us our former diligence, that we at other times have been careful and active; or (3.) by setting before us the greater negligence of those that are below us. The meaning of both which insinuations is to this one purpose, that we may make bold with some omissions, without any great hazard of our religious intentions, or scandal and offence to others. Now if he can by any of these ways bring us to any abatement of our wonted care and exercise, he will then still press for more, and from fervency of spirit to a cold moderation; from thence he will labour to bring us down to seldom performances; from thence, to nothing. The spiritual sluggard that will be overcome to some neglects, shall be found a companion at last to a waster, Prov. xviii. 9, and will be brought to a total neglect of all. The church of Ephesus, Rev. ii. 4, 5, may sadly give proof of this; they left their first love, and from thence declined so far that at last God was provoked to 'remove the candlestick out of its place.'

[6.] Sixthly, Satan puts tricks upon men in order to the hindering of duty, by putting us from a service *presently needful, with the proposal of another, in which, at that time, we are not so concerned.* In several duties of Christianity there is a great deal of skill required to make a right choice, for present or first performance; and to have a right judgment to discover the times and seasons of them, is matter of necessary study. Our adversary observing our weaknesses in this, when no other art will prevail, endeavours to put us upon an inconvenient choice, when he cannot make us neglect all. As (1.) by engaging us in a less duty, that we may neglect a greater; he is willing that we, as the Pharisees, should ' tithe mint and anise,' upon condition that we 'neglect the greater things of the law.' This was the fault of Martha, Luke x. 41, who busied herself in making entertainment for Christ's welcome, and in the meantime neglected to hear his preaching: which, as he notes, was the only necessary duty of that time; 'one thing' is necessary. She is not blamed for doing that which was simply evil in itself—for the thing she did was a duty—but for not making a right choice of duty; for that rebuke, ' Mary hath chosen the better part,' is only a comparative discommendation; as Austin interprets, *Non tu malam, sed illa meliorem,* The thing thou doest is not evil, if it had not put thee upon a neglect of a greater good. (2.) He sometimes puts men upon what is good and necessary, but such as they cannot come at without sin. Thus sacrificing in itself was a necessary duty; and such was Saul's condition, that it concerned him at that time to make his peace with God, and to inquire his mind. Yet when the devil upon that pretence put him upon offering a sacrifice, he put him upon no small transgression, 1 Sam. xiii. 13. The like game Satan sometimes plays with private Christians, who are persuaded beyond their station and capacity in refer-

[1] Query, ' most part'?—ED.

ence to some ordinances of God. (3.) He sometimes puts men upon dangerous undertakings in pursuit of their fancy, of gaining an advantage for some service; and so are they turned out of the way of present obedience, in grasping at opportunities of duty out of their reach. Saul spared the sheep and oxen of the Amalekites for sacrifice, 1 Sam. xv. 15, 22, when obedience had been more acceptable than sacrifice. (4.) There is a further cheat in the choice of duty, when Satan employs them to provide for duties to come, to the neglect of duties presently incumbent upon them; whereas we are more concerned in that which at present is necessary, than in that which may be so for the future; which is a mistake, like that of caring for the morrow, while we use not what God puts in our hand for to-day.

CHAPTER XVIII.

Satan's second grand design against duties is to spoil them. (1.) In the manner of undertaking, and how he effects this. (2.) In the act or performance, by distracting outwardly and inwardly. His various ways therein, by vitiating the duty itself. How he doth that. (3.) After performance, the manner thereof.

The chief of Satan's ways for the hindering and preventing of duty have been noted; what he comes short in this design he next labours to make up, by spoiling and depraving them: and this he doth endeavour three ways:—

I. 1. First, By putting us upon services *in such a manner as shall render them unacceptable and displeasing unto God, and unprofitable to us*: as by a careless and rash undertaking of service. We are commanded to 'take heed' to ourselves 'how we hear' or pray; and to 'watch' over our hearts, that they be in a fit posture for meeting with God, because the heart in service is that which God most looks at, and our services are measured accordingly. If then by a heedless undertaking we adventure upon them, not keeping our 'foot when we go into the house of God,' Eccles. v. 1, we offer no other than 'the sacrifice of fools,' and give occasion to God to complain that we do but 'draw near to him with our lips, while our hearts are far from him.'

2. Secondly, The like spoil of duty is made when we adventure upon it *in our own strength, and not in the strength of Christ*. Satan sees the pride of our heart, and how much our gifts may contribute to it, and how prone we are to be confident of a right performance of what we have so often practised before; and therefore doth he more industriously catch at that advantage to make us forget that our 'strength is in God,' and that we cannot come to him acceptably but by his own power. Christians are often abused this way. When their strength is to seek, duty is oft perversely set before them, that they may act as Samson did when his locks were cut, who thought to 'shake himself, and to go out as at other times,' and so fell into the hands of the Philistines, [Judges xvi 20.]

3. Thirdly, If he can substitute *base ends and principles, as motives to duty, instead of these that God hath commanded,* he knows the service will become stinking and loathsome to God. Fasting, prayers, alms, preaching, or any other duty may be thus tainted, when they are performed upon no better grounds than ' to be seen of men,' or out of envy, or to satisfy humour, or when from custom, rather than conscience. How frequently did the prophets tax the Jews for this, that they fasted to themselves! and brought forth fruit to themselves! How severely did Christ condemn the Pharisees upon the same account! telling them that in hunting the applause of men, by these devotions, they had got all the reward they were like to have.

4. Fourthly, When we do our services *unseasonably,* not only the grace and beauty of them is spoiled; but often are they rendered unprofitable. There are times to be observed, not only for the right management of common actions, but also for duties. What is Christian reproof, if it be not rightly suited to season and opportunity? The same may be said of other services.

5. Fifthly, Services are spoiled, when men set upon them *without resolutions of leaving their sins.* While they come with their ' idols in their heart,' and ' the stumbling-block of their iniquity before their face, God will not be inquired of by them,' Ezek. xiv. 3. He requires of those that present their services to him, that at least they should not affront him with direct purposes of continuing in their rebellions against him; nay, he expects from his servants that look for a blessing in their duties, that they come with their ' hearts sprinkled from an evil conscience, and their bodies washed with pure water,' Heb. x. 22. If they come to hear the word, they must ' lay aside all filthiness, and superfluity of naughtiness,' James i. 21; if they pray, they must ' lift up pure hands,' 1 Tim. ii. 8; if they come to the Lord's Supper, they must eat that feast ' with the unleavened bread of sincerity and truth,' 1 Cor. v. 8. And albeit, he may accept the prayers of those that are so far convinced of their sins—though they be not yet sanctified—that they are willing to lay down their weapons, and are touched with a sense of legal repentance; for thus he heard Ahab, and regarded the humiliation of Nineveh: yet while men cleave to the love of their iniquity, and are not upon any terms of parting with their sins, God will not look to their services, but abhor them. For thus he declares himself, Isa. i. 11, ' To what purpose is the multitude of your sacrifices? Bring no more vain oblations. I cannot away with them, it is iniquity, even the solemn meeting,—my soul hateth them, they are a trouble to me, I am weary to bear them: when you spread forth your hands, I will hide mine eyes from you; yea, when you make many prayers, I will not hear.' The ground of all this is, that their heart was no way severed from the purposes of sinning, ' Your hands are full of blood,' ver. 15. Satan knowing this so well, he is willing that they engage in the services of God, if they will keep up their allegiance to him, and come with intentions to continue wicked still; for so, while he cannot prevent the actual performance of duty,—which yet notwithstanding he had rather do, because he knows not but God may by that means some time or other rescue these slaves of Satan out of his hand,

—he makes their services nothing worth, and renders them abominable to God.

6. Sixthly, In the manner of undertaking duties are spoiled, when men have not *a submissive ingenuity*[1] *in them, by giving themselves up to the direction and disposal of the Almighty;* but rather confine and limit God to their wills and desires. Sometimes men by attempting of services to God, think thereby to engage God to humour them in their wills and ways. With such a mind did Ahab consult the prophets about his expedition to Ramoth-Gilead; not so much seeking God's mind and counsel for direction, as thinking thereby to engage God to confirm and comply with his determination. With the same mind did Johanan and the rest of the people consult the Lord concerning their going down to Egypt, Jer. xlii. 5. Though they solemnly protested obedience to what God should say, 'whether it were good or evil;' yet when the return from God suited not with their desires and resolutions, they denied it to be the command of God; and found an evasion to free themselves of their engagement, Jer. xliii. 2. Such dealings as these being the evident undertakings of a hypocritical heart, must needs render all done upon that score to be presumptuous temptings of God; no way deserving the name of service.

II. Secondly, Not only are services thus spoiled in those wrong grounds and ways of attempting, or setting about them, but in *the very act or performance of them.* While they are upon the wheel—as a potter's vessel in the prophet—they are often marred; and this Satan doth two ways. (1.) By disturbing our thoughts, which should be attentive and fixed upon the service in hand. (2.) By vitiating the duty itself.

1. First, *By distracting or disturbing our thoughts.* This is a usual policy of Satan. Those fowls which came down upon Abraham's sacrifice are supposed by learned expositors to signify those means and ways by which the devil doth disorder and trouble our thoughts in religious services, Gen. xv. 12. And Christ himself compares the devil stealing our thoughts from duty, to the 'fowls of the air,' that gather up the seed as soon as it is sown, Mat. xiii. 4. There are many reasons that may persuade us that this is one of his masterpieces of policy. As (1.) in that the business of distraction is oft easily done. Our thoughts do not naturally delight in spiritual things, because of their depravement; neither can they easily brook to be pent in or confined so strictly as the nature of such employments doth require; so that there is a kind of preternatural force upon our thoughts, when they are religiously employed; which as it is in itself laborious, like the stopping of a stream, or driving Jordan back, so upon the least relaxing of the spring, that must bend our thoughts heavenward, they incline to their natural bend and current; as a stone rolled up a hill, hath a *renitentia*, a striving against the hand that forceth it, and when that force slackens it goes downward. How easily then is it for Satan to set our thoughts off our work! If we slacken our care never so little, they recoil and tend to their old bias; and how easy is it for him to take off our hand, when it is so much in his power to inject

[1] 'Ingenuousness.'—G.

thoughts and motions into our hearts, or to present objects to our eyes, or sounds to our ears, which by a natural force raiseth up our apprehension to act, for in such cases *non possumus non cogitare;* we cannot restrain the act of thinking, and not without great heedfulness can we restrain the pursuit of those thinkings and imaginations. (2.) Satan can also do it insensibly. Our distractions or rovings of thoughts creep and steal upon us silently, we no more know of it when they begin than when we begin to sleep, or when we begin to wander in a journey, where oft we do not take ourselves to be out of the way, till we come to some remarkable turning. (3.) And when he prevails to divide our thoughts from our duty, he always makes great advantage, for thus he hinders at least the comfort and profit of ordinances. While we are busied to look to our hearts, much of the duty goeth by, and we are but as those that in public assemblies are employed to see to the order and silence of others, who can be scarce at leisure to attend for their own advantage. Besides, much of the sweetness of ordinances are abated by the very trouble of our attendance. When we are put to it, as Abraham was, to be still driving away those fowls that come down upon our sacrifice, the very toil will eat out and eclipse much of the comfort. Thus also he at least provides matter to object against the sincerity of the servants of God; and will assuredly find a time to set it home upon them to the purpose, that their hearts were wandering in their services. Thus he further gets advantage for a temptation to leave off their duty, and will not cease to improve such distractions as we have heard to an utter overthrow of their services. Nay, if he prevail to give us such distractions as wholly takes away our minds and serious attentions from the service, then is the service become nothing worth, though the outward circumstances of attendance be never so exact and saint-like. Who could appear in a more religious dress than those in Ezek. xxxiii. 31, who came and sat, and were pleased with divine services, as to all outward discovery, as God's people; yet was all spoiled with this, that their hearts were after their covetousness?

Now this distraction Satan can work two ways.

(1.) First, *By outward disturbances.* He can present objects to the eyes on purpose to entice our thoughts after them. The closing of the eyes in prayer is used by some of the servants of God to prevent Satan's temptations this way. And we find, in the story of Mr Rothwel, that the devil took notice of this in him, that he 'shut his eyes to avoid distraction in prayer;'[1] which implies a concession in the devil, that by outward objects he useth to endeavour our distraction in services. The like he doth by noises and sounds. Neither can we discover how much of these disturbances, by coughings, hemmings, tramplings, &c., which we hear in greater assemblies, are from Satan, by stirring up others to such noises. We are sure the damsel that had an unclean spirit, Acts xvi., that grieved and troubled Paul, going about these duties with her clamours, was set on by that spirit within her, to distract and call off their thoughts from the services which they were about to undertake. Besides the common ways of giving trouble to the servants of God in outward disturbances, he sometimes,

[1] '*Vide* Clark's Lives. [As before.—G.]

though rarely, doth it in an extraordinary manner; thus he endeavoured to hinder Mr Rothwel from praying for a possessed person, by rage and blaspheming. The like hindrance we read he gave Luther and others; and truly so strict an attendance in the exercise of our minds, spiritual senses and graces, is required in matters of worship, and so weak are our hearts in making a resistance or beating off these assaults, that a very small matter will discompose us, and a smaller discomposure will prejudice and blemish the duty.

(2.) Secondly, He distracts or disturbs us also *by inward workings, and injections of motions, and representations of things to our minds:* and as this is his most general and usual way, so doth he make use of greater variety of contrivance and art in it. As,

[1.] First, *By the troublesome impetuousness and violence of his injections, they come upon us as thick as hail.* No sooner do we put by one motion but another is in upon us. He hath his quiver full of these arrows, and our hearts, under any service, swarm with them; we are incessantly infested by them and have no rest. At other times, when we are upon worldly business, we may observe a great ease and freedom in our thoughts; neither doth he so much press upon us; but in these Satan is continually knocking at our door, and calling to us, so that it is a great hazard that some or other of these injections may stick upon our thoughts, and lead us out of the way; or if they do not, yet it is a great molestation or toil to us.

[2.] Secondly, He can so order his dealings with us, that he provokes us sometimes *to follow him out of the camp, and seeks to ensnare us by improving our own spiritual resolution and hatred against him;* even as courage, whetted on and enraged, makes a man venture some beyond the due bounds of prudence or safety. To this end he sometimes casts into our thoughts hideous, blasphemous, and atheistical suggestions, which do not only amaze us, but oftentimes engage us to dispute against them, which at such time is all he seeks for; for whereas in such cases we should send away such thoughts with a short answer, 'Get thee behind me, Satan,' we by taking up the buckler and sword against them are drawn off from minding our present duty.

[3.] Thirdly, He doth sometimes seek to allure and draw our thoughts to the object *by representing what is pleasant and taking.* (1.) He will adventure to suggest good things impertinently and unseasonably, as when he puts us upon praying while we should be hearing; or while we are praying, he puts into our hearts things that we have heard in preaching. These things, because good in themselves, we are not so apt to startle at, but give them a more quick welcome. (2.) He also can allure our thoughts by the strangeness of the things suggested. Sometimes we shall have hints of things which we knew not before, or some fine and excellent notions, so that we can scarce forbear turning aside after them to gaze at them; and yet when all is done, except we wholly neglect the duty for them, they will so vanish, that we can scarce remember them when the duty is over. (3.) Sometimes he suits our desires and inclinations with the remembrances of things that are at other times much in our love and affection; and with these we are apt to comply, the pleasure of them making us forget our present duty. Thoughts of estates, honours, relations, delights, recreations, or whatever else we are set upon at other times, will more easily prevail for audience now.

[4.] Fourthly, He hath a way to betray and circumvent us *by heightening our own jealousies and fears against him;* and here he outshoots us in our own bow, and by a kind of overdoing makes us undo our desired work. For where he observes us fearful and watchful against wandering, he doth alarm us the more: so that (1.) instead of looking to the present part of duty, we reflect upon what is past, and make inquiries whether we performed that aright, or whether we did not wander from the beginning. Thus our suspicions that we have miscarried bring us into a miscarriage: by this are we deceived, and put off from minding what we are doing at present. Or (2.) an eager desire to fix our thoughts on our present service doth amaze and astonish us into a stupid inactivity, or into a saying or doing we know not what; as ordinarily it happens to persons, that out of a great fearfulness to offend in the presence of some great personages, become unable to do anything right, or to behave themselves tolerably well; or as an oversteady and earnest fixing the eye weakens the sight, and renders the object less truly discernible to us.

[5.] Fifthly, Sometimes *the exercise of fancy acting or working according to some mistake which we have entertained as to the manner of performance, doth so hold our thoughts doing, that we embrace a cloud or shadow when we should have looked after the substance.* I will give an instance of this in reference to prayer, which, I have observed, hath been a snare and mistake to some, and that is this: because in that duty the Scripture directs us to go to God, and to set him before us, therefore have they thought it necessary to frame an idea of God in their thoughts, as of a person present to whom they speak. Hence their thoughts are busied to conceive such a representation; and when the shadow of imagination vanisheth, their thoughts are again busied to inquire whether their hearts are upon God. Thus by playing with fancy, they are really less attentive upon their duty.

[6.] Sixthly, Satan can lay *impressions of distraction upon men before they come to religious services,* which shall then work and shew their power to disturb and divide our hearts, which is by a strong prepossession of the heart with anything that we fear, or hope, or desire, or doth any way trouble us. These will stick to us, and keep us company in our duties, though we strive to keep them back. And this was the ground of the apostle's advice to the unmarried persons, to continue in single life,—times of persecution and distress nearly approaching,—that they might 'attend upon the Lord without distraction,' 1 Cor. vii. 37; implying that the thoughtfulness and more than ordinary carefulness which would seize upon the minds of persons under such straits and hazards, would unavoidably follow them in their duties, and so distract them.

2. Secondly, The other way, besides this of distraction, by which Satan spoils our duties in the act of performance, is *by vitiating duty itself;* and this he commonly doth three ways.

(1.) First, *When he puts men upon greater care for the outward garb and dress of a service than for the inward work of it.* He endeavours to make some devotionaries deal with their duties, as the pharisees did with their cups, washing and adorning the outside, while the inside is altogether neglected. Thus the papists generally are for the outward pomp and beauty of services, being only careful that all things should have their external bravery, as the tombs of the prophets were painted and beautified, which yet were full of rottenness. And the generality of Christians are more taken up with this than with the service of the heart. Paul was so sensible of this snare in the work of preaching, where ordinarily men cared for 'excellency of speech or wisdom,' 1 Cor. ii. 2, that he determines another course of preaching; not notions, or rhetoric, and enticing words, but the doctrine of Christ crucified in sincerity and plainness, 1 Cor. ii. 2. It is not indeed the outward cost and fineness of ordinances that God regards. 'Incense from Sheba, and the sweet cane from a far country,' Jer. vi. 20, are not to any purpose where the heart doth not most design a spiritual service; for these are rather a satisfaction to the humours of men than to please God: an offering to themselves rather than to him. And therefore is it, that what Jeremiah confessed they did, (chap. vi. 20,) in buying incense and the sweet cane, Isaiah (chap. xliii. 24) seems to deny, 'Thou hast bought me no sweet cane with money'—that is, though thou didst it, yet it was to thyself, rather than to me: I accepted it not, and so was it all one as if thou hadst not done it.

(2.) Secondly, Duties and services are more apparently vitiated by *human additions:* a thing expressly contrary to the second commandment, and yet is there a strange boldness in men this way, which sometimes riseth to such a height, that the plain and clear commands of God are violated under the specious pretence of decency, order, and humility; and nothing doth more take them than what they devise and find out. Satan knows how displeasing this is to God, and how great an inclination there is in men to be forward in their inventions and self-devised worship, that he can easily prevail with the incautious. This was the great miscarriage of the Jewish nation all along the Old Testament; and of the pharisees, who, though they declined the idolatries of their fathers, yet were so fond upon their traditions, that they made their worship vain, as Christ tells them. And this humour also in Paul's time was insinuating itself into Christians, managed by a great deal of deceit [Col. ii. 8] and 'show of wisdom,' ver. 23, which accordingly he doth earnestly forewarn them of. There are indeed several degrees of corrupting a service or ordinance by human additions, according to which it is more or less defiled: yet the least presumption this way is an offence and provocation.

(3.) Thirdly, Duties are vitiated *in their excess.* Natural worship, which consists in fear, love, faith, humility, &c., can never be too much, but instituted worship may. Men may preach too much, and pray too long—a fault noticed by Christ in the pharisees; they made 'long prayers'—Even in duties, a man may be righteous overmuch. Timothy was so in his great pains and over-abstemious life, to the wasting of his strength—which the apostle takes notice of, and adviseth against it, 'Drink no longer water,' &c., [1 Tim. v. 23.] The Corinthians were so, when out of a high detestation of the miscarriage of the incestuous person, they were backward to forgive him, and to receive him into the church again. Peter is another instance to us of excess, John xiii. 8. First, in a modest humility, he refuseth to let Christ 'wash his feet;' but after understanding the meaning of it, then he runs to the other extreme, and offers not 'only his feet, but his hands and his head.' When the servants of God are conscious of defects in their services, as if they would make amends for these by the length and continuance of their services, they are easily drawn into an excess every way disadvantageous to themselves and the service.

III. Thirdly, When Satan's designs do not take to spoil the duties, either by the manner of the attempt or in the act, he then seeks to play an after-game, and endeavours to spoil them *by some after-miscarriage of ours in reference to these services*. As,

(1.) First, *When he makes us proud of them.* We can scarce perform any service with a tolerable suitableness, but Satan is at hand to instil thoughts of applause, vainglory, and boasting: and we readily begin to think highly of ourselves and performances; as if we were better than others, whom we are apt to censure as low and weak in comparison of ourselves. Though this be an apparent deceit, yet it is a wonder how much the minds, even of the best, are apt to be tainted with it; even where there are considerable endeavours for humility and self-denial, these thoughts are apt to get too much entertainment. Now though we run well, and attain some comfortable strength and watchfulness in the services of God; yet if they be afterward fly-blown with pride, or if we think to embalm them with praises, or reserve them as matter of ostentation; though they be angels' food, yet, like the manna of the Israelites when kept too long, they will putrify and breed worms, and so be good for nothing, after that we have been at the pains of gathering it.

(2.) Secondly, When well-performed services are perverted *to security*, then are they also spoiled. We are ready to say of them, as the rich man of his abundance, 'Soul, take thine ease: thou hast much laid up for many years,' [Luke xii. 19.] Satan is willing, for a further advantage, that we think ourselves secure from him; and as after a full meal we are apt to grow drowsy, so after services we are apt to think ourselves out of harm's way. The church after a high feast with Christ, presently falls asleep, and highly miscarries in security and neglect, Cant. v. 2. By this means do the best of saints sometimes lose the things they have wrought, and throw down what they formerly built up.

NOTE.

Agreeably to Note at the beginning, there will be found below * the more specific title-page of Part II.—G.

DÆMONOLOGIA SACRA:

OR, A

TREATISE

OF

Satans Temptations:

The Second Part.

CONTAINING

The manifold Subtilties and Stratagems of Satan, for the corrupting of the minds of Men with Errour; and for the destruction of the Peace and Comfort of the Children of God.

By *R. G.*

London, Printed by *J. D.* for *Richard Randel,* and *Peter Maplisden,* Booksellers in *New Castle* upon *Tine,* 1677.

PART II.

CHAPTER I.

That it is Satan's grand design to corrupt the minds of men with error—The evidences that it is so—And the reasons of his endeavours that way.

Next to Satan's deceits in tempting to sin and against duty, his design of *corrupting the minds of men by error* calls for our search; and indeed this is one of his principal endeavours, which takes up a considerable part of his time and diligence. He is not only called in Scripture an 'unclean spirit,' but also a 'lying spirit,' [1 Kings xxii. 22,] and there are none of these cursed qualifications that lie idle in him. As by his uncleanness we may easily conjecture his attempts upon the will and affections to defile them by lust; so by his lying we may conclude that he will certainly strive to blind the understanding by error. But a clear discovery of this we may have from these considerations :—

I. 1. First, *From God's interest in truth, in reference to his great designs of holiness and mercy in the world.* Truth is a ray and beam of him who is the Father of lights.[1] All revealed truths are but copies and transcripts of that essential, archetypal truth. Truth is the rod of his strength, Ps. cx. 2, the sceptre of his kingdom, by which he doth subdue the hearts of men to his obedience and service in conversion. Truth is that rock upon which he hath built his church, the foundations are the prophets and apostles, Eph. ii. 20—that is, the doctrine of the prophets and apostles, in the Scriptures of the Old and New Testament. Truth is that great *depositum* committed to the care of his church, which is therefore called the pillar of truth, 1 Tim. iii. 15; because as princes or rulers put their proclamations on pillars for the better information of their subjects, so doth his church hold out truth to the world. Holiness is maintained by truth, our ways are directed by it, and by it are we forewarned of Satan's devices, John xvii. 17. Now the prince of darkness carrying

---

[1] Deus est prima veritas essentialis, verbum Dei prima veritas normalis.—*Mac. Distinc. Theol.* cap. i. [The quotation is from the posthumous work of Maccovius ' Distinctiones et Regulas Theologicas et Philosophicas.' Amstel: 1656, and various subsequent editions.—G.]

himself in as full an opposition to the God of truth as he can in all his ways, God's interest in truth will sufficiently discover the devil's design to promote error; for such is his hatred of God, that, though he cannot destroy truth, no more than he can tear the sun out of the firmament, yet he will endeavour by corrupting the copy to disgrace the original. Though he cannot break Christ's sceptre, yet by raising error he would hinder the increase of his subjects; though he cannot remove the rock upon which the church is built, he will endeavour to shake it, or to interrupt the building, and to tear down God's proclamation from the pillar on which he hath set it to be read of all; and if we can conceive what a hatred the thief hath to the light, as it contradicts and hinders his designs, we may imagine there is nothing against which the devil will use greater contrivances than against the light of truth. He neither can nor will make a league with any, but upon the terms that Nahash propounded to the men of Jabesh-Gilead—that is, that he may 'put out their right eye,' and so 'lay it for a reproach upon the Israel of God,' 1 Sam. xi. 3. It is the work of the Holy Spirit 'to lead us into truth,' and by the rule of contraries it is the devil's work to lead into error.

2. Secondly, Though the Scripture doth charge the sin and danger of delusion and error upon those men that promote it to the deception of themselves and others, yet doth it chiefly blame Satan for *the great contriver of it, and expressly affirms him to be the grand deceiver.* Instruments and engineers he must make use of to do him service in that work, but still it is the devil that is a lying spirit in their mouths; it is he that teacheth and prompts them, and therefore may they be called, as Elymas was by Paul, the children of the devil, Acts xiii. 10, or, as Cerinthus of old, the first-born of Satan, πρωτότοκον τοῦ Σατανᾶ.

The church of Corinth, among other distempers, laboured under dangerous errors, against which when the apostle doth industriously set himself, he doth chiefly take notice, (1.) Of the false teachers, who had cunningly wrought them up to an aptitude of declining from the 'simplicity of the gospel.' These he calls false apostles, as having no commission from God, and Satan's ministers, 2 Cor. xi. 13, 15; thereby informing us who it is that sends them out and employs them upon this errand. (2.) He especially accuseth Satan as the great contriver of all this evil. If any shut their eyes against the light, he gives this for the principal cause, that 'the god of the world blinded their minds,' 2 Cor. iv. 4. If any stumbled at the simplicity of the gospel, he presently blames the 'subtlety of the old serpent' for it, 2 Cor. xi. 3. When false doctrine was directly taught, and varnished over with the glorious pretexts of truth, still he chargeth Satan with it, ver. 14, 'No marvel, for Satan himself is transformed into an angel of light;' where he doth not only give a reason of the corrupting or the adulterating the word of God by false apostles, as vintners do their wines by mixtures; a metaphor which he makes use of, chap. ii. 17, καπειλεύοντα; that they learned it of Satan, 'who abode not in the truth, but was a liar from the beginning;' but also, he further points at Satan, to furnish us with a true account of the ground of that cunning craft which these deceitful workers used, while they metamorphosed themselves, by an imitation of the way and manner, zeal and diligence of the apostles of Christ, they were taught by one who had exactly learned the art of imitation, and who could, to all appearance, act to the life the part of an angel of light. And to take away all objection or wonder, that so many with such seeming earnestness and zeal should give up themselves to deceive by false doctrine, he tells us that this hath been the devil's work from the first beguiling of Eve, ver. 3, and that as he then made use of a serpent for his instrument, so ever since in all ages he hath made so often and so much use of men as his emissaries, that it should now neither seem a marvel, nor a great matter to see the devil at this work by his agents, οὐ θαυμαστόν, οὐ μέγα, ver. 14, 15.

3. Thirdly, That this is Satan's great design, may be further cleared from *the constant course of his endeavours.* The parable of the tares, Mat. xiii. 25, shews that Satan is as busy in sowing tares, as the master of the field is in sowing wheat. That by tares, not errors in the abstract, but men are to be understood, is evident from the parable itself; but that which makes men to be tares is sin and error; so that, in a complex sense, we are taught how diligent the devil, who is expressly signified by the enemy, ver. 39, is in that employment: much of his time hath been taken up that way. 'There were false prophets,' saith Peter, 2 Epist. ii. 1, ' and there shall be false teachers;' that is, so it was of old, and so it will be to the end. The shortest abstract of Satan's acts in this matter would be long and tedious; judge of the rest by a few instances.

In the apostles' times how quickly had the devil broached false doctrine. That it was necessary to be circumcised, was early taught, Acts xv. 1. In Col. ii. 8, the vain deceit of philosophy, traditions, and the elements of the world, which were the body of Mosaical ceremonies, are mentioned as dangerous intrusions; and in ver. 18, the worshipping of angels, as it seems, was pleaded for, with no small hazard to the church. The denial of the resurrection is expressly charged upon some of the Corinthian church, 1 Cor. xv. 12; and that 'the resurrection is past already,' 2 Tim. ii. 18, is affirmed to have been the doctrine of Hymeneus, Philetus, and others. But these are comparatively little to that gross error of denying Christ, Jude 4, or ' that Jesus is the Christ,' 1 John ii. 22, or 'Jesus Christ is come in the flesh,' 1 John iv. 3, which are branded for antichristian errors, and were boldly asserted by many false prophets that were then ' gone out into the world;' and to such a height came they at last, that they taught the lawfulness of 'committing fornication, and to eat things offered to idols,' Rev. ii. 20. All these falsehoods took the boldness to appear before all the apostles were laid in their graves: and if we will believe what Austin tells us [*De Hæres.*] from Epiphanius and Eusebius, there were no less than ten sorts of heretical Antichrists in the apostle John's days, the Simonians, Menandrians, Saturnalians, &c. This was an incredible increase of false doctrine in so short a time, and in the times and preachings of the apostles themselves, whose power and authority, one would think, might have made Satan ' fall before them as lightning.' What progress, then, in this work of delusion might be expected when they were all removed out of the world! They left, indeed, behind them sad predictions of the power of delusion in after times: 'Of yourselves shall men arise, speaking perverse things.' 'After my departing shall grievous wolves enter,' &c., Acts xx. 30. 'The Spirit speaketh expressly, that in the latter times some shall depart from the faith,' 1 Tim. iv. 1; and Paul, 2 Thes. ii. 3, prophesies of a general apostasy, upon the revealing of 'the man of sin,' and the 'mystery of iniquity,' and that these should be 'perilous times,' 2 Tim. iii. 1. To the same purpose, John mentions the coming of the great Antichrist as a thing generally known and believed, 1 John ii. 18. But before all these, Christ also had fully forewarned his servants of false Christs, the power and danger of their delusion, and of the sad revolt from the faith which should be before his second coming, Mat. xxiv. 24. And as we have heard, so have we seen; all ages since the apostles can witness that Satan hath answered the prophecies that were concerning him. What a strange increase of errors hath been in the world since that time! Irenæus and Tertullian made catalogues long since; after them Epiphanius and Eusebius reckoned about eighty heresies; Austin, after them, brings the number to eighty-eight. Now though there be just exceptions against the largeness of their catalogues, and that it is believed by many that there are several branded in their rolls for heretics that merely suffer upon the account of their name and nation, for Barbarism, Scythism, Hellenism are mustered in the front; and others also stand there for very small matters, as the *quarto-decimani*, &c., and that some ought altogether to be crossed out of their books; yet still it will appear that the number of errors is great, and that all those hard names have this general signification, that the devil hath made a great stir in the world by error and opinion. Aftertimes might also be summoned in to speak their evidence, and our own knowledge and experience might, without any other help, sufficiently instruct us, if it were needful, of the truth of this, that error is one of Satan's great designs.

II. Secondly, Let us next look into *the reasons which do so strongly engage Satan to these endeavours of raising up errors*. If we set these before us, it will not only confirm us in our belief that this is one of his main employments—for if error yield him so many advantages for the ruin of men and the dishonour of God, there can be no doubt of his readiness to promote it. This also may be of use to put us in mind who it is that is at work behind the curtain, when we see such things acted upon the stage, and consequently may beget a cautious suspicion in our minds against his proceedings. The reasons are such as these:—

1. First, *Error is sinful*, so that if Satan should be hindered in his endeavours for any further mischief than the corrupting of any particular person, yet he will reckon that he hath not altogether lost his labour. Some errors, that overturn fundamentals of faith, are as deadly poison, and called expressly 'damnable' by the apostle, 2 Pet. ii. 1. These heresies are by Paul, Gal. v. 20, recounted among 'the works of the flesh,' of which he positively affirms, that 'they that do such things cannot inherit the kingdom of God.' Those that are of a lower nature, that do not so extremely hazard the soul, can only be

capable of this apology, that they are less evil; yet as they are oppositions to truth, propounded in Scripture for our belief and direction, they cease not to be sins, though they may be greater or less evils, according to the importance of those truths which they deny, or the consequences that attend them; and if we go yet a step lower, to the consideration of those rash and bold assertions about things not clearly revealed, though they may possibly be true, yet the positiveness of avouchments and determinations in such cases, where we want sufficient reason to support what we affirm—as that of the pseudo-Dionysius for the hierarchy of angels, and some adventurous assertions concerning God's secret decrees, and many other things of like nature—are by the apostle, Col. ii. 18, most severely taxed for an unwarrantable and unjust presumption, in setting our foot upon God's right; as if such men would by violence thrust themselves into that which God hath reserved for himself—for so much the word intruding—$\dot{\epsilon}\mu\beta\alpha\tau\epsilon\acute{\nu}\epsilon\iota\nu$—imports. The cause of this he tells us is the arrogancy of corrupt reason, the fleshly mind—suitable to that expression, Mat. xvi. 17, 'Flesh and blood hath not revealed it.' The bottom of it is pride, which swells men to this height; and the fruit, after all these swelling attempts, is no other than as the apples of Sodom, dust and vanity, 'intruding into those things which he hath not seen, vainly puffed up by his fleshly mind.' If then Satan do but gain this, that by error, though not diffused further than the breast of the infected party, truth is denied, or that the heart be swelled into pride and arrogancy, or that he hath hope so to prevail, it is enough to encourage his attempts.

2. Secondly, But error is a sin *of an increasing nature, and usually stops not at one or two falsehoods, but is apt to spawn into many others*—as some of the most noxious creatures have the most numerous broods; for one error hath this mischievous danger in it, that it taints the mind to an instability in every truth; and the bond of steadfastness being once broken, a man hath no certainty where he shall stay: as a wanton horse, once turned loose, may wander far. This hazard is made a serious warning against error: 2 Pet. iii. 17, 'Beware lest ye, being led away with the error of the wicked, fall from your own steadfastness.' One error admitted, makes the heart unsteady; and besides this inconvenience, error doth unavoidably branch itself naturally into many more, as inferences and conclusions resulting from it, as circles in water multiply themselves. Grant but one absurdity, and many will follow upon it, so that it is a miracle to find a single error.[1] These locusts go forth by bands, as the experience of all ages doth testify, and besides the immediate consequences of an error, which receive life and being together with itself, as twins of the same birth, we may observe a tendency in errors, to others that are more remote, and by the long stretch of multiplied inferences, those things are coupled together that are not very contiguous. If the Lutherans—it is[2] Dr Prideaux his observation—admit universal

[1] ἑνὸς δοθέντος ἀπάτου, τ'ἄλλα πολλὰ συμβαίνει.
[2] Si Wittenbergenses admittant universalem gratiam, Huberiani introducent universalem electionem, Pucciani fidem naturalem, naturalistæ explodent Christum et scripturas.—*Prid., Lect.* iii. p. 34. [The *Lectiones 'Theologicæ'* of John Prideaux: Oxon. 1651, &c.—G.]

grace, the Huberians introduce universal election, the Puccians natural faith, the Naturalists explode Christ and Scriptures at last as unnecessary. This is then a fair mark for the devil to aim at; if he prevails for one error, it is a hundred to one but he prevails for more.

3. Thirdly, Satan hath yet a further reach in promoting error, he knows *it is a plague that usually infects all round about;* and therefore doth he the rather labour in this work, because he hopes thereby to corrupt others, and infected persons are commonly the most busy agents, even to the 'compassing of sea and land to gain proselytes' to their false persuasions. This harvest of Satan's labour is often noted in Scripture. 'They shall deceive many,' Mat. xxiv. 24; 'Many shall follow their pernicious ways,' 2 Pet. ii. 2. How quickly had this leaven spread itself in the church of Galatia, even to Paul's wonder! Gal. i. 6, 'I marvel that you are so soon removed from him that called you into the grace of Christ unto another gospel.' Instances of the spreading of error are frequent. Pelagianism rose about the year 415, but presently spread itself in Palestine, Africa, Greece, Italy, Sicily, France, and Britain. Arianism, like fire in straw, in a little time brought its flame over the Christian world, and left her wondering at herself that she was so suddenly become Arian. Socinianism had the like prevalency; Lælius privately had sowed the seeds, and after his death, Faustus Socinus, his nephew, did so bestir himself, that within ten years after his confident appearing, whole congregations in Sarmatia submitted themselves to his dictates, as Calovius affirms,[1] and within twenty or thirty years more several hundreds of churches in Transylvania were infected, and within a few years more the whole synod was brought over to subscribe to Socinianism. We have also instances nearer home. After the Reformation, in the reign of Edward VI., how soon did popery return in its full strength when Queen Mary came to the crown! which occasioned Peter Martyr, when he saw young students flocking to mass, to say, 'that the tolling of the bell overturned all his doctrine at Oxford,' *Hæc una notula omnem meam doctrinam evertit.* And of late we have had the sad experience of the power of error to infect. No error so absurd, ridiculous, or blasphemous, but, once broached, it presently gained considerable numbers to entertain it.

4. Fourthly, Error is also eminently serviceable to Satan for the bringing in *divisions, schisms, rents, hatreds, heart-burnings, animosities, revilings, contentions, tumults, wars, and whatsoever bitter fruits, breach of love, and the malignity of hatred can possibly produce.* Enough of this might be seen in the church of Corinth. The divisions that were amongst themselves were occasioned by it, and a great number of evils the apostle suspected to have been already produced from thence, as debates, envyings, wraths, strifes, backbitings, whisperings, swellings, tumults, 2 Cor. xii. 20. He himself escaped not from being evilly entreated by those among them that were turned from the simplicity of the gospel. The quarrelsome exceptions that they had raised against him he takes notice of. They charged him with levity, in neglecting his promise to come to them, 2 Cor. i. 17. They

[1] Consid. Th. Soc. Proemial, p. 65.

called him carnal, one that walked according to the flesh, chap. x. 2: they taunted him as a contemptible fellow, ver. 10. They undervalued his ministry, which occasioned, not without great apology, a commendation of himself; nay, they seemed to call him a false apostle, and were so bold as to challenge him for a proof of Christ speaking in him, 2 Cor. xiii. 3.

If the devil had so much advantage from error that was but in the bud, and that in one church only, what may we imagine hath he done by it, when it broke out to an open flame in several churches! What work do we see in families when an error creeps in among them! The father riseth up against the son, the son against the father, the mother against the daughter, the daughter against the mother. What sad divided congregations have we seen! what fierceness, prejudices, slanders, evil surmises, censurings, and divisions hath this brought forth! what bandying of parties against parties, church against church, hath been produced by this engine! How sadly hath this poor island felt the smart of it! The bitter contests that have been betwixt presbyterian and independent, betwixt them and the episcopal, makes them look more like factious combinations, than churches of Christ. The present differences betwixt conformists and nonconformists, if we take them where they are lowest, they do daily produce such effects as must needs be very pleasing and grateful to the devil, both parties mutually objecting schism, and charging each other with crime and folly. What invectives and railings may be heard in all companies, as if they had been at the greatest distances in point of doctrine! But whosoever loseth, to be sure the devil gains by it. Hatreds, strife, variance, emulations, lyings, railings, scorn, and contempt, are all against the known duty of brotherly kindness, and are undoubted provocations against the God of love and peace. What can we then think of that can be so useful to Satan as error, when these above-mentioned evils are the inseparable products of it? The modestest errors that ever were among good men are still accompanied with something of these bitter fruits. The differences about meats and days, when managed with the greatest moderation, made the strong to despise the weak as silly, wilful, factious humorists; and, on the contrary, the weak judged the strong as profane, careless, and bold despisers of divine institutions; for so much the apostle implies, Rom. xiv. 3, 'Let not him that cateth despise him that eateth not; and let not him which eateth not, judge him that eateth.' But should we trace error through the ruins of churches, and view the slaughters and bloodshed that it hath occasioned, or consider the wars and desolations that it hath brought forth, we might heap up matter fit for tears and lamentations, and make you cease to wonder that Satan should so much concern himself to promote it.

5. Fifthly, The greatest and most successful stratagem for the hindering a reformation, is that of *raising up an army of errors*. Reformation of abuses, and corruptions in worship or doctrine, we may well suppose the devil will withstand with his utmost might and policy, because it endeavours to pull that down which cost him so much labour and time to set up, and so crosseth his end. They who are called out by God to 'jeopard their lives in the high places of the

field,' Judges v. 18, undertake a hard task in endeavouring to check the power of the mighty, whose interest it is to maintain those defilements which their policy hath introduced, to fix them in the possession of that grandeur and command which so highly gratifies their humours, and self-seeking aspiring minds. But Satan knowing the strength of that power which hath raised them up to oppose, with spiritual resolution, the current of prevailing iniquity, usually provides himself with this reserve, and comes upon their backs with a party of deluded, erroneous men, raised up from among themselves, and by this means he hopes either to discourage the undertakers for reformation, by the difficulty of their work, which must needs drive on heavily when they that should assist prove hinderers, or at least to straiten and limit the success; for by this means, (1.) He divides the party, and so weakens their hands. (2.) He strengthens their enemies, who not only gather heart from these divisions, seeing them so fair a prognostic of their ruin, but also improve them, by retorting them as an argument, that they are all out of the way of truth. (3.) The erroneous party in the rear of the reformers do more gall them with their arrows, even bitter words of cursed reviling, and more hazard them with their swords and spears of opposition, than their adversaries in the front against whom they went forth. In the meanwhile, they that stand up for truth are as corn betwixt two millstones—oppressed with a double conflict, beset before and behind.

This hath been Satan's method in all ages. And indeed policy itself could not contrive anything that would more certainly obstruct reformation than this. When the apostles, who in these last days were first sent forth, were employed to reform the world, to throw down the ceremonies of the Old Testament and heathen worship, Satan had presently raised up men of corrupt minds to hinder their progress. What work these made for Paul at Corinth, and with the Galatians, the epistles to those churches do testify. The business of these men was to draw disciples after them from the simplicity of the gospel, nay, to another gospel; and this they could not do but by setting up themselves, boasting of the Spirit, carrying themselves as the apostles of Christ, and contemning those that were really so, insinuating thereby into the affections of the seduced, as if they zealously affected them, and that Paul was but 'weak and contemptible,' nay, their very 'enemy, for telling them the truth,' [Gal. iv. 16.] What unspeakable hindrance must this be to Paul! What grief of heart, what fear and jealousy must this produce! He professeth he was afraid lest he had 'bestowed upon them labour in vain,' Gal. iv. 11; and that he did no less than 'travail of them in birth the second time,' ver. 19. If one Alexander could do Paul so much evil by 'withstanding his words,' that he complains of him, and cautions Timothy against him, 2 Tim. iv. 24; if one Diotrephes, by 'prating against John with malicious words,' prevailed with the church, that they 'received him not, nor the brethren,' 3 John 10, what hurt might a multitude of such be able to do!

In the primitive times of the church, after the apostles' days, when those worthies were to contest with the heathen world, the serpent 'cast out of his mouth water, as a flood, after the woman,'—which most interpret to be a deluge of heresies, and some particularly understand it of the Arian heresy,—that he might hinder the progress of the gospel; which design of his did so take, that many complaints there were of hindering the conversion of the heathens, by the errors that were among Christians. Epiphanius tells us that pagans refused to come near the Christians, and would not so much as hear them speak, being affrighted by the wicked practices and ways of the Priscillianists. Austin complains to the same purpose, that loose and lascivious heretics administered matter of blaspheming to the idolatrous heathens.

In after-times, when religion grew so corrupt by popery, that God extraordinarily raised up Luther, Calvin, and others in the fifteenth and sixteenth centuries, to discover those abominations, and to bring back his people from Babylon, the devil gave them no small trouble by a growth of errors, so that they were forced to fight against the papists before and those Philistines behind; insomuch that reformation attained not that height and universality which might rationally have been expected from such blessed undertakings. This was the conjecture of many, particularly of our countryman Dr Prideaux,[1] that if these fanatic enthusiasts, which with so great a scandal to the gospel then brake forth, had not retarded and hindered those glorious proceedings, that apocalyptical beast of Rome had been not only weakened and wounded, but utterly overthrown and slain. In particular cities, where any of the faithful servants of Christ endeavoured to detect the errors of popery, these instruments of Satan were ready to join with the common adversary in reproaches and disturbances. How they opposed Musculus at Augusta, and with what fierceness they called him viper, false prophet, wolf in sheep's clothing, &c., you may see in those that write his life. How these men hindered the gospel at Limburg against Junius, at Zurich against Zuinglius, at Augsburg against Urbanus Regius, you may also see in their lives.[2] In all which, and others of like nature, you will still find, (1.) That there was never a reformation begun, but there were erroneous persons to hinder and distract the reformers; (2.) That these men expressed as great hatred against the reformers, and oftentimes more, than against the papists; and were as spitefully bitter in lies, slanders, and scorns against them, as the papists themselves.

6. Sixthly, Satan can also make use of error either to *fix men in their present mistaken ways and careless course, or as a temptation to atheism.* Varieties of opinions and doctrines do amuse and amaze men. While one cries, 'Lo, here is Christ,' and another, 'Lo, he is here,' men are so confounded that they do not know what to choose. It is one of the greatest difficulties to single out truth from a crowd of specious, confident pretences, especially seeing truth is modest, and oftentimes out-noised by clamorous, bold error; yea, sometimes out-vied by the pretensions of spirit and revelation in an antiscriptural falsehood. At what a loss is an unskilful traveller where so many waves[3] meet! While one party cries up this, another that, mutually charging one another with error, they whose hearts are anything

---

[1] Excitata a Luthero bestia apocalyptica, et non irritata tantum, sed sauciata multorum venabulis, ultimum fere omnium bonorum judicio, efflasset spiritum, nisi spiritus isti inauspicati tam heroicos distraxissent et retardassent impetus.—*Prid[eaux], Orat. de Spir. Seduct.*, p. 95. [As before.—G.]   [2] Melch. Adam. in vita Theol.
[3] Query, 'ways'?—ED.

loosened from a sense and reverence of religion, are easily tempted to disbelieve all. Thus error leads to atheism, and lays the foundation for all those slanderous exceptions against Scripture by which godless men usually justify themselves in their religion. Now though all wicked men are not brought to this, because the consciences of some do so strongly retain the sentiments of a deity, that all Satan's art cannot obliterate those characters; yet the consideration of the multitude of errors doth rivet them in the persuasion of the truth and goodness of that way of religion wherein they had been educated. Papists are hardened by this; and though they have no reason to boast of their unity among themselves, as they have been often told, and now of late by Dr Stillingfleet,[1] who hath manifested that their divisions among themselves are as great, and managed with as great animosity, as any amongst us; yet are their ears so beaten with the objection of sects and schisms elsewhere, that they are generally confirmed to stay where they are. Besides, this is a stumbling-block which the devil throws in the way of poor ignorant people. If they are urged to a serious strictness in religion, they are affrighted from it by the consideration of sects and parties, and the woeful miscarriages of some erroneous persons that at first pretended to strictness, imagining that strictness in religion is an unnecessary, dangerous thing, and that the sober, godly Christians are but a company of giddy, unsettled, conceited, precise persons, who will in a little time run themselves into madness and distraction, or into despair. And thus out of fear of schism or error, they dare not be religious in good earnest; but content themselves with 'drawing near to God with their mouths, and confessing him with their lips, whilst their hearts are far from him, and in their works they deny him,' [Titus i. 16.]

There is such a propensity in the hearts of men to be staggered by the multitude and boldness of errors, that the apostle Paul expresseth a sense of it, and seems tenderly careful to avoid that blow, which he knew Satan would readily give through that consideration, by the apology that he makes for God in his holy, wise, providential permission of them, 1 Cor. xi. 19, 'There must be heresies among you.' His intent is not barely to put them off with this, that heresies are unavoidable, but to satisfy them that there is a necessity of them, and that they are useful, as God's furnace and fan, to purify and to cleanse, that 'they which are approved may be made manifest.' The like care he hath in 2 Tim. ii. 19, 20, upon the mention of the error of Hymeneus and Philetus, where he obviateth the offence that might arise by reason of their apostasy, partly by removing the fears of the upright, in affirming their safety whatever became of other men, seeing 'the foundation of God standeth sure,' and partly by declaring it no more suitable or dishonourable for God to permit the rise of errors in his church, than for great men to have in their houses not only 'vessels of gold and silver, but also of wood and of earth; some to honour, and some to dishonour.' By these very apologies it appears that Satan by this device of error designs to shake men's faith and to drive them from their religion.

[1] 'Discourse of the Idolatry of the Church of Rome.' [Works. 1710. 6 vols., folio.—G.

7. Seventhly, Neither can this, *that corrupt doctrines bring forth corrupt practices*, be of any less weight with Satan, or less engaging for the pursuit of this design, than any of the forementioned reasons.

Corrupt doctrines are embraced as the very truth of God by the deluded; and one way or other, directly or consequentially, they lead on practice, and that with the highest security and confidence, as if they were very truths indeed.

The devil then hath this great advantage by error, that if he can but corrupt the minds of men, especially in the more weighty and fundamental points of religion, then by a great ease and without any more labour he hath gained them to the practice of whatsoever these corrupted principles will lead unto. No course can be taken that with greater expedition and prevalency can introduce profane debaucheries than this. Thus he conquers parties and multitudes, as a victorious general takes cities and whole countries, by surrender; whereas his particular temptations to sin are but inconsiderable, less successful *picqueerings*[1] in comparison; and when he hath once corrupted the understandings of men, he hath by that means a command over their consciences, and doth not now urge to evil in the notion of a devil or tempter, but as an angel of light, or rather as a usurper of divine authority. He requires, he commands these wicked practices as necessary duties, or at least gives a liberty therein, as being harmless allowances. This difference was of old observed in Satan's management of persecution and error, that in the former he did compel men to deny Christ, but by the latter he did teach them. *In persecutione cogit homines negare Christum, nunc docet.*

That the lives and practices of men are so concerned by corrupt doctrines, may appear to any that are but indifferently acquainted with Scripture or history. We are told by the apostle Paul that faith and conscience stand so related to each other that they live and die together, and that when the one is shipwrecked the other is drowned for company, 1 Tim. i. 19. In Phil. iii. 2, he seems severely harsh against those of the concision; he calls them dogs, 'Beware of dogs; beware of evil workers.' The reason of which expression I apprehend lies not so much in these resemblances, that dogs spoil the flock by devouring, or that they are fawning creatures, or that they are industrious in prosecution of their prey,—though in all these particulars false teachers may be compared to dogs, for they spare not the flock, they compass sea and land to gain disciples, and they entice them with fair speeches,—but rather he intends the similitude to express the profane life and carriage of these seducers, for dogs are filthy creatures, to a proverb, 'The dog to his vomit.' And common prostitutes, for their uncleanness, were called dogs in the Old Testament. So some expound Deut. xxiii. 18, 'The hire of a whore, or the price of a dog.' And we have full and clear descriptions of seducers from their wicked and abominable practices: 2 Peter ii. 10, 'They that walk after the flesh, in the lust of uncleanness, and despise government; presumptuous are they, self-willed, they are not afraid to speak evil of dignities: ver. 14, 'Having eyes full of adultery, and that can-

---

[1] 'Pickeer' in Spanish means to 'rob or pillage;' a 'gipsy' in English dialect [Sussex] is called a 'picker' or tramp, *e.g.*, Shakespeare, Hamlet, iii. 2.—G.

not cease from sin; an heart exercised with covetous practices; cursed children:' ver. 18, 'They allure through the lusts of the flesh, through much wantonness.' Jude 4, 'There are certain men crept in unawares, who were before of old ordained to this condemnation; ungodly men, turning the grace of God into lasciviousness:' ver. 16, 'These are murderers, complainers, walking after their own lusts,' &c. 2 Tim. iii. 2–5, 'Men shall be lovers of their own selves; covetous, boasters, proud, blasphemers, disobedient to parents, unthankful, unholy, without natural affection, truce-breakers, false accusers, incontinent, fierce, despisers of those that are good, traitors, heady, high-minded, lovers of pleasures more than lovers of God; of this sort are they which creep into houses.' All which do set forth heretical persons as the most scandalous wicked wretches that we shall meet with; grossly filthy in themselves, corrupted in all the duties of their relations, natural and civil; defiled in all the ways of their converse with men.

Neither are these wicked practices issuing from gross errors to be looked upon as rare, accidental, or extraordinary effects thereof, but as the natural and common fruits of them; for Christ makes this to be the very special property and note whereby false prophets may be discovered, Mat. vii. 16, 'Ye shall know them by their fruits. Do men gather grapes off thorns, or figs off thistles?' &c. These fruits were not their doctrines, but their lives; for to know false prophets by false doctrines is no more than to know false doctrine by false doctrine. If any object that many false teachers appeared in the shape of seeming holiness and strictness of life, they may be answered from Christ's own words; for there he tells us, to avoid mistakes, that their first appearance, and it may be the whole lives of some of the first seedsmen of any error, is under the form of sanctity: 'They come to you in sheep's clothing,' in an outward appearance of innocency and plausible pretences; but then he adds, that their fruits afterward will discover them. A tree at its first planting is not discovered what it is, but give it time to grow to its proper fruitfulness, and then you may know of what kind it is; so that we need not affirm that damnable doctrines produce wicked lives in all that entertain them at the very first. It is enough for discovery if there be a natural consequential tendency in such doctrines to practical impieties, or that at last they produce them, though not in all, yet in many.

And that this matter hath been always found to be so, all history doth confirm. Such there were in the apostles' days, as is evident by their complaints. Such there were in the church of Pergamos: Rev. ii. 14, 'Thou hast them that hold the doctrine of Balaam; who taught Balak to cast a stumbling-block before the children of Israel; to eat things sacrificed unto idols, and to commit fornication.' There were also the Nicolaitans, of whom Christ declares his abhorrency, ver. 15. In the church of Thyatira there was the 'woman Jezebel, who taught and seduced many' of that church to the like abominable doctrines and practices, ver. 20. Besides these, the apostle John was troubled with the abominable Gnostics, [and] the filthy Carpocratians, who taught that men must sin and do the will of all the devils, or else they could not evade principalities and powers, who would no otherwise be pleased to suffer them to escape to the superior heavens. Of these men and their licentious doctrine doth he speak, 1 John iii. 6, &c., that they that are born of God indeed, must not, dare not, cannot give themselves up to a liberty in such abominations.

The same fruits of corrupt doctrine appeared after the apostles' days. What was Montanus, but an impure wretch? What were his two companion prophetesses, Priscilla and Maximilla, but infamous adulteresses? The Priscillianists, the Manichees, and abundance more, left the stink of their profaneness behind them, by reason of whom, according to Peter's prophecy, 2 Peter ii. 2, 'The way of truth was evil spoken of.'

Later times have also given in full evidence of this truth. How shameful and abominable were the lives of John of Leyden and the rest of those German enthusiasts! Who reads the story of Hacket and Coppinger without detestation of their wicked practices! What better have the Familists and libertines of New and Old England been! Some were turned off to highest ranting, in all profaneness of swearing, drinking, adultery, and the defying of a godly life; and this, under the unreasonable boast of spirit and perfection.[1] The heavens may blush and the earth be astonished at these things! But in the meantime Satan hugs himself in his success, and encourageth himself to further attempts in propagating error, seeing it brings in so great a harvest of sin.

8. Eighthly, In this design of false doctrine Satan is never altogether out; if he cannot thus defile their lives, yet it is a thousand to one but *he obstructs their graces by it.* What greater hindrance can there be to conversion than error! The word of truth is the means by which God, through his Spirit, doth beget us; it is part of that image of God that is implanted in us: it is God's voice to the soul to awaken it. It cannot then be imagined that God will give the honour of that work to any error; neither can truth take place or have its effect upon a soul forestalled with a contrary falsehood. Falsehood in possession will keep truth at the door. Neither is conversion only hindered by such errors as directly contradict converting truths, but also by collateral non-fundamental errors; as they fill the minds of men with prejudice against those that profess another persuasion, so that for their own beloved error's sake men will not entertain a warning or conviction from those that dissent from their opinions: they first account them enemies, and then they despise their message. It is no small matter in Satan's way to have such an obstruction at hand in the grand concern of conversion. Yet this is further serviceable to him, to hinder or weaken the graces of the converted already. If he can set God's children a-madding upon error, or make them fond of novelties, he will by this means exhaust the vigour and strength of their hearts, so that the substantials of religion will be neglected. For as hurtful plants engross all the moisture and fatness of the earth where they stand, and impoverish it into an inability for the nourishment of those that are of greater worth, so doth error possess itself of the strength of the spirit, and in the meantime neglected graces dwindle into emptiness, and 'fade as a

[1] See the story of Mr Copp[inger.]

leaf.' The most curious questions and opinions that are, contribute nothing to the establishment of the heart; it is only grace that doth that: Heb. xiii. 9, 'The heart is established with grace,' and not with disputes about meats; nay, they do grace a prejudice, in that they make it sick and languishing—for to that sense is the original, in 1 Tim. vi. 4, ' Doting about questions,' or growing diseased, because of the earnest prosecution of opinions, Νοσῶν περὶ ζητήσεις.

9. Ninthly, Error hath yet another mischief in it, which makes it not a little desirable to Satan; and that is *the judgment or punishment that it brings.* So that it every way answers the devil's hatred against both soul and body. The blessings of prosperity and peace do attend the triumphal chariot of truth: Ps. lxxxv. 11, 12, 'Truth shall spring out of the earth, and righteousness shall look down from heaven.' And then it follows, that 'the Lord shall give that which is good, and our land shall yield her increase.' But on the contrary, error doth more provoke God than men are aware. How often did God desolate the Israelites, set a fire in their cities, and gave them into the hands of their enemies, because of their changing the truth of God into a lie, and worshipping and serving the creature more than the Creator! God left not the church of Pergamos and Thyatira without severe threatenings for the error of the Nicolaitans: Rev. ii. 16, 'Repent, or else I will come unto thee quickly.' Ver. 22, 'I will cast them into great tribulation, except they repent of their deeds, and I will kill her children with death.' And accordingly God fulfilled his threatening upon them, by bringing in the Saracens to desolate them, and to possess their land—as he also brought the Goths upon the empire for the Arian heresy. How is Satan pleased to labour in a design that will kindle the wrath of the Almighty!

CHAPTER II.

Of the advantages which Satan hath, and useth, for the introduction of error; as (1.) *From his own power of spiritual fascination. That there is such a power, proved from Scripture, and from the effects of it.* (2.) *From our imperfection of knowledge; the particulars thereof explained.* (3.) *From the bias of the mind. What things do bias it, and the power of them to sway the understanding.* (4.) *From curiosity.* (5.) *From atheistical debauchery of conscience.*

That Satan may the better speed in his design, he carefully takes notice of, and diligently improves all advantages. Indeed all his stratagems are advantages taken against us; for so the apostle, in his caution to the Corinthians, calls his devices, 'lest Satan should get an advantage of us,' 2 Cor. ii. 11. But here I only understand those that are more general, which are the grounds and encouragements to his particular machinations against men, and which also direct him in his procedure. These are,

1. First, Satan's own power of *spiritual fascination*, by which he

infatuates the minds of men, and deludes them, as the external senses are deceived by enchantments or witchcraft.

That Satan is a cunning sophister, and can put fallacies upon the understanding; that by subtle objections or arguments he can obtrude a falsehood upon the belief of the unskilful and unwary; that he can betray the judgment by the affections, are things of common practice with him. But that which I am now to speak of is of a higher nature, and though it may probably take in much of his common method of ordinary delusion, yet in this it differs, at least that it is more efficacious and prevalent; for as his power over the children of disobedience is so great that he can 'lead them captive at his will,' except when he is countermanded by the Almighty, so hath he, by special commission, a power to lead those to error effectually, without missing his end, that have prepared themselves for that spiritual judgment by a special provocation; and for aught we know, as he hath an extraordinary power which he exerts at such times, so may he have an extraordinary method which he is not permitted to practise daily, nor upon all.

That such a power as this the devil hath, is believed by those whose learning and experience have made their judgments of great value with serious men; and thus some do describe it: It is a delusion with a kind of magical enchantment; so Calvin, Gal. iii. 1: a satanical operation whereby the senses of men are deluded; thus Perkins, who after he had asserted that Satan can corrupt the fantasy or imagination, he compares this spiritual witchcraft to such diseases of melancholy, that make men believe that they are, or do, what they are not or do not, as in the disease called *lycanthropia;* and to the enchantments of Jannes and Jambres, who deluded the senses of Pharaoh. Others more fully, call it 'a more vehement operation of the great impostor, whereby he obtrudes some noxious error upon the mind, and persuades with such efficacy that it is embraced with confidence, defended strenuously, and propagated zealously.'[1]

A particular account of the way and manner by which the devil doth this, is a task beyond sober inquiry. It may suffice us to know that such power he hath, and this I shall confirm from Scripture, and from the effects of such delusion.

(1.) First, There are several scriptures which assert a power in Satan to bewitch the minds of men into error, from which I shall draw such notes as may confirm and in part explain this truth in hand.

And I shall begin with that of Gal. iii. 1, 'O foolish Galatians, who hath bewitched you, that you should not obey the truth?' &c. The word which the apostle here useth for bewitching, as grammarians and critics note,[2] is borrowed from the practice of witches and sor-

[1] Fascinatio est spiritus impostoris vehementior operatio, qua noxium aliquem errorem in dogmate vel praxi—doctrinæ sanæ contrarium, sed sophisticis præstigiis depictum—pro veritate incautis hominibus obtendit, iisque efficaciter persuadet, ut errorem eum confidenter amplectantur, strenuè defendant, et zelo, non secundum Deum, propagant.—*Dickson, Therapeut. Sacra,* lib. iii. cap. 7.

[2] Βασκαίνω, Grammaticis dictum esse placet quasi φασκαίνω, id est, τοῖς φάεσι τι καίνειν, quo pertinet illud, *Virg., ec.* iii. Nescio quis teneros, &c. *Vide* Piscator, *in loc.,* and Leigh. Crit. Sac.

cerers, who use by secret powers to bind the senses, and to effect mischiefs. It is true he speaks of false apostles, but he intends Satan as the chief workman; and this he transfers to signify Satan's power upon the mind, in blinding the understanding for the entertainment of error. Neither can anything be objected why this place should not prove a fascinating power in Satan, such as we have been speaking of, but this, that it may be supposed to intend no more than an ordinary powerful persuasion by arguments. Yet this may be answered, not only from the authority of learned interpreters, who apprehend the apostle and his expression to intend more, but also from some concomitant particulars in the text. He calls them 'foolish Galatians,' as we translate it, but the original goes a little higher, to signify a madness; and withal he seems to be surprised with wonder at the power of Satan upon them, which had not only prevailed against the truth, but against such evident manifestations of it as they had when they were so plainly, fully, and efficaciously instructed; for 'before their eyes Jesus Christ had been evidently set forth;' which expressions and carriage cannot rationally be thought to befit a common ordinary case.[1]

Next to this, let us a little consider that famous scripture in 2 Thes. ii. 9–11, 'Whose coming is after the working of Satan, with all power. . . . and for this cause, God shall send them strong delusions, that they should believe a lie.' I shall from this place observe a few things, which if put together will clear the truth we speak of: As, first, In this delusion here mentioned, the apostle doth not only set down extraordinary outward means, as signs and lying wonders, but also suits these extraordinary means with a suitable concomitant inward power; for by 'power' I do not understand, as some, [Piscator and Sclater,] a power of shewing signs and doing wonders, as if the apostle had said, ἐν δυνάμει σημείων καὶ τεράτων, with the power of signs and wonders—for the words will not well bear that without some unnatural straining; but I understand by it a power, distinct from the signs and wonders, by which he moves their hearts to believe, by an inward working upon their minds, striking in with the outward means of lying miracles propounded to their senses. And we may the better satisfy ourselves in this interpretation, if we compare it with Rom. xv. 19,[2] where not only the power of doing wonders is expressed by a phrase, proper and different from this of the text in hand, 'through mighty signs and wonders,' or in the power of signs and wonders, but it is also clearly distinguished from the power of the Spirit of God, in working upon the hearts, to make those wonders efficacious and persuasive; so that, as in the Spirit of God we observe a power to do wonders, and a power to work upon the heart by these wonders, we may conclude that this wicked spirit hath also, in order to sin and delusion, this twofold power. But secondly, I note further, That this power is called a special energy of peculiar force and efficacy in its working—κατ' ἐνέργειαν τοῦ Σατανᾶ. The strange inexpressible

---

[1] Neque tantum quod se decipi passi fuerint eos arguit, sed quadam veluti magica incantatione deludi.—*Calvin, in loc.* Ἀνόητοι mente alienati—eorum lapsum magis dementiæ esse quam stultitiæ, arguens.—*Calvin.*

[2] ἐν δυνάμει σημείων καὶ τεράτων, ἐν δυνάμει πνεύματος Θεοῦ.

strength of it seems to stand in need of many words for explanation. He calls it 'all power'—ἐν πάσῃ δυνάμει—which as well notes the degree and height, as the variety of its operations, and then the energy, the virtue, operativeness, and strength of power. Thirdly, It is also to be observed that Satan's success and exercise of this power of delusion depends upon the commission of God, and that therefore it is extraordinary, and not permitted to him but upon special occasions and provocation, 'for this cause God shall send,' &c. Fourthly, The success of this power when exercised is certain. They are not only strong delusions, in regard of the power from whence they come, but also in regard of the event; those upon whom they come cannot but believe. Infatuation and pertinaciousness are the certain fruits of it.[1] Fifthly, The proof of all is manifest in the quality of the errors entertained, for they are palpable gross lies, and yet believed as the very truths of God, and they are in such weighty points as do evidently determine the soul to ruin, 'lies to be damned,' which two things are sufficient proofs of spiritual fascination; it being unimaginable that rational men, and especially such as were instructed to a belief of a contrary truth, should so far degenerate from the light of reason as to be deluded by gross and apparent lies, and of such high importance, except their minds had been blinded in some extraordinary way. Some further confirmation may be added to this truth from 1 Kings xxii. 21, 'And there came forth a spirit and stood before the Lord, and said, I will persuade him. . . . I will go forth, and I will be a lying spirit in the mouth of all his prophets. And he said, Thou shalt persuade him, and prevail also.' I might here take notice of Satan's readiness in this work, as wanting neither skill nor will, if he were but always furnished with a commission; as also the powerful efficacy of spiritual witchcraft, where it pleaseth the Lord to permit to Satan the exercise of his power, 'Thou shalt persuade, and prevail also.' But that which I would observe here, is something relating to the manner of his proceeding in these delusions. He attempted to deceive the false prophets, and by them to delude Ahab; and both, by being a lying spirit in the mouth of the prophets, which necessarily, as Peter Martyr observes, implies, (1.) That Satan had a power so strongly to fix upon their imaginary[2] faculty the species, images, or characters of what was to be suggested, that he could not only make them apprehend what he presented to their minds, but also make them believe that it was a divine inspiration, and consequently true; for these false prophets did not speak hypocritically what they knew to be false, but what they confidently apprehended to be true, as appears by the whole story. (2.) He could irritate and inflame their desires to publish these their persuasions to the king, after the manner of divine prophecies. (3.) He had a further power of persuading Ahab that his prophets spake truth.[3]

That passage of Rom. i. 28, 'God gave them over to a reprobate mind,' doth give some account how men are brought by the devil into

[1] Sclater, *in loc.* [1627. 4to.—G.]   [2] 'Imaginative.'—G.]
[3] Licet ei (Deo concedente) species, imagines et simulacra rerum falsarum effingere in imaginaria hominum facultate, ita ut falsa pro veris eis demonstrentur, deinde potest incendere atque inflammare appetitum eorum ad ea incredibili alacritate prædicanda, &c. Pet. Martyr, *in loc.* Reynolds, Treat. of Passions, chap. 4, p. 27, [as before.—G.]

these false persuasions. A reprobate mind is a mind injudicious, a mind that hath lost its power of discerning—Νοῦς ἀδόκιμος. It is plain then that he can so besot and blind the mind that it shall not be startled at things of greatest absurdity or inconveniency.

If any yet further inquire how he can do these things; we must answer, that his particular ways and methods in this case we know not: only it may be added, that, Eph. iv. 17, Paul tells us he can make their 'minds vain, and darken their understandings.' By mind, Νοὸς, the seat of principles is commonly understood. By understanding, Διάνοια, the reasoning or discursive faculty, which is the seat of conclusions: so that his power seems to extend to the obliterating of principles, and can also disable them to make right inferences, insomuch that he wants nothing that may be necessary to the begetting of strong persuasions of any falsehood which he suggests, according to what is intimated, Gal. v. 3, 'This persuasion cometh not of him that called you'—that is, not of God, but of the devil.

From all these scriptures then it appears that this spiritual fascination is a power in Satan, which he exerts, by special commission, upon those that receive not the truth in the love of it, by which he can so strongly imprint falsehoods upon their minds, that they become unable to discern betwixt truth and a lie, and so by darkening their understanding, they are effectually persuaded to believe an error.

(2.) Secondly, There is yet another proof of this spiritual witchcraft, from the consideration *of the effects of it upon the deluded, and the uncouth, strange, unnatural way of its proceeding.* Let all particulars of this kind be put together, and it will not be found possible to give any other rational account of some errors than that of extraordinary delusion.

[1.] First, Let us take notice of the *vileness and odiousness of some errors that have prevailed upon men.* Some have been plainly sottish, so evidently foolish that it cannot be imagined that men that entertained them had at that time the use of reason, or any competent understanding. This very consideration the prophet Isaiah insists upon largely, chap. xliv. 9–21, where he taxeth them smartly for the senseless doltishness of their error in worshipping idols. He tells them the matter of it is the work of nature, a cedar, oak, or ash, that they themselves possibly had planted, and the rain did nourish it, ver. 14. He tells them also that the form of it was from the art of the workman, the smith, or carpenter: ver. 12, 13, 'The smith with the tongs both worketh in the coals, and fashioneth it with hammers, and worketh it with the strength of his arms. . . . The carpenter stretcheth out his rule; he marketh it out with a line; he fitteth it with planes, and he marketh it out with a compass.' He further minds them, that without any reverence they make use of the residue of the materials out of which they formed their idol to common services of dressing their meat and warming themselves. 'He burneth part thereof in the fire; with part thereof he eateth flesh; he roasteth roast, and is satisfied; yea, warmeth himself, and saith, Aha, I am warm, I have seen the fire,' ver. 16. Then he accuseth them of sottishness, in that the 'residue thereof he maketh a god, even his graven image: he falleth down to it, and worshippeth it, and prayeth unto it, and saith, Deliver me; for thou art my god,' ver. 17. And from all this he concludes, that seeing this is so directly contrary to common reason and understanding—which in the ordinary exercise of it would easily have freed them from such a dotage; for if they had but 'knowledge or understanding to say, I have burnt part of it in the fire; I have baked bread, and shall I make the residue an abomination?' ver. 19, they could not have been so foolish. It must, then, of necessity be a spiritual infatuation. 'Their eyes were shut that they cannot see, and their hearts, that they cannot understand,' ver. 18. 'A deceived heart hath turned him aside,' ver. 20. Other errors there are that lead to beastly and unnatural villanies, such as directly cross all the sober principles of mankind, the natural principles of modesty, the most general and undoubted principles of religion and holiness, as when adulteries, swearing, ranting, going naked, cruelties, murders, outrageous confusions and madness, are clothed with pretences of spirit, revelation, freedom in the use of the creature, exercise of love, and having all things common, &c.: of which sad instances have been given more than once. Let any sober man consider how it could come to pass, that men that have reason enough to defend them against such furies, and the knowledge of Scripture, which everywhere—with the greatest happiness imaginable and highest earnestness—doth prohibit such practices as most abominable, and doth direct to a sober, just, modest, humble, inoffensive life, should entertain notwithstanding, such errors as transform men into beasts, monsters, or rather devils, and religion into the grossest impieties; and all this as the perfection and top of religious attainment commanded in the word of God or by his Spirit, and well-pleasing to most holy and pure divine majesty! Let it, I say, be left to the consideration of men how it should be, without some such extraordinary cause as hath been mentioned.

[2.] Secondly, Let it be observed also, that some errors bring with them some *extraordinary, strange, unnatural, unusual actions*, and put men into such odd garbs, postures, and behaviours, that it is easy to see they are acted by a force or power not human. Some have been carried to do things beyond whatsoever might have been expected from the age and capacities of the parties; as ecstasies, trances, and quakings of little children; their prophesying and speaking Scripture threatenings after such fits. Some have been acted in a way of ecstatical fury; as Montanus, of whom Eusebius witnesseth,[1] that 'sometimes he would be seized upon by a kind of malignant spirit, and would suddenly break forth into a rage and madness, and presently utter rash and bold speeches, strange, unusual voices, with prophesyings; insomuch that he was judged by those that saw him to be acted by the devil.' Others have been as in a more sober spiritual rapture; an instance whereof I shall give you from Mr Baxter in these words: 'I have heard from an ancient godly man that knew Arthington and Coppinger, that they were possessed with the spirit of the Grundletonians. The same man affirmed that he went but once among them

[1] Ferunt quendam nomine Montanum—spiritu quodam maligno abripi, et de repente furore et mentis insania exagitatum bacchari; atque mox non solum temere garrire, sed peregrinas quasdem voces fundere et prophetare—Nonnulli illum tanquam insano spiritu præditum, dæmonio agitatum increpabant. Ita Christopher. interp. *Euseb. Histor. Eccles.*, lib. v. cap. 15.

himself, and after prayer they breathed on him as giving him the Holy Ghost; and he was so strangely transported for three days that he was not the same man, and his family wondered what was the matter with him: he had no confession of sin, but an elevated strain in prayer, as if he had been in strange raptures; and after three days he was as before, and came no more at them.'[1] Some have been carried into childish and ridiculous actions: such was the behaviour of Jo. Gilpin in his delusion at Kendal in Westmoreland; as his going to the fiddler's house, playing upon a bass viol in token of spiritual melody; his creeping up the streets upon hands and knees in token of bearing his cross; his making marks on the ground, and beating it, as his mortification of sin; and a great many more things of like nature.[2]

Such things as these are as spiritual marks and characters engraven upon errors, by which a diabolical power, moving and acting such deluded creatures, like so many puppets, is evidently discovered.

[3]. Thirdly, When we see not only idiots, and those whose defect of understanding might put them under the power of an ordinary cheat, thus imposed upon, *but men otherwise intelligent, rational, and serious*, blinded with follies, taken with apparent dotages, admiring trifles, and carried away with things which common reason would teach them to abhor, it is more than suspicious that it is not any probability of truth or excellency in the error that prevails with them, but a spiritual power that doth bewitch them. When we consider that such a learned man as Tertullian begins to admire such a wretch as Montanus; or such a one as Arthington led away with Hacket and Coppinger; or such a man as Kneperdollin seduced by John of Leyden; and especially such numbers of wise and seemingly sober and religious persons, going down the stream after irrational and plainly irreligious errors,—what else can be apprehended to be the cause but a powerful satanical delusion?

[4.] Fourthly, Add we to these the consideration of *the suddenness of the prevalency of such errors against plain and evident truths*, which is a circumstance taken notice of by the apostle: Gal. i. 6, ' I marvel that ye are so soon removed from him that called you into the grace of Christ unto another gospel.' In which case we may observe it usually falls out that men's affections prevent their discoveries; at the first view they are taken, before they understand what the error is, and they are persuaded before they know.

[5.] Fifthly and lastly, That *the earnestness of the prosecution by which they maintain and propagate the error is a kind of unnatural fury, which hurries men with violence into an unyielding stiffness, to the stifling of all kind of charity and consideration.* These things put together, I say, makes the matter in hand evident; when men otherwise rational are at first touch highly enamoured with, and violent in the pursuit of errors that are sottish or devilish, we can resolve it into nothing less than into that of the apostle, 'Who hath bewitched you?' The improvement of this first and great advantage for the introduction of errors is more than can be well expressed; but he hath besides other advantages which he noway neglects: among which,

---

[1] Baxter's 'Confession of Faith,' p. 3, in the margin, [1655. 4to.—G.]
[2] See his story called the 'Quaker Shaken.'

2. Secondly, *Our imperfection in knowledge* is none of the least. If our knowledge had been perfect, it would have been a task too hard for the devil to make us erroneous; for men do not err but so far as they are ignorant. To impose upon men against clear and certain knowledge is impossible. Men cannot believe that to be true which they know to be false. It would be as silly for Satan to make such attempts as for a juggler to endeavour the deception of those that know and see the ways of his conveyances as well as himself. That our knowledge is imperfect, I shall prove and explain in the following particulars:—

[1.] First, *The Scripture plainly asserts it.* The greatest number of men which are in an unregenerate estate are expressly called foolish, blind, ignorant—men that are in darkness, men that do not know nor consider, that perish through ignorance. Others that, in comparison to these, are called 'children of the light,' and such as 'see with open face,' are notwithstanding, when compared to a state of perfection, represented to be in the non-age of their knowledge, unripe, imperfect. The apostle doth so express it, 1 Cor. xiii. 9, 'We know in part, we prophesy in part.' In the explanation of this, he compares our attainments in this world to the understanding, thoughts, and speakings of children, ver. 11: concludes, ver. 12, that all our knowledge gives us but a dark, imperfect reflection of things: 'we see through a glass darkly.'

[2.] Secondly, *Men that have had the clearest heads, and have been at the greatest pains in their inquiries to find out truths, have brought back the clear conviction of their own ignorance.* Austin confesseth that in the Scriptures—which he made his chief study—the things which he knew not were more than the things he understood.[1] Chytræus, in humble modesty, goes a little further: 'My dearest knowledge,' saith he, 'is to know that I know nothing;' and it will be a clear demonstration of that man's ignorance that boasts of his knowledge; his own mouth will prove against him that 'he knows nothing as he ought to know,' [1 Cor. viii. 2.]

[3.] Thirdly, The consideration of *the nature of the things which are the objects upon which we employ our search* will sufficiently convince us that we do comprehend but very little. For though the Scripture hath expressed the main concerns of eternal life so fully that they are as clear as light, and need no such stretch of the brain but that the meanest capacities may as certainly understand them as they understood anything of common business; as, that Christ died for sinners; that without faith it is impossible to please God; that without holiness no man shall see his face, &c. Yet, as Peter speaks, 2 Pet. iii. 16, 'There are many things that are hard to be understood,' δυσνόητά τινα. There are difficulties, depths, and mysteries. Some things, whereof we have but dark touches in Scripture, though enough to let us know that such things there are, and, to humble us for our ignorance, are in their own nature sublime, bounded on all sides with rocks and precipices, where our near and bold approaches are prohibited: such are those things that concern the decrees of God, the Trinity, &c. Other things are dark and uncertain to us, from their

[1] Plura nescio quam scio.—Epist. 119, cap. 21. Melch. Adam in vita.

very proximity to us—as some are pleased to fancy the reason. Such are the nature, faculties, and workings of our own souls within us—which we cannot directly see, as the eye sees not itself, and do but, as it were, guess by dark reflections. Some things in Scripture are accidentally obscure to us that were plain to those that heard them first, to whom they were spoken and written; for now to the understanding of a great many passages there is necessary the knowledge of the tongues in which they were dictated, of the histories of those times to which they severally related; as also of the particular customs of the Jewish nation, which gave a mould and form to a great many Scripture assertions; all which were easy and familiar to those that knew the exact propriety of such languages, were acquainted throughly with such histories, customs, usages, and manner of speakings; and besides all these, the application of general rules to particular cases—where a little circumstance may make a great alteration—is full of puzzle and intricacy; insomuch that some have thought that there are several cases of conscience that are not yet fully determined, and that are like so to remain.[1]

[4.] Fourthly, Neither is *the nature of knowledge itself* without an argument to prove the insufficiency of our knowledge. To know is properly to understand things by their causes, or at least by their effects, and to make a right result of particulars from a general maxim. Such a kind of knowledge is necessary in religion, for setting aside some particulars of mysterious height, about which God hath set bounds, lest men in presumptuous boldness should adventure to 'break through unto the Lord to gaze;' and some things which are the principles of nature, or their next results, which are, upon that score, beyond all need of inquiry—in all which it is enough to believe that what the Scripture saith is true, without asking a further account; yet in other things the Scripture gives us the grounds, reasons, and proofs of what it declares or asserts, as may appear by infinite examples; so that to know Christ died, or that we are justified by faith, or that Christ shall come to judgment, without a knowledge of the grounds and reasons of these things, is indeed but gross ignorance. The like may be said of the knowledge of general precepts, without the knowledge of their necessary application.

But how few are there that do thus know! The greatest part of men satisfy themselves with the bare affirmations of Scripture, and they resolve all into this, that the word of God saith so, or that it is the will of God it should be so, without further inquiry.

And as for others, though they may know the reasons of many things, yet are there a vast number of particulars whose reasons we know not, though the Scripture may contain them; and as for consequences, and the application of general rules, their just limitation, and the enumeration of the cases wherein they are true or false, it is that that keeps the wits of men upon the rack perpetually.

[5.] Fifthly, *The unsuitableness of our capacities to those objects of knowledge* may be particularly considered as a further confirmation of our ignorance. The incapacity of the vulgar is generally observed. Some we find so grossly ignorant, that they are incapable to comprehend the easiest matters; and this makes their persuasion to some

---

[1] D'Espagne, Popular Errors, sec. 2, cap. 12. [As before.—G.]

plain truths so very difficult, that when they are, as it were, 'brayed in a mortar' by a multitude of unreasonable[1] arguments, yet their ignorance 'departs not from them,' but they will stubbornly hold the conclusion of their own fancy, whatever become of the premises. Those that are of a higher form, and seem to understand a great many particulars in religion, are ordinarily unable to conjoin all truths into one entire proportionable body: they heap up several notions that they hear here and there, but know not their consistencies; insomuch that they either are like children, who know all the letters of the alphabet, without the skill to frame words or sentences out of them, being unable to give an account how their notions are related one to another, or to the whole; or if they attempt such a thing, they hang inconsistent things on the same thread, and do but *humano capiti cervicem jungere equinam.* If these instances, and a great many more of like kind, were not at hand, yet the very condescensions of our great prophet the Lord Jesus, and of his disciples in their ways of teaching, do evince that the capacities of men are low—that they are 'dull of hearing, children in understanding.' The course they took was to instruct them in a plain, familiar way, by parables and examples. Thus were they 'fed as babes in Christ,' according to the apostle's similitude, with 'milk, and not with strong meat, because they were not able to bear it,' 1 Cor. iii. 1. And yet Christ sometimes complained that this would not do. For so he speaks, John iii. 12, 'If I have told you earthly things,' that is, divine truth in earthly and common similitudes, 'and ye believe not,' *i.e.*, cannot apprehend them, 'how shall ye believe if I tell you of heavenly things?' How unable, then, would you be to understand these truths if I should speak in language and expression properly suited to their natures? A great check to our slowness of apprehension.

But possibly some may expect higher matters from those that are exalted above the common rank of men by the repute they have of learning. And indeed it cannot be denied but such have very great advantages for the widening of their capacities; yet are they not such as wholly take away the distemper, but still so much incapacity may be seen in them as will sufficiently justify the charge of imperfection in knowledge against the most learned. Let us bring in some instances, and it will be evident:

(1.) *The greatest errors that have most disturbed the church in all ages have had their rise from learned men.* The names of their authors are marked upon their foreheads. These known errors are so many, that they fill whole volumes. The result of which consideration will be this, that learned men have often been very dangerously mistaken.

(2.) *The present contentions and disputes of men,* managed on all hands with so much earnestness, wherein one party triumphs over another, and all, in their own apprehensions, are victorious. Instead of conquests by arguments and answers, each party is but more confirmed in its own apprehensions; and yet the one-half is certainly wrong, and perhaps in many things both parties are mistaken. This, I say, sufficiently shows the incapacities of the learned; for if every capacity were truly correspondent to truth, there would be no more disputes nor differences.

[1] Query, 'unanswerable'?—ED.

(3.) *The most learned find the business of their own persuasion and satisfaction in many truths, in which common people have no scruple nor doubt, very difficult;* because they see more objections to be answered, and more of the weakness of arguments than others do; but this shews their capacities are not so large as some would think.

(4.) Let us once for all consider *that which seems to be the highest evidence for knowledge and understanding in the learned, and we shall find, upon just examination, it is no more than an argument of their ignorance.* What is there wherein they seem more acute and eagle-eyed than in their distinctions, by which they would give us the most minute differences of things, and appear so exact as if they would divide an atom, and give everything its just weight and measure? But let us consider that, though all distinctions are not unprofitable, their multitude is become oppressive and troublesome, and more time must be spent in learning terms and words of art than things; and their nicety and subtlety so great, that they rather darken truth, and give occasion to bold spirits to undertake the defence of any paradox. Nay, if we could sever these clearly from their abuses, yet, seeing it is certain there are more distinctions of terms than things, they will evince that our knowledge is more verbal than real, and that often for a mountain of words we have but a molehill of substantial matter. Nay, seeing we make but a sorry shift at best by these artifices to come to some rude conceptions of things, which otherwise we cannot in any tolerable manner comprehend, it is as great a proof of our imperfection in knowledge, as the necessary use of staves and crutches is an evidence of lameness. If I should pass from this to the consideration of the multitude beyond all number of books that are written, we shall find them but so many proclamations of our ignorance; for if we could believe them all to contain so many wholesome precepts of necessary truth, which yet we cannot rationally imagine, this would imply that the greatest part wanted these informations; and that common ignorance is not only a general distemper, but also a distemper hard to be cured, that stands in need of such multitudes of instructors and such varieties of helps. But if we believe that among this infinite number of volumes there are thousands of lies, millions of unproved conjectures, millions of millions of idle, unprofitable fancies, then do we in express terms pronounce them guilty of ignorance, and of ignorance so much the more dangerous, by how much the more bold it is to avouch itself in the light, and to obtrude itself upon the belief of others, who, instead of being better informed by it, shall but increase their own blindness. Were there nothing to be said but this, that there are such a vast multitude of commentators upon the Bible, which do all pretend to expound and explain it, it would of necessity admit of these conclusions:—[1.] That the Bible hath in it things so dark, or at least our capacities are so dull, that there is need of great endeavours to explain the one, or assist the other. [2.] That the knowledge of men is imperfect; for if all or most men could certainly interpret the Scripture, there needed not so many volumes, but that one or two might have signified as much as now whole libraries can do.

The imperfection of our knowledge being thus laid open, it is easy to see what advantages the devil may make out of it for the promoting of error; for it must now become our wonder, not that any man errs, but that all do not. We find it easy to impose anything upon children; it is an easy matter for a trifle to cheat them out of all they have. Surely then Satan may do as much by men, who are but 'children in understanding.' The apostle, Eph. iv. 14, puts us in mind of this hazard under that very similitude, 'that we henceforth be no more children, tossed to and fro, and carried about with every wind of doctrine.' How fitly doth he resemble us to children! Their weaknesses are, [1.] Want of discerning; they see not the true worth of things. [2.] Credulity; they believe all fair speeches and specious promises: and the hazard of both these is in this, that it makes them unconstant, uncertain, and fickle; and such are we made by our ignorance, so little do we truly discern, so apt are we to believe every pretence, for the simple believes every word, Prov. xiv. 15; that, as the apostle's metaphors do tell us, we are easily tossed from one conceit or opinion to another, as a ship is by the waves, or a feather in the wind. κλυδονιζόμενοι καὶ περιφερόμενοι.

3. Thirdly, A third advantage which the devil takes against us in his design of error, is *the bias of the mind*. Were our understandings purely free, in a just and even balance toward all things propounded to its deliberation and assent, though it were imperfect in its light, the danger were the less; but now, in regard of the bent and sway it is under, it is commonly partial, and inclined to one side more than to another, and yet the matter were the less, if only one or two noted things had the power of setting up a false light before the mind; but there are many things that are apt to do us this mischief, which have the same effect upon us that bribes have upon persons interested in judgment, which not only tempts them to do wrong, but so blinds their eyes that they know not they do so, or at least not in so great a measure. The mind is biassed,

(1.) First, *Naturally to error rather than truths*. The corruption of our nature is general, and doth not only dispose the will and affections to practical iniquities, but doth also incline the understanding to error and misapprehension. And that seems to be the ground of Christ's assertion against the Jews: John v. 43, 'I am come in my Father's name, and ye receive me not: if another shall come in his own name, him ye will receive.' Which implies that men are naturally more prone to believe an impostor, than one that speaks the most certain and profitable verities; and besides this general inclination to vanities and lies, there are, if some think right, some errors that are formally engraven in the nature of fallen man—as that opinion to be saved by works.[1] For not only do all men that have any apprehensions of a future eternal state resolve that question of obtaining salvation into works as the proper cause,—and indeed no other could have been imagined, if the Scripture had not revealed the redemption by the blood of Jesus—but the Jews in John vi. 28, when they propound that question, 'What shall we do, that we might work the works of God?' take it for granted, that works of some kind or other are the causes of happiness. Possibly some impression of that notion,

[1] D'Espagne, Popular Errors, sec. 2, chap. 4. [As before.—G.]

while it was a truth, as in the state of innocency it was, may yet remain upon our natures, though by the fall the case is altered with us.

(2.) Secondly, The mind is biassed *by bodily temper and complexional inclination.* The varieties of complexions introduce varieties of humours and dispositions; and the understanding being necessitated to look through these, as so many coloured glasses, is apt to judge, that is, to misjudge, according to the misrepresentation of objects.

(3.) Thirdly, Sometimes *habitual acquirements have the same influence upon the understanding that natural humours have.* The arts and sciences we study, our ways of education and employment, are but so many prejudicate prepossessions that do secretly taint the mind.

(4.) Fourthly, There are also *accidental inclinations,* which, though not customary, have the force of a second nature, because their working is violent and impetuous, and these, which are from a wounded conscience or excesses of melancholy, have a bias more than ordinary; they lay violent hands upon the understanding, and with a mighty torrent run it down. So that if an error be offered that is suitable to such fears or misapprehensions, it can scarce miss of success. The extraordinary turbulences of some other passions, as anger, love, &c., have the like effect.

(5.) Fifthly, *Vicious habits* do so much bias the mind, that the understanding must needs be defiled by them. Nothing can more prepare the mind to a wicked error than a wicked life. An error of indulgence being so grateful to corruption may readily find favour with the understandings of those that know not to do good, because they have accustomed themselves to do evil.

(6.) Sixthly, There are *external things* that have no less power on the understanding than any of the foregoing; and these are custom, education, and interest. These stick so close, and work so subtly, that though there are few that are not, in disputable cases, influenced by them, yet none are able or willing to take notice how and by what steps they do engage them to pass sentence against truth. And indeed that man must have a singular measure of suspicious watchfulness and clear integrity that is not deceived by them. And the best way to keep clear of the mischief that these may do us, is to be severe in our suspicions on that side to which custom and interest have their tendencies.

(7.) Seventhly, I might note that there is something considerable to this purpose *in the nature of spirits.* Some spirits are unfixed and volatile, and these are soon altered by their own unsteadiness. Others are tenacious and unflexible; and if such be first set wrong, it is not an easy thing that will reduce them to truth. Others are soft and ductile, persuaded by good words as soon as strong arguments. And again, some are of such a rough, sour, contradictious temper, that they will sooner choose to run wrong than comply with the persuasions of those that offer truth, even for that reason, because they are persuaded to it; so that the truth which, if none had minded them, they of themselves would have embraced, they will now refuse when it is pressed upon them, out of a cross and thwarting humour, because they hate nothing more than to do as they are bidden.

To come a little nearer, let us consider how these things shew their power upon the mind to sway and incline it. It is indeed true, that in things that are clearly and strongly propounded to the understanding, it cannot but judge according to the evidence of truth, and cannot be guided by the will to judge contrary; nay, the will—though in things purely speculative it may retain its averseness, as also in things practical, while they are considered only as what may be done before the understanding hath come up to its final resolve, determining that such things must or ought to be done—cannot but follow the light and information of the understanding, and that according to the proportion of its conviction; so that though in some cases a man would have things otherwise than he believes them to be, yet he cannot believe what he will, neither can he refuse to will what is certainly represented to be good and necessary. *Tantum quisque vult, quantum intelligit se velle debere.* Notwithstanding all this, the forementioned particulars may so bias the mind that it shall not act truly and steadily, as we may see in these three particulars:

[1.] First, *In things clearly demonstrated to the understanding*, though the will cannot directly oppose, nor prevail to have them judged false, yet it can indirectly hinder the procedure of the understanding, and divert it from fixing its consideration upon the truth, or from working itself into positive determinations for bringing it into practice. *Intellectus sequitur voluntatem quoad exercitium, non quoad specificationem.* Thus many that cannot but believe there is a God, and that his law is true, being biassed by their lusts, the power of pleasures or interest, &c., do prevail upon their understandings to take up other objects of consideration; so that they are said to forget God, and to cast his commandments behind their backs, as also not to remember their latter end, though they cannot but believe that they shall die. Truth may be imprisoned and fettered, where it cannot be slain. We read of 'holding the truth in unrighteousness,' Rom. i. 18, which was this, that those heathens of whom the apostle speaks, by reason of their vicious inclinations and practices, though they could not obliterate those notices of equity and religion that were imprinted on their minds, yet they kept them at under, as captives in a dungeon, and suffered them not to rise up in a just practical improvement. Now the wrong that is done to truth this way is not only by rendering it unfruitful and useless at present, but hereby the devil hath his advantage in the gaining of time to gather together more forces against that truth, and by frequent onsets of contrary arguings, especially upon the advantage of the mind's indifferency and remissness, begot by long and often diversions, to set another face upon it, and by degrees to overturn former persuasions. This was the very case of the heathens in the place last cited, who, being first swayed by their impieties, became unwilling to give way to those dictates of light and justice which they had; and having thus gratified their lusts, the devil further prevailing with them to find evasions from the power of those truths, they began to make unsuitable inferences from these premises, which they could not deny, and so became sottish and vain in their reasonings, 'changing the glory of the uncorruptible God, into an image made like unto corruptible man.' And by such practices against truth, they at last changed the truth into a lie, ver. 25, and at long-run obliterated the knowledge of God out of their minds. This is Satan's old method of overturning truth at last, by diverting the mind from receiving the present powerful impressions of those principles.

[2.] Secondly, But in things doubtful, where there is not a clear certainty what is truth, but contrary opinions strive with such equal confidence, that it is difficult to determine which hath the conquest, there the mind may be so swayed by its bias that it *may give approbation to error; nay, where, upon a fair and indifferent trial, truth hath the greater appearance of strength, and error nothing else than little shadows or appearances of reason to shelter itself under;* yet that way may the mind be inclined by the aforesaid things. We have a more easy and facile belief for what we would have than for what we would not. Though there is nothing more noted by common experience than this, that men are usually drawn aside by humours, inclinations, interests, and education, &c., to judge well of that which an unprejudiced person would easily see to be weak, unjust, ridiculous, or unreasonable; yet how these considerations and tempers do exert their force upon the understanding to draw it into a compliance, or by what secret art they can heighten probabilities, and lessen objections; or by what insensible progress they move, that men thus carried do not perceive that they are under such a force, is not so very discernible. How often may we observe men, that are rational enough to discover the pitiful shifts and poor allegations of others, with such gravity and confidence, where their own interests are concerned, to offer such low reasonings and extravagant impertinences, that all that hear them are ready to laugh at their folly; and yet they themselves entertain no less than persuasions of the invincibleness of their arguings. They so eagerly desire what they would establish, that they think anything is enough to justify it, and are apt to imagine that their shifts and excuses appear as strong to others as to themselves. I have known some that, by the sway of interest, have changed their opinions in religious matters, and have really become otherwise persuaded than they had been formerly, and not as some who, for advantage, will knowingly take up what they cannot believe to be true, and have not been able to say that they have met with new arguments or new answers to objections, but I know not how arguments, which they had contemned, and laid by for weak, began to look big upon them. The arguments by which their former persuasion was upheld grew insensibly feeble in their hands; the one revived, gathered strength, after they had a little cherished them, by thinking there might be something in them, though before they knew all the particulars, and could not instance in anything which they had not formerly notified and answered; and the other sort of arguments grew weaker and weaker, till at last they parted with all good conceit of them; so that such a change was but as the turning of the tables. That which acted behind the curtain, and wrought this change of the fancy, could be no other than some of the forementioned things that biassed their mind; for where the arguments, *pro* and *con*, were the same, the alteration of opinion, where men are not so wicked as to go directly against their own light, must of necessity be imputed to the different positions of external things, and the different humours and inclinations begot by them, even as the different stations of men in the prospect of some pictures represent them variously; one way they give the shape of a beautiful face, another way they express the ugly deformity of a devil; or as different reflections of the sunbeams upon the same object clothe it with several colours. The Scripture doth also give us notice of this advantage which the devil takes from the inclinations of men to lead them into mistakes. That of Micah ii. 11, 'If a man, walking in the spirit of falsehood, do lie, saying, I will prophesy unto thee of wine and of strong drink; he shall even be the prophet of this people,' hath this for its foundation, that, let the error be never so gross and palpable, as if a man should prophesy a liberty for drunkenness, if it be suitable to the sway of people's humours, it will readily enough be embraced, 'he shall be a prophet to this people,' that is, such a prophet will easily prevail with such a people; their vicious inclinations fit them for any impression of a suitable error. The apostle Paul also found this too true in the heresies of his own times; for he tells us that seducers had learned that cunning from the devil to draw men to error by the sway of their lusts: 2 Tim. iii. 6, 'They creep into houses, and lead captive silly women laden with sins, and led away with divers lusts;' as also 2 Tim. iv. 6, he prophesies of the future use of this stratagem, 'After their own lusts shall they heap to themselves teachers.' So that the usual prevalency of error was and is from the underground working of lusts, humours, habits, and inclinations, which make men willing to entertain an opinion, which can but gratify them with a suitableness or fitness.

[3.] Thirdly, Where the forementioned particulars of inclination, natural or acquired humours, custom, education, &c., do neither divert the understanding, nor engage it to close with error; yet often do they discover how powerfully they can bias the mind, in that these prevail with men *to modify and mould a truth according to the bent or form of their inclinations;* as a bowl which is skilfully aimed at a mark, goes nevertheless by a compass which its bias forceth it unto, according to the risings or fallings of the ground it meets with in the way. Men may arrive at real truth in the main, and yet may shape it according to their humours. For instance, let us consider the different modes or forms in which the same truth is represented under the workings of different tempers. A melancholy person conceives of all things under such reflections as fear and sadness do usually give. If he consider God, he looks upon him in the notion of greatest severity and justice; if upon the ways of duty, he colours them all in black, and can scarce account anything piety which is not accompanied with sadness and mourning; if he calls his soul to a reckoning, his conclusions concerning himself are sad, doleful, or at best suspicious. On the contrary, a hilarious, cheerful temper censures all sadness for sullenness, and is apt to accuse those that go mourning in their way for unthankful murmurers and unbelieving complainers; it interprets God's favourable condescensions to the weak in the greatest latitude, and is easily persuaded to those things that are upon the utmost brink of liberty, to which others of a more timorous disposition dare not approach for fear of offending. This puts a higher excellency upon the duties of praise, as the other upon fasting and mourning. Those men that are morose and severe, they are apt to think that God 'is such an one as themselves;' and though they acknowledge there is such a grace as charity, yet under a pretence of strictness they cannot believe they are bound to exercise it towards any that are under any failing of which they judge themselves to be free; and therefore such men are usually very difficult in all cases wherein condescension is to be used; they are hard to be reconciled, and after the miscarriage of any person, are not easily satisfied of their repentance; and in cases of dissent from their way and practice of religion, they are commonly censorious, and conclude the worst. They again that are naturally mild and gentle, under a pretence of charity and meekness, are apt to become remiss in their carriages towards any brother; and because 'charity thinks not evil,' they model their acknowledged duty into the form of their own disposition, and so think they must 'see, and yet not perceive;' and instead of covering the 'infirmities' of a brother, they have a mantle to cast over every transgression. At the same rate also do they frame their conceptions of God, as if he was so merciful that he would scarce reckon any abomination to be above the height of an ordinary infirmity. These are apt to think that the mercies of God, so much praised in Scripture, signify little less than an indulgence in transgression far above what precisians are apt to imagine; and that it is as easy to obtain forgiveness from God for any offence, as it is to say, 'The Lord be merciful to me a sinner.' Those that accustom themselves to the delights of the senses are apt to bend the way of their religion to that humour; and think that nothing can be solemn in worship that is not set out with garnishings that may please the eye or ear. Nay, it is observable enough that religion borrows some taint or shape from the various studies and sciences of men; in some, as in many of the fathers, we may see religion dipped in Platonism or Peripateticism. Some introduce the distinctions and definitions of philosophy, others compel all scriptures to submit to the laws of strict logical analysis. Thus, according to the various mediums that men look through, are truths discoloured and dressed up in several shapes. It is easy from these instances to imagine that Satan must have a great advantage against us, in point of error, from the bias of the mind.

4. Fourthly, *Adventurous curiosity* is another general advantage by which he works. This ariseth partly from a desire of knowledge, and partly from pride; and both these make way for his design.

A desire after knowledge is natural, and withal very bewitching. *Divinum est scire quam-plurima*, To know hath something in it more than ordinary. This is noted in Job xi. 12, 'Vain man would be wise, though man be born like a wild ass's colt.' Though he be foolish, yet he affects wisdom, and the very delight of knowing doth engage men to curious prying searches, though with much labour and hazard. Of this temper were the Athenians: Acts xvii. 21, 'They spent their time in nothing else, but either to tell or to hear some new thing;' not barely in telling news, but in inquiries after new notions and discoveries, and this made them willing to hear Paul, as 'a setter forth of strange gods, and a new doctrine.'

When this desire after knowledge is animated with pride, as oft it is, for 'knowledge puffeth up,' then it is more dangerous. When men are upon a design to seem higher than others, to be singular, to see more than what all men see, to be admired, to out-talk their neighbours, what adventures will they not make! How fair do they lie open to any conceit that may serve this end!

That Satan labours to improve this curiosity is without doubt; he carefully affords fuel to this burning, and diligently blows it up into a flame. The first temptation had that ingredient in it, 'Ye shall be as gods, knowing good and evil,' [Gen. iii. 5.] And we see it was a great enticement to Eve: that which would make 'one wise' was therefore desirable. The blame of Israel's first idolatry seems to be laid at this door: Deut. xxxii. 17, 'They sacrificed to gods whom they knew not,' to new gods that came newly up; implying that they were drawn aside from their old established way of worship by a curiosity to try the new ways of the heathens. And so great a hand hath this generally in errors, that Paul, 2 Tim. iv. 3, makes this itch after novelty the great ground of that defection from truth which he foresaw was coming, 'They shall heap to themselves teachers, having itching ears,' *Pruritus aurium est scabies ecclesiarum.* This itch of the ear is the usual forerunner of a scab in the church, because it doth dispose men to receive any kind of teacher. God indeed doth sometimes take the advantage of our natural curiosity for our good. By this means many of John's hearers, who went out into the wilderness to him, as to a 'strange sight,' as those words imply, 'What went ye out into the wilderness to see?' [Mat. xi. 7,] were converted. By this means, the gospel afterwards made a large progress, as we see commonly new teachers affect most at first; for when men grow acquainted with their gifts, their admiration decays, and the success of their labours is not so great many times. The devil also observing the prevalency of curiosity, and that men are more pleased with new notions than with old truths he endeavours also to plough with this heifer, and oft makes a great harvest by it. There is yet another advantage more that he sometimes useth, and that is,

5. Fifthly, *Atheistical debauchery.* When men by long custom in sinning have arrived to habitual carelessness and presumption, then they become practical atheists. Their vicious habits work upon their understandings to obliterate all principles. When men are gone so far, they are fit engineers for Satan; for while they disbelieve all things, they can, to serve a design or to head a party, take up any opinion, and pretend the greatest seriousness in the propagating it, though in the meantime they secretly laugh at the credulity of the vulgar.

These men let out themselves and all their parts to the devil, and he knows how to make use of them, to bring on the delusion and deception of others. Many ages have given examples of such. Those seducers mentioned in the New Testament were, some of them, of this rank, and therefore called 'deceitful workers,' [2 Cor. xi. 13.] Such as were not really under those persuasions which they thought to fix upon others, but upon design, transformed themselves into the apostles of Christ; such as served not our Lord Jesus Christ, but their own bellies, and yet by good words and fair speeches deceived the hearts of the simple: Rom. xvi. 18, 'Who, through covetousness, with feigned words, made merchandize of men,' 2 Pet. ii. 3. Balaam was such, and the woman Jezebel, that called herself a prophetess, Rev. ii. 20. Such was the Archbishop of Spalato,[1] who for advantage could at pleasure take up and lay down his religion. Such a one was the false Jew, not so long since discovered in this place, who being a Romish emissary, pretended to be a Jew converted; and seeking a pure church, under that vizor, designing to overthrow, by private insinuations, the faith of the simple, uncautious admirers![2] By such instruments Satan works where he hath opportunity.

CHAPTER III.

Of Satan's improving these advantages for error: 1. *By deluding the understanding directly: which he doth* — (1.) *By countenancing error from Scripture. Of his cunning therein.* (2.) *By specious pretences of mysteries; and what these are. Of personal flatteries.* (3.) *By affected expressions. Reason of their prevalency.* (4.) *By bold assertions. The reasons of that policy.* (5.) *By the excellency of the persons appearing for it, either for gifts or holiness. His method of managing that design.* (6.) *By pretended inspiration.* (7.) *By pretended miracles. His cunning herein.* (8.) *By peace and prosperity in ways of error.* (9.) *By lies against truth, and the professors of it.*

What are the general advantages which Satan hath to forward his design of error we have seen. It now remains that we take an account of the various ways by which he improves those advantages, and those may be referred to two heads: (1.) They are such stratagems as more directly work upon the understanding to delude and blind it. Or, (2.) They are such as indirectly by the power of the will and affections do influence it.

1. First, Those stratagems that more immediately concern the understanding are the use of such *arguments, which carry in them a probability to confirm an error*, though indeed they are but fallacies, sophisms, or paralogisms, of which the apostle speaks, Col. ii. 4, 'Lest any beguile you,'—that is, lest they impose upon you by 'false reasonings.' His usual way of proceeding in this case is:

(1.) First, When he hath to do with men that are brought up with profession and belief of Scripture, he is then careful *to give an error some countenance or pretence from Scripture*. It is not his course to decry the Scriptures with such men, but to suppose their truth and authority, as the most plausible way to his design; for by this means he doth not only prevent a great many startling objections which would otherwise rise up against him—seeing men brought up with Scripture cannot easily be brought to call them false—but with consi-

---

[1] M. Anthony de Dominis, who became Dean of Windsor. Died 1624.—G.
[2] See the narration called 'The False Jew.'

derable advantage he doth thereby authorise and justify his error, for nothing can give more boldness or confidence to a mistake than a belief that it is backed with Scripture.

That this is one of his grand stratagems may be sufficiently evinced from the infinite number of errors that pretend to Scripture warrant. Those that are above or beyond Scripture, which acknowledge no dependence upon it, are but few and rare, and indeed among Christians error cannot well thrive without a pretence of Scripture. Men would have enough to do to persuade themselves to such errors, but it would be impossible to make a party or persuade others. Such errors would presently be hissed out of the world. Upon this account is it that atheism skulks and conceals itself, except where generally tolerated profaneness gives it more than ordinary encouragement, which is not to be ascribed to any shame-faced modesty that atheisms can be supposed to nourish, but to the general dislike of others, who so stick to the authority of the Bible that they reject all direct contradictions to it with great abhorrency. Hence also it is that some erroneous persons are forced to contradictions in their practice against their professed principles, because they find it impossible to propagate their errors without some pretence or other to Scripture. They that would undermine those sacred records are forced to make use of their authority for proof of what they would say. The papists have a quarrel at them, and envy them the title of perfection and perspicuity, upon design to introduce traditions, and to set up the pope's judicial authority in matters of faith; and when they have said all they can to subject the Scriptures to the pope's determination, they are forced at last to be beholden to the Scriptures to prove the pope's determination. They would prove the Scriptures by the church, and then the church by the Scriptures, which is a circle they have been often told of, and of which some of the wiser sort among themselves are ashamed. Others also that will not allow the Scriptures to be a general standing rule are yet forced to make it, in some cases, a rule to themselves, and eagerly plead it to be so to others. They that pretend to be above ordinances, and decry outward teachings as unnecessary or hurtful, yet they teach outwardly, because they see they are not able to enlarge the empire of error without such teaching. Those very errors that make it their chief business to render the Scriptures no better than an old almanack, they yet seek to Scripture to countenance their blasphemous assertions; and if they get any scrap or shred of it that may by their unjust torture be wrested to speak any such thing, or anything toward it, they think all their follies are thereby patronised, 2 Pet. iii. 16; and commonly such men either fix upon such places as give warning of the necessary concomitances of the spirit and heart with the outward act of service; and from hence, separating what God hath joined together, they set up spiritual sabbaths, spiritual baptism, spiritual worship, to cry down and cashier the external acts of such ordinances, or they pretend kindred to Scripture, as prophesying or foretelling those new administrations which they are about to set up. Let H. Nicholas be an instance of this, who, though he decried the service of the law under God the Father, and the service of the belief under Christ, and in the room of both these would set up another administration under the Spirit; yet, that he might be the better believed, he applied several scriptures to his purpose, as prophetically foretelling H. Nicholas and his services, and would have men imagine that he was that 'angel flying in the midst of heaven with the everlasting gospel,' Rev. xiv. 6; and that prophet inquired after by the Jews: John i. 21, 'Art thou that prophet?' and that 'man ordained to judge the world,' Acts xvii. 31; and that the times of his dispensation were the times of perfection and glory spoken of in 1 Cor. xiii. 9, and Heb. vi. 1. The like pretences for new administrations had Saltmarsh and several others.

Satan, fixing his foot upon this design, and taking advantage of men's ignorance, curiosity, and pride, &c., it is impossible to tell what he may do. He hath introduced many heresies already, and none knows what may be behind. Many passages of Scripture are dark to the wisest of men, a great many more are so to the common sort of Christians. A great many wits are employed by him as adventurers for new discoveries, and a small pretence is ground enough for a bold undertaker to erect a new notion upon; and a new notion in religion is like a new fashion in apparel, which bewitcheth the unsteady with an itch to be in it before they well understand what it is; so that it is alike impossible to stint the just number of errors, as to adjust the various pretences from Scripture upon which they may be countenanced. Leaving, therefore, this task to those that can undertake it, I shall only note a particular or two of Satan's cunning in affixing an error upon Scripture.

[1.] First, In any grand design of error, he endeavours *to lay the foundation of it as near to truth as he can;* but yet so that, in the tendency of it, it may go as far from it as may be, as some rivers, whose first fountains are contiguous, have notwithstanding a direct contrary course in their streams. For instance, in those errors that tend to overthrow the doctrine of the gospel concerning Christ and ordinances — and these are things which the devil hath a great spite at—he begins his work with plausible pretences of love and admiration of Christ and grace; he proceeds from thence to the pretence of purer enjoyments; from thence to a dislike of such preachers and preaching as threaten sin and speak out the wrath of God against iniquity, and these are presently called legal preachers, and the doctrine of duty a legal covenant. Having them once at this point, they easily come to immediate assistances and special gifts, which they pretend to have above others. Being thus set up, they are for free grace and the enjoyment of God in spirit. From thence they come to Christian liberty, and by degrees duties are unnecessary. There is no Christ but within them; and being freed from the law, whatever they do is no transgression. This is a path that Satan hath trodden of old, though now and then he may vary in some circumstances, and be forced to stop before he come to the utmost of his journey. You may observe this method in the late errors of New England,[1] in the Familists of Germany, and in those of Old England; in all which at the long-run men are led as far from Scripture as darkness is from light. Now this is not only to be seen in a progressive multiplication of errors, but often may we perceive

[1] See the book called 'Wonder-working Providence for New England.'

the same subtlety of Satan in a simple error, as when he takes up part of a truth which should stand in conjunction with another, and sets it up alone against its own companion, where we shall have the name and pretence kept up, but the thing quite destroyed. God requires services of men, and prescribes to their use prayer, hearing, sacraments; but because in these God is dishonoured when men only draw near with their lips, he further tell us, 'that he is not a Jew which is one outwardly, neither is that circumcision which is of the flesh,' &c., [Rom. ii. 28.] This part are some men so fixed upon, that they think they are discharged of the other, and in practice go quite from these duties; and yet still they profess they are for ordinances and the worship of God. Just so are some men for Christ, but then it is but the name, not the thing; they own Christ, they say, but then it is Christ in them, and Christ come in their flesh, but not that Christ that died at Jerusalem as a sacrifice for the sins of men.

[2.] Secondly, Satan takes great care that an error be, in all the ways of its propagation, *clothed with Scripture phrases;* and the less the error can pretend to any plausible ground of Scripture, the more doth he endeavour to adorn it with Scripture language: I understand this chiefly of such errors as are designed for the multitude: so that though Scripture be not used to prove the error, yet are deceivers taught to express their conceptions by it, and to accommodate the words and sentences of it to their purposes; for besides pride and confidence, scriptural eloquence is a necessary ingredient to make a powerful deluder. Observe the ringleaders of errors, and you shall find that ordinarily such have at first been studious of the Scriptures; and though never able to digest them, yet when they turned their ears from truth, they have carried their Scripture language, which they had before brought themselves unto by long custom, away with them, and still retain it, and express their opinions by it.

Now this is a great advantage to Satan. For, *first,* By this means *the ignorant multitude are often caught without any more ado.* If they hear Scripture expressions, they are apt to think that all is truth which is spoken by them; and they the rather believe it, because they will imagine such teachers to be well versed in Scripture, and consequently either so honest or so knowing that they neither can nor will delude them. *Secondly,* There is a majesty in Scripture which, in some sense, *doth stick to the very expressions of it.* Men may perceive that generally hearers are more affected with Scripture eloquence than with play-book language. It hath, as it were, a charm in the words, which makes the ear attentive more than a quaint discourse, starched up in the dress of common rhetoric. One gives us an observation to that purpose of his own preaching,[1] and so may many others. While, then, men hear such language, they have a reverence to it. And as physicians cover their pills with gold that the patient might more willingly take them, so do men often swallow down error without due consideration, because conveyed to them in a language which they respect.

(2.) Secondly, Satan's second care for the advancement of error, after he hath given it all the countenance he can from Scripture, is to gild

[1] Savonarola, 'Triumph. Crucis,' lib. ii. cap. 2, [*i.e.,* 'De Veritate Fidei.' Florent. 1497. Folio.—G.]

it over with *specious pretences.* He sets it off with all the bravery he can, and then urgeth that as an argument of its truth. Men are apt to judge that what doth better their spiritual condition cannot be a lie or delusion; and the argument were the more considerable, if the advantages were such as he pretends them to be; but the very noise and boast of advantages please the unwary, without a due inquiry into their reality. The apostle, in Rom. xvi. 18, reduceth all this policy of the deceiver to two heads: (1.) Good words, χρηστολογίας—words that set out the profit and advantage of the thing; (2.) And fair speeches, εὐλογίας—speeches that flatter the condition of the party. His art, as to the first of these, is to tell them that the notions offered to them are special discoveries, rare mysteries, which have been hidden from others; and thence infers, that it must of necessity conduce much to their happiness and spiritual perfection to know and embrace them. Those that troubled the church in Paul's days with false doctrines, used this sleight of boasting, as appears by that expression in 1 Tim. vi. 20, 'oppositions of science.' It seems they called their opinions, though they were but profane and vain babblings, by the name of 'science' or 'knowledge,' implying that all others, even the apostles themselves, were in the dark, and came short of their illumination. The like we have in Rev. ii. 24 of that abominable prophetess Jezebel, who recommended her blasphemous, filthy doctrines under the name of 'depths,' profundities or hidden knowledge, though the Spirit of God told that church they were not such; but if depths, they were 'depths of Satan'—as it is added there by way of correction—and not of the Spirit of God. We may trace these footsteps of Satan in all considerably prevailing errors; for what hath been more common than to hear men speak of the designs they have been carrying on under the specious titles of Christ's coming to set up a righteous kingdom, the church's coming out of Babylon and out of the wilderness, the dawning of the day of the Lord, the day of reformation, 'the time of the restitution of all things,' with abundance of brags of the same kind? I shall add no particular instance of this nature, but a few strains of H. Nicholas, with whom such high promising vaunts were ordinary. His service of love he compares to the 'most holy;' whereas John's doctrine of repentance was but a preparation to the holy, and the service of Christ he allowed to be no more than as the holy of the temple. This his service he calls 'the perfection of life, the completion of prophecies, the perfect conclusion of the works of God, the throne of Christ, the true rest of the chosen of God, the last day, the sure word of prophecy, the new Jerusalem,' and what not.

If we make further inquiry into the nature of these fair promising mysteries, we shall find that Satan most frequently pitcheth upon these three :—

[1.] *First,* He befools men into a belief that the Scriptures do, under the veil of their words and sentences, contain *some hidden notions* that are of purpose so disguised that they may be locked up from the generality of men, at least from learned and wise men; and that these rarities cannot be discerned from the usual significations of the words and phrases, as we understand other books of the same language, but they fancy these sacred writings to be like the writings of the Egyptians,[1] by which they absconded[2] their mysteries, especially like that kind of writing, whereby under words of common known sense they intended things which the words themselves could not signify; and that which occasions this imagination is this, that we read frequently of 'mysteries' in [the] Scriptures, and 'hidden wisdom,' and the 'special revelation' of them to God's children, which are very great truths, but yet not to be so understood as this delusion supposeth; for these expressions in Scripture intend no more than this, that the design of God to save man by Christ is in itself a 'mystery,' which never would have been found out without a special revelation; and that though this 'mystery' is now revealed by the gospel, yet as to the application of it to the hearts of men in conversion by the operation of the Spirit, it is yet a 'mystery.' But none of these intend any such suggestion, that there are private notions of truth or doctrine that are lying under ground, as it were, in Scripture words, which the words in the common language will not acquaint us withal; nay, the contrary is expressly affirmed when we are told that all is plainly laid open to the very simple, so that from the Scriptures they may as well understand the fundamental principles of religion, as they may understand any other thing which their language doth express to them. However, in this Satan takes advantage of men's pride and curiosity to make them forward in the acceptation of such offers, especially when such things are represented as the only saving discoveries, which a man cannot be ignorant of but with hazard of damnation.

[2.] *Secondly*, In this boast of mystery, Satan sometimes takes another course somewhat differing from the former, and that is to put men upon *allegorical reflections and allusions*, by which the historical passages of Scripture are made, besides the import of the history, resemblances of spiritual truths, which supposeth the letter of Scripture to be true, but still as no better than the first rudiments to train up beginners withal, yet withal that the spiritual meaning of it raiseth the skilful to a higher form in Christ's school. At this rate all are turned into allegories. If they fall upon the first of Genesis, they think they then truly understand it when they apply the light and darkness, and God's separating of them, with such other passages, to the regeneration of the soul. The like work make they with the sufferings of Christ. But then the crafty adversary at last enticeth them on to let go the history, as if it were nothing but a parable, not really acted, but only fitted to represent notions to us. Allegories were a trap which the devil had for the Jews, and wherein they wonderfully pleased themselves. How much Origen abused himself and the Scriptures by this humour is known to many; and how the devil hath prevailed generally by it upon giddy people in later times I need not tell you.

The pretence that Satan hath for this dealing is raised from some passages of the New Testament, wherein many things of the Old Testament are said to have had a mystical signification of things expressed or transacted then, and some things are expressly called allegories. Hence papists determine the Scripture to have, besides the grammatical sense, which all of us do own, and besides the tropological sense,

---

[1] As *Ibis a scarabeo accipitris pulchritudinem participat;* by which they signified the moon borrowing its light from the sun. [2] 'Concealed.'—G.

which is not diverse or distinct from the grammatical, as when from histories we deduce instructions of holy and sober carriage, an allegorical and analogical sense; in which dealing men consider not that the Spirit of God his interpreting a passage or two allegorically, will never justify any man's boldness in presuming to do the like to any other passage of Scripture; and beside, when any hath tried his skill that way, another may with equal probability carry the same scripture to a different interpretation, and by this means the Scripture shall not only become obscure, but altogether uncertain and doubtful, and unable to prove anything; so that this doth extremely dishonour Scripture, by making it little less than ridiculous. Porphyry and Julian made themselves sport with it upon the occasion of Origen's allegorizing; and no wonder, seeing that humour, as one calls it,[1] is no better than a learned foolery. Notwithstanding this, men are sometime transported with a strange delight in turning all into allegories, and picking mysteries out of some by-passages and circumstances of Scripture where one would least expect them; which I can ascribe to no second cause more than to the working and power of fancy, which, as it can frame ideas and images of things out of that that affords no real likeness or proportion, as men that create to themselves similitudes and pictures in the clouds or in the fire, so doth it please itself in its own work; and with a kind of natural affection it doth kiss and hug its own baby. It hath been my wonder sometimes to see how fond men have been of their own fancies, and how extremely they have doted upon a very bauble. I might note you examples of this, even to nauseousness, in all studies, as well as in this of religion. Those that affect the sublimities of chemistry do usually by a strange boldness stretch all the sacred mysteries of Scripture, as of the Trinity, of regeneration, &c., to represent their secrets and processes, as may be seen sufficiently in their writings. One of them I cannot forbear to name, and that is Glauber, who doth so please himself with some idle whims about *sal* and *sol*, that at last he falls in with Bernardinus Gomesius, whom he cites and approves, who in this one word, ἅλς, which signifies *salt*, finds the Trinity, the generation of the Son, the two natures of Christ, the calling of the Jews and Gentiles, the procession of the Spirit, and the communications of the Spirit in the law and gospel; and all this he gathers from the shapes, strokes, and positions of these three letters—a very subtle invention.[2] Not unlike to this were some of the dotages of the Jewish Cabala, which they gathered from the different writing of some letters in the sacred text, from the transposing of them, and from their mystical arithmetic. R. Ellis from the letter *aleph*, mentioned six times in Gen. i. 1, collected his notion of the world's continuance for six thousand years, because that letter א stands for a thousand in the Hebrew computation. Another Rabbi,

---

[1] Whitaker, Def. lit. sententia adv. Duræum., lib. ii. p. 88. Parum a docta quadam insania discrepat. [The title of this famous book is as follows: 'Responsionis ad Decem illas Rationes, quibus fretus Edmundus Campianus certamen Ecclesiæ Anglicanæ ministris obtulit in causa fidei. Defensio contra Confutationem. Joannis Duræi, Scoti, Presbyteri, Jesuitæ. London, 1583, 8vo. Richard Stock translated the 'Controversy,' 1606, 4to.—G.]

[2] *Vide* Lumen Chymicum Crollii Basil. Chymic. in prefatione. Glauber de signatura Salium, p. 31, 38.

mentioned by Lud. Cappellus,[1] hath a profound speculation concerning the first letter of Genesis, which, as he saith, doth therefore begin with *beth*, and not with *aleph*, to shew the unexceptionable verity of God's word, against which no mouth can justly open itself; and this he gathers from the manner of the pronunciation of that letter ב, which is performed by the closure of the lips. It were not possible to imagine that wise men should be thus carried away with childish follies, if there were not some kind of enchantment in fancy, which makes the hit of a conceit, though never so silly, intoxicate them into an apprehension of a rare discovery. And doubtless this is the very thing that doth so transport the allegorizers and inventors of mysteries, that they are ravished either with the discovery of a new nothing or with the rare invention of an enigmatical interpretation.

[3.] Thirdly, The devil hath yet another way of coining mysteries, and that is a pretence of *a more full discovery of notions and ways;* which, as he tells those that are willing to believe him, are but glanced at in the Scripture; and this doth not only contain his boast of unfolding prophecies, and the dangerous applications of them to times and places that are no way concerned—which hath more than once put men upon dangerous undertakings,—but also his large promise of teaching the way of the Lord more perfectly, and of leading men into a full comprehension of those tremendous mysteries, wherein the Scripture hath as industriously concealed the reasons, way, and manner of their being, as it hath fully asserted that they are: such are the decrees of God, the Trinity, &c.; as also of unfolding and teaching at large those things that the Scripture seems only to hint at. In all which points we have instances enough at hand which will shew us how the devil hath played his game, either by making men bold in things not revealed, or by drawing men to dislike solid truths, and by puffing them up with notions, till at last they were prepared for the impression of some grand delusion. All this while I have only explained the first head of Satan's specious pretences, which consists in the promise of discoveries and mysteries—χρηστολογίαι, good words.

The next head of pretences are those that relate to the *persons* enamoured with these supposed mysteries—εὐλογίαι, fair speeches. With these he strokes their heads, and causeth them to hug themselves in a dream of an imaginary happiness. For if they have the knowledge of mysteries which are locked up from other men, they cannot avoid this conclusion, that they are the only favourites of heaven, that they only have the Spirit, are only taught of God, &c. Such swelling words of vanity have ever accompanied delusion. And indeed we shall find the confidence of such men more strong, and their false embracements more rapturous, than ordinarily the ways of truth do afford, upon this account, that in such cases fancy is elevated, and the delights of a raised fancy are excessive and enthusiastical. It is a kind of spiritual frenzy, which extends all the faculties to an extraordinary activity, the devil doing all he can to further it by his utmost contributions. Joy, delight, hope, love, are all raised to make a hubbub in the heart; whereas, on the contrary, truth is modest,

---

[1] Lud. Cappelli, Spec. in Eph. vi. 19. [Spicilegio post messem ... Geneva, 1632, 4to.—G.]

humble, sober, and affords a more silent joy, though more even and lasting.

Here might I set error before you in its rant, and give you a taste of the high-flown strains of it. Montanus, as vile as he was, had the confidence to call himself 'the comforter.' Novatus and his brother would be no less than Moses and Aaron. The Gnostics called themselves the *Illuminati*. The Swinkfieldians assumed the title of the Confessors of the glory of Christ. The Family of Love had their *Evangelium regni*, the gospel of the kingdom. The *Fratricelli* distinguished themselves from others by the term spiritual. Muntser asserted, that all of his opinion were God's elect, and that all the children of their religion were to be called the children of God, and that all others were ungodly and designed to damnation. H. Nicholas affirms, that there was no knowledge of Christ nor Scripture, but in his family. To this purpose most of them speak that forsake the ways of truth; and though these swellings are but wind and vapour, yet those heights are very serviceable to the devil's purposes: who by this means confirms those whom he hath already conquered, and then fits them out with the greater confidence to allure others; and men are apt enough to be drawn by fair shows and confident boastings. But I proceed.

(3.) The third stratagem of Satan for promoting error, is to *astonish men with strange language and affected expressions*. It was an old device of Satan to coin an unintelligible gibberish as the proper vehicle of strange enthusiastics' doctrine, and this he artificially suits to his pretended mysteries. Without this, his rare discoveries would be too flat and dull to gain upon any man of competent understanding. For if these dotages were clothed in plain words, they would either appear to be direct nonsense, or ridiculous folly. It concerns him when he hath any feats of delusion in hand, to set them off with a canting speech, as jugglers use their hard words of *Ailif, casyl, zaze, presto, millat*, &c., to put their ignorant admirers into a belief of some unknown power by which they do their wonders. And this is in some sort necessary. Extraordinary matters are above expression, and such wild expressions put men into an expectation of things sublime. This knack Satan hath constantly used. Montanus had his strange speeches; and all along, downward to our times, we may observe that error hath had this gaudy dress. The Familists especially abound with it. You may read whole books full of such a kind of speaking, as the book called *Theologia Germanica*, or German divinity,[1] the books of Jacob Behmen, 'The Bright Morning Star,' &c. Neither are the papists free; one of late hath taken the pains to shew them this and other follies.[2] Among them you may find such talk as this: of being 'beclosed in the midhead of God, and in his meekhead; of being substantially united to God, of being one'd to God; as also of the abstractedness of life, of passive unions, of the deiform fund of the soul; of a state of introversion; of a super-essential life, a state of nothingness,' &c. Just like the ravings of H. Nicholas,

---

[1] It is painful to find Gilpin thus indiscriminately condemning John Tauler's '*Theologia Germanica*:' which, by Miss Winkworth's recent translation, has entered on a new lease of deserved popularity.—G.   [2] Dr Stillingfleet, 'Idolatry of the Church of Rome.'

David George, and others, who confidently discourse of being 'godded with God,' of being 'consubstantiated with the Deity,' and of God's 'being manned with them.'

I have oft considered what reason might be given for the takingness of such expressions, and have been forced to satisfy myself with these: *First*, Many mistake the knowledge of words for the knowledge of things. And well may poor ignorant men believe they have attained, no man knows what, by this device; when among learned men the knowledge of words is esteemed so great a pitch of learning, and they nourish a great many controversies that are only verbal. *Secondly*, Some are pleased to be accounted understanders by others, and rest in such high words as a badge of knowledge. *Thirdly*, Some are delighted with such a hard language upon a hope that it will lead them to the knowledge of the things at last; they think strange expressions are a sign of deep mysteries. I knew one that set himself to the reading of Jacob Behmen's books, though at present he confessed he was scarce able to make common sense of three lines together, upon a secret enticement that he had from the language, to come to some excellent discovery by much pains and reading. *Fourthly*, Some that have their fancies heated, have by this means broken, confused impressions of strange things in their imaginations, and conceive themselves to know things beyond what common language can express; as if with Paul, rapt up into the third heaven, 'they hear and see wonders unutterable.' But what reason soever prevails with men to take up such a way of speaking, Satan makes them believe that it contains a rich mine or treasury, not of common truths, but of extraordinary profundities.[1]

(4.) Fourthly, Instead of argument to confirm an error, sometimes we have only *bold assertions that it is truth, and a confident condemning the contrary as an error*, urging the danger of men's rejecting it, backed with threatening of hell and damnation; and all this in the words of Scripture. To be sure, they are right, and all other men are wrong. This kind of confidence and fierceness hath been still the complexion of any remarkable way of delusion; for that commonly confines their charity to their own party, which is a great token of an error. Not only may you observe in such extraordinary proclamations of wrath against those that will not believe them: a practice used by the mad fanatics of Munster, who, as our Quakers were wont to do, go up and down the streets, crying, 'Wo, wo; repent, repent; come out of Babylon; the heavy wrath of God; the axe is laid to the root of the tree;' but in their more settled teaching they pronounce all to be antichrist, and of the carnal church, that do oppose them. Take for this H. Nicholas his words: 'all knowledge' besides his, 'is but witchery and blindness, and all other teachers and learners are a false Christianity, and the devil's synagogue; a nest of devils and wicked spirits; a false being, the antichrist, the kingdom of hell, the majesty of the devil,' &c. This piece of art, not only our Quakers, to whom nothing is more familiar than to say to any opposer, 'Thou art damned, thou art in the gall of bitterness, the lake of fire and brim-

---

[1] Dicas eos mera tonitrua sonare, nam communi sermone spreto, exoticum nescio quid idioma sibi fingunt, visi sunt suos discipulos supra coelum rapere. —*Calvin in Jude* 13.

stone is prepared for thee,' &c., but also the papists commonly practise, who shut all out of heaven that are not of their church; and when they would affright any from protestantism, they make not nice to tell him that there is no possibility of salvation but in their way.

The reasons of this policy are these: (1.) The heart is apt to be startled with threatenings, and moved by commands; especially those that are of a more tender and frightful spirit; and though they know nothing by themselves, yet these beget fears which may secretly betray reason, and make men leave the right way because of affrightment. (2.) The confidence of the assertors of such things hath also its prevalency; for men are apt to think that they would not speak so if they were not very certain, and had not real experience of what they said, and thus are men threaped[1] out of their own persuasions. (3.) The native majesty of Scripture, in a business of so great hazard, adds an unexpressible force to such threatenings; and though, being misapplied, they are no more Scripture threatenings, yet, because God hath spoken his displeasure in those words, men are apt to revere them—as men cannot avoid to fear a serpent or toad, though they know the sting and poison were taken out, because nature did furnish them with a sting or venom.

(5.) Fifthly, It is a usual trick of Satan to *derive a credit and honour to error, from the excellencies, supposed or real, of the persons that more eminently appear for it.* So that it fetcheth no small strength from the qualities of those that propagate it. The vulgar, that do not usually dive deep into the natures of things, content themselves with the most superficial arguments, and are sooner won to a good conceit of any opinion by the respects they carry to the author, than by the strongest demonstration.

The excellencies that usually move them are either their gifts or their holiness. If the seedsman of an error be learned, or eloquent and affectionate in his speaking, men are apt to subscribe to anything he shall say, from a blind devotional[2] admiration of the parts wherewith he is endowed. And often, where there is no learning, or where learning is decried, as savouring too much of man, if there be natural fluency of speech, with a sufficient measure of confidence, it raiseth them so much the higher in the esteem of the common sort, who therefore judge him to be immediately taught of God, and divinely furnished with gifts. At this point began the divisions of the church of Corinth. They had several officers severally gifted; some were taken with one man's gift, others with another man's; some are for Paul, as being profound and nervous in his discourses; others for Apollos, as eloquent; a third sort were for Cephas, as, suppose, an affectionate preacher. Thus upon personal respects were they divided into parties: and if these several teachers were of different opinions, their adherents embraced them upon an affectionate conceit of their excellencies. And generally Satan hath wrought much by such considerations as these. This he urgeth against Christ himself, when he set up the wisdom and learning of the rulers and pharisees, as an argument of truth in their way of rejecting such a Messias: John

---

[1] 'Out-contradicted' or 'argued.'—G. [2] 'Devoted,' = over-attached.—G.

vii. 48, 'Have any of the rulers, or of the Pharisees believed on him?' There is no insinuation more frequent than this: these are learned, excellent, able men, and therefore what they say or teach is not to be disbelieved; and though this be but *argumentum stultum*, a foolish argument, yet some that would be accounted wise do make very great use of it. The crack[1] ' of learned doctors among the papists' is one topic of persuasion to popery, and so to other errors, as appears by this, that all errors abound with large declamations of the praises of their founders and teachers: and the most illiterate errors usually magnify the excellent inspirements and gifts of utterance of their leaders.

But the other excellency of holiness in the teachers of error is more generally and more advantageously improved by Satan, to persuade men that all is true doctrine which such men profess. Of this delusion Christ forewarned us, 'They shall come in sheep's clothing'— that is, under the mask of seeming holiness, at least at first; notwithstanding, 'beware of them,' Mat. vii. 15. Those complained of by Paul, 2 Cor. xi. 15, though they were Satan's ministers, yet that they and their doctrine might be more plausibly entertained, they were 'transformed as the ministers of righteousness.' This cunning we may espy in heretics of all ages. The Scribes and Pharisees used a pretence of sanctity as a main piece of art to draw others to their way. Their alms, fastings, long prayers, strict observations, &c., were all designed as a net to catch the multitude withal. The lying doctrines of Antichrist were foretold by Paul, to have their success from this stratagem; all that idolatry and heathenism which he is to introduce must be, and hath been, through the hypocrisy of a painted holiness, 1 Tim. iv. 2; and where he intends most to play the dragon, Rev. xiii. 11, he there most artificially counterfeits the innocency and simplicity of the lamb. Arch-heretics have been arch-pretenders to sanctity, and such pretences have great influence upon men; for holiness and truth are so near of kin, that they will not readily believe that it can be a false doctrine which a holy man teacheth. They think that God that hath given a teacher holiness will not deny him truth. Nay, this is an easy and plausible measure which they have for truth and error. To inquire into the intricacies and depths of a disputation is too burdensome and difficult for ordinary men, and therefore they satisfy themselves with this consideration, which hath little toil in it, and as little certainty: that surely God will not leave holy men to a delusion. It would be endless to give all the instances that are at hand in this matter. I shall only add a few things of Satan's method in managing this argument, as,

[1.] First, When he hath a design of common or prevailing delusion, he mainly endeavours *to corrupt some person of a more strict, serious, and religious carriage, to be the captain and ringleader;* such men were Pelagius, Arius, Socinus, &c. He mainly endeavours to have fit instruments. If he be upon that design of blemishing religion, and to bring truth into a disesteeem, then, as one observes,[2] he persuades such into the ministry as he foresees are likely to be

---

[1] 'Talk,' or 'report.'—G.
[2] Acontius' 'Stratagema Satanæ,' lib. viii. p. 406, Oxon. [1631. 8vo.—G.]

idle, careless, profane, and scandalous; or doth endeavour to promote such ministers into more conspicuous places, and provokes them to miscarriage, that so their example may be an objection against truth, while in the meantime he is willing that the opposers of truth should continue their smooth carriage; and then he puts a two-edged sword into the hands of the unstable: Can that be truth where there is so much wickedness? and can this be error where there is so much holiness?

[2.] Secondly, In prosecution of this design he usually puts men upon some more than *ordinary strictness, that the pretence of holiness may be the more augmented.* In this case a course of ordinary sanctity is not enough, they must be above the common practice; some singular additions of severity and exactness above what is written, are commonly affected to make them the more remarkable. Christ notes this in the Pharisees, concerning all their devotions, and the ways of expressing them; their phylacteries spoken of, Mat. xxiii. 5, as some think,[1] were not intended by that text of Deut. vi. 8, but only that they should remember the law, and endeavour not to forget it, as they do that tie a thread or such like thing about their finger for a remembrancer; according to Prov. iii. 3, 'Bind them about thy neck, write them upon the table of thine heart.' However, if they were literally enjoined, they would have them, as Christ tells them, broader than others, as an evidence of their greater care. The *Cathari* boasted of sanctity and good works, and rejected second marriages; the *Apostolici* were so called from a pretended stricter imitation of the singular holiness of the apostles. The *Valesians* made themselves eunuchs, according to the letter, 'for the kingdom of God.' The *Donatists* accounted that no true church where any spot or infirmity was found. The *Messalians*, or *Euchytæ*, were for constant praying, the *Nudipedales* for going barefoot, &c. The papists urge canonical hours, whippings, penances, pilgrimages, voluntary poverty, abstinence from meats and marriage in their priests and votaries. In a word, all noted sects have something of special singularity, whereby they would difference themselves from others, as a peculiar character of their greater strictness; and for want of better stuff they sometimes take up affected gestures, devotional looks, and outward garbs; all which have this note, that what they most stand upon, God hath least, or not at all, required at their hands—their voluntary humility, or neglecting of the body being but will-worship, and a self-devised piece of religion.

[3.] Thirdly, When once men are set in the way of exercising severities, Satan endeavours, by working upon their fancies, to *press them on further to a delight and satisfaction in these*[2] *ways* of strictness, so that the practisers themselves are not only confirmed in these

---

[1] Jerome, Theophylact, Lyra, &c.

[2] Atque hac ratione seducta est, astu Satanæ, innumera hominum multitudo, quæ ut viam vitæ ambularet, arctam illam ingressa est, quæ instinctu Satanæ per humanas est ad-inventiones inducta, [maxime eorum qui in monasteriis vixerunt.] Postea quam vidit Satan viam suam quæ ad mortem ducit, traduci, eò quòd sit lata, et quod multi per illam ambulent, cœpissentque quidam arctam et strictam quærere, quæ non tereretur a multis, callido consilio effecit, ut pro vera via vitæ, arriperetur ea, quæ quidem esset stricta via, verò vitæ non esset, &c.—*Musculus in Mat.* vii. 13. [1548. Folio.—G.]

usages, and the opinions that are concomitant with them, but others are the more easily drawn to like and profess the same things. Any serious temper, under any profession of religion, easily comes to be devout, and readily complies with opportunities of evincing its devotion by strictness. And therefore we shall find among heathens a great devotional severity, and such as far exceeds all of that kind which the papists do usually brag of. The Magi abstained from wine, ate not the flesh of living creatures, and professed virginity. The Indian Brachmans did the like, and besides used themselves to incredible hardship; they laid upon skins, sustained the violence of the sun and storms, and exercised themselves therewith; some spending thirty-seven years in this course, others more. We read strange things of this nature concerning the Egyptian priests, and others. The Mohammedans are not without their religious orders, which pretend a more holy and austere life than others; and though of some, as of the *torlachs* and *dervizes*, several private villainies are reported, yet of others, as of the order of *calender*, we are assured from history that they profess virginity, and expose themselves to hardship, and a stricter devotion in their way; and generally it is said of all of them, that they go meanly clad, or half naked; some abstinent in eating and drinking, professing poverty, renouncing the world. Some can endure cutting and slashing, as if they were insensible; some profess perpetual silence, though urged with injuries and tortures; others have chains about their necks and arms, to shew that they are bound up from the world, &c. If such things may be found among heathens, no wonder that error boasts of them, for in both there is the same reason of men's pleasing themselves in such hardships, which is from a natural devotion, assisted by Satan's cunning, and the same design driven on by it; for the devil doth confirm heathens and Mohammedans in their false worship by the reverence and respect they carry to such practices.

[4.] Fourthly, Because religious holiness hath a beauty in it, and is very lovely, he doth all he can *to affect men with the highest reverence for these pretences of religious strictness;* so that they that will not be at pains to practise them, can bestow an excessive respect and admiration upon those that are grown famous in the use of such things; and by that means being almost adored, they are without doubt persuaded that all they teach or do is right, and in a doting fondness they multiply superstitious errors. Idolatry is supposed to have a great part of its rise from this. While men endeavoured to express their thankful and admiring remembrances of some excellent persons by setting up their pictures, their posterity began to worship them as gods. Pilgrimages were first set on foot by the respects that men gave to places that were made famous by persons and actions of more than ordinary holiness;[1] and because the devil found men so very apt to please themselves in paying such devotional reverences, he wrought upon their superstitious humour to multiply to themselves the occasions thereof, and by fabulous traditions sent them to places no otherwise made memorable than by dreams and impostures. Much of this you might see if you would accompany a caravan from Cairo

[1] Purchas' Pilg., lib. i. cap. 10, out of Eusebius, [as before.—G.]

to Mecca and Medina, where you would see the zealous pilgrims, with a great many orisons and prayers, compassing Abraham's house, kissing a stone which, they are told, fell from heaven; blessing themselves with a relic of the old vesture of Abraham's house, washing themselves in the pond, which, as their tradition goes, the angel shewed to Hagar; saluting the mountain of pardon, throwing stones in defiance of the devil, as their legend tells them Ishmael did; their prayers on the mountain of health, their visit to the prophet's tomb at Medina, &c.[1] The like might you observe among the papists, in their pilgrimages to Jerusalem and the sepulchre, to the Lady of Loretto's chapel, and other places. By such devices as these the unobservant people are transported with a pleasure, insomuch that they not only persuade themselves they are very devout in these reverences, but they also become unalterably fixed to these errors that do support these delightful practices, or as consequences do issue from them.

(6.) Sixthly, A more plausible argument for error than the learning and holiness of the persons that profess it, is that of *inspiration*, in which the devil soars aloft and pretends the highest divine warrant for his falsehoods; for 'God is truth,' and 'we know that no lie is of the truth.' Now to make men believe that God by his Holy Spirit doth in any manner dictate such opinions, or certainly reveal such things for truths, is one of the highest artifices that he can pretend to, and such a confirmation must it be to those that are so persuaded, that all disputes and doubtings must necessarily be silenced.

That the devil can thus 'transform himself into an angel of light,' we are assured from Scripture, which hath particularly cautioned us against this cheat. The apostasy of the later times, 1 Tim. iv. 1, the apostle foretells should be carried on by the prevalency of this pretence: 'Some shall depart from the faith, giving heed to seducing spirits.' That by 'spirits' there, doctrines are intended rather than doctors, is Mr Mede's interpretation;[2] but it will come all to one if we consider that the word 'spirit' carries more in it than either doctrine or doctor; for to call either the one or the other 'a spirit' would be intolerably harsh, if it were not for this, that that 'doctor' is hereby supposed to pretend an infallibility from the Spirit of God, or, which is all one, that he received his doctrine by some immediate revelation of the Spirit; so that by 'seducing spirits' must be men or doctrines that seduce others to believe them, by the pretence of the Spirit or inspiration; and that text of 1 John iv. 1 doth thus explain it: 'Believe not every spirit, but try the spirits whether they are of God,' which is as much as if he had said, Believe not every man or doctrine that shall pretend he is sent of God and hath his Spirit; and the reason there given makes it yet more plain, because many 'false prophets are gone out into the world;' so that these 'spirits' are 'false prophets,' men that pretend inspiration. And the warning, 'Believe not every spirit,' tells us that Satan doth with such a dexterity counterfeit the Spirit's inspirations, that holy and good men are in no small hazard to be deceived thereby. Most full to this purpose is that of 2 Thes. ii. 2, 'That ye be not soon shaken in mind, or be troubled, neither by spirit,

---

[1] *Vide* Purchas' Pilg., iii. chap. 5.   [2] 'Apostasy of the Latter Times,' p. 7.

nor by word, nor by letter as from us, as that the day of Christ is at hand;' where the several means of seduction are particularly reckoned as distinct from the doctrine and doctors, and by 'spirit' can be meant no other than a pretence of inspiration or revelation.[1]

It is evident then that Satan by this artifice useth to put a stamp of divine warrant upon his adulterate coin; and if we look into his practice, we shall in all ages find him at this work. Among heathens he frequently gained a repute to his superstitious idolatrous worship by this device. The men of greatest note among them feigned a spiritual commerce with the gods. Empedocles endeavoured to make the people believe that there was a kind of divinity in him, and affecting to be esteemed more than a man, cast himself into the burnings of Mongebel, that they might suppose him to have been taken up to the gods.[2] Pythagoras his fiction of a journey to hell was upon the same account. Philostratus and Cedrenus report no less of Apollonius, than that he had familiar converses with their supposed deities; and the like did they believe of their magi and priests; insomuch that some cunning politicians, observing how the vulgar were under a deep reverence to such pretences, gave it out that they had received their laws by divine inspirations. Numa Pompilius feigned he received his institutions from the nymph Ægeria, Lycurgus from Apollo; Minos the lawgiver of Candia boasted that Jupiter was his familiar. Mohammed also speaks as high this way as any; his Alcoran must be no less than a law received from God, and to that end he pretends a strange journey to heaven, and frequent converse with the angel Gabriel.

If we trace Satan in the errors which he hath raised up under the profession of the Scriptures, we may observe the same method. The Valentinians, Gnostics, Montanists talked as confidently of the Spirit as Moses or the prophets could do, and a great deal more; for some of them blasphemously called themselves the Paraclete or Comforter. Among the monsters which later ages produced, we still find the same strain: one saith he is Enoch, another styles himself the 'great prophet,' another hath raptures, and all immediately inspired. The papists have as much of this cheat among them as any other; and some of their learned defenders avouch their *lumen propheticum*, and *miraculorum gloria*, prophesies and miracles, to be the two eyes, or the sun and moon of their church; nay, by a strange transportment of folly, to the forfeiture of the reputation of learning and reason, they have so multiplied revelations that we have whole volumes of them, as the revelations of their St Bridget and others; and by wonderful credulity they have not only advanced apparent dreams and dotages to the honour of inspirations or visions, but upon this sandy foundation they have built a great many of their doctrines, as purgatory, transubstantiation, auricular confession, &c. By such warrants have they instituted festivals and founded several orders. The particulars of these things you may see more at large in Dr Stillingfleet and others. And that there might be nothing wanting that might make

[1] Prideaux, 'Orat. X. de spir. Seductoribus,' [as before.—G.]
[2] Mt. Ætna: Diog. Laert., viii. 67, 69-71: Horace, *ad Pizon*, 464, &c. Cf. Karsten, Empedocl's Agrigent. Carm. Reliquæ, p. 36, &c., and Apollon. ap Diog. Laert., viii. 52.—G.

them shamelessly impudent, they are not content to equal their fooleries with the Scriptures of God, as that the rule of their St Francis—for I shall only instance in him, omitting others for brevity sake—was not composed by the wisdom of man, but by God himself, and inspired by the Holy Ghost, but they advance their prophets above the apostles, and above Christ himself. Their St Benedict, if you will believe them, was rapt up to the third heavens, where he saw God face to face, and heard the choir of angels; and their St Francis was a nonsuch for miracles and revelations. Neither may we wonder that Satan should be forward in urging this cheat, when we consider,

[1.] First, *What a reverence men naturally carry to revelations, and how apt they are to be surprised with a hasty credulity.* An old prophecy, pretended to be found in a wall, or taken out of an old manuscript, of I know not what uncertain author, is usually more doted on than the plain and infallible rules of Scripture. This we may observe daily; and foreigners do much blame the English for a facile belief of such things; but it is a general fault of mankind, and we find even wise men forward in their persuasions upon meaner grounds than those that gain credit to old prophecies. For their antiquity and strangeness of discovery, especially at such times wherein the present posture of affairs seem to favour such predictions with a probability of such events, are more likely to get credit than these artificial imitations of the ways and garbs of the old prophets, and the cunning legerdemain of those that pretend to inspirations by seeming ecstasies, raptures, and confident declarations, &c.; nevertheless arrant cheats have by these ways deceived no mean men. Alvarus acknowledgeth that he honoured a woman as a saint that had visions and raptures as if really inspired—and the same apprehensions had the bishop and friars—who was afterward discovered to be a naughty woman.[1] Who shall then think it strange that the unobservant multitude should be deluded by such an art?

[2.] Secondly, Especially if we consider that *God himself took this course to signify his mind to men.* His prophets were divinely inspired, and the Scriptures were not of 'any private interpretation,' ἰδίας ἐπιλύσεως. The words that the penmen of Scriptures wrote were not the interpretations of their own private thoughts, 'for the prophecy came not in old time by the will of man, but holy men of God spake as they were moved by the Holy Ghost,' 2 Pet. i. 20, 21. Now though the prophecies of Scripture are sealed, and no more is to be added to them upon any pretence whatsoever, yet seeing there are promises left us of the 'giving of the Spirit,' of 'being taught and led by the Spirit,' it is an easy matter for Satan to beguile men into an expectation of prophetic inspirations, and a belief of what is pretended so to be; for all men do not or will not understand that these promises of the Spirit have no intendment of new and extraordinary immediate revelations, but only of the efficacious applications of what is already revealed in Scripture. This kind of revelation we acknowledge and teach, which is far enough from enthusiasm, that is, a pretended revelation of new truths, and we have reason to assert that

---

[1] Lib. ii. cap. 45, p. 87. [Diego Alvarez?—G.]

internal persuasions without the external word are to be avoided as Satan's cozenages.[1] But for all this, when men's minds are set a-gadding, if they meet with such as magnify their own dreams, and call their fancies visions, the suitableness of this to their humour makes them to reject our interpretations of these promises as false, and to persuade themselves that they are to be understood of such inspirations as the prophets of old had; and then they presently conclude they are to believe them, lest otherwise they should resist the Holy Ghost.

[3.] Thirdly, But *the advantage which the devil hath to work delusion upon by this pretence is a high motive to him to practise upon it.* For inspirations, visions, voices, impulses, dreams, and revelations are things wherein wicked impostors may by many ways and artifices play the counterfeits undiscovered. It is easy to prophesy false dreams, and to say, thus saith the Lord, when yet they do but lie, and the Lord never sent them nor commanded them, Jer. xxiii. 31; nay, it is easy, by tricks and illusions, to put that honour and credit upon their designs which they could not by their bare assertions, backed with all their art of seeming seriousness. The inventions of men that have been formerly successful in this deceit being now laid open to our knowledge, may make us more wary in our trust. Among the heathens you may find notable ways of deceits of this nature. The story of Hanno and Psappho is commonly known; they tamed birds and learned them to speak, 'Hanno and Psappho are gods,' and then set them at liberty, that men hearing such strange voices in the woods from birds, might imagine that these men were declared gods by special discovery. Mohammed's device of making a dove to come frequently to his ear, which he did by training her up to a use of picking corn out of it, served him for an evidence among the vulgar beholders, who knew not the true cause of it, of his immediate inspiration by the angel Gabriel, who, as he told them, whispered in his ear in the shape of a dove. The like knavery he practised for the confirmation of the truth of his Alcoran, by making a bull, taught before to come at a call or sign, to come to him with a chapiter upon his horns. Hector Boetius tells us of a like stratagem of a king of Scots, who, to animate his fainting subjects against the Picts that had beaten them, caused a man clothed in the shining skins of fishes, and with rotten wood, which, as a glow-worm in the night, represents a faint light, to come among them in the dark, and through a reed or hollow trunk, that the voice might not appear to be human, to incite them to a vigorous onset: this they took to be an angel bringing them this command from heaven, and accordingly fought and prevailed. Crafty Benedict, who was afterward pope under the name of Boniface VIII., made simple Celestine V. give over the popedom by conveying to him a voice through a reed to this purpose: Celestine, Celestine, renounce the papacy, give it over, if thou wouldst be saved, the burden is beyond thy strength, &c. The silly man, taking this for a revelation from heaven, quitted his chair and left it for that crafty fox Benedict.

[1] Whitaker, Di[sputatio de Sacra] Script. contra [Robertum Bellarminum et] Stapletonum, lib. i. cap. 10, p. 121, [1588, 4to, has been translated and edited for the Parker Society by Professor Fitzgerald, 1849, 8vo.—G.]

Not very many years since the same trick was played in this country to a man of revelations—Paul Hobson—who called himself David in spirit. When he had wearied his entertainer with a long stay, he quitted himself of his company, as I was credibly informed, by a policy which he perceived would well suit with the man's conceitedness, for through a reed in the night-time he tells him that he must go into Wales, or some such country, and there preach the gospel; the next morning the man avouches a revelation from God to go elsewhere, and so departs. These instances shew you how cunningly a cheating knave may carry on a pretence of revelation or vision. And yet this is not all the advantage which the devil hath in this matter, though it is an advantage which he sometime makes use of when he is fitted with suitable instruments. But he works most dangerously when he so acts upon men that they themselves believe they have visions, raptures, and revelations, for some are really persuaded that it is so with them. Neither is it strange that men should be deluded into an apprehension that they hear and see what they do not; in fevers, frenzies, and madness we clearly see it to be so; and who can convince such persons of their mistakes, when with as high a confidence as may be they contend that they are not deceived? Shall we think it strange that Satan hath ways of conveying false apprehensions upon men's minds? No, surely. Do we not see that the senses may be cheated, and that the fancies of men may be corrupted? Is it not easy for him to convey voices to the ear, or shapes and representations to the eye? and in such cases, what can ordinarily hinder a belief that they hear or see such things? But he needs not always work upon the fancy by the senses. If he hath the advantage of a crazy distempered fancy, as commonly he hath in melancholy persons, he can so strongly fix his suggestions upon them, and so effectually set the fancy on work to embrace them, that without any appearance of madness they will persuade themselves that they have discoveries from God, impulses by his Spirit, scriptures set upon their hearts, and what not; and because they feel the workings of these things within them, it is impossible to make them so much as suspect that they are deceived. Do but consider the power of any fancy in a melancholic person, and you may easily apprehend how Satan works in such delusions. Melancholy doth strangely pervert the imagination, and will beget in men wonderful misapprehensions, and that sometimes doth bewitch them into peremptory, uncontrollable belief of their fancy. It is a vehement, confident humour, what way soever it takes; the imagination thus corrupted hath an enormous strength, so that if it fix upon things never so absurd or irrational, it is not reducible by the strongest reasons. If such a man conceits himself dead, or that he is transformed to a wolf or cat, or that he is made of glass, as many in this distemper have done, there is no persuasion to the contrary that can take place with him. Now if this humour be taken up with divine matters, as usually it doth, for it hath a natural inclination to religious things, it still acts with fierceness and confidence, and there are many things often concomitant to such actings, that if it misconceit inspiration or prophecy, the parties themselves are not only bound up under that persuasion, but even unwary spectators are deluded. For sometime a melancholy imagination is not wholly corrupt, but only in respect of some one or two particulars, whilst in other things it acts regularly, and then neither they nor others, that are unacquainted with such cases, are so apt to suspect that they are mistaken in these things, while they act rationally and soberly in other matters. Sometime they have vehement fits of surprisal—for the humour hath its ebbings and flowings—and this gives them occasion to apprehend that something doth supernaturally act or raise them, and then when the things they speak are for the matter of them of religious concern and odd notions—for the humour flies high and bounds not itself with ordinary things—and withal uttered in Scripture rhetoric and with fervency and urgency of spirit—when these things concur, there is such an appearance of inspiration that the parties themselves and others rest fully persuaded that it is so.

(7.) Seventhly, *Pretended and counterfeit miracles the devil makes much use of to countenance error, and this is also one of his strongholds;* for he suggests that God himself bears witness by these signs, wonders, and miracles to such erroneous doctrine as seems to be concerned[1] by them.

That the devil cannot work a true miracle hath been discoursed before, but that he can perform many strange things, and such as may beget admiration, none denies; and that by such unwonted actions he usually endeavours to justify false doctrines, and to set them off with the appearance of divine approbation, we are sufficiently forewarned in the Scriptures.[2] Jannes and Jambres resisted Moses by false miracles. In Deut. xiii. 1, God speaks of the signs and wonders of false prophets, who would' by that means seek to seduce the people to follow after other gods. Christ also, in Mat. xxiv. 24, foretells that 'false Christs and false prophets shall arise, and shew great signs and wonders, insomuch that, if it were possible, they shall deceive the very elect,' and puts a special note of caution upon it: 'Behold, I have told you before.' And to the same purpose is that of Paul concerning Antichrist, 2 Thes. ii. 9, where he tells us of powerful 'signs and wonders by the working of Satan,' who doth all the while only lie and cheat that he may draw men to error.

If we make inquiry how Satan hath managed this engine, we shall observe not only his diligence in using it on all occasions to countenance all kind of errors both in paganism and Christianity, but also his subtle dexterity by cheating men with forgeries and falsehood.

Heathenish idolatry, among other helps for its advancement, wanted not this. The oracles and responses, which were common before the coming of Christ, were esteemed as miraculous confirmations of the truth of the deities which they worshipped; the movings and speakings of their statues[3] were arguments that the operative presence of some celestial *Numen* was affixed to such an image. In some places the solemn sacrifices are never performed without a seeming miracle. As in Nova Zembla, where the priest's trances, his running a sword

---

[1] Query, 'confirmed'?—G.
[2] Miraculum voco, quicquid arduum aut insolitum, supra spem aut facultatem mirantis apparet.—*Aug. de utilitat. cred. contra Manich.*, cap. xvi.
[3] Spelled 'statuas.'—G.

into his belly, his making his head and shoulder fall off his body into a kettle of hot water by the drawing of a line, and then his reviving again perfect and entire, without maim or hurt, are all strange, astonishing things to the beholders.[1] But besides such things as these, which are standing constant wonders, we read of some that have had, as it were, a gift of miracles, that they might be eminently instrumental to promote and honour paganism. All histories agree that Simon Magus did so many strange things at Rome—as the causing an image to walk, turning stones into bread, transforming himself into several shapes, flying in the air, &c.—that he was esteemed a god. Philostratus and Cedrenus[2] report great things of Apollonius [of Tyana,] as that he could deliver cities from scorpions, serpents, earthquakes, &c., and that many miracles were wrought by him. This man Satan raised up in an extraordinary manner to revive the honour of paganism, that it might at least vie with Christianity. And though few ever attained to that height which Apollonius and Simon Magus reached unto, yet have we several instances of great things done now and then by some singular persons upon a special occasion, which Satan improved to his advantage. Vespasian cured a lame and blind man.[3] Adrianus cured a blind woman; and which is more, after he was dead, by the touch of his body, a man of Pannonia who was born blind received his sight.[4] Valerius Maximus tells of many strange things, and particularly of a vestal virgin that drew water into a sieve. As Livy tells of another, Claudia by name, who with her girdle drew the ship to the shore which carried the mother of their gods, when neither strength of men nor oxen could do it.[5]

Errors under profession of Christianity have been supported and propagated by the boast of miracles. A clear instance for this we have in popery, that religion being a perpetual boast of wonders. To let pass their great miracle of transubstantiation, which, as one hath lately demonstrated, is a bundle of miracles, or contradictions rather,[6] because it appears not to the senses of any man, and consequently is not capable of being an argument to prove any of their opinions. We have abundance of strange things related by them, as proofs of some doctrines of theirs in particular, as purgatory, invocation of saints, transubstantiation, &c., and of their profession in the general, devils cast out, blind and lame cured, dead raised, and what not; it would be endless to recite particulars. It would take a long time to tell what their St Francis hath done—how he fetched water out of a rock, how he was homaged by fowls and fishes, how he made a fountain in Marchia run wine, and how far he exceeded Christ himself in wonderful feats. Christ did nothing which St Francis did not do, nay, he did many more things than Christ did: Christ turned water into wine but once, but St Francis did it thrice; Christ was once transfigured, but St Francis twenty times; he and his brethren raised above a thousand to life, cast out more than a thousand devils,

---

[1] Johnson's relat. in Hakluyt, tom. i.
[2] Misprinted 'Cedremus,' instead of Cedrenus Georgius. See Smith's 'Dictionary,' *sub nomine.*—G.   [3] Cornel. Tacit. Histor., lib. iv.
[4] Ætius Spartianus *in vit.* Adriani.   [5] De secundo bello Punico.
[6] Mr Baxter, 'Full and Easy Satisfaction, [which is the true and safe Religion.' 1674. 4to.—G.] cap. 4.

&c.[1] Their Dominicus raised three dead men to life. Their Zeverius,[2] while he was alive, did many miracles, and after he was dead his body lay fifteen months sweetly smelling, without any taint of corruption. It is irksome to repeat their stories; abundance of such stuff might be added out of their own writings, the design of all which is to prove, to those that are so prodigal of their faith as to believe them, that they only are the true church, and that by this note among others they may be known to be so.

But let us turn aside a little to observe Satan's cunning in this pretence of miracles; let things be soberly weighed, and we may see enough of the cheat. This great boast is, as Austin hath it, resolved into one of these two—either the figments of lying men, or the craft of deceitful spirits: *Vel figmenta hominum mendacium, vel portenta fallacium spirituum.*

As to the first of these, it is evident that a great many things that have been taken by the vulgar for mighty wonders, were nothing but the knaveries of impostors, who in this matter have used a threefold cunning.

[1.] First, *By mere juggling and forgery in confederacies and private contrivances they have set upon the stage persons before instructed to act their parts, or things aforehand prepared, to pretend to be what they were not, that others might seem to do what they did not, and all to amaze those that know not the bottom of the matter.* Of this nature was Mohammed's dove and bull, who were privately trained up to that obedience and familiarity which they used to him. The pagan priests were not altogether to seek in this piece of art. Lucian tells us of one Alexander, who nourished and tamed a serpent, and made the people of Pontus believe that it was the god Æsculapius, and doubtless the idol priests improved their private artificial contrivances: as of the movings of their images, as that of Venus made by Dædalus, which by the means of quicksilver enclosed could stir itself;[3] their eating and drinking, as in the story of Bel in the Apochryphal adjections to the Book of Daniel; their responses, and several other appearances; as of the paper head of Adonis or Osiris, which, as Lucian reports, comes swimming down the river every year from Egypt to Byblos, &c.; these and such like they improved as evidences of the power, knowledge, and reality of their gods. And though in the prevalency of idolatry, where there was no considerable party to oppose, their cheats were not always discovered, yet we have no reason to imagine that the priests of those days were so honest that they were only deceived by the devil's craft, and did not in a villainous design purposely endeavour the delusion of others. If we had no other grounds for a just suspicion in these cases, the famous instances of the abuse of Paulina at the temple of Isis in Rome, in the reign of the emperor Tiberius, by the procurement of Mondus, who corrupted the priest of Anubis to signify to her the love of their god, and under that coverture gratified the lust of Mondus, mentioned by Josephus.[4] And that of Tyrannus,

---

[1] Nihil fecit Christus quod Franciscus non fecit, imo plura fecit quam Christus.—*Barthol. de Pisis lib. conformitat.*, fol. 1149.

[2] Query, Xavier, often spelled Xavierus?—G.

[3] Arist., lib. i. de anima.

[4] Antiquitat. Judæ., lib. xviii. cap. 14.

priest of Saturn in Alexandria, who by the like pretence of the love of Saturn, adulterated most of the fairest dames of the city, mentioned by Ruffinus.[1] These would sufficiently witness that the priests of those times were apt enough to abuse the people at the rate we have been speaking of. In popery nothing hath been more ordinary. Who knows not the story of the holy maid of Kent and the boy of Bilson? How common is it with them to play tricks with women troubled with hysterical distempers; and to pretend the casting out of devils, when they have only to deal with a natural disease. Not very many years since they practised upon a poor young woman at Durham, and made great boasts of their exorcisms, relics, and holy water against the devil, with whom they would have all believe she was possessed, when the event discovered that her fits were only the fits of the mother. I myself, and some others in this place, have seen those fits allayed by the fume of tobacco blown into her mouth, to the shame and apparent detection of that artifice. I might mention the legerdemain of Antonius of Padua, who made his horse adore the host, for the conversion of a heretic; the finding of the images of St Paul and St Dominic in a church at Venice, with this inscription for Paul, 'By this man you may come to Christ;' and this for Dominic, 'But by this man you may do it easilier:' and the honour put upon Garnet, by his image on straw,[2] found at his execution, in all probability by him that made it and threw it down, or by his confederate: but these are enough to shew the honesty of these kind of men.

[2.] Secondly, *They have also a cunning of ascribing effects to wrong causes, and by that means they make those things wonders that are none.* Mohammed called his fits of falling-sickness ecstasies or trances. Austin tells us the heathens were notable at this: the burning lamp in the temple of Venus, though only the work of art, was interpreted to be a constant miracle of that deity.[3] The image which, in another temple, hung in the air, by ignorant gazers was accounted a wonder, when indeed the loadstone in the roof and pavement, though unseen, was the cause of it. The Sidonians were confirmed in their constant annual lamentations of Adonis, by a mock miracle of the redness of the river Adonis at one time of the year constantly; they take it to be blood, when it is nothing else but the colouring of the water by the dust of red earth or *minium*, which the winds constantly at that time of the year from mount Libanus do drive into the water.[4] Neither are the papists out in this point. I will only instance in that observation of Dr Jenison, to confirm the doctrine and practice of invocation:[5] they take the advantage of sovereign baths and waters, and where they espy any fountain good against the stone, or other diseases, presently there is the statue or image of some saint or other erected by it, by whose virtue the cure and miracle must seem to be done; or some chapel is erected to this or that saint, to whom prayers before and thanks after washing must be offered.

[3.] Thirdly, where the two former fail, men that devote themselves

---

[1] Eccles. Hist., lib. xi. cap. 25.   [2] See Lathbury's 'Guy Fawkes.' 1840.—G.
[3] De Civitate Dei, lib. xxi. cap. 6.
[4] Purchas, 'Pilg.' Asia, lib. i. cap. 17.   Heylin, 'Cosmography,' p. 689.
[5] 'Height of Israel's Idolatry,' cap. 12.

to this kind of service *imitate their father the devil, and fall to plain lying and devised fables.* Idolatry was mainly underpropped by fabulous stories; and no wonder, when they esteemed it a pious fraud to nourish piety towards the gods, in which case, as Polybius saith, though their writers speak monsters, and write childish, absurd, and impossible things, yet are they to be pardoned for their good intent.[1] Among the papists what less can be expected, when the same principle is entertained among them? Canus, and Ludovicus Vives mentioned by him,[2] as also some few others, do exceedingly blame that blind piety of coining lies for religion, and feigning histories for the credit of their opinions; but while they with great freedom and ingenuity do tax the fables of their own party, they do plainly acknowledge that they are too much guilty of feigning, insomuch that not only the author of the Golden Legend is branded with the characters of a brazen face and a leaden heart, but also Gregory's Dialogues and Bede's History are blamed by him, as containing narrations of miracles taken upon trust from the reports of the vulgar.[3] And indeed the wonders they talk of are so strange, so unlikely, so ridiculous and absurd some of them, that except a man offer violence to his reason, and wilfully shut his eyes against the clear evidences of suspicion, he cannot think they are anything else than dreams and fables, no better than Æsop's. You may meet with several catalogues of them in protestant writers:[4] as their St Swithin's making whole a basket of broken eggs by the sign of the cross; Patricius his making the stolen sheep to bleat in the thief's belly after he had eaten it; their St Bridget's bacon, which in great charity she gave to a hungry dog, was found again in her kettle; Dionysius after he was beheaded carried his head in his hand three French miles; St Dunstan took the devil by the nose with his tongs till he made him roar; Dominicus made him hold the candle till he burnt his fingers; St Lupus imprisoned the devil in a pot all night; a chapel of the Virgin Mary was translated from Palestine to Loretto; a consecrated host, being put into a hive of bees to cure them of the murrain, was so devoutly entertained that the bees built a chapel in the hive, with doors, windows, steeple, and bells, erected an altar and laid the host upon it, sung their canonical hours, and kept their watches by night, as monks used to do in their cloisters, &c. Who would ever imagine that men of any seriousness could satisfy themselves with such childish fopperies? These are the usual ways by which men of design have raised the noise of miracles.

The other part of Satan's coming[5] relates to himself and his own actions. When his agents can go no further in the trade of miracle-making, he as a spirit doth often make use of his power, knowledge, and agility, by which he can indeed do things incredible and to be wondered at: *Portenta fallacium spirituum.* It is nothing for him, by his knowledge of affairs at a distance, of the private endeavours or expressed resolves of princes, to prognosticate future events. By

---

[1] Hist., lib. xvi.
[2] Loc., lib. xi. cap. 6. [Query, Camus, Bp. of Belley—the reference being to his 'Agathonphile.' Rouen, 1641?—G.]
[3] *Vide* Chamier, Panst., tom. 5, lib. ii. cap. 15.
[4] Prideaux, Orat. de impost. mendaciis; Rome's Triumphs; Mr Baxter's 'Safe Religion,' p. 168. [1657. 8vo.—G.]   [5] Query, 'cunning'?—ED.

his power over the bodies of men, he can, with the help of inclinations and advantages, do much to bring a man into a trance, or take the opportunity of a fit of an apoplexy, and then, like a cunning juggler, pretend, by I know not what nor whom, to raise a man from death. He knows the secret powers and virtues of things, and by private applications of them may easily supply spirits, remove obstructions, and so cure lameness, blindness, and many other distempers, and then give the honour of the cure to what person or occasion may best fit his design; so that either by the officious lies of his vassals, or the exerting of his own power on suitable objects at fit times, he hath made a great noise of signs and wonders in the world. And this stratagem of his hath ever been at hand to gain a repute to false doctrine. And the rather doth he insist upon this,

First, Because true miracles are a divine testimony to truth. As Nicodemus argued, John iii. 2, 'No man could do these miracles that thou doest except God be with him.' And there were solemn occasions wherein they were necessary; as when God gave public discoveries of his mind before the Scriptures were written; and also when he altered the economy of the Old Testament and settled that of the New. In these cases it was necessary that God should confirm his word by miracles. But now, though these ends of miracles are ceased, though God hath so settled and fixed the rule of our obedience and worship that no other gospel or rule is to be expected, and consequently no need of new miracles, where the certain account of the old miracles are sufficient attestations of old and unalterable truths; nay, though God have expressly told us, Deut. xiii. 1, that no miracle—though it should come to pass, and could not be discovered to be a lie—should prevail with us to forsake the established truths and ways of Scripture, or to entertain anything contrary to it; yet doth Satan exercise herein a proud imitation of the supreme majesty, and withal doth so dazzle the minds of the weaker sort of men—who are more apt to consider the wonder than to suspect the design—that, without due heed given to the cautions which God hath laid before us in that particular, they are ready to interpret them to be God's witness to this or that doctrine, to which they seem to be appendant.

Secondly, Because Satan hath a more than ordinary advantage to feign miracles; he doth more industriously set himself to pretend them and to urge them for the accomplishment of his ends. It is an easy work to prevail with men that are wholly devoted to their own interest, under the mask of religion to say and do anything that may further their design; and the business of miracles is so imitable by art, through the ignorance and heedlessness of men, that with a small labour Satan can do it at pleasure. The secret powers of nature—such as that of the loadstone—by a dexterous application brought into act in a fitly-contrived subject, will seem miraculous to those that see not the secret springs of those actions. There have been artificial contrivances of motions which, had they been disguised under a religious form, and directed to such an end, might have passed for greater miracles than many which we have mentioned. Such was the dove of Archyas, which did fly in the air as if it had been a living creature.[1]

---

[1] [Gellius, x. 12.—G.] Heylin, 'Cosmographie,' p. 399, [1666 folio.—G.]

Such was the fly of Regiomontanus, and the eagle presented to the Emperor Maximilian, which, in the compass of their little bodies, contained so many springs and wheels as were sufficient to give them motion, and to direct their courses as if they had been animated. Albertus Magnus his artificial man, and the silver galley and tritons made by a goldsmith at Paris,[1] were rare pieces of art—their motions so certain and steady, that they seemed to have life and understanding. If art can do all this, how much more may we suppose can Satan do! how easily can he make apparitions, present strange sights to the eye and voices to the ear, and, by putting out his power, do a thousand things astonishing and wonderful!

(8.) Eighthly, *Sometimes Satan pleads for error, from the ease, peace, or other advantages which men pretend they have received since they engaged in such a way or received such a persuasion.* This is an argument from the effect, and frequently used to confirm the minds of men in their opinions. Hence they satisfy themselves with these reasonings: 'I was before always under fears and uncertainties; I never was at peace or rest in my mind. I tried several courses, followed several parties, but I never had satisfaction or comfort till now, and by this I know that I am in a right way.' Others argue after the same manner from their abundance and outward prosperity: 'I met with nothing but crosses and losses before, but now God hath blessed me with an increase of substance, prospered my trade and undertakings,' &c. These, though apparently weak and deceitful grounds, are reputed strong and conclusive to those that are first resolved upon an error. For men are so willing to justify themselves in what they have undertaken, that they greedily catch at anything that hath the least appearance of probability to answer their ends.

This plea of satisfaction is commonly from one of these two things:

1. First, *From inward peace and contentment of mind.* Satan knows that peace is the thing to which a man sacrificeth all his labours and travail. This he seeks, though often in a wrong way, and by wrong means. He knows also that true peace is only the daughter of truth, 'the ways whereof are pleasantness, and the paths whereof are peace;' neither is he ignorant of the delights which a man hath, by enjoying himself in the sweet repose of a contented mind, that he may charm the hearts of the erroneous into a confidence and assurance that they have taken a right course; he doth all he can to further a false peace in them, and to this purpose he commonly useth this method:—

[1.] First, He doth all he can to *unsettle them from the foundation of truth upon which they were bottomed.* He labours to render things suspicious, doubtful, or uncertain. This some have noted from 2 Thes. ii. 2, where Satan's first attempts are to shake their minds, not only by disquiet, of which we are next to speak, but by alteration of their judgment; for mind is sometimes taken for sentence, opinion, judgment, as 1 Cor. ii. 16, 'We have the mind of Christ;' and 1 Cor. i. 10, 'In the same mind, and in the same judgment.'[2]

[2.] Secondly, His second approach is to *raise a storm of restless*

---

[1] For all above, see Heylin, as before.—G.
[2] Sclater in loc. νοῦς for γνώμη, [as before.—G.]

disquiet upon that uncertainty; and in order to his intended design, he usually fills them with the utmost anxiety of mind, and makes their thoughts, like a tempestuous sea, dash one against another. This piece of his art is noted in the fore-cited place, that 'ye be not shaken in mind, or troubled:' the word signifies a great perplexity, θροεῖσθαι. And this is a usual method which the false teachers among the Galatians practised; they first troubled them, and then endeavoured by the advantage of that trouble to pervert the gospel of Christ, Gal. i. 7, and v. 12. To effect both these, he doth amuse them with all the objections that can be raised. If he can say anything of the antiquity of the error, the number, wisdom, learning, or authority of those that embrace it, they are sure to hear of these things to the full. The danger of continuing as they were, and the happiness of the new doctrine, are represented with all aggravating circumstances; and these so often, that their thoughts have no rest: and if this restlessness does wound or weaken them, he pursues with a high hand. These ways of disturbing the unsettled mind are hinted to us in the aforesaid place—spirit, word, letter, anything that carries a seeming authority to unsettle, or power to amaze and distress. And we may here further note, that where the minds of men are discomposed with other fears or disquiets, Satan is ready to improve them to this use, so that commonly when the word of God begins to work at first upon the consciences of men, to awaken them to the consideration of their sin and danger, the adversary is then very busy with them to inveigle them into some error or other.

[3.] Thirdly, Having thoroughly prepared the mind with restless fears, he then advanceth forward with the *proffers of peace and comfort in the way of error which he proposeth;* and in this case error will boast much, 'Come to me, and ye shall find rest for your souls.' How grateful and welcome the confident proffers of ease and satisfaction are to a tossed and disquieted mind, any man will easily imagine. It is usually thus: men that are tired out will easily embrace anything for ease. A man in this case may be wrought upon like wax, to receive any impression; he will fasten on anything, true or false, that doth but promise comfort.

[4.] Fourthly, The completement of his method is *to please the man in the fruition of the peace promised;* and this he labours to do, not only to fix the man in his delusion, but to make that man brag of ease, to be a snare to others. And it is easy for the devil to do this: for, *first,* The novelty of a new opinion doth naturally please, especially if it give any seeming commendation for discovery or singularity. We see men are fond of their own inventions, and delighted to be lifted up above others. *Secondly,* Satan can easily allay the storm which he himself raised: he gives over to molest with anxious thoughts—on the the contrary, he suggests thoughts of satisfaction. *Thirdly,* And whatever he can do in a natural way to raise up our passions of joy and delight, he will be sure to do it now, to ravishment and excess if he can; and then he not only makes these men sure—for what argument can stand before such a confidence?—but hath an active instrument for the allurement of such as cannot discover these methods.

2. Secondly, *Outward prosperity* is the other common plea for

error. Though successes, plenty, and abundance of worldly comforts argue of themselves neither love nor hatred, truth nor falsehood—because the wise providence of God, for holy ends and reasons often undiscerned by us, permits often the tabernacles of robbers to prosper, and permits those that 'deal treacherously' with the truths of God 'to be planted, to take root, to grow, yea, to bring forth fruit'—nevertheless if in a way of error they meet with outward blessings, they are apt to ascribe all to their errors, and to say as Israel, Hosea ii. 5, 'I will go after my lovers that gave me my bread and my water, my wool and my flax, mine oil and my drink,' without any serious consideration of God's common bounty, which upon far other accounts, 'gives them corn, and wine, and oil, and multiplies their silver and gold,' which they prepared for Baal, ver. 8. I shall not need to add anything further for the proof and explanation of this than what we have in Jer. xliv. 17, 18, where the Jews expressly advance their idolatrous worship as the right way, and confirm themselves even to obstinacy in the pursuit of it, upon this reason: 'We will certainly do whatsoever thing goeth out of our own mouth, to burn incense to the queen of heaven . . . . for then had we plenty of victuals, and were well, and saw no evil: but since we left off to burn incense to the queen of heaven, and to pour out our drink-offerings unto her, we have wanted all things, and have been consumed by the sword and by the famine.'

(9.) Ninthly, Instead of better arguments, Satan usually makes *lies his refuge:* and these respect either the truth which he would cry down, or the errors which he would set up.

Those lies that are managed against truth are of two sorts: mistakes and misrepresentations of its doctrines, or calumnies against the persons and actions of those that take part with it.

Those lies that are proper to bespatter a truth withal are such as tend to render it unlovely, inconvenient, or dangerous. Satan hath never been a-wanting to raise up mists and fogs to eclipse the shining beauty of truth. Sometime he persuades men that it is a novelty, and contrary to the tradition of the fathers; and then, if an error had been once upon the stage before, and had again been hissed out of the world, when it peeps out again into the world, its former impudency is made an argument for its antiquity, and truth is decried as novel. Or if it be but an error of yesterday, and hath only obtained an age or two, then the ghosts of our forefathers are conjured up as witnesses, and the plea runs current, What has become of your fathers? or, are you wiser than your fathers? are they all damned? These were insisted on by the heathens: the gods of the country and the worship of their fathers, they thought, should not be forsaken for Christianity, which they judged was but a novelty in comparison of paganism. Of the same extract is that old song of the papists, 'Where was your religion before Luther?' and to this purpose they talk of the succession of their bishops and popes. And other errors grow a little pert and confident, if they can but find a pattern or sample for themselves among the old heresies. Sometime he endeavours to bring truth into suspicion, by rendering it a dangerous encroachment upon the rights and privileges of men, as if it would turn all upside down, and introduce factions and confusions. This clamour was raised against the gospel, that it would subvert the doctrine of Moses and the law. Sometimes he clothes the opinions of truth with an ugly dress, and misrepresents it to the world as guilty of strange inferences and absurdities, which only arise from a wrong stating of the questions; and where it doth really differ from error, he endeavours to widen the differences to an inconvenient distance, so that if it go a mile from error, Satan will have it to go two: if truth teach justification by faith, error represents it as denying all care of holiness and good works; if truth say bare moral virtues are not sufficient without grace, error presently accuseth it as denying any necessary use of morality, or affirming that moral virtues are obstructions and hindrances to salvation. It were easy to note abundance of such instances.

As for calumnies against the persons and actions of those that are assertors of truth, it is well known for an old threadbare design, by which Satan hath gained not a little. Machiavel borrowed the policy from him, and formed it into a maxim; for he found by experience that where strong slanders had set in their teeth, though never so unjustly, the wounds were never throughly healed; for some that heard the report of the slander never heard the vindication, and those that did were not always so unprejudiced as to free themselves from all suspicion, but still something remained usually upon their spirits for ever after; and that, like a secret venom, poisons all that could be said or done by the persons that wrongfully fell under their prejudice, and did not a little derogate from the authority and power of the truths which they delivered.

The friends of truth have always to their cost found it so. Christ himself escaped not the lies and censures of men when he did the greatest miracles; they raised this calumny against him, that 'he cast out devils by Beelzebub, the prince of devils,' John viii. 48. When he shewed the most compassionate condescensions, they called him 'a man gluttonous, a wine-bibber, a friend of publicans and sinners;' and at last, upon a misinterpretation of his speeches, 'I will destroy this temple, and in three days I will build it up,' Mat. xxvi. 61, they arraigned and condemned him for blasphemy; and his servants have, according to what he foretold, drunk of the same cup: the more eminent in service the greater draught. Paul, a chosen vessel, met with much of this unjust dealing: he was accused, Acts xxi. 28, as speaking against the people, the law, and the temple, and, chap. xxiv. 5, called 'a pestilent fellow, a mover of sedition, a profaner of the temple.' Neither can we wonder at this, that the greatest innocency or highest degree of holiness is no armour or proof against the sharp arrows of a lying tongue; when we read this as one of Satan's great characters, that he is 'the accuser of the brethren,' and that his agents are so perfectly instructed in this art that they are also branded with the same mark of 'false accusers,' Jude 10. It is well known how the primitive Christians were used: they were accounted 'the filth and offscouring of all things;' there could be nothing that could render them odious or ridiculous but they were aspersed with it; as that they 'sacrificed infants, worshipped the sun, and used promiscuous uncleanness;' nay, whatever plague or disaster befell their neighbours, they were sure to carry the blame. And we might trace this stratagem down to our own days. Luther in his time was the common butt for all the poisoned arrows of the papists' calumny; which so exceeded all bounds of sobriety and prudence that they devised a romance of his death, how he was choked of the devil; that before he died he desired his corpse might be carried into the church and adored with divine worship; and that after his death the excessive stench of his carcase forced all his friends to forsake him. All this and more to this purpose they published while he was alive; whose slanders, worthy only of laughter, he refuted by his own pen. The like fury they expressed against Calvin by their Bolsecus, whom they set on work to fill a book with impudent lies against him. Neither did Beza, Junius, or any other of note escape without some slander or other. How unjustly the Arians of old accused Athanasius of uncleanness, and of bereaving Arsenius of his arm, is sufficiently known in history.[1]

But the devil's malice doth not always run in the dirty channel of odious calumnies. He hath sometimes a more cleanly conveyance for his lies against holy men. In prosecution of the same design, it is a fair colour for error if he can abuse the name and credit of renowned champions of truth, by fathering an error upon them which they never owned. By this means he doth not only grace a false doctrine with the authority of an eminent person, whose estimation might be a snare to some well-meaning persons, but weakens the truth, by bringing a faithful assertor of it into suspicion of holding, at least in some points, dangerous opinions; by which many are affrighted from entertaining anything that they write or preach. For though they may be confessedly sound in the most weighty doctrines, yet if it be once buzzed abroad that they are in anything unsound, this dead fly spoils all the precious ointment. And the matter were yet the less if there were any just cause for such a prejudice; but such is Satan's art, that if a man explains the same truth, but in different words and forms of speech than those that others have been used unto; or if he casts it into a more convenient mould, that, by laying aside doubtful or flexible expressions, it may be more safely guarded from the exceptions of the adversaries; especially if he carefully choose his path betwixt the extremes on either hand,—this is enough for Satan to catch at, and presently he bestows upon him the names of the very errors which he most strenuously opposeth; nay, sometimes if he mention anything above the reach or acquaintance of those that hear him, it is well if he escapes the charge of heresy, and that he meets not with the lot of Virgilius, bishop of Salzburg, who was judged no less than heretical for venting his opinion concerning the antipodes.[2] I know men do such things in their zeal; but while they do so they are concerned to consider how Satan doth abuse their good meaning to the disservice of truth.

As Satan's design in bespattering the actions and doctrines of good men is to bring the truth they profess into a suspicion of falsehood, and to advance the contrary errors to the place and credit of truth, so doth he use a skill proportionable to his design. And though he be

---

[1] Theod. Hist., [*sub nominibus.*—G.]
[2] *Vide* Harvæi, Præfat. in Sang. Circulo; and Heylin, Cosmogr. p. 399.

so impudent that he will not blush at the contrivance of the most gross and malicious lie, yet withal he is so cunning that he studiously endeavours some probable rise for his slanders, and commonly he takes this course:—

[1.] First, He doth all he can *to corrupt the professors of truth.* If riches or honours will tempt them to be proud, high-minded, contentious, or extravagant, he plies them with these weapons; if the pleasures of the flesh and world be more likely to besot them, or to make them sensual, earthly, or loose, he incessantly lays those baits before them; if fears and persecutions can affright them out of duty, if injuries and provocations may prejudice them into a froward or wayward temper, he will certainly urge them by such occasions; and when he hath prevailed in any measure, he is sure to aggravate every circumstance to its utmost height, and upon that advantage to make additions of a great many things beyond what they can be justly accused of. This old device Paul, in Rom. ii. 24, takes notice of concerning the Jews, whose breach of the law so dishonoured God that 'the name of God was blasphemed among the Gentiles through them.' The Jews lived wickedly, and their wicked lives was a current argument among the Gentiles to confirm them in paganism; for they judged the law of God could not approve itself to be better than their own, when the professors of it were so naught. To prevent this mischief, we are seriously warned to be carefully strict in all our stations, 'that the name of God and his doctrine be not blasphemed,' 1 Tim. vi. 1; Titus ii. 5.

[2.] Secondly, *Whatever miscarriages any professor of truth is guilty of, Satan takes care that it be presently charged upon all the profession.* If any one offend, it is matter of public blame; much more if any company or party shall run into extravagances, or do actions strange and unjustifiable; those that agree with them in the general name of their profession, though they differ as far from their wild opinions and practices as their enemies do, shall still be upbraided with their follies. We see this practised daily by differing parties; according to what was foretold in 2 Pet. ii. 2, 'false prophets' seduce a great number of Christians to follow their pernicious ways, and by reason of their wild, ungodly behaviour, 'the whole way of truth was evil spoken of.'

[3.] Thirdly, *The least slip or infirmity of the children of truth the devil is ready to bring upon the stage;* and they that will not charge themselves as offenders for very great evils, will yet object, to the disparagement of truth, the smallest mistakes of others: a mote in the eye of the lovers of truth shall be espied when a beam in the eye of falsehood shall pass for nothing.

[4.] Fourthly, *Slanderous aspersions are sometimes raised from a simple mistake of actions, and their grounds or manner of performance, and sometimes from a malicious misrepresentation.* The devil seldom acts from a simple mistake; but he will either suborn the passionate opposers to a wilful perverting of the true management of things, or will by a false account of things take the advantage of their prejudice, to make men believe that such things have been said or done, which indeed never were. The Christians in the primitive times were reported to be bloody men, and that they did kill men in sacrifice, and did eat their flesh and drink their blood; and this was only occasioned by their doctrine and use of the sacrament of the body and blood of Christ. They were accused for promiscuous uncleanness with one another, and this only because they taught that there was no distinction of male and female in respect of justification, and that they were all brethren and sisters in Christ. This account Tertullian gives of the calumnies of those times, and others have noted the like occasions of other abuses of them.[1] They were reported to worship the sun, because they in times of persecution were forced to meet early in the fields, and were often seen undispersed at sunrising. They were reported to worship Bacchus and Ceres, because of the elements of bread and wine in the Lord's supper. If they met in private places, and in the night, it was enough to occasion surmises of conspiracy and rebellion: so ready is Satan to take occasion where none is given.

[5.] Fifthly, But if none of these are at hand, then *a downright lie must do the turn, according to that of Jer.* xviii. 18, 'Come and let us devise devices against Jeremiah;' and when once the lie is coined, Satan hath officious instruments to spread it: Jer xx. 10, 'Report, say they, and we will report it.'

These were the lies raised against truth; but besides this endeavour, he useth the same art of lying to enhance the credit of error. Lying inspirations, lying signs and wonders we have spoken of; I shall only mention another sort of lying, which is that of forgery, an art which error hath commonly made use of. Sometimes books and writings erroneous have been made to carry the names of men that never knew or saw them. The apostles themselves escaped not these abuses: you read of the counterfeit Gospels of Thomas and Bartholomew, the Acts of Peter and Andrew, the Apostolical Constitutions, and a great many more. Later writers have by the like hard usage been forced to father the brats of other men's brains. I might be large in these, but they that please may see more of this in authors that have of purpose discovered the frauds of spurious, supposititious books.[2] The design is obvious: error would by this means adorn itself with the excellent names of men of renown, that so it might pass for good doctrine with the unwary.

[1] Apolog., cap. 7–9, 39.
[2] Coci Censura Patrum, [Query, the *Thesaurus Catholicus* of Joan. Coccius.—G.]; Dr James, De Corrupt. Scrip. Concilior, [1688, 8vo, and re-edited by Cox, 1843, 8vo]; Prideaux, De Pseudo-Epigraphis, [as before.—G.]

CHAPTER IV.

Of Satan's second way of improving his advantages, which is by working upon the understanding indirectly by the affections.—This he doth—(1.) *By a silent, insensible introduction of error. His method herein.* (2.) *By entangling the affections with the external garb of error, a gorgeous dress, or affected plainness.* (3.) *By fabulous imitations of truth. The design thereof.* (4.) *By accommodating truth to a compliance with parties that differ from it. Various instances hereof.* (5.) *By driving to a contrary extreme.* (6.) *By bribing the affections with rewards, or forcing them by fears.* (7.) *By engaging pride and anger.* (8.) *By adorning error with the ornaments of truth.*

The usual arguments by which Satan doth directly blind the understanding to a persuasion to accept darkness for light, we have now considered. It remains that some account be given of the second way of prevailing upon the understanding, and that is *by swaying it through the power and prevalency of the affections.* In order to this he hath many devices, the principal whereof are these :—

1. First, *By silent and insensible procedure he labours to introduce errors;* and lest men should startle at a sudden and full presentment of the whole, he thinks it policy to insinuate into the affections, by offering it in parcels. Thus he prevents wonderment and surprisal, lest men should boggle and turn away, and doth by degrees familiarise them to that which at first would have been rejected with abhorrency. We read in the parable of the tares that the envious man which sowed them, who was Satan, took his opportunity 'while men slept,' and then went away in the dark; insomuch that the discovery was not made at the sowing, but at their coming up. In pursuance of this policy, we find the principal instruments of Satan have followed the footsteps of their master; they 'creep in unawares,' Jude 4; they 'privily bring in damnable heresies,' 2 Pet. ii. 1; and, as if they were guilty of some modest shamefacedness, they '*creep* into houses,' 2 Tim. iii. 6. The steps by which the devil creeps into the bosoms of men to plant error in the heart are these :—

[1.] First, He endeavours to gain the heart by *the ingenuous, sweet, and delightful society of those that are corrupted already.* Error hath a peculiar art to woo the good-will before it disclose itself. It first steals the ear and affections to the person, and thence insensibly derives it to the opinion. Truth is masculine, and persuades by teaching, but error doth often teach by persuading. It is very difficult to affect the person, and not to bestow upon the error better thoughts than it deserves. Those therefore that are cunning in the art of seduction, make extraordinary pretences of affectionate kindness, and, as the apostle noted concerning the seducers of his time, Gal. iv. 17, 'they zealously affect' those whom they would delude, 'but not well.' Their art doth also teach them not to be over-hasty in propounding their opinions, nor so much as to touch upon them, till they perceive they have gained a firm persuasion of their amity, and of the reality of those kindnesses which they have made show of; but when they have once gained this point of advantage, they take opportunity more freely to propound and press their doctrines. Thus are men at last beguiled 'with enticing words.'

It is also part of the same design that Satan sometimes makes use of women seducers: For, (1.) They are more apt to be deluded themselves: 'silly women' are soon 'led captive.' (2.) Being deceived, they are most earnestly forward in the heat of zeal to propagate their opinions. (3.) And by the advantage of their nature they are most engaging; their affectionate persuasions usually have a peculiar prevalency. The daughters of Moab, through Balaam's counsel, were made choice of as the fittest instruments to seduce Israel to idolatry. Solomon, though a wise man, was prevailed with by the importunity of his wives, against his former practice and knowledge, to favour false worship. The woman Jezebel, Rev. ii. 20, was Satan's under-agent 'to teach and seduce God's servants to commit fornication, and to eat things sacrificed to idols.' (4.) Besides, they have a greater influence upon their children to leaven them with their own opinions.

[2.] Secondly, Satan also observes *a gradual motion in fixing any particular error*. If he attempt it immediately, without an external agent, he first puts men upon the reading or consideration of some dark passages that seem to look favourably upon his design; then he starts the notion or objection; then begets a scruple or questioning. Having once proceeded thus far, he follows his design with probable reasons, till he have formed it into an opinion. When it is come to this, a little more begets a persuasion, that persuasion he ripens into a resoluteness and obstinacy, and then at last fires it with zeal for the deluding of others. Having thus laid the foundation by one error, he next endeavours to multiply it, and then brings in the inferences that unavoidably follow; for as one wedge makes way for another, so from one falsehood another will easily force itself, and from two or three who knows how many? And though the consequences are usually more absurd than the principles, yet are they with a small labour brought into favour where the principles are first confidently believed; so that those errors, which because of their ugly look Satan durst not at first propound, lest he should scare men off from their reception, he can now with an undaunted boldness recommend. It cannot be imagined that ever men would at first have entertained opinions of contempt of ordinances and libertinism, and therefore we may observe they usually come in the rear of other opinions, which by a long tract of art prepare their way.

Yet may we note, that though Satan usually is forced to wait the leisure of some men's timorousness and bashfulness, and therefore cannot ripen error to a hasty birth as he desires, hence is it that one man often doth no more for his time, but only brew it, or, it may be, makes only the rude draught of it, and another vents and adorns it; for so it was betwixt Lælius and Faustus Socinus, betwixt David George and his successors. And though he be so confined to the first principles of error which he hath instilled that he cannot at present enlarge them beyond their own just consequences; yet there are some choice principles of his which, if he can but fasten upon the mind, they presently open the gap to all kind of errors imaginable. They are like the firing a train of gunpowder, which in a moment blows up the whole fabric of truth. Such are the delusions of enthusiasm, inspirations, and prophetic raptures. Let these be once fixed, and then there is nothing so inhuman, irreligious, mad, or ridiculous, but Satan can with ease persuade men to it, and also under the highest pretences of religion and certainty. The experience of all ages hath made any further proof of this altogether needless.

This is his way when he acts alone. But if he use instruments, though he is also gradual in his procedure, yet it is in a different method; for there he sometimes proceeds from the abuse of something innocent and lawful, by the help of a long tract of time, to introduce the grossest falsehood. Thus may we conceive he brought idolatry to its height: first men admired the wisdom or famous acts of their progenitors or benefactors; next they erected pillars or images of such persons to perpetuate the names, honour, and memory of them and their actions. Another age, being at a greater distance from the things done, and consequently greater strangers to the true ends and reasons of such practices, which being, as it usually falls out in such cases, abused by false reports or misrepresentations of things—for time covers things of this nature with so thick a mist that it is difficult to discover the true metal of an original constitution—they in a devout ignorance gave the images a greater respect than was at first intended. Then did they slide into a conceit they were not of the ordinary rank of mortals, or at least they were exalted to a condition which ordinary mortals were not capable of. Thus they supposed them deities, and gave them worship of prayers and sacrifices. Hence they went further, and multiplied gods, and that of several sorts, according to the natures of things that were good or hurtful to them; and then at last consulting how mean their offerings were, and how unlikely to please their godships, they concluded human sacrifices most suitable, especially to expiate greater provocations, and in times of great calamity.

The burdensome heap of ceremonious superstitions in popery was the work of several ages; they were not brought in all at once. One in a devotional heat fancied such a ceremony as a fit testimony of zeal, or a proper incitement of his affections; another deviseth a second, and so all along. As the minds of men were best pleased with their own inventions, and had so much credit or authority to recommend them to others, they increased the sum by new additions, till at last they are become a burden not to be borne; and still as they receded from the primitive purity, and became more careless and corrupt in their lives—for from good bishops they declined to but tolerable archbishops, till at last they are become incurable Babylonians—so they departed gradually from the simplicity of the gospel, and abounded in contrivances of ceremonies.[1]

[3.] Thirdly, *In corrupting established truths*. Satan's proceedings are not by sudden and observable leaps, but by lingering and slow motions—as flowers and plants grow insensibly, and as men gradually wax old and feeble. Violent and hasty alterations he knows would beget observation, dislike, and opposition; neither will he make such

---

[1] Matth[ias] Prideaux, Introduct. Histories. [1655. 4to.—G.]

attempts but where he is sure of a strong prevalent party, which by force and power is able to carry all before it. In this case he is willing to enforce error by fire and sword. Thus he propagated Mohammedanism at first, and still continueth to do so by the conquering arms of the Turks; but where he hath not this advantage, he betakes himself to another course, and studieth to do his work so that he may not be observed. The possibility of such a change, with the manner of effecting it, we may observe in many churches that have declined from the doctrine which they at first received, but most of all in the church at Rome, which at first was a pure church, as the apostle testifieth, but now so changed from the truths upon which they were bottomed in their first constitution, as if she had not been the same church. They boast indeed that as they were at first, so they are now; but nothing is more evident than the contrary; and the possibility of their insensible corruption is as demonstrable as the alteration of doctrine in any other church. The manifold ways that Satan takes in this matter, in the abuse of Scripture, by raising perverse interpretations and unnatural inferences, and the advantages of a long succession in authority; of the negligence and ignorance of the common people; of the crafty subtlety of the teachers, especially when religion began to be abused to secular interest, is described by Acontius and others.[1] If we should single out any of their noted errors, and follow up the history of it to its first original, we shall find that whatever strong current it hath now gotten, it was very small and inconsiderable in the fountain. The invocation of saints, though it be now an established article among them, yet its first rise was from the unwary *prosopopœias* of the ancients, and the liberty of their oratorical declamatory style. These gave occasion to some private opinions, these opinions to some private devotional liberty in practice, and from private opinions and practices, at last it obtained so strong a party that it procured a public injunction. The like method was used for the doctrine of transubstantiation, whose beginning was from the abuse of such sentences as this in ancient writers, that 'after consecration it was no more bread and wine, but the body and blood of Christ;' by which expression the authors intended no more than this, that the bread and wine in the sacrament were relatively altered, and were more than ordinary bread and wine, because they were representatives of the body and blood of Christ: however, this gave them courage to interpret literally and strictly these words of Christ, 'This is my body;' and thus by degrees from the opinion of a few it became the judgment of many, and from the toleration of a private opinion of some doctors, and unimposed, it obtained at last a canon to make it authentic public doctrine.

[4.] Fourthly, This insensible proceeding is in nothing more evident than *in the power of custom and education*. Custom doth by degrees take off the startling of conscience; and those opinions or practices which at first look affright it, are by a little familiarity made more smooth and tolerable. The dissents of men by frequent seeing and hearing become tame and gentle; but the force of education is incomparably great, for this makes an error to become as it were na-

[1] Stratagema Satanæ, lib. iv., [as before.—G.]

tural; they suck it in with their milk, and draw it in with their air. This general advantage the devil hath over all the children of erroneous parents, especially where countries or nations are of the same persuasion; insomuch that Turks have as great belief of their Alcoran as we of the Bible, and think as reverently of Mohammed as Christians do of Christ. The children of idolatrous pagans have as great a confidence of the truth of their way of heathenish worship, as we have of God's ordinances and institutions.

[5.] Fifthly, We may see something of this stratagem of silent entanglement *in Satan's surprisals;* for sometimes he inveigles men at unawares, and engageth them in error while they know not what they are doing. Weak heads cannot see the far end of a smooth-faced doctrine, and they usually embrace it by wholesale, for some particular that strikes upon their fancy, or gratifies their humour. If they read a book that hath some good things in it, or is affectionate, for the sake of these they swallow all the rest, though never so dangerous doctrine, without further examination. The like advantage he hath from actions that are bad or tolerable, according to the various respects which they have to the ends or consequences that lie before them; for he frequently doth interest men in an erroneous consequence, by concerning them in actions that lead that way; and having thus beguiled them into an evil mistake, instead of drawing their foot out of the snare, he pusheth them forward to maintain their ground, and to justify their proceedings. This was the case of some of the Corinthians; when the heathens had offered a sacrifice to an idol, part of the sacrifice was reserved, and either sold at the shambles, or used in a feast, to which the heathens sometimes invited their Christian acquaintance or relations. Those that went, knowing that ' an idol was nothing,' ate what was set before them without any regard to the idol, and ' making no question for conscience sake;' by their example others that ' had not that knowledge,' 1 Cor. viii. 7, were emboldened, not only to eat against their scruples and doubts of conscience,—which is all that many interpreters think to be intended in that place,—but also—as the words make probable—with some positive regard to the idol; so that by the examples of those that sat in the idol's temple, eating what was set before them as common meat, others misinterpreting their actions, proceeded to eat with a conscience of the idol, as if the idol had been something indeed, and deserving a conscientious regard. Not unlike to this was that art of Julian, mentioned by Sozomen, whereby he endeavoured to twist something of paganism with actions and things that were lawful or necessary.[1] He caused the images of Mars and Mercury to be placed by his own, so that the respects that were payed to the emperor's picture, seemed to carry a concomitancy of reverence to those idols. He also, in prosecution of the same policy, caused their meats and drinks to be sprinkled or mixed with the lustral water, that so every one that used them might be inured to give some regard to his idols; and that some, at least, might be engaged to a justification of that and such other practices.

All these are but instances of Satan's silent insinuation, by which

[1] Sozom. Eccl. Hist., lib. v. cap. 16.

he secretly steals the affections, and through these taints the judgment. Next follows,

A second plot upon the affections, which is an endeavour to entangle them by *the external garb of error*. In this he works by two contrary extremes, that he may the better prevail with men's different dispositions.

[1.] First, He sometimes *clothes a false doctrine with the most pompous, gorgeous, delightful attire*, that, like Solomon's harlot, it may entice those that are pleased with the highest gratifications of the senses, 'I have decked my bed with coverings of tapestry, with fine linen of Egypt,' &c. Most men that are given up to an animal life cannot be pleased with any religion but such as may most please the senses. They so disrelish the simplicity of the gospel—which is, notwithstanding, its particular mark and honour, 2 Cor. xi. 3—that they cannot persuade themselves they do anything in religious worship except they abound in costly ceremonious observances. Thus do some interpret that fear of the heathens, which first put them upon images and outward representations of their gods. They were afraid they should not have any religion to their own satisfaction, except they proceeded in such a course as might make their senses sure that they were doing something, *primus in orbe deos timor fecit*. The devil, knowing well the force of external beauties in religion, prepared the way to idolatry by it. They had their costly temples, some of them admirable for antiquity and magnificence, enriched with gifts and offerings, excellent for matter and workmanship, adorned with images, lamps, beds, and tables of gold, beautified by art, and natural pleasantness of situation; they had also their groves in the most pleasant and delightful places, as that of the Daphne, besides [1] Antiochia, which was environed with tall cypress trees ten miles about, and within adorned with the sumptuous temples of Apollo and Diana's sanctuary. In these places they had their music and solemn festivals, which were sometimes extraordinary for cost and continuance. Antiochus at Daphne continued an incredible solemnity, with a vast train and costly preparation, for thirty days' together; and that nothing might be wanting, they had their annual feasts, sacrifices, rites, the adornments of their priests, their white garments, their coats of divers colours, their mitres, &c.; in a word, nothing was lacking that might please the eye or ear. And doubtless the devil found this course very successful to win the affections of men to Gentilism. And if it were not for this consideration, it might be admired that the Jews, who were instructed in the true worship of God, should, notwithstanding, be so prone to idolatry, and so hardly drawn from it; but surely their strong inclinations that way proceeded from a natural delight that men have in a sensual religion, which, by a powerful witchcraft, doth enchant them to an excess of love. The same method the devil takes in popery. The chief enticement lies in its glorious external appearance. All their religious places are dressed up in the highest bravery, they are beautified with images and pictures, with lights and costly adornments; they abound in rites, ceremonies, gestures, and obser-

[1] 'Beside' Antioch in Syria. Cf. Libanius, Monod. de Daphnæo Templo, iii. 334.—G.

vances, and all this is but to dazzle the eyes, and to win a reverence in men to their worship ; and accordingly they practise in these exterior things on purpose to ravish men's affections ; their children are brought up to a confirmed delight and resolution for popery, by pleasing them with shows, pictures, representations, processions, and grateful observances. If a stranger of another religion come among them, then, as their first essay, they shew them all their play-things, that their affections may be tickled with the outward pomp and ornament of their way, for they know by experience that a glittering outside and a great deal ado of bodily labour is the all of most men's religion. If it have but body enough, they never inquire whether it have spirit or life within. A dead carcase in robes, that may put them to the exercise of their postures and ceremonious compliments, doth make up a more grateful religion for a carnal man than a living, spiritual service, that necessarily will put them upon inward care and watchfulness in the constant exercise of holy spiritual graces, without affording any considerable gratification to the senses. Hence is it truly more difficult, and yet inwardly more beautiful and glorious, to pray in faith and humility, even in short breathings after God, than to say a thousand Ave Marias, or to perform a task of ordinary penance. But as those that have no children of their own delight themselves in playing with a monkey or baboon, so those that know not how to worship God in spirit and truth seek to satisfy themselves in the performance of external gesture and ceremony.

[2.] Secondly, On the other hand he sometimes is willing that an error should affect *an excess of plainness and simplicity.* In this he takes advantage of those expressions in Scripture, wherein the gospel is commended for its simplicity ; and the inventions of men, under the pretences of wisdom, humility, and neglecting of the body, are condemned. Upon this ground he runs men upon such an excess of dotage, that they never think the things of God are rightly managed but when they are brought down to a contemptible silliness. By this means he arms conceited ignorant men with exceptions against learning, and the necessary decencies of language in preaching ; and with them they are the only preachers, and most likely to be inspired, that use least study and preparation for their work. It is indeed very true that the affected fooleries of a bombast style or starched discourse, and needless citations of sentences for ostentation, without any true advantage to the matter in hand, are things very pedantic, and exceedingly unsuitable to the gravity of the work of the ministry, and renders it very ungrateful to a pious mind ; but this contrary folly makes the solemn ordinances of God so nauseous and contemptible, that it often makes way, by Satan's cunning improvement of the temptation, to an atheistical rejection of all worship. In the meantime it is wonderful to observe how some persons please themselves with this conceit, that their way of worship is plain, and that they speak what immediately comes into their mind ; and though it be nonsense or contradictions, which sufficiently evidenceth that it is nothing of kin to the Spirit's inspirations, which they utter, yet it is argument enough to them that their opinions and ways are right, because they proceed in a designed neglect of all necessary order, and under pretence of the simplicity of the gospel they reduce all they do to childish silliness. Neither is this all the mischief which the devil raiseth out of this conceit, for the contempt and disuse of the sacraments may in great part be ascribed to it. Those erroneous ways of worship that are most noted for decrying those institutions of Christ, have this for their plea, that the worship which God is best pleased with is spiritual, and that all bodily services and external observations are things that God stands not upon, such as profit little, and were no further in use, but to recommend an internal spiritual communion with God; so that the more they reject these things, they persuade themselves they have a more true understanding of the design of God in religion. Either of these ways Satan makes use of for the befooling of men into a humour of pleasing themselves with error. But,

[3.] Thirdly, He hath of old endeavoured *to cloud and enervate the doctrine of the Bible by traditionary fables.* We meet with many passages to this purpose. Sometimes he sets up unwritten traditions, not only of equal authority to the written word, but as completions and perfections of it. This he practised among the Jews with such success, that the traditions of the elders were of greater force with them than the commands of God, as Christ himself noted of them, Mat. xv. 13. Of these unwritten traditions, which they called ' the law by the word of mouth,' feigned by them to be given to Moses when he was in the mount, and so delivered from hand to hand, the apostles gave many warnings, and signified the hazards that truth stood in by them through the cunning of Satan; as Col. ii. 8, ' Beware lest any man spoil you through the traditions of men;' 1 Tim. i. 4, ' Neither give heed to fables, and endless genealogies;' Titus i. 14, ' Not giving heed to Jewish fables, and commandments of men;' 2 Tim. iv. 4, ' And they shall turn away their ears from the truth, and shall be turned unto fables.'

The papists at this day give the same entertainment to this device that the Jews did of old; they boast as high of their traditions, and are every whit as fabulous and foolish in them as they were. Satan in his attempts upon the Gentiles to confirm them in their false worship, though he kept up the substance of this design, yet he was necessitated to alter the scene a little, that he might more handsomely accommodate it to their condition; and therefore he set up amongst them fabulous imitations of the truths and ordinances of the Scripture, insomuch that there is scarce any grand mystery or remarkable history or ordinance mentioned in the Scripture but we may find something among the heathens in tradition or practice that doth allude to it. What traditionary imitations had they of the creation recorded in the book of Genesis! That of Ovid concerning the chaos and first beginning of things is known to every schoolboy. The Phœnicians in their theology give an odd account of it from their Taautus, to this purpose:[1] ' That the first beginnings of all things were a dark, disordered chaos, and the spirit of the dark air; hence proceeded *moth*, that is, mire, from thence issued the seeds and generation of all creatures in earth

---

[1] Purchas, Pilg., lib. i. cap. 17, [as before.—G.]

and heaven,' &c. The wickedness of men before the flood—mentioned Gen. vi. 1, 2—is fabulously related in an ancient book, falsely ascribed to Enoch, wherein the watchmen or angels are reported to take them wives of the daughters of men, and that from thence was the race of giants.[1] For the description of paradise, the heathens had the poetical fiction of the Elysian fields; as they had the story of Deucalion, instead of Noah's ark and the deluge. The story of Lot's wife was abused by the fiction of Orpheus his wife, suddenly snatched from him for looking back. The history of Samson was turned into their story of Hercules and his ten labours. From the sun standing still in Joshua and Hezekiah's time, came that fiction of Jupiter's doubling the night, that he might enjoy Alcmena. In some of these disguises of sacred story, they go so near in name and circumstances, that it is past doubt they imitated the true history, which they corrupted. For instance, Herodotus relates that Sethon, king of Egypt and priest of Vulcan, was helped by his god from heaven against Sennacherib, which plainly relates to Hezekiah king of Judah, and the wonders that God did for him.[2] So in imitation of Uriah's letters to Joab for his own destruction, we have in Homer and others the story of Prœtus sending letters to Jobatas by Bellerophon, wherein his death was commanded; the near affinity of the names Joab and Jobatas, shews with what heifer the devil ploughed. The history of Abraham's offering up Isaac is by Porphyry applied to Saturn, who saith he was by the Phœnicians called Israel; he had by Anobreth one only son called Jeud,—an evident allusion, saith Godwyn, [Antiq., lib. iv. cap. 3,] to Gen. xxii. 2, where Isaac is in the Hebrew called Jechid, that is, an only-begotten,—him he offered up on an altar purposely prepared. Here not only the matter, but the names, do clearly shew that Abraham's story is imitated in this. The like imitation I might shew to have been among the heathen of doctrinal truths, as of the sacred mystery of the Trinity. In Peru they worship the father, son, and brother; as also their Tangatauga, which they say was one in three, and three in one.[3] But their imitation of ordinances is everywhere remarkable, so that I need say nothing of their temples, priests, sacrifices, and other religious rites; only the devil's imitation of the sacraments of the New Testament deserves particular observation. Instances of an apish imitation of baptism are everywhere obvious, and that of the Lord's supper or Christian communion was frequently resembled in the chief Peruvian feasts, where they carried small loaves of bread in great platters of gold, of which all present received and ate little pieces, and this as a sign of honour and profession of obedience to their gods and the ingua.[4] Not unlike to this were those morsels of paste which the Mexicans used in their religious feasts, which they laid at their idol's feet, consecrating them by singing and other ceremonies, and then they called them the flesh and bones of their god Vitziliputzli, alluding directly to that of our Saviour, 'This is my body,' &c., insomuch that Acosta thought

---

[1] Vide Scaligeri notas in Euseb. Chron., p. 244.
[2] Lib. ii.; mentioned also by Josephus, Antiq. Jews, lib. x. cap. 1.
[3] Purchas, Pilg. America, lib. ix. cap. 12, [as before.—G.]
[4] Purchas, Pilg. America, lib. ix. cap. 12. [Inca or Incas.—G.]

the devil mocked their transubstantiation by it. This was distributed among all, and was eaten with a great deal of reverence, fear, and devotion.[1]

We may see by those instances that in these fabulous imaginations of truth the devil hath industriously traded, and that which he aimed at in this design may easily be conjectured to be,

[1.] *The despiting and discrediting of truth.* He renders it by this means suspicious of some forgery; as if the Scripture were no better than an uncertain tradition, as if, at the best, it were doubtful whether Scripture or these traditionary fables had better authority.

[2.] He further intends *the entanglement of the affections to error by this device;* for he doth, as it were, take the spoils of the tabernacle to adorn his Dagon withal; and without doubt the heathens were very much hardened in Gentilism by these traditionary stories. Hence one observes,[2] the devil imitated the history of the miracle done in favour of Hezekiah, that the Scriptures might lose their credit and authority, and that the glory of such a wonder might be transferred to their idols; and the consequence of both these is,

[3.] *To deprive the truth of its convincing power upon the consciences of men.* The principles of Scripture convince by the evidence of their truth. If that truth be questioned by the substitution of another competitor, it presently loseth its force, and the commands thereof are disregarded upon a supposition of its uncertainty.

[4.] Another of his ways to betray the understanding by the affections, is by *putting men upon an accommodation of truth to a compliance with parties differing from it.* And this hath been so much the more successful, because it hath begun, and been carried on, upon the most specious pretences. The avoiding of offences, the smoothing of the way of religion for the gaining of the contrary minded, the preservation of peace and unity, are pleas very plausible; and really, upon the account of these things, the Scripture, both by its precepts and examples, hath recommended to us condescensions and brotherly forbearances. The Jews, who were dissatisfied at the first publication of the liberty from the yoke of Mosaical ceremonies purchased for us by Christ, were indulged in the use of circumcision, and observance of the difference of meats for a long time, till they might be the better satisfied in the truth. These pretences the devil makes use of to undermine truth. And pleasing his agents with the honour of a pious design—and it may be at first really so intended by them—he prevails with them, not only for a present condescension to men of contrary practice, but to cast the principles of truth into such a fixed mould that they may carry a more near resemblance to those opinions which they do most directly oppose. The appearance of sanctity, peaceableness, prudence, and successfulness in such an undertaking, doth exceedingly animate the well-meaning designers, which Satan, in the meantime, carries them beyond all bounds, and so dangerously fixeth an unnatural representation of truth, that it loseth its own splendour,

---

[1] Purchas, Pilg. America, lib. viii. cap. 13, [as before.—G.]
[2] Ita diabolus hoc egit, ut divinum miraculum in Judæa editum vilesceret, fidem et authoritatem amitteret, et tanti operis gloria ad turpissima idola rediret.—*Bucholcer.*

and settles at last upon unsafe notions. Thus by the continuance of such a compliance, error begins to recruit its forces, and is as likely to draw over truth wholly to its side—by the argument of resemblance, and the consequences following thereupon—as truth is wholly to extirpate and conquer error. And if it do not that, succeeding ages, that minded not the first design, finding things so continued to them, in deep reverence to their predecessors, form their prudential condescensions into perverse opinions.

If we follow the tract of time from the first preaching of the gospel, we may find Satan's footsteps all along. In the apostles' times, when the believing Jews were tolerated necessarily till time and experience might fully convince them in their observation of the law of Moses, which was certainly given of God, and so might very easily occasion an opinion of the continuance of it, Acts xv. 1, 5, though the apostles did not at all accommodate the standing precepts of the New Testament to carry a perpetual resemblance of that opinion, neither did they still countenance that practice, but did seasonably and fully declare against it, exhorting Christians ' to stand in the liberty wherewith Christ hath made them free,' Gal. v. 1, 2, yet Satan was busy to take advantage of the present forbearances, which the Holy Ghost had directed them unto; insomuch that instead of convincing all the dissenters by that lenity, some dissenters waxed bold to persuade the Christians ' to another gospel.' But after their days the devil pursued this design with greater scope; for instance, in Constantine's time, when the Gentiles flocked into the church with dirty feet and in their old rags, they were tolerated in some old customs of Gentilism, and upon a design to win them, they made bold to bend the doctrine of the gospel toward their former usages; they thought indeed it was best to wink at things, and not to bear too hard upon them at first, but that, tolerating a lesser evil, they might avoid a greater inconvenience; and withal they deemed they had done great service to the church and Christian religion, if they could any way divert the heathen from worshipping their idols. And to effect this the easilier, they seemed to cherish their customs and rites of worship, as consonant in the general to the principles of Christianity, only they excepted against the object of their worship as unlawful, so that upon the matter they did no more than change the name. The manifold inconveniences that followed this kind of dealing, they did not discover at first; but besides the infecting the simplicity of Christian religion with the dirt and dregs of paganism, which they might easily have seen, time hath since discovered that here the devil secretly laid the chief foundations of popery.

Whosoever shall impartially compare the rites, customs, usages, and garbs of popery, with those of paganism, will to his admiration find such an exact agreement and consonancy, that he must necessarily conclude that either paganism imitated popery, or popery imitated paganism; but the latter is true, and that these corruptions in religion by popery came in by a designment of conforming Christianity to heathenism, though it may be upon pious intentions at first, is no difficult thing to evince; for besides that the rites of paganism were more ancient, and so could not be borrowed from popery, which came long after, the Scripture did foretell a great defection from truth which should be in the 'last days,' and this under a profession of religion; and the things particularised are such as shew that the defection should carry an imitation of paganism: for no less seems to be signified by 1 Tim. iv. 1, 'The Spirit speaketh expressly, that in the latter times some shall depart from the faith, giving heed to seducing spirits, and doctrines of devils;' that is—as Mr Mede, whose interpretation I follow,[1] doth prove—doctrines concerning devils or demons: as in Heb. vi. 2, we have the phrase of 'doctrines of baptisms,' which must needs signify doctrines concerning baptisms; the Gentile theology of demons is the thing which Paul prophesies should be introduced into Christianity. How clearly this relates to popery may be evident to any that doth not wilfully blind himself by prejudice. Their doctrine of demons was this: they supposed two sorts of gods, supreme and inferior; the supreme they supposed did dwell in the heavenly lights, sun, moon, and stars, without change of place; these they judged were so sublime and pure, that they might not be profaned with the approach of earthly things, and that immediate approaches to them were derogatory to their sovereignty. The inferior order of gods they imagined were of a middle sort, betwixt the supreme beings and men, as participating of both. These they called mediators and agents, and supposed their business was to carry up men's prayers to God, and to bring down blessings from God upon men. These were in Scripture called Baalim, and by the Greeks demons; to this purpose Austin and others speak.[2]

Now these demons they supposed were the souls of dead men, that had been more than ordinarily famous in their generation. Thus Ninus made an image to his father Belus after he was dead, and caused him to be worshipped. Hermes confesseth that Æsculapius, grandfather to Asclepius, and Mercury, his own grandfather, were worshipped as gods of this order. Abundance of instances I might produce to this purpose; but to go on, these demons, because to them was committed the care of terrestrial affairs, as Celsus argues against Origen, and because of the help and advantage that men might receive from them, they supposed it gratitude and duty to worship them, and this worship they performed at their images, sepulchres, and relics. To this purpose Plutarch tells us of Theseus his bones, and Plato of the θῆκαι or shrines of their demons.[3]

How evident is it that the papists in their doctrine and practice about the invocation of saints and angels, have writ after this copy, and that they are the men that have introduced this doctrine of demons, the thing itself declares without further evidence. Had the heathens their dead heroes for agents betwixt the supreme gods and men? so have the papists their dead saints to offer up their prayers. Did the heathen expect more particular aids from some of these demons in several cases than from others? so do the papists. Instead of Diana for women in labour, and Æsculapius for the diseased, they

---

[1] Apostasy of the Latter Times. [Works, 1677, folio, pp. 623, seq.—G.]
[2] De Civitate Dei, lib. viii. cap. 14, 18.
[3] Vide Du Plessis, Of the Trueness of Christian Religion, cap. 22; Origen, Cont. Cels., lib. viii. p. 416; Plutarch in Vita Thesei et Demetrii.

have their St Margaret and St Mary for travailing; Sebastian and Roch against the pestilence; Apollonia against the toothache; St Nicholas against tempests, &c. Did the heathen pray to these demons for their aid? so do the papists to their saints, as their breviaries, rosaries, and Lady's psalters testify. Had the heathen their feasts, their *statas ferias* to their demons? so have the papists. Had they their *Februalia et Proserpinilia* with torches and lights? so have the papists their Candlemas with lights. Did the heathen erect images and pillars, or keep the ashes and shrines of their demons? so do the papists; the one had processions and adorations, so have the other; and a great many more things there are wherein popery keeps a correspondence with heathenism. To this purpose you may read enough in Monsieur de Croy, ' Of the Three Conformities.'

To make it yet more clear that the corruptions in religion by popery came in by the design of suiting Christian religion to paganism, I shall in a testimony or two shew you that they professedly avouched the design. Gregory the Great writes chidingly to Serenus, bishop of Marseilles, who it seems was no forward man in this matter to this purpose,[1] ' Thou shouldst have considered that thou didst converse chiefly with the Gentiles, to whom pictures are instead of reading, to the end that no offence be given them under colour of lawful zeal, wherewith thou art not cunningly endued.' And in another epistle to Mellitus,[2] he adviseth, ' That the honours and offerings which the heathens gave to their demons should be transferred to the martyrs and their relics,' and gives this reason for it, ' It is impossible,' saith he, ' to cut off all at once from stubborn minds.'[3] Eusebius also endeavours to persuade to Christianity by this argument, that the Christians' custom of honouring the memories of the martyrs, and solemnly assembling at their sepulchres, did agree with the custom of the Gentiles of doing the like honour to their demons, and having mentioned what Hesiod speaks concerning Plato's opinion, that their champions became demons after death, helpers and protectors of men— for which cause they were worshipped at their sepulchres as gods; he adds to this purpose, that ' if these honours had been given to the favourites of God, and champions of true religion, it had been well enough;' and for this shews the example and custom of Christians then to go to the tombs of martyrs, there to pray in honour of their blessed spirits.' And although at first they might be more modest in honouring the martyrs than now they are, according to that of Austin, ' These observances at the tombs of martyrs,' saith he, ' are only ornaments of their memories, not sacrifices to them as to gods.'[4] Yet this soon slid into greater abuse, insomuch that Lud. Vives,[5] in his notes on that chapter, blames those of his own time for worshipping saints as gods, and tells us he cannot see the difference betwixt the opinion concerning saints, as generally practised, and that of the

---

[1] Lib. ix. Epist. 9.   [2] Lib. ix. Epist. 71.
[3] Nam duris mentibus simul omnia abscindere impossible est. *Vide* Perkins's Prepar[atives] to Demonst. of the Prob[leme of the forged Catholicisme or Universalitie of the Romish Religion, 1613, folio.—G.], cap. 3; [Eusebius] Præpar. Evan., lib. xiii. cap. 7.
[4] De Civit. Dei, lib. viii. cap. 27. Ornamenta sunt memoriarum, non sacrificia mortuorum.
[5] Non video in multis quid sit discrimen inter eorum opinionem de sanctis et id quod Gentiles putabant de diis suis.

heathens concerning their gods. I might add the positive acknowledgment of Beatus Rhenanus, Jacobus de Voragine, concerning the burning of candles to the Virgin Mary, which custom they confess was borrowed from the heathens, with a respect to the frowardness of paganism, and a design not to exasperate them, that they might gain them.

I might also shew that the mischief of this design, of accommodating truth to a compliance with different parties, hath not only shewn itself in introducing strange actions and ceremonies, but hath also discovered itself in leavening men's judgments in reference to opinion. Calvin conjectures [1] that those confident assertions of the powers of nature were first occasioned by an over-officious willingness to reconcile the doctrine of the Scripture with the opinions of philosophy; and that men being unwilling to run the hazard of the scorn which they might meet with in contradicting the general received principles of philosophers, were willing to form the doctrine of truth relating to human ability accordingly. Abundance of instances of this kind may be given. Whence came the doctrine of purgatory, but from hence? It is but Plato's philosophy Christianised by the Roman synagogue.[2] He divided all men into three ranks: the virtuous, who are placed by him in the Elysian fields; the desperate ungodly, these he adjudgeth to everlasting fire; and a third sort, betwixt the perfectly virtuous and the desperately wicked, he sendeth to Acheron, to be purged by punishment. All of this Eusebius makes mention of at large.[3] That the papists derived their purgatory from hence is generally affirmed by protestants—nay, not only in these cases, but in very many more, corruptions have entered into Christianity by an over-eager endeavour to make the doctrine of the Scriptures to run even with the sayings and assertions of the schools of philosophers; a thing complained of old by Tertullian, who plainly affirmed the philosophers to be the patriarchs of the heretics.[4] To which agrees that observation of Dr Owen, that those who either apologised for Christians, or refuted the objections of the heathens against Christianity, frequently cited the opinions or sentences of the philosophers, and accommodated them to their purpose, that so they might beget in their adversaries more friendly persuasions towards the Christian religion, by evidencing that the mysteries thereof were not absurd, nor dissonant from reason, seeing they might be justified by the sayings of their own philosophers. And 'here was laid, in this design and its prosecution, (and surely it pleased its undertakers not a little,) the foundation of that evil which religion hath since groaned under, that men made bold with the tremendous mysteries of Christianity, to accommodate them unwarily to the notions of the Gentiles.'[5] And this the apostle Paul foresaw in that caution he gave, Col. ii. 8, 'Beware lest any man

---

[1] [Ex quibus] veteres mihi videntur hoc consilio vires humanas sic extulisse, ne, si impotentiam diserte essent confessi [primum] philosophorum [ipsorum] cachinnos, [quibus cum tunc certamen habebant,] excuterent. . . . Scripturæ doctrinam cum philosophiæ dogmatibus dimidia ex parte conciliare studium illis fuit.—*Institut.*, lib. ii. cap. 2, sec. 4.
[2] Plato, lib. x., de Rep. Dial.   [3] De Præpar. Evang., lib. xi. cap. ult.
[4] Chemnitii, Exam. Concil. Trident, p. 3, in Hist. Purgator., cap. 1.
[5] Hinc prima mali labes, dum cœlestia mysteria et tremenda Christianorum sacra Gentilium notionibus et vanis ceremoniis attemperare voluerint.—*Owen's Disser. De Verbo*, sec. 16.

spoil you through philosophy and vain deceit, after the tradition of men, after the rudiments of the world, and not after Christ.' Certainly the snare is neither unusual nor weak, where the caution is so serious. It is a thing naturally pleasing, to be the inventor of any new thing, or to make new discoveries in religion, to raise new hypotheses, or to adventure in unbeaten paths, for a reconcilement of religion to any notion or practice famous for its antiquity, or pretence to beauty and decency. Men hug themselves when they can make several things to hit right, and an exact suiting of parallels is instead of demonstration. By this foolish delight the devil makes men bold to make essays; and what doth answer their humour passeth current for undoubted truth.

[5.] He doth sometime blind the understanding, *by working up the affections to such an earnest opposition to some error, that in a forward haste they cast the mind upon a contrary extreme;* so that through a hasty, violent avoidance of one error, they are cast upon a contrary, and, it may be, as dangerous as that they fly from. And this the devil doth with great ease, having the plausible pretence of zeal and care to truth, wherein the affections being highly engaged, the mind in a careless confidence doth easily overshoot the truth, which commonly lies in the middle, and thinks it doth well enough if it gives the greatest contradiction to the error now to be abominated. Men in this case, having their eyes only fixed upon what they would avoid, consider not so much whither they are going, as from what they go. So that seeking, as men in a fright, to avoid the pit that is before them, they run backward into another behind them.

This is such a noted stratagem of Satan, that all men take notice of it in the general, though all men do not improve the discovery for their own particular caution. The wisest of men are often so befooled by their violent resistance of an untruth, that they readily overshoot themselves and miss the mark. The fathers, in the heat of dispute, said many things so inconveniently, that those who come after do see and lament these hasty oversights, and have no other way to salve their credit but by giving this observation in excuse for them. And it may be observed that some errors which have risen from this root at first have so strongly fixed themselves, that they have grown up to the great annoyance of the truth; while the contrary errors that did occasion them are forgotten, and their memories are perished. I shall but instance in one instead of many, and that shall be Arianism. How sadly prevalent that hath been in its time, all men know that know anything of church history. The Christian world once groaned under it. But that which gave the first occasion to Arius to fix himself in that error was the doctrine of Alexander, who, discoursing of the unity in the Trinity too nicely, seemed to justify the error of Sabellius, who had taught, as also Noetus before, that there was but one person in the Trinity, called by divers names of Father, Son, and Spirit, according to different occasions; the Trinity, according to his doctrine, being not of persons, but of names and functions. While Arius was dissatisfied with this account of the Trinity, he ran to a contrary extreme; and that he might give the highest proof of a Trinity of persons, he affirmed that Jesus Christ had a beginning, and that there was a time when he was not, &c. Thus Socrates speaks of the rise of that heresy.[1]

We might further follow the footsteps of this device, and trace it in most opinions; where we might find the humour of running to a contrary extreme hath still either set up a contrary error, or at least leavened the truth with harsh and unjustifiable expressions and explanations. The disputes betwixt faith and works have been thus occasioned and aggravated. Some speak so of faith, as if they slighted works; others so urge a necessity of works, as if they intended to make faith useless. Some talk of grace, to an utter contempt of morality; others, on the contrary, magnify morality to the annihilating of grace. Some in their practice acquiesce in the outward performance of ordinances: if they pray or receive the sacraments, though never so formally, they are at peace, supposing they have done all that is required; others observing the mistake, and knowing that God looks more to the performance of the soul and spirit than to the act of the body, upon a pretence of worshipping God in spirit, throw off the observation of his ordinances altogether. Neither is there anything that doth more generally and apparently undo us in the present dissensions, as many have complained, than men's violent overdoing and running to contrary extremes.

[6.] Satan *makes use of rewards or punishments, on the one hand to bribe, or on the other to force the affections, and they being strongly possessed, easily prevail with the understanding to give sentence accordingly.* Men are soon persuaded to take that for truth which they see will be advantageous to them. Some men indeed take up with a profession of truth, which yet their hearts approve not; but the advantages they have by their profession, do silence their dissatisfactions; these are said to use the profession of truth as 'a cloak of covetousness,' 2 Thes. ii. 5. But others go further, and are really brought to an approbation of that doctrine or way that makes most for their profit, their minds being really corrupted by a self-seeking principle. They persuade themselves, where there is any contest about doctrines, that that doctrine is true which is gainful, and will accordingly dispute for it. Hence that expression in 1 Tim. vi. 5, 'supposing that gain is godliness.'

To this may be added, that the affections are quickly sensible of the ease and sensual gratifications of any doctrine, and these are usually thrown into the same scale to make more weight. Men have naturally a good liking to that doctrine that promiseth fair for ease, liberty, gain, and honour; and this hath made it a usual piece of Satan's business in all ages to gild an error with outward advantages, and to corrupt the mind by secret promises of advancement.

On the other side, he labours as much to prejudice truth, by representing it as hazardous and troublesome to the professors of it. And this not only affrights some from an open confession of the truth they believe, but also, by the help of the affections, doth persuade some to believe that to be an error, which unavoidably brings persecution with it. By this engine are the minds of men turned about to think well or ill of a doctrine presented to them. This is so well known,

[1] Socr[ates] Eccles. Histor., lib. i. cap. 3.

that I shall forbear a further prosecution of this head, and go to the next course that Satan takes to corrupt the judgment by the affections; which he doth,

[7.] *By stirring up some particular passions, which in opinions do usually more influence the understanding.* And here I shall only insist upon these two, pride and anger, with the peculiar means that Satan hath to engage them in his service.

That pride and anger are the two usual firebrands of contention and fountains of error, all ages have acknowledged and bewailed. These two companions in evil do so darken the mind, that the miserable captive in whom they domineer is carried blindfold, he knows not whither, nor how. Pride usually begins, and anger follows with all its forces, to justify what pride hath undertaken. Hence the apostle, in 1 Tim. vi. 4, rakes up all the concomitant filth of error, as envy, strife, railings, evil surmisings, and perverse disputings of men, and lays them at the door of pride: 'He is proud, knowing nothing.'

For the engaging of these two thieves, that rob the understanding of its light, Satan hath many artifices in readiness. Pride, which is forward enough of itself, is soon excited by laying before it an opportunity of a seeming rare discovery, or of advancing the glory of knowledge above the common pitch, of being seen and admired as more excellent than others, &c.: for upon such unworthy grounds have some dared to adventure upon strange notions; yet there is nothing that doth more firmly engage it than contention or dispute: for though the proper end of disputation be the sifting out of truth, yet such is man's pride, and Satan's advantage by it, that it seldom attains its true end in those that are engaged. Bystanders that keep their minds calm and unbiassed, may receive more satisfaction than the contenders themselves; and there needs no other evidence of this than the common experience which men have of our frequent contentions; where we have confutations, answers and replies, and yet still all parties continue in their opinions without conviction. So that they that would unfeignedly seek truth, in my mind, take not the best course in their pursuit, that presently engage themselves in a public dispute; for the usual heats that are begot in a contention alienate their minds from a just impartiality, and the dust they raise blinds their eyes, that they discern not truly. Let us look into this artifice of engaging pride by disputation, and by it the judgment. First we find that when a humour of contending is raised, certain truths are neglected, as to their improvement and practice; for so much of the strength of the soul is laid out upon disputable questions, that little is left for more weighty matters. Secondly, In disputes men's credit is so concerned, that it is a most difficult thing to preserve a faithful regard to verity, especially where they are managed with affronts and contumelies. They that by calm handling might be induced to acknowledge a mistake, will scarce come near that point of ingenuity, when they must be called fool, knave, or ass for their labour. Hence ordinarily, though they profess otherwise, men seek rather victory than truth. Thirdly, In disputes pride and passion are usually heightened, and the stronger the passions are the weaker is the judgment. Eager altercations bring a confusion, both upon the matter of which they dispute and upon the understanding that should judge. Fourthly, In the heat of disputation, when the mind is inflamed, men usually behave themselves like those in a fray, where they snatch and throw anything that comes to hand, and never mind where it hits; they will affirm or deny anything that may seem any way to bring them off. Fifthly, These assertions being once affirmed must be maintained, and so errors and contentions increase without end. Disputes fix a man in his persuasion, and do, as it were, tie him to the stake, so that right or wrong he will go through with it. Sixthly, Some dispute in jest against their present judgment, and yet at last dispute themselves into a belief of what they wantonly at first affirmed; as some tell lies so long, that at length they believe them to be true. Seventhly, A sadder mischief often follows a disputing humour, which is a hazard of the loss of all truth. Men dispute so long till they suspect all things, and after a long trade of scepticism turn atheists.[1]

After the same manner doth the devil engage anger in all disputes and controversies, for it keeps company with pride, wherever there is a provocation. And besides this, anger stirring up injuries and wrongs, hath often engaged men, as it were in revenge, to change their opinion, and to take up another way or doctrine. Nay, often that simple mixture of pride and anger which we call emulation, hath privately tainted the integrity of mind, and prepared it for the next fair opportunity of error. This is noted of Arius, by Theodoret, that when Alexander was chosen bishop of Alexandria, he envied him the preferency, and from thence sought occasions of contention, which after a little while the devil brought to his hand, as we have heard.[2]

So great is the power of these two passions over the understanding, that we have cause to wonder at their success. Seldom or never can it be shewn that any ringleader in error was not visibly tainted with pride, or not apparently soured with discontents and emulation.

[8.] To these ways of blinding the understanding by the affections I shall add but one more, which is this: Satan endeavours mainly to *adorn an error with truth's clothing.* He takes its ornaments and jewels to dress up a false doctrine, that it may look more lovely and dutiful; I mean that he designs, where errors are capable of such an imitation, to put them into the way, method, garb, and manner which truth doth naturally use. If truth be adorned with zeal, order, strictness, or have advantageous ways of managing itself, error must straightway imitate it in all these things; and though he that looks near may easily discern that it is not the natural complexion of error, but an artificial varnish, and such as doth no more become it than a court dress doth become a coarse, clownish, country person—for you may at first look usually discover the wolf under sheep's clothing, and under the garb of the apostles of Christ you may see the ministers of Satan—yet are the credulous usually affected with these appearances. If they find a professed strictness, a seeming severity, an imitation of

---

[1] Contentionibus amittitur veritas, et multi eo adiguntur, ut postea nihil constitui posse certi sibi persuadeant, atque ita religionis omne studium abjiciant.—*Acontius, Strat[agema] Satanœ,* lib. i. p. 23. [2] Theod. Eccles. Hist., lib. i. cap. 2.

the ways of truth, or of the fruits thereof, they commonly seek no further, but judge that to be truth which doth the things that truth doth; and if error can handsomely stand in competition with truth, upon a pretence of being as effectual in good works, and doing things of themselves lovely and of good report, it doth much gain upon the good liking of those whose consideration leads them not much further than fair appearances. I shall only exemplify this by the art and policy which Julian used to set up paganism, and to ruin Christianity; and those who have observed the ways which he took to gain his end, will readily acknowledge he was as well skilled in advancing error and suppressing truth as any whosoever, and knew exactly to suit his designs to men's inclinations. He observing that Christian religion had some particular things in its practice and way which made its face to shine, as that it had persons solemnly set apart by ordination for teaching the mysteries of the gospel, and for managing the public worship of God; that these persons were to be grave in their carriage, and exemplary in a strict holy conversation; that the constitutions of religion appointed certain necessary and effectual ways of discipline, for punishment, and restoring of offenders, and bringing them to repentance; that it took care of the comfortable maintenance of those that had given up themselves to the ministry of the word and prayer; that it also enjoined a relief of the poor and strangers, &c.: taking notice, I say, of these excellencies in Christianity, and how lovely they were in the eyes of their enemies, he appointed the like constitutions for paganism, and ordained that the idol temples should be suited in conveniency and comeliness to Christian churches: that there should be seats and desks for the chief doctors and readers of Gentilism, who at set times were to exhort the people and pray with them; and that colleges and monasteries should be erected for them, and for the relief of the poor and strangers; he commanded discipline and penances for the chastisement of offenders; he required that their priests should seriously give up themselves to the worship of God, as also their families, that they should not frequent shows and taverns, nor practise any infamous trade and art. Thus Sozomen reports him,[1] and gives us a copy of his letter to Arsacius, high priest of Galatia, to this purpose; and all this he did to bring Gentilism into credit with the vulgar, whom he had observed to be affected to Christianity for its order, strictness, and government.

Yet is not this the only instance that may be given in this kind: for observe but any error that by schism sets up for itself in a distinct party, and you shall see that though it departs from the truth of the church, and from its communion, yet still, as the Israelites did with the Egyptians, it carries away with it these jewels of the church, and keeps to some considerable part of the church's way, though modified according to its own bent, that it might have a lustre with it, to make it taking with others.

These eight particulars are the most remarkable ways of Satan whereby the affections are gained to a good liking of error, and by them the judgment secondarily corrupted to call it truth.

[1] Sozom. Eccles. Hist., lib. v. cap. 15.

CHAPTER V.

*Satan's attempts against the peace of God's children evidenced—
(1.) By his malice; (2.) From the concernment of peace to God's
children; what these concerns are, explained. (3.) From the
advantages which he hath against them by disquieting their minds
—1. Confusion of mind; 2. Unfitness for duty, and how; 3. Rejection of duty; 4. A stumbling-block to others; 5. Preparation of
the mind to entertain venomous impressions, and what they are;
6. Bodily weakness; 7. Our miseries Satan's contentment.*

We have viewed the ways of Satan by which he tempts to sin, by which he withdraws men from duty and service, by which he corrupts the mind through error. It only now remains that something be spoken of his attempts against the peace and comfort of the children of God.

That it is also one of Satan's chief designs to cheat us of our spiritual peace, may be fully evinced by a consideration of his malice, the great concern of inward comfort to us, and the many advantages which he hath against us by the disquiet of our minds.

1. First, Whosoever shall seriously consider the devil's *implacable malice, will easily believe that he so envies our happiness that he will industriously rise up against all our comforts.* It is his inward fret and indignation that man hath any interest in that happiness from which he irrecoverably fell, and that the Spirit of God should produce in the hearts of his people any spiritual joy or satisfaction in the belief and expectation of that felicity; and therefore must it be expected that his malice—heightened by the torment of his own guilt, which, as some think, are those 'chains of darkness' in which he is reserved at present 'to the judgment of the great day,' [2 Peter ii. 4,]—will not, cannot leave this part of our happiness unattempted. He endeavours to supplant us of our birthright, of our blessing, of our salvation, and the comfortable hopes thereof. From his common employment in this matter, the Scripture hath given him names, importing an opposition to Christ and his Spirit in the ways they take for our comfort and satisfaction. Christ is our advocate that pleads for us; Satan is $\delta\iota\acute{\alpha}\beta o\lambda o\varsigma$, a calumniator. The Spirit intercedes for us; Satan is $\kappa\alpha\tau\acute{\eta}\gamma o\rho o\varsigma\ \tau\hat{\omega}\nu\ \dot{\alpha}\delta\epsilon\lambda\phi\hat{\omega}\nu$, 'the accuser of the brethren, who accuseth them before God night and day,' Rev. xii. 10. The Spirit is our comforter; Satan is our disturber, a Beelzebub who is ever raking in our wounds, as flies upon sores. The apostle Paul had his eye upon this when he was advising the Corinthians to receive again the penitent incestuous person; his caution was most serious: 2 Cor. ii. 11, 'Lest Satan get advantage of us,' lest he deceive and circumvent us; for his expression relates to men cunningly deceitful in trade, that do overreach and defraud the unskilful, $\pi\lambda\epsilon o\nu\epsilon\kappa\tau\eta\theta\hat{\omega}\mu\epsilon\nu$; and the reason of this caution was the known and commonly experienced subtlety of Satan, 'for we are not ignorant of his devices,' implying that he will, and frequently doth lie at catch to take all advantages against us. Some indeed restrain these advantages to ver.

10,[1] as if Paul only meant that Satan was designing to fix the Corinthians upon an opinion, that backsliders into great sins were not to be received again, or that he laid in wait to raise a schism in the church upon the account of this Corinthian. Others[2] restrain this advantage which he waited for to ver. 7, where the apostle expresseth his fear lest the excommunicated person should 'be swallowed up of too much sorrow;' but the caution being not expressly bound up to any one of these, seems to point at them all, and to tell us that Satan drives on many designs at once, and that in this man's case Satan would endeavour to put the Corinthians upon a pharisaical rigour, or to rend the church by a division about him, and to oppress the penitent by bereaving him of his due comfort; so that it appears still that it is one of his designs to hinder the comfort and molest the hearts of God's children.

2. Secondly, Of *such concern is inward spiritual peace to us*, that it is but an easy conjecture to conclude from thence that so great an adversary will make it his design to rob us of such a jewel; for,

[1.] Spiritual comfort is the *sweet fruit of holiness*, by which God adorns and beautifies the ways of religious service, to render them amiable and pleasant to the undertakers: 'Her ways are ways of pleasantness, and all her paths are peace,' Prov. iii. 17; and this is the present 'rest and refreshment' of God's faithful servants under all their toil, that when they have 'tribulation from the world,' yet they have 'peace in him,' John xvi. 33; and that, being 'justified by faith, they have peace with God,' and sometimes 'joy unspeakable and full of glory,' 1 Peter i. 8; and this they may the more confidently expect, because 'the fruits of the Spirit are love, joy, peace,' &c., Gal. v. 22.

[2.] Spiritual comfort is not only our satisfaction, but our *inward strength and activity; for all holy services doth depend upon it*. By this doth God strengthen our heart and gird up our loins 'to run the ways of his commandments.' It doth also strengthen the soul to undergo afflictions, to glory in tribulations, to triumph in persecutions. The outward man is also corroborated by the inward peace of the mind: 'A merry heart doth good like a medicine, but a broken spirit drieth the bones,' Prov. xvii. 22; all which are intended by that expression, Neh. viii. 10, 'The joy of the Lord is your strength;' it is strength to the body, to the mind, and that both for service and suffering; the reason whereof the apostle doth hint to us, Phil. iv. 7, 'The peace of God, which passeth all understanding, shall keep your hearts and minds'—that is, peace doth so guard us as with a garrison, $\varphi\rho o \nu \rho \acute{\eta} \sigma \epsilon \iota$—for so much the word imports—that our affections, our hearts, being entertained with divine satisfactions, are not easily enticed by baser proffers of worldly delights, and our reasonings, our minds, being kept steady upon so noble an object, are not so easily perverted to a treacherous recommendation of vanities.

[3.] Joy and peace are propounded to our careful endeavours, for attainment and preservation, *as a necessary duty of great importance to us*. Rejoicings are not only recommended as seemly for the upright, but enjoined as service, and that in the constant practice: 'Rejoice evermore;' 'In everything give thanks,' 1 Thes. v. 16, 18;

---

[1] Piscator, *in loc.*   [2] Calvin, *in loc.*

'Rejoice in the Lord alway; and again I say, rejoice,' Phil. iv. 4. In the Old Testament, God commanded the observation of several feasts to the Jews. These, though they had their several respective grounds from God's appointment, yet the general design of all seems to have been this, that 'they might rejoice before the Lord their God,' Lev. xxiii. 40; as if God did thereby tell them that it was the comely complexion of religion, and that which was very acceptable to himself, that his children might always serve him in cheerfulness of heart, seeing such have more cause to rejoice than all the world besides. They are then much mistaken that think mournful eyes and sad hearts be the greatest ornaments of religion, or that none are serious in the profession of it that have a cheerful countenance and a rejoicing frame of spirit. It is true, there is a joy that is devilish, and a mirth which is madness, to which Christ hath denounced a woe: 'Woe be to them that laugh now, for they shall mourn and weep,' [Luke vi. 25]; but this is a joy of another nature, a carnal delight in vanity and sin, by which men fatten their hearts to ruin; and whatsoever is said against this can be no prejudice to spiritual, holy joy in God, his favour and ways.

[4.] Spiritual comfort is also *a badge of our heavenly Father's kindness*. As Joseph, the son of his father's affections, had a special testimony thereof in his parti-coloured coat, so have God's favourites a peculiar token of his good-will to them when he gives them 'the garments of praise for the spirit of heaviness,' [Isa. lxi. 7.] If spiritual comfort be so advantageous to us, it will be no wonder to see Satan so much rage against it. It would be a satisfaction to him to tear these robes off us, to impede so needful a duty, to rob us of so much strength, and to bereave us of the sweet fruits of our labours.

3. Thirdly, It further appears that Satan's design is against the comforts of God's children, *by the many advantages he hath against them, from the trouble and disquiet of their hearts*. I shall reckon up the chief of them; as,

[1.] From the trouble of the spirit *he raiseth confusions and distractions of mind*; for, (1.) It is as natural to trouble to raise up a swarm of muddy thoughts as to 'a troubled sea to cast up mire and dirt;' and hence is that comparison, Isa. lvii. 20; a thousand fearful surmises, evil cogitations, resolves, and counsels immediately offer themselves. This disorder of thoughts Christ took notice of in his disciples when they were in danger, 'Why do thoughts arise in your hearts?' Luke xxiv. 38. And David considered it as matter of great anxiety, which called for speedy help: Ps. xciv. 19, 'In the multitude of my thoughts within me, thy comforts delight my soul.' Sometimes one fear is suggested, then presently another; now this doubt perplexeth, then another question is begot by the former; they think to take this course, then by and by they are off that, and resolve upon another, and as quickly change again to a third, and so onward, one thought succeeding another, as vapours from a boiling pot. (2.) Such thoughts are vexatious and distracting, the very thoughts themselves, being the poisonous steams of their running sores, are sadly afflictive, and not unfitly called *cogitationes onerosæ*, burdensome thoughts.

But as they wrap up a man in clouds and darkness, as they puzzle him in his resolves, nonplus him in his undertakings, distract him in his counsels, disturb and hinder him in his endeavours, &c., so do they bring the mind into a labyrinth of confusion. What advantage the devil hath against a child of God when his heart is thus divided and broken into shivers, it is easy to imagine. And David seems to be very sensible of it when he put up that request, Ps. lxxxvi. 11, 'Unite my heart to fear thy name.'

[2.] By disquiet of heart the devil *unfits men for duty or service.* Fitness for duty lies in the orderly temper of body and mind, making a man willing to undertake, and able to finish his work with comfortable satisfaction. If either the body or mind be distempered, a man is unfit for such an undertaking; both must be in a suitable frame, like a well-tuned instrument, else there will be no melody. Hence, when David prepared himself for praises and worship, he tells us his 'heart was ready and fixed,' and then 'his tongue was ready also,' so was his hand with psaltery and harp; all these were awakened into a suitable posture, Ps. xlv. 1, 2, and cviii. 1, 2. That a man is or hath been in a fit order for service may be concluded from—(1.) His alacrity to undertake a duty. (2.) His activity in the prosecution. (3.) His satisfaction afterward, right grounds and principles in these things being still presupposed. This being laid as a foundation, we shall easily perceive how the troubles of the spirit do unfit us for duty. For,

First, These do take away all *alacrity and forwardness of the mind, partly by diverting it from duty.* Sorrows when they prevail do so fix the mind upon the present trouble, that it can think of nothing but its burden; they confine the thoughts to the pain and smart, and make a man forget all other things, as David in his trouble 'forgot to eat his bread,' [Ps. cii. 4]; and sick persons willingly discourse only of their diseases; partly by indisposing for action. Joy and hope are active principles, but sorrow is sullen and sluggish. As the mind in trouble is wholly employed in a contemplation of its misery, rather than in finding out a way to avoid it, so if it be at leisure at any time to entertain thoughts of using means for recovery, yet it is so tired out with its burden, so disheartened by its own fears, so discouraged with opposition and disappointment, that it hath no list to undertake anything. By this means the devil brings the soul into a spiritual catoche,[1] so congealing the spirits, that it is made stiff and deprived of motion.

Second, Disquiets of heart unfit us for duty, *by hindering our activity in prosecution of duty.* The whole heart, soul, and strength should be engaged in all religious services, but these troubles are as clogs and weights to hinder motion. Joy is the dilatation of the soul, and widens it for anything which it undertakes; but grief contracts the heart, and narrows all the faculties. Hence doth David beg an 'enlarged heart,' as the principle of activity: Ps. cxix. 32, 'I will run the way of thy commandments, when thou shalt enlarge my heart;' for what can else be expected when the mind is so distracted with fear and sorrow, but that it should be uneven, tottering, weak, and

---

[1] An 'apoplexy,' Gr. κατοχη.—G.

confused? so that if it do set itself to anything, it acts troublesomely, drives on heavily, and doth very little with a great deal ado; and yet, were the unfitness the less, if that little which it can do were well done, but the mind is so interrupted in its endeavours that sometimes in prayer the man begins, and then is presently at a stand, and dare not proceed, his words are 'swallowed up, he is so troubled that he cannot speak,' Ps. lxxvii. 4. Sometimes the mind is kept so employed and fixed on trouble, that it cannot attend in hearing or praying, but presently the thoughts are called off, and become wandering.

Third, Troubles hinder *our satisfaction in duty, and by that means unfit us to present duties, and indispose us to future services of that kind.* Our satisfaction in duty ariseth, (1.) Sometimes from its own lustre and sweetness, the conviction we have of its pleasantness, and the spiritual advantages to be had thereby; these render it alluring and attractive, and by such considerations are we invited to their performance, as Isa. ii. 3, 'Come ye, let us go up to the mountain of the Lord; and he will teach us of his ways, and we will walk in his paths.' Hosea vi. 1, 'Come, and let us return unto the Lord: for he hath torn, and he will heal us; he hath smitten, and he will bind us up;' but trouble of spirit draws a black curtain over the excellencies of duty, and presents us with frightful thoughts about it, so that we judge of it according to our fears, and make it frightful to ourselves, as if it would be to no purpose—rather a mischief than an advantage. (2.) Sometime our satisfaction ariseth from some special token of favour which our indulgent Father lets fall upon us while we are in his work, as when he gives us more than ordinary assistance, or puts joy and comfort into our hearts. And this he often doth to make us come again, and to engage afresh in the same or other services, as having 'tasted and seen that the Lord is gracious,' [1 Pet. ii. 3,] and that there is a blessedness in waiting for him. As in our bodies he so orders it that the concocted juices become a successive ferment to those that succeed from our daily meat and drink: so from duties performed doth he beget and continue spiritual appetite to new undertakings. But oh how sadly is all this hindered by the disquiet of the heart! The graces of faith and love are usually obstructed, if not in their exercise, yet in their delightful fruits, and if God offer a kindness, inward sorrow hinders the perception: as when Moses told the Israelites of their deliverance, 'they hearkened not for hard bondage,' [Exod. vi. 9.] If a message of peace present itself in a promise, or some consideration of God's merciful disposition, yet usually this is not credited. Job confesseth so much of himself: Job xix. 16, 'If I had called and he had answered me, yet would I not believe that he had hearkened unto my voice.' David also doth the like: Ps. lxxvii. 2, 3, 'My soul refuseth to be comforted; I remembered God, and was troubled.' Matter of greatest comfort is often so far from giving ease, that it augments the trouble. However, the heart is so hurried with its fears, and discomposed with grief, that it cannot hearken to, nor consider, nor believe any kind offer made to it.

By all these ways doth the devil, through the disquiet of mind, unfit the Lord's people for duty; and what a sad advantage this is against us cannot easily be told. By this means he may widen the distance betwixt God and us, keep our wounds open, make us a reproach to religion; and what not? But (3.) By these disquiets he pusheth us on to reject all duties; for when he hath tired us out by wearisome endeavours, under so great indispositions and unfitness, he hath a fair advantage to tempt us to lay all aside. Our present posture doth furnish him with arguments, he forgeth his javelins upon our anvil, and they are commonly these three:—

[1.] That duties are *difficult*. And this is easily proved from our own experience; while we are broken or bowed down with sorrows, we make many attempts for duty, and are oft beat off with loss; our greatest toil helps us but to very inconsiderable performances; hence, he infers, it is foolishness to attempt that which is above our strength, better sit still than toil for nothing.

[2.] That they are *unfruitful;* and this is our own complaint, for troubled spirits have commonly great expectations from duties at first, and they run to them, as the impotent and sick people to the pool of Bethesda, with thoughts of immediate ease as soon as they shall step into them; but when they have tried, and waited a while, stretching themselves upon duty, as Elisha's servant laid the staff upon the face of the Shunammite's son, and yet there is no voice nor hearing, no answer from God, no peace, then are they presently dissatisfied, reflecting on the promises of God and the counsels of good men, with this, Where is all the pleasantness you speak of? what advantage is it that we have thus run and laboured, when we have got nothing? And then it is easy for the devil to add, And why do you wait on the Lord any longer?

[3.] His last and most dangerous argument is, that they are *sinful*. Unfitness for duty produceth many distractions, much deadness, wandering thoughts, great interruptions, and pitful performances. Hence the troubled soul comes off from duty wounded and halting, more distressed when he hath done than when he began; upon these considerations, that all his service was sin, a mocking of God, a taking his name in vain, nay, a very blasphemous affront to a divine majesty. Upon this the devil starts the question to his heart, Whether it be not better to forbear all duty, and to do nothing? Thus doth Satan improve the trouble of the mind, and often with the designed success. For a dejected spirit doth not only afford the materials of these weapons which the devil frames against it, but is much prepared to receive them into its own bowels. The grounds of these arguments it grants, and the inferences are commonly consented to, so that ordinarily duty is neglected, either, 1. Through sottishness of heart; or, 2. Through frightful fears; or, 3. Through desperateness; bringing a man to the very precipice of that atheistical determination, 'I have cleansed my hands in vain,' [Ps. lxxiii. 13.]

Fourth, Satan makes use of the troubles of God's children as a *stumbling-block to others*. It is no small advantage to him, that he hath hereby an occasion to render the ways of God unlovely to those that are beginning to look heavenward; he sets before them the sighs, groans, complaints, and restless outcries of the wounded in spirit, to scare them off from all seriousness in religion, and whispers this to them, 'Will you choose a life of bitterness and sorrow? can you eat ashes for bread, and mingle your drink with tears? will you exchange the comforts and contents of life for a melancholy heart and a dejected countenance? how like you to go mourning all the day, and at night to be scared with dreams and terrified with visions? will you choose a life that is worse than death, and a condition which will make you a terror to yourselves and a burden to others? can you be in love with a heart loaden with grief, and perpetual fears almost to distraction, while you see others in the meantime enjoy themselves in a contented peace? Thus he follows young beginners with his suggestions, making them believe that they cannot be serious in religion, but at last they will be brought to this, and that it is a very dangerous thing to be religious overmuch, and the highway to despair; so that if they must have a religion, he readily directs them to use no more of it than may consist with the pleasures of sin and the world, and to make an easy business of it, not to let sin lie over-near their heart, lest it disquiet them; nor overmuch to concern themselves with study, reading, prayer, or hearing of threatening, awakening sermons, lest it make them mad; nor to affect the sublimities of communion with God, exercises of faith and divine love, lest it discompose them and dash their worldly jollities out of countenance. A counsel that is readily enough embraced by those that are almost persuaded to be Christians; and the more to confirm them in it, he sticks not sometime to asperse the poor troubled soul with dissimulation—where that accusation is proper, for the devil cares not how inconsistent he be with himself, so that he may but gain his end—affirming all his seriousness to be nothing but whining hypocrisy. So that whether they judge these troubles to be real or feigned, his conclusion is the same, and he persuades men thereby to hold off from all religious strictness, holy diligence, and careful watchfulness.

Fifth, A further use which the devil makes of these troubles of spirit is, *to prepare the hearts of men thereby to give entertainment to his venomous impressions.* Distress of heart usually opens the door to Satan, and lays a man naked, without armour or defence, as a fair mark for all his poisoned arrows; and it is a hundred to one but some of them do hit. I shall choose out some of the most remarkable, and they are these:—

[1.] *After long acquaintance with grief he labours to fix them in it.* In some cases custom doth alleviate higher griefs, and men take an odd kind of delight in them; *Est quædam etiam dolendi voluptas.* It is some pleasure to complain, and men settle themselves in such a course, their finger is ever upon their sore, and they go about telling their sorrows to all they converse with—though to some this is a necessity, for real sorrows, if they be not too great for vent, will constrain them to speak—yet in some that have been formerly acquainted with grief, it degenerates at last into a formality of complaining; and because they formerly had cause so to do, they think they must always do so. But besides this, Satan doth endeavour to chain men to their mourning upon two higher accounts[1]: 1. By a delusive contentment

---

[1] Collins 'Cordial,' part ii. p. 154. [Misprint for Collinges, whose 'Cordial for a Fainting Soul' (1649, 4to) is one of the richest of Puritan experimental treatises; and not less so his 'Intercourses of Divine Love,' (2 vols. 4to. 1673-83.)—G.]

in sorrow, as if our tears paid some part of our debt to God, and made amends for the injuries done to him. 2. By an obstinate sullenness and desperate resolvedness they harden themselves in sorrow, and say as Job, chap. vii. 11, 'I will not refrain my mouth, I will speak in the anguish of my spirit, I will complain in the bitterness of my soul. Am I a sea, or a whale, that thou settest a watch over me?'

[2.] Another impression that men's hearts are apt to take, is, *unthankfulness for the favours formerly bestowed upon them.* Their present troubles blot out the memory of old kindnesses. They conclude they have nothing at all, because they have not peace. Though God heretofore hath sent down from on high, and taken them out of the great waters, or out of the mire and clay where they were ready to sink; though he hath sent them many tokens of love, conferred on them many blessings; yet all these are no more to them, so long as their sorrows continue, than Haman's wealth and honour was to him, so long as Mordecai the Jew sat at the king's gate. Thus the devil oft prevails with God's children, to deal with God as some unthankful persons deal with their benefactors; who, if they be not humoured in every request, deny the reality of their love, and despise with great ingratitude all that was done for them before.

[3.] By inward griefs, the heart of the afflicted are prepared to entertain *the worst interpretation that the devil can put upon the providences of God.* The various instances of Scripture, and the gracious promises made to those that 'walk in darkness and see no light,' do abundantly forewarn men from making bad conclusions of God's dealings, and do tell us that God in design, for our trial and for our profit, doth often hide his face 'for a moment,' when yet his purpose is to 'bind us up with everlasting compassions.' Now the devil labours to improve the sorrows of the mind to give a quite contrary construction. If they are afflicted, instead of saying, 'Sorrow may endure for a night, but joy will come in the morning,' [Ps. xxx. 5,] or that 'for a little while God hath hidden himself,' he puts them to say, 'this darkness shall never pass away.' If the grief be little, he drives them on to a fearful expectation of worse; as he did with Hezekiah, Isa. xxxviii. 13, 'I reckoned till morning, that, as a lion, so will he break all my bones; from day even to night wilt thou make an end of me.' If God purpose to teach us by inward sorrows our pride of heart, carelessness, neglect of dependence upon him, the bitterness of sin, or the like, the devil will make us believe, and we are too ready to subscribe to him, that God proclaims open war against us, and resolves never to own us more. So did Job, chap. xix. 6, 'Know now that God hath overthrown me, and compassed me with his net;' how often complained he, 'thou hast made me as thy mark, thou hast broken me asunder, thou hast taken me by my neck and shaken me to pieces'! So also Heman, Ps. lxxxviii. 14, 'Why castest thou off my soul? why hidest thou thy face from me?'

[4.] Upon this occasion the devil is ready to envenom the soul *with sinful wishes and execrations against itself.* Eminent saints have been tempted in their trouble to say too much this way. Job solemnly cursed his day: Job iii. 3, 'Let the day perish wherein I was born, and the night in which it was said, There is a man-child conceived,'

&c. So also Jeremiah, chap. xx. 14, 'Cursed be the day wherein I was born: let not the day wherein my mother bare me be blessed. Cursed be the man who brought tidings to my father, saying, A manchild is born unto thee; and let that man be as the cities which God overthrew, and repented not.' Strange rashness! what had the day deserved? or wherein was the messenger to be blamed? Violent passions hurried him beyond all bounds of reason and moderation. When troubles within are violent, a small push sets men forward; and when once they begin, they are carried headlong beyond what they first intended.

[5.] On this advantage the devil sometimes emboldens them to *quarrel God himself directly.* When Job and Jeremiah cursed their day, it was a contumely against God indirectly; but they durst not make bold with God at so high a rate as to quarrel him to his face. Yet even this are men brought to often when their sorrows are longlasting and deep. The devil suggests, Can God be faithful, and never keep promise for help? can he be merciful, when he turns away his ears from the cry of the miserable? where is his pity, when he multiplies his wounds without cause? Though at first these cursed intimations do a little startle men, yet when by frequent inculcating they grow more familiar to the heart, the distressed break out in their rage with those exclamations, Where is the faithfulness of God? where are his promises? hath he not forgotten to be gracious? are not his mercies clean gone? And at last it may be Satan leads them a step higher, that is—

[6.] *To a despairing desperateness.* For when all passages of relief are stopped up, and the burden becomes great, men are apt to be drawn into rage and fury when they think their burden is greater than they can bear, and see no hope of ease; in a kind of revenge they express their anger against the hand that wounded them. The devil is officiously ready with his advice of 'Curse God and die,' [Job. ii. 9,] and they, being full of anguish, are quickly made to comply with it.

[7.] When it is at this height, the devil hath but one stage more, and that is the suggesting of *irregular means for ease.* Rage against God doth not quench the inward burning, blasphemies against heaven easeth not the pain, the sore runs still and ceaseth not, the trouble continues, the man cannot endure it longer, all patience and hope is gone. What shall he do in this case? The devil offers his service; he will be the physician, and commonly he prescribes one of these two things: (1.) That it is best to endeavour to break through all this trouble into a resolved profaneness; not to stand in awe of laws, not to believe that there is a God that governs in the earth, but that this is only the bitter fruit of melancholy and unnecessary seriousness, and therefore it is best ' to eat, drink, and be merry.' If a man can thus escape out of his trouble, the devil needs no more; but oft he cannot, the wounds of conscience will not be thus healed. Then, (2.) He hath another remedy, which will not fail, as he tells them, that is, to ' destroy themselves,' to end their troubles with their lives. How open are the breasts of troubled creatures to all these darts! and were it not that God secretly steps in and holds the afflicted with his right hand, it is scarce imaginable but that wounded consciences should by Satan's subtle improvement of so fair an advantage be brought to all this misery.

[8.] Satan can afflict the *body by the mind*. For these two are so closely bound together that their good and bad estate is shared betwixt them. If the heart be merry the countenance is cheerful, the strength is renewed, the bones do flourish like an herb. If the heart be troubled the health is impaired, the strength is dried up, the marrow of the bones wasted, &c. Grief in the heart is like a moth in the garment, it insensibly consumeth the body and disordereth it. This advantage of weakening the body falls into Satan's hands by necessary consequence, as the prophet's ripe figs, that fell into the mouth of the eater. And surely he is well pleased with it, as he is an enemy both to body and soul. But it is a greater satisfaction to him in that as he can make the sorrows of the mind produce the weakness and sickness of the body, so can he make the distemper of the body, by a reciprocal requital, to augment the trouble of the mind. How little can a sickly body do! It disables a man for all services; he cannot oft pray, nor read, nor hear; sickness takes away the sweetness and comfort of religious exercises. This gives occasion for them to think the worse of themselves. They think the soul is weary of the ways of God, when the body cannot hold out. All failures which weariness and faintness produce are ascribed presently to the bad disposition of the mind, and this is like oil cast upon the flame. Thus the devil makes a double gain out of spiritual trouble.

[9.] Let it be also reckoned among the advantages which Satan hath against men from trouble of spirit, that it is *a contentment to him to see them in their miseries*. It is a sport to him to see them, as Job speaks, take their flesh in their teeth, and cry out in the bitterness of their souls, [Job. xiii. 14.] Their groanings are his music. When they wallow in ashes, drown themselves in tears, roar till their throat is dry, spread out their hands for help, then he gluts his heart in looking upon their woes. When they fall upon God with their unjust surmises, evil interpretations of providence, questioning his favour, denying his grace, wishing they had never been born, then he claps his hands and shouts a victory. The pleasantest sight to him is to see God hiding himself from his child, and that child broken with fears, torn in pieces with griefs, made a brother to dragons, a companion to owls, under restless anxieties, perpetual lamentations, feeble and sore broken, their strength dried like a potsherd, their throat dry, their tongue cleaving to their jaws, their bowels boiling, their bones burnt with heat, their skin black upon them, their flesh consumed, their bones sticking out, chastened with strong pain upon their bed. This is one of Satan's delightful spectacles, and for these ends doth he all he can to bereave them of their comfort, which we may the more certainly persuade ourselves to be true, when we consider the grounds forementioned, his malicious nature, the advantages of spiritual peace, and the disadvantages of spiritual trouble.

CHAPTER VI.

Of the various ways by which he hinders peace—1. Way by discomposures of spirit. These discomposures explained, by shewing, (1.) What advantage he takes from our natural temper, and what tempers give him this advantage. (2.) By what occasions he works upon our natural tempers. (3.) With what success. [1.] These occasions suited to natural inclinations, raise great disturbance. [2.] They have a tendency to spiritual trouble. The thing proved, and the manner how discovered. [3.] These disturbances much in his power. General and particular considerations about that power.

Having evidenced that one of Satan's principal designs is against the peace and comfort of God's children, I shall next endeavour a discovery of the various ways by which he doth undermine them herein. All inward troubles are not of the same kind in themselves, neither doth Satan always produce the same effects out of all; some being in their own nature disquiets, that do not so directly and immediately overthrow the peace and joy of believing, and the comforts of assurance of divine favour, as others do. Yet seeing that by all he hath no small advantage against us as to sin and trouble, and that any of them at the long run may lead us to question our interest in grace and the love of God, and may accordingly afflict us, I shall speak of them all; which that I may do the more distinctly, I shall rank these troubles into several heads, under peculiar names—it may be not altogether so proper but that the curious may find matter of exception to them—that by them and their explanation the differences may the better appear. I distinguish therefore of a fourfold trouble that the devil doth endeavour to work up upon the hearts of men. They are, 1. Discomposures. 2. Affrightments. 3. Dejections of sadness. 4. Distresses of horror. Of all which I shall speak in their order. And,

1. *Of discomposures of soul.* These are molestations and disturbances by which the mind is put out of order and made unquiet. The calm in which it should enjoy itself, and by which it should be composed to a regular and steady acting, being disturbed by a storm of commotion, and in which the conscience or the peace of it is not presently concerned. This distinction of the trouble of soul from the trouble of conscience is not new. Others have observed it before,[1] and do thus explain it: Trouble of soul is larger than trouble of conscience; every troubled conscience is a troubled soul, but every troubled soul is not a troubled conscience; for the soul may be troubled from causes natural, civil, and spiritual, according to variety of occasions and provocations, when yet a man's inward peace with God is firm; and in some cases, as in infants and in men distracted with fevers, &c., there may be passions and disturbances of soul when the conscience is not capable of exercising its office: nay, the soul of Christ was troubled—John xii. 27, 'Now is my soul troubled'—when

---

[1] Differunt inter se casus animæ ægræ et casus conscientiæ ægræ, &c.—*Dickson, Therap. Sacr.*, lib. i. cap. 2. [Edinburgh, 1656, 8vo.—G.]

it was not possible that sin or despair should have the least footing in him.

For the opening of these discomposures of soul I shall—1. Shew upon what advantage of natural temper the devil is encouraged to molest men. 2. By what occasions he doth work upon our natural inclinations. 3. And with what success of disturbance to the soul.

(1.) As to our natural dispositions, Satan, as hath formerly been noted, *takes his usual indications of working from thence.* These guide him in his enterprises; his temptations being suited to men's tempers, proceed more smoothly and successfully. Some are of so serene and calm a disposition, that he doth not much design their discomposure; but others there are whose passions are more stirring —fit matter for him to work upon: and these are,

[1.] *The angry disposition.* How great an advantage this gives to Satan to disturb the heart, may be easily conceived by considering the various workings of it in several men, according to their different humours. It is a passion that acts not alike in all; and for the differences, so far as we need to be concerned, I shall not trouble the schools of philosophers, but content myself with what we have in Eph. iv. 31, where the apostle expresseth it by three words, not that they differ essentially, declaring thereby the various ways of anger's working. The first is πικρία, which we translate *bitterness.* This is a displeasure smothered; for some when they are angry cover it, and give it no vent, partly for that they are sometimes ashamed to mention the ground as trivial or unjust, partly from sullenness of disposition, and oft from a natural reservedness; while the flame is thus kept down, it burns inwardly, and men resolve[1] in their minds many troublesome, vexatious thoughts. The second word is θυμὸς, *wrath;* this is a fierce, impetuous anger. Some are soon moved, but so violent that they are presently transported into rage and frenzy, or are so peevishly waspish that they cannot be spoken to. The third is ὀργὴ, translated here *anger*, but signifies such a displeasure as is deep, entertaining thoughts of revenge and pursuit, settling itself at last into hatred. Any of these is enough to bereave the heart of its rest, and to alarm it with disturbances.[2]

[2.] Others have an *envious nature, always maligning and repining at other men's felicity;* an evil eye that cannot look on another's better condition without vexation. This turns a man into a devil. It is the devil's proper sin, and the fury that doth unquiet him, and he the better knows of what avail it would be to help on our trouble.

[3.] Some are *of proud tempers*, always overvaluing themselves, with the scorn and contempt of others. This humour is troublesome to all about them, but all this trouble doth at last redound to themselves. These think all others should observe them, and take notice of their supposed excellencies, which if men do not, then it pines them or stirs up their choler to indignation. Solomon, Prov. xxx. 21, mentioning those things that are greatly disquieting in the earth, instanceth in 'a servant when he reigneth; and the handmaid that is heir to her mistress,' intending thereby the proud, imperious insolency of those that are unexpectedly raised from a low estate to wealth or honour.

[1] Query, 'revolve'?—Ed.   [2] Bayne, *in loc.*

He that is of 'a proud heart stirreth up strife,' Prov. xxviii. 25; and as he is troublesome to others, so doth he create trouble to himself; for he not only molests himself by the working of his disdainful thoughts, while he exerciseth his scorn towards others: Prov. xxi. 24, 'The haughty scorner deals in proud wrath;' but this occasions the affronts and contempt of others again, which beget new griefs to his restless mind.

[4.] Some have a natural *exorbitancy of desire, an evil coveting;* they are passionately carried forth toward what they have not, and have no contentment or satisfaction in what they do enjoy. Such humours are seldom at ease, their desires are painfully violent; and when they obtain what they longed for, they soon grow weary of it, and then another object takes up their wishes, so that these 'daughters of the horse-leech are ever crying, Give, give,' Prov. xxx. 15.

[5.] Others have *a soft effeminate temper, a weakness of soul that makes them unfit to bear any burden, or endure any hardness.* These, if they meet with pains or troubles—and who can challenge an exemption from them?—they are presently impatient, vexing themselves by a vain reluctancy to what they cannot avoid; not but that extraordinary burdens will make the strongest spirit to stoop, but these cry out for the smallest matters, which a stout mind would bear with some competent cheerfulness.

[6.] And there are other dispositions that *are tender to an excess of sympathy,* so that they immoderately affect and afflict themselves with other men's sorrows. Though this be a temper more commendable than any of the former, yet Satan can take advantage of this, as also of the fore-named dispositions, to discompose us, especially by suiting them with fit occasions, which readily work upon these tempers. And this was,

(2.) The second thing to be explained, which shall be performed by a brief enumeration of them, the chief whereof are these:

[1.] *Contempt or disestimation.* When a man's person, parts, or opinion are slighted, his anger, envy, pride, and impatience are awakened, and these make him swell and restless within. Even good men have been sadly disturbed this way. Job, as holy a man as he was, and who had enough of greater matters to trouble his mind, yet among other griefs complains of this more than once: Job xii. 4, 'I am as one mocked of his neighbour: the just upright man is laughed to scorn;' chap. xix. 15, 'They that dwell in mine house, and my maids, count me for a stranger. I called my servant, and he gave me no answer. Yea, young children despised me; I rose up and they spake against me.' Thus he bemoans himself, and, which is more, speaks of it again with some smartness of indignation: Job xxx. 1, 'Now they that are younger than I have me in derision, whose fathers I would have disdained to have set with the dogs of my flock.' David also, who had a stout heart under troubles, complains that he could not bear reproaches: Ps. lxix., 'Reproach hath broken mine heart; I am full of heaviness.' What these reproaches were, and how he was staggered with them, he tells us: ver. 10, 'I chastened my soul with fasting, that was to my reproach. I made sackcloth my garment; and I became a proverb to them. They that sit in the gate speak against me ; and I was the song of the drunkards.' With these he was so stounded that if he had not catched hold on God by prayer, as he speaks, ver. 13, he had fallen, ' But as for me, my prayer is unto thee, O Lord,' &c. ; and he afterward speaks of his support under reproaches as a wonder of divine assistance : Ps. cxix. 51, ' The proud have had me in derision : yet have I not declined from thy law.'

[2.] *Injury* is another occasion by which the devil works upon our tempers to disquiet us. Wrongs of injustice and oppression are hard to bear. This is a common ground of trouble. Good men cannot always acquit themselves in this case as they ought. Jeremiah, when smitten by Pashur, and put in the stocks, Jer. xx. 2, 8, falls into a sad passion : ' I am a derision daily, every one mocketh me. I cried out, I cried violence and spoil,' imitating the passionate affrightments of those that cry, Murder, murder, &c. No wonder, seeing Solomon gives it as an axiom built upon manifold experience, Eccles. vii. 7. Oppression doth not only make a man unquiet, but mad in his unquietness; and not only those that are foolish and hasty, but the most considerate and sedate persons : ' Oppression makes a wise man mad.'

[3.] Another occasion of men's discomposure is, *the prosperity of the wicked*. Their abundance, their advancements to honours and dignity, hath always been a grudge to those whose condition is below them, and yet suppose themselves to have better grounds to expect preferment than they. This astonished Job even to trembling : Job xxi. 7, ' When I remember, I am afraid, and trembling taketh hold on my flesh ;' and the matter was but this, ' Wherefore do the wicked live, become old, yea, and mighty in power ?' &c. The trouble that seizeth on men's hearts on this occasion is called fretting, a vexation that wears out the strength of the soul, as two hard bodies waste by mutual attrition or rubbing. And it takes its advantage from our envy chiefly, though other distempers come in to help it forward : Ps. xxxvii. 1, ' Fret not thyself because of evil-doers, neither be thou envious against the workers of iniquity.' David confesseth that he was apt to fall into this trouble, Ps. lxxiii. 3, ' I was envious at the foolish, when I saw the prosperity of the wicked.' Against this disquiet we have frequent cautions, Prov. xxiv. 1, 19, and Ps. xlix. 16, ' Be not afraid when one is made rich, when the glory of his house is increased.' All which shew our proneness to this disease.

[4.] *Crosses and afflictions give Satan an opportunity to work upon our passions ;* as disappointments of expectations, loss of friends, of estate, persecutions and sufferings for conscience sake, &c. None of these in their own nature are 'joyous, but grievous ;' and what use they have been of to the devil to discompose the minds of the sufferers, is evidenced by common experience. The tears, sad countenances, and doleful lamentations of men are true witnesses of the disquiet of their hearts. Every one being pressed with the sense of his own smart is ready to cry out, ' Is there any sorrow like my sorrow ? I am poor and comfortless ; my lovers and my friends have forsaken me, and there is none to help.' Some grow faint under their burden, while their eyes fail in looking for redress, especially when new unexpected troubles overwhelm their hopes : ' When I looked for good, then evil came ; and when I waited for light, there came darkness,' Job xxx. 26.

'Why hast thou smitten us, and there is no healing for us? We looked for peace, and there is no good; and for the time of healing, and behold trouble,' Jer. xiv. 19; and here they sink, concluding there is no hope. Others that bear up better in a blessed expectation of spiritual profit, having that of David in their eye, 'Blessed is the man whom thou afflictest, and teachest in thy law;' yet they cannot forbear their complaints even to God; Ps. xxv. 17, 'The troubles of mine heart are enlarged; oh bring thou me out of my distresses; look upon mine affliction and my pain.' Nay,[1] those that have had the highest advantages of heavenly support, whose hearts have been kept in peace, counting it all joy that they have fallen into these trials—and God doth more this way for those that suffer for the gospel's sake than ordinarily for others; yet have not these been under a stoical senselessness of their trouble. Though they were not 'distressed,' they were 'troubled on every side;' though 'not in despair,' yet they were 'perplexed,' 2 Cor. iv. 8; though their afflictions were light, yet were they afflictions still.

[5.] To these may be added, *the pain or anguish of sickness and bodily distemper*. Though there are various degrees of pain, and that some sicknesses are less afflictive than others, yet none of them forbear to pierce the mind. The whole man is discomposed. He that is exercised with 'strong pains upon his bed,' cries out in the bitterness of his soul; and he that by insensible degrees languisheth, grows ordinarily peevish, and his mind bleeds by an inward wound, so that he 'spends his days in sighing,' and his years in mourning. And others there are who, being before acquainted with bodily pains, grow very impatient in sickness, and are able to bear nothing. And besides the present sense of pain, the expectation of death puts some into great commotion; the fears of it, for it is naturally dreadful, fills them with disquiet thoughts; and those that approach to the grave by slow steps, under consumption or languishing sicknesses, they are habituated to sadness, and can think of nothing cheerfully—except they have great assurance of salvation, and have well learned to die—because the coffin, grave, and winding-sheet are still presented to them. These, though they be very suitable objects for meditation, and, well improved, of great advantage for preparation to death, yet doth Satan thereby, when it is for his purpose, endeavour to keep men under grief, and to bereave them of their peace.

[6.] Satan takes an advantage of trouble from *the miseries of others*. Sympathy is a Christian grace; and to bear one another's burdens, to mourn with those that mourn, shews us to be fellow-feeling members of the same body; for 'if one member suffer, all the members suffer with it,' [1 Cor. xii. 26.] Yet are some men naturally of so tender a constitution, that Satan overdrives them herein. Every common occasion will wound them. The usual effects of God's ordinary providence on the poor, lame, or sick, are deeply laid to heart by them; and instead of being not unsensible of other men's miseries, they are not sensible of anything else, neither do they enjoy their own mercies. And here, as Satan can every moment present them with objects of pity, ordinary or extraordinary, so upon a religious pretence of merciful consideration,

---

[1] Misprinted 'may.'—G.

they are made cruel to themselves, refusing their own peace, because other men are not at ease.

(3.) The third particular promised to be explained for the discovery of these discomposures of soul was this, that by *a concurrence of these and such like occasions to such tempers, the hearts of men are disturbed, and their inward peace broken.* This I shall evidence of these three things: 1. That these occasions meeting with such dispositions, do naturally raise great disturbances in their present working; 2. That they have a tendency to further trouble; 3. That Satan doth design, and hath it ordinarily in his power, to discompose the hearts of men hereby.

[1.] That these occasions meeting with such dispositions, do naturally raise *great disturbances*. This is evident from what hath been said already; for (1.) *All these dispositions carry as much fire in their own bosoms, as is sufficient to burn up the standing corn of any man's peace.* What is anger, but an inward burning, a restless confusion of the spirits? sometime a frenzy, a distraction, a troubled sea full of rage, a wild beast let loose. Envy, that is a fretful peevishness, a vexatious repining, needing no other tormentors but its own furies, recoiling upon him that bred it, because it cannot wreak its spite upon its objects. An envious person is a self-murderer, by the verdict of Eliphaz: Job v. 2, 'Wrath killeth the foolish man, and envy slayeth the foolish one.' This is not barely to be understood of its provoking the judge of all the earth to send down its deserved destruction; but also, if not chiefly, of its own corroding temper, which by long continuance wastes the strength and consumes the body. Pride is a perpetual vexation, creating its troubles from its own fancy. Irregular covetings keep a man still upon the rack; they make a man like the Tantalus of the poets; they give a man a *caninus appetitus*, a strong appetite with excessive greediness, and restless pursuit, and constant dissatisfactions; he is ever gaping, and never enjoying. Impatience is a wearisome conflict with a burden which it can neither bear nor yet shake off; where all the fruit of the vain labour amounts to no better account than this, that the impatient makes his burden the greater, the bands that tie it on the stronger, and the strength that should bear it the weaker. Lastly, An excess of pity multiplies 'wounds without cause.' It hinders a man to be happy so long as there are any that are miserable. He is always, in reference to his quiet, at the mercy of other men. The afflicted can torment him at a distance; and, by a kind of magic, make him feel the torments that are inflicted upon his image. Who can deny but that men that are ridden by such vexatious dispositions must lead an unquiet life, and always be tossed with inward tempests? Especially, (2.) When we consider *how fit the fore-mentioned occasions are to draw out these humours to their tumultuary extravagances.* A lighted match and gunpowder are not more exactly suited to raise a shaking blast, than those occasions and tempers are to breed an inward annoyance. Some of these humours are so troublesome, that rather than they will want work, they will fight with their own shadows, and, by a perverseness of prejudicated fancy, will create their own troubles; and the best of them, which seem sometime to take truce and compose themselves to rest, while occasions are out of the way; yet they are quickly awakened, like sleeping dogs that are roused with the least noise. What work, then, may we expect they will make when they are summoned to give their appearance upon a solemn occasion? But (3.) If we should deal by instances, and bring upon the stage the effects that have been brought forth by these concurring causes, it will appear that they make disturbances in good earnest. Let us either view *the furious fits that have been, like sudden flashes, soonest gone,* or their more lasting impressions, and we shall find it true. As to violent fits raised by such occasions and dispositions, examples are infinite. What rages, outrages, madnesses, and extravagances have men run into! Some, upon provocations, have furiously acted savage cruelties, and for small matters have been carried to the most desperate revenges. Others have been brought to such violent commotions within themselves, that the frame of nature hath been thereby weakened and overthrown. As Sylla, who in a strong passion vomited choler till he died. Some in their fury have acted that which hath been matter of sorrow to them all their days. But, omitting the examples of heathens and wicked men, let us consider the wonderful transports of holy men. Moses, a man eminent beyond comparison in meekness, was so astonished with a sudden surprise of trouble at the sight of the golden calf, that he threw down the tables of the law, and brake them. Some indeed observe from thence a significancy of Israel's breaking the law and forfeiting God's protection as his peculiar people; but this is more to be ascribed to the designment of divine providence, that so ordered it, than to the intendment of Moses, who no doubt did not this from a sedate and calm deliberation, as purposing by this act to tell Israel so much; but was hurried by his grief, as not considering well what he did, to break them. Asa, a good man, when he was reproved by the prophet, instead of thankful acceptance of the reproof, grows angry, falls into a rage, and throws the prophet into prison. Elias, discomposed with Jezebel's persecution, desires that God would take away his life. Jonah, in his anger, falls out with God, and justifies it when he hath done. Surely such fits as these proceeded from great inward combustion. Would wise, sober, holy men have said or done such things if they had not been transported beyond themselves? and though in such cases the fits are soon over, yet we observe that some are apt to fall into such fits often, and are so easily irritated, that, like the epileptic person possessed by the devil, upon every occasion, they are by him 'cast into the fire or into the water,' [Mat. xvii. 15,] and by the frequent return of their distemper are never at rest.

As to others, whose tempers are more apt to retain a troublesome impression, it is very obvious that their discomposures have as much in length and breadth as the other had in height. You may view Haman tormented under his secret discontent, which his pride and envy formed in him, for the want of Mordecai's obeisance. The king's favour, a great estate, high honour, and what else a man could wish to make him content, are all swallowed up in this gulf, and become nothing to him. You see Amnon, vexed and sick for his sister Tamar, waxing lean from day to day. You see Ahab, though a king, who had enough to satisfy his mind, in the same condition for Naboth's vineyard. If you say these were wicked men, who rid their lusts without a bridle, and used the spur; look then upon better men and you will see too much. Rachel so grieves and mourns for want of children, that she professeth her life inconsistent with her disappointment: 'Give me children, else I die,' [Gen. xxx. 1.] Hannah upon the same occasion weeps and eats not, and prays in the bitterness of her soul, and the abundance of her complaint and grief. Jeremiah, being pressed with discouragements from the contradiction of evil men, calls himself 'a man of strife and contention to the whole earth,' Jer. xv. 10; his sorrows thence arising, had so imbittered his life, that he puts 'a woe' upon his birth: 'Woe is me, my mother, that thou hast born me a man of strife.' Paul had a noble courage under manifold afflictions; he could glory in the cross and rejoice in persecutions; nevertheless the greatness of his work, the froward perverseness and unsteadiness of professors, which put him under fears, jealousies, and new travail, the miseries of Christians, and the care he had for the concerns of the gospel—2 Cor. xi. 2; Gal. vi. 19—which was a constant load upon his mind, his heart,—like old Eli's, trembling still for the ark of God, made him complain as one worn out by the troubles of his heart: 2 Cor. xi. 27, 'In weariness and painfulness, in watchings often, in hunger and thirst, in fastings often, in cold and nakedness. Besides those things that are without, that which cometh upon me daily, the care of all the churches. Who is weak, and I am not weak?' &c. For the Jews he had great heaviness and continual sorrow in his heart; and for the Gentiles he had perpetual fears, Rom. ix. 2. Now though he had a great share of divine comforts intermixed, and a more than ordinary assistance of the Spirit to keep him from sinful discomposure of spirit, at least to such a height as it ordinarily prevails upon others, yet was he very sensible of his burden, and doubtless the devil laboured to improve these occasions to weary out his strength. For by these and such like things he frequently vexeth the righteous souls of the faithful ministers of the gospel from day to day; so that their hearts have no rest, and their hands grow often feeble, and they cry out, Oh the burden! oh the care! being ready to say, as Jeremiah, chap. xx. 7, 'O Lord, thou hast deceived me, and I was deceived: I am a derision daily, every one mocketh me.' Thus say they, Did we ever think to meet with such disappointments, such griefs, from the wilfulness, pride, weakness, ignorance, pettishness, inconstancy, negligence, and scandals of friends? and such hatred, contradictions, scorns, and injuries from enemies? Were we free, what calling would we not rather choose? what place would we not rather go to, where we might spend the remainder of our days in some rest and ease? Were it not better to work with our hands for a morsel of bread? for so might our sleep be sweet to us at night, and we should not see these sorrows. At this rate are good men sometime disturbed, and the anguish of their spirit makes their life a burden.

[2.] Yet is not this all the disturbance that the devil works upon our hearts by these things, though these are bad enough, but they have a tendency *to further trouble*. Discomposures of spirit, if they continue long, turn at last into troubles of conscience. Though there is no affinity betwixt simple discomposure of soul and troubles of conscience in their own nature—the objects of the former being things external, no way relating to the soul's interest in God and salvation, which are the objects of the latter—yet the effects produced by the prevalency of these disturbances are a fit stock for the engrafting of doubts and questionings about our spiritual condition. As Saul's father first troubled himself for the loss of his asses, and sent his son to seek them; but when he stayed long, he forgot his trouble, and took up a new grief for his son, whom he feared he had lost in pursuit of the asses; so is it sometime with men, who, after they have long vexed themselves for injuries or afflictions, &c., upon a serious consideration of the working and power of these passions, leave their former pursuit, and begin to bethink themselves in what a condition their souls are, that abound with so much murmuring, rage, pride, or impatience, and then the scene is altered, and they begin to fear they have lost their souls, and are now perplexed about their spiritual estate. To make this plain I will give some instances, and then add some reasons, which will evidence that it is so, and also how it comes to be so.

For instances, though I might produce a sufficient number to this purpose from those that have written of melancholy, yet I shall only insist upon two or three from Scripture.

Hezekiah, when God smote him with sickness, at first was discomposed upon the apprehension of death, that he should so soon be deprived of the 'residue of his years, and behold man no more with the inhabitants of the world,' as he himself expresseth it, Isa. xxxviii. 10; afterward his trouble grew greater, 'He chattered as a crane or swallow, and mourned as a dove;' he was in 'great bitterness,' ver. 17; and sadly oppressed therewith, ver. 14. That which thus distressed him was not simply the fear of death. We cannot imagine so pious a person would so very much disquiet himself upon that single account; but by the expressions which he let fall in his complainings, we may understand that some such thoughts as these did shake him: that he apprehended God was angry with him, that the present stroke signified so much to him, all circumstances considered—for he was yet in his strength, and Jerusalem in great distress, being at that time besieged by Sennacherib's army,[1] and for him to be doomed to death by a sudden message at such a time, seemed to carry much in it—and that surely there was great provocation on his part; and it seems, upon search, he charged himself so deeply with his sinfulness, that his apprehensions were no less than that, if God should restore him, yet in the sense of his vileness he should never be able to look up; 'I shall go softly all my years in the bitterness of my soul,' ver. 15; which expression implies a supposition of his recovery, and a deep sense of iniquity, and accordingly when he was recovered, he takes notice chiefly of God's love to his soul and the pardon of his sin, which evidently discover where the trouble pinched him: 'Thou hast in love to my soul delivered it from the pit of corruption, for thou hast cast all my sins behind thy back,' ver. 17.

Job's troubles were very great, and his case extraordinary. Satan

[1] 2 Kings xx. 6. *Vide* Lightfoot, Harm. *in loc.*

had maliciously stripped him of all outward comforts; this he bore with admirable patience: Job i. 21, 'Naked came I out of my mother's womb, and naked shall I return thither: the Lord gave, and the Lord hath taken away; blessed be the name of the Lord.' The devil, seeing now himself defeated, obtains a new commission, wherein Job is wholly put into his hand—life only excepted, chap. ii. 9. He sets upon him again, and in his new encounter labours to bring upon him spiritual distresses, and accordingly improves his losses and sufferings to that end, as appears by his endeavours and the success; for as he tempted him by his wife to a desperate disregard of God that had so afflicted him, 'Curse God and die,' so he tempted him also by his friends to question the state of his soul and his integrity, and all from the consideration of his outward miseries. To that purpose are all their discourses. Eliphaz, chap. iv. 5–7, from his sufferings and his carriage under them, takes occasion to jeer his former piety, as being no other than feigned, 'It is come upon thee, and thou faintest: is not this thy fear, thy confidence, thy hope, and the uprightness of thy ways?—that is, Is all thy religion come to this? and also concludes him to be wicked, 'Who ever perished, being innocent? and where were the righteous cut off?' Bildad, chap. viii. 6, 13, chargeth him with hypocrisy upon the same ground, and while he makes his defence, Zophar plainly gives him the lie, chap. xi. 3; and at this rate they go their round; and all this while Satan, whose design it was to afflict his conscience with the sense of divine wrath, secretly strikes in with these accusations, insomuch that though Job stoutly defended his integrity, yet he was wounded with inward distresses, and concluded that these dealings of God against him were no less than God's severe observance of his iniquity; as is plain from his bemoaning himself in chap. x. 2, 'I will say unto God, Do not condemn me: shew me wherefore thou contendest with me;' ver. 16, 17, 'Thou huntest me as a fierce lion, thou renewest thy witnesses against me,' &c.

David was a man that was often exercised with sickness and troubles from enemies, and in all the instances almost that we meet with in the psalms of these his afflictions, we may observe the outward occasions of trouble brought him under the suspicion of God's wrath and his iniquity; so that he was seldom sick, or persecuted, but this called on the disquiet of conscience, and brought his sin to remembrance; as Ps. vi., which was made on the occasion of his sickness, as appears from ver. 5, wherein he expresseth the vexation of his soul under the apprehension of God's anger; all his other griefs running into this channel, as little brooks, losing themselves in a great river, change their name and nature. He that was at first only concerned for his sickness, is now wholly concerned with sorrow and smart under the fear and hazard of his soul's condition; the like we may see in Ps. xxxviii. and many places more.

Having made good the assertion that discomposures of soul upon outward occasions, by long continuance and Satan's management, do often run up to spiritual distress of conscience, I shall next, for further confirmation and illustration, shew how it comes to be so.

(1.) Discomposures of spirit *do obstruct, and at last extinguish the inward comforts of the soul;* so that if we suppose the discomposed person at first, before he be thus disordered, to have had a good measure of spiritual joy in God's favour, and delight in his ways, yet the disturbances,

[1.] *Divert his thoughts from feeding upon these comforts, or from the enjoyment of himself in them.* The soul cannot naturally be highly intent upon two different things at once, but whatsoever doth strongly engage the thoughts and affections, that carries the whole stream with it, be it good or bad, and other things give way at present. When the heart is vehemently moved on outward considerations, it lays by the thoughts of its sweetness which it hath had in the enjoyment of God; they are so contrary and inconsistent, that either our comforts will chase out of our thoughts our discomposures, or our discomposures will chase away our comforts. I believe the comforts of Elias, when he lay down under his grief, and desired to die; and of Jeremiah, when he cried out of violence, run very low in those fits of discontent, and their spirits were far from an actual rejoicing in God. But this is not the worst; we may not so easily imagine that upon the going away of the fit, the wonted comforts return to their former course. For,

[2.] The mind being distracted with its burden, is *left impotent and unable to return to its former exercise.* The warmth which the heart had, being smothered and suspended in its exercise, is not so quickly revived, and the thoughts which were busied with disturbance, like the distempered humours of the body, are not reduced suddenly to that evenness of composure as may make them fit for their old employment. And,

[3.] If God should *offer the influences of joyful support, a discomposed spirit is not in a capacity to receive them,* no more than it can receive those counsels that by any careful hand are interposed for its relief and settlement. Comforts are not heard in the midst of noise and clamour. The calmness of the soul's faculties are presupposed as a necessary qualification towards its reception of a message of peace. Phinehas his wife being overcome of grief for the ark's captivity and her husband's death, could not be affected with the joyful news of a son, [1 Sam. iv. 19, *seq.*] But,

[4.] Sinful discomposures *hinder these gracious and comfortable offers; if we could possibly, which we cannot ordinarily, receive them, yet we cannot expect that God will give them.* The Spirit of consolation loves to take up his lodging in a 'meek and quiet spirit,' and nothing more grieves him than bitterness, wrath, anger, clamour, and malice, which made the apostle, Eph. iv. 30, 31, subjoin his direction of 'putting these away' from us, with his advice of 'not grieving the Spirit by which we are sealed unto the day of redemption.' And then,

[5.] *The former stock of comfort, which persons distempered with discomposures might be supposed to have, will soon be wasted,* for our comforts are not like the oil in the cruse, or meal in the barrel, which had, as it were, their spring in themselves. We are comforted and supported by daily communication of divine aid, so that if the springhead be stopped, the stream will quickly grow dry. It is evident then that inward consolations in God will not ripen under these shadows, nor grow under these continual droppings, seeing a discomposed spirit is not capable to receive more, nor able to keep what comfort it had at first. We may easily see how it comes to pass that these disturbances may in time bring on spiritual troubles; for if our comforts be once lost, trouble of conscience easily follows. Where there is nothing to fortify the heart, the poison of malicious suggestions will unavoidably prevail.

(2.) *Discomposures of soul afford the devil fit matter to work upon.* They furnish him with strong objections against sincerity of holiness, by which the peace of conscience, being strongly assaulted, is at last overthrown. The usual weapons by which Satan fights against the assurance of God's children, are the guilt of sins committed and the neglect of duty; and the disturbed soul affords enough of both these to make a charge against itself: for,

[1.] *Where there is much discomposure there is much sin.* If in the multitude of words there wants not iniquity, then much more in the multitude of unruly thoughts. A disturbed spirit is like troubled water; all the mud that lay at the bottom is raised up and mixeth itself with the thoughts. If any injury or loss do trouble the mind, all the thoughts are tinctured with anger, pride, impatience, or whatsoever root of bitterness was in the heart before. We view them not singly as the issues of wise providence, but ordinarily we consider them as done by such instruments, and against ourselves, as malicious, spiteful, causeless, ungrateful wrongs; and then we give too great a liberty to ourselves to rage, to meditate revenge, to threaten, to reproach, and what not. And if our disposition have not so strong a natural inclination to these distempers, yet the thoughts by discomposure are quickly leavened. It is the comparison used by the apostle, 1 Cor. v. 8, to express the power of malice, which is a usual attendant in this service, to infect all the imaginations with a sharpness, which makes them swell into exorbitancy and excess; hence proceed revilings, quarrellings, &c. When the tongue is thus fermented, it is 'a fire, a world of iniquity,' producing more sins than can be reckoned, 'it defileth the whole body,' engaging all the faculties in heady pursuit, James iii. 6.

[2.] *Discomposures obstruct duties.* This is the inconvenience which the apostle, 1 Pet. iii. 7, tells us doth arise from disturbances among relations. If the wife or husband do not carry well, so that discontents or differences arise, their prayers are hindered. Duties then are obstructed, 1. *In the act.* When the heart is out of frame, prayer is out of season, and there is an averseness to it; partly because all good things are, in such confusions, burdensome to the humour that then prevails, which eats out all desire and delight to spiritual things; and partly because they dare not come into God's presence, conscious of their own guilt, and awe of God hindering such approaches. 2. They obstruct the *right manner of performance*, straitening the heart and contracting the spirit, that if anything be attempted it is poorly and weakly performed, 3. And also *the success of duty* is obstructed by discomposure. God will not accept such services, and therefore Christ adviseth to 'leave the gift before the altar,' though ready for offering, where the spirit is overcharged with offences or angry thoughts, and 'first to go and be reconciled to our brother,' and then to 'come and offer the gift,' it being lost labour to do it before, [Mat. v. 24.] From these sins of omission and commission Satan can, and often doth, frame a dreadful charge against those that are thus concerned, endeavouring to prove by these evidences that they are yet, notwithstanding pretence of conversion, in 'the gall of bitterness and bond of iniquity,' [Acts viii. 23,] whereby the peace of conscience is much shaken; and the more because also,

[3.] These discomposures of soul give Satan *a fit season for the management of his accusation.* Strong accusations do often effect nothing when the season is unsuitable. Many a time he hath as much to say against the comforts of men, when yet they shake all off, as Paul did the viper off his hand, and feel no harm, [Acts xxviii. 3.] But that which prepares the conscience to receive the indictment is a particular disposition which it is wrought into by suspicious credulity and fearfulness. These make the heart, as wax to the seal, ready to take any impression that Satan will stamp upon it. Now, by long disturbances, he works the heart into this mould very often, and upon a double account he gains himself a fit opportunity to charge home his exceptions. 1. In that he sets upon the conscience with his accusations after the heart hath been long molested and confused with its other troubles; for then the heart is weakened, and unable to make resistance as at other times. An assault with a fresh party after a long conflict disorders its forces, and puts all to flight. 2. In that long and great discomposures of mind bring on a distemper of melancholy; for it is notoriously known by common experience that those acid humours producing this distemper, which have their rise from the blood, may be occasioned by their violent passions of mind, the animal spirits becoming inordinate by long discomposures of sadness, envy, terror, and fretful cares, and the motion of the blood being retarded, it by degrees departs from its temperament, and is infected with an acidity, so that persons no way inclined naturally to melancholy may yet become so by the disquiets of their troubled mind.

Both these ways, but chiefly melancholy, the devil hath his advantage for disturbing the conscience. Melancholy most naturally inclines men to be solicitous for their souls' welfare; but withal disposeth them so strongly to suspect the worst—for it is a credulous, suspicious humour in things hurtful—and afflicts so heavily with sadness for what it doth respect, that when Satan lays before men of that humour their miscarriages under their discontents, their impatience, unthankfulness, anger, rash thoughts, and speeches against God or men, &c., withal suggesting that such a heart cannot be right with God, after serious thoughts upon Satan's frequently repeated charge, they cry out, Guilty, guilty; and then begins a new trouble for their unregenerate estate, and their supposed lost souls.

[4.] In this case usually Satan hath greater *liberty to accuse, and by his accusations to molest the conscience,* in that men of discomposed spirits, by the manifold evils arising thence, provoke God to desert them, and to leave them in Satan's hand to be brought into an hour of temptation. Satan's commission is occasioned by our provocations, and the temptations arising from such a commission are usually dreadful. They are solemn temptations, and called so after a singular manner; for of these I take those scriptures to be meant, 'Watch and pray, that ye enter not into temptation, Mat. xxvi. 41; 'And lead us not into temptation,' Mat vi. 13. Such temptations are not common temptations, and are of unknown force and hazard to the soul, which way soever they are designed, either for sin or terror. For several things do concur in a solemn temptation. As, 1. Satan doth in a special manner challenge a man to the combat, or rather he challenges God to give him such a man to fight with him, as he did concerning Job. This Christ tells us of, Luke xxii. 31, 'Simon, Satan hath desired to have you.' The word signifies a challenging or daring—$\dot{\epsilon}\xi\alpha\iota\tau\epsilon\hat{\iota}\sigma\theta\alpha\iota$; and it seems the devil is oft daring God to give us into his hand, when we little know of it. 2. There is also a special suitableness of occasion and snare to the temper and state of men. Thus he took Peter at an advantage in the high priest's hall; and in the case we now speak of he takes advantage of men's provocations and melancholy. 3. There is always a violent prosecution, which our Saviour expresseth under the comparison of sifting, which is a restless agitation of the corn, bringing that which was at the bottom to the top, and shuffling the top to the bottom, so that the chaff or dirt is always uppermost. 4. And to all this there is divine permission, Satan let loose, and we left to our ordinary strength, as is implied in that expression, 'He hath desired to have you that he might sift you.' Now then, if the devil have such ground to give God a challenge concerning such men, and if God do, as he justly may, leave such men, whose bitterness of spirit hath been as 'a smoke in his nostrils all the day,' [Isa. lxv. 5,] in Satan's hand, he will so shake them that their consciences shall have no rest. And this he can yet the more easily effect, because,

[5.] Discomposures of spirit have a particular tendency *to incline our thoughts to severity and harshness*, so that those who have had long and great disturbances upon any outward occasions—of loss, affliction, or disappointment, &c.—do naturally think, after a solemn review of such troubles, harshly of God and of themselves. They are ready to conclude that God is surely angry with them in that he doth afflict them, or that they have unsanctified hearts in that their thoughts are so fretful and unruly upon every inconsiderable petty occasion. It is so ordinary for men under the weight of their trouble, or under the sense of their sin, to be sadly apprehensive of God's wrath and their soul's hazard, that it were needless to offer instances: let David's case be instead of all. That his troubles begot such imaginations frequently, may be seen throughout the book of the Psalms. We never read his complaints against persecuting enemies, or for other afflictions, but still his heart is afraid that God is calling sin to remembrance. In Ps. xxxviii. he is under great distress, and tells how low his thoughts were: he was 'troubled,' greatly 'bowed down;' he 'went mourning all the day long;' he expresseth his thoughts to have been that 'God had forsaken him,' ver. 21: and his hopes, though they afterward revived, were almost gone; he cries out of his sins as having 'gone over his head,' and become 'a burden too heavy for him,' ver. 4, and therefore sets himself to confess them, ver. 18. He trembles at God's anger, and feels the 'arrows of God sticking fast in him,' ver. 2. But what occasioned all this? The psalm informs us, God had visited him with sickness, ver. 7. Besides that—for one trouble seldom comes alone—his friends were perfidious, ver. 11; his enemies also were busy laying snares for his life, ver. 12. Now his thoughts were to this purpose, that surely he had some way or other greatly provoked God by his sins, and therefore he fears wrath in every rebuke, and displeasure in every chastisement, ver. 1. The like you may see in Ps. cii., where the prophet upon the occasion of sickness, ver. 3, 23, and the reproach of enemies, ver. 8, is under great trouble, and ready to fail except speedy relief prevent, ver. 2: the reason whereof was this, that he concluded these troubles were evident tokens of God's indignation and wrath; 'because of thine indignation and thy wrath,' ver. 10. From these five particulars we may be satisfied that it cannot be otherwise, and also how it comes to be so, that sometime trouble of conscience is brought on by other discomposing troubles of the mind. For if these take away the comforts which supported the soul, and afford also arguments to the devil to prove a wicked heart, and withal 'a fit season,' to urge them to a deep impression, God in the meantime standing 'at a distance,' and the thoughts naturally inclined to conclude God's wrath from these troubles, how impossible is it that Satan should miss of disquieting the conscience by his strong, vehement suggestions of wickedness and desertion!

In our inquiries after Satan's success in working these discomposures of mind, we have discovered, 1. That the disturbances thence arising are great; 2. That they have a tendency to trouble of conscience. There is but one particular more to be spoken of, relating to his success in this design, and that is,

(3.) These disturbances are *much in Satan's power*. Ordinarily he can do it at pleasure, except when God restrains him from applying fit occasions, or when, notwithstanding these occasions, he extraordinarily suspends the effect, which he frequently doth when men are enraged under suffering upon the account of the gospel and conscience; for then, though they be bound up under affliction and iron, yet the 'iron enters not into the soul;' though they are troubled, they are not distressed. These extraordinaries excepted, he can as easily discompose the spirits of men as he can by temptation draw them into other sins; which may be evidenced by these considerations:

[1.] We may observe that those *whose passionate tempers do usually transport them into greater vehemencies, are never out of trouble.* Their fits frequently return, they are never out of the fire, and this is because Satan is still provided of occasions suitable to their inclinations.

[2.] Though God, out of his common bounty to mankind, hath allowed him a comfortable being in the world, yet we find that generally the sons of men, under their various occupations and studies, are wearied out *with vexations of spirit.* This Solomon, in Ecclesiastes, discovers at large in various employments of men, not exempting the pursuit of wisdom and knowledge: chap. i. 18, 'In much wisdom is much grief; and he that increaseth knowledge increaseth sorrow:' nor pleasures nor riches, for by all these he shews that a man is obnoxious to disquiets; so that the general account of man's life is but this: chap. ii. 23, 'All his days are sorrows, and his travail grief; yea, his heart taketh not rest in the night.' That it is so, is testified by common experience past denial; but how it comes to be so, is the inquiry. It is either from God, or from Satan working by occasions upon our tempers. That it is not from God, is evident; for though sorrow be a part of that curse which man was justly doomed unto, yet hath he appointed ways and means by which it might be so mitigated that it might be tolerable without discomposure of spirit; and therefore Solomon, designing in his Ecclesiastes to set forth the chief good, shews that felicity consists not in the common abuse of outward things, because that brings only vexation, but in the fear of God leading to future happiness, and in the meantime in a thankful, comfortable use of things present without anxiety of mind. Hence doth he fix his conclusion, as the result of his experience, and often repeats it: 'There is nothing better for a man than that he should eat and drink, and that he should make his soul enjoy good in his labour,' chap. ii. 24, iii. 12, 13, and v. 18, 19. Not that Solomon plays the epicure, giving advice 'to eat and drink, for to-morrow we die,' nor that he speaks deridingly to those that seek their felicity in this life, as if he should say, 'If ye do terminate your desires upon a terrene felicity, there is nothing better than to eat and drink,' &c. But he gives a serious positive advice of enjoying the things of this life with cheerfulness, which he affirms proceeds from the sole bounty of God as his singular gift: 'It is the gift of God,' chap. iii. 13; 'it is our portion'—that is, our allowance, chap. v. 19, for these two expressions, 'our portion,' and 'God's gift,' they are of the same signification with Solomon here; and when a man hath power to enjoy this allowance in comfort, it is God that 'answereth him in the joy of his heart,' ver. 20. It is plain, then, that God 'sows good seed in his field;' the springing up, therefore, of these tares of vexation, which so generally afflict the sons of men, must be ascribed to this, 'the enemy hath done it,' [Mat. xiii. 28.]

[3.] It is also a considerable ground of suspicion that Satan can do much in discomposures of spirit, in that sometimes those whose tempers are *most cool and calm, and whose singular dependence upon, and communion with God, must needs more strengthen them against these passionate vexations, are notwithstanding precipitated into violent commotions.* Moses was naturally meek above the common disposition of men, and his very business was converse with God, whose presence kept his heart under a blessed awe; yet, upon the people's murmuring, he was so transported with sullenness and unbelief, at the waters of Meribah, Num. xx. 10-12, that 'it went ill with him;' which David thus expresseth, Ps. cvi. 33, 'They provoked his spirit, so that he spake unadvisedly with his lips.' Who can suppose less in this matter than that Satan, having him at advantage, hurried him to this rashness—specially seeing such vehemencies were not usual with Moses, and that his natural temper led him to the contrary? This hath some affinity with the next consideration, which is,

[4.] That when *men most foresee the occasions of their trouble, and do most fear the trouble that might thence arise, and most firmly design to keep their hearts quiet, yet are they oft forced, against all care and resolution, upon extravagant heats.* David resolved and strenuously endeavoured to possess his soul in serenity and patience;—for what could be more than that solemn engagement? Ps. xxxix. 1, ' I said I will look to my ways;' and what endeavours could be more severe than to keep himself ' as with bit and bridle'? what care could be more hopeful to succeed than to be ' dumb with silence'?—yet for all this he could not keep his heart calm nor restrain his tongue: ver. 3, 'My heart waxed hot within me; while I was musing the fire burned: then spake I with my tongue.' Who suspects not the hand of Satan in this?

[5.] It is also remarkable, that when we have *least reason to give way to discomposure, when we have most cause to avoid all provocations, yet then we have most occasions set before us.* When we would most retire from the noise of the world for private devotion, when we would most carefully prepare ourselves for a solemn ordinance, if we be not very watchful, we shall be diverted by business, disturbed with noises, or some special occasion of vexation shall importune us to disquiet ourselves—when yet we shall observe, if we have not these solemn affairs to wait upon, we shall have fewer of these occasions of vexation to attend us. This cannot be attributed to mere contingency of occasions, nor yet to our tempers solely; for why they should be most apt to give us trouble when they are most engaged to calmness, cannot well be accounted for. It is evidently, then, Satan that maliciously directs these occasions—for they have not a malicious ingenuousness to prepare themselves, without some other chief mover—at such times as he knows would be most to our prejudice.

These general considerations amount to more than a suspicion, that it is much in Satan's power to give disturbances to the minds of men; yet, for the clearer manifestation of the matter, I shall shew that he can do much to bring about occasions of discomposure, and also to stir up the passions of men upon these occasions.

1. That occasions are much in his hand, I shall easily demonstrate. For,

First, There being *so many occasions of vexation to a weak, crazy mind, we may well imagine that one or other is still occurring;* and while they thus offer themselves, Satan needs not be idle for want of an opportunity.

Second, But if common occasions do not so exactly suit his design, *he can prepare occasions;* for such is his foresight and contrivance, that he can put some men—without their privity to his intentions, or any evil design of their own—upon such actions as may, through the strength of prejudice, misinterpretation, or evil inclination, be an offence to others; and, in like manner, can invite those to be in the way of these offences. I am ready to think there was a contrivance of Satan—if we well consider all circumstances—to bring David and the object of his lust together; while Bathsheba was bathing, he might use his art in private motions to get David up to the roof of his house. But more especially can the devil prepare occasions that do depend upon the wickedness of his slaves; these are servants under his command, he can 'say to one, Go, and he goes; and to another, Come, and he comes.' If contempt or injury, affronts or scorns, &c., be necessary for his present work against any whom he undertakes to disturb, he can easily put his vassals upon that part of the service; and if he have higher employment for them, he ever finds them forward. And hence was it, that when Satan designed to plunder Job, he could quickly perform it, because he had the Chaldeans and Sabeans ready at a call.

Third, If both these should fail him, he can easily awaken in us *the memory of old occasions that have been heretofore a trouble to us.* These being raised out of their graves will renew old disturbances, working afresh the same disquiets which the things themselves gave us at first.

If Satan's power were bounded here, and that he could do no more than set before men occasions of vexation, yet we might justly, on that single account, call him the troubler of the spirits of men; considering that naturally the thoughts of men are restless, and their imaginations ever rolling. If men sequester themselves from all business, if they shut themselves up from commerce with men, turn Eremites—as Jerome did—on purpose to avoid disquiet, yet their thoughts would hurry them from place to place, sometimes to the court, sometimes to the market, sometimes to shows and pastimes, sometimes to quarrellings; sometimes they view fields, buildings, and countries; sometimes they fancy dignities, promotions, and honours; they are ever working upon one object or other, real or supposed, and according to the object such will the affections be, high or low, joyful or sorrowful; so that if the utmost of what Satan could do were no more than to provide occasions, discomposures would follow naturally. The evil dispositions of men would thereby be set a-working, though Satan stood by as an idle spectator. The serpent—in our breasts, as Solomon tells us, Eccles. x. 11—would 'bite without enchantment,' that is, except it were charmed. But Satan can do more than tempt objectively, when he hath provided the fuel he can also bring fire. For,

2. *He can also set our passions on work, and incense them to greater fury than otherwise they would arrive at.* We see persons that are distempered with passion may be whetted up to a higher pitch of rage by any officious flatterer, that will indulge the humour and aggravate the provocation. Much more then can Satan do it by whispering such things to our minds as he knows will increase the flame; and therefore is it, that where the Scripture doth caution us against anger—as the proper product of our own corruption, calling it our wrath, Eph. iv. 26, 27—there also it warns us against the devil, as the incendiary, that endeavours to heighten it. And where it tells us of the disorders of the tongue,—which, though a little member, can of itself do great mischief, James iii. 6—there it also tells us that the devil brings it an additional fire from hell: 'It is set on fire of hell.' And there are several ways by which Satan can irritate the passions. As,

[1.] By *presenting the occasions worse than they are, or were ever intended, unjustly aggravating all circumstances.* By this means he makes the object of the passions the more displeasing and hateful. This must of necessity provoke to a higher degree.

[2.] *He can in a natural way move, as it were, the wheels, and set the passions a-going, if they were of themselves more dull and sluggish,* for he hath a nearer access to our passions than every one is aware of. I will make it evident thus: our passions in their workings do depend upon the fluctuations, excursions, and recursions of the blood and animal spirits, as naturalists do determine.[1] Now that Satan can make his approaches to the blood, spirits, and humours, and can make alterations upon them, cannot be denied by those that consider what the Scripture speaks in Job's case, and in the cases of those that were by possession of the devil made dumb, deaf, or epileptic; for if he could afflict Job with grievous boils, chap. ii. 7, it is plain he disordered and vitiated his blood and humours, which made them apt to produce such boils or ulcers; and if he could produce an epilepsy, it is evident that he could infect the *lympha* with such a sharpness as by vellicating the nerves might cause a convulsion; and these were much more than the disorderly motions of blood, spirits, or humours, which raise the passions of men. If any object to this, that then, considering Satan's malicious diligence, we must expect the passions of men would never be at rest; it is answered, that this power of Satan is not unlimited, but oft God prohibits him such approaches, and without his leave he can do nothing; and also grace in God's children, working calmness, submission, and patience, doth balance Satan's contrary endeavour. For as hurtful and vexatious occasions, being represented by the sense to the imagination, are apt to move the blood and spirits; so, on the contrary, the ballast of patience and other graces doth so settle the mind, that the blood and spirits are kept steady in their usual course.

[3.] *When the passions are up, Satan can by his suggestions make them more heady and violent.* He can suggest to the mind motives and arguments to forward it, and can stir up our natural corruption, with all its powers, to strike in with the opportunity. Thus he not only kindles the fire, but blows the flame.

[4.] *And he can further fix the mind upon these thoughts, and keep them still upon the hearts of men.* And then they eat in the deeper, and like poison diffuse their malignity the further. We see that men, who are at first but in an ordinary fret, if they continue to meditate upon their provocation, they increase their vexation; and if they give themselves to vent their passions by their tongues, though they begin in some moderation, yet as motion causeth heat, so their own words whet their rage, according to Eccles. x. 13, 'The beginning of the words of his mouth is foolishness, but the latter end of his talk is mischievous madness.' The same advantage hath Satan against men by holding down their thoughts to these occasions of discomposure.

If occasions be so much in Satan's power, and he have also so great a hand over men's passions, it is too evident that he can do very much to discompose the spirits of men that are naturally obnoxious to these troubles, except God restrain him, and grace oppose him. Thus have I spoken my thoughts of the first sort of troubles, by which Satan doth undermine the peace of men's hearts.

[1] *Vide* Willis de anima brut., cap. 8, 9.

CHAPTER VII.

Of the second way to hinder peace.—Affrightments, the general nature and burden of them, in several particulars.—What are the ways by which he affrights: 1. *Atheistical injections. Observations of his proceeding in them;* 2. *Blasphemous thoughts;* 3. *Affrightful suggestions of reprobation. Observations of his proceedings in that course;* 4. *Frightful motions to sin;* 5. *Strong immediate impressions of fear;* 6. *Affrightful scrupulosity of conscience.*

The next rank of troubles by which the devil doth endeavour to molest us, I call *affrightments.* It is usual for those that speak of temptations, to distinguish them thus: Some are, they say, enticements, some are affrightments; but then they extend these affrightments further than I intend, comprehending under them all those temptations of sadness and terror, of which I am next to speak. But by affrightments, I mean only those perplexities of spirit into which Satan casts men, by overacting their fears, or astonishing their minds, by injecting unusual and horrid thoughts against their consents.[1] Some there are that have thought those temptations, of which the apostle complains, 2 Cor. xii. 7, 'There was given me a thorn in the flesh, the messenger of Satan to buffet me,' were of this kind—that is, horrid injections frequently repeated, as men deal their blows in fighting. Gerson, speaking of these, tells us they sometime come from the sole suggestion of Satan troubling the fancy, and saying, Deny God, curse God; and then adds, such was the thorn in the flesh given to the apostle.[2] But whether this was the trouble of the apostle, or some other thing—for several things are conjectured, and nothing can be positively proved—we are sure, from the sad experience of many, that such troubles he doth often give; which I shall first explain in the general, and then give a particular of these frightful injections.

1. To explain the nature and burden of this kind of trouble, I shall present you with a few observations about them. As,

[1.] These astonishing thoughts are purely *injections*, such as *Satan casts into the mind, and not what the mind of itself doth produce;* as one expresseth it, they are more darting than reflecting. Not but that our natural corruption could of itself beget blasphemous or atheistical thoughts; but when they have their rise from ourselves solely, they do not so startle us. Having some share at least of our consent going along with them, they appear not so strange. But in this case in hand, Satan is the agent, and men are the sufferers, their understandings and souls being busied all the while to repel them, with the utmost of their reluctances. And to those that do thus strive against them, making resistance with all their strength, with tears and prayers, they are only their afflictions, but not their sins. For the thoughts are not polluted by the simple apprehension of a sinful object, no more than the eye is defiled by beholding loathsome and filthy things; for

---
[1] Irritamenta, terriculamenta.
[2] In calce, tom. iv. p. 973. Talis stimulus datus fuit apostolo.

then should the mind of Christ have been defiled, when Satan propounded himself blasphemously as the object of his worship; his mind as truly apprehended the meaning of that saying, 'fall down and worship me,' as ours can do, when he casts such a thing immediately into our thoughts. Which is a consideration to be observed diligently by those that meet with such sad exercise. If they do truly apprehend that they are but their sufferings, and that God will not charge the sin upon them, they will more easily bear and overcome the trouble.

These injections are commonly impetuous and sudden, frequently compared to lightning; and this is usually made a note of distinction betwixt wicked, blasphemous thoughts rising from our natural corruption, and darted in by Satan; the former being more leisurely, orderly, and moderate, according to the usual course of the procedure of human thoughts, the latter usually accompanied with a hasty violence, subtly and incoherently shooting into our understandings, as lightning into a house; so that all the strength we have can neither prevent them nor expel them, nor so much as mitigate the violence of them.

[3.] They are also for the most part *incessant and constant troublers where they once begin.* Though Satan hath variety, in regard of the matter of these amazing injections—for sometimes he affrights one man with blasphemous thoughts, another with atheistical thoughts, a third with grievous, unusual temptations to sin, as murder, &c.—yet usually he fixeth his foot upon what he first undertakes. And as cunning huntsmen do not change their game that they first rouse, that they may sooner speed in catching the prey; so what frightful thought Satan begins the trouble with, that he persists in, and is withal so vehement in his pursuit, that he gives little intermission. He makes these unwelcome thoughts haunt them like ghosts, whithersoever they go, whatsoever they do; he will give solemn onsets it may be twenty or forty times in a day: and at this rate he continues, it may be for some considerable time, so that they are not quit of the trouble for several months, or it may be years.

[4.] The matter of these affrightments are things *most contrary to the impressions of nature or grace, and therefore most odious and troublesome.* When he is upon this design, things that are most contrary to the belief and inclination of men are best for his purpose; as men that intend to affright others choose the most ugly vizors, the strangest garbs and postures, and make the most uncouth, inhuman noises; and the more monstrous they appear, the better they succeed in their purposes. Yet Satan doth not always choose the very worst, for then most of the troubles of this kind would be about the same thing; but he considers the strength of our persuasions, our establishment in truths, the probability or improbability of an after game with us; and accordingly sometimes refuseth to trouble us with injections, contrary to what we are most firmly rooted in, choosing rather that which, though contrary to our thoughts and resolves, we have not been fixed in without a great deal of labour, and which, if there be occasion, might most fitly be charged upon us as our own, so that, whereas other suggestions would be slighted as apparent malice and scarecrows, these are most afflicting, as being an assault against such a fort which costs us much to rear, and which we are most afraid to lose, and most liable to his accusation after a long continuance, as being the issue of our own unsettledness.

[5.] The first and most obvious effects of these injections are *the utmost abhorrency of the mind*—which presently startles at the appearance of such odious things—*and the trembling of the body, sometimes to an agony and fainting.* The invasion of one single injection hath put some into such a heart-breaking affrightment, that they have not recovered themselves in a whole day's time. This trembling of the body and agony of the mind are the usual consequences of anything that is surprising, strange, and fearful; and therefore is trembling of the body made by divines a mark to discover that these hideous, blasphemous thoughts are cast in by Satan, and have not their rise from our own hearts; for the horror of the mind is usually so great, when it is spoken to in this language, that it cannot bear up under its astonishment and trouble. Yea, those very men that are otherwise profane, and can with boldness commit great iniquities, cannot but shake, and inwardly conceive an unspeakable hatred at these monstrous suggestions.[1]

[6.] *These affrightments are more common than men are usually aware of.* They are by some thought to be rare and extraordinary; but this mistake ariseth from the concealment of these kind of troubles. Those that are thus afflicted are often ashamed to speak to others what they find in their own hearts; but if all would be so ingenuous as to declare openly what fearful imaginations are obtruded upon them, it would appear that Satan very frequently endeavours to trouble men this way.

[7.] *These are very grievous burdens, and hard to be borne upon many accounts.*

First, Who can well express *the inward torture and molestation of the mind,* when it is forced against its own natural bent and inclination to harbour such monsters within itself! How would nature reluct and abominate the drinking down of noisome puddled water, or the swallowing of toads and serpents! And hence was it that persecutors in their devilish contrivances invented such kind of tortures. And what less doth the devil do when he forceth blasphemies upon their thoughts, and commits a rape by a malicious violence upon their imaginations? David, under these temptations, Ps. lxxiii. 21, cries out, 'Thus my heart was grieved, and I was pricked in my reins:' and it cannot be otherwise, for the reason already mentioned. Nature abhors to be forced to what is most contrary to itself, and so doth grace. Now the things by which Satan works these affrightments are contrary to nature or grace, or both together; and as they will strive to the utmost of their ability to cast out what is so opposite to them, so must the devil to the utmost of his ability, if he would carry his design, strengthen himself in his force, and from hence, as when fire and water are committed to-

---

[1] Horrore sui sic implent animum, ut tantum non pectus ipsum expectorare videantur,—ad quorum præsentiam natura vel depravatissima contremiscit.—*Arowsmith. Tract. Sacr.,* lib. ii. cap. 7, sec. 6. [For 'Tract' read 'Tactica Sacra.' Cambridge, 1657, 4to.—G.]

gether, ariseth a most troublesome conflict; and indeed if there were a compliance of our consent, there would be no affrightment; neither can this kind of temptation be managed except there be the utmost dissent of the mind. If any think there is no great ground for these temptations, because some of the particulars by which he is said to affright men are natural to us, as, for instance, atheistical thoughts, which are by some called the master-vein of our original corruption, and by others said to be in the heart of every man naturally, and then consequently not so troublesome as is imagined, &c.; I answer, that when divines call these or blasphemous thoughts natural, they do not mean that they are natural impressions engraven on us by creation,—for they assert the contrary; that it is a natural and unextinguishable impression upon every man that there is a God, &c., and usually give in this for proof, that the greatest atheists in fear and extremity will manifest a secret belief of a deity, by calling out, O God, &c.,[1] or by some other posture, as Caligula by hiding himself when it thundered,—but they mean only that our natural corruption may produce these thoughts, and that they are the natural issues thereof; and therefore Perkins, in answer to a question of this nature, tells us that these two thoughts, 'there is a God,' and 'there is no God,' may be, and are both, in the same heart.[2] Now as this will give us the reason why Satan doth make choice of these thoughts to trouble us withal, which may also rise from ourselves—which I have hinted before, and shall presently again touch upon—so it tells us still that whether these thoughts arise from our own corruption or from Satan, our natural impressions are strong against them, and withal that they cannot be so affrightful but when Satan doth manage them, and when the contrary impressions of nature are awakened to give strong resistance, and then that struggling must be as the tearing of our bowels, and still the worse in that we are incessantly pursued, Satan still casting back with unwearied labour the same thoughts as they are repulsed and rejected, as soldiers that besiege cities use to cast over the walls their fired grenades.

Second, These are also grievous, *as they set the mind upon the rack, and stretch it under laborious and doubtful inquiries after the grounds or causes of this kind of trouble*, for the heart, astonished with such cursed guests against his will, presently reflects upon God and itself, What have I done, and wherefore am I thus disquieted with monsters? why doth the righteous Lord suffer Satan to break open my heart, and fill me with such fearful thoughts? But when men's inquiries are not so high, but detained in a consideration of the nature of the trouble and manner of its working, without looking up to the providence of God, then are their troubles increased.

Third, As these injections necessitate men, in their own defence, *to oppose and every way to resist, it is an increase of the burden*. What pleadings are they put to, what defiances, what endeavours to call off the thoughts! and all to little purpose; while the trouble continues they are forced to lie in their armour, and to be constantly in their ward.

[1] Perkins, Cases of Conscience, lib. i. cap. 10, sec. 2.
[2] 'Treatise of Imaginations,' cap. 3.

Fourth, And yet are they further troublesome *in the after-game that Satan plays by these thoughts*. It is not all of his design to affright men, but he usually hath another temptation to come in the rear of this, and that is to turn these affrightments into accusations, and by urging them long upon the hearts of men, to make them believe that they are their own thoughts, the issues of their own natural corruption; and after men are by continual assaults weakened, their senses and memory dulled, their understanding confounded, &c., they easily conclude against themselves. The tempter imputes all the horrid blasphemy to them, boldly calls them guilty of all; and because their thoughts have dwelt long upon such a subject, and withal knowing that corrupt nature of itself will lead men to such horrid blasphemies or villainies—which makes it probable that it might be their own fault, and for this reason Satan makes choice of such injections as may in the accusation seem most likely to be true—being strongly charged as guilty, they yield; and then begins another trouble more fearful than the former.[1] Oh, what sad thoughts have they then of themselves, as the most vile blasphemous wretches! sometimes they think that it is impossible that other men's hearts should entertain such intolerable things within them as theirs, and that none was ever so bad as they; sometimes they think that if men knew what vile imaginations and monstrous things are in their minds, they would in very zeal to God and religion stone them, or at least exclude them from all commerce with men; sometimes they think their sin to be the sin against the Holy Ghost; sometimes they think God is engaged in point of honour to shew upon them some remarkable judgment, and they verily look for some fearful stroke to confound them, and live under such a frightful expectation. These and many more to this purpose are their thoughts, so that these temptations are every way troublesome, both in their first and second effects.

Thus I have in the general expressed the nature of these affrightments. What the particular injections are by which he studies to affright men, I shall next declare. They are principally six:

1. *Atheistical thoughts.* By injecting these into the mind he doth exceedingly affright men, and frequently for that end doth he suggest that there is no God, and that the Scriptures are but delusive contrivances, &c. Concerning these I shall note a few things; as,

[1.] Though there be an observable difference betwixt *atheistical injections and temptations to atheism*, not only in the design—Satan chiefly intending seduction in the latter, and affrightment by the former—but also in the manner of proceeding—(for when he designs chiefly to tempt to atheism, he first prepares his way by debauching the conscience with vicious or negligent living,—according to Ps. xiv. 1, that which makes men 'say in their hearts there is no God,' is this, that 'they are corrupt, and have done abominable works'—and in this method was famous Junius tempted to atheism: but when he chiefly intends to affright, he sets upon men that by a watchful and strict conversation cut off from him that advantage)—yet he doth so manage himself that he can turn his course either way, as he finds probability of success after trial; for he presseth on upon men most

[1] *Vide* Dickson, Therap. Sacra., lib. iii. cap. 26, sec. 7.

where he finds them most to yield, so that those who were but at first affrighted may at last be solemnly persuaded and urged to believe the suggestion to be true if they give him any encouragement for such a procedure.[1]

[2.] *Contemplative heads and great searchers* are usually most troubled in this manner, partly because they see more difficulties than other men, and are more sensible of human inability to resolve them, and partly because God, who will not suffer his children to be tempted 'above what they are able,' doth not permit Satan to molest the weaker sort of Christians with such dangerous assaults.

[3.] *Persons of eminent and singular holiness may be, and often are, troubled with atheistical thoughts, and have sad conflicts about them*, Satan labouring, where he cannot prevail for a positive entertainment of atheism, at least to disquiet their minds by haunting them with his injections, if not to weaken their assent to these fundamental truths, in which he sometimes so prevails, that good men have publicly professed that they have found it a harder matter to believe that there is a God than most do imagine.

[4.] *Satan lies at the catch in this design, and usually takes men at the advantage, suddenly setting upon them, either in the height of their meditations and inquiries into fundamental truths*—for when they soar aloft, and puzzle themselves with a difficulty, then is he at hand to advise them to cut the knot which they cannot unloose—*or in the depth of their troubles*—for when men cannot reconcile the daily afflictions and sufferings which they undergo, with the love and care of God toward his children, then it is Satan's season to tell them that there is no supreme disposer of things. In both these cases the devil leaps upon them unawares, like a robber out of a thicket, who, if he do not wound them by the dart of atheistical injection, at least he is sure to astonish them, and to confound them with amazement. For,

[5.] *Sometimes he pursues with wonderful violence, and will dispute with admirable subtlety, urging the inequality of providence, the seeming contradictions of Scripture, the unsuitableness of ordinances to an infinite wisdom and goodness, with many more arguments of like kind;* and this with such unexpected acuteness and seeming demonstration, that the most holy hearts and wisest heads shall not readily know what to answer, but shall be forced to betake themselves to their knees, and to beg of God that he would rebuke Satan, and uphold them that their faith fail not. Nay, he doth not only dispute, but by urging, and with unspeakable earnestness threaping,[2] the conclusion upon men, doth almost force them to a persuasion, so that they are almost carried off their feet whether they will or no; which was the very case of David when the devil pursued him with atheistical thoughts on the occasion of the prosperity of wicked men, and his daily troubles: Ps. lxxiii. 2, 'My feet were almost gone, my steps had well-nigh slipped.'

[6.] Yet for all this he sometimes *lays aside his sophistical subtlety, and betakes himself to an impudent importunity;* for sometimes he

---

[1] The construction of this paragraph is involved and inaccurate, but the thought is sufficiently plain, when from 'for when he designs,' &c., down to 'advantage,' is placed in parenthesis.—G.   [2] Arguing against contradiction.—G.

insists only on one argument, not changing that which he first took up, nor strengthening his suggestion with variety of arguments, but by frequent repetition of the same reason persists to urge his injected atheism. This gives no discovery of any deep reach if he designed to persuade—for it is scarce rational to imagine that serious men, who by many arguments are fully persuaded there is a God, should readily lose their hold upon the appearance of one objection—but it shews that he purposeth only to molest. And this appears more evidently, when he contents himself with weak and trivial arguments, which the afflicted party can answer fully, and yet cannot for all that quit themselves of the trouble; for instance, it is not very many years since a serious and pious person came to me, and complained that he could not be at rest for atheistical thoughts that perpetually haunted him; and upon a particular inquiry into the cause and manner of his trouble, he told me the first rise of it was from his observation, that I had interpreted some scriptures otherwise than he had heard some others to have done; but withal he added that he knew the reason of his perplexity was but silly, and that which he could easily answer; this being no just charge against the Scripture, whose sense and truth might for all that be one, and uniform to itself, but only an implication of human weakness appearing in the different apprehensions of expositors; yet notwithstanding he affirmed he could not shake off the trouble, and that his thoughts were ever urged with the same thing for a long time together. Nay, such is his impudency in this kind of trouble, that those who know it is the best way not to dispute fundamentals with Satan, but with abhorrency to reject him—after the example of Christ, with a 'get thee behind me, Satan'—and accordingly do with their utmost strength reject them, yet they find that he doth not readily desist.

How sad is this trouble! how are pious persons affrighted to see the face of their thoughts made abominably ugly and deformed by these violent and unavoidable injections! It is not only wearisome to those that know it to be solely Satan's malice, but it often proves to be an astonishing surprisal—like that of a traveller who, while he passeth on his way without foresight or thought of danger, is suddenly brought to the top of a great precipice, where, when he looks down to the vast deep below, his head swims, his heart pants, his knees tremble, and the very fear of the sudden danger so confounds him that he is through excessive dread ready to fall into that which he would avoid; so are these amazed at so great hazards before them. Satan could not by all his art prevail with them to abandon the holy ways of God in exchange for the pleasures of sin, and now they seem to be in danger to lose all at once; and yet it is more affrightful by far to those that charge, through Satan's cunning, all this atheism upon themselves.

2. Another affrightful injection is that of *blasphemous thoughts*, as that God is not just, not compassionate; that scriptures and ordinances are but low and sorry things, &c.

That Satan doth delight to force such thoughts upon men, is evident,

[1.] *From his nature.* He is a blasphemous spirit, and withal so malicious, that whatsoever is in his cursed mind he will be ready to vent upon all occasions.

[2.] *From his practice;* for where he can obtain the rule over men's imaginations, as in some distracted persons, and those that are distempered with fevers, he usually makes them vomit forth oaths, cursings, and blasphemies, and this he doth to some that, while they have had the use of their reason, have not been observed to give their tongue the liberty of swearing or cursed speaking.

[3.] *From his professed design in the case of Job,* concerning whom he boasted to God himself that he would make him curse him to his face, and accordingly tempted him by his wife to curse God and die.

[4.] *From the sad experience of those that have suffered under this sad affliction:* for many have complained of blasphemous thoughts; and those whom he cannot conquer he will thus trouble. Neither need we think it strange that the devil can impress blasphemies upon the imaginations of men against their wills, when we consider that he could make Saul, in his fits, to behave himself like an inspired person, and cause him to utter things beyond and unsuitable to his disposition, after the rate and manner of those raptures which idolatrous priests used to be transported withal. *Bacchatur vates.* [Virgil.][1] This, in 1 Sam. xviii. 10, is called Saul's prophesying, when the 'evil spirit from the Lord vexed him;' and is the same with that which is spoken concerning Baal's priests: 1 Kings xviii. 29, 'They prophesied until the time of the offering of the evening sacrifice'—that is, they were exercised with trances and rapturous furies, in which they uttered strange sounds and speeches. How easily, then, may Satan possess the fancies of men with blasphemies! so that the unwilling may be troubled with them, and those that are deprived of the benefit of reason, may, from the power of the impression upon their imagination, vent them with a kind of unwillingness.

Melancholy persons do very frequently meet with this kind of trouble, Satan having a great power upon their imagination, and great advantages, from the darkness of that humour, to make the fear arising from such thoughts the more astonishing, and to delude them into an apprehension that they are guilty of all that passeth through their thoughts, and also to work this perplexity to more dismal effects. In these kind of men he doth play the tyrant with such injections, abusing them to such a height as if they were his vassals and slaves, whose thoughts and tongues were in his and not their own keeping; and so strongly doth he possess them with this perplexity sometimes, that all the counsels, reasonings, or advice of others cannot in the least satisfy or relieve them; yet, notwithstanding, I have known several under this affliction who, when by physic the state of their bodies hath been altered, have found themselves at ease immediately, the trouble gradually and insensibly ceasing of itself.

Others there are that have great vexation from these thoughts, and these are commonly such as by some long and grievous pain, sickness, or other crosses, have their spirits fretted and imbittered; then is Satan ready to suggest that God is cruel or regardless of his people; and these thoughts are the more dreadful because fretting and murmuring spirits have a natural tendency to think harshly of God; so that Satan in this case doth with the more boldness obtrude these

[1] 'Immanis in antro Bacchatur vates,' Æneid, iv. 6, 78.—G.

suggestions upon them, finding so great a forwardness toward such imaginations, and also with greater severity he doth reflect upon them, as being in some likelihood compliant and consenting.

When other persons—not so concerned as these two sorts of men above mentioned—are assaulted with blasphemous thoughts, the fits are less permanent, and, because they easily discover the design and author of them, not highly affrightful, though still troublesome.

The burden of these injections are much like the former, very sadly afflicting. For who can easily bear the noise of Satan while he shouts continually into their ears odious calumnies and blasphemous indignities against God? David could not hear wicked men blaspheme God but it was 'as a sword in his bones,' exceeding painful. The impressions of nature, that teach us to revere and honour God; the power of education, that confirms these impressions; the persuasion of faith, that assures us of the reality and infinite excellency of a Godhead; and the force of love, that makes us more sensibly apprehensive of any injury or dishonour done to him whom we love above all;—all these do suffer by these violent incursions of Satan, and the sufferer finds himself to be pained and tortured in these noble parts. How grievous must it be to a child of God to have his ear chained to these intolerable, ingrateful reproaches!—especially when we consider that the devil will in this case utter the most dreadful blasphemies he can devise, which will still add to the affliction—for even those men that through habit can well bear ordinary petty oaths, will yet startle at outrageous prodigious swearing—and therefore whatever covert and consequential blasphemies may be to some men, these impudent, hideous abuses of the holy and just God must needs sadly trouble those that are forced to hear them. And the more constant the greater trouble. Who would not be weary of their lives that must be forced to undergo this vexation still without intermission? And yet the devil can advance the trouble a little higher by the apparatus or artificial[1] dread which he puts upon the temptation in the manner of the injection; as the roaring of the lion increaseth terror in the beasts of the field, who without that would tremble at his presence; and as the thundering and lightning at the giving of the law increased the fear of Israel, so when Satan is upon this design, he shakes as it were the house, and makes a noise that the fright may be increased.

3. *Suspicious fears of being excluded out of God's eternal decree of election is another of his affrightments.* This is when Satan boldly takes upon him to determine God's secret counsel concerning any man; peremptorily asserting that he is none of God's elect. In which case he often doth only inject the suspicion confidently, without offer of proof; or if he use arguments, they never amount to a proof of his assertion; neither is it possible they should, for these are among 'God's secrets,' and out of Satan's reach, though possibly they may prove the person to be not converted at present. So that this kind of trouble differs exceedingly from those disquiets of temptation which frequently men suffer about their state of regeneration. And indeed the question should not be confounded, it being of great concern to men when their peace is assaulted to be able to observe the difference

[1] 'Artful' = unreal.—G.

betwixt these two assertions, 'Thou are not elected,' and 'Thou art not yet regenerated.' Seeing—the latter being granted—there yet remains a hope of the probability or possibility of that man's conversion afterwards. The suspicions of non-conversion are more common, and not so dangerous; nay, in unregenerate persons the fears of their being yet in that condition, being joined with diligence and care to avoid the danger, are necessary and advantageous; but the former being granted, all hopes are, together with that concession, laid off, which must needs make the affrightment intolerable. In this we may observe,

[1.] That Satan, for the better management of this design, doth not only inject these suspicions *in the most dreadful language*—as, 'Thou art a lost and damned wretch, hopelessly miserable to all eternity; God hath not elected thee to life, but prepared for thee, as a vessel of wrath, the lake of fire and brimstone for ever,' &c.—but also he doth assert them with the highest peremptoriness imaginable, as if he had authority from God to pronounce a sentence of condemnation against a man. This must needs amaze the afflicted unspeakably.

[2.] In this he also *observes his advantages;* for there are some men so sadly suited to this design, that Satan comes better to speed upon them than others. Usually he fixeth his eyes,

First, Upon young persons at their first serious attendances upon, and considerations of, Scripture truths. Their hearts are then tender. Youth hath a natural tender-heartedness. We find them coupled together in Rehoboam's character: 2 Chron. xiii. 7, 'When Rehoboam was young and tender-hearted.' And they are apt to receive strong impressions. When those who were formerly mindless of their spiritual concern begin to be serious, they can no sooner fall upon a consideration of those weighty doctrines, that there are sheep and goats, some saved and some damned, that the blessed are few in comparison of the many that take the broad way to destruction, and that these were from eternity ordained unto life, and these only, &c.; no sooner, I say, begin they to ponder these things, but Satan is ready with his suspicion, 'And what dost thou know but thou art one of these excluded wretches? If but few are saved, a thousand to one thou art none of them; for why should God look upon thee more than another?' These are his first essays[1] with young men beginning to be serious, in which afterward he proceeds with greater boldness as he seeth occasion.

Secondly, He also doth this to persons that are *some way quickened to a devotional fear of God and care of their souls, but withal are ignorant, and not able distinctly to apprehend and orderly to range the doctrines of the Scriptures into a due consistency with one another.* Their careful fears make them inquire into what God hath said concerning the everlasting state of men; and before they can be able to digest the principles of religion, Satan sets some truths edgeways against them, which put them into great affrightment; while, through their ignorance, other truths, appointed and declared for the satisfaction of the minds of those that hunger and thirst after righteousness, cannot come in to their relief. How startling must the truths of

[1] Spelled 'assays.'—G.

God's election be when they stand forth alone, and are not accompanied with the invitations of the gospel, that promise pardon and acceptance to all that will come in and submit to Christ! Satan usually holds such kind of men to the consideration of those truths that have the most dismal aspect; and while they are stopped there, they can draw forth no other conclusions than these, that they are in hazard, and, for aught they know, utterly lost.

Third, Satan hath also this plot against those that by some *grievous iniquity, or long continuance in sin, have highly provoked the Lord.* Here he useth arguments from the heinousness of their iniquity: Thou art a reprobate, because thou hast committed these great evils, these are marks of damnation, &c.; which arguments, though they be of no value, and no way proving that for which they are brought, yet Satan injecting suspicions, and their own consciences in the meantime justly accusing, they so sink under their fear that they suffer Satan to make what conclusion he will, and then they subscribe to it.

Fourth, Above all, *melancholy persons give the devil the greatest advantage to raise affrightments.* That distemper naturally fills men with sad thoughts, and is credulous of the worst evil that can be objected against him that hath it. Of itself, it can create the blackest conceits and saddest surmises, and then believes its own fancy. When Satan strikes in with this humour—*finguntque creduntque*—they are the more confirmed in their suspicions; and the fright is the greater, because they are as incredulous of what is good, if it be told them, as they are apt to believe what is evil, and to believe it, because they fear it, *dum timet credit*,—though no other reason were offered: but much more when Satan, in a prophetic manner, foretells their misery, and assures them they must never be happy.

[3.] The suspicions which the devil hath by these advantages *raised up, he doth endeavour to increase, and to root them deeply in the minds of them upon whom he hath thus begun.* And indeed, by frequent inculcating the same thing, with his continued peremptoriness of asserting the certainty of their non-election, he at last brings up very many to a full persuasion that it is so; and besides other arts that he may have, or exercise in this particular, he commonly practiseth upon men by perverting the true intendment and use of the doctrine of election. That there is such a thing as election, and that of a determinate number, are truths undeniable; and the end of their discovery in the gospel is the comfort and confirmation of the converted. Here they may see God's unchangeable love to them—how much they stand engaged for the freeness of grace, and that the foundation of God is sure, &c.; for to this purpose doth our Saviour improve these doctrines, John xvii. 6, 7, 9, 12, 15, 16. But nothing of this is spoken to discourage any man from his endeavours, neither can any man prove that he or any other is excluded out of the decree of election, except in case of the sin against the Holy Ghost; neither is it possible for the devil to prove any such thing against any man; neither ought any to suppose himself not elect; but on the contrary, if he is willing to forsake sin, and desirous to be reconciled to God, he ought to apprehend a probability that he is elected, because the proffer of

Christ is made to all that will receive him. And therefore should men stop their ears against such suggestions, and not dispute that with Satan, but rather hearken to the commands, exhortations, and promises of Scripture, it being most certain that these 'secret things belong to God,' Deut. xxix. 29, and are no man's rule to walk by, seeing 'revealed things only belong to us;' all this the devil perverts, for he endeavours to make election the immediate object of our faith, and our rule to walk by, as if it were necessary that every man knew God's eternal purpose concerning him before he begin his endeavours. And as he argues some men into a perverse carelessness upon the ground of election, making them to conclude that if they are ordained to life, they shall be saved, though they live wickedly; if they be not, they shall be damned, though they endeavour never so much to the contrary; so he also argues some, from this doctrine, into terrible fears of damnation, because they cannot be assured aforehand that their names are written in heaven. And these dreadful suspicions he doth labour to strengthen by some men's unwary handling of the doctrine of non-election. When some preachers unskilfully urge the dangerous signs of reprobation, or speak severely of God's decrees, without due caution and promise of mercy to all penitent sinners; or when some, unskilful in the methods of comforting the distressed in conscience, because they are not able to shew the afflicted their condition, or to speak 'a word in season' to quiet their minds, and to direct them what course to take, do usually refer them to God's decree, and tell them, If God have decreed them to salvation, they shall be saved; Satan doth industriously hold them there; by this means he leads them from their promises and their duty, and keeps them musing and poring upon election till they are bewildered, and cannot find the way out. Thus have several continued under their affrightments for many years.

[4.] We may observe, That when Satan hath brought them into this snare, *he doth tyrannically domineer over them.* He doth deride them under their trouble, and mock at them when their fear comes upon them. And because now the very thought or hearing of election is as a dagger to the heart, and a 'dreadful sound in their ears,' he delights to repeat it to them; for the very naming of the word becomes as dreadful as the sentence of condemnation to a malefactor, being always accompanied with this reflection, Oh how miserable am I that have no part nor portion in it! Besides, he doth busy their minds with imaginary representations of hell, and sets before them, as in a scheme, the day of judgment, the terrors of the damned, the sentence against the goats on the left hand, the intolerable pains of everlasting burnings, and that which is the misery of all these miseries, the eternity of all. Thus he forceth their meditations, but still with application to themselves; neither doth he suffer them to rest in the night, but they are terrified with sad dreams, and the visions of the night do disquiet them.

[5.] *How grievous this affrightment is,* I should next observe; but that is partly expressed in the aforegoing particulars, and may yet more fully appear by a consideration of these three things:

First, That a man hath nothing dearer to him than his soul. Alas!

that cannot be counterbalanced by the gaining of the whole world, and to have no hope or expectancy of its salvation must needs be terribly affrightful!

Second, These suspicions of non-election prevailing, all promises and comforts are urged in vain, and they commonly return them back again to those that offered them with this reply, ' They are true and useful to those unto whom they appertain, but they belong not unto me.' Nay, all means are rejected as useless. If such be advised to pray or read, they will in their fit of affrightment refuse all; upon this reason, that they are not elected. And then to what purpose, say they, is prayer, or any endeavours? For who can alter his decree? And, indeed, if their affrightments continued at a height without intermission, they would never do anything; but this is their help, that some secret underground hopes which they espy not, do revive, at least sometimes, and put them upon endeavours which, through God's blessing, become means of better information.

Third, Though Satan's injections of non-election be altogether unproveable, and withal so terrifying, that it might be supposed men should not be forward in their belief of so great an unhappiness; yet can he prevail so far *that the persons above named—especially the melancholy—are made to believe him, and this chiefly by possessing their imaginations with his frequent confident affirmations.* We see it is a common practice to teach birds musical notes and sounds, which is only by constant repetition, till a strong impression is made upon their fancy; and thus may one man impose upon the imagination of another with his songs or sayings; for what we hear often we cannot forbear to repeat in our thoughts, being strongly fixed upon our fancy. No wonder, then, if Satan, by often repeating, 'Thou art not elected, thou art damned,' &c., do form so strong an impression upon the imagination, that poor amazed creatures learn to say after him, and then take the echoes of their fancy to be the voice of conscience condemning them. Now, then, if the unhappiness suspected be the greatest beyond all comparison, if these suspicions entertained cut off all succours of comfort that may arise from the promises of God and the endeavours of man, if Satan can prevail with men to entertain them with any persuasion—as we see he can—how dreadfully will these persuasions recoil upon a man! And thus will his thoughts run, 'I am persuaded I am not elected; and if not elected, then comforts and prayers are all in vain; and if these be in vain, there is no possibility of salvation, nor the least hope of a *who knows,* or a *peradventure;* and if that, oh unspeakably miserable!' Under these astonishing thoughts doth Satan exercise their hearts by suspicions of non-election. But,

4. Sometimes he takes another course to affright men, and that is by *injecting motions of some abominable sin or evil into their minds, to the commission whereof he seems strongly to solicit;* yet not with any full intention or expectation of prevalency, but with a purpose to molest and disquiet. And for that end, he commonly chooseth such sins as are most vile in their own nature, and most opposite to the dispositions of men. Thus he injects thoughts of uncleanness to a chaste person; thoughts of injustice and wrong to

a just man; thoughts of revenge and cruelty to a weak man; thoughts of rejoicing in the loss and misery of others to the merciful man. Or else he injects motions to such sins wherein formerly men have been overtaken, but have been made bitter by deep repentance; the very thoughts whereof are now become most loathsome. And sometimes he pursues men with thoughts of self-murder, even while there is nothing of discontent or trouble in their minds to second such a temptation. By this manner of proceeding he creates great affrightments to the hearts of men. For,

[1.] *These are strange surprisals;* and persons under this kind of trouble cannot but be amazed to find such thoughts within them, which are most contrary to their dispositions, or their most serious resolves. The chaste person tempted to uncleanness, or the just man to revenge; the humble person urged to the same sin that cost him so dear, &c.; they wonder at their own hearts, and while they mistake these temptations, by judging them to be the issues of their own inclination, with astonishment they cry out, Oh, I had thought that I had mortified these lusts, but what a strange heart have I! I see sin is as strong in me as ever! And I have cause to fear myself, &c.

[2.] And this is yet a greater trouble, because usually Satan takes them *at some advantage of an offered occasion or opportunity*, then he gives them a sudden push, and with importunity urgeth them to take the time. This often affrights them into trembling, and their fears do so weaken their purposes that their hazards are the greater, in that they are astonished into an inactivity. So that in this case the men of might do not readily find their hands.

[3.] Neither are these motions *sudden and transient glances, which perish as soon as they are born*, though it be a very frequent thing with Satan to cast in motions into the heart for trial sake, without further prosecution; but he, in this case, pursues with frequent repetitions, following hard after them, to the increase of the affrightment. So that for a long time together men may be afflicted with these messengers of Satan to buffet them; and though they may pray earnestly against them that they may be removed, yet they find the motions continue upon them. Which must needs be a hateful annoyance to an upright heart, that doth know it to be only Satan's design to affright; much more must it afflict those that do not perceive the contriver and end of such motions, but judge them to be the natural workings of their own evil heart.

5. Satan can also affright men *by immediate impressions of fear upon their minds.* He can do much with the imagination, especially when persons are distempered with melancholy, for such are naturally fearful, and any impressions upon them have the deepest, most piercing operation. They are always framing to themselves dismal things, and abound with black and dark conceits, surmising still the worst, and always incredulous of what is good. Hence it is that sometimes men are seized upon by fearfulness and trembling, when yet they cannot give any tolerable account of a cause or reason why it should be so with them. And others are excessively astonished with the shadows of their own thoughts upon the meanest pretences imaginable.

That this is the work of Satan doth appear by unquestionable evidence. This was that 'evil spirit' which God sent between Abimelech and the men of Shechem, Judges ix. 23. God permitted Satan, for the punishment of them both, to raise fears and jealousies in the heart of Abimelech against the men of Shechem, and in the hearts of the men of Shechem against Abimelech. They were mutually afraid of one another, and these fears wrought so far, that they were, for the prevention of a supposed danger, engaged in treacherous conspiracies, to the real ruin of them both. The 'evil spirit' that vexed Saul, 1 Sam. xvi. 14, was nothing else but sudden and vehement fits of terror and inward fear, which the devil raised by the working up of his melancholy. For we may observe these fits were allayed by music; and also we might see by his disposition out of his fits, and by his carriage in them, that inward fears were his tormentors; for, 1 Sam. xviii. 9, it is noted that Saul eyed David, that is, his jealous fears began to work concerning David, of whom it is said expressly, ver. 12, 'that he was afraid because the Lord was with him,' and when the evil spirit came upon him his heart was exercised with these fears, and accordingly he behaved himself when he cast the javelin at David with a purpose to slay him. Upon any occasion, of trouble especially, the devil was at hand to heighten his affrightment, insomuch that when the supposed Samuel told him of his death, 1 Sam. xxviii. 20, he was afraid to such a height that he 'fell straightway all along on the earth, and there was no strength in him.' Neither must we suppose that Satan in this kind of working is confined only to wicked men; for there is nothing in this manner of affrightment which is inconsistent with the condition of a child of God, especially when God gives him up to trial or correction. Nay, many of God's servants suffer under Satan's hand in this very manner. Let us consider the troubles of Job, and we shall find that though Satan endeavoured to destroy his peace by discomposure of spirit, by questioning his integrity, by frightful injections of blasphemous thoughts, yet all these he vanquished with an undaunted courage, the blasphemy he rejected with abhorrency, his integrity he resolved he would not deny so long as he lived, his losses he digested easily with a sober composed mind, blessed God that gives and takes at pleasure; and yet he complains of his fears, and his frequent surprisals thereby, insomuch that his friends take notice that most of his trouble arose from thence: chap. xxii. 10, 'A sudden fear troubleth thee;' and he himself confesseth as much, ix. 34, 'Let not his fear terrify me . . . . but it is not so with me.' So that it appears that Job's inward distress was mostly from strong impressions of affrighting fears.

These fears impressed upon the mind must needs be an unexpressible trouble. There is nothing that doth more loosen the sinews and joints of the soul, to the weakening and utter enfeebling of it in all its endeavours, than fears; it scatters the strength in a moment. And besides the present burden, which will bow down the backs of the strongest, these fears have a special kind of envious magnanimity in them. For (1.) they come by fits, and have times of more fierce and cruel assaults, yet in their intervals they leave the heart in a trembling fainting posture; for the devil gives not over the present fit till he hath rent them sore, and left them, as he did the man's son in Mark

ix. 26, 'as one dead': so that it is no more to be reckoned compassion and gentleness in Satan toward the afflicted that their fits are not constant, than it can be accounted tenderness or kindness in a tyrant who, when he hath racked or tormented a man as much as strength will bear without killing out of hand, gives over for a time that the party might be reserved for new torments. (2.) These fits usually return at such times as the party afflicted seems to promise himself some little ease, being designed to give the greater disappointment in intercepting his expected comforts. Sleep and meat are the two great refreshments of the distressed; these times Satan watcheth for his new onsets. Job found it so in both cases; his meal times were times of trouble: chap. iii. 24, 'My sighing cometh,' that is, the fits of sighing return, 'before I eat, and my roarings are poured out like the waters.' And his sleeping-times were no better: vii. 13, 'When I say, My bed shall comfort me, my couch shall ease my complaint; then thou scarest me with dreams, and terrifiest me through visions: so that my soul chooseth strangling, and death rather than life.' (3.) These fears do make them feel the weight, not only of real present evils, but of all others which the imagination can represent to them. So that the sight or hearing of any sad thing afflicts them with surmises that this will be their case. Hence are they full of misgiving thoughts. Sometimes they fear that they shall at last fall off from God into some scandalous sin, to the dishonour of God and religion, as that they shall be apostates, and turn openly profane; sometimes they fear they shall meet with some signal devouring judgment by which they shall one day perish, as David said in the like case, 'I shall one day perish by the hand of Saul,' [1 Sam. xxvii. 1.] Thus are they crucified betwixt their present burden and future expectations of evil.

6. The last, and indeed the meanest, engine for the working of affrightment, is *scrupulosity of conscience*. Satan vexeth the conscience and distracteth the mind, by raising up *needless, groundless fears concerning a man's practice*. Where the ignorance of men or their timorous dispositions do encourage Satan to this enterprise, there he multiplies scruples upon them; so that, though they assent to the doing of anything as good or lawful, yet are they constantly affrighted from it by a suspicious fear that it may be otherwise.

This kind of trouble takes in almost all kind of actions. It extends to the way of a man's calling, the way of his management of it, the rates he takes and the prices he gives for his commodities; our very natural actions of sleeping, eating, drinking, company, recreation, are not unconcerned. In all which the devil affrights the timorous conscience that, *it may be* he hath offended: if he buys or sells, he is disquieted with a *maybe* that he hath sold too dear, or bought too cheap; if he eats or sleeps, he fears he hath been excessive, a sluggard or a glutton: thus are some men molested in everything they do.

Neither is this kind of affrightment to be despised; for though often it is a groundless fear, and so appears to be to discerning Christians, yet those that are under this molestation think it bad enough. Though it be not as a rack, that afflicts with violent pains, yet it is as those kinds of punishments which at first are nothing, but by continuance do tire men out with little ease, and so at last become intolerable.

Besides, this is a multiplying trouble; for one scruple begets another, and by continuance of scrupling, the conscience grows so weak and unsteady, that everything is scrupled, and the man brought to a continual affrightment of doing wrong in every action. Neither can all men make use of the remedy that is prescribed for the cure of this distemper, which is, that when such scruples cannot be removed by reason, then either men should forbear the thinking upon such things from whence scruples are apt to arise, or they should break them down by violence, and go over the belly of their scruple to the performance of their action. I deny not but that something may be done and endeavoured this way; but any may see that it is not easy for every one to do either of these: so that this is also a troublesome evil, from which it is not easy to be discharged.

CHAPTER VIII.

Of Satan's third way to hinder peace, by spiritual sadness.—Wherein, 1. Of the degrees of spiritual sadness. 2. Of the frequency of this trouble, evidenced several ways. Of the difference betwixt God and Satan in wounding the conscience. 3. Of the solemn occasions of this trouble. 4. The engines by which Satan works spiritual sadness. (1.) His sophistry. His topics enumerated and explained. [1.] Scriptures perverted. [2.] False notions. [3.] Misrepresentations of God. [4.] Sins: how he aggravates them. [5.] Lessening their graces: how he doth that. (2.) His second engine, fear: how he forwards his design that way.

Besides the troubles already mentioned under the heads of discomposures of spirit and affrightments, there is a third kind of trouble which Satan gives to the children of God, and this may, for distinction sake, be called *spiritual sadness*. These spiritual sadnesses *are troubles raised in the mind, relating to the conscience and spiritual state or condition of men.* They differ exceedingly from the two former sorts of trouble: for, (1.) These troubles wholly concern the conscience in point of regeneration, and men's suitableness thereunto; whereas simple discomposures of spirit firstly relate to outward things. (2.) In these the conscience is immediately concerned, but in other troubles the conscience is either wholly untouched, or wounded only secondarily, by continuance and progress of the discomposure of the spirit. (3.) In these troubles, conscience is the great instrument by which the devil works; whereas, in the trouble of affrightments, the devil acted alone, the heart being in the meantime uncompliant and resisting. For the opening of this trouble I shall explain—

1. *The several degrees thereof.* It is a trouble of conscience unduly aggravated by Satan, wherein he confines himself to the operations of conscience. But then, as he suggests the troubles of men by the voice of conscience, so he doth all he can to make it irregular in its actings, and excessive in that irregularity. So that in this case the conscience is evil, and employs itself in that mistake, to inquire into

men's regeneracy or holiness, always being either a neuter or an adversary, and the devil helps this forward all he can.

The apostle, in Heb. x. 22, makes mention of an 'evil conscience,' and that chiefly as it doth occasion fear, hindering our comfortable access to God. This the conscience doth when it doth not execute its office aright, either in 'not excusing' when it ought, or in 'accusing' when it should not; and these false accusations cause different sorts of troubles according to the variety of the matter for which it doth condemn. Hence is it that there are three degrees of trouble of conscience below the trouble of despair:—

[1.] The lowest degree is when *a regenerate person doth not positively determine the case of his soul, whether he be regenerate or not, but is only kept in suspense betwixt hope that he is, and fear that he is not, the conscience in the meantime forbearing to witness for him, though it hath just cause to excuse him.* This we may call a doubting or questioning conscience; and though it comes far short of these distresses in which some men are plunged upon the account of their souls, yet is it a trouble, for their peace is hereby hindered and their desires of satisfaction frustrated, which in matters of so great concern, as are these of everlasting life and everlasting misery, must be very disquieting. When the affections are earnest, their satisfaction cannot be delayed without trouble; for 'hope deferred makes the heart sick,' Prov. xiii. 12; not only doth it faint under its doubts, but is by that means so weak in its purposes that it is easily drawn to admit of greater inconveniences, which may lay the foundation of more perplexing disturbances.

That the conscience may be in such a distemper that it will not witness for a man, when yet it cannot witness against him, is the observation of those that have treated of the nature of conscience.[1] Sometimes it will not make application of God's promises. Though it will believe that he that forsakes sin is regenerate, that he that truly repents shall be pardoned, yet it will not affirm for a man that he forsakes sin or repents, though he really do so; or if it cannot deny that, yet it will sometimes refuse to make that conclusion which one would think would follow of itself by natural consequence, and so refuseth to judge the person regenerate or pardoned, though it cannot deny but that he forsakes sin and repents. The greatness of the blessing, the remainders of unbelief, the deep sense of unworthiness, with other considerations, do keep off the heart from making, as I may say, so bold with the promises; but all this while the devil is doing his utmost to aggravate these considerations, affrighting the conscience from that just absolution which it ought to give.

[2.] Another degree of trouble arising from an evil conscience, is when *the condition of a regenerate person is determined by conscience, but falsely, to be very bad.* I must here, as some others have done,[2] for want of better terms, distinguish betwixt the state of regeneracy and a man's condition in that state, though the words *state* and *condition* are used promiscuously the one for another. A man may be in a regenerate state, and yet his condition in that state may be very

---
[1] Ames, 'Case Consc.,' lib. i. cap. 9.
[2] Dickson, Therap. Sacra, lib. iii. cap. 1.

bad and blameworthy, as not walking worthy of so holy a calling; as a person may be a man, and yet unhealthy or languishing. Thus many of the Asian churches were true churches, and yet in a bad condition; some 'lukewarm;' some had 'a name to live,' and yet were comparatively 'dead,' because their works were not full or 'perfect before God;' and others had 'left their first love.' To this purpose is that of the apostle, 2 Cor. xiii. 5, 'Know ye not your own selves, how that Jesus Christ is in you, except ye be reprobates?'—εἰ μή τι ἀδόκιμοί ἐστε—where the word 'reprobate' is not to be taken in the strict, severe sense for one 'not elected,' but for one whose conversation is not so sound and approved as it should be: for this relates not to their being in Christ, but to their assurance of being in that state, which the apostle affirms they might know, except the fault lay in their negligent, careless conversation.

This kind of trouble then is of this nature: the conscience doth not accuse a man to be unregenerate, yet it condemns him for a carriage unsuitable to the gospel; and this sometimes when his actions are not absolutely evil, but partly good, partly bad. When the conscience condemns the actions as altogether sinful, because of some mixture of infirmities, in which case we should imitate the apostle, in Rom. vii., who when by reason of the remainders of sin in him, he could not do the good he would—that is, in such a manner and degree as he desired, nor avoid the evil which he would so clearly and fully as he wished, some imperfections in his best endeavours still cleaving to him; yet his conscience took a right course, he was humbled for his imperfections, but withal acquits himself in point of integrity; his conscience testified, ver. 16, that he 'consented to the law as good;' and ver. 22, that he 'delighted in the law of God, after the inward man.' But in this case of spiritual trouble, the conscience takes all in the worst sense; it only fixeth upon the imperfections, and makes them to serve for proofs against the sincerity. Thus if a man in praying be troubled with wandering thoughts, then a distempered conscience condemns that prayer as a sinful profanation of the name of God. If the great concern of God's glory run along in such a way as is also advantageous to the person in outward things, then will such a conscience condemn the man for self-seeking, though his main design were truly the honour of God. In all actions where there is infirmity appearing with the most serious endeavours, or where God's glory and man's good are twisted together, the disordered conscience will be apt to take part with Satan, accusing and condemning the action. Yea, very often when the actions are very good, no way justly reprovable, the conscience shall condemn. If he have had peace, he shall be judged for security; if he have faith in God's promises, it will call it presumption; if he have a zeal for God, it will be misinterpreted for carnal rigour; if he have joy, it shall be misjudged to be natural cheerfulness or delusion; in a word, all his graces shall be esteemed no better than moral virtues. At this rate are the children of God put to great trouble, losing, as I may say, the things they have wrought, sadly bemoaning their hardness of heart, or want of faith and love, when in their carriage and complainings, they give very high proofs of all. In this also Satan is busy to nourish the conscience in its jealousies, and doth suggest many objections to confirm it in its distemper. The conscience is not always of a peevish or perverse humour; for sometimes it will smite a man for a miscarriage,—as it did to David when he cut off the lap of Saul's garment,—and yet not break his peace: which is a sufficient evidence that it is put, in this case, far out of order; which advantage Satan works upon to disquiet the heart, to make men unthankful for the mercies they have received, and to incapacitate them for more. This, for distinction sake, we may call the trouble of a grieved or dejected conscience, according to that of Ps. xlii. 5, 11, 'Why art thou cast down, O my soul? and why art thou disquieted within me?' Though such men are under God's favour, yet they misdeem it, and think God is angry with them; their heart pants, their soul thirsts, their tears are their meat, they are ready to say unto God, 'My rock, why hast thou forsaken me?' and though they have some hopes for the future, that God 'will command his loving-kindness,' and that they 'shall yet praise him;' yet their present apprehension of their spiritual wants and weaknesses, and of the displeasure of God, which they suppose they are under, makes them go mourning all the day.

[3.] The third degree of trouble of conscience is when the conscience *peremptorily denies the state of regeneration*. Hereby a man that is really regenerate, is concluded to be yet 'in the gall of bitterness, and bond of iniquity;' his former hopes are taxed for self-delusion, and his present state to be a state of nature. This trouble is far greater than the two former, because the party is judged to be in greater hazard, and by many degrees more remote from hope. It is the frequent and sad thought of such, that if death should in that estate cut off their days, oh, then they were for ever miserable! The fears and disquiets of the heart on this account are very grievous, but yet they admit of degrees, according to the ignorance of the party, the distemper of the conscience, the strength of the objections, or severity of the prosecution, in regard the conscience is now sadly out of order. We may call this degree of grief, for distinction, ' a wounded spirit;' which how hard it is to be borne Solomon tells us, Prov. xviii. 14, by comparing it with all other kind of troubles, which the spirit of a man can make some shift to bear, making this heavier than all, and above ordinary strength.

Some make inquiry what may be the difference betwixt a wounded spirit in the regenerate and the reprobate? To which it may be answered, (1.) That in the party's apprehension there is no difference at all; both of them may be compassed about with the sorrows of death, and suppose themselves to be in the belly of hell. (2.) Neither is there any difference in the degree of the trouble; a child of God may be handled with as much seeming severity, as he whom God intends for a future Tophet. (3.) Neither is there any such remarkable difference in the working of the spirits of the one and other, that they themselves at present, or others that are bystanders, can easily observe. Yet a formal difference there is; for grace being in the heart of the one, will in some breathing or pulse discover its life. And though sometimes it acts so low or confusedly that God only can distinguish, yet often those that are experienced observers will discover some real breathings after God, and true loathing of sin, and other traces of faith and love, that are not so discernible to the parties themselves. (4.) But in God's design the difference is very great; the wicked lie under his lash as malefactors, but the regenerate are as patients under cure, or children under discipline. (5.) And accordingly the issue doth determine, that God's intention in wounding their spirits were not alike to both; the one at last coming out of the furnace as gold, the other still remaining as reprobate silver, or being consumed as dross. Thus have ye seen the nature and degree of spiritual sadness.

2. For the further explanation whereof I shall next shew you that this is a usual trouble to the children of God.

Which, (1.) I might evidence from several *instances of those that have suffered much under it;* as David, whose complaints in this case are very frequent, and Heman, who left a memorial of his griefs in Ps. lxxxviii. Jonah also, in the belly of the whale, had a sharp fit of it, when he concluded that he was 'cast out of God's sight,' and his 'soul fainted within him,' Jonah ii. 4, 7. Neither did Hezekiah altogether escape it, for though his disquiet began upon another ground, it ran him into spiritual trouble at last. But besides these, innumerable instances occur. One shall scarce converse with any society of Christians but he shall meet with some who, with sad complaints, shall bemoan the burden of their hearts, and the troubles of their conscience.

(2.) *The provisions which God hath made in his word for such, is an evidence that such distempers are frequent.* He that in a city shall observe the shops of the apothecaries, and there take notice of the great variety of medicines, pots, and glasses full of mixtures, confections, and cordials, may from thence rationally conclude, that it is a frequent thing for men to be sick, though he should not converse with any sick person for his information. Thus may we be satisfied from the declarations, directions, and consolations of Scripture that it is a common case for the children of God to stand in need of spiritual physicians and spiritual remedies to help them when they are wounded and fainting. Solomon's exclamation, 'A wounded spirit who can bear?' shews that the spirit is sometimes wounded. The prophet's direction, 'He that walks in darkness and sees no light, let him trust in the Lord,' [Isa. l. 10,] clearly implies that some there are that walk in darkness. God's creating the 'fruit of the lips, Peace, peace;' his promises of restoring 'comforts to mourners;' his commands to others to comfort them; do all inform us that it is a common thing for his children to be under such sadnesses of spirit, that all this is necessary for their relief.

(3.) *The reasons of this trouble* do also assure us of the frequency of it; for of them we may say, as Christ speaks of the poor, [Mat. xxvi. 11,] 'we have them always with us;' so that the grounds of spiritual sadness considered, it is no wonder to find many men complaining under this distemper. The reasons are,

[1.] *The malice of Satan,* who hath no greater revenge against a child of God, when translated from the power of darkness to the kingdom of Christ, than to hinder him of the peace and comfort of that condition.

[2.] *The many advantages which Satan hath against us.* For the effecting of this we cannot imagine that one so malicious as he is will suffer his malice to sleep, when so many fair opportunities of putting it in practice do offer themselves. For, *first, The questions to be determined for settling the peace of the soul are very intricate, and often of greater difficulty than doctrinal controversies.* How hard is it to conclude what is the *minimum quod sic,* the lowest degrees of true grace! or the *maximum quod sic,* the highest degree of sin consistent with true grace! To distinguish betwixt a child of God at the lowest, and a hypocrite or temporary believer at the highest, is difficult. In mixed actions, to be able to shew how the soul doth manage its respect to God, when the man hath also a respect to himself, especially when it is under any confusion, is not easy. And in these actions, where the difference from others of like kind lies only in the grounds and motives of the undertaking, or where the prevailing degree must distinguish the act in reference to different objects that are subordinate to one another—as our loving God above the world or ourselves, our fearing God above men, &c.—it is not every one that can give a satisfactory determination. *Second,* As the intricacies of the doubts to be resolved give the devil an advantage to puzzle us, so is the advantage heightened exceedingly *by the great injudiciousness and unskilfulness of the greatest part of Christians.* These questions are in their notion difficult; more difficult in their application to particular persons, where the ablest Christian may easily be nonplussed; but most difficult to the weak Christians. These Satan can baffle with every poor objection, and impose what he will upon them. *Third,* Especially having the advantage of *the working guilt of conscience,* which he can readily stir up to present to a man's remembrance all his failings and miscarriages of what nature soever. And when guilt rageth in an unskilful heart, it must needs create great disquiet. *Fourth,* But most of all when our *natural fears are awakened;* as when a man hath been under any great conviction, though he be cured of his trouble, yet it usually leaves a weakness in the part, as bruises and maims do in any member of the body, which at the change of weather or other accidental hurt will renew their old trouble; and then when fresh guilt begins to press hard upon the conscience, not only do the broken bones ache, by the reviving of former fears, but the impressions of his old suspicions, bad conceit of himself, and jealousies of the deceitfulness of his heart, which had then fixed themselves by a deep rooting, do now make him most fearful of entertaining any good thought of himself. So that if any consideration tending to his support be offered, he dare not come near it, suspecting his greatest danger to lie on that hand. These advantages considered, we should not think it strange that any child of God is driven to spiritual sadness, as some do, but may rather wonder that this is not the common condition of all Christians.

[3.] Another reason that must be assigned for these troubles is *divine dispensation.* Such are his children, some so careless, others proud, others stubborn, many presumptuous, that God is forced to correct them by this piece of discipline, and to cure them by casting them into a fever. Others of his children he thus exerciseth for other ends, sometimes to take occasion therefrom of making larger discoveries of his love; sometimes thereby preventing them from falling under some grievous miscarriage, or for the trial and exercises of their graces. We may observe, accordingly, that there are three sorts of men that usually have exercises of this kind.

(1.) Those who at their conversion are either *ignorant, melancholy, or were grossly scandalous, are usually brought through with great fear and sadness.* And this is so observable, that by the mistake of men it is made a general rule that none are converted but they are under great and frightful apprehensions of wrath and dismal terrors. This indeed is true of some, but these ordinarily are the scandalous, melancholy, and ignorant sort—though sometimes God may deal so with others, for who can limit him? Yet are there many whose education hath been good, and their instruction aforehand great, whose conversion is so gradual and insensible, that they are strangers to these troubles of conscience, and profess that if these heights of fear be necessary to conversion, they must be at a loss; neither can they give an account of the time of their conversion, as others may.

(2.) Those whose conversion was easy, when after their conversion *they miscarry by any great iniquity, they meet with as great a measure of terror and fear, and some think far greater, as those whose new birth was more difficult.* David's greatest troubles of soul came upon him after he began to appear more public in the world; for then he met with many temptations, and great occasions for God's exercising his discipline over him. I believe, when he kept his father's sheep, his songs had more of praises and less of complainings than afterward. It is the opinion of some that God's dealing in this kind of dispensation, even when miscarriage is not the cause, is more sharp usually to those whose conversion hath been most easy.

(3.) *There is another sort of men, to whom God vouchsafes but seldom and short fits of spiritual joy, as breathing times, betwixt sharp fits of soul-trouble, for necessary refreshment and recovery of strength;* but the constant course which God holds with them is to exercise them under fears, while he hides his face from them, and suffers Satan to vex them, by urging his objections against their holiness and integrity. Heman was one of this rank, and the great instance which God hath given in his word for the support of others that may be in the same case. For he testifies, Ps. lxxxviii., that he suffered the terrors of God almost to distraction, and this from his youth up. It is not fit for us too narrowly to question why God doth thus to his children, seeing his 'judgments are unsearchable,' and his 'ways past finding out;' but we may be sure that God sees this dealing to be most fit for those that are exercised therewith. It may be to keep pride from them, or to prevent them from falling into some greater inconvenience or sin, unto which he takes notice of a more than ordinary proneness in their disposition; or for the benefit of others, who may thereby take notice what 'an evil and bitter thing it is' to sin against God, and what a malicious adversary they have to deal with. Whoso shall consider these reasons of spiritual sadness, must needs confess, that seeing the advantages which men give to a malicious devil to vex their consciences are so many and great, and the weakness of God's children so hazardous, for the prevention whereof, a wise, careful Father will necessarily be engaged to exercise his discipline, it cannot be expected.

but that spiritual troubles should be very frequent among the servants of God.

Quest. Here it is requisite that I give satisfaction to this query. Seeing that God doth sometime wound the consciences of his children, and that Satan also wounds them, what are the differences betwixt God and Satan in inflicting these wounds?

Ans. For the right understanding of this question I shall propound two things:

(1.) That it is a truth that *God doth sometimes wound the consciences of his children;* and this,

[1.] *Before conversion:* but in order to it, as preparatory to that change, men are then in their sins, walking in the vanity of their minds. To translate them from this estate he awakens the conscience, shews them their iniquities, and the danger of them, that at present they are ' in their blood,' ' children of wrath, as well as others,' and that without Christ they are miserable. The effect of this must needs be serious consideration, deep thoughts of heart, with some trouble; only as to the measure and degree there is great difference. God doth not in the particular application of these things to the conscience tie up himself exactly to the same manner and measure of proceeding, though he keep still to his general method. Hence is it that some, in regard of God's gentle, leisurely dealing, and the frequent interposure of encouragements, are, if compared with the case of others, said to be allured and ' drawn with cords of love.' But others have a remarkable measure of trouble, sharp fits of fear and anguish; and those most commonly are such whose conversion is more quick, and the change visible from one extreme to another, as Paul, when converted in the midst of his persecuting rage, or those whose ignorance or melancholy makes their hopes and comforts inaccessible for the present. These troubles God owns to be the work of his Spirit. The same Spirit, which is a ' Spirit of adoption' to the converted, is a ' spirit of bondage' to these, Rom. viii. 16. And accordingly we find it was so to the converts in Acts ii., who being ' pricked in their hearts' by Peter's sermon, ' cried out, Men and brethren, what shall we do?' The like did the jailor. And the promise which God makes of calling the Jews, Zech. xii. 10, doth express God's purpose of dealing with them in this very method: ' They shall look upon him whom they have pierced, and shall mourn for him as one that mourneth for his only son, and shall be in bitterness for him; . . . in that day shall be a great mourning.'

[2.] God also sometimes wounds the conscience of his children *after conversion;* and this he doth to convince and humble them for some miscarriage which they become guilty of.[1] As when they grow secure, carnally confident of the continuance of their peace—when they are carelessly negligent of duty and the exercises of their graces—when they fall into gross and scandalous sins, or wilfully desert the ways of truth, and in many more cases of like kind. When his children make themselves thus obnoxious to divine displeasure, then God hides his face from them, takes away his Spirit, signifies his anger to their consciences, threatens them with the danger of that condition, from

[1] *Vide* Goodwin's ' Child of Light.' [As before.—G.]

whence follows grief and fear in the hearts of his people. In this manner God expressed his displeasure to David, as his complaints in Ps. li. do testify: 'Make me to hear joy and gladness, that the bones which thou hast broken may rejoice. Hide thy face from my sins. Cast me not away from thy presence, and take not thy Holy Spirit from me. Restore unto me the joy of thy salvation,' &c.

(2.) Notwithstanding all this, there is *a great difference betwixt God and Satan in this matter*, which mainly appears in two things:—

[1.] *God doth limit himself in all the trouble which he gives his children, to his great end of doing them good, and healing them*, and consequently stints himself in the measure and manner of his work to such a proportion as his wisdom sees will exactly suit with his end. So that his anger is not like the brawlings of malicious persons that know no bounds. He will not 'always chide;' his debates are in measure, and this 'lest the spirit should fail before him,' Isa. lvii. 16. So that when he wounds the conscience before conversion, it is but to bring them to Christ, and to prevent their taking such courses as might through delusion make them take up their stand short of him. So much of mourning and fear as is requisite for the true effecting of this, he appoints for them, and no more. When he wounds after conversion, it is but to let them feel that it is an evil and bitter thing to sin against him, that their 'godly sorrow may work repentance' suitable to the offence, and that they may be sufficiently cautioned for the time to come to 'sin no more, lest a worse thing befall them.' He that afflicts not willingly, will put no more grief upon them than is necessary to bring them to this. But Satan, when he is admitted—and God doth often permit him in subservience to his design, to wound the conscience—he proceeds according to the boundless fury of his malice, and plainly manifests that his desire is to destroy and to tread them down that they may never rise again. This though he cannot effect, for God will not suffer him to proceed further than the bringing about his holy and gracious purpose, yet it hinders not but that still his envious thoughts boil up in his breast, and he acts according to his own inclination. For it is with Satan as it is with wicked men. If God employ them for the chastisement of his children, they consider not who sets them on work, nor what measures probably God would have them observe, but they propose to themselves more work than ever God cut out for them; as Assyria, when employed against Jerusalem, Isa. x. 7, had designs more large and cruel than was in God's commission. God had stinted him in his holy purpose; yet the 'Assyrian meant not so, neither did his heart think so; but it was in his heart to destroy and cut off nations not a few.' So that when God is 'a little displeased,' as he speaks, Zech. i. 15, they do all that lies in them to help forward the affliction. Thus doth the devil endeavour to make all things worse to God's children than ever God intended. Here is one difference betwixt God and Satan, in the wounding of consciences. But,

[2.] They are yet further differenced, in that all that God doth in this work is still *according to truth*. For if he signify to the unconverted that they are in a state of nature, liable to the damnation of hell, unless they accept of Christ for salvation upon his terms, this is no more than what is true. God doth not misrepresent their case to them at that time. Again, if he express his displeasure to any of his converted children that have grieved his Spirit by their follies, by setting before them the threatenings of his word, or the examples of his wrath, he doth but truly tell them that he is angry with them, and that *de jure*, according to the rigour of the law and the demerit of their offence he might justly cast them off; but he doth not positively say that, *de eventu*, it shall infallibly be so with them. But Satan, in both these cases, goes a great way further. He plainly affirms to those that are in the way to conversion, that God will not pardon their iniquities, that there is no hope for them, that Christ will not accept them, that he never intended the benefit of his sufferings for them. And when the converted do provoke God, he sticks not to say the breach cannot be healed, and that they are not yet converted. All which are most false assertions. And though God can make use of Satan's malice, when he abuseth his children with his falsehoods to their great fear, to carry on his own ends by it, and to give a greater impression to what he truly witnesseth against them; yet is not God the proper author of Satan's lying, for he doth it of his own wicked inclination. The effect of these desperate false conclusions, which is the putting his children into a fear in order to his end, may be ascribed to God; but the falsehood of these conclusions are formally Satan's work and not God's; for he makes use of so much of Satan's wrath as may be to his praise, and the 'remainder of his wrath he doth restrain,' [Ps. lxxvi. 10.]

I have discovered the nature and degrees of these spiritual troubles, and that it is a common thing for the children of God to fall under them. For the further opening of them I shall next discover,

3. The usual solemn occasions that do, as it were, invite Satan to give his onset against God's children; and they are principally these six:—

[1.] *The time of conversion.* He delights to set on them when they are in the straits of a new birth, for then the conscience is awakened, the danger of sin truly represented, fear and sorrow, in some degree, necessary and unavoidable. At this time he can easily overdrive them. Where the convictions are deep and sharp, ready to weigh them down, a few grains more cast into the scale will make the trouble, as Job speaks, 'heavier than the sand,' [chap. vi. 3;] and where they are more easy or gentle, yet the soul being unsettled, the thoughts in commotion, they are disposed to receive a strong impression, and to be turned, as wax to the seal, into a mould of hopelessness and desperation. That this is one of Satan's special occasions, we need no other evidence for satisfaction than the common experience of converts. Many of them do hardly escape the danger, and after their difficult conquest of the troubles of their heart—which at that time are extraordinarily enlarged—do witness that they are assaulted with desperate fears that their sins were unpardonable, and sad conclusions against any expectation of favour from the Lord their God. These thoughts we are sure the Spirit of God will not bear witness unto, because false, and therefore we must leave them at Satan's door.

[2.] Another occasion which Satan makes use of, is the time of *solemn repentance for some great sin committed after conversion.* Sometimes God's children fall, to the breaking of their bones. What great iniquities they may commit through the force of temptation, I need not mention. The adultery and murder of David; the incest of the Corinthian; Peter's denial of Christ, with other sad instances in the records of the Scriptures, do speak enough of that. These sins—considering their heinousness, the scandal of religion, the dishonour of God, the grieving of his Spirit, the condition of the party offending against love, knowledge, and the various helps which God affords them to the contrary, with other aggravating circumstances—being very displeasing to God, their consciences at least, either compelled to examination by God immediately, or mediately by some great affliction, or voluntarily awakening to a serious consideration of what hath been done, by the working of its own light, assisted thereunto by quickening grace, 1 Cor. xi. 31, 32,—call them to a strict account. Thence follow fear, shame, self-indignation, bitter weeping, deep humiliation. Then comes Satan; he rakes their wounds, and by his aggravations makes them smart the more. He pours in corrosives instead of oil, and all to make them believe that their 'spot is not the spot of God's children,' [Deut. xxxii. 5;] that their backslidings cannot be healed. An occasion it is, as suitable to his malice as he could wish; for ordinarily God doth severely testify his anger to them, and doth not easily admit them again to the sense of his favour. At which time the adversary is very busy to work up their hearts to an excess of fear and sorrow. This was the course which he took with the incestuous Corinthian, taking advantage of his great transgressions to 'overwhelm him with too much sorrow,' 2 Cor. ii. 7, 11.

[3.] Satan watcheth *the discomposures of the spirits of God's children, under some grievous cross or affliction.* This occasion also falls fit for his design of wounding the conscience. When the hand of the Lord is lifted up against them, and their thoughts disordered by the stroke, suggesting at that time God's anger to them and their sins, he can easily frame an argument from these grounds, that they are not reconciled to God, and that they are dealt withal as enemies. David seldom met with outward trouble, but he at the same time had a conflict with Satan about his spiritual condition or state, as his frequent deprecations of divine wrath at such times do testify; 'Lord, rebuke me not in thy wrath,' &c. There is indeed but a step betwixt discomposure of spirit and spiritual troubles, as hath been proved before.

[4.] *When Satan hath prepared the hearts of God's children by atheistical or blasphemous thoughts, he takes that occasion to deny their grace and interest in Christ,* and the argument at that time seems unanswerable. Can Christ lodge in a heart so full of horrid blasphemies against him? Is it possible it should be washed and sanctified, when it produceth such filthy, cursed thoughts? All the troubles of affrightment, of which before, are improvable to this purpose.

[5.] Another spiritual occasion for spiritual trouble is *melancholy.* Few persons distempered therewith do escape Satan's hands. At one time or other he casts his net over them, and seeks to stab them with his weapon. Melancholy indeed affords so many advantages to him, and those so answerable to his design, that it is no wonder if he make much of it. For, 1. Melancholy affects both head and heart; it affords both fear and sadness, and deformed, misshapen, delirious imaginations to work upon, than which nothing can be more for his purpose.[1] For where the heart trembles and the head is darkened, there every object is misrepresented. The ideas of the brain are monstrous appearances, reflected from opaque and dark spirits, so that Satan hath no more to do but to suggest the new matter of fear. For that question, Whether the man be converted, &c., being once started, to a mind already distempered with fear, must of itself, it being a business of so high a nature, without Satan's further pursuit, summon the utmost powers of sadness and misreprehension[2] to raise a storm. 2. Besides, the impressions of melancholy are always strong. It is strong in its fears, or else men would never be tempted to destroy themselves; it is strong in its mistakes, or else they could never persuade themselves of the truth of foolish, absurd, and impossible fancies; as that of Nebuchadnezzar, who by a delusive apprehension, believing himself to be a beast, forsook the company of men, and betook to the fields to eat grass with oxen. The imaginations of the melancholic are never idle, and yet straitened or confined to a few things; and then the brain, being weakened as to a true and regular apprehension, it frames nothing but bugbears, and yet with the highest confidence of certainty. 3. These impressions are usually lasting, not vanishing as an early dew, but they continue for months and years. 4. And yet they have only so much understanding left them as serves to nourish their fears. If their understanding had been quite gone, their fears would vanish with them, as the flame is extinguished for want of air; but they have only knowledge to let them see their misery, and sense to make them apprehensive of their pain.[3] And therefore will they pray with floods of tears, unexpressible groanings, deepest sighing, and trembling joints, to be delivered from their fears. 5. They are also apt after ease of their troubles to have frequent returns. What disposition, all these things being considered, can be more exactly shaped to serve Satan's turn? If he would have men to believe the worst of themselves, he hath such imaginations to work upon as are already misshapen into a deformity of evil surmising. Would he terrify by fears or distress by sadness? he hath that already, and it is but altering the object, which oftentimes needs not—for naturally the serious melancholic employs all his griefs upon his supposed miserable estate of soul, and then he hath spiritual distress. Would he continue them long under their sorrows, or take them upon all occasions at his pleasure, or act them to a greater height than ordinary? still the melancholic temper suits him. This is sufficient for caution, that we take special care of our bodies, for the preventing or abating of that humour by all lawful means, if we would not have the devil to abuse us at his will.

[6.] *Sickness or death-bed* is another solemn occasion which the devil seldom misseth with his will. Death is a serious thing; it represents the soul and eternity to the life. While they are at a distance, men look slightly upon these; but when they approach near to them,

---

[1] Willis, de anima Brut., cap. 9, de Melancholia.
[2] Query, 'misapprehension'?—G.
[3] Fæl. Plateri prox. med., cap. 3, de mentis alienatione.

men usually have such a sight of them as they never had before. We may truly call sickness and death-bed an hour of temptation, which Satan will make use of with the more mischievous industry, because he hath but 'a short time' for it. That is the last conflict, and if he miss that, we are beyond his reach for ever. So that in this case Satan encourageth himself to the battle with a *now or never*. And hence we find that it is usual for the dying servants of God to undergo most sharp encounters. Then to tell them, when the soul is about to loose from the body, that they are yet 'in their blood' 'without God and hope,' is enough to affright them into the extremest agonies, for they see no time before them answerable to so great a work, if it be yet to do. And withal they are under vast discouragements from the weariness and pains of sickness, their understandings and faculties being also dull and stupified, so that if at this last plunge God should not extraordinarily appear to rebuke Satan and to pluck them out of these great waters, as he often doth, by the fuller interposition of the light of his face, and the larger testimony of his Spirit, after their long and comfortable profession of their faith and holy walking, their light would be 'put out in darkness,' and they would 'lie down in sorrow.' Yet this I must note, that as desirous as Satan is to improve this occasion, he is often remarkably disappointed, and that wherein he, it may be, and we would least expect, I mean in regard of those who, through a timorous disposition or melancholy, or upon other accounts, are, as I may so say, 'all their lifetime subject to bondage.' Those men who are usually exercised with frequent fits of spiritual trouble, when they come to sickness, death-bed, and some other singular occasions of trouble, though we might suspect their fears would then be working, if ever, yet God, out of gracious indulgence to them, considering their mould and fashion, or because he would prevent their extreme fainting, &c., doth meet them with larger testimonies of his favour, higher joys, more confident satisfactions in his love, than ever they received at any time before, and this, to their wonder, their high admiration, making the times which they were wont to fear most, to be times of greatest consolation. This observation I have grounded not upon one or two instances, but could produce a cloud of witnesses for it. Enough it is to check our forward fears of a future evil day, and to heal us of a sighing distemper, while we afflict ourselves with such thoughts as these: If I have so many fears in health, how shall I be able to go through the valley of the shadow of death?

4. I have one thing more to add for these discoveries of these spiritual troubles, and that is to shew you *the engines by which Satan works them*, and they are these two, sophistry and fears.

I. *As to his sophistry*, by which he argues the children of God into a wrong apprehension of themselves, it is very great. He hath a wonderful dexterity in framing arguments against their peace; he hath variety of shrewd objections and subtle answers to the usual replies by which they seek to beat him off. There is not a fallacy by which a cunning sophister would seek to entangle his adversary in disputation, but Satan would make use of it; as I might particularly shew you, if it were proper for a common auditory. Though he hath so much impudence as not to blush at the most silly, contemptible reason that can be offered, notwithstanding he hath also so much wit as to urge, though never true, yet always probable arguments. How much he can prevail upon the beliefs of men, in cases relating to their souls, may be conjectured by the success he hath upon the understandings of men, when he argues them into error, and makes them believe a lie. We usually say, and that truly, that Satan cannot in any case force us properly to consent; yet considering the advantages which he takes, and the ways he hath to prepare the hearts of men for his impressions, and then his very great subtlety in disputing, we may say that he can so order the matter that he will seldom miss of his aim. It would be an endless work to gather up all the arguments that Satan hath made use of to prove the condition or state of God's children to be bad. But that I may not altogether disappoint your expectations in that thing, I shall present to your view Satan's usual topics, the commonplaces or heads unto which all his arguments may be reduced. And they are,

[1.] *Scripture abused and perverted.* His way is not only to suggest that they are unregenerate, or under an evil frame of heart, but to offer proof that these accusations are true. And because he hath to do with them that profess a belief of Scriptures as the oracles of God, he will fetch his proofs from thence, telling them that he will evidence what he saith from Scripture. Thus sometimes he assaults the weaker, unskilful sort of Christians, Thou art not a child of God; for they that are so are enlightened, translated from darkness, they are the children of the light; but thou art a poor, ignorant, dark, blind creature, and therefore no child of God. Sometimes he labours to conclude the like from the infirmities of God's children, abusing to this purpose that of 1 John iii. 9, 'He that is born of God doth not commit sin,' and 'he cannot sin, because he is born of God.' Thus he urgeth it, Can anything be more plainly and fully asserted? Is not this scripture? Canst thou deny this? Then he pursues, But thou sinnest often; that is thine own complaint against thyself, thy conscience also bearing witness to the truth of this accusation; therefore thou canst be no child of God. Sometimes he plays upon words that are used in divers senses—a fit engine for the devil to work by— for what is true in one sense will be false in another; and his arguing is from that which is true to that which is false. I remember one that was long racked with that of Rev. xxi. 8, 'The fearful and unbelieving,' &c., 'shall have their part in the lake which burns with fire and brimstone.' From whence the party thus argued: The proposition is true, because it is scripture, and I cannot deny the assumption. 'Fearful I am, because I am doubtful of salvation; and unbelieving I am, for I cannot believe that I am regenerate, or in a state of grace, and therefore I cannot avoid the conclusion.' To the same purpose he disputes against some from 1 John iv. 18, 'There is no fear in love: but perfect love casteth out fear; but thou art full of fears, therefore thou lovest not God.' Sometimes he makes use of those scriptures that make the prevailing degree of our love and respects to God above the world and the things of this life, to be the characters of true grace; as that of John, 'If any man love the world, the love of the Father is not in him;' and that of Christ, 'If a man love anything more than me, he is not worthy of me: he that forsakes not all for me cannot be my disciple,' &c. Then he urgeth upon them their love of the world, and unwillingness to part with their estates; and so brings the conclusion upon them. Instances might be infinite; but by these you may judge of the rest. Let us now cast our eye upon his subtlety in managing his arguments against men. 1. He grounds his arguments on Scripture, because that hath authority with it, and the very troubled conscience hath a reverence to it. 2. He always suits his scriptures, which he thus cites, to that wherein the conscience is most tender. If there be anything that affords matter of suspicion or fear, he will be sure to choose such an arrow out of the quiver of Scripture as will directly hit the mark. 3. Though in the citation of Scripture he always urgeth a sense which the Holy Ghost never intended, yet there will be always something in those scriptures which he makes use of, which, in words at least, seem to favour his conclusion; as appears in the instances now given. For when he would conclude a man not to be a child of God because of his ignorance, something of his argument is true: it may be the man is sensible that his knowledge is but little, compared with the measures which some others have; or that he is at a loss or confused in many doctrinal points of religion; or hath but little experience in many practical cases, &c. This as it is true, so it is his trouble; and whilst he is poring upon his defect, Satan claps an arrest upon him of a far greater debt than God chargeth upon him, and from scriptures that speak of a total ignorance of the fundamentals of religion, as that there is a God, that Christ Jesus is God and man, the Redeemer of mankind by a satisfaction to divine justice, &c., or of a wilful ignorance of the worth of the proffer of the gospel, or its reality, which is discovered in the refusal of the terms thereof, he concludes him to be in a state of darkness; whereas the ignorance which the man complains of is not the ignorance which those scriptures intend. So in the next instance, the sins which a child of God complains of are those of daily incursion, which he labours and strives against; but that committing sin mentioned in the text hath respect to the Gnostics, who taught a liberty in sinning, and fancied a righteousness consistent with the avowed practice of iniquity. Hence doth John, 1 Epist. iii. 7, directly face their opinion in these terms, 'Little children, let no man deceive you; he that doth righteousness is righteous;' and, 'He that is born of God' neither doth nor can avouch a liberty of sinning, it being contrary to the principles of the new nature. So that the miscarriages of infirmity which the child of God laments in himself are not the same with that of the text, upon which Satan grounds the accusation. The like may be said of the third instance, from Rev. xxi. 18. The threatening there is against such a fear to lose the comforts of the world, that they dare not believe the gospel to be true, and accept it accordingly; which is nothing to those fears and doubtings that may be in a child of God, in reference to his happiness. Thus in all the rest the fallacy lies in misapplying the Scripture, to suit them to that wherein the conscience is tender, under a sense which was never intended by them; yet in another sense, the thing charged upon the conscience is true. (4.) Yet is Satan so subtle, that when he disputes by such fallacious arguments, he chiefly endeavours to draw off the defendant's eye and consideration from that part of the argument wherein its weakness lies, which in this case is always in the abuse of the scripture to a wrong sense. This he doth, partly from the advantage which he hath from the reverence that they carry to Scripture; they believe it to be true, and are not willing to suspect the sense; and many are so weak that if they should, Satan is so cunning that he can easily baffle them in any distinction that they can make. And partly from the sense they have of that whereof they are accused, they feel themselves so sore in that place, and for that very end doth Satan direct his scripture to hit it, that they readily take it for granted that the hinge of the controversy turns upon it, and that the whole dispute rests upon it. Now Satan having these fair advantages, by a further improvement of them hides the weakness of his argument. For, [1.] He takes that sense of the Scripture, in which he misapplies it, for granted, and that with great confidence, making as if there were no doubt there. [2.] He turns always that part of the argument to them which they can least answer, pressing them eagerly with the matter of charge, which they are as ready to confess as he is to accuse them of, and aggravating it very busily. And because the unskilful have no other direction for the finding the knot of the controversy than Satan's bustle—though he, like the lapwing, makes the greatest noise when he is furthest from his nest, on purpose to draw them into a greater mistake—they look no further; and then, not being able to answer, they are soon cast, and striking in with the conclusion against themselves, they multiply their sorrows, and cry out of themselves as miserable.

[2.] Another piece of his sophistry is, the improving certain *false notions, which Christians of the weaker sort have received, as proofs of their unregeneracy or bad condition.* As there are vulgar errors concerning natural things, so there are popular errors concerning spiritual things. These mistakes in a great part have their original from the fancies or misapprehensions of unskilful men. Some indeed have, it may be, been preached and taught as truths, others have risen without a teacher from mere ignorance, being the conclusions and surmises which weak heads have framed to themselves, from the sayings or practices of men, which have not been either so cleared from the danger of mistake, or not so distinctly apprehended as was necessary. These false inferences, once set on foot, are traditionally handed down to others, and in time they gain among the simple the opinion of undoubted truths. Now, wherever Satan finds any of these that are fit for his purpose—for to be sure whatever mistake we entertain, he will at one time or other cast it in our way—he will make it the foundation of an argument against him that hath received it, and that with very great advantage. For a falsehood in the premises will usually produce a falsehood in the conclusion. And these falsehoods being taken for granted, the devil is not put to the trouble to prove them. If then he can but exactly fit them to something in the party which he cannot deny, he forthwith carries the cause, and condemns him by his own concessions, as out of his own mouth.

It is scarce possible to number the false notions which are already entertained among Christians relating to grace and conversion, much less those that may afterward arise. But I shall mention some that Satan frequently makes use of as grounds of objection.

First, It is a common apprehension among the weaker sort, that conversion *is always accompanied with great fear and terror.* This is true in some, as hath been said, and though none of the preachers of the gospel have asserted the universality of these greater measures of trouble, yet the people, taking notice that many speak of their deep humiliations in conversion, and that several authors have set forth the greatness of distress that some have been cast into on that occasion—though without any intention of fixing this into a general rule—have from thence supposed that all the converted are brought to their comforts through the flames of hell. Upon this mistake the devil disquiets those that have not felt these extreme agonies of sorrow in themselves, and tells them that it is a sure sign that they are not yet converted. Though it is easy for a man that sees the falsehood of the notion to answer the argument, yet he that believes it to be true cannot tell what to say, because he finds he never was under such troubles, and now he begins to be troubled because he was not troubled before, or, as he supposeth, not troubled enough.

Second, Another false notion is, that a convert can *give an account of the time and manner of his conversion.* This is true in some, as in Paul and some others, whose change hath been sudden and remarkable, though in many this is far otherwise; who can better give account that they are converted, than by what steps, degrees, and methods they were brought to it. But if any of these receive the notion, they will presently find that Satan will turn the edge of it against them, and will tell them that they are not converted, because they cannot nominate the time when, nor the manner how, such a change was wrought.

Third, Some take it for granted that conversion is accompanied with a *remarkable measure of gifts for prayer and exhortation;* and then the devil objects it to them, that they are not converted, because they cannot pray as others, or speak of the things of God so readily, fluently, and affectionately as some others can. Thus the poor, weak Christian is baffled for want of abilities to express himself to God and men.

Fourth, False notions about *the nature of faith are a sad stumbling-block to some.* Many suppose that saving faith is a certain belief that our sins are pardoned, and that we shall be saved, making faith and assurance all one. This mistake is the deeper rooted in the minds of men because some have directly taught so, and those men of estimation, whose words are entertained with great reverence by well-meaning Christians. For whom notwithstanding this may be pleaded in excuse, that they have rather described faith in its height than in its lowest measures. However it be, those that have no other understanding of the nature of faith can never answer Satan's argument, if he takes them at any time at the advantage of fear or doubting: for then he will dispute thus, Faith is a belief that sins are pardoned, but thou dost not believe this, therefore thou hast no faith. Oh, what numbers of poor doubting Christians have been distressed with this argument!

Fifth, Some take it for a truth that *growth of grace is always visible, and the progress remarkable.* And then because they can make no such discovery of themselves, the devil concludes their grace to be counterfeit and hypocritical.

Sixth, Of like nature are some *mistaken signs of true grace, as that true grace fears God only for his goodness.* And then if there be any apprehension of divine displeasure impressed upon the heart, though upon the necessary occasion of miscarriage, they, through the devil's instigation, conclude that they are under 'a spirit of bondage,' and their supposed grace not true, or not genuine at least, according to that disposition which the New Testament will furnish a man withal. It is also another mistaken sign of grace, that it doth direct a man to love God singly for himself, without the least regard to his own salvation; for that, they think, is but self-love. Now, when a child of God doth not see his love to God so distinct, but that his own salvation is twisted with it, Satan gets advantage of him, and forceth him to cast away his love as adulterate and selfish. Like to this mistake, but of a higher strain, is that of some, that where grace is true, it is so carried forth to honour God, that the man that hath it can desire God may be honoured though he should be damned. God doth not put us to such questions as these, but upon supposition that this is true, the grace of most men will be shaken by the objection that Satan will make from thence; he can and will presently put the mistaken to it, Canst thou say thou art willing to go to hell, that God may be glorified? If not, where is thy grace? From such mistakes as these he disputes against the holiness of the children of God; and it is impossible but that he should carry the cause against those who grant these things to be true. Satan can undeniably shew them that their hearts will not answer such a description of a convert or gracious heart as these false notions will make. So long then as they hold these notions they have no relief against Satan's conclusions; no comfort can be administered till they be convinced that they have embraced mistakes for truths. And how difficult that will be in this case, where the confidence of the notion is great, and the suspicion strong, that the defect is only in the heart, hath been determined by frequent experience already.

[3.] The third piece of Satan's sophistry from whence he raiseth false conclusions, is his *misrepresentation of God.* In this he directly crosseth the design of the Scriptures, where God in his nature and dealings is so set forth, that the weakest, the most afflicted and tossed, may receive encouragement of acceptance, and of his fatherly care over them in their saddest trials. Yet withal, lest men should turn his grace into wantonness, and embolden themselves in sin because of his clemency, the Scriptures sometimes give us lively descriptions of his anger against those that wickedly presume upon his goodness, and continue so to do. Both these descriptions of God should be taken together, as affording the only true representation of him. He is so gentle to the humbled sensible sinner, that 'he will not break their bruised reed, nor quench their smoking flax,' [Mat. xii. 20.] And so careful of health that, for their recovery, he will not leave them altogether unpunished, nor suffer them to ruin themselves by a surfeit upon worldly comforts; yet with 'the froward he will shew himself froward,' Ps. xviii. 26. And 'as for such as turn aside unto their crooked ways, the Lord shall lead them forth with the workers of iniquity,' Ps. cxxv. 5. He will 'put out the candle of the wicked,' for he sets them in 'slippery places, &c., so that they are cast down into destruction, and brought into desolation as in a moment; they are consumed with terrors,' [Ps. lxxiii. 19.] Now Satan will sometimes argue against the children of God, and endeavour to break their hopes by turning that part of the description of God against them, which is intended for the dismounting of the confidence of the wicked, and the bringing down of high looks. By this means he wrests the description of God to a contrary end, and misrepresents God to a trembling afflicted soul. This he doth,

First, By misrepresenting *his nature*. Here he reads a solemn lecture of the holiness and justice of God, but always with reflection upon the vileness and unworthiness of the person against whom he intends his dart. And thus he argues: Lift up thine eyes to the heavens, behold the brightness of God's glory: consider his unspotted holiness, his infinite justice. The heavens are not clean in his sight; how much more abominable and filthy then art thou! His eyes are pure, he cannot wink at nor approve of the least sin; how canst thou then imagine, except thou be intolerably impudent, that he hath taken such an unclean wretch into his favour? He is a jealous God, and will by no means acquit the guilty; canst thou then with any show of reason conclude thyself to be his child? He beholds the wicked afar off; he shuts out their prayer; he laughs at their calamity; he mocks when their fear comes; and therefore thou hast no cause to think that he will hear thy cry, though thou shouldst make many prayers. It cannot be supposed that he will incline his ear. It is his express determination, that if any man regard iniquity in his heart, the Lord will not hear his prayer. This, and a great deal more will he say. And while Satan speaks but at this rate, we may call him modest, because his allegations are in themselves true, if they were applied rightly. Sometimes he will go further, and plainly belie God, speaking incredible falsehoods of him: but because these properly appertain to a higher sort of troubles, of which I am next to speak, I shall not here mention them. However, if he stops here, he saith enough against any servant of God that carries a high sense of his unworthiness. For being thus brought to the view of these astonishing attributes, he is dashed out of countenance, and can think no other, but that it is very unlikely that so unworthy a sinner should have any interest in so holy a God. Thus the devil affrights him off, turning the wrong side of the description of God to him; and in the meantime hiding that part of it that speaks God's wonderful condescensions, infinite compassions, unspeakable readiness to accept the humble, brokenhearted, weary, heavy-laden sinner, that is prostrate at his footstool for pardon. All which are on purpose declared in the description of God's nature, to obviate this temptation, and to encourage the weak.

Second, He misrepresents God *in his providence*. If God chastise his children by any affliction, Satan perversely wrests it to a bad construction, especially if the affliction be sharp, or seem to be above their strength, or frequent, and most of all if it seem to cross their hopes and prayers; for then he argues, These are not the chastisements of sons. God indeed will visit their transgressions with rods, but his dealing with thee is plainly of another nature, for he 'breaketh thee with his tempests.' And whereas he corrects his sons that serve him in measure, thou art bowed down with thy trouble to distress and despair: but he will lay no more upon his sons than they are able to bear. He will not always chide his servants; but thou art afflicted every morning. And besides, if thou wert pure and upright, surely now he would awake for thee, and make the habitation of thy righteousness prosperous: for to his sons he saith, 'Call upon me in the day of trouble, I will deliver thee; and thou shalt glorify me,' Ps. l. 15. Hence comes the complaint of many, that they are not regenerated, because they think God deals not with them as with others. Oh, say they, we know God chastiseth 'every son whom he receiveth;' but our case is every way different from theirs, our troubles are plagues, not rods; our cry is not heard, our prayers disregarded, our strength faileth us, our hearts fret against the Lord, so that not only the nature and quality of our affections, but the frame of our heart under them, in not enduring the burden,—which is the great character of the chastisement of sons, Heb. xii. 7,—plainly evinceth that we are under God's hatred, and are not his children. This objection, though it might seem easy to be answered by those that are not at present concerned, yet it will prove a difficult business to those that are under the smart of afflictions. How much a holy and wise man may be gravelled by it, you may see in Ps. lxxii., where the prophet is put to a grievous plunge upon this very objection; ver. 14, 'All the day long have I been plagued, and chastised every morning.'

And yet in all this Satan doth but play the sophister, working upon the advantages which the nature of the affliction and the temper of men's hearts do afford him. For, 1. Afflictions are a great depth, one of the secrets of God, so that it is hard to know what God intends by them. 2. The end of the Lord is not discovered at first, but at some distance, when the fruits thereof begin to appear. 3. The mind of the afflicted cannot always proceed regularly in making a judgment of God's design upon them: especially at first, when it is stounded by the assault, and all things in confusion; faith is to seek, patience awanting, and love staggering. After it hath recollected itself, and attained any calmness to fit it for a review of the ways of God and of the heart, it is better enabled to fix some grounds of hope: Lam. iii. 19–21, 'This I recall to my mind, therefore have I hope.' 4. Afflictions have a light and a dark side, and their appearances are according to our posture in which we view them: as some pictures, which if we look upon them one way, they appear to be angels, if another way, they seem devils. 5. Some men in affliction do only busy themselves in looking upon the dark side of affliction. Their disposition, either through natural timorousness or strong impressions of temptation, is only to meditate terrors, and to surmise evils. These men out of the cross can draw nothing but the wormwood and the gall, while others, that have another prospect of them, observe mixtures of mercy and gentleness, and do melt into submission and thankfulness. These, considered together, are a great advantage to Satan in disputing against the peace of God's afflicted children, and it often falls out, that as he doth misrepresent God's design, so do they, urged by temptation, upon that account misjudge themselves.

Third, He also misrepresents God *in the works of his Spirit.* If God withdraw his countenance, or by his Spirit signifies his displeasure to the consciences of any, if he permit Satan to molest them with spiritual temptations, presently Satan takes occasion to put his false and malignant interpretation upon all ; he tells them that God's hiding his face is his casting them off ; that the threatenings signified to their conscience are plain declarations that their present state is wrath and darkness ; that Satan's molestations by temptations shew them to be yet under his power ; that the removal of their former peace, joy, and sensible delight which they had in the ways of God is beyond contradiction an evidence that God hath no delight in them, nor they in him ; that their faith was but that of temporaries, their joy but that of hypocrites, which is only for a moment. How often have I heard Christians complaining thus : We cannot be in a state of grace ; our consciences lie under the sense of God's displeasure, they give testimony against us, and we know that testimony is true, for we feel it. It is true, time was when we thought we had a delight in hearing, praying, meditating, but now all is a burden to us, we can relish nothing, we can profit nothing, we can remember nothing. Time was when we thought we had assurance, and our hearts rejoiced in us ; sometimes we have thought our hearts had as much of peace and comfort as they could hold, now all is vanished, and we are under sad fears ; if God had had a favour to us, would he have dealt thus with us ? Thus are they cheated into a belief that they never had any grace ; they take all for granted that is urged against them ; they cannot consider God's design in hiding his face, nor yet can they see how grace acts in them under these complainings ; how they express their love to God in their desires and pantings after him, in their bewailing of his absence, in abhorring and condemning themselves, &c. ; but their present feeling—and an argument from sense is very strong—bears down all before it.

Thus doth Satan frame his arguments from misrepresentations of God, which, though a right view of God would easily answer them, yet how difficult it is for a person in an hour of temptation to dispel, by a right apprehension of the ways of the holy God, doth abundantly appear from Ps. lxxvii., where the case of Asaph, or whoever else he was, doth inform us—1. That it is usual for Satan, for the disquieting of the hearts of God's children, to offer a false prospect of God. 2. That this overwhelms their hearts with grief, ver. 3. 3. That the more they persist in the prosecution of this method, under the mists of prejudice, they see the less, being apt to misconstrue everything in God to their disadvantage, ver. 3, ' I remembered God, and was troubled.' 4. The reason of all that trouble lies in this, that they can only conclude wrath and desertion from God's carriage toward them. 5. That till they look upon God in another method, and take up better thoughts of him and his providences, even while they carry the appearance of severity, they can expect no ease to their complainings. For before the prophet quitted himself of his trouble, he was forced to acknowledge his mistake, ver. 10, in the misconstruction he made of his dealings, and to betake himself to a resolve of entertaining better thoughts of God, ver. 7. His interrogation, 'Will the Lord cast off for ever?' &c., shews indeed what he did once think, being misled by Satan, but withal that he would never do so again. 'Will the Lord cast off for ever?' is not here the voice of a despairing man, but of one that, through better information, hath rectified his judgment, and now is resolved strongly to hold the contrary to what he thought before: as if he should say, It is not possible that it should be so; he will not cast off for ever, and I will never entertain such perverse thoughts of God any more. 6. But before they can come to this, it will cost them some pains and serious thoughts. It is not easy to break these fetters, to answer this argument, but they that will do so must appeal from their present sense to a consideration of the issues of these dealings upon other persons, or upon themselves at other times; for the prophet, ver. 5, 'considered the days of old, and the years of ancient times;' and ver. 6, he also made use of his own experience, calling to remembrance that after such dealings as these, God by his return of favour gave him 'songs in the night.'

[4.] Another common head from whence this great disputant doth fetch his arguments against the good condition and state of God's servants, is their *sin and miscarriages*. Here I shall observe two or three things in the general concerning this, before I shew how he draws his false conclusions from thence. As,

First, That with a kind of *feigned ingenuity*[1] he will grant a difference betwixt sin and sin—betwixt sins reigning and not reigning, sins mortified and not mortified; betwixt the sins of the converted and the unconverted; and upon this supposition he usually proceeds. He doth not always, except in case of great sins, argue want of regeneration from one sin; for that argument, This is a sin, therefore thou art not a convert, would be easily answered by one that knows the saints have their imperfections; but he thus deals with men: These sins whereof thou art guilty are reigning sins, such as are inconsistent with a converted estate, and therefore thou art yet unregenerated.

Second, He produceth usually, for the backing of his arguments, such scriptures as *do truly represent the state of men unsanctified*; but then his labour is to make the parties to appear suitable to the description of the unregenerate. And to that purpose he aggravates all their failings to them; he makes severe inquiries after all their sins, and if he can charge them with any notorious crime, he lays load upon that, still concluding that a regenerate person doth not sin at such a rate as they do.

Third, This is always a *very difficult case;* it is not easy to answer the objections that he will urge from hence; for, (1.) If there be the real guilt of any grievous or remarkable scandal which he objects, the accused party, though never so knowing, or formerly never so holy, will be hardly put to it to determine anything in favour of his

[1] 'Ingenuousness.'—G.

estate. [1.] The fact cannot be denied. [2.] The Scripture nominates particularly such offences as render a man unfit for the kingdom of God. [3.] Whether in such cases grace be not wholly lost, is a question in which all are not agreed. [4.] However, it will be very doubtful whether such had ever any grace. The Scripture hath given no note of difference to distinguish betwixt a regenerate and unregenerate person in the acts of murder, adultery, fornication, &c. It doth not say the regenerate commits an act of gross iniquity in this manner, the unregenerate in that, and that there is a visible distinction betwixt the one and the other, relating to these very acts. And whatever may be supposed to be the inward workings of grace in the soul, while it is reduced to so narrow a compass as a spark of fire raked up in ashes, yet the weight of present guilt upon the soul, when it is charged home, will always poise it toward the worst apprehensions that can be made concerning its state. Former acts of holiness will be disowned under the notion of hypocrisy; or if yet owned to be true, they will be apt to think that true grace may be utterly lost. Present acts of grace they can see none, so that only the after-acts of repentance can discover that there is yet a being and life of grace in them, and till then they can never answer Satan's argument from great sins. But, (2.) In the usual infirmities of God's children the case is not so easy. For the Scriptures give instances of some whose conversations could not be taxed with any notorious evils; who, though they were not 'far from the kingdom of God,' yet were not 'of the kingdom of God,' [Mark xii. 34:] a freedom then from great sins is not pleadable as an undoubted mark of grace. And if others that are not converted may have no greater infirmities than some that are, the difference betwixt the one and the other must depend upon the secret powers of grace giving check to these infirmities and striving to mortify them; and this will be an intricate question. The apostle, Rom. vii. 15, notes indeed three differences betwixt the regenerate and unregenerate in this case of sins of infirmity. [1.] Hatred of the sin before the commission of it: 'What I hate, that do I.' [2.] Reluctancy in the act: 'What I would, that do I not.' [3.] Disallowance after the act: 'That which I do, I allow not.' Yet seeing natural light will afford some appearances of disallowance and reluctancy, it will still admit of further debate whether the principles, motives, degrees, and success of these strivings be such as may discover the being and power of real grace.

While Satan doth insist upon arguments from the sins of believers for the proof of an unconverted estate, he only aims to make good this point, that their sins are reigning sins, and consequently that they cannot be in so good a condition as they are willing to think. And to make their sins to carry that appearance, his constant course is to aggravate them all he can. This is his design, and the means by which he would effect it. His great art in this case is to heighten the sins of the regenerate. This he doth many ways. As,

(1.) *From the nature of the sin committed, and the manner of its commission;* and this he chiefly labours, because his arguments from hence are more probable, especially considering what he fixeth upon usually is that which may most favour his conclusion: as, [1.] If any have fallen into a great sin which a child of God doth but rarely commit, then he argues against him thus: They that are in Christ do mortify the flesh with the affections and lusts, they cast away the works of darkness; and these works of the flesh are manifest, Gal. v. 19, 'Adultery, fornication, uncleanness, lasciviousness, idolatry, witchcraft, hatred, variance, emulations,' &c. 'Because of these things cometh the wrath of God upon the children of disobedience.' 'Be not therefore partakers with them;' 'have no fellowship with the unfruitful works of darkness,' Eph. v. 6, 11. But thou hast not put these away, nor mortified them, as thy present sin doth testify, therefore thou art no child of God. [2.] If any do more than once or twice relapse into the same sin, suppose it be not so highly scandalous as the former, then he pleads from thence that they are backsliders in heart, that they have broken their covenant with God, that they are in bondage to sin. Here he urgeth, it may be, that of 2 Pet. ii. 19, 20, 'Of whom a man is overcome, of the same is he brought in bondage. . . . The dog is returned to his vomit.' [3.] Or if any have by any offence more remarkably gone against their knowledge or violated their conscience, then he tells them that they sin wilfully, that they reject the counsel of the Lord, that they are the servants of sin; 'for his servants ye are to whom ye obey,' Rom. vi. 16; 'and that where there is grace, though they may fall, yet it is still against their wills,' &c. [4.] If he have not so clear ground to manage any of the former charges against them, then he argues from the frequency of their various miscarriages. Here he sets their sins in order before them, rakes them all together, that he may oppress them by a multitude, when he cannot prevail by an accusation from one or two acts; and his pleading here is, Thou art nothing but sin, thy thoughts are evil continually, thy words are vain and unprofitable, thy actions foolish and wicked, and this in all thy employments, in all relations, at all times. What duty is there that is not neglected or defiled? what sin that is not some way or other committed? &c. Can such a heart as thine be the temple of the Holy Ghost? For the temple of the Lord is holy, and his people are washed and cleansed, &c.

These are all of them strong objections, and frequently made use of by Satan, as the complaints of the servants of God do testify, who are made thus to except against themselves: If our sins were but the usual failings of the converted, we might comfort ourselves, but they are great, they are backslidings, they are against conscience, they are many; what can we judge but that we have hitherto deceived ourselves, and that the work of conversion is yet to do? The objections that are from great sins, or from recidivation[1] or wilful violation of conscience, do usually prevail for some time against the best that are chargeable with them; they cannot determine that they are converted, though they might be so, so long as they cannot deny the matter of fact upon which the accusation is grounded. Till their true repentance give them some light of better information, they are in the dark, and cannot answer the argument. Jonah being imprisoned in the whale's belly for his stubborn rebellion, at first concluded himself a castaway: chap. ii. 4, 'Then I said, I am cast out of thy sight.'

[1] 'Relapse.'—G.

Neither could he think better of himself till, upon his repentance, he recovered his faith and hope of pardon: 'Yet will I look again toward thy holy temple.' Yea, those objections that are raised from the multitude and frequency of lesser failings, though they may be answered by a child of God while his heart is not overshadowed with the mists and clouds of temptation, yet when he is confused with violent commotions within, his heart will fail him, and till he can bring himself to some composure of spirit, he hath not the boldness to assert his integrity. David was gravelled with this objection: Ps. xl. 12, 'Innumerable evils have compassed me about, mine iniquities have taken hold upon me, so that I am not able to look up; they are more than the hairs on my head, therefore my heart faileth me.'

(2.) He aggravates the sinfulness of our condition from *the frequency and violence of his own temptations.* It is a usual thing for him to give young converts incessant onsets of temptation to sin. Most commonly he works upon their natural constitution; he blows the coals that are not yet quite extinguished, and that have greater forwardness, from their own inclination, to kindle again, as lust and passion. The first motions of the one, though it go no further than those offers and risings up in the heart, and is there damped and kept down by the opposing principle of grace; and the occasional outbreakings of the other, which he provokes by a diligent preparation of occasion from without, and violent incitations from within, furnish him with sufficient matter for his intended accusations; and sometimes— being, as it were, wholly negligent of the advantages which our tempers give him, or not being able to find any such forwardness to these evils in our constitution as may more eminently serve his ends—he satisfies himself to molest us with earnest motions to any sins indifferently; and all this to make us believe that sin is not crucified in us, which some are more apt to believe, because they observe their temptations to these sins to importune them more, and with greater vehemency, than they were wont to do before; and this doth yet the more astonish them, because they had high expectations that, after their conversion, Satan would fall before them, and their temptations abate; that their natures should be altered, and their natural inclinations to these sins wholly cease; but now, finding the contrary, they are ready to cry out—especially when Satan violently buffets them with this objection— We are yet in our sins, and under the dominion thereof; neither can it be that we are converted, because we find sin more active and stirring than formerly; it is not then surely mortified in us, but lively and strong. Though in this case it be very plain that temptations are only strong, and sin weak, and that grace is faithfully acting its part against the flesh, arguing, not that grace is so very weak, but that Satan is more busy than ordinary. The sins are not more than formerly, but the light that discovers them more is greater, and the conscience that resents the temptation is more tender. Yet all this doth not at first give ease to the fears that are now raised up in the mind. They find sin working in them; their expectations of attaining a greater conquest on a sudden, and with greater ease, are disappointed, and the desire of having much makes a man think himself poor; and withal they commonly labour under so much ignorance or perverse credulity, that they conclude they consent to everything which they are tempted to, insomuch that it is long before these clouds do vanish, and the afflicted brought to a right understanding of themselves.

(3.) From some *remarkable appearances of God doth Satan aggravate our sinful condition.* If God shew any notable act of power, he makes the beams of that act reflect upon our unworthiness with a dazzling light. When Peter saw the power of Christ in sending a great multitude of fishes into his net, having laboured all night before and caught nothing, it gave so deep an impression to the conviction of his vileness, that he was ready to put Christ from him, as being altogether unfit for his blessed society: 'Depart,' saith he, 'from me, for I am a sinful man,' [Luke v. 8.] If God discover the glorious splendour of his holiness, it is enough to make the holiest saints, such as Job and Isaiah, to cry out they are undone, being 'men of unclean lips,' Isa. vi. 5; and to 'abhor themselves in dust and ashes,' Job xlii. 6. The like may be said of any discovery of the rest of the glorious attributes of God. Of all which Satan makes this advantage, that the parties tempted should have so deep a consideration of their unworthiness as might induce them to believe—as if it were by a voice from heaven—that God prohibits them any approaches to him, and that they have nothing to do to take God's name within their mouths. And though these remarkable discoveries of God, either by his acts of power and providence, or by immediate impressions upon the soul, in the height of contemplation, have ordinarily great effects upon the hearts of his children, but not of long continuance; yet where they strike in with other arguments, by which they were already staggered as to their interest in God, they mightily strengthen them, and are taken for no less than God's own determination of the question against them.

But this is not all the use that Satan makes of them; for from hence he sometimes hath the opportunity to raise new accusations against them, and to tax them with particular crimes, which, in a particular manner, seem to prove them unregenerate. For what would seem to be a clearer character of a man dead in trespasses and sins than a hard heart, that can neither be sensible of judgments nor mercies? This he sometimes chargeth upon the children of God, from the great disproportion that they find in themselves betwixt the little sense that they seem to have—and that which is disproportionable, they reckon to be nothing—and the vast greatness of God's mercy or holiness. I have observed some to complain of utter unthankfulness and insensibleness of heart—from thence concluding confidently against themselves—because, when God hath remarkably appeared for them in deliverances from dangers, or in unexpected kindnesses, they could not render a thankfulness that carried any proportion to the mercy. While they were in the highest admiration of the kindness, saying, 'What shall I render to the Lord?' they were quite out of the sight of their own sense and feeling, and thought they returned nothing at all, because they returned nothing equivalent to what they had received. Others I have known, who, from the confusion and amazement of their spirit, when they have been overwhelmed with troubles, have positively determined themselves to be senseless, stupid, past feeling, hardened to destruction; when, in both cases, any might have seen the working of their hearts to be an apparent [1] contradiction to what Satan charged them withal. For they were not unapprehensive either of mercies or judgments; but, on the contrary, had only a greater sense of them than they were able to manage.

(4.) To make full measure, Satan doth sometimes aggravate the miscarriages of those whom he intends to accuse, *by comparing their lives and actions with the holy lives of some eminent servants of God, especially such as they have only heard of and not known personally.* For so they have only their virtues represented, without their failings. Here Satan takes a liberty of declaiming against them: and though he could never spare a saint a good word out of respect, yet that others might be put out of heart and hope, he will commend the holiness, strictness, care, constancy of dead saints to the skies. And then he queries, Art thou such a one? Canst thou say thou art anything like them, for a heavenly heart, a holy life, a contempt of the world, a zeal for God, for good works, for patient suffering? &c. All this while not a word of their weaknesses. These, saith he, were the servants of the Most High: their examples thou shouldst follow, if thou expectest their crown. Had they any more holiness than they needed? And if thou hast not so much, thou art nothing. What can humility, modesty, and sense of guilt speak in such a case? They go away mourning, their fears increase upon them, and what God hath set before them, in the examples of his servants, for the increase of their diligence, they take to be as a witness against them, to prove them unconverted.

[5.] The last part of Satan's sophistry is to lessen their *graces, that so he may altogether deny them.* In this he proceeds upon such scriptures as do assert the fruits of the Spirit, and urgeth for his foundation that none are the children of God but such as ' are led by the Spirit,' [Rom. viii. 14;] and that he that hath ' not the Spirit of Christ is none of his,' [Rom. viii. 9.] The necessity of faith, love, patience, humility, with the fruits of these and other graces, he presseth; but still in order to a demonstration, as he pretends, that such are not to be found in those whose gracious state he calls into question, and consequently that they are not the children of God.

The rule by which he manageth himself in this dispute is this: The more graces are heightened in the notions, that must give an account of their nature and beings, the more difficult it will be to find out their reality in the practice of them. His design then hath these two parts: 1. He heightens grace in the notion, or abstract, all he can; 2. He lessens it in the concrete, or practice, as much as is possible, that it may appear a very nullity, a shadow and not a substance. I shall speak a little of both.

(1.) As to the first part of his design, he hath many ways by which he *aggravates grace in the notion.* We may be sure, if it lie in his way, he will not stick to give false definitions of grace, and to tell men that it is what indeed it is not. He is a liar, and in any case

---

[1] ' Evident.'—G.

whatsoever he will lie for his advantage, if he have hope his lie may pass for current; but he cannot always use a palpable cheat in this matter, where the nature of any grace is positively determined in Scripture, except it be with the ignorant, or where the nature of grace is made a business of controversy among men. I will not make conjectures what Satan may possibly say in belying the nature of grace, to make it seem to be quite another thing than it is; but shall rather shew you the more usual plausible ways of deceit which herein he exerciseth; and they are these that follow:—

First, As the same graces have different *degrees in several persons, and these different degrees have operations suitable:* some acts being stronger, some weaker, some more perfected and ripened, others more imperfect and immature; so when Satan comes to describe grace, he sets it forth in its *highest excellencies and most glorious attainments.* You shall never observe him to speak of graces at their lowest pitch, except where he is carrying on a design for presumption, and then he tells men that any wishing or woulding is grace; and every formal 'Lord forgive me' is true repentance; but, on the contrary, he offers the highest reach of it that any saint on earth ever arrived at, as essentially necessary to constitute its being; and tells them if they have not that, they have nothing. Let us see it in the particulars.

[1.] Grace sometimes hath its *extraordinaries*, as I may call them. We have both precept and example of that nature in Scripture, which are propounded, not as the common standard by which the being and reality of grace is to be measured, but as patterns for imitation, to provoke us to emulation, and to quicken us in pressing forward. Of this nature I reckon to be the example of Moses, desiring to be blotted 'out of God's book,' [Exod. xxxii. 32,] whatever he meant by it, in his love to the people; and the like of the apostle Paul, wishing himself to be 'accursed from Christ for his brethren's sake,' [Rom. ix. 3.] Of this nature also we have many precepts; as, 'rejoice evermore,' [1 Thes. v. 16,] of 'waiting and longing for the appearance of Christ,' [2 Thes. iii. 5,] of 'rejoicing when we fall into divers temptations,' [James i. 2,] and many more to this purpose, all which are heights of grace that do rarely appear among the servants of God at any time.

[2.] Grace hath sometimes its *special assistances*. This is when the occasion is extraordinary; but the grace befitting that occasion is promised in ordinary, and ordinarily received. When God calls any to such occasions, though compared with that measure of grace which usually is acted by the children of God upon ordinary occasions, it is a special assistance of the Spirit. Of this nature is that boldness which the servants of Christ receive, to confess Christ before men in times of persecution, and to die for the truth, with constancy, courage, and joy.

[3.] There are also singular *eminences of grace*, which some diligent, careful, and choice servants of God attain unto, far above what the ordinary sort arrive at. Enoch had his conversation so much in heaven, that he was said to 'walk with God,' [Gen. v. 24.] David's soul was often full of delight in God. Some in the height of assurance rejoice in God with 'joy unspeakable, and full of glory,' [1 Pet. i. 8.] Moses was eminent in meekness, Job in patience, the apostle Paul in zeal for promoting the gospel, &c. Now Satan, when he comes to question the graces of men, he presents them with these measures; and if they fall short, as ordinarily they do, he concludes them altogether graceless.

Second, Satan also can do much to heighten the *ordinary work and usual fruits of every grace*. His art herein lies in two things. [1.] He gives us a description of grace as it is *in itself*, abstracted from the weakness, dulness, distraction, and infirmities, that are concomitant with it, as it comes forth to practice. He brings to our view grace in its glory, and without the spots by which our weakness and Satan's temptation do much disfigure it. [2.] He presents us with grace in its *whole body*, completed with all its members, faith, love, hope, patience, meekness, gentleness, &c. From both these he sets before those whom he intends to discourage a complete copy of an exact holy Christian; as if every true Christian were to be found in the constant practice of all these graces at all times, on all occasions, and that without weakness or infirmity. Whereas indeed a true Christian may be found sometimes evidently practising one grace, and weak, or at present defective, in another. And sometimes the best of his graces is so interrupted with temptation, so clogged with infirmity, that its workings are scarce discernible.

Third, He hath a policy in heightening those *attainments and workings of soul*, in things relating to God and religion, which are to be found in *temporary believers*; which, because they sometimes appear in the unconverted as well as in the converted, though all unconverted men have them not, are therefore called common graces. This he doth that he may from thence take occasion to disprove the real graces of the servants of God; of whom 'better things, and things that accompany salvation,' that is, special saving graces, are to be expected, Heb. vi. 9. His way herein is, [1.] To shew the utmost *bravery of these common graces*; how much men may have, how far they may go, and yet at last come to nothing. For gifts, they may have powerful eloquence, prophecy, understanding of mysteries, faith of miracles. For good works, they may give their estates to relieve the poor. In moral virtues they may be excellent, their illumination may be great; they may taste the 'good word of God, and the powers of the world to come,' Heb. vi. 4. Their conversation may be 'without offence,' and their conscience honest, as Paul's was before his conversion. [2.] With these heights of common grace, he compares *the lowest degree of special grace*. And because the principles, motives, and ends which constitute the difference betwixt these two, are, as it were, underground, remote from sense and observation, and oftentimes darkened by temptation; he takes the boldness to deny the truth of grace, upon the account of the small, inconsiderable appearance that it makes, confidently affirming that special grace must of necessity make a far greater outward show than these common graces. In what manner, and to what end, Satan doth heighten grace in the abstract, we have seen. It remains that we discover—

(2.) How he doth *lessen grace in the concrete*. This is the centre of his design. He would not extol grace so much, but that he hopes thereby to 'condemn the generation of the just,' and to make it appear that there are few or none that are truly gracious. When he comes to apply all this to the condition of any child of God, he deals treacherously: and his cunning consists of three parts :—

[1.] He compares *the present state of any one with whom he deals, to the highest attainments and excellencies of grace ;* allowing nothing to be grace, but what will answer these descriptions he had already given. Here the tempter doth apparently make use of a 'false balance, and a bag of deceitful weights.' For thus he puts them to it: Thou sayest thou hast grace, but thou dost altogether deceive thyself, for indeed thou hast none at all. Compare thyself with others that were in Scripture noted as undoubtedly gracious, and thou wilt see that in the balance thou art lighter than vanity. Abraham had faith, but he believed above hope. Moses and Paul had love, but they manifested it by preferring their brethren's happiness before their own. David was a saint, but he had a heart ravished with God. The martyrs spoken of in Heb. xi., they could do wonders ; they were above fears of men, above the love of the world ; they loved not their lives to the death: how joyfully took they the spoiling of their goods ! how courageously did they suffer the sharpest torments ! Besides, saith he, all the children of God are described as sanctified throughout, abounding with all fruits of righteousness ; their faith is working ; their love still laborious ; their hope produceth constant patience: what art thou to these ? That in thee which thou callest faith, or love, or patience, &c., it is not fit to be named with these. Thy fears may tell thee that thou hast no faith, and so may thy works ; thy murmurings under God's hand is evidence sufficient that thou hast no patience. The little that thou dost for God, or especially wouldest do, if it were not for thy own advantage, may convince thee that thou hast no love to him ; thy weariness of services and duties, thy confessed unprofitableness under all, do proclaim thou hast no delight in God nor in his ways. He further adds, for the confirmation of all this: Consider how far temporaries may go, that shall never go to heaven. Thou art far short of them ; thy gifts, thy works, thy virtues, thy illumination, thy conversation, thy conscientiousness, are nothing like theirs: how is it possible then that such a one as thou, a pitiful, contemptible creature, shouldest have anything of true grace in thee ? Thus he makes the application of all the discovery of grace which he presented to them. Though he needs not urge all these things to every one, any one of these particulars frequently serves the turn. When a trembling heart compares itself with these instances, it turns its back, yields the argument, and is ashamed of its former hopes, as those are of their former confidence who flee from battle. Hence then do we hear of these various complaints: one saith, Alas ! I have no grace, because I live not as other saints have done, in all exactness. Another saith, I have no faith, because I cannot believe about[1] reason, and contrary to sense, as Abraham did. A third cries out, he hath no love to God, because he cannot find his soul ravished with desire after him. Another thinks, he hath a hard heart, because he cannot weep for sin. Another concludes against himself, because he finds not a present cheerful resolve, while he is not under any question for

[1] Query, 'above'?—ED.

religion, to suffer torments for Christ. Some fear themselves, because temporaries in some particulars have much out-gone them. You see how complaints may upon this score be multiplied without end; and yet all this is but fallacy. Satan tells them what grace is at the highest, but not a word of what it is at lowest; and so unskilful is a tossed, weak Christian, that he in examining his condition looks after the highest degrees of grace, as affording clearer evidence, and not after the sincerity of it, which is the safest way for trial, where graces are weak. In a word, this kind of arguing is no better than that of children, who cannot conclude themselves to be men, because their present stature is little, and they are not as tall as the adult.

[2.] Another part of his cunning in lessening the real graces of God's children, is to take them at an advantage, *when their graces are weakest, and themselves most out of order.* He that will choose to measure a man's stature while he is upon his knees, seems not to design to give a faithful account of his height. No more doth Satan, who, when he will make comparisons, always takes the servants of God at the worst. And indeed many advantages do the children of God give him, insomuch that it is no wonder that he doth so oft baffle them, but rather a wonder that they at any time return to their comforts. *First*, Sometimes he takes them to task while they are yet young and tender, when they are but newly converted, before their graces are grown up, or have had time to put forth any considerable fruit. *Second*, Or when their graces are tired out by long or grievous assaults of temptation, for then they are not what they are at other times. *Third*, When their hearts are discomposed or muddied with fear, for then their sight is bad, and they can so little judge of things that differ, that Satan can impose almost anything upon them. *Fourth*, Sometimes he comes upon them when some grace acts his part but poorly, as not having its perfect work, and is scarce able to get through, sticking, as it were, in the birth. *Fifth*, Or when the progress of grace is small and imperceptible. *Sixth*, Or while in the absence of the sun, which produceth flowers and fragrancy, and is the time of the singing of birds, Cant. ii. 11, 12, it is forced to cast off its summer fruits of joy and sensible delights, and only produceth winter fruits of lamenting after God, longing and panting after him, justifying of God in his dealings and condemning itself, all this while 'sowing in tears' for a more pleasing crop. *Seventh*, Or while expectations are more than enjoyments: the man it may be promised himself large incomes of greater measures of comforts, ease, or strength, under some particular ordinances or helps which he hath lately attained to, and not finding things presently to answer what he hoped for, is now suspicious of his case, and thinks he hath attained nothing, because he hath not what he would. *Eighth*, Sometimes Satan shews them his face in this glass when it is foulest, through the spots of some miscarriage. *Ninth*, Or he takes advantage of some natural defects, as want of tears, which might be more usual in former times, but are now dried up; or from the ebbings and uncertainty of his affections, which are never sure rules of trials. *Tenth*, Or in such acts that are of a mixed nature in the principles and motives, where it may seem to be uncertain to which the act must be ascribed as to the true parent. The heart of a gracious person being challenged upon any of these points, and under so great a disadvantage, being called out to give a proof of himself, especially in the view of grace set forth in all its excellency and glory, shall have little to plead, but will rather own the accusation. And the rather because,

[3.] It is another part of Satan's cunning to urge them, whilst they are thus at a stand, *with a possibility, nay, a probability of their mistaking themselves, by passing too favourable an opinion formerly of their actions.* To confirm them in this apprehension, *first,* He lays before them the consideration of the deceitfulness of the heart, Jer. xvii. 6, which, being so above all things, and desperately wicked beyond ordinary discovery, makes a fair way for the entertainment of a suspicion of self-delusion in all the former hopes which a man hath had of himself. Satan will plainly speak it: Thou hast had some thoughts and workings of mind towards God, but seeing they carry so great a disproportion to rule and example, and come so far short of common graces, it is more than probable that such poor, weak, confused appearances are nothing. How knowest thou that thine adherence to and practice of the command and services of God are any more than from the power of education, the prevalency of custom, or the impressions of moral suasion? How dost thou know that thy desires after God, and thy delight in him, are any more than the products of natural principles, influenced by an historical faith of Scripture doctrine? It is oftentimes enough for Satan to hint this. A suspicious heart, as it were greedy of its own misery, catcheth at all things that make against it; and hence complains that it hath no grace, because it sees not any visible fruits, or makes not a sufficient appearance at all times when opposed or resisted; or because it wants sensible progress, or gives not the summer fruits of praises, rejoicings, and delights in God; or because it seems not to meet with remarkable improvements in ordinances; or because it cannot produce tears and raise the affections; and because the party doth not know but his heart might deceive him in all that he hath done. Which the devil yet further endeavoureth to confirm, *second,* By a consideration of the seeming holiness and graces of such as believed themselves to be the children of God, and were generally by others reputed so to be, who yet, after a glorious profession, turned apostates. This being so great and undeniable an instance of the heart's deceitfulness, makes the poor tempted party conclude that he is certainly no true convert.

Thus have we seen Satan's sophistry in the management of those five grand topics from whence he draws his false conclusions against the children of God, pretending to prove that they are not converted; or at least if they be in a state of grace, that they in that state are in a very bad, unsuitable condition to it. For if his arguments fall short of the first, they seldom miss the latter mark. This was his first engine. Now follows,

II. The other engine by which he fixeth these conclusions, which, though it be not argumentative, yet it serves to sharpen all his fallacies against the comforts of God's children—this is *fear,* which, together with his objections, he sends into the mind. That Satan can raise a storm and commotion in the heart by fear, hath been proved before. I shall now only in a few things shew how he doth forward his design by astonishing the heart with his frightful thunderings.

[1.] *His objections being accompanied with affrightments, they pass for strong undeniable arguments, and their fallacy is not so easily detected.* Fear, as well as anger, darkens reason, and disables the understanding to make a true, faithful search into things, or to give a right judgment. As darkness deceives the senses, and makes every bush affrightful to the passenger, or as muddied waters hinder the sight, so do fears in the heart disable a man to discover the silliest cheat that Satan can put upon it.

[2.] They are also very *credulous*. When fear is up, any suggestion takes place. As suspicious incredulity is an effect of joy,—the disciples at first hearing that Christ was risen, 'for joy believed it not'—so suspicious credulity is the effect of fear. And we shall observe several things in the servants of God that shew a strange inclination, as it were a natural aptitude, to believe the evil of their spiritual estate which Satan suggests to them. As, *first*, There is a great forwardness and precipitancy in the heart to close with evil thoughts raised up in us. When jealousies of God's love are injected, there is a violent hastiness forthwith—all calm deliberation being laid aside—to entertain a belief of it. This is more than once noted in the Psalms. In this case, David acknowledgeth this hasty humour, ' I said in my haste,' Ps. xxxi. 22, and cxvi. 11. This hasty forwardness to determine things that are against us without due examination, Asaph calls a great weakness: ' This is my infirmity,' Ps. lxxvii. 10. *Second*, There is observable in those that are under spiritual troubles, a great kind of delight, if I may so call it, to hear threatenings rather than promises, and such discourses as set forth the misery of a natural state, rather than such as speak of the happiness of the converted ; because these things, in their apprehension, are more suitable to their condition, and more needful for them, in order to a greater measure of humiliation, which they suppose to be necessary. However, thus they add fuel to the flame. *Third*, They have an aptitude to hide themselves from comfort, and with a wonderful nimbleness of wit and reasoning, to evade and answer any argument brought for their comfort, as if they had been volunteers in Satan's service to fight against themselves. *Fourth*, They have also so great a blasting upon their understanding, that Satan's tempting them to doubt of their good estate is to them a sufficient reason to doubt of it ; and that is ground enough for them to deny it, because Satan questions it.

[3.] These fears make all Satan's suggestions *strike the deeper;* they point all his arrows and make them pierce, as it were, ' the joints and marrow ;' they poison and envenom them, to the great increase of the torment and hindrance of the cure ; they bind the objections upon them, and confirm them in a certain belief that they are all true.

We have now viewed Satan's engines and batteries against the servants of the Lord, for the destruction of their joy and peace, by spiritual troubles ; but these are but the beginnings of sorrows, if compared with those distresses of soul which he sometimes brings upon them. Of which next.

CHAPTER IX.

Of his fourth way to hinder peace, by spiritual distresses. 1. *The nature of these distresses; the ingredients and degrees of them. Whether all distresses of soul arise from melancholy.* 2. *Satan's method in working them; the occasions he makes use of, the arguments he urgeth, the strengthening of them by fears.* 3. *Their weight and burden explained in several particulars.—Some concluding cautions.*

The last sort of troubles by which Satan overthrows the peace of the soul, are *spiritual distresses.* These are more grievous agonies of soul, under deepest apprehensions of divine wrath, and dreadful fears of everlasting damnation, differing in nature and degree from the former sorts of troubles; though in these Satan observes much-what the same general method which he used in spiritual troubles last mentioned. For which cause, and also that these are not so common as the other, I shall speak of them with greater brevity. Herein I shall shew—1. Their nature; 2. Satan's method in working them: 3. Their weight and burden.

1. The nature of spiritual distresses will be best discovered by a consideration of those ingredients of which they are made up, and of the different degrees thereof.

(1.) As to the ingredients, there are several things that do concur for the begetting of these violent distresses. As,

[1.] There is usually a *complication of several kinds of troubles.* Sometimes there are outward troubles and inward discomposures of spirit arising from thence; sometimes affrightments of blasphemous thoughts long continued, and usually spiritual troubles, in which their state or condition have been called to question, have gone before. Heman, who is as famous an instance in this case as any we meet withal in Scripture, in Ps. lxxxviii., seems not obscurely to tell us so much; his 'soul was full of troubles,' ver. 3; and in ver. 7 he complains that God had afflicted him 'with all his waves.' And that these were not all of the same kind, though all concurred to the same end, he himself explains, ver. 8, 18, where he bemoans himself for the unkindness of his friends: 'Thou hast put away mine acquaintance; lover and friend hast thou put far from me.'

[2.] These troubles drive at *a further end than any of the former;* for their design was only against the present quietness and peace of God's children, but these design the ruin of their hopes for the future. They are troubled, not for that they are not converted, but for that they expect never to be converted. This is a trouble of a high nature, making them believe that they are eternally reprobated, cut off from God for ever, and under an impossibility of salvation.

[3.] These troubles have *the consent and belief of the party.* In some other troubles Satan disquieted the Lord's servants by imposing upon them his own cursed suggestions, violently bearing in upon them temptations to sin and blasphemy, or objections against their state of regeneration, while in the meantime they opposed and refused to give consent; but in these Satan prevails with them to believe that their case is really such as their fears represent it to be.

[4.] They are troubles of *a far higher degree than the former;* the deepest sorrows, the sharpest fears, the greatest agonies. Heman, Ps. lxxxviii. 15, 16, calls them 'terrors even to distraction:' 'While I suffer thy terrors, I am distracted; thy fierce wrath goeth over me, thy terrors have cut me off.'

[5.] There is also God's deserting of them in a greater measure than ordinary, by withdrawing his aids and comforts. And, as Mr Perkins notes, 'If the withdrawing of grace be joined with the feeling of God's anger, thence ariseth the bitterest conflict that the soul of a poor creature undergoes.'[1]

(2.) As to the different degrees of spiritual distresses, we must observe—That according to the concurrence of all or fewer of these ingredients, for they do not always meet together, though most frequently they do; and according to the higher or lower degrees in which these are urged upon the conscience, or apprehended and believed by the troubled party, *these agonies are more or less; and accordingly we may distinguish them variously.* As,

[1.] Some are desperate terrors *of cursed reprobates under desperation.* These terrors in them are, in the greatest extremity, the very pit of misery, of the same nature with those of the damned in hell, 'where the worm that never dies,' is nothing else but the dreadful vexation and torment of an accusing conscience.[2] They are commonly accompanied with blaspheming of God, and an utter rejection of all means for remedy; and though they sometimes turn to a kind of secure desperation,—by which, when they see it will be no better, they harden themselves in their misery, and seek to divert their thoughts—as Cain did, betaking himself to the building of cities; and Esau, when he had sold his birthright, despised it, and gave himself up to the pursuit of a worldly interest;—yet sometimes these terrors end in self-murder, as in Judas, who being smitten with dread of conscience, went and hanged himself. We have many sad instances of these desperate terrors. Cain is the first we read of; and though the account the Scriptures give of him be but short, yet it is sufficient to let us see what his condition was—Gen iv. 11-16. First, He was cursed from the earth. Of this part of his curse there were two branches: 1. That his labour and toil in tillage should be great and greatly unsuccessful; for thus God himself explains it, ver. 12, 'When thou tillest the ground, it shall not henceforth yield unto thee her strength.' The earth was cursed with barrenness before to Adam, but now to Cain it hath a double curse. 2. That he should be a man of uncertain abode in any place: 'A fugitive and a vagabond shalt thou be in the earth;' not being able to stay long in a place by reason of the terrors of his conscience. His own interpretation of it, ver. 14, shews that herein lay a great part of his misery: 'Thou hast driven me out this day from the face of the earth.' By which it appears that he was to be as one that was chased out of all society, and as one that thought himself safe in no place. Secondly, He was 'hid from the face of God'— that is, he was doomed to carry the inward feeling of God's wrath,

---

[1] Treat. of Desertions. [2] Ames, 'Cases of Consc.,' lib. i.

without any expectation of mercy. Thirdly, His mind being terrified under the apprehension of that wrath, he cries out that his 'sin was greater than it could be pardoned,' or that his 'punishment was greater than he could bear;' for the word in the original signifies both sin and punishment, עון. Take it which way you will, it expresseth a deep horror of heart. If in the former sense, then it signifies a conviction of the greatness of his sin to desperation; if in the latter sense, then it is no less than a blasphemous reflection upon God, as unjustly cruel. Fourthly, This horror was so great, that he was afraid of all he met with, suspecting everything to be armed with divine vengeance against him: 'Every one that findeth me shall slay me.' Or if that speech was a desire that any one that found him might kill him, as some interpret,[1] it shews that he preferred death before that life of misery. It seems, then, that God smote him with such terror and consternation of mind, and with such affrightful trembling of body, for his bloody fact, that he was weary of himself, and afraid of all men, and could not stay long in a place. By these tokens, or some other way, God sets his mark upon him, as upon a cursed miscreant, to be noted and abhorred of all. Such another instance was Lamech, of whom the same chapter speaks: 1. The sting of conscience was so great, that he is forced to confess his fault—the interpretations of those that take it interrogatively, 'Have I slain?' or, 'If I have, what is that to you?' &c., are upon many accounts improper, much more are those so that take it negatively—which, whether it were the abomination of polygamy, as some think, by which example he had destroyed more than Cain did; or if it were murder in a proper sense, as the words and context plainly carry it, it is not very material to our purpose. However, God smote him with horror, that he might be a witness against himself. 2. He accuseth himself for a more grievous sinner and more desperate wretch by far than Cain: 'If Cain,' ver. 24, 'shall be avenged sevenfold, truly Lamech seventy and sevenfold.' Which is as much as to say, that there was as much difference betwixt his sin and Cain's, as betwixt seven and seventy-seven. 3. It seems also, by his discourse to his wives, that he was grievously perplexed with inward fears, suspecting, it may be, his very wives as well as others might have private combinations against him; for the prevention whereof, he tells them by Cain's example of God's avenging him. These two early examples of desperation the beginning of the world affords; and there have been many more since, as Esau and Judas. Of late years we have the memorable instance of Francis Spira, one of the clearest and most remarkable examples of spiritual horror that the latter ages of the world were ever acquainted with. Yet I shall not dare to be confident of his reprobation, as of Cain's and Judas's; because the Scripture hath determined their case, but we have no such certain authority to determine his.

[2.] *There are also distresses from melancholy;* which may be further differenced according to the intenseness or remissness of the distemper upon which they depend. For sometimes the imagination is so exceedingly depraved, the fears of heart so great, and the sorrows so deep, that the melancholy person, crying out of himself that he is

---
[1] Lightfoot, Harm. *in loc.*

damned, under the curse of God, &c., appears to be wholly besides himself, and his anguish to be nothing else but a delirious, irrational disturbance. There are too many sad instances of this. Some I have known that for many years together have laboured under such apprehensions of hell and damnation, that they have at last proceeded to curse and blaspheme God in a most dreadful manner, so that they have been a terror to all their friends and acquaintance. And though sometimes they would fall into fits of obstinate silence, yet being urged to speak, they would amaze all that were about them with the confident averment of their damnation, with horrible outcries of their supposed misery and torments, and with terrible rage against heaven. Some in this distemper will fancy themselves to be in hell already, and will discourse as if they saw the devils about them and felt their torture. Such as these give plain discovery by their whole carriage under their trouble, and some concomitant false imaginations about other things —as when they fancy themselves to be in prison or sentenced to death, and that torments or fire are provided for them by the magistrate, &c. —that it is only melancholy perverting their understanding that is the cause of all their sorrow. Others there are who are not altogether irrational, because in most other things their understanding is right; yet being driven into melancholy upon the occasion of crosses or other outward afflictions, they at last fix all their thoughts upon their souls; and now their fancy becoming irregular in part, the whole of the irregularity appears only in that wherein they chiefly concern themselves. Hence they misjudge themselves, and condemn themselves to everlasting destruction; sometimes without any apparent cause; and sometimes they accuse themselves of such things as they never did. They fear and cry out they are damned, but they cannot give a particular reason why they should entertain these fears, neither can they shew any cause why they should refuse the comforts of the promises that are offered; but they say they know or are persuaded it is so, upon no better account than this, It is so, because it is so. Or if they give reasons of their imagination, they are commonly either feigned or frivolous; and yet in all other matters they are rational, and speak or act like men in their right minds. Of both these kinds of desperation I shall speak nothing further. It is enough to have noted that such there are, because the cure of the former is impossible, and the cure of the latter doth wholly depend upon physic.

Quest. Some may possibly question, Whether all extraordinary agonies of soul, upon the apprehension of eternal damnation, be not the fruits of melancholy? And if not, then what may the difference be betwixt those that proceed from melancholy, and those that are properly the terrors of conscience?

Ans. As to the first part of the question, I answer, *First, That all spiritual distresses are not to be ascribed to melancholy.* For,

[1.] There are some melancholy persons who are never more free from spiritual troubles—though frequently accustomed to them at other times—than when, upon the occasion of some special trouble, or sickness threatening death, there is *greatest cause to fear such onsets upon the increase of melancholy.* Some such I have known.

[2.] Sometimes these distresses come *suddenly,* their conscience *smiting them in the very act of sin;* and these persons sometimes such as are not of a melancholic constitution. Spira was suddenly thunderstruck with terrors of conscience upon his recantation of some truths which he held; and so were some of the martyrs.

[3.] Sometimes terrors that have continued long, and have been very fierce, *are removed in a moment.* Now it is not rational to say that melancholy only occasioned all such troubles, wherein bodies that are not naturally of that complexion—and some such have been surprised with terrors of conscience; if we will take a liberty to suppose an accidental melancholy, we must of necessity allow some time; and, usually, some precedaneous[1] occasion to mould them into such a distemper. Neither do the fears of melancholy cease on a sudden, but abate gradually, according to the gradual abatement of the humour. To say that Cain's or Judas's despair were the invasions of strong melancholy, is not only beyond all proof, but also probability. Neither is it likely that David, whose ruddy countenance and inclination to music are tokens of a sanguine complexion, was always melancholic under his frequent complaints of spiritual trouble.

[4.] They that read the story of Spira, and observe *his rational serious replies* to the discourses that were offered him for his comfort and his carriage all along, will have no cause to conclude his trouble to be only melancholy; neither did the sober judicious bystanders ascribe his distress to any such cause.

[5.] *The agony of Christ upon the cross,* under the sense of divine wrath for our sins, though it were without desperation, is an undeniable proof that there may be deep sense of God's displeasure upon the soul of man, which cannot be ascribed to melancholy.

Second, I answer, That it is not to be denied but that God *may make use of that humour as his instrument, for the increase and continuance of terrors upon the consciences of those whom he thinks fit to punish, for any provocation, with spiritual desertion,* as he made use of that distemper to punish Saul and Nebuchadnezzar. I speak not here of those distresses which are nothing else but melancholy, such as those before mentioned, of which physicians have given us frequent histories,[2] though in this case the secret ways of God's providences are to be adored with humble silence; but of those terrors of conscience which have a mixture of melancholy to help them forward, yet so as that the judgment and reason are not thereby perverted. Spira, when his case was hastily concluded by an injudicious friend to be a strong melancholy, made this reply, Well, be it so, seeing you will needs have it so; for thus also is God's wrath manifested against me. Which shews, [1.] That he believed God doth sometimes manifest his wrath against man by melancholy. And [2.] That he denied this to be his condition; for he still concluded that God sent the terrors of his wrath immediately upon his conscience, as the sentence of his just condemnation for denying Christ. Now when God doth make use of melancholy, as his instrument in Satan's hand, to make the soul of man more apprehensive of his sin and God's wrath—though he doth not always make use of this means, as hath been said—while he still

---

[1] 'Preceding,' or 'inviting.'—G.
[2] *Vide* Fel. Plateri. observ., lib. i., in mentis alienatione.

preserves the understanding from false imaginations, the distress is still rational, and we have no cause to make any great difference betwixt these troubles that have such a mixture of melancholy, and such as have not. Neither must we say that then it is in the power of the physician to remove or mitigate such spiritual distresses. For if God see it fit to make use of melancholy for such a purpose, he can suspend the power of physic, so that it shall not do its work till God hath performed all his purpose. And the unsuccessfulness of remedies in this distemper, while it seems to be wonderfully stubborn in resisting all that can be done for cure, is more to be ascribed, in some cases, to God's design, than every physician doth imagine.

As to the latter part of the question, *How the terrors of melancholy and those of conscience are to be distinguished?* I shall only say this; that, as I said, we are not much concerned to make any distinction where the distressed party acts rationally. It is true something may be observed from these mixtures of melancholy; and thence may some indications be taken by the friends of the distressed, which may be of use to the afflicted party. Physic in this case is not to be neglected, because, though God may permit that distemper in order to the terror of the conscience, we are not of God's counsel, to know how high he would have it to go, nor how long to continue; but it is our duty, with submission to him, to use all means for help. However, seeing the physician is the only proper judge of the bodily distemper, it were improper to speak of the signs of melancholy in these mixed cases, to those that cannot make use of them. And as for these distresses of melancholy that are irrational, they are of themselves so notorious, that I need not give any account of them. There is usually a constitution inclining that way, and often the parents or friends of the party have been handled in the same manner before; or if their natural temper do not lead them that way, there is usually some cross, trouble, disappointment, or the like outward affliction, that hath first pressed them heavily, and by degrees hath wrought them into melancholy, and then afterward they come to concern themselves for their souls; as that woman in Plater's observations, who being long grieved with jealousy upon grounds too just, at last fell into grievous despair, crying out that God would not pardon her, that she was damned, that she felt hell already and the torments of it, &c.[1] Or there are some concomitant deliriums, imaginations apparently absurd or false, &c., all which give plain discoveries of irrational distresses. And if there remained any doubt concerning them, the consideration of all circumstances together, by such as are sober and judicious, would easily afford a satisfaction.

(3.) Having now confined the discourse to the spiritual distresses of God's children, that are not so oppressed with melancholy as to be misled with false imaginations, I must next, concerning these distresses, offer another observable distinction, which is this: *That they are either made up of all the five forementioned ingredients, or only of some of them, and so may be called total or partial,* though in each of these there may be great differences of degrees.

[1.] *Sometimes then the children of God may be brought into total*

[1] Lib. i. de mentis alienatione.

distresses of conscience, even with desperation, and, that which is more hideous, with blasphemy, if Mr Perkins his observation hold true, who tells us, ' that they may be so overcharged with sorrow as to cry out they are damned, and to blaspheme God:'[1] and we have no reason to contradict it, when we observe how far David went in his haste more than once. And whatever may be the private differences betwixt these and the reprobates in their agonies—as differences there are, both in God's design, and their hearts, though not visible—yet if we compare the fears, troubles, and speeches of the one and the other together, there appears little or no difference which bystanders can certainly fix upon. If it seems harsh to any that so horrid a thing as despair should be charged upon the elect of God, in the worst of their distresses, it will readily be answered: *First, That if we suppose not this, we must suppose that which is worse.* If we like not to say that God's children may fall into despair, we must conclude, very uncharitably, that they that fall into despair are not God's children. *Second,* It is easy to imagine a difference *betwixt partial and total despair, betwixt imaginary and real.* The children of God, under strong perturbation of spirit, may imagine themselves to do what they do not, and so may bear false witness against themselves—professing that all their hope of salvation is lost, when yet the root of their hope may still remain in their hearts undiscovered. The habit may be there when all visible acts of it are at present suspended, or so disguised in a crowd of confused expressions that they cannot be known; or, if they have real distrust of their salvation, yet every fit of real diffidence is not utter desperateness; neither will it denominate a man to be totally desperate, any more than every error, even about fundamentals, will denominate a man a heretic.[2] For as it must be a pertinacious error in fundamentals that makes a heretic, so it must be a pertinacious diffidence that makes a man truly desperate. *Third,* But *sometimes the children of God have only partial distresses.* That is, they may have a great measure of some of the ingredients, without mixture of the rest. Particularly, they may have a great measure of the sense of divine wrath and desertion, without desperation. The possibility of this is evident, beyond exception, in the example of our blessed Saviour, when he cried out, ' My God, my God, why hast thou forsaken me?' [Mat. xxvii. 46.] None can ascribe desperation to him without blasphemy; and if they should, the very words, ' *My* God, *my* God'—expressing his full and certain hope—do expressly contradict them. Such an instance of spiritual distress without desperation I take Heman to be. How high his troubles were is abundantly testified in Ps. lxxxviii.; and yet that his hope was not lost appears not only by his prayer for relief in the general— for hope is not utterly destroyed where the appointed means for help are carefully used—but by the particular avouchment of his hope in God, in the first verses of that psalm, ' O Lord God of my salvation, I have cried day and night before thee.'

(4.) The last difference of spiritual distresses which I shall observe is this, that some are more *transient fits and flashes of terror under a present temptation, which endure not long; others are more fixed and*

---

[1] Treatise 'Of Desertions.' [2] Ames, ' Cases of Consc.,' lib. iv. cap. 9.

permanent. The less durable distresses may be violent and sharp while they hold. Temptations of diffidence may strongly possess a child of God, and at first may not be repelled; and then before their faith can recover itself, they vent their present sad apprehensions of their estate, as Jonah did, chap. ii. 4, 'I said, I am cast out of thy sight.' Many such fits David had, and in them complained at this rate, 'Why hast thou forsaken me? why castest thou off my soul?' Ps. xxxi. 22, 'I said in my haste, I am cut off from before thine eyes.' Ps. cxvi. 11, 'I said in my haste, All men are liars;' which was a great height of distrust, and too boldly reflecting upon God's faithfulness, considering the special promises that God had made to him. Such sharp fits were those of Bainham and Bilney, martyrs, whose consciences were so sorely wounded for recanting the truth which they professed, that they seemed to feel a very hell within them.

The more fixed distresses, as they are of longer continuance, so they are often accompanied with the very worst symptoms; for when in these agonies, no sun nor star of comfort appears to them for many days, all hope that they shall be saved seems to be taken away, [Acts xxvii. 20;] and being tired out with complaints and importunities, without any answer, they at last reject the use of means. Some have lain many years—as the paralytic man at the pool of Bethesda—without cure; some from their youth up, as Heman complains. Some carry their distresses to their death-bed, and it may be are not eased till their souls are ready to depart out of their bodies, and then they often end suddenly and comfortably. Some I could tell you of, who on their death-bed, after grievous terrors, and many outcries concerning their miseries of 'blackness and darkness for ever,' lay long silent; and then on a sudden brake out into raptures of joy and adoring admiration of the goodness of God, using that speech of the apostle, Rom. xi. 33, 'Oh the depth of the riches both of the wisdom and knowledge of God! how unsearchable are his judgments, and his ways past finding out!' Others go out of the world in darkness, without any appearance of comfort. Such an instance was Mr Chambers, as the story of his death testifies, mentioned by Mr Perkins, in his treatise 'Of Desertions,' of whom this account is given: that in great agonies he cried out, 'he was damned,' and so died. The case of such is surely very sad to themselves, and appears no less to others; yet we must take heed of judging rashly concerning such. Nay, if their former course of life hath been uniformly good—for who will reject a fine web of cloth, as one speaks, for a little coarse list[1] at the end—especially if there be any obscure appearance of hope—as that expression of Mr Chambers, 'Oh that I had but one drop of faith!' is by Mr Perkins supposed to be—we ought to judge the best of them. We have seen the nature of spiritual distresses in the ingredients and differences thereof. We are now to consider,

2. Satan's method in procuring them: which consists, (1.) In the occasions which he lays hold on for that end. (2.) In the arguments which he useth. (3.) In the working up of their fears, by which he confirms men in them.

[1] 'Selvage,' or border.—G.

(1.) *As to the occasions*, he follows much *the same course which hath been described before in spiritual troubles;* so that I need not say much, only I shall note two things:—

[1.] That it makes much for Satan's purpose, if the party against whom he designs *have fallen into some grievous sins.* Sins of common magnitude do not lay a foundation suitable to the superstructure which he intends. He cannot plausibly argue reprobation or damnation from every ordinary sin; but if he finds them guilty of something extraordinary, then he falls to work with his accusations. The most usual sins which he takes advantage from, are, as Mr Perkins observes, those against the third, sixth, and seventh command; sometimes those against the ninth. Murder, adultery, perjury, and the wilful denial of truth against conscience, are the crimes upon which he grounds his charge, but most usually the last. Upon this, the distressed Spira, and some of the martyrs. As for the other, the more private they are, Satan hath oft the more advantage against them, because God's secret and just judgment will by this means 'bring to light the hidden things of darkness,' [1 Cor. iv. 5,] and force their consciences to accuse them of that which no man could lay to their charge, that he might manifest himself to be 'the searcher of the hearts, and trier of the reins,' [Rev. ii. 23.] Thus have many been forced to disclose private murders, secret adulteries, and to vomit up, though with much pain and torture, that which they have by perjury or guile extorted from others.

[2.] Where Satan hath not these particular advantages, he doth endeavour to prepare men for distresses, *by other troubles long continued.* All men that are brought to despair of their happiness, must not be supposed to be greater sinners than others. Some are distressed with fears of eternal damnation, that are in a good measure able to make Job's protestation in these cases, chap. xxxi. 9, &c., that their 'heart hath not been deceived by a woman;' that they have not laid wait at their neighbour's door; that they have not lift up their hand against the fatherless, when they saw their help in the gate; that their land doth not cry against them, nor the furrows thereof complain; that when they saw the sun when it shined, or the moon walking in brightness, their heart hath not been secretly enticed, nor their mouth kissed their hand; that they rejoiced not in the destruction of him that hated them, nor lift up themselves when evil found him, &c. Notwithstanding all which, their fears are upon and prevail against them. But then before Satan can bring them to consent to such dismal conclusions against themselves, they must be extraordinarily fitted to take the impression; either tired out under great afflictions, or long exercised with fears about their spiritual estates, without intermixture of comfort or ease, or their faculties broken and weakened by melancholy. Any of these give him an advantage equivalent to that of great sins. For though he cannot say to these, Your sins are so enormous, that they are, considered themselves together with their circumstances, sad signs of reprobation; yet he will plead that God's carriage towards them doth plainly discover that he hath wholly cast them off, and left them to themselves, without hope of mercy.

(2.) *As for the arguments which he useth*, they are much-what from the same topics which he maketh choice of in bringing on spiritual troubles. Only as he aims at the proof of a great deal more against God's children, than that they are not converted; so accordingly he screws up his mediums for proof to a higher pin. His arguments are,

[1.] *From scriptures wrested or misapplied.* His choice of scriptures for this purpose, is of such places as either seem to speak most sadly the dangerous and fearful estate of men, according to the first view and literal representation of them, through the unskilfulness of those that are to be concerned; or of such places as do really signify the miserable unhappiness of some persons, who through their own fault have been cut off from all hope, and the possibility of the like to some others for the future. So that, in framing arguments from Scripture, the devil useth a twofold cunning. *First,* There are some scriptures which have the word *damnation* in them, applied to some particular acts and miscarriages of men, when yet their intendment is not such as the word seems to sound, or as he would make them to believe. Now when he catcheth a child of God in such acts as are there specified, if he finds that his ignorance or timorousness is such as may render the temptation feasible, he presently applies damnation to them, by the authority of those texts. For instance, that text of Rom. xiv. 23, hath been frequently abused to that end, 'He that doubteth, is damned if he eat.' The word 'damned' there, strikes deep with a weak, troubled Christian that is not skilful in the word of righteousness. For whether Satan apply it to sacramental eating, as sometimes he doth to the ignorant, though contrary to the purpose of the text, or to doubting in the general, he makes this conclusion out of it: 'Thou doubtest, or thou hast eaten the sacrament doubtingly, therefore there is no hope for thee; thou art damned.' Whereas all this while, the devil doth but play the sophister in the abuse of the signification of words. For that scripture evidently relates to the difference that then was in the church, about eating those meats that were unclean by Moses's law; in which case the apostle doth positively declare, that the difference betwixt clean and unclean meats is taken away; so that a Christian might with all freedom imaginable eat those meats that were formerly unclean, with this proviso, that he were 'fully persuaded in his own mind,' [Rom. xiv. 5.] The necessity of which satisfaction, he proves from this, that otherwise he should offend his own conscience, which in that case must needs condemn him, and that is the damnation that is there spoken of; as is more evident by comparing this verse with the next foregoing, 'Happy is he that condemneth not himself.' But he that doubteth, doth condemn himself, because 'he eats not of faith,'—that is, from full persuasion of the lawfulness of the thing. This scripture then hath nothing at all in it to the purpose for which Satan brings it. It doth not speak of any final sentence of condemnation passed upon a man for such an act; all and the utmost that it saith, is only this, that it is a sin to go against the persuasion of conscience, and consequently it puts no man further off salvation than any other sin may do; for which, upon repentance, the sinner may be pardoned.

Another text which Satan hath frequently abused, to the very great prejudice of many, is that of 1 Cor. xi. 29, 'He that eateth and drinketh unworthily, eateth and drinketh damnation to himself.' With this scripture he insults over the humble, fearful Christian, who is sensible of his unworthiness of so great a privilege. Sometimes he keeps him off long from the sacrament of the Lord's supper, upon this very score that such an unworthy wretch ought not to make such near and familiar approaches to Christ. And if at last he is persuaded to partake of this ordinance, then, taking advantage of the party's consciousness of his great vileness, and the very low thoughts which he entertains of himself, he endeavours to persuade him that now he hath destroyed himself for ever, and run upon his own irrecoverable damnation. Thus he pleads it, Can anything be more plain than that thou hast eaten and drunken unworthily? Thy own conscience tells thee so; and can anything be more positively asserted than this, that he that doth so, eateth and drinketh damnation to himself? What then canst thou think of thyself, but that thou art a damned wretch? Neither do I speak barely what may be supposed Satan would say in this matter, but what may be proved by many instances he hath said and urged upon the consciences of the weak, who have from hence concluded, to the great distress of their souls, that by unworthy receiving of the sacrament they have sealed up their own condemnation; and all this by abusing and perverting the sense of this text. For the unworthy receiving doth relate to the miscarriages which he had taxed before, and it implies a careless, profane eating; such as might plainly express the small or unworthy esteem that they had in their hearts for that ordinance. And the damnation there threatened is not final and irrevocable damnation, but temporal judgment; as the apostle himself doth explain it in the next verses; 'For this cause many are sickly. . . . And if we would judge ourselves we should not be judged.' That is, as he further explains it, we should not be thus chastened or afflicted; and the word translated 'damnation' doth signify judgment—$\kappa\rho\hat{\iota}\mu\alpha$. At the furthest, if we should take it for the condemnation of hell, all that is threatened would be no more than this: that such have deserved, and God in justice might inflict the condemnation of hell for such an offence; which is not only true of this sin but of all others, which still do admit of the exception of repentance. All this while this is nothing to the poor humbled sinner, that judgeth himself unworthy in his most serious examination and greatest diligence. Satan here plays upon the unexactness of the translation, and the ignorance of the party in criticisms; for it is not every one that can readily answer such captious arguments.

[2.] But he hath another piece of cunning, which is this: *He doth by a singular kind of art, threap upon men some scripture that really speaks of eternal condemnation, without any sufficient evidence in matter of fact for the due application of them, only because they cannot prove the contrary.* His proceeding herein is to this purpose. First, After he hath prepared his way, by forming their minds to a fearful suspicion of their estate, he sets before them such scriptures as these: God hardened the heart of Pharaoh: he hath prepared 'vessels of wrath, fitted for destruction.' Christ prayed not 'for the world:' and that concerning the Jews, 'He hath blinded their eyes, and hardened their hearts.' Secondly, He confidently affirms that they are such. Thirdly, He puts them to prove the contrary, and herein he sends them to the search of God's eternal decrees; in which art Satan, like an *ignis fatuus*, leads them out of the way. And though he cannot possibly determine what he affirms, he shifts off the positive proof from himself, and leaves it upon them to make out, that they are not thus determined of by God's unchangeable purpose. And because the tempted, under so great a cloud, have no such persuasion of their present graces as may enable them to make sure their election by the fruits of their vocation, they are beaten off from their hold, and are brought to believe that the argument is unanswerable. Because they cannot say they are converted, they conclude they must be damned, overlooking the true answer that they might make, by keeping close to the possibility or probability that they may be converted, and so escape the damnation of hell. This general hope being of such high concern to the distressed, for it is the first thing that must relieve them till better evidence come in, it is Satan's great policy to cheat them of it, which he often doth by this method now declared.

(2.) Satan doth mainly endeavour *to misrepresent God to troubled souls, and from thence he draweth out arguments against them.* In the former case of spiritual troubles, he misrepresents God, in that he represents only some attributes of his, not only distinct from, but in opposition to others, by which he labours to conceal the sweet and beautiful harmony that is among them; and also to make one attribute an argument against the comfortable supporting considerations which another would afford. He insists upon God's justice without respect of mercy, upon his holiness without any regard of his gracious condescensions to the infirmities of the weak. But when it is his business to bring any under spiritual distresses, he then misrepresents God at a higher rate, and sticks not to asperse him with abominable falsehoods. There are two lies which he commonly urgeth at this time:—

[1.] He represents God as *a cruel tyrant, of a rigorous, unmerciful disposition, that delights himself in the ruin and misery of men.* To this purpose he rakes together the harshest passages of the Scripture, that speak of God's just severity against the wilful obstinate sinners, that stubbornly contemn his offers of grace. God indeed hath cleared himself of this aspersion, by solemn oath, Ezek. xxxiii. 11, 'As I live, saith the Lord God, I have no pleasure in the death of the wicked, but that the wicked turn from his way and live.' Yet the tempted will sooner believe Satan's suggestion than God's oath; partly because the sense of their vileness doth secretly sway them to think there is reason that he should be so; partly because their fears incline them to suspect the worst; and partly the uneasy tossings of their mind long continued reviveth the natural frowardness of the spirit against God. Which, how apt it is, when fretted with vexation, to entertain harsh thoughts of God, may be seen in the answer of the slothful servant to his lord, who returned his talent back again unimproved, with a reflection importing that his master was such as none could please; so severe that he was discouraged from making any attempt of serving him acceptably: Mat. xxv. 24, he said, 'Lord, I knew thee that thou art an hard man, reaping where thou hast not sown, and gathering where thou hast not strawed.'

[2.] He belies God further, by representing him as *designing the ruin and misery of the tempted person in particular*. He would make him believe that God had a particular spleen, as it were, against him above other men, and that in all his dealings with, or concerning him, he is but as a 'bear lying in wait, and as a lion in secret places,' [Lam. iii. 10,] ready to take any advantage to cut him off. And accordingly he gives no other interpretation of all the ways of God but such as make them look like tokens of final rejection of those that are concerned in them. If there be upon them outward afflictions, he tells them these are but the forerunners of hell; if they lie under inward sense of wrath, he calls that the first-fruits of everlasting vengeance; if any particular threatening be impressed upon their consciences by the Spirit of God, in order to their humiliation and repentance, he represents it as God's final sentence and absolute determination against them. If for caution God see it fit to set before them the examples of his wrath, as it is very frequent for him to do, lest we 'should fall after the same example of unbelief,' 1 Pet. ii. 6; 1 Cor. x. 6, Satan perverts this to that which God never intended, for he boldly asserts that these examples prognosticate their misery, and that God signifies by them a prediction of certain unavoidable unhappiness.

This must be observed here, that these misrepresentations of God are none of Satan's primary arguments; he useth them only as fresh reserves to second others. For where he finds any wing of his battalions ready to be beaten, he comes up with these supplies to relieve them. For indeed these considerations of God's severity in the general, or of his special resolve against any in particular, are not of force sufficient to attack a soul that is within the trenches of present peace; they are not of themselves proper mediums to produce such a conclusion. Though we suppose God severe, except we should imagine him to be a hater of mankind universally, we cannot thence infer the final ruin of this or that individual person. And besides that these are unjustifiable falsehoods, they cannot make the final damnation of any one so much as probable till the heart be first weakened in its hopes by fears or doubtings, raised up in it upon other grounds. Then indeed men are staggered, either by the deep sense of their unworthiness, or some sad continuing calamity, and the seeming neglect of their prayers. If Satan then tell them of God's severity, or that, all his providences considered, he hath set them up as a 'mark for the arrows of his indignation,' they are ready to believe his report, it being so suitable to their present sense and feeling.

[3.] Satan also fetcheth arguments from *the sins of God's children, but his great art in this is by unjust aggravations to make them look like those offences which by special exception in Scripture are excluded from pardon*. The apostle, 1 John v. 16, tells us of a 'sin that is unto death;' that is, a sin which, if a man commits, he cannot escape eternal death, and therefore he would not have such a sinner prayed for. That the popish distinction of venial and mortal sins is not here intended, some of the papists themselves do confess.[1] What he means by that sin he doth not tell us, it being a thing known sufficiently from other scriptures. The note of unpardonableness is indeed affixed to sins under several denominations; the sin against the Holy Ghost Christ pronounceth unpardonable, Mat. xii. 31. Total apostasy from the truth of the gospel hath no less said of it by the apostle when he calls it 'a drawing back to perdition,' Heb. x. 39. Whether these be all one, or whether there is any other species of sin irremissible besides that against the Holy Ghost, it is not to our purpose to make inquiry. Whatever they are in themselves, Satan in this matter makes use of the texts that speak of them distinctly, as we shall presently see. But, besides these, the Scriptures speak of some that were ' given up to vile affections, and to a reprobate mind,' Rom. i. 26, 28. And of others that were given up ' to hardness of heart,' Mat. xiii. 14; Acts xxviii. 26. Now whosoever they are of whom these things may be justly affirmed, they are certainly miserable, hopeless wretches. Here then is Satan's cunning, if he can make any child of God believe that he hath done any such act, or acts of sin, as may bring him within the compass of these scriptures, then he insults over them, and tells them over and over again that they are cut off for ever.

To this purpose he aggravates all their sins. And,

First, If he find them guilty of any *great iniquity*, *he fixeth upon that, and labours all he can to make it look most desperately, that so he may call it the sin against the Holy Ghost;* and in this he hath a mighty advantage, that most men are in the dark about that sin, all men being not yet agreed whether it be a distinct species of sin, or a higher degree of wilfulness relating to any particular sin. Upon this score Satan can lay the charge of this sin upon those that apostatize from the truth, and through weakness have recanted it. Thus he dealt with Spira, with Bilney, with Bainham, and several others. There is so near a resemblance in these sins of denying truths to what is said of the unpardonable sin, that these men, though they were scholars and men of good abilities, yet they were not able to answer the argument that the devil urged against them, but it prevailed to distress them. Upon others also hath Satan the advantage to fix this accusation; for let the species of the sin be what it will, if they have anything of that notion, that the sin against the Holy Ghost is a presumptuous act of sin under temptation, they will call any notorious crime the sin against the Holy Ghost, because of the more remarkable aggravating circumstances that have accompanied such a fact.

Second, He aggravates the sins of God's children from the wilfulness of their sinning. It is a thing often too true that a child of God may be carried by a violent impetus, or strong inclination of affection, to some particular iniquity, where the forwardness of desires that way, by a sudden haste, do stifle those reluctancies of mind which may be expected from one endowed with the Spirit of God, whose power upon them doth ordinarily sway them ' to lust against the flesh.' But it is more ordinary to find a temptation to prevail, notwithstanding that an enlightened mind doth make some resist-

[1] Lorinus *in loc.;* Barth. Petrus *in loc.*

ance; which, because it is too feeble, is easily borne down by the strong importunities of Satan, working upon the inclinations of the flesh. Both these cases are improved against them over whom Satan hath got any advantage of doubting of their estate. If they have resisted but ineffectually, or not resisted at all, he chargeth them with the highest wilfulness, and will so aggravate the matter that they shall be put in fear, not only that there can be no grace—where sin hath so much power as either to control so much light and endeavours, or hath so subjected the heart to its dominion that it can command without a contradiction—but that they can have no hope; that they that sin with so high a hand should ever enter into God's rest. And to this purpose he commonly sets before them that text of Heb. x. 26, 'If we sin wilfully after that we have received the knowledge of the truth, there remaineth no more sacrifice for sins.' Or that of Heb. vi. 4, 'It is impossible for those who were once enlightened, . . . if they fall away, to renew them again to repentance.' Both which places speak indeed, at least, such a difficulty as in common use of speech is called an impossibility, if not an utter absolute impossibility, of repentance and pardon. But then the sinning wilfully or falling away there mentioned, is only that of total apostasy; when men that have embraced the gospel, and by it have met with such impressions of power and delight upon their hearts, which we usually call common grace, do notwithstanding reject that gospel as false and fabulous, and so rise up against it with scorn and utmost contempt, as Julian the apostate did. If now the true intendment of those scriptures were considered by those that are distressed with them, they might presently see that they were put into fear, where no such cause of fear was. But all men have not this knowledge, nor do they so duly attend to the matter of the apostle's discourse as to be able to put a right interpretation upon it. Upon such Satan imposeth his deceitful gloss, and tells them: Wilful sinners cannot be restored to repentance; but you have sinned wilfully; when sin was before you, you rushed into it without any consideration, as the horse into the battle; or when God stood in your way with commands and advice to the contrary, when your consciences warned you not to do so great wickedness, yet you would do it. You were as those that break the yoke and burst the bonds. Upon this supposition, that these texts speak of wilful sinning in the general, how little can be said against Satan's argument! How many have I known that have been tortured with these texts, judging their estate fearful, because of their wilfulness in sinning! who upon the breaking of the snare of Satan's misrepresentation, have escaped as a bird unto the hill.

Third, When either of the two former ways will not serve the turn— that is, when he meets with such against whom he hath nothing of notorious wickedness to object, or such as have a better discerning of Scripture than so to be imposed upon—he labours *to make a charge against them, from the number of their miscarriages.* Here he takes up all the filth he can, and lays it upon one heap at their door. It is indeed an easy thing for Satan to set the sins of a child of God in order before him, and to bring to mind innumerable evils, especially to one that is already awakened with a true discovery of the corruption of nature and the vileness of sin. In which case the more a man considers, the more he will discover; and sins thus set in battle array, though they be not more than ordinary heinous, yet being many, have a very dismal appearance. Satan's design in this is to bring men under the affrightments which seem most proper to be raised from a perverse aspect of the third rank of scriptures, which a little before I pointed at. For the word of God, speaking of the final estate of men, doth not only discover the hopeless condition of some as to eternal life from some particular acts of sin, but also the sad estate of others from the manner, degrees, and frequency of sinning. The heathens, because they improved not the knowledge of God, which they had from the works of creation, neither making those inferences in matters relating to his worship, which those discoveries did direct them unto, nor behaving themselves in full compliance to those rules of virtuous conversation which they might have drawn from these principles, and unto which in point of gratitude they were obliged: Rom. i. 21, 'They glorified him not as God, neither were thankful; therefore God gave them to a reprobate mind.' And generally, concerning all others, the Scripture teacheth us that a return to a profane fleshly life, after some reformation, hath a greater hazard in it than ordinary, as appears by the parable in Mat. xii. 45, 'Seven more wicked spirits re-enter;' where one that was cast out is received again; and 'the last state of that man is worse than the first.' So also 2 Pet. ii. 20. To this purpose is that of Solomon concerning the danger of continuance in sin, after many reproofs: Prov. xxix. 1, 'He that being often reproved hardeneth his neck, shall suddenly be destroyed, and that without remedy.' These, and many such like scriptures, Satan hath in readiness, which he plies home upon the consciences of those that are troubled with the sense of sin; telling them that their hearts and ways being continually evil, notwithstanding all the courses that God hath taken to reclaim them; that they having so long neglected so great salvation, or that after having seemed to entertain it, became more sinful than before—which they will easily believe, because they are now more sensible of sin, and more observant of their miscarriages than formerly—there can be no question but they are given up to vile affections; and like the ground that bears nothing but 'briars and thorns, they are rejected, and nigh unto cursing, whose end is to be burned,' [Heb. vi. 8.] The wound that is made with this weapon is not so easily healed as some others already mentioned; because though Satan do unduly wrest these passages to such failures in the children of God as have little or no affinity with them, for they only speak of falling into open profaneness with contumacy, yet they that have deep convictions, accompanied with great fears, do usually think that there are none worse than they are. And though they will grant that some others have more flagitious lives, yet they think they have hearts so desperately wicked, that they must needs be under as great hazards as those whose lives seem to be worse.

[4.] There is but one argument more that carries any probability of proof for everlasting condemnation, and that is from *a hard and impenitent heart*. How Satan will manage himself to make a child of God believe that he hath such a heart, is our last observation relating to his sophistry. And it is this: he unjustly aggravates the discomposures of the spirits of those that are troubled for sin, and from thence draws his arguments of irrecoverable damnation, pleading that their hearts are seared, hardened, uncapable of repentance, and consequently of heaven. That final impenitency will conclude damnation is certain; and that some have been given up to such a judicial hardness long before death, that they could not repent, may not only be evidenced from the threatening of God to that purpose, Mat. xiii. 15, 'Make the heart of this people fat,' &c, but also from the sad instances of Pharaoh, of whom it is said, that 'God hardened his heart;' and the Jews who were blinded, Rom. xi. 8, 'God hath given them the spirit of slumber, eyes that they should not see, and ears that they should not hear.' But still the art lieth in this, How to make a child of God believe that it is so with him. For this purpose he must take him at some advantage, he cannot terrify him with this argument at all times. While he is acting repentance with an undisturbed settled frame of heart, it is not possible to make him believe he doth not, or cannot repent; for this were to force him contrary to sense and experience. But he must take him at some season which may, with some probability, admit of his plea, and nothing is more proper for that design than a troubled heart; so that he hath in this case two things to do:

First, He disquiets the soul into as great a height of confusion as he can. That, *second*, when he hath melted it into heaviness, and torn it into pieces, he may work upon its distractions.

There are many things that fall out in the case of great anxiety of mind, that are capable of improvement for the accomplishment of this design. As, 1. *Distracting troubles bring the heart under the stupidity of amazement.* Their thoughts are so broken and disjointed, that they cannot unite them to a composed, settled resolution in anything; they can scarce join them together to make out so much as might spell out their distinct desires or endeavours; they scarce know what they are doing, or what they would do. 2. *They also poison the thoughts with harsh apprehensions against God.* Great distresses make the thoughts sometimes recoil against the holy Lord with unseemly questionings of his goodness and compassion; and this puts men into a bad sullen humour of untowardness, from whence, through Satan's improvement, arise the greatest plunges of despair. 3. Most usually in this case *the greatest endeavours are fruitless and dissatisfactory.* Satan, though he be no friend to duty, doth unseasonably urge them to repent and pray; but it is because they cannot do either with any satisfaction, and then their failures are matter of argument against them. For if they resolve to put themselves upon a more severe course of repentance, and accordingly begin to think of their sins, to number them, or to aggravate them, they are usually affrighted from the undertaking by the heinous appearance of them. They cannot, they dare not think of them; the remotest glimpse of them is terrible to an affrighted conscience; the raising of them up again in the memory, like the rising of a ghost from the grave, is far more astonishing than the first prospect of them after commission. So true is that of Luther, 'If a man could see sin perfectly, it would be a perfect hell.' If they set themselves to beg their pardon by earnest prayer, they are so distracted and confused in prayer, that their prayers please them not; they come off from the duty more wounded than when they began. Or if in any measure they overcome these difficulties, so that they do pray and confess their iniquities, then they urge and force a sorrow or compunction upon themselves, but still to a greater dissatisfaction. For it may be—and this usually happens in greater distresses—they cannot weep, nor force a tear, or if they do, still they judge their sorrow is not deep enough, nor any way suitable to the greatness of their sin. 4. To all these Satan sometimes makes a further addition of trouble, *by injecting blasphemous thoughts.* Here he sets the stock, with an intention to graft upon it afterward. When all these things are thus in readiness, then comes he to set fire to the train, and thus he endeavours to blow up the mine. Is not thy heart hardened to everlasting destruction? How canst thou deny this? Art thou not grown stupid, and senseless of all the hazards that are before thee? Here he insists upon the amazement and confusion of their spirit; and it is very natural for those that are drunk with the terrors of the Almighty, to think themselves stupid, because of the distraction of their thoughts. I have known several that have pleaded that very argument to that purpose. Satan goes on: What greater evidence can there be of a hardened heart than impenitency? Thou canst not mourn enough. Thou hast not a tear for thy sins, though thou couldst weep enough formerly upon every petty occasion; nay, thou canst not so much as pray for pardon. Is not this not only a heart that doth not, but that cannot repent? Besides, saith he, thou knowest the secret thoughts that thy heart is privy to; do they not boil up in thy breast against God? Art thou not ready to tax him for dealing thus with thee? What is this untowardness, but desperate obdurateness? And if with all these there be blasphemous injections, then he tells him it is a clear case that he is judicially hardened; in that he acts the part of the damned in hell already. By all, or some of these deceits, the devil doth often prevail so far with men, that they conclude their heart to be so obstinate, so stupid, that it is impossible that it should be ever mollified or brought into a penitential frame, and consequently that there is no hope of their salvation.

(3.) There is but one thing more, besides the occasions which he takes, and the arguments which he makes use of, relating to Satan's method for the procurement of spiritual distresses, and that is his endeavour to strengthen these arguments by the *increase of fears in their hearts.*

What Satan can do in raising up misgiving, tormenting fears, hath been said; and how serviceable this is to his design, I shall shew in a few particulars, having only first noted this in the general, that as his design in these distresses is raised to express his utmost height of malice against men—in pushing them forward to the greatest mischief, by excluding them totally from the lowest degree of the hope of happiness, and by persuading them of the inevitable certainty of their eternal misery—so he doth endeavour, by the strongest impressions of fear, to terrify them to the utmost degree of affrightful amazement, and consequently the effects of that fear are most powerful; for,

[1.] By this means *the spirits of men are formed and moulded into a frame most suitable for the belief and entertainment of the most dismal impressions that Satan can put upon them.* For strong fears, like fire, do assimilate everything to their own nature, making them naturally incline to receive the blackest, the most disadvantageous interpretations of all things against themselves, so that they have no capacity to put any other sense upon what lies in their way, but the very worst. Hence are they possessed with no other thoughts but that they are remediless wretches, desperate miscreants, utterly forsaken of God. They are brought into such a woeful partiality against their own peace, that they cannot judge aright of any accusation, plea, or argument that Satan brings for a proof of their unhappiness; but being filled with strong prejudices of hell, they think every sophism a strong argument, every supposition a truth, and every accusation conclusive of no less than their eternal damnation; insomuch that their fears do more to discomfit them than all Satan's forces. 'A dreadful sound being in their ears,' [Job xv. 21,] their strength fails them at the appearance of any opposition; as when fear comes upon an army they throw away their weapons, and, by an easy victory, give their backs sometimes to an inconsiderable enemy.

[2.] Men thus possessed with fear do not only receive into their own bowels every weapon which Satan directs on purpose to the wounding and slaying of their hopes, but by a strange kind of belief *they imagine everything to be the sword of an enemy.* All they hear or meet with turns into poison to them, for they think everything is against them—promises as well as threatenings, mercies as well as judgments, and that by all these, one as well as another, God, as with a flaming sword turning every way, doth hinder their access to the tree of life. Bilney the martyr, as Latimer in his sermons reports of him, after his denial of the truth, was under such horrors of conscience, that his friends were forced to stay with him night and day. No comforts would serve. If any comfortable place of Scripture was offered to him, it was as if a man should cut him through with a sword. Nothing did him good; he thought that all scriptures made against him, and sounded to his condemnation. Neither is it so rare a thing for fears to form the imagination into such misshapen apprehensions, as that we should think such instances to be only singular and unusual; but it is a common effect of terror, which few or none escape that are under spiritual distresses. The blackness of their thoughts make the whole Scripture seem black to them. The unfit medium through which they look doth discolour every object. So that the book of life, as Mrs Kath. Bretterge in the like case expressed herself concerning the Bible, seems to be nothing else but a book of death to them.[1]

[3.] From hence it follows *that no counsel or advice can take place with them.* Excessive fears do remove their souls so far from peace, that they will not believe there is any hope for them, though it be told them. The most compassionate, serious admonitions of friends, the strongest arguments against despair, the clearest discoveries of the hopes that are before them, &c., effect but little. While they are spoken, it may be, they seem to relieve them a little; but the comfort

[1] *Vide* her story in Clark's Lives. [As before.—G.]

abides not with them, it is soon gone. Though they cannot answer the arguments brought for them, yet they cannot believe them; as if their souls were now deprived of all power to believe anything for their good: suitable to that expression of Spira, in answer to his friends that laboured to comfort him, 'I would believe comfort, but cannot; I can believe nothing but what is contrary to my comfort.' Nay, when they are told that many others have been under the like dreadful apprehensions of everlasting misery who have at last been comforted—and by manifold experience we find that it is the greatest ease to distressed souls to hear, especially to speak with some that have been in the like case, for this will oft administer some hope that they also may be at last comforted, when the most comfortable promises of the Scripture are a terror to them;—yet this doth [not] effect the least ease for them sometimes, because some are so wholly possessed with unalterable prejudice against themselves, that they think none are or ever were like them. They compare themselves to Judas and Cain, and think their iniquity to be aggravated by many circumstances far beyond the pitch of them. Thus Spira judged of himself: ' I tell you,' saith he, 'my case is mine own, it is singular, none like it.'

[4.] Though fears make the soul unactive to anything of comfort, because they wholly destroy its inclination and alter its bias to hope, yet, on the contrary, *they make it very nimble and active to pursue the conclusions of misery which they have helped to frame,* for the spring of all the faculties of the soul are bent that way. Hence it is that those who are possessed with these agonies will eagerly plead against themselves, and with an admirable subtlety will frame arguments against their peace, coin distinctions, and make strange evasions to escape the force of any consolation that may be offered to them. Their understandings are, as it were, whetted by their fears to an unimaginable quickness. Who would not wonder to hear the replies that some will give to the arguings of their friends that labour to comfort them! What strange answers Spira gave to those that pleaded with him! How easily he seemed to turn off the example of Peter denying Christ, and those scriptures that speak of God's love to mankind, &c., may be seen at large in his narrative.

[5.] Fears by a strange kind of witchcraft do not only make them believe that they shall be unhappy, but also will at last persuade them *that they feel and see their misery already.* How astonishingly doth Spira speak to this purpose: ' I find he daily more and more hardens me; I feel it.' Answerable to this, I remember, was the case of one who was long imprisoned in deep distresses. He told me that he verily believed that scripture of Isa. lxvi. 23, 24 was fulfilled upon him, 'From one sabbath to another shall all flesh come to worship before me, and they shall go forth and look upon the carcases of the men that have transgressed against me; for their worm shall not die, neither shall their fire be quenched, and they shall be an abhorring to all flesh.' To his own feeling he had the torments of conscience, and the sense of divine wrath was as a burning fire within him, and to his apprehension every look from others was a gazing upon him as a monster of misery, ' abhorred of all flesh.'

The nature of spiritual distresses, and Satan's method in working them, being explained, the last thing promised is now to be opened. This is,

3. The burden and weight of these distresses, which how grievous, how intolerable it is, may be sufficiently seen in what hath been already said, and may be further evidenced in the particulars following :—

[1.] *Those that are wounded with these fiery darts do at first usually conceal their wound and smother their grief, being ashamed to declare it,* partly because some great transgression, it may be, hath kindled all this fire in their bosoms, and this they are unwilling to declare to others; partly because they suspect—though no one remarkable sin hath occasioned these troubles—that the discovery of their case will expose them to the wonder and censures of all that shall hear of them. By this means the fire burns with greater vehemency. Their sore runs continually, and having none to speak a word in season for the least relief, it becomes more painful and dangerous; as bodily distempers, concealed by a foolish modesty from the physician, increase the trouble and hazard of the patient. Here have they many strugglings within themselves, many attempts to overcome their fears, but all in vain. They sit alone and keep silence, they flee the company and society of men, they labour after solitary places where they may weep with freedom, if their tears be not yet dried up, or at least where they may pour out their complaints against themselves. They meditate nothing but their misery, they can fix their thoughts upon nothing else, they 'chatter as a crane or swallow, they mourn as a dove,' they are as 'a pelican in the wilderness, as an owl in the desert,' but still without ease. They are but as those that are 'snared in dens and prison-houses,' who the longer they lie there have the less patience to bear the present unhappiness, and the less hope to be delivered from it.

[2.] *When they are tired out with private conflicts, and have no rest or intermission of trouble, then at last they are forced to speak; and having once begun to open their troubles, they care not who knows it.* If there be any heinous sin at the bottom, their consciences are forced to confess it. Wickedness, that was once sweet in his mouth, 'is turned in his bowels, it is the gall of asps within him,' Job xx. 14, 15. Thus doth God make men to vomit up what they had swallowed down. Terrors chase away all shame, they can now freely speak against their sin with the highest aggravations. And if their consciences have not a heinous crime to accuse them of in particular, yet in the general they will judge and condemn themselves as the most stubborn, sinful, or hardened wretches, justly branded with indelible characters of the wrath of God. However, the distress becomes greater; if they truly accuse themselves of any particular sin, that vomit is not without a violence offered to nature which otherwise would cover its shame. It cannot be done without sickness, straining, and torture; and when it is done, they take it for granted that every one passeth the same judgment upon them which they do upon themselves; and the frequent speaking doth confirm their minds in their fearful expectations. For what men do accustom themselves to assert, that they do more confidently believe. If they only complain of themselves in the general, with any intentions of procurement of pity, as is usual for the distressed to do, yet while they cry out to others, 'Is this nothing to you, all you that pass by? Is there any sorrow like to my sorrow?' &c., [Lam. i. 12,] still they think their 'stroke is heavier than their groaning,' [Job xxiii. 2;] and their cry to others doth strongly fix this apprehension in themselves, that none can be more miserable than they. Thus are they brought to Job's condition: chap. xvi. 6, 'Though I speak, my grief is not assuaged; and though I forbear, what am I eased?'

[3.] All this while they are under *an expressible*[1] *sense of divine wrath.* Heman speaks his apprehensions of it under the similitude of the most hideous and dismal comfortless imprisonment: Ps. lxxxviii. 6, 'Thou hast laid me in the lowest pit, in darkness, in the deeps.' David, in Ps. cxvi. 3, compares it to the 'sorrows of death,' and—the highest that human thoughts can reach—'the pains of hell.' 'The sorrows of death compassed me, and the pains of hell gat hold upon me; I found trouble and sorrow.' Well might they thus judge, all things considered; for sin, that then lies heavy upon them, is a great weight, 'a burden,' saith David, 'greater than I can bear,' especially when it is pressed on by a heavy hand: 'Thy hand presseth me sore.' Sin makes the greatest wound, considering the conscience, which is wounded by it, is the tenderest part, and of exquisite sense. Hence the grief of it is compared to the pain of a running, fretting ulcer, that distempers the whole body: 'My wounds stink and are corrupted; my sore ran in the night, and ceased not.' Or to the pain of broken and shattered bones: Ps. xxxviii. 3, 'There is no soundness in my flesh, because of thine anger; neither is there any rest in my bones, because of my sin.' The instrument also that makes the wound is sharp, and cuts deep: 'It is sharper than a two-edged sword,' [Heb. iv. 12;] but when the weapon is poisoned,—and Satan hath a way to do that,—then it burns, making painful, malignant inflammations. The wrath of God, expressed to the conscience, brings the greatest terror: 'Who knows the power of thine anger?' Ps. xc. 11. It is impossible for the most trembling conscience, or most jealous fears, to go to the utmost bounds of it; neither can we apprehend any torture greater. The rack, tortures, fire, gibbets, &c., are all nothing to it. Hence it is that those who were afraid of suffering for truth, when by this means they were brought under these distresses, could then be willing to suffer any torment on the body; yea, and heartily wish to suffer much more, so that these tortures might be ended. Thus it was with Bainham martyr,[2] who, in the public congregation, bewailed his abjuration of the truth; and prayed all his hearers 'rather to die by and by, than do as he had done.' But that of Spira seems almost beyond belief. Thus speaks he to Vergerius, 'If I could conceive but the least spark of hope of a better estate hereafter, I would not refuse to endure the most heavy weight of the wrath of that great God, yea, for twenty thousand years, so that I might at length attain to the end of that misery.' What dreadful agonies were these that put him to these wishes! But it is less wonder, if you observe what apprehensions he had of his present trouble, he judged it worse than hell itself. And if

---

[1] Query, 'inexpressible'?—G.   [2] [Foxe,] Acts and Mon., cap. 8, p. 938.

you would have a lively exposition of David's expression, 'The pains of hell,' &c., you may fetch it from this instance: 'My present estate,' saith he, 'I now account worse than if my soul, separated from my body, were with Judas and the rest of the damned; and therefore I desire rather to be there than thus to live in the body.' So that if you imagine a man crushed under the greatest weight, wounded in the most tender parts, and those wounds provoked by the sharpest corrosives, his bones all disjointed and broken, pined also with hunger and thirst, and in that case put under the highest tortures; yet you have but a very shadow of divine wrath. Add to all these, according to Spira's wish, twenty thousand years of hell itself, yet all is nothing to that which a distressed mind supposeth; while the word *eternity* presents the soul with the total sum of utmost misery all at once. Oh, unexpressible burden of a distressed mind! who can understand it truly, but he that feels it? How terribly is the mind of man shaken with terrors, as the wilderness by a mighty wind! which not only produceth violent motions, but also hideous noise, murmur, and howling.

[4.] This burden upon the mind *forceth the tongue to vent its sorrow in the saddest accent of most doleful outcries.* Their whole language is lamentation; but when the pangs of their agonies come upon them, for their distresses have their fits, then they speak in the bitterness of their souls. Oh, said Bainham, I would not for all the world's good feel such a hell in my conscience again. One, formerly mentioned, in these distresses cries out, 'Woe, woe, woe, a woeful, a wretched, a forsaken woman!'[1] It would surely have made a man's hair to stand upright for dread to have heard Spira roaring out that terrible sentence, 'How dreadful is it to fall into the hands of the living God!' [Heb. x. 31.] Or to have heard his reply to him that told of his being at Venice: 'O cursed day!' saith he, 'O cursed day! Oh that I had never gone thither, would God I had then died!' &c. The like outcries had David often: Ps. xxi. 1, 'My God, my God, why hast thou forsaken me? Why art thou so far from helping me, and from the words of my roaring?' And Heman, Ps. lxxxviii. 14, 'Lord, why castest thou off my soul, why hidest thou thy face from me?' It is true David's and Heman's words have a better complexion than those others last mentioned; but their disquiet of heart seems, at some times, to have urged their expressions with impetuous violence; as those passages seem to say, Ps. xxxviii. 8, 'I have roared by reason of the disquietness of my heart;' Ps. xxxii. 3, 'My bones waxed old through my roaring all the day long;' Job iii. 24, 'My roarings are poured out like water.' If their lamentations were turned into roarings, and those roarings were like the breaking in of a flood, and that flood of so long continuance that it dried up the marrow of the bones, we may safely imagine that they were not so much at leisure to order their words, but that their tongues might speak in that dialect which is proper to astonishment and distress.

[5.] Though the mind be the principal seat of these troubles, *yet the body cannot be exempted from a co-partnership in these sorrows.* Notwithstanding, this is so far from abating the trouble, that it increaseth it by a circulation. The pains of the body, contracted by

[1] Mrs K. B. [Mrs Katherine Bretterge, as before.—G.]

the trouble of the mind, are communicated again to the fountain from whence they came, and reciprocally augment the disquiet of the mind. The body is weakened, their 'strength poured out like water;' they are 'withered like grass,' pined as 'a skin,' become as a 'bottle in the smoke.' Thus David frequently complains: Ps. xxii. 14, he describes himself as reduced to a skeleton, 'I am poured out like water, and all my bones are out of joint: my heart is like wax; it is melted in the midst of my bowels. My strength is dried up like a potsherd; my tongue cleaveth to my jaws; and thou hast brought me to the dust of death.' Neither is this his peculiar case, but the common effect of spiritual distresses: Ps. xxxix. 11, 'When thou with rebukes dost correct man for iniquity, thou makest his beauty to consume away like a moth.'

[6.] Being thus distressed for their souls, they cast off *all care of their bodies, estates, families, and all their outward concerns whatsoever.* And no wonder, for being persuaded that they have made shipwreck of their souls, they judge the rest are not worth the saving.

[7.] Giving all for lost, they usually cast about for some ease to their minds, *by seeking after the lower degrees of misery, hearing or supposing that all are not tormented alike, they endeavour to persuade themselves of a cooler hell.* This, if they could reach it, were but poor comfort, and little to their satisfaction; but, as poor as it is, it is usually denied to them, for while they judge themselves to be the greatest sinners, they cannot but adjudge themselves to the greatest torments; and these endeavours being frustrated, they return back to themselves, as now hopeless of the least ease, worse than before. Now they fix themselves upon the deep contemplations of their misery. Oh, think they, how great had our happiness been if we had been made toads, serpents, worms, or anything but men; for then should we never have known this unhappiness; and this begets a thousand vain wishes. Oh that we had never been born! or that death could annihilate us! or that as soon as we had been born, we had died! as Job speaks: chap. iii. 11, 12, 'Why died I not from the womb? why did I not give up the ghost when I came out of the belly?' for then had we not contracted so much guilt. 'Or that the mountains and hills could fall upon us, and cover us from the face of our judge,' [Rev. vi. 16.]

[8.] When all their hopes are thus dashed, and, like a shipwrecked man on a plank, they are still knocked down with new waves, all their endeavours being still frustrated, they seem to themselves to be able to hold out no longer; then they *give over all further inquiries, and the use of means, they refuse to pray, read, hear.* They perceive, as Spira said, that they pray to their own condemnation, and that all is to no purpose. They are 'weary of their groanings,' Ps. vi. 6; their 'eyes fail with looking up;' their 'knees are feeble;' their hands hang down; and as Heman: Ps. lxxxviii. 4, 5, 'They count themselves with those that go down to the pit, free among the dead, like the slain that lie in the grave, whom God remembereth no more.' Thus they lie down under their burden, and while they find it so hard to be borne, it is usual for them to come to the utmost point of desperateness, Satan suggesting and forwarding them. Sometimes they open their mouths with complaints against God, and blaspheme. And, as the last part of the tragedy, being weary of themselves, they seek to put an end to their present misery, by putting an end to their lives.

I have presented you with Satan's stratagems against the peace of God's children. The remedies against these and other subtleties of our grand enemy I shall not offer you, because many others have done that already, to whose writings I must refer you. Some principal directions I have pointed at in the way, and in the general, have done this for the help of the tempted, that I have endeavoured to shew them the methods of [the] tempter, which is no small help to preserve men from being thus imposed upon, and to recover out of his snare those that are. It is a great preservative from sickness, and no mean advantage to the cure, to have a discovery of the disease, and the causes of it. I shall conclude these discoveries with a caution or two.

[1.] *Let none think worse of the serious practice of holy strictness in religion, because these spiritual distresses do sometimes befall those that are conscientiously careful in the ways of God, while the profane and negligent professors are strangers to such trials.* These troubles are indeed very sad, but a senseless, careless state is far worse. These troubles often end very comfortably, whereas the other end—except God make them sensible by conviction of their sin and danger—in that real misery, the fears whereof occasion these sorrows to God's children. And the danger of spiritual troubles is not so great as is that of a hardened heart; nay, God frequently makes use of them to prevent eternal ruin—for one that goes roaring to the pit, there are thousands that go laughing to hell.

[2.] *Let none slight or scoff at these tremendous judgments.* It is too common with men, either to ascribe spiritual troubles to melancholy, as if none were ever thus concerned, but such, as by too much seriousness in religion, are become mad—a fair pretence for carelessness—or to a whining dissimulation. To the former I have said something before, and as for the latter I shall only reply, in the words of Spira, to one that objected hypocrisy to him: 'I am a castaway, a vessel of wrath; yet dare you call it dissembling and frenzy, and can mock at the formidable example of the heavy wrath of God that should teach you fear and terror. But it is natural to the flesh to speak, either out of malice or ignorance, perversely of the work of God.'

[3.] *Let none be afraid of this Goliath, let no man's heart faint because of him.* A fear of caution and diligence to avoid his snares is a necessary duty—'Be sober, be vigilant; because your adversary the devil,' &c., [1 Pet. v. 8]—but a discouraging, distrustful fear is a dishonourable reflection upon God's power and promises to help us, and upon the captain of our salvation, who goeth out before us. Let us hold on in the practice of holiness, and not be afraid. 'The God of peace shall tread down Satan under our feet shortly,' [Rom. xvi. 20.] Amen.

NOTE.

Agreeably to Note at beginning, there will be found below* the more specific title-page of Part III.—G.

* *DÆMONOLOGIA SACRA:*

OR, A

TREATISE

OF

Satans Temptations.

The Third Part.

CONTAINING

An Account of the Combate betwixt Christ and Satan, in *Matth.* 4. Wherein the deep Subtilty of Satan, in managing those Temptations, is laid open, as the grand Instance of the Sum of his Policy in all his Assaults upon Men; Leading to a consideration of many Temptations in particular, and of special directions for Resistance.

By *R. G.*

Heb. 4. 15.
—*He was Tempted in all points like as we are, yet without Sin*.

London, Printed by *J. D.* for *Richard Randel*, and *Peter Maplisden*, Booksellers in *New-Castle* upon *Tine*, 1677.

PART III.

Then was Jesus led up of the Spirit into the wilderness, to be tempted of the devil.—MAT. iv. 1.

CHAPTER I.

The first circumstance of the combat—The time when it happened—The two solemn seasons of temptation—The reasons thereof.

I SHALL here consider the great temptation which it pleased our Lord Christ to submit unto, as a most famous instance for confirmation and illustration of the doctrine of temptations already handled.

The first verse sets down several remarkable circumstances of this combat, all of them matter of weight and worth: as,

1. First, *The time when this fell out;* not as a loose and accidental emergency, but as particularly made choice of both by God and Satan, being most fit and proper for the design which each of them were carrying on. This is expressly noted in Mat. iv. 1, ' Then was Jesus led up;' but more full in Mark i. 12, '*Immediately* the Spirit driveth him into the wilderness;' manifestly directing us to expect something worthy of our observation in that circumstance. Neither can we miss of it, when the things unto which this directs us are so fully related immediately before. For we find in both these evangelists, which speak so exactly of the time of these temptations, that Christ was baptized of John. This was in order to the fulfilling the righteousness of his office. As the priests under the law, when they came to be thirty years old, entered upon their function by washings, or baptizings and anointings:[1] so Christ, that he might answer his type, beginning to be about thirty years of age, was solemnly inaugurated into the great office of the mediatorship by baptism, and the extraordinary descending of the Holy Ghost, by which he was ' anointed with the oil of gladness above his fellows.' To this solemn instalment the Father adds an honourable testimony concerning him, ' This is my beloved Son, in whom I am well pleased,' Luke iii. 23. Immediately after this was he carried to the place of combat. Hence we may infer,

Obs. 1. *That our entering upon a special service for God, or re-*

[1] Numb. iv. 3. *Vide* Lightfoot, ' Temple Service and Harmony.' Lev. viii. 6, 12.

ceiving a special favour from God, are two solemn seasons which Satan makes use of for temptation. Often these two seasons meet together in the same person at the same time. Paul, after his rapture into the third heaven, 2 Cor. xii. 2, 7, which, as some conceive, was also upon his entrance upon the ministry, was buffeted by 'the messenger of Satan.'

Sometime these two seasons are severed; yet still it may be observed that the devil watcheth them. When any servant of God is to engage in any particular employment, he will be upon him. He assaulted Moses by persecution, when he was first called to deliver Israel. As soon as David was anointed, immediately doth he enrage the minds of Saul and his courtiers against him. It was so ordinary with Luther, that he at last came to this, that before any eminent service he constantly expected either a fit of sickness, or the buffetings of Satan. He is no less sedulous in giving his assaults when any child of God hath been under peculiar favours or enjoyments. The church, after a high entertainment with Christ, is presently overcome by a careless, sleepy indisposition, Cant. v. 1, 2.

Though this may seem strange, yet the harshness of such a providence on God's part, and the boldness of the attempt on Satan's part, may be much taken off by the consideration of the reasons hereof.

(1.) First, *On Satan's part.* It is no great wonder to see such an undertaking, when we consider his fury and malice. The more we receive from God, and the more we are to do for him, the more doth he malign us. So much the more as God is good, by so much is his eye evil.

(2.) Secondly, There are in such cases as these several advantages, which, through our weakness and imperfection, we are too apt to give him; and for these he lieth at the catch.

[1.] As first, *Security.* We are apt to grow proud, careless, and confident, after or upon such employments and favours; even as men are apt to sleep or surfeit upon a full meal, or to forget themselves when they are advanced to honour. Job's great peace and plenty made him, as he confesseth, so confident, that he concluded he should 'die in his nest,' chap. xxix. 18. David enjoying the favour of God in a more than ordinary measure, though he was more acquainted with vicissitudes and changes than most of men, grows secure in his apprehension, that he 'should never be moved,' Ps. xxx. 6; but he acknowledgeth his mistake, and leaves it upon record as an experience necessary for others to take warning by, that when he became warm under the beams of God's countenance, then he was apt to fall into security; and—this it seems was usual with him in all such cases—when he was most secure, he was nearest some trouble or disquiet. 'Thou didst hide thy face'—and then to be sure the devil will shew his—' and I was troubled.' Enjoyments beget confidence; confidence brings forth carelessness; carelessness makes God withdraw, and gives opportunity to Satan to work unseen. And thus, as armies after victory growing secure, are oft surprised; so are we oft after our spiritual advancements thrown down.

[2.] Secondly, *Discouragement and tergiversation* is another thing the devil watcheth for. By his assaults he represents the duty difficult, tedious, dangerous, or impossible, on purpose to discourage us, and to make us fall back. No sooner doth Paul engage in the gospel than the devil is upon him, suggesting such hazards as he knew were most prevalent with our frail natures, if he had not been aware of him, and refused to hearken to what flesh and blood would have said in the case, Gal. i. 16. When God honoured Moses with the high employment of delivering Israel, the hazard and danger of the work was so strongly fixed upon his thoughts, that he makes many excuses: one while pleading his inability and insufficiency, ' Who am I, that I should go to Pharaoh?' Exod. iii. 11. Another while he urgeth Israel's unbelief, and a seeming impossibility to satisfy them of his commission, Exod. iv. 1. After that he deviseth another shift, ' I am not eloquent,' ver. 10. And when all these subterfuges were removed, Satan had so affrighted him with the trouble and difficulty of this undertaking, that he attempts to break away from his duty: ver. 13, ' Send by the hand of him whom thou wilt send;' that is, spare me and send another: and till the anger and displeasure of God was manifested against him, he submitted not. In Jonah the temptation went higher. He, upon the apprehensions mentioned, ran away from his service, and puts God to convince him by an extraordinary punishment. And when Satan prevails not so far as wholly to deter men by such onsets, yet, at least, he doth dishearten and discourage them, so that the work loseth much of that glory, excellency, and exactness, which a ready and cheerful undertaking would put upon it.

[3.] Thirdly, *The fall or miscarriage of the saints at such times is of more than ordinary disadvantage*, not only to others—for if they can be prevailed with to lay aside their work, or to neglect the improvement of their favours, others are deprived of the benefit and help that might be expected from them—but also to themselves. A prevailing temptation doth more than ordinarily prejudice them at such times. The greatness of the disappointment under special service, the unworthy neglect and unanswerableness to special favours, are extraordinary provocations, and produce more than ordinary chastisements, as we see in Jonah's affliction, and the spouse's desertion.

(2.) Secondly, As we have seen the reason of Satan's keenness in taking those opportunities, so may we consider the reasons of *God's permission*, which are these:—

[1.] First, Temptations at such seasons are permitted for more eminent *trial of the upright*. On this account was Job tempted.

[2.] Secondly, *For an increase of diligence, humility, and watchfulness*. If these privileges and mercies will not discourage Satan, what will? And if Satan so openly malign such enjoyments, we may be awakened to hold them faster and set a double guard upon them.

[3.] Thirdly, *For a plentiful furniture of experience*. Temptation is the shop of experience. Luther was so great a gainer by this, that he became able so to speak to the consciences and conditions of his hearers, that the thoughts of their hearts were manifested by his speaking, as if he had had an intelligencer in their own bosoms. Hence did he commend prayer, meditation, and temptation as necessary requisites for the accomplishment of a minister.

Applic. This may administer matter of counsel to us in both cases aforementioned, if we be put upon eminent employments or receive eminent favours.

1. First, *We must not be so secure as to think Satan will be asleep that while, or that we are beyond danger.* While we are receiving kindnesses, he is devising plots and laying snares. With privileges and mercies expect exercises and hazards.

2. Secondly, in particular, *We may receive something of advice from this consideration in reference to both cases.*

(1.) If God is about to employ us in any service,

[1.] We have little need to be *confident of our abilities or performance*, when we know that temptations wait for us.

[2.] We must not only be sensible of our weakness, that we be not confident; but we must be *apprehensive of the strength and power of God to carry us through*, that we be not discouraged.

[3.] We must see our *opposition*, that we may be watchful; and yet must we refuse to give it the least place of consideration in our debates of duty, lest it sway us against duty or dishearten us in it.

(2.) If God be pleased to honour us with peculiar favours, then,

[1.] Though we must improve them to the full, yet must we not feed on them without fear.

[2.] We must not stay in the enjoyment or play with the token, but look to the tendency of such favours and improve them to duty, as to their proper end.

CHAPTER II.

The second circumstance, Christ's being led by the Spirit.—What hand the Spirit of God hath in temptations.—And of running into temptation when not led into it.

2. The second circumstance acquaints *how Christ was carried to the combat.* In solemn combats and duels, the persons undertaking the fight were usually carried to the place with great solemnity and ceremony. Christ in this spiritual battle is described as having the conduct of the Spirit, ' He was led up of the Spirit,' &c. What this Spirit was is, though by a needless and over-officious diligence, questioned by some; but we need not stay much upon it, if we consider the phrase of the evangelists, who mention *Spirit* without any note of distinction—which of necessity must have been added if it had intended either his proper spirit as man, or the wicked spirit Satan—directing thereby to understand it of him to whom the word Spirit is more peculiarly attributed, viz., the Holy Ghost. Or if we observe the close connexion in Luke betwixt that expression of Christ's being ' full of the Holy Ghost,' and his being ' led by the Spirit,' it will be out of controversy that the Holy Spirit is here intended. Hence was it that Beza translates it more fully, ' Jesus being full of the Holy Ghost, was led, *eodem Spiritu*, of the same Spirit;' and the Syriac, in Matthew, doubts not to express it by the Holy Spirit. And what else can be imagined, when in this text the Spirit that led him up, and the

devil that tempted, are mentioned in so direct an opposition? 'He was led of the Spirit into the wilderness to be tempted of the devil.' The manner of his being carried thither is expressed by such words as signify, though not an external rapture like that of Philip, a strong inward motion and impulse upon him. The Spirit driveth—ἐκβάλλεν —him, saith Mark. The Spirit 'led him'—ἤγετο—saith Luke, using the same word by which the Scripture elsewhere expresseth the power of the Spirit upon the children of God, who are said to be 'led' by him.

Obs. 2. Hence note *that the Spirit of God hath a hand in temptations.* Christ was led by the Spirit to be tempted. This must not be understood as if God did properly tempt any to sin, either by enticing their hearts to evil, or by moving and suggesting wicked things to their minds, or by infusing evil inclinations, or by any proper compliance with Satan to undermine and delude us by any treachery or deceit. None of these can be imagined without apparent derogation to the holiness of God, 'who tempteth no man, neither can he be tempted with evil,' [James i. 13.] But what we are to understand by the Holy Spirit's concerning himself in temptations, is included in these particulars:—

1. First, God gives *commission to Satan*, without which his hand would be sealed up under an impossibility of reaching it out against any.

2. Secondly, *Opportunities and occasions do depend upon his providence*, without which nothing comes to pass. Neither we nor anything else do or can move without him.

3. Thirdly, The Spirit *oversees the temptation as to measure and continuance.* The length and breadth of it is ordered by him.

4. Fourthly, *The issue and consequences of every temptation are at his appointment.* The ways of its working for our exercise, humiliation, or conviction, or for any other good and advantage whatsoever, they all belong to his determination.

So that it is not improper to assert that God and Satan do concur in the same temptation, though the ways of proceeding, with the aims and intentions of both, be directly different and contrary. Hence is it that the temptation of David, 1 Sam. xxiv. 1, and 1 Chron. xxi. 1, are upon several regards attributed both to God and Satan.

Appl. 1. This note is of use to remove those harsh interpretations which poor tempted Christians meet withal, commonly from such as have not touched their burdens with the least of their fingers. Men are apt in these cases to judge,

(1.) First, *The ways of religion, as being ways, at least in the more serious and rigid practice of them, of intolerable hazard and perplexity*, and only upon an observation that those who most addict themselves to a true and strict observance of duty and command usually complain of temptations, and express sometimes their fears and distress of heart about them. This is your reading, your praying, and hearing. Such preaching, say they, leads men to despair and perpetual disquiet; and upon the whole they conclude it dangerous to be religious above the common rate of those that prosecute it in a slow and careless indifferency.

(2.) Secondly, The like severity of censure do they use in reference to *the spiritual state of the tempted*, as if they were vessels of his hatred, and such as were by him given up to the power of this ' wild boar of the forest' to devour and tear. All kind of distresses are obnoxious to the worst of misjudgings from malevolent minds. The sufferings of Christ produced this censorious scoff, ' Let God deliver him, if he will have him,' [Mat. xxvii. 43.] David's troubles easily induced his adversaries to conclude that ' God had forsaken him, and that there was none to deliver him,' Ps. lxxi. 11. But in troubles of this nature, where especially there are frightful complainings against themselves, men are more easily drawn out to be peremptory in their uncharitable determinations concerning them, because the trouble itself is somewhat rare, and apt to beget hideous impressions; and withal the vent which the afflicted parties give by their bemoaning of their estate, in hope to ease themselves thereby, is but taken as a testimony against themselves, and the undoubted echoes of their real feelings.

(3.) Thirdly, *Their sins are upon this ground misjudged and heightened.* Unusual troubles with common apprehension argue unusual sins. The viper upon Paul's hand made the barbarians confident he was a man of more than ordinary guilt and wickedness, Acts xxviii. 4. David's sickness was enough to give his enemies occasion to surmise that it was the punishment of some great transgression. ' An evil disease,' say they, ' cleaveth to him,' Ps. xli. 8. Those that were overwhelmed by the fall of the tower of Siloam, and those whose blood Pilate mixed with their sacrifices, were judged greatest sinners, Luke xiii. 4. But in inward temptations, this misjudging confidence is every way more heightened; and those that are most molested are supposed to have given more away to Satan.

(4.) Fourthly, Temptations are also misjudged *to be worse than they are.* They are indeed things to be trembled at; but they are not properly of an astonishing, amazing, or despairing consideration, as men are apt to think that view the workings of them at a distance.

Against all those unrighteous surmises, the poor afflicted servants of Christ may have relief from this truth in hand, that the Holy Spirit of God hath a hand in temptations: and therefore it is impossible that everywhere they should be of such a signification. Were they in themselves no way serviceable to God's glory in the gracious exercise of his children, the Spirit of wisdom and holiness would not at all have a hand in them. If under Satan's assaults you meet with those that by such a harshness of censure would aggravate your troubles, and so grieve those whom God hath saddened, you may boldly appeal from them to him that judgeth righteously. And indeed, if men would but consider, in the saddest case of this nature, either,

[1.] *The end of the Lord in permitting temptations*, which, if seen, would give a high justification of his dealing, and force men to applaud and magnify his wisdom, rather than to censure it. Or,

[2.] If they could but see the *secret ways of God's support*, how he acts his part in holding them by the hand, in counterworking of Satan, and confounding him under the exercise of his highest malice, and also in the ways of his preservation and deliverance. Or,

[3.] *If the harmlessness of temptations, when their sting is taken out, were but weighed,* men would change their minds as readily as the barbarians did, when they saw the viper not effect that mischief they supposed upon Paul; and would see cause to stand amazed at the contrivances of so much power and wisdom, as can turn these to quite other ends and uses, than what they of themselves seem to threaten.

Applic. 2. This consideration will further express its usefulness *in comforting us under temptations.* It might have been Paul's great discouragement, that in his answer before Nero no man stood with him, 2 Tim. iv. 16; but this was his support, that God was with him. The like encouragement we have under all assaults of Satan, that we are not left to ourselves, but the Spirit of God is with us, and that he concerns himself on a design to oversee and overrule his work, and to put a check upon him when there is need. So that he cannot tempt as he will, nor when he will, nor in what he would, nor as long as he would; but that in all cases, we may rely upon the great master-contriver, for relief, help, mitigation, or deliverance, as there is need.

Obs. 3. In that the evangelists do not say that Christ cast himself upon a temptation, neither did go to undertake it till he was led to it, we note, *that whatever may be the advantage of a temptation by the Spirit's ordering of it, or what security from danger we may promise to ourselves upon that account, yet must we not run upon temptations; though we must submit when we are fairly led into them.* The reasons of this truth are these:—

(1.) First, There is so much of *the nature of evil in temptations that they are to be avoided if possible.* Good they may accidentally be, that is, beyond their proper nature and tendency, by the overruling hand of God; but being in their own natural constitution evil, it is inconsistent with human nature to desire them as such.

(2.) Secondly, *To run upon them would be a dangerous tempting of God;* that is, making a bold and presumptuous trial, without call, whether he will put forth his power to rescue us or not. Now he that runs upon a temptation hath no promise to be delivered out of it. And besides, runs upon so desperate a provocation, that in all probability he shall miscarry in it, as a just punishment of his rashness.

Quest. But inquiry may be made, When do men run uncalled and unwarrantably upon temptation? I answer, many ways. As,

Ans. [1.] First, When men engage themselves *in sin and apparent wickedness, in the works of the flesh.* For it can never be imagined that the holy God should ever by his Spirit call any to such things as his soul abhors.

[2.] Secondly, When men run upon *the visible and apparent occasions and causes of sin.* This is like a man's going to the pest-house. Thus do they, that though they design not to be actors in evil, yet will give their company and countenance to persons actually engaged in evil.

[3.] Thirdly, When men *unnecessarily, without the conduct either of command or urging an unavoidable providence, do put themselves, though not upon visible and certain opportunities, yet, upon dangerous and hazardous occasions and snares.* Peter had no errand in the high-priest's hall; his curiosity led him thither; he might easily have foreseen a probable snare; but confidently putting himself forward, where his danger was more than his business, he ran upon the temptation, and accordingly fell. The like did Dinah, when she made a needless vagary to see the daughters of the land; where she met with her sin and shame, Gen. xxxiv. 1. Neither do they otherwise, who dare adventure themselves in families—whilst yet they are free and may otherwise dispose of themselves—where they see snares and temptations will be laid before them. The case indeed is otherwise to those that are under the necessary engagement of relation, natural or voluntary, if it be antecedent to the hazard, to live in such places or callings; they have a greater promise of preservation than others can lay claim to, Ps. xci. 11 ; Prov. x. 29.

[4.] Fourthly, Those run upon temptation, that adventure *apparently beyond their strength, and put themselves upon actions good or harmless, disproportionably to their abilities.* The apostle gives the instance in marriage abstinence, 1 Cor. vii. 5, which he cautions may not be undertaken at a careless adventure for fear of a temptation: and by this may we judge other things of like nature.

[5.] Fifthly, They are also guilty that design an *adventure unto the utmost bounds of lawful liberty.* Those that have a mind to try conclusions, how near they may make their approaches to sin, and yet keep off from the defilement, such as would divide a hair betwixt good and evil, have at best but a hair's breadth betwixt them and sin ; but how easily are they brought over that. Like a man that walks upon the utmost verge of a river's brink, ofttimes meets with hollow ground and a dangerous slip before he is aware.

[6.] Sixthly, Those also may be reckoned in the number of such as rush upon their danger, *who go abroad without their weapons, and forget in the midst of daily dangers the means of preservation.* Thomas, by his neglect, slid into a greater unbelief than the rest of the apostles. David's unwatchful heart was easily smitten by the intelligence which his eyes brought him. They that would plead their innocency against temptation had need to carry their arms and preservatives still with them.

Applic. This truth is a sufficient caution against the *rash adventurousness of those who forwardly engage themselves in matters of temptation.* As the former observation told us, temptations are not to be feared, so this also tells they are not to be slighted. The carriage of the Philistines when the ark came among them is matter of imitation to us. We may tremble justly when we hear of their approach, but our hazard should be the whetstone of our courage, and our danger should bring us to resolves of a more stout resistance, that we may 'quit ourselves like men.'

The apostle, Gal. vi. 1, seems to imply, when he tells those that were more severe and careless of others, that 'they may also be tempted,' that the best of men do little know what a change a temptation may make upon them; a small temptation may be too strong for them, and may carry them to what they never thought of; nay, may break down the strongest of their resolves, and snap their purposes as a thread in a flame. It did so with Peter, who was quickly overcome by that which he had with so much confidence undervalued.

CHAPTER III.

The third circumstance, the place of the combat.—The advantage given to temptations by solitude.

3. The third circumstance next to be considered is *the place of this combat, 'the wilderness.'* To inquire what or where this wilderness was, is not only impertinent and useless, as to anything we can observe from it in reference to temptation, but also a matter of mere uncertain conjecture; only they that would understand it of a place more thinly peopled are expressly contradicted by Mark i. 13, where it is said, 'he was with the wild beasts;' noting thereby a desolate and dangerous solitude, far remote from human society and comfort.

It is much more our concern to seek after the reasons of his choice of that place, or rather among those many that are given, to satisfy ourselves with what may have the greatest appearance of truth. They that think Christ hereby designed to shew the uncertain changes and vicissitudes of outward things in this life, or to point at the future low estate of his church in the world, that it should sojourn in a wilderness; or to direct those that have dedicated themselves to God to withdraw from the blandishments and allurements of the earth, with a great many more hints of instruction and document of that kind; they, I say, that offer no other, seem not to attend to the true design of the choice of this place, which notwithstanding is evidently discovered to have been done in order to the temptation.[1] 'He was led into the wilderness *to be tempted.*' The place then was subservient to the conflict, as the proper theatre on which so great a contest was to be acted. And if we shall but mind what special consideration was to be had of such a place,—a howling desolate wilderness,—we may with ease pitch upon these following reasons:—

(1.) First, It pleased God to have an eye to *the glory of Christ's conquests*, when in a single combat he should so remarkably foil the devil, without any the least advantage on his part, there being none that might be the least support or encouragement to him.

(2.) Secondly, The condition of the place *gave rise to the first temptation.* For in that he 'hungered' in a barren wilderness, it gave occasion to Satan to tempt him more strongly to 'turn stones into bread.'

(3.) Thirdly, In the choice of such a place God seems to offer Satan a special *advantage in tempting*, which was the solitude and danger of his present condition.

To omit the two former considerations, as not altogether so useful,

[1] Spanheim, Dub. Evan. *in loc.*

further than what I shall be engaged to speak to afterwards, this last affords this observation:

Obs. 4. *That solitude affords a great advantage to Satan in the matter of temptation.* This advantage ariseth from solitude two ways:

(1.) First, *As it doth deprive us of help.* So great and many are the blessed helps arising from the society and communion of such as fear the Lord, as counsel, comfort, encouragement from their graces, experiences, and prayers, &c., that the woe pronounced to him 'that is alone' is not groundless, Eccles. iv. 10. Christians in a holy combination can do more work, and so have a good reward for their labour. They can mutually help one another when they fall; they can mutually heat and warm one another; they can also strengthen one another's hands to prevail against an adversary. He then that is alone, being deprived of these advantages, lieth more open to the stroke of temptation.

(2.) Secondly, *Solitude increaseth melancholy,* fills the soul with dismal apprehensions; and withal doth so spoil and alter the temper of it that it is not only ready to take any disadvantageous impression, but it doth also dispose it to leaven and sour those very considerations that should support, and to put a bad construction on things that never were intended for its hurt.

Applic. This may warn us to take heed of giving Satan so great an advantage against us, *as an unnecessary solitude may do.* I know there are times and occasions that do justly require us to seek a solitary place for the privacy of duty, or for secret lamentations, as Jeremiah desired, chap. ix. 1, 2, or to avoid the trouble and snare arising from our mixing with an assembly of treacherous and wicked men. This is no more than care and watchfulness. But when these reasons urge not, or some of like nature, but either out of pettish discontent or a mopish reservedness, we withdraw from those aids and comforts which are necessary for our support, we do strengthen Satan's hands against us and weaken our own.

CHAPTER IV.

The fourth circumstance, the end wherefore Christ was led to the wilderness.—Holiness, employment, privileges, exempt not from temptation.—Of temptations that leave not impressions of sin behind them.—How Satan's temptations are distinguished from the lusts of our own heart.

4. The fourth circumstance was *the end.* There was no other design in the main of Christ's being led up and into the wilderness, but that he might be 'tempted.' In this two things seem to be matter of equal wonder:—

(1.) First, *Why Christ would submit to be tempted.* For this many great and weighty reasons may be given. As,

[1.] First, Thus was Christ *evidenced to be the second Adam, and the seed of the woman.* His being tempted, and in such a manner, doth clearly satisfy us that he was true man ; and that in that nature he it was that was promised ' to break the serpent's head.'

[2.] Secondly, This was a fair *preludium and earnest of that final conquest over Satan, and the breaking down of his power.*

[3.] Thirdly, There was a more peculiar aim in God by these means of temptation to qualify him with *pity and power to help,* ' For in that he suffered being tempted, he is able to succour them that are tempted,' Heb. ii. 18. And having experience of temptation himself, he became a merciful high-priest, apt to be ' touched with the feeling of our infirmities,' Heb. iv. 15.

[4.] Fourthly, *The consequence of this experimental compassion in Christ,* was a further reason why he submitted to be tempted, to wit, that we might have the greater comfort and encouragement in the expectancy of tender dealing from him. Hence the apostle, Heb. iv. 16, invites to ' come boldly to the throne of grace at any time of need.'

[5.] Fifthly, A further end God seemed to have in this, viz., *to give a signal and remarkable instance to us of the nature of temptations;* of Satan's subtlety, his impudency, of the usual temptations which we may expect ; as also to teach us what weapons are necessary for resistance, and in what manner we must manage them.

(2.) Secondly, It seems as strange that Satan would *undertake a thing so unfeasible and hopeless as the tempting of Christ.* What expectation could he have to prevail against him, who was ' anointed with the oil of gladness above his fellows' ? [Ps. xlv. 7.] Some answer,

[1.] First, That Satan might possibly *doubt whether Christ were the Son of God or no.* But the improbability of this I shall speak of afterwards.

[2.] Secondly, Others attribute it to his *malice,* which indeed is great, and might possibly blind him to a desperate undertaking. But,

[3.] Thirdly, We may justly apprehend *the power of sin over Satan to be so great that it might enforce him to the bold attempt of such a wickedness.* We see daily that wicked men, by the force of their own wicked principles, are restlessly hurried upon acts of sin, though they know the prohibition, and are not ignorant of the threatened danger. Satan is as great a slave to his own internal corrupt principles as any. And whatsoever blind fury is stirred up in man by the power of his lust, we may very well suppose the like in Satan.

[4.] Fourthly, *There is a superior hand upon the devil, that sways, limits, and orders him in his temptations.* He cannot tempt when he would, neither always what he would, but in his own cursed inclinations and the acting of them, he is forced to be subservient to God's designs. And in this particular, whatever might be Satan's proper end or principle, it is evident that God carried on a gracious design for the instruction and comfort of his children.

The end of Christ's going to the wilderness being that he might be tempted, if together with this the holiness and dignity of Christ in respect of his person and office be considered, we may note from it,

Obs. 5. *That neither height of privilege, nor eminency of employment, nor holiness of person, will discourage Satan from tempting, or secure any from his assaults.* The best of men in the highest attainments may expect temptations. Grace itself doth not exempt them.

(1.) For first, None of these privileges *in us, nor eminencies of grace, want matter to fix a temptation upon.* The weaknesses of the best of men are such that a temptation is not rendered improbable, as to the success, by their graces. Nay, there are special occasions and inclinations in them, to encourage temptations of pride and neglect. He found indeed nothing in Christ that might offer the least probability of prevalency; but in the best of men, in their best estate, he can find some encouragement for his attempts.

(2.) Secondly, None of us are beyond *the necessity of such exercises.* It cannot be said that we need them not, or that there may not be holy ends wherefore God should not permit and order them for our good. Temptations, as they are in God's disposal, are a necessary spiritual physic. The design of them is to humble us, to prove us, and to do us good in the latter end, Deut. viii. 16. Nothing will work more of care, watchfulness, diligence, and fear in a gracious heart, than a sense of Satan's designment against it. Nothing puts a man more to prayer, breathing after God, desiring to be dissolved, and running to Christ, than the troublesome and afflictive pursuits of Satan. Nothing brings men more from the love of the world, and to a delight in the ordinances of God, than the trouble which here abides them unavoidably from Satan. This discipline the best have need of. There are such remainders of pride and other evils in them, that if God should not permit these pricks and thorns to humble them, and thereby also awaken them to laborious watchfulness, they would be careless, secure, and sadly declining. This made Augustine conclude that it was no way expedient that we should want temptations,[1] and that Christ taught us as much when he directed us not to pray that we should 'not be tempted,' but that we might not be 'led into the power and prevalency of temptation.'

(3.) Thirdly, *The privileges and graces of the children of God do stir up Satan's pride, revenge, and rage against them.* And though he hath no encouragement to expect so easy a conquest over these as he hath over others, who are captivated by him at pleasure; yet hath he encouragements to attempt them, for the singular use and advantage he makes of any success against them, the difficulty of the work being recompensed by the greatness of the booty. For the fall of a child of God, especially of such as are noted above others, is as when 'a standard-bearer fainteth,' [Isa. x. 18;] or as the fall of an oak, that bears down with it the lower shrubs that stand near it. How the hearts of others fail for fear, lest they should also be overcome; how the hearts of some grow thereby bold and venturesome; how a general disgrace and discredit thereby doth accrue to religion, and the sincere profession of it, are things of usual observation. If such men had not in them something of special prey in case of conquest, his pride would not so readily carry him against the heads and chief of the people, while he seems to overlook the meaner and weaker. Out-houses, though more accessible, are not the objects of the thief's design, but the dwelling-house, though stronger built and better guarded, because it affords hopes of richer spoil, is usually assaulted. Neither do pirates so much

---

[1] Non nobis expedit esse sine tentationibus; non rogamus ut non tentemur, sed ne inducat in tentationem.—*Aug. in Ps.* lxxiii.

set themselves to take empty vessels, though weakly manned, but richly laden ships, though better able to make resistance, are the ships of their desire.

Applic. 1. This may be applied for *the encouraging of those that think it strange that temptations do so haunt them,* especially that they should, in their apprehension, be more troubled by him when they fly furthest from him. The consideration of this will much allay these thoughts, by these inferences which it affords:—

(1.) First, *There is nothing unusual befalls these complainants.* Satan frequently doth so to others; they cannot justly say their case is singular, or that they are alone in such disturbances; it is but what is common to man. If they urge the uncessantness of the devil's attempts, Christ and others have felt the like. If they object the peculiar strangeness and horridness of the temptation, as most unsuitable to the state of an upright soul, Christ met with the like. He was tempted to self-destruction, to distrust, to blasphemy itself in the highest degree.

(2.) Secondly, *There is a good advantage to be made of them:* they are preservations from other sins that would otherwise grow upon us.

(3.) Thirdly, These temptations to the upright do but argue Satan's *loss of interest in them, and their greater sensibility of the danger.* The captivated sinners complain not so much, because they are so inured to temptation that they mind not Satan's frequent accesses. He that studies humility is more sensible of a temptation to pride than he that is proud.[1]

2. Secondly, This is also of use to those that are apt to be *confident upon their successes against sin through grace.* Satan, they may see, will be upon them again; so that they must behave themselves as mariners, who, when they have got the harbour, and are out of the storm, mend their ship and tackling, and prepare again for the sea.

Lastly, If we consider the unspotted holiness of Christ, and his constant integrity under these temptations, that they left not the least of taint or sinful impression upon him, we may observe,

Obs. 6. *That there may be temptations, without leaving a touch of guilt or impurity behind them upon the tempted.*

It is true this is rare with men. The best do seldom go down to the battle, but in their very conquests they receive some wound; and in those temptations that arise from our own hearts, we are never without fault; but in such as do solely arise from Satan, there is a possibility that the upright may so keep himself, that the wicked one may not so touch him as to leave the print of his fingers behind him.

Quest. But the great difficulty is, How it may be known when temptations are from Satan, and when from ourselves?

Ans. To answer this I shall lay down these conclusions:—

(1.) First, The same sins which *our own natures would suggest to us, may also be injected by Satan.* Sometimes we begin by the forward working of our own thoughts upon occasions and objects presented to us from without, or from the power of our own inclination, without the offer of external objects, and then Satan strikes in with it.

---

[1] Tentationem experiuntur ac sentiunt hi, qui ex animo pietati student.—*Musculus, in loc.*

Sometimes Satan begins with us, and by his injected motions endeavours to excite our inclinations; so that the same thing may be sometime from ourselves, and sometimes from Satan.

(2.) Secondly, *There is no sin so vile, but our own heart might possibly produce it without Satan.* Evil thoughts of the very worst kind, as of murders, adulteries, thefts, false witness, and blasphemies may, as Christ speaks, Mat. xv. 19, be produced naturally from our own hearts; for seminally all sins, the very greatest of all impieties, are there. So that from the greatness and vileness of the temptation we cannot absolutely conclude that it is from Satan, no more than from the commonness of the temptation, or its suitableness to our inclination, we can conclude infallibly that its first rise is from ourselves.

(3.) Thirdly, There are many cases wherein it *is very difficult, if not altogether impossible, to determine whether our own heart or Satan gives the first life or breathing to a temptation.* Who can determine, in most ordinary cases, when our thoughts are working upon objects presented to our senses, whether Satan or our own thoughts do run faster? Yea, when such thoughts are not the consequent of any former occasion, it is a work too hard for most men to determine which of the parents, father or mother, our own heart or Satan, is first in the fault. They are both forward enough, and usually join hand in hand with such readiness, that he must have a curious eye that can discover certainly to whom the first beginning is to be ascribed.

The difficulty is so great, that some have judged it altogether impossible to give any certain marks by which it may be determined when they are ours and when Satan's.[1] And indeed the discoveries laid down by some are not sufficient for a certain determination; and so far I assent, that neither the suddenness of such thoughts—for the motions of our own lusts may be sudden—nor the horridness of the matter of them, are sufficient notes of distinction. That our own corrupt hearts may bring forth that which is unnatural and terrible, cannot be denied. Many of the sins of the heathens mentioned in Rom. i. were the violent productions of lust against natural principles; and to ascribe these to the devil, as to the first instigator, is more than any man hath warrant to do. Yet though it be confessed that in some cases it is impossible to distinguish, and that where a distinction may be made, these notes mentioned are not fully satisfactory, there may, I believe, be some cases wherein there is a possibility to discover when the motions are from Satan, and that by the addition of some remarkable circumstances to the fore-named marks of difference.

(4.) Fourthly, Though it be true, which some say,[2] that in most cases it is needless altogether to spend our time in disputing whether the motions of sin in our minds are firstly from ourselves or from Satan, our greatest business being rather to resist them than to difference them; *yet there are special cases wherein it is very necessary to find out the true parent of a sinful motion,* and these are when tender consciences are wounded and oppressed with violent and great temptations, as blasphemous thoughts, atheistical objections, &c. For here Satan in his furious molestations aims mainly at this, that such afflicted and tossed souls should take all these thoughts which are

---

[1] Capel, 'Tempt.,' part 1, cap. 4, sec. 1.   [2] *Ibid.*, part 1, cap. 4.

obtruded upon their imaginations, to be the issue of their own heart. As Joseph's steward hid the cup in Benjamin's sack, that it might be a ground of accusation against him, so doth the devil first oppress them with such thoughts, and then accuseth them of all that villainy and wickedness, the motions whereof he had with such importunity forced upon them; and so apt are the afflicted to comply with accusations against themselves, that they believe it is so, and from thence conclude that they are given up of God, hardened as Pharaoh, that they have sinned against the Holy Ghost, and finally that there is no hope of mercy for them. All this befalls them from their ignorance of Satan's dealings, and here is their great need to distinguish Satan's malice from their guilt.

(5.) Fifthly, Setting aside ordinary temptations, wherein it is neither so possible nor so material to busy ourselves to find out whether they are Satan's or ours;—in extraordinary temptations, such as have been now instanced, we may discover if they proceed from Satan, though not simply from the matter of them, not from the suddenness and independency of them, yet from *a due consideration of their nature and manner of proceeding, compared with the present temper and disposition of our heart.* As,

[1.] First, *When unusual temptations intrude upon us with a high impetuosity and violence, while our thoughts are otherwise concerned and taken up.*[1] Temptations more agreeable to our inclination, though suddenly arising from objects and occasions presented, and gradually proceeding, after the manner of the working of natural passions, may throng in amidst our thoughts or actions that have no tendency that way, and yet we cannot so clearly accuse Satan for them; but when things that have not the encouragement of our affections are by a sudden violence enforced upon us, while we are otherwise concerned, we may justly suspect Satan's hand to be in them.

[2.] Secondly, While such things are borne in upon us, against the *actual loathing, strenuous reluctancy, and high complainings of the soul, when the mind is filled with horror and the body with trembling at the presence of such thoughts.*[2] Sins that owe their first original to ourselves, may indeed be resisted upon their first rising up in our mind; and though a sanctified heart doth truly loathe them, yet they are not without some lower degree of tickling delight upon the affections; for the flesh in those cases presently riseth up with its lustings for the sinful motion; but when such unnatural temptations are from Satan, their first appearance to the mind is a horror without any sensible working of inclination towards them; and the greatness of the soul's disquiet doth shew that it hath met with that which the affections look not on with any amicable compliance.

[3.] Thirdly, Our hearts may bring forth that which is *unnatural in itself, and may give rise to a temptation that would be horrid to*

---

[1] Illæ plerumque suggerunt, quæ naturæ gratiora, idque placide et gradatim, ita ut mens sui compos maneat in ipso æstu, hæ autem impetu plusquam humano irruentes, fulguris instar, ocyus quam solent passiones dianoeticæ, &c.—*Arrowsmith, Tactica [Sacra] I.,* lib. ii. cap. 7, sec. 6.

[2] Horrore sui si implent animum, ut tantum non pectus ipsum expectorare videantur, dum ea perpetim dictitari sentit, et dolet, ad quoque præsentiam, natura vel depravatissima contremiscet.—*Idem, Ibid.*

the thoughts of other men, but that it should of its own accord, without a tempter, on a sudden bring forth that which is directly contrary to its present light, reason, or inclination; as for a man to be haunted with thoughts of atheism, while he is under firm persuasions that there is a God; or of blasphemy, while he is under designs of honouring him, is as unimaginable as that our thoughts should of themselves contrive our death, while we are most solicitous for our life; or that our thoughts should soberly tell us it is night when we see the sun shine. Temptations that are contrary to the present state, posture, light, and disposition of the soul are Satan's. They are so unnatural as to its present frame, that the production of them must be from some other agent.

[4.] Fourthly, Much more evident is it that such proceed from Satan, when they are of *long continuance and constant trouble*, when they so incessantly beat upon the mind, that it hath no rest from them, and yet is under grievous perplexities and anxieties of mind about them.

Applic. The consideration of this is of great use to those that suffer under the violent hurries of strange temptations.

(1.) First, In that sometime they can justly complain of *the affliction of such temptation*, when they have no reason to charge it upon themselves as their sin. It is one thing to be tempted, and another to consent or comply. To be tempted, and not to be brought into temptation, is not evil. Satan only barks when he suggests, but he then bites and wounds when he draws us to consent.[1]

(2.) Secondly, That not only the *sin but the degree also*, by just consequence, is to be measured by the consent of the heart. If we consent not, the sin is not ours, and the less degree of consent we give, the less is in the sin.

CHAPTER V.

And when he had fasted forty days and forty nights, he was afterwards an hungered.—Mat. iv. 2.

Of Christ's fast, with the design thereof.—Of Satan's tempting in an invisible way.—Of his incessant importunities, and how he flies when resisted.—Of inward temptations, with outward afflictions.—Several advantages Satan hath by tempting in affliction.

I am next to explain *the fast of Christ, the end and design whereof,* because it is not expressly mentioned, is variously conjectured. Not to insist in this discourse, which is designed for practice, on the controversy about the Quadragesimal fast, that which I shall first consider is the opinion of Musculus,[2] who, upon this ground that his fast was not the principal thing for which the Spirit led him into the wilderness; for he was not led to fast, but to be tempted—thereupon concludes,

---

[1] Aliud est tentari, aliud tentationem recipere. Tentari et non in tentationem ferri non est malum.—*Aug., De Bono Persever.*, lib. ii. cap. 6. Mordet Satan cum ad consensum trahit, latrat solum cum suggerit.—*Bernard.* [2] Musculus, *in loc.*

that this was only a consequent of his solitary condition in the wilderness, and no other thing than what befell Moses and Elias, who being engaged by God to attend him in such a service, where the ordinary means of the support of life were wanting, were therefore kept alive by him in an extraordinary way without them. Thus he thinks the fasting was not, at least principally, designed, but that he being to undergo a temptation in a desolate wilderness where he had no meat to eat, there God restrained his hunger, so that he neither desired nor needed any. If we acquiesce in this, it will afford this doctrine:—

Doct. 1. *That when God leads forth his children to such services as shall unavoidably deprive them of the ordinary means of help or supply, there God is engaged to give extraordinary support, and his people may expect it accordingly.*

This is a great truth in itself, and a great and necessary encouragement to all the children of God that are called out to straits; but I shall not insist on this as the genuine product of this fast.

If we look further amongst protestant divines, we shall observe it taken for granted, that Christ fasted upon design, and this is generally reduced to those two heads:—

(1.) First, Either for *instruction*: as to shew that he was *God, by fasting so long*, and that under the trouble of molesting and disquieting temptations; whereas the fasts of like date in Moses or Elias were accompanied with the quiet repose of their thoughts; or to shew that he was *man, in that he really felt the natural infirmities of the human nature, in being hungry;* or to teach us *the usefulness of fasting in the general*, when fit occasions invite us thereto; or,

(2.) Secondly, *For confirmation of his doctrine*, to put an honour and dignity upon his employment;[1] as Elias fasted at the restoring of prophecy, and at the Reformation. As Moses fasted at the writing of the law, so Christ began the gospel of the kingdom with fasting. However, that these things cannot be spoken against, being conclusions warrantably deducible from this act of Christ's; yet these seem not, in my apprehension, to come fully up to the proper end of this undertaking of his; which seems not obscurely to be laid before us in that passage of Luke iv. 2, 'being forty days tempted of the devil; and in those days he did eat nothing;' where we see that his being 'tempted forty days' was the principal thing, and that his fasting had a plain reference and respect to his temptation. Thus far, I suppose, we may be secure, that we have the design in the general, that his fasting was in order to his temptation. But then whether this was designed as an occasion of the temptations, or as a remedy against them, it is not so easy to determine. That one of those, at least, was intended, cannot be denied by those that will grant that his fast related to the combat; and it seems not to labour of any repugnacy or absurdity, if we say that it is possible that both these ends might be aimed at, and accordingly I shall proceed to observe upon them. There are only some other things to be first despatched out of the way: as

The continuance of the fast, why it was forty days, neither more nor less. Though some adventure to give reasons for it,[2] not only papists, who, according to their wont, are ridiculous and trifling in

---

[1] *Vide* Lightfoot, Harm. *in loc.*   [2] Spanheim, Dub. Evan. *in loc.*

this matter; but also protestants, supposing that some regard was, or ought to be, had to his fulfilling the times of the fasts of Moses and Elias; yet I think it is neither pertinent nor safe to determine anything about it, only it observes to us that the continuance of this was a considerable time.

We are more concerned to inquire whether Christ was under any conflict of temptation all that time;[1] which although some deny, lest they should favour a seeming contradiction among the evangelists, yet the words of Luke are so express, 'being forty days tempted of the devil,' Luke iv. 2, that no tolerable evasion can be found to cast these temptations to the end of the forty days; for he tells us, he was not only tempted after the expiration of the forty days, but that he was tempted during the continuance of the forty days beside; only there was a difference in the kinds of these temptations, in regard of the way wherein Satan managed them, and this also is fully set down by Matthew, 'And when the tempter came to him,' which with the other expression of Luke compared, shews us, that during the space of the forty days Satan tempted Christ, and yet came not to him till afterward—that is, he managed those temptations in an invisible way. Hence we may note,

Doct. 2. *That Satan doth usually tempt in an invisible way and manner.* To explain this a little, I shall evidence it by a few considerations. As,

(1.) First, *That he hath a hand in all sins first or last, and then it must needs be in an invisible way.* His work is to tempt, to go about laying snares to draw men to sin. Wicked men are 'of their father the devil,' John viii. 44, and do his works. Carnal desires are 'his lusts;' giving way to anger is 'giving place to the devil,' Eph. iv. 26, 27, and resisting of sin is called in the general, 'a resisting of the devil,' &c., James iv. 7. In all this work of Satan, men do not see him. When he puts evil motions into their hearts they do not perceive him, and therefore doth he his work in an invisible way.

(2.) Secondly, We have sufficient discoveries of these private paths of his: for, [1.] Sometime he tempts by *friends:* he tempted Job by his wife, Christ by Peter. [2.] Sometime by *external objects*, as he drew out Achan's covetousness, and David's uncleanness, by the eye. [3.] Sometime by *injecting thoughts and motions* to our mind. [4.] Sometime by exercising an *invisible power upon our bodies*, in stirring up the humours thereof, to provoke to passion or excessive mirth. All these ways, of which I have discoursed before more largely, are secret and invisible, and by such as these he most usually tempts.

(3.) Thirdly, *The wiles, depths, secrets, and devices of Satan*, which the Scripture tells us are his most familiar ways and courses, they in their own nature imply a studied or designed secrecy and imperceptibility.

(4.) Fourthly, He hath peculiar *reasons of policy* for his invisible way of dealing; for the less visible he is, the less suspicious are his designs, and consequently the less frightful and more taking. By this way he insinuates himself so into our bosoms, that he gets a party in us against ourselves before we are aware; whereas in vain he knows

[1] Spanheim, *in loc.*

he should spread his net if his designs and enmity were discovered to us.

Applic. This must teach us to suspect Satan where we see him not, and so to converse with objects and occasions as still fearing that there may be *anguis in herba,* a secret snare laid for us to entrap us at unawares.

If we again cast our eyes upon what hath been said, that Christ was tempted 'all the forty days,' it will then give us this observation:—

Doct. 3. *That Satan is sometime incessant in temptations, and sets upon us with continued importunities.*

Here we may note a distinction of temptations, besides that of invisible and visible, of which I have spoken, that some are moveable and short fits, and as it were skirmishes, in which he stays not long, and others are more fixed and durable. We may call them solemn temptations, in which Satan doth, as it were, pitch down his tents, and doth manage a long siege against us. Of these last sort is this observation.

Thus he tempted Paul, continuing his assault for some time before he departed, 2 Cor. xii. 8. Thus also he dealt with Joseph, who was solicited day by day for a long time together, Gen. xxxix. 10. Of these I shall note a few things. As,

(1.) First, Such temptations are not without a *special commission.* He cannot indeed tempt at all without leave, but in the ordinary course of his temptations he hath a general commission under such restraints and limitations as pleaseth the Most High to put upon him; but in these he must have a special order, as we see in Job's case.

(2.) Secondly, Such temptations have also *a special ground.* Either the present state and posture of our condition is such as Satan apprehends highly advantageous for his design, and therefore he desires to have the winnowing of us at such a season; or there are more than ordinary dispositions and inclinations in our heart to what we are directly tempted to, or to some other consequent design. These animate and encourage him to high resolves of prosecuting us more closely, upon an expectation that a continued solicitation is most likely to prevail at the long run.

(3.) Thirdly, It is possible that such temptations *may stand out against the endeavours of many prayers,* and that we shall find they are not so easily shaken off as the viper that was upon Paul's hand. Paul, 2 Cor. xii. 8, prayed thrice against the messenger of Satan, that is, as Estius and others interpret, he prayed often and fervently, and yet it departed not.

(4.) Fourthly, Such temptations give *no rest nor intermission;* men are haunted and dogged by them; what way soever they go, they still hear the same things, and cannot command their thoughts to give an exclusion to his motions, but still by renewed disputes and arguings, or by clamorous importunities, they are vexed and tormented: which surely shews a high degree of earnestness and impudency in Satan.

(5.) Fifthly, These are consequently *very burdensome, exceeding irksome and tiresome to us.* Paul calls them 'buffetings,' for their trouble and molestation. Satan so molested Job in his affliction by inward accusations and troubles of terror, that, as an overwearied man, he cries out he had no quiet, and that he was disappointed of his hope of ease in sleep, because he was then 'scared with dreams and terrified with visions,' [Job vii. 14.]

(6.) Sixthly, These are also upon a special design *on God's part, either to find us work and to keep us doing, or to prevent sin and miscarriage;* to keep down our pride, lest we should be 'exalted above measure,' [2 Cor. xii. 7;] to awaken us from slothfulness and security, lest we should 'settle upon our lees,' [Jer. xlviii. 11;] or to be an occasion of his grace, and an evidence of his power in our preservation, satisfying us and others, that in the greatest shocks of our spiritual battle his 'grace is sufficient for us,' [2 Cor. xii. 9.] Upon these, and such like designs as these, doth the most wise God permit it.

(7.) Seventhly, Satan doth not attempt temptations of this kind but upon *a special design*, and that either because he hopes by a violent and pertinacious impetuosity at length to prevail, or that he would please himself to molest us; for surely the cries and complainings of God's children are music in his ears; or at least upon a design to discourage us in our services, and to make way for other temptations of murmuring, blasphemy, despair, &c., which are as a reserve or ambushment laid in wait for us. The inferences from hence are these two:—

Applic. 1. That the children of God under such temptations may be encouraged under a patient expectation, by considering that Christ did undergo the like assaults from Satan. It is in itself tedious and disheartening, but they may see,

(1.) First, That this way of trouble *is usual, and that to the best;* and therefore they should not faint under it.

(2.) Secondly, That grace *is sufficient to preserve from the prevalency of the most earnest temptations* even there, where our heavenly Father thinks it not fit to preserve us from the trouble of them. When Paul gives the highest security that the faithfulness of God can afford, that temptations shall not be above strength, 1 Cor. x. 13, or the ability that shall be given them, he tells them they are not to expect always such aids as shall presently drive away the temptation, that it must immediately vanish, or that their temptations shall become light and contemptible, but that God's faithfulness will be no further engaged in the general, than [1.] to make their temptations tolerable, that they 'may be able to bear them,' though not without much to do. [2.] That the 'way of escape' shall be concurrent with the continuance of the temptation, that though the temptation abide, yet we shall be aided under it. [3.] That yet he is as careful of our help in temptations as he is ready to commissionate them, when need requires. His resolves that we should be tempted, and his resolves that we should be succoured, they bear the same date. 'With the temptation he will make a way to escape.'

(3.) Thirdly, That such temptations do not argue [1.] either a likelihood, much less a necessity, that they should prevail; nor [2.] any want of care and love in God; nor [3.] do they always evidence a more than ordinary proneness and inclination in us; for Christ, who was most averse to the least of sin, who was highest in God's love, against whom there was no possibility he should prevail, yet was thus tempted.

Applic. 2. Secondly, In such continued violences it will concern us to *make stout resistances;* according to the counsel of James, chap. iv. 7, 'Resist the devil, and he will fly.'

Obj. But I have done so, and yet the temptation is the same, and still continues.

Ans. (1.) First, It is not enough *to resist, but we must continue to do so.* Some make limited resistances, as besieged persons that set a time for their holding out, and then if they be not relieved at that time, they yield; but we must resolve a perpetual resistance, as long as the temptation lasts. When one hand is beaten off, we must hold by another; when both are beaten off, we must, as it were, hold by our teeth.

(2.) Secondly, In a faithful resistance, we may *cast the whole matter upon God*, and engage him in the quarrel; as David: 'I will say unto God, Why hast thou forsaken me?' &c.

Obj. But how is it consistent with truth that the temptation should continue, when James tells us that Satan will fly upon resistance?

Ans. (1.) It may be *the resistance is not as it ought, and so the blame is ours.* If we be not serious, as some who defy the devil in words, and resist him by crossing themselves, things which doubtless the devil laughs at; or if in the confidence of a presumptuous bravado, or if not with that humility and care that is requisite, it will be no wonder if he depart not.

(2.) Secondly, *He doth fly at every resistance more or less;* he doth give back, and is discouraged, and is a loser by every opposition.

(3.) Thirdly, Though the scripture say that he shall fly,—that is, sooner or later,—yet it doth not say *that he shall do so immediately*, though most usually he doth so where he is peremptorily rejected. But in some cases time must be allowed; for the devil, as it is in Chrysostom's comparison, stands like a fawning dog scratching and waving his tail, and if anything be given him, it makes him importunate for more; yet though we give him nothing, we cannot expect that the first or second denial should make him cease his trouble: as he hath been encouraged by former compliances, so will he not be discouraged but with many and continued denials.

If we consider the fast of Christ as an occasion designed by God for an advantage to the temptation, and then look upon his condition in the wilderness, being under hazards from wild beasts, in want of necessaries, and without a possibility of supplies in a usual way, and also under the discomforts of cold and long nights,—for according to the conjectures of some this was about our October and November [1]—then we may observe,

Doct. 4. *That it is Satan's way to second outward distresses and afflictions with inward temptations.* We see the like carriage of Satan toward Job. His affliction was followed with many temptations. All his friends, in urging him with hypocrisy, were no other than parties to Satan's design, though they knew it not apparently. His

[1] Lightfoot, Harm. *in loc.*

wife is set on by the tempter, as the serpent against Eve, to provoke him to 'curse God and die.' Besides all this, whosoever shall consider what inward workings of heart, spiritual trouble and conflict, his words frequently express, they will quickly find that when God put Job into Satan's hand, under that only limitation of not touching his life, he gave Satan a liberty to pursue him with inward temptations as well as outward vexations. When Israel was pinched with the straits of the wilderness, Satan was most busy with them to put them upon distrust, murmuring, revolt, disobedient oppositions, idolatry, and what not. David gives in his experience to confirm this truth. He never met with outward troubles but he had also inward temptations with them, as fretting, disquiet, sad apprehensions of God's wrath, haste, distrust, fear, &c., as the relation of his several straits do testify. And besides these, the generality of God's children find it so. Outward afflictions seldom pass alone. When they have 'fightings without,' they have 'fears within' usually. Seldom have they a sickness, or meet with a sad providence, but they have Satan busy with their souls, molesting their peace, or endeavouring to ensnare them. Thus their feet are never in the stocks but the iron enters into their soul. And for this reason is it that outward afflictions and troubles are called temptations in Scripture, because temptations usually accompany them, and they are indeed the solemn seasons that Satan desires to improve for that end; and for that is it that Luke expresseth that which we translate a time of temptation by $καιρὸς\ πειρασμοῦ$, which signifies an occasion or opportunity of temptation, Luke viii. 13; 1 Peter i. 6; 2 Peter ii. 9.

The temptations that Satan drives on, upon the advantage of an afflicted estate, are these:—

(1.) First, To drive men upon *impatient outbreakings against God*, as the Israelites in the wilderness turn upon Moses with this, 'Hast thou brought us into the wilderness to slay us?' [Exod. xiv. 11.] To this tended Job's temptation by his wife, 'Curse God, and die,' as it is in our translation, which cannot in anywise admit of the excuse that Beza makes for her, as if she gave wholesome advice, 'to die blessing of God,' because he reproves her sharply as having spoken foolishly and wickedly; but at best it is an ironical scoff at Job's integrity, 'Dost thou bless God while thou art killed by his displeasure?' if it be not a direct suggestion of revengeful despite. At such times men are too apt to entertain cruel thoughts of God, and sadly reflective upon his mercy or justice.

(2.) Secondly, In this posture of affliction he strives to put them *upon direful conclusions against themselves*, as if God called solemnly their sin to remembrance, and that they are forsaken of God, and marked out for destruction, the pledge and earnest whereof they take these troubles to be. We may observe that David's afflictions awakened his conscience to object guilt and miscarriage, so that he is as earnest to deprecate the marking and remembrance of his sin as he is to pray against his troubles. For this see Ps. xxv. 6, 7, xxxviii. 1, 4.

(3.) Thirdly, He pusheth them usually upon *contempt of religion, and abandoning the ways of God*. We are too apt to blame religion for all our troubles; and as we expect that our owning the ways of God should secure us from outward affliction, so when we find it otherwise we are too forward to say, 'We have washed our hands in vain,' &c., [Ps. lxxiii. 13.]

(4.) Fourthly, *The sin of distrust is another evil that he drives at;* he would have men conclude that God cannot or will not deliver. 'Can God prepare a table in the wilderness?' said the Israelites, by the power of temptation, when they were distressed, [Ps. lxxviii. 19.]

(5.) Fifthly, Another evil aimed at in such a case, is to put us upon *indirect courses and ways to escape from our troubles. Flectere si nequeo superos,* &c. Saul went to the witch of Endor when God answered him not. Distresses naturally prompt such things, and a little temptation makes us comply, as is noted by the wise man's desire, 'Give me not poverty, lest I put out my hand and steal,' [Prov. xxx. 9.] Distresses of poverty put men upon theft and unlawful ways.

The reasons of Satan's tempting the afflicted are these:—

(1.) First, That outward afflictions are *a load and burden.* This gives a probability that his designs may the better take place. It is easy to overthrow those that are bowed down, to break those that are bruised, to master those that are weary and weak-handed.

(2.) Secondly, An afflicted estate is *a temptation of itself, and naturally dictates evil things.* It is half of his design brought to his hand, it affords variety of matter for a temptation to work on.

(3.) Thirdly, Such a condition *strongly backs a temptation, and furnisheth many arguments for a prevalency;* for troubles are serious things; they speak to the heart, and what they speak, they speak fiercely; they represent things otherwise than common discovery can do, and for the most part they shew an ingenuity in multiplying fears, and aggravating hazard, and ascertaining suspected events, so that Satan can scarce desire a fairer hit than what these offer him.

(4.) Fourthly, They also give him the advantage *of darkness;* for to such their 'way is hid,' Job iii. 23, and God hath hedged them in; they neither know where they are, whether their trouble be a chastisement of sin, or for trial, or for prevention of miscarriage, or to make way for more comfortable manifestations; and as little know they how to behave themselves in their trouble, or how and when to get out of it. In such groping uncertainties, it is scarce possible but they should be put wrong.

(5.) Fifthly, An afflicted condition brings *on weakness and indisposition to duty;* it makes the hands weak, and the knees feeble. This made Job to faint, chap. iv. 5; this dried up David's strength. The first assault of an affliction doth stound the soul, and put it into such a confusion, that hope turns back, and faith is to seek, and every grace so out of order, that a man shall be unable to do anything of duty in a comfortable manner.

(6.) Sixthly, In this case men are apt to conclude *their prayers are not heard:* 'I cry in the day-time, and thou hearest not,' [Ps. xxii. 2,] says David; 'Hath the Lord forgotten to be gracious?' [Ps. lxxvii. 9.] And with such seeming probability is this urged upon us by affliction, that Job professeth he could not believe his own sense and knowledge in such a case. 'If I had called, and he had answered me; yet would I not believe that he had hearkened unto my voice,' Job ix. 16.

(7.) Seventhly, Afflictions strongly *fix guilt upon us*, and represent God 'searching out our iniquities, and inquiring after our sin,' Job x. 6.

(8.) Eighthly, They *imbitter the spirit*, and beget impressions upon the mind, of very hard thoughts of God.

(9.) Ninthly, They violently push men on *to speak unadvisedly*. There is such a swelling ferment of the old leaven of impatience and distrust in the mind, that it is matter of pain and difficulty to be silent: 'Their belly is as wine that hath no vent; it is ready to burst like new bottles,' and they are 'weary with forbearing and cannot stay, and must speak let come on them what will,' Job xxxii. 19.

All these advantages doth an afflicted condition bring to Satan; and who can think that he who is so studious of our ruin will be willing to miss so fair an opportunity?

Applic. (1.) First, This must teach us to have *a watchful eye over affliction*. Though at all times we must expect Satan's stratagems, yet in troubles especially prepare for them; according to the wise man's advice, 'In a day of adversity, consider,' [Eccles. vii. 14.]

(2.) Secondly, Seeing Satan takes advantage of the sharp humours of impatience and distrust, we must be particularly careful not *to touch too much upon the harshness of our troubles*, because this is that that sets fretting and distracting thoughts on work. Afflictions, like the pillar of the cloud and fire in the wilderness, have a light and darkness; and accordingly, those that converse with the dark side of troubles envenom their imaginations, and poison their thoughts with dark and hideous conclusions, and, in a word, draw forth nothing but the wormwood and the gall; whereas those that study and view the light side of them are full of praise and admiration for the gracious mixtures, comfortable mitigations, encouraging supports, &c., which they observe. It is wisdom then to keep upon the right side of them.

Though it be the design of God to turn the dark side of the cloud to us, yet may we have a competent light to guide us if we would improve it. When the sun is set, the moon may be up. Nay, it is our duty to strive to recover the right side of the cloud. He hides that we may seek.

If this fast of Christ's be considered as a remedy against temptations, then may we observe *that solemn temptations are to be resisted with fastings and prayers*. Of this I shall forbear to speak, till I come to speak of Christ's answer, and the repulse of Satan.

CHAPTER VI.

And when the tempter came to him, he said, If thou be the Son of God, command that these stones be made bread.—Mat. iv. 3.

That Christ's temptations were real and not in vision.—That temptation is Satan's employment, with the evidences and instances thereof.—Of Satan's tempting visibly, with the reasons thereof.

Next follows a particular account of those more eminent temptations wherewith Christ was assaulted by Satan. Before I speak of these, I must necessarily remove this stumbling-block out of the way, viz., whether Christ was really tempted, or only in a vision. That this was but visionary hath been supposed; not only by some, whose conceits in other things might justly render their supposals in this matter less worthy of a serious consideration,[1] but also by very grave and serious men,[2] whose reasons, notwithstanding, are not of that weight as to sway us against the letter and history of these temptations, which give us a full account of these things as really transacted, without the least hint of understanding them as done only in a vision. For,

(1.) First, It is a dangerous thing to depart from *the literal sense of what is historically related*. If we take such a liberty, we may as well understand other historical passages after the same rate, and so bring the history, not only of Christ's suffering to a visionary and fantastical cross, but also of all the New Testament to a very nothing.[3]

(2.) Secondly, *The circumstances of the temptation are so particularly set down*—as the devil's coming to him, leaving him, taking him to the temple, &c.—that if we may expect in anything to secure ourselves from a visionary supposition, we may do it in this history.[4]

(3.) Thirdly, This imagination doth wholly *enervate and make void the very end and design of Christ's being tempted;* for where were the glory of this victory over Satan, if it were only a visionary temptation, and a visionary conquest? or where were the comfort and encouragement which believers—from the apostle's authority, Heb. ii. 18, and iv. 16—might reap from this, that Christ imagined himself to be tempted, when really he was not so? Nay, how impossible is it to make that expression of the apostle, 'He was tempted in all points like as we are,' to agree to an imaginary temptation? except we also say that we are only tempted visionarily and not really?

(4.) Fourthly, Neither is it a plea of any value against this truth, that it seems to *derogate too much from the honour and authority of our Saviour, that Satan should so impudently assault him with temptations to worship him, and should carry him at pleasure from place to place,* when we find that he voluntarily submitted to higher indignities from Satan's instruments, and 'turned not away his cheek' from those

---

[1] Hobbes's Leviathan, cap. 45, p. 354. [2] Calvin, Scultetus.
[3] Tenison Hobbes's 'Creed Exam.,' p. 65. [4] Spanheim, Dub. Evan. *in loc.*

that 'smote' him, spit upon him, and contumeliously mocked him, and at last submitted to death, even the death of the cross.[1]

As for those objections from πτερύγιον ἱεροῦ, the pinnacle of the temple, upon which Scultetus thinks it was impossible for Christ to stand; as also the objection of the impossibility to shew the kingdoms of the world from any mountain, I shall answer them in their proper place. In the meantime I shall return to the verse in hand, in which I shall first pitch upon the general *prooemium*, or introduction to these special temptations, which is this, 'The tempter came to him.'

In this we are to take notice of the name given to Satan, and also the way and manner of the assault, in that expression, 'he came to him.'

There are three distinct names given to him in these temptations. [1.] His name 'Satan' shews his malice and fury, which is the ground and fountain whence all that trouble proceeds which we meet with from him. [2.] He is styled 'the tempter,' and that signifies to us how he puts forth this malice, his way and exercise in the exerting of it. [3.] He is called 'the devil' or accuser, expressing thereby the end and issue of all. From this name, then, here given, we may observe:—

Obs. 1. First, *That it is Satan's work and employment to tempt men.* We need not here dispute whether it be proper to Satan to tempt—that is, *an soli, et semper competat*, whether it agree to him only and always, which some indeed affirm in such a sense as this, that men do tempt men as Satan's instruments, the world tempts as it is the object and matter of temptations, but Satan tempts as the proper author and engineer of temptations. Others there are that think that men can and do properly tempt themselves, according to James i. 'Every man is tempted, when he is drawn away of his own lust.'[2] But the question is altogether needless as to us; though we and others may be true and proper tempters, yet this hindereth not but that it is most true, that Satan makes temptation his very work and business. And therefore not only here, but in 1 Thes. iii. 5, the devil is described by his employment, 'Lest by any means the tempter,' or he that tempteth, 'hath tempted you:' which the ordinary gloss doth thus explain, *Diabolus, cujus est officium tentare*. This name, then, is put upon Satan, κατ' ἐξοχήν, by way of eminency. Implying, [1.] That though there be never so many tempters, yet Satan is the chief. [2.] That he makes temptation his proper employment.

That Satan doth so, I shall evidence by these few notes:—

[1.] First, Temptation is in itself *a business and work*. For if we consider either the work of any one temptation, where Satan is oft put to it, after suggestion to persuade, and after persuasion to instigate and provoke; or if we consider what furniture, tools, means, and instruments are requisite, and what it may cost to bring all things together into fit order and method; or if we think of the various ways and manners of temptation, that some are mediate, some immediate;

---

[1] Non mirum est Christum permisisse se circumduci a diabolo, qui permisit se a membris sui crucifigi.—*Gregorius*.

[2] Aquinas, Sum. part 1, q. 114, art. 2. Homines instrumentaliter, mundus materialiter, Satanas efficienter.—*Sclater on* 1 *Thes.* iii. 5.

some inward, some outward; some moveable, some fixed and solemn; some enticements to evil, some affrightments from duty, others invasions of our peace and joy; or lastly, if we call to mind what study, what art, what fetches and contrivances the devil is sometimes put upon, we shall easily see that it keeps him doing, and that he eats not the bread of idleness that hath that employment to follow.

[2.] Secondly, Satan *gives up himself unto it, is wholly in it.* He 'walks to and fro,' 'goes about' seeking advantages of this nature, 'compasseth sea and land' to proselyte men to his slavery, useth all means, upon all men, at all times, with all diligence. Hence was it that Latimer, in his homely way of speaking, called him 'a busy bishop in his diocese,' and excited the sluggish to learn laboriousness of the devil.

[3.] Thirdly, *He takes a delight in it, not only from a natural propensity, which his fall put upon him, whereby he cannot but tempt—* as an evil tree cannot but bring forth evil fruits—but also from the power of a habit acquired by long exercise, which is accompanied with some kind of pleasure; and further, whatever pleasure may be supposed to arise from revengeful pride or companionship in evil, he hath of that in full measure, pressed down, and running over. *Solamen miseris,* &c.

[4.] Fourthly, All other things in Satan, or in his endeavours, have either a *subserviency, or some way or other a reference and respect to temptation.* His power, wisdom, malice, and other infernal qualifications, render him able to tempt; his labour and diligence in other things are but the work of one that prepares materials and occasions; his other business of accusing, affrighting, destroying, tormenting, are but the ends and improvements of tempting.

[5.] Fifthly, *He cares not how it goes on, so that it go on;* as a man that designs to be rich, cares not how he gets it; which shews that tempting in general is his design. Of this we have many instances, as [1.] He sticks not to lie and dissemble; he will tell them of the 'kingdoms of the world, and the glory of them,' and a thousand fair promises which he never intends. [2.] He will tempt for a small matter; if he can but gain a little, or but molest us, yet he will be doing. [3.] He will not give over for a foil or disappointment. [4.] He is not ashamed to tempt contradictory things: he tempted Christ against the work of redemption, 'Master, spare thyself,' [Mat. xvi. 22.] He tempted Judas to further it in betraying him. [5.] Any temptation that he sees will hold, he takes up. Hence is it that he tempts not the Jews now to idolatry, because he hath them fast in another snare, being strongly led to an opposition and contempt of Christ. [6.] He will sometime tempt where he hath not probability to prevail, even against hope. Thus he tempted Christ and Paul.

Applic. (1.) The use of the observation is this, *If it be his business to tempt, it must be our work to resist.*

[1.] First, To resist *is a labour.* It is not an idle formality, consisting in words of defiance, or a few ridiculous crossings and sprinklings of holy water, or spitting at the name of him, as ignorant people are wont to do.

[2.] Secondly, *We must give up ourselves to this work*, always fighting and opposing.

[3.] Thirdly, It will be necessary to *make use of all helps*, as prayer, fasting, the counsel and support of holy and experienced men.

[4.] Fourthly, *We must also cast off all hindrances.* Whatsoever in us is apt to take fire or give advantage must be laid off, as pride, which doth prognosticate a fall, and security, which betrays the best, or presumption, which provokes God to leave those of highest attainments, Neh. xiii. 16.

2. Secondly, In this general introduction, we may cast our eye upon *the way and manner of the assault.* When it is said, 'the tempter came unto him,' we are unavoidably forced to suppose another manner of coming than that whereby he tempted him for forty days together. And when we call to mind that at his coming here mentioned, he carried Christ to the temple, and from thence to a high mountain, and there propounded himself an object of worship; we can imagine no less than that Satan here came visibly to him. But in what shape or manner of appearance it is altogether uncertain, though it is most probable it was not in the form of a brute, but in some lustre of majesty or glory, as an angel, because a deformed or base appearance had been unsuitable to the boast of giving 'the kingdoms of the world,' or to his desire that Christ should 'fall down and worship him.' Hence we may observe :—

Obs. 2. *That Satan sometimes tempts in a visible appearance, and by voice.*

[1.] First, The possibility of this is evident from *the apparitions of angels.* Satan is still an angel, and there is nothing of a natural incapacity in him as to an outward appearance to our eyes and senses, more than in glorified spirits.[1]

[2.] Secondly, *In the first temptation he did no less, when he used the serpent as a trunk to speak through, and an instrument to act by.* In possessions he speaks audibly, and evidenceth a real presence.

[3.] Thirdly, *Undoubted instances may be given of Satan's tempting and molesting visibly.* I deny not but there are a great many idle stories of this kind, and a number of ridiculous figments; but it would be unreasonable and highly prejudicial to the truth of history, and the common faith of mankind, to refuse credit to the serious accounts of sober men, because of some foolish and unwarrantable fables.

What is related of Luther and his several troubles from Satan this way, is evident in the story of his life. Cyrillus tells us of one Eusebius, disciple of Jerome, who when he was dying, cried out of the devil's appearing to him. The like is storied of St Martin and others, and of these, you may read more collected by Mr Clark.[1]

If we would inquire into the reasons of Satan's appearing thus, we cannot more fitly pitch upon any other than these :—

---

[1] Piscat., *in loc.*

[2] O Fratres adjuvate me, ne peream, nonne videtis Dæmonum agmina, qui me debellare, et ad Tartara ducere festinant, quid hic astas cruenta bestia ?—*Cl.* Senarclæus in Epist. ad M. Bucerum, &c., tells of a country man, at Tribury, ['Friburg'—G.] in Germany, to whom the devil appeared in the shape of a tall man, claiming his soul, and offering to set down his sins in a scroll.

[1.] First, Either he thinks a great affrightment necessary in some cases, and for that end appears. Or,

[2.] Secondly, He sees his appearance needful, to give a greater evidence and certainty to the reality of the pleasures of sin which he promiseth. That is the common ground of his appearing in the ways and designs of witchcraft.

[3.] Or thirdly, In the height of rage, when he perceives other ways not available, and when he hath to do with persons not ignorant of his devices, where he sees he hath no need of a visor, or covert ways of dealing, then he sticks not, if permitted, to tempt or molest openly.

This must teach us not to wonder at such temptations, much less to judge those that may be so molested, as if Satan had a greater share in them, seeing Christ was thus tempted.

CHAPTER VII.

The general view of these temptations.—Of Satan's gradual proceeding in temptations.—Of reserving a great temptation last.—What a great temptation is; in what cases to be expected.—Of Satan's using a common road, in comparing these temptations with the ordinary temptations of men.—Of the advantage Satan takes of natural appetite, sense, and affections.

I have done with the *proœmium* to the temptations. Yet before I open them particularly, I shall take a general view of them. First, By comparing these with the other temptations of Christ during the forty days. Secondly, By comparing these with the temptations of men.

1. First then, If we compare these with the former temptations, and observe that we have no account given us of those temptations, but only in the general, 'that he was tempted,' whereas these are particularly set down and recorded, we cannot apprehend less than this, *that these last temptations were certainly greater and more remarkable temptations.* Hence note,

Obs. 3. *That it is Satan's method to be gradual in his temptations, and that he keeps his greatest temptations to the latter end.*

That Satan is gradual in his temptations; this is true of him, if we regard,

(1.) First, *The manner of his proceeding*, that he drives slowly, entreats gently, and is very careful that he do not over-drive men, but after they are accustomed to his way, he puts on imperiousness and commands them.

(2.) Secondly, *If the matter of temptation be regarded*, he is gradual there also. He tempts to little sins first, then to greater.

I shall illustrate both these particulars by the example of Thomas Savage, apprentice to Mr Collins, vintner at the Ship Tavern, in Ratcliffe, who suffered in *anno* 1660, for murdering his fellow-servant. He confesseth that the devil took this course with him: he first tempted him to neglect of duty, then to contempt of ordinances and profanation of the Sabbath, then to drinking, then to fornication, then to rob and steal from his master, and last of all to murder; and takes particular notice that in this last temptation, to kill his fellow-servant, there was a violent and more than ordinary power of Satan upon him, to instigate him to that wickedness. All this you may read at large in the printed narration of his life.

(1.) The reasons of his gradual proceedings are,

[1.] First, *He would discover no more of himself in any temptation than he is necessitated unto for the gaining his end*, lest he cross his own design, and instead of drawing men to wickedness, scare or affright them from it.

[2.] Secondly, *Sins are mutually preparatory to each other.* Smaller proffers and temptations do insensibly prepare and incline the heart to greater.

(2.) Secondly, That he keeps his greatest temptations last, is a consequence of the former; for which, besides what is now spoken, these reasons may be given:—

[1.] First, *There is provocation given him in refusing his lesser assaults.* His 'head is bruised' by every refusal, he is set at defiance, which calls him out to stronger opposition. He perceives by often repulses that those with whom he hath to do are not subjects of his kingdom, and that his 'time is short,' and therefore no wonder is it, if he assault most furiously and with all his strength.

[2.] Secondly, *There is also policy in it.* When he hath brought down our strength and weakened our courage, then a violent onset is fair to procure him a victory.

But because I mention a great temptation, it may not be amiss both for the further explaining of the text, and illustration of the matter, to shew what is a great temptation. These were great temptations to Christ, and there are several things remarkable in them, which, wherever they appear, they will denominate the temptation great, and the more of them are conjoined together, and in higher degree, it may justly be called still the greater. As,

(1.) First, In these temptations, we may note there were *external objects as well as insinuated suggestions.* Inward motions are real temptations, but when they have the objects and things presented to the eye or the senses, then do they strongly urge. At this advantage the devil tempted Eve. He urged her when the fruit was within the view. Thus he tempted Achan, when the gold and garment were in his eye.

(2.) Secondly, *These temptations were complex*, consisting of many various designs, like a snare of many cords or nooses. When he tempted to turn stones to bread, it was not one single design, but many, that Satan had in prosecution. As distrust on one hand, pride on another, and so in the rest. The more complicated a temptation is, it is the greater.

(3.) Thirdly, *These were also perplexing, entangling temptations.* They were dilemmatical,[1] such as might ensnare, either in the doing or refusal. If he had turned stones into bread, he had too much honoured Satan by doing it at his motion. If he did not, he seemed

[1] Putting into a 'dilemma.'—G.

to neglect his own body, in not making necessary provisions for himself, being now hungry.

(4.) Fourthly, *These temptations proceeded upon considerable advantages.* His hunger urged a necessity of turning stones into bread. His present straits, and the lowness of his condition, seemed to speak much for the reasonableness of giving proof of his divine nature, by casting himself down from the temple, and of doing anything that might tend to a more plentiful being and support in the world. Advantages strengthen temptations.

(5.) Fifthly, *These temptations were accompanied with a greater presence and power of Satan.* He appeared visibly in them, and was permitted to touch and hurry the body of Christ, and to depaint and set forth the glory of the world, doubtless in the most taking way, to the eye of Christ.

(6.) Sixthly, *The matter of these temptations,* or the things he tempted Christ to, *were great and heinous abominations:* a distrust of providence, a presumption of protection, and a final renunciation of the worship due to him, and transferring it to the most unworthy object, God's professed enemy; and yet were they seconded by the strongest, most powerful, and most prevailing means, as his present straits, his infallible assurance of sonship, pleasure, and glory. Where the matter is weighty, and the medium strong and pressing, there is the temptation great.

(7.) Seventhly, *All these temptations pretended strongly to the advantage and benefit of Christ,* and some of them might seem to be done without any blame, as to turn stones to bread, to fly in the air. The more kindness a temptation pretends to us, it is the stronger.

(8.) Eighthly, *Satan urged some of them in a daring, provoking way;* 'If thou be the Son of God?' as if he had said, I dare thee to shew thyself what thou pretendest to be. These kind of provocations are very troublesome to the most modest and self-denying, who can scarce forbear to do what they are urged unto at such times.

(9.) Ninthly, *These temptations seem to be designed for the engagement of all the natural powers of Christ;* his natural appetite in a design of food; his senses in the most beautiful object, the world in its glory; the affections, in that which is most swaying, pride, and delight in extraordinary testimonies of divine power and love, in supporting him in the air, &c.

(10.) Tenthly, *Some of these warranted as duty, and to supply necessary hunger, others depending upon the security of a promise,* 'He shall give his angels charge,' &c. The greater appearance of duty, or warrantableness, is put upon sin, the greater is the temptation.

By these ten particulars may we, as by a standard, judge when any temptation is great or less.

Applic. 1. *Let us then take heed of small temptations, or the smoother proceedings of Satan, as we would avoid the greater attempts that are to follow.* Where he is admitted to beat out our lusts with a rod or a staff, he may be suspected to bring the wheel over them at last, [Isa. xxviii. 27, *seq.*]

Let us also after our assaults expect more and greater, because the greatest are last to be looked for. This holds true in three cases. [1.] In solemn temptations, where Satan fixeth his assaults, there the utmost rage is drawn out last. [2.] In the continuance and progress of profession, the further we go from him and the nearer to God, be sure of the highest measure of his spite. [3.] At the end of our race: for if he miss his prey then, it is escaped for ever, as a bird unto its hill.

Obj. But some may say, I am but a messenger of sad tidings; and that by bringing such a report of giants and walled cities, I may make the hearts of the people to faint.

Ans. I answer; This is bad news only to the sluggish, such as would go to heaven with ease, and in a fair and easy way; but to the laborious resolute soldiers of Christ this is no great discouragement: for, [1.] It doth but tell them of their work, which as they are persuaded of, so it is in some measure their delight, as well as their expectation. [2.] It doth but tell them, Satan's malice and fury, which they are assured of, and are most afraid of it sometimes, when it seems to lie idle and as asleep. [3.] It doth tell them that Satan's thoughts concerning them are despairing, he fears they are going, or gone from him. If they were his willing servants, there would be no hostility of this nature against them.

I have thus compared these special temptations with those wherewith our Lord Christ was exercised during the forty days. I shall,

Secondly, Compare these temptations of Christ with those that usually befall his members, in which there is so much suitableness and agreement both in matter and manner, that it cannot be unuseful to take notice of it, which will the better appear in instances. First, then, let us consider the first temptation of Eve: Gen. iii. 6, 'And when the woman saw that the tree was good for food, and that it was pleasant to the eyes, and a tree to be desired to make one wise,' &c. Here are all the arguments and ways summed up by which Satan prevailed upon her. It was 'good for food;' here he wrought upon the desire of the natural appetite. It was 'pleasant to the eyes;' here he took the advantage of the external senses. It was 'to be desired to make one wise;' here he inflamed the affections. Let us again call to mind the general account of temptations in 1 John ii. 16, 'All that is in the world, the lust of the flesh, the lust of the eyes, and the pride of life;' where the apostle designedly calls all off from a love of the world, because of the hazard and danger that we lie open unto, from the things of the world, striking upon and stirring up our lusts; which he ranks into three general heads, according to the various ways whereby these outward things do work upon us, in exciting our natural powers and apprehensions to sinful lustings; and these are so fully agreeing with those three in Eve's temptation, that I need not note the parallel. Let us now cast our eyes upon these temptations, and the suitableness of Satan's ways and dealings will immediately appear. When he tempted Christ to turn stones into bread, there he endeavoured to take advantage of the 'lust of the flesh,' which in 1 John ii. I understand in a more restrained sense, not for the lustings of corrupt nature, but for the lustings of the body in its natural appetite, acccording to that expression of Christ, 'The spirit is willing, but the flesh'—or body—'is weak.' And if we should not so restrain it in this place, the lust of the flesh would include the lust of the eyes and the pride of life, contrary to the clear scope of the text, for these are also the lustings of corrupt nature. When he further tempted him 'to cast himself down,' he pushed him upon 'the pride of life;' when he shewed him 'the kingdoms of the world, and the glory of them,' he attempted to gain upon him by the 'lust of the eyes.' From this proportion and suitableness of temptation to Christ and his members, observe,

Obs. 4. *That Satan usually treads in a beaten path, using known and experienced methods of temptation.* It is true, in regard of circumstances, he useth unspeakable varieties in tempting, and hath many more devices and juggles than can be reckoned up; yet in the general he hath digested them into method and order, and the things upon which he works in us are the same. Thus he walks his round, and keeps much-what the same track, not only in different persons, but also in the same men, using the same temptations over and over; and yet this argues no barrenness of invention or sluggishness in Satan; but he hath these reasons for it:—

[1.] First, Because the same temptations being suited to human nature in general, will, with a small variation of circumstance, suit all men: their inclinations generally answering to one another, as face answers to face in water.

[2.] Secondly, These standing methods are famous with him, as generally powerful and taking; and it can be no wonder if Satan practise most with these things that have the largest *probatum est* of experience to follow them.

[3.] Thirdly, The more experienced he is in any temptation, the more dexterously and successfully still he can manage it; so that we may expect him more cunning and able in what he most practiseth.

Applic. This may be some satisfaction to those that are apt to think of themselves and their temptations as Elias did in his persuasion, 'I alone am left,' [1 Kings xix. 14.] Where Satan useth anything of vigour and fierceness, we are apt to say, 'None are tempted as we,' none in like case, we are singular, they are peculiar and extraordinary temptations, &c.; but it is a mistake. Even that of Solomon may be applied to these, 'There is nothing new,' [Eccles. i. 9,] nor anything befallen us which others have not undergone before us; and would but Christians be so careful to observe the way of the serpent upon their hearts as they might, and so communicative of their experiences as they ought, the weak and heavy laden would not go so mourning under such apprehensions as commonly affright them, that none were ever so tempted as they are. It would be some support at worst, when the most hellish furies do oppress them, to know that others before them were in these deeps, and as fearful of being overwhelmed as themselves, and yet were delivered. The deliverances of those that have escaped the danger, is ground of hope to those that are at present under it.

Obs. 5. *The usual advantages that Satan takes against us is from our natural appetite, our external senses, or our passions and affections.* All these are usual ways by which Satan works against us, as appears from what hath been said; neither are any of them so mean and contemptible, but that we have cause to fear the power and influence of them. Hence the Scripture cautions descend to the eyes: 'Look not upon the wine when it is red in the cup,' [Prov. xxiii. 31;] 'Be sober, be vigilant,' &c., [1 Peter v. 8.] The appetite is not so easily kept in, but that it may prevail to gluttony and drunkenness; and some are so powerfully carried by this, that they are said 'to make their bellies their god,' [Phil. iii. 19.] Of the power of sense and affection, elsewhere hath been spoken.

CHAPTER VIII.

The rise of Christ's first temptation.—Of Satan's suiting his temptations to the conditions of men.—Of tempting men upon the plea of necessity.—The reasons and cheats of that plea.—His pretences of friendship in tempting, with the danger thereof.

Having thus considered these temptations as they lie before us in their general prospect, I shall now speak of this first special temptation in particular, in which—(1.) The rise, or occasion; (2.) The temptation itself; (3.) The argument by which Satan would enforce it, are to be distinctly noted.

1. First, *As to the rise of it,* it is questioned by some why Satan begins with this first. The cause they assign, in part at least, is from his first success against Eve, in a temptation about eating, as if this were the chief and most hopeful arrow in his quiver. But we need not go so far, when the evangelist is so punctual in setting it down, in the latter end of the former verse, 'he was an hungered.' This the devil took notice of, and from hence took the rise of his temptation, that by 'turning stones to bread,' for the satisfaction of his present hunger, he might be induced to make way for the secret stratagems which he had prepared against him on this occasion. Here I note,

Obs. 6. *That where Satan hath a design against any, he doth take the advantage of their condition, and suits his temptation accordingly.* Thus, if men be in poverty, or in the enjoyments of plenty, in sickness or health, if in afflictions, under wrongs, in discontents, or carried to advancements and honours, or whatever else may be considerable relating to them, he observes it, and orders his designs so as to take in all the advantages that they will afford. That it is his concern and interest so to do, we may imagine, upon these grounds:—

(1.) First, *Our consent must be gained.* This he cannot properly and truly force, but must entice and deceive us to a compliance with him.

(2.) Secondly, *If our condition speak for him, and lie fair for the furtherance of any device of his, our consent is upon the matter half gained.* It is much, if so powerful an advocate, as is our present state, do not influence us to an inclination.

(3.) Thirdly, *This doth his work easily and effectually.* He more generally prevails by this course, and with less labour.

Applic. This policy of Satan should advantage us by *suggesting fit memorials to us in our expectations of temptation.* Though we know not all Satan's thoughts, yet may we know where and how he will usually make an onset. Our condition will tell us what to look for. The distressed and afflicted may expect a temptation suited to their condition, as of murmuring, repining, revenge, distrust, use of indirect means, despairings, &c. They that have peace and plenty may be sure they shall be tempted suitably, to pride, boasting, covetousness, oppression, contempt of others, security, or whatever may be fit to be ingrafted on that stock. The like may be said of any other different condition. How fairly are we forewarned, by an observation made upon Satan's proceeding upon these advantages, where to expect him, and how to provide against him.

Let us proceed to a further inquiry, *How the devil managed this advantage of Christ's hunger.* He plainly urgeth him with a necessity of providing supplies for himself, spreading before him his desire to eat, and the impossibility of help, in a barren and desolate wilderness: as if he had said, 'The want of the body is to be provided for; nature and religion consents to this; the wilderness affords no help, ordinary means fail; there is therefore a necessity that some extraordinary course be taken, therefore turn stones to bread; this is not unsuitable to the condition and power of him who is the Son of God.' At this rate he pleads.

Obs. 7. Observe then, *That Satan usually endeavours to run his temptations upon the plea of necessity, and from thence to infer a duty.*

When he cannot pretend a fair and direct way to irregular practices, he would break a door and force a way by necessity.

Under this notion of necessity, the devil marshals all those pretences that seem to be of more than ordinary force, in their usual prevalencies. Thus he teacheth men to think they are necessitated, if they be carried by a strong inclination of their own, or if there be an urgency and provocation from others, or if they be in straits and dangers; and sometime he goes so high as to teach men that a necessity is included in the very fabric of their natural principles, by which they presumptuously excuse themselves in being sinful, because by nature they are so, and cannot be changed without special grace. Scarce shall we meet any man with seasonable reproof for his iniquity, but he will plead such kind of necessities for himself,—I could not help it; I was strongly carried; or, I was compelled; I must do so, or else I could not escape such a danger, &c.

The reasons of this policy are these:—

(1.) First, *He knows that necessity hath a compulsive force*, even to things of otherwise greatest abhorrencies. A treasury of instances is to be had in famines and besieged places, where it is usual to eat unclean things, not only creatures that are vile, but even dung and entrails; nay, so tyrannical is necessity, that it makes inroads into, and conquests upon nature itself, causing 'the tender and delicate woman, which would not adventure the sole of her foot upon the ground for delicateness and tenderness, to have an evil eye towards the husband of her bosom, towards her son, and towards her daughter,' Deut. xxviii. 56. A like force doth it exercise upon the minds and consciences of men. It makes them rise up against their light, it engageth men to lay violent hands upon their own convictions, to stifle and extinguish them. How many mournful examples have we of this kind! How many have apostatized from truth, being terrified by the urging necessities of danger, contrary to the highest convictions of conscience!

(2.) Secondly, *Necessity can do much to the darkening of the understanding, and change of the judgment, by the strong influence it hath upon the affections.* Men are apt to form their apprehensions according to the dictates of necessity. What they see to be hazardous, they are inclinable to judge to be evil. Men in straits not only violate their reason, but sometime by insensible steps, unknown to themselves, slide into a contrary judgment of things, directly cross to what they have believed and professed. Which persuasion they owe not to any further accession of light, or new discovery of argument; for ofttimes the same arguments which, in the absence of trouble, they have contemned as weak, by the appearance of danger, put on another face and seem strong; but to the prevalency of their fears. And thus many in all ages have altered their judgments and thoughts, not because they knew more, but because they feared more.

The like necessities do men form to themselves from exorbitant and greedy hopes and expectations of a better condition, compared to that wherein they at present are; and the like influence it hath in the alteration of their judgments. Let the bishop of Spalato be an example of this, who loathed the Romish religion first, and in England, whither he came for refuge, writ against it; but saw a necessity, from the disappointment of expectation, to change his mind, returned to Rome again, and persuaded himself that that was true which he had formerly pronounced false; and so writ against the church of England, as before he had done against the church of Rome. To him we may add Ecebolius,[1] of whom Socrates reports, that, according to the various appearings of hazards, he changed his religion several times. Under Constantine, he was a Christian; under Julian, a pagan; and under Jovinian, a Christian again.

(3.) Thirdly, *Necessity offers an excuse, if not a justification, of the greatest miscarriages.*[2] Lot offered to expose his daughters to the raging lust of the Sodomites for the preservation of his angel-strangers, which surely he would in no wise have done, but that he thought the present necessity might have excused him. Esau profanely sells his birthright, but excuseth the matter so, 'Behold, I am at the point to die; and what profit shall this birthright do to me?' Gen. xxv. 32. Aaron produceth a necessity, from the violent resolves of the people, in justification of himself in the matter of the golden calf, 'Thou knewest that this people are set on mischief,' [Exod. xxxii. 22.]

(4.) Fourthly, *Necessity is a universal plea*, and fitted to the conditions of all men in all callings, and under all extravagancies. The tradesman, in his unlawful gains or overreachings, pleads a necessity for it from the hardness of the buyer in other things; the poor

---

[1] Eccles. Hist., lib. iii. cap. 11.
[2] Antiochus put Eleazer and the Maccabees in mind of this excuse, If it be a sin to do contrary to your law, compulsion doth excuse it.—*Josephus on the lives of the Maccabees.*

man pleads a necessity for stealing, and the rich pleads the same necessity for revenge, and thus it serves all with a pretext.

These considerations, discovering this course so hopeful as to this design of the devil, he will be sure to put us to this pinch where he can. But, besides this, we may observe three cheats in this plea of necessity :—

[1.] First, *Sometimes he puts men upon feigning a necessity where there is none.* Saul sacrificed upon a needless supposal that, Samuel not coming at the time appointed, there was a necessity for him to do it. He spared also the cattle upon the like pretence, that it was a necessary provision for sacrifice. And thus would the devil have persuaded Christ, that there was an absolute necessity to turn stones to bread, when in truth there was no such need.

[2.] Secondly, *Sometimes he puts men upon a necessity of their own sinful procurement.* Herod sware to gratify the daughter of Herodias, and this is presently pleaded as a necessity for the cutting off John Baptist's head. Saul forbade the tasting of meat, and sealed the penalty by an oath and curse, and this is by and by made a necessity for the taking away of Jonathan's life,—who had tasted honey not knowing his father's curse,—had not the people rescued him, [1 Sam. xiv. 24, *seq.*]

[3.] Thirdly, *Sometime he stretcheth a necessity further than it ought.* He knows that God hath such a regard to real necessities, that upon that ground he will dispense with his Sabbath and the present performance of duty. These instances he lays before men, and endeavours to persuade them, that in like manner God will, upon a necessity, dispense with sins, as well as with the present opportunity of service. What a covering, in all ages, men have made of necessity for their highest outrages and extravagancies, and with what confidence they have managed such pleas, would be endless to relate.

Applic. This must warn us *not to suffer ourselves to be imposed upon by the highest pretences of necessity.* Whatever it may dispense with, as in some cases it will suspend a present service, and warrant the performance of a duty, besides the common rule and way wherein it ought ordinarily to be managed, it must never be pleaded to give warranty to anything in its own nature sinful. Necessity will not justify lying, stealing, covetousness, adulteries, &c., *Ferenda magis omnis necessitas quam perpetranda aliqua iniquitas.*—Aug[ustine.]

Besides, we must be wary in judging what is a necessity. Men are apt to plead a necessity where there is none; and if we give way to a facile admittance of excuses of this kind, we shall presently multiply necessities, and have them to serve us at every turn. Some would warrant sin by necessity, others would turn off duty and rule by pretending a necessity where none is; both are to be avoided as snares of Satan.

Once more, before we dismiss this rise of the temptation of Christ in hand, let us observe that, in persuading him to turn stones to bread, he seems to express a great deal of care and tenderness to Christ, with an invidious reflection upon the love and providence of God: as if he should say, ' I see thou art hungry, and this wilderness affords nothing to eat, and God hath not taken care to spread a table for thee; I therefore, pitying thy condition, as a friend, advise thee to turn stones to bread.'

Obs. 8. Note, *That Satan manageth his most cruel designs under the highest pretences of friendship.* He did so with Eve, 'The Lord knoweth that ye shall be as gods,' [Gen. iii. 5 ;] as if he had a greater regard to them than God himself. He tempted Christ in the mouth of Peter to 'spare himself,' under the show of great kindness, [Mat. xvi. 22 ;] and no less are his common pretences to all men. This is a deep policy, for by this means the mischief intended is the better concealed, and the less care and provision made against it; and besides, the affections and desires are stirred up to a hasty embracement of the motion, and an eager swallowing of the bait.

So great a subtlety is in this manner of dealing, that those who affect the name of great politicians in the world have learned from Satan to shew greatest respects and a most friendly countenance to those whom they most hate and intend to ruin. Thus our Richard the Third of England constantly dealt with those for whose blood he lay in wait ; and the precepts of Machiavel are fitted to this, that it is wisdom ' to hug those whom we desire to destroy.' Ehud's present made way for his dagger, [Judges iii. 22.] Joab's sword could not so well have despatched its errand upon Abner, if he had not ushered it in with a kiss, [2 Sam. xx. 9.]

Applic. This should make us most *suspect those temptations that offer us most kindness and advantage, and such as are most gratifying to our humours and desires.* For can it be imagined in good earnest that Satan intends us a real good ? Can the gifts of enemies pass for courtesies and favours with any,[1] but such as are bewitched into a blockish madness ? Satan is more to be feared when he flatters than when he rageth ; and though such offers may be looked upon by some as more benign, and less odious temptations, as some kind of familiar spirits are more kindly treated by some, under the notion of white devils, yet may we say of them, as Cornelius Agrippa speaks of some unlawful arts and ways of Thurgia,[2] *Eò sunt perniciosiora, quò imperitis diviniora,* They have the greatest danger that pretend the highest friendship. Thus much for the rise of the temptation.

CHAPTER IX.

A particular consideration of the matter of the first temptation, what Satan aimed at in bidding him turn stones into bread.—Of Satan's moving us to things good or lawful.—The end of such a motion.—How to know whether such motions are from Satan or the Spirit.—What to do in case they be from Satan.—Of his various aims in one temptation.—What they are, and of his policy therein.—Of his artificial contrivement of motions to make one thing infer another.

Next follows the temptation itself, ' Command that these stones be made bread.' There is no great difficulty in the words. The Greek indeed hath a remarkable suitableness to the supposition, on which

[1] Timeo Danaos et dona ferentes.   [2] Query : ' Thaumaturgia' ?—G.

Satan insists, taking Christ to be the Son of God. It is very pertinently spoken, 'Say or speak'—εἰπέ—that these stones be made bread; for if God speak, it must be done.

It is not worth the while to insist upon so small a variety of expression as is betwixt this evangelist, who hath it 'these stones,' and Luke, who speaks it in the singular number, 'this stone;' for besides that, as some suppose, this expression of Luke might, for anything that appears to the contrary, be Satan's lowering his request to one stone, when Christ had denied to turn many into bread upon his first asking; *this* one stone in Luke, taken collectively for the whole heap, will signify as much as *these* stones in Matthew; or the phrase 'these stones,' in Matthew, by an imitation of a common Hebraism, may be no more but one of these stones, or this stone, as it is in Luke; as it is said, Jephthah was buried in the cities of Gilead, that is, in one of the cities.[1]

The thing urged was the turning or changing the form of a creature, which is a work truly miraculous and wonderful, and such as had neither been unsuited to the power of Christ, nor unlawful in itself. It is from hence justly questioned where the sting of this suggestion lay, or in what point was the temptation couched.

(1.) First, It was not in *the unlawfulness or sinfulness of the thing mentioned.* For Christ did as much as would amount to all this when he turned water into wine, and when he fed multitudes by a miraculous multiplication of a few loaves and fishes.

(2.) Secondly, *It was not unsuitable to his condition, as hungry;* for so it seemed a duty to provide for himself, and which Satan took for granted.

(3.) Thirdly, Neither seemed it *any derogation to his power and divine nature, but rather an advantage and fit opportunity to give a full proof of it,* to the stopping of Satan's mouth for ever.

Notwithstanding these, there was poison and malignity enough in the suggestion, and under these green leaves of plausible pretences lay hid many snakes. For [1.] By this was he secretly tempted to admit of a doubting of the truth of the divine testimony, lately declaring him to be the Son of God. [2.] As also further to question his Father's providence and love; [3.] and unnecessarily to run out of the ordinary way of supply, and to betake himself to indirect means or extraordinary courses. [4.] And all this to the abuse and undervaluing of his power, in prostituting it to Satan's direction or persuasion; and the devil had gained a considerable advantage if he could have prevailed with him to do such a thing by his instigation. [5.] It may be he further thought this might entice to a high esteem of himself, and so make way for a vain ostentation of his power and interest in God. All or most of these seem to be the design that the devil was driving forward. Several things are hence observable.

Obs. 9. That *where Satan doth not judge it his present interest to suggest to us things in their own nature sinful, he will move us to things good in themselves, in hopes thereby to lead us into evil.* This way of tempting is from a more refined policy than downright motions to sin, and doubtless it is less suspected, and consequently more taking.

[1] Spanheim, Dub. Evan. *in loc.*, and Lightfoot, Harm. *in loc.*

The evils that Satan would introduce by this method are such as these:—

(1.) First, Sometime when he tempts us to that which is good, it is that he might *affright us from it.* His approbation is enough to put a discredit and disgraceful suspicion upon anything. Such a design had he when he gave testimony for Christ, 'that he was the Son of God,' Mat. viii. 29; or for the apostles, that they were the 'servants of the most high God,' Acts xvi. 17. It was not his intention to honour him or them by bearing them witness, but to bring them under suspicion and trouble.

(2.) Secondly, *There are a great many ways to miscarry in a lawful action*, either by propounding bad ends, or by failures in the manner of performance, or by a misimprovement of the whole. These miscarriages, and the possibility and probability of them, Satan carries in his mind; yet doth he not at first propound them, but moving us unto the thing, he hath an expectation that we will slide into them of ourselves, or be inclined by some suitable touches of suggestion upon our minds, together with the tendency or improvableness of the thing or action to such evils as are properly consequent to it. Satan did not here tempt Christ to these sinful ends directly, but to an action which he hoped might insensibly produce them.

(3.) Thirdly, Another evil hereby aimed at is *the hindrance of a greater good, not only as a diversion to turn us off a better or more profitable occasion, but also as an unseasonable interruption of something at present more concerning us.* Thus he makes the suggestion of good things the hindrance of prayer or hearing.

Quest. Some will say, This is a perplexing case, that in things good or lawful in themselves, men should be in such dangers, and will thereupon desire to know how they may distinguish Satan's contrivances and motions from those that have no dependence upon him, or are from the Spirit of God?

Ans. In answer to this:—

[1.] Let us, when we fear thus to be circumvented, look well *to what impressions are upon our spirit when we are moved to what may be lawful.* For together with the motion, if it be Satan's, we shall find either a corrupt reason and end privately rising up in our mind, or we may observe that our hearts are out of order and perversely inclined. This is oft unseen to ourselves. When the disciples moved Christ to bring down 'fire from heaven,' if they had considered the present revengeful selfish frame of their spirits, which our Lord tells them they were ignorant of, they might easily have known that the motion had proceeded from Satan.

[2.] Secondly, *The concurrent circumstances of the thing or action are to be seriously weighed*, for from thence we may take a right measure of the conveniency or inconveniency of the proceeding in it. What is from Satan it will be either unseasonable as to the time, place, and person, or some other thing will appear that may give a discovery. As here Christ refuseth to turn stones to bread, because not only the way and manner of the proposal doth sufficiently lay open the design, but also the circumstances of Christ's condition at that time shewed the motion to be unseasonable and inconvenient; for if Satan had urged the necessity of it for the satisfaction of his hunger, Christ could have answered, that the experience that he had of God's support for forty days together, was sufficient to engage him to rely yet further upon him. If he had urged further, that by this means he might have had a full proof of God's love and care, or of his sonship, it was at hand to tell him that it was needless to seek a further evidence when God had given one so full a little before. If again he had pleaded it to have been a useful occasion to give a testimony of his power to the satisfaction of others, he could have told him that it had been impertinent to have done it then, when he was in the wilderness, where none could have the benefit of it. So that nothing Satan could have propounded as a reason for that miracle, but it might have been repelled from a consideration of his present condition.

Applic. The instruction that may be gathered from this is, *that we must not entertain thoughts of doing lawful things without a due inquiry into the temper of our own hearts, and a full consideration of all circumstances round about, with the probable tendencies and consequences of it.*

Quest. But, may some say, if I judge such a motion to be a thing lawful, which doth proceed from Satan, what am I to do?

Answ. I answer, [1.] Consider whether the good be necessary or not. If it be necessary, it is a duty and not to be forborne, only the abuses are to be watched against and avoided.

[2.] Secondly, If it be a duty, consider whether it be seasonable or unseasonable, necessary or not, as to the present time; if it be not, it may be suspended, and a fitter opportunity waited for.

[3.] Thirdly, If it be only lawful and not necessary, we ought to abstain from it wholly, after the example of David, Ps. xxxix. 2, who 'abstained even from good,' that is, from lawful bemoanings of himself or complainings against Absalom, that had rebelled against him; because it was not necessary, and, the circumstances of his condition considered, very dangerous, lest vent and way being given, he might have been easily drawn to speak passionately or distrustfully against God, and foolishly against providences.

That the thing unto which Satan moved Christ was lawful, hath been noted. Next, let us consider *what end Satan might propound to himself in this motion*, and we shall see, as hath been said, that he did not so narrow and contract his design as that only one thing took up his intentions, but several. Hence have we this observation:—

Obs. 10. *That in one single temptation Satan may have various aims and designs.*

Temptation is a complicated thing, a many-headed monster. Satan hath always many things in his eye.

[1.] First, In every temptation there is *a direct and principal design, a main thing that the devil would have.*

[2.] Secondly, There are several things *subservient to the main design*, as steps, degrees, or means leading to it; the lesser still making way for the greater. If Satan design murder, he lays the foundation of his work in inward grudgings and hatreds; next he gives provocations, by reproachful words, or disdainful carriages and behaviours, as our Saviour notes in the expressions of *raca* and *fool*, Mat. v. 22, and so by degrees enticeth on to murder. The like we may observe in the lusts of uncleanness, and other things.

[3.] Thirdly, Besides these there are usually *reserves, something in ambushment to watch our retreats;* for Satan considers what to do in case we repel and refuse his motion, that so he may not altogether labour in vain. A contrary extreme watcheth those that fly from a temptation; pride, security, self-confidence, and boasting are ready to take them by the heel. So truly may it be said of Satan, that he knoweth the way that we take: if we go forward, he is there; if backward, we may also perceive him; on the left hand, he is at work; and on the right hand, he is not idle. All these we may particularly see in this temptation in hand. He had a main design, of which more presently; he prepares means and seconds to help it forward; such were those pleas of necessity and conveniency which the hunger and want of Christ did furnish him withal, and there wanted not the reserves of presumption and self-neglect in case he resisted the motion.

The reasons of this policy are these:—

(1.) First, *When Satan tempts, he is not certain of his prevalency, even when the probabilities are the greatest;* and therefore doth he provide himself with several things at once, that if the tempted party nauseate one thing, there may be another in readiness that may please his palate. God gives this advice to the spiritual seedsman, 'In the morning sow thy seed, and in the evening withhold not thine hand; for thou knowest not what shall prosper, whether this or that,' [Eccles. xi. 6.] Satan, that seedsman of the tares, imitates this; and because he knows not what shall prosper, therefore doth he use variety.

(2.) Secondly, *Where many things are at once designed, it is a hundred to one they will not all return empty.* It is much if many snares miss; he that hath broken one or two, may not only be enticed with a third temptation—as being either wearied out with the assaults, or made pliable with the allurements of the former, but may also sit down secure, as having, in his supposal, passed all the danger, and so unawares fall into an unseen or unsuspected trap.

Applic. This may [1.] by way of caution, assure us that we have no cause to think that all fear is over, when we have avoided the more obvious and conspicuous designments of a temptation, but rather to suspect some further train than we yet have discovered. [2.] That there is a necessity for us to be circumspect every way, and, Janus-like, to have an eye before and behind, that we may make timely discoveries of what Satan intends against us.

As we have taken a view of the various designments of Satan in one temptation, so it is also remarkable, that these various ways of his in this temptation, do give strength one to another, and have as close a connexion as stones in an arch. Christ was pleased to commend the wisdom of the unjust steward, though he intended not the least approbation of his dishonesty. So we may turn aside and observe the cunning artifice of the devil, in the management of this argument against Christ, which is to this purpose, as if he had thus proceeded: 'If thou art the Son of God,' as the voice from heaven lately testified, it can be no inconvenience, but every way an advantage to give a further proof of it. Thy present condition of want and hunger seem to contradict it; for how strange and unbeseeming is it for the Son of God to be in such straits! yet if thou beest what thou sayest thou art, it is easy for thee to help thyself. God, that made the world of nothing, by the power of his command, can much more change the forms of things that are made already; it is but speaking, and these stones that are before thee will be turned into bread; and besides that, in so doing thou mayest seasonably vindicate thyself from the eclipse of thy present condition. Necessity and duty—for it is duty to supply the want of the body, which cannot be supported without its proper nourishment—compel thee unavoidably to it, except thou fearest not to contract the guilt of self-destruction, especially seeing I do not urge thee to provide delicacies, but only bread, and such as is needful to keep in the lives of the poorest men, in the poorest manner.

Obs. 11. Hence note, *Satan in driving on a temptation, useth such an artificial contrivement of motives and things, that still one doth infer another, one strengthens another.* Temptations are like a screw, which if once admitted, will improve its first hold to draw in all the rest. By these arts doth Satan, like a cunning serpent, wriggle himself into the affections of men.

CHAPTER X.

Of Satan's chief end in this temptation; his skill in making the means to sin plausible.—The reasons of that policy, with his art therein.—Men's ignorance his advantage.—Of the differences of things propounded to our use.

The various aims of Satan, and their close dependence one upon another, having contributed to us their several observations, it r ꞉ that we ask after the main and chief thing that Satan principally intended. And to make way to this, it must be noted, that in grand temptations especially, the main design of Satan comprehends these two: the chief end, and the chief means conducing to that end. About these, some authors conjecture variously, whose differences we have no great occasion to mention, seeing the text gives so great a satisfaction in this matter.

1. For first, The main end of Satan we have not obscurely expressed to us in these words, 'If thou be the Son of God,' which if we compare with Mat. iii. 17, 'This is my beloved Son, in whom I am well pleased,' we shall easily apprehend that here Satan doth but echo to that voice which came down from heaven; as he did with Eve. God had said, of the tree in the midst of the garden, ye shall not eat, [Gen. iii. 3.] Satan, having as it were the sound of this yet in his ears, in a clear reference to it saith, 'Yea, hath God said, Ye shall not eat?' ver. 1. So here is also an evident respect to God's testimony concerning Christ, as if he had said, 'Hath God said thou art his Son? If thou beest indeed such as he testified, give some proof of it,' &c. By which it appears that his design was to undermine this testimony, or some way or other to defeat it. Neither need it pass for an objection against this,

that Satan doth not directly mention his doubt or distrust, nor positively suggest to Christ a questioning or misbelief of his sonship, for it was not suitable to his policy so to lay open his main end. That must have been expected afterward, as the last in execution, if it had taken effect, though it were first in intention.

2. Secondly, The chief means by which he would have brought this end about, may be understood from Christ's answer to the temptation; for it cannot but be imagined that Christ knew the bottom of Satan's policy, and that his answer must fully confront the means by which Satan endeavoured to ensnare him. His answer was, 'Man lives not by bread alone, but by every word that proceedeth out of the mouth of God.' If we can then come to a certain understanding of this scripture, which is not difficult, we shall evidently know the mind of the temptation, to which this is a direct answer.

These words are cited out of Deut. viii. 3, which some interpret to this sense,[1] as if Christ had said, Man hath not only a life of the body —which is mentioned[2] by bread—to look after, but another life of the soul, which is of so great concernment, that the bodily life is to be neglected, rather than that of the soul to be endangered. This is a truth in itself, but is apparently besides the meaning of Deut. viii. Neither doth it afford so full and particular an answer as doubtless Christ intended. But let us consider the text, and we shall find more in it; for Moses first sets down God's dealing with Israel in the wilderness, in that he suffered them to hunger, and took from them the ordinary means of life, which, as the latter part of the verse shews, is to be understood of ordinary bread; and then to supply that want, he fed them by an extraordinary means, such as they had never heard of before; this was by manna. Next he makes an inference from this way of God's proceeding, improving this particular to a general rule, 'That he might make thee know that man lives not by bread only, but by every word that proceedeth out of the mouth of the Lord doth man live;' which is clearly of this import, that man lives not by ordinary means only, but that God can provide for his life in an extraordinary way, by appointing anything to that end, through his mighty and powerful word and good pleasure. So that things never so unusual, or unfit in themselves for nourishment, will become strengthening to us, if he shall give out his command. Christ then applying this in this sense, did, as it were, thus say to Satan, 'Though I want ordinary means of life, which is bread, yet I know God can make anything which he pleaseth to nourish me instead of it. So that I will not cast off a dependence upon the providence of God in this strait, and without warrant run to an extraordinary course for supply.' Hence it is evident that to bring about his main end, which was to distrust of his relation to God, he used this means, that by reason of his strait in the failure of ordinary supply, he should distrust providence, and without warrant provide for himself. Observe,

Obs. 12. *That where Satan carries on a main design and end, he bestows most of his pains and skill in rendering the means to that end*

---

[1] *Vide* Lightfoot, Harmon. in Mat. iv. Pool Synopsis, in Deut. viii.
[2] Query, 'Maintained'?—ED.

plausible and taking. The end is least in mention, and the means in their fit contrivance takes up most of his art and care. The reasons whereof are these:—

(1.) First, *The end is apparently bad, so that it would be a contradiction to his design to mention it.* It is the snare and trap itself, which his wisdom and policy directs him to cover. His ultimate end is the destruction of the soul. This he dare not openly avouch to the vilest of men; he doth not say to them, 'Destroy your souls,' 'Bring eternal miseries upon yourselves,' but only tempts them to that which will bring this misery upon them; and as for those intermediate ends, which are the formal acts of sin, he useth also a kind of modesty in their concealment. He doth not usually say, Go and murder, or, Commit adultery; but rather puts them upon ways or means that will bring them up to those iniquities, except that he sometime have to deal with those that are so hardened in sin, that they make a sport to do wickedly, and then he can more freely discover his ends to such in the temptation.

(2.) Secondly, The means to such wicked ends have not only an innate and natural tendency in themselves, which are apt to sway and bias men that way, but are also capable *of artificial improvement, to a further enticement to the evils secretly intended; and these require the art and skill for the exact suiting and fitting of them.* The end cannot be reached without the means, and means so ordered, without the aid of grace, will scarce miss of the end.

(3.) Thirdly, The means are capable of *a varnish and paint.* He can make a shift to set them off and colour them over, that the proper drift of them cannot easily be discovered; whereas the ends to which these lead cannot receive, at least so easily with some, such fair shows. It is far easier to set off company-keeping, with the pleasurable pretences of necessity or refreshing divertisement, than to propound direct drunkenness, the thing to which company-keeping tends, under such a dress.

Query. If it be demanded, How and by what arts he renders the means so plausible? I shall endeavour a satisfaction to that query, by shewing the way that Satan took to render the means he made use of in this temptation, plausible to Christ, which were these:—

[1.] First, He represents it as *a harmless or lawful thing in itself.* Who can say it had been sinful for the Son of God to have turned stones into bread, more than to turn water into wine?

[2.] Secondly, He gives the motion a further pretext of *advantage or goodness.* He insinuated that it might be a useful discovery of his sonship, and a profitable supply against hunger.

[3.] Thirdly, He seems also to put *a necessity upon it*, that other ways of help failing, he must be constrained so to do, or to suffer further want.

[4.] Fourthly, He forgets not to tell him that to do this was but *suitable to his condition*, and that it was a thing well becoming the Son of God to do a miracle.

[5.] Fifthly, He doth urge it at the rate of *a duty*, and that being in hunger and want, it would be a sinful neglect not to do what he could and might for his preservation.

The same way doth he take in other temptations; in some cases pleading all, in some most of these things, by which the means conducing thereunto may seem plausible. If he presents to men occasions of sinning, he will tell them ordinarily that they may lawfully adventure upon them, that they are harmless, nay, of advantage, as tending to the recreating of the spirits and health of the body; yea, that it is necessary for them to take such a liberty, and that in doing so, they do but what others do that profess religion. And often he hath such advantage from the circumstances of the thing, and the inclination of our heart, that he makes bold to tell us it is no less than duty. Such did the outrage of Demetrius seem to him, when he considered how much his livelihood did depend upon the Diana of the Ephesians. Paul's zeal made him confident that persecution of Christians was his duty; neither is there anything which can pretend to any zeal, advantage, or colourable ground, but presently it takes the denomination of duty.

If any wonder that such poor and shallow pretences are not seen through by all men, they may know that this happens from a fourfold ignorance:—

(1.) First, *From an ignorance of the thing itself.* How easily may they be imposed upon, who know not the nature or the usual issues of things! As children are deluded to put a value upon a useless or hurtful trifle, so are men deceived and easily imposed upon in what they do not understand. And for this cause are sinners compared to birds, who are easily enticed with the bait proposed to their view as profitable and good for them, because they know not the snare that lies hid under it. This ignorance causing the mistake mentioned, is not only a simple ignorance, but also that ignorance which owes its rise to a wilful and perverse disposition,—for there are some that are willingly ignorant,—doth often lay those open to a delusion, who, through prepossession or idleness, will not be at pains to make full inquiries.

(2.) Secondly, This also comes to pass from *an ignorance of our spirits:* for while we either engage in the things proposed by Satan upon the general warranty of a good intention, or that we have no evil meaning in it, we are kept from a discovery of the intended design. Hence Paul saw nothing, in his persecuting the church of God, of what Satan aimed at; or while upon the pretence of a good intention, our secret corrupt principles do indeed move us underhand to any undertaking, we are as little apt to see the ends of Satan in what he propounds to us. Jehu and the disciples, Luke ix. 55, pretending a zeal for God, but really carried on by their own furious tempers, did as little as others see what the devil was doing with them.

(3.) Thirdly, The means of a temptation are rendered less suspicious, from *an ignorance of the circumstances and concomitants that do attend them.*

(4.) Fourthly, As also from *an ignorance of our own weakness and inclination.* While we are confident of greater strength to resist than indeed we have, of a greater averseness than is in us to the evil suspected, we contemn the danger of the means as below us, and so grow bold with the occasions of iniquity, as pretending no hazard or danger to us.

Applic. This may teach us a piece of wisdom in the imitation of the devil. We see his malice appears in the bloody and destructive aims or intendments which he discovers against us, but his skill and cunning in a suitable disposal and ordering of the means. So should we learn to employ all our care and watchfulness about those plausible ways or introductions to sin that Satan puts in our hand; and as his eager desire of gaining his end makes him industrious about the offering of means fit to compass it, so our fear of his design and end should make us jealous of every overture propounded to us. They that from wilfulness or neglect shall admit the means of evil, cannot expect to avoid the evil to which they lead, or if they may, unexpectedly, be rescued from the end, while they use the means,—by grace interposing, as between the cup and the lip,—it is no thanks to them, and often they come not off so clear, but that some lameness or other sticks by them.

Quest. I may suspect this will be retorted back as an advice scarce practicable: for if all means leading to sin are to be avoided, then can we use nothing, but rather, as the apostle saith in another case, 'we must go out of the world,' [1 Cor. v. 10,] seeing everything may lead to evil?

Ans. I answer, We are not by any command of God put into any such strait. Things that are or may be improveable against us, may be used by us with due care and watchfulness; yet all things are not alike neither, for we must look upon things under a threefold consideration.

[1.] First, If that which is propounded or laid before us as a means to sin, be in itself sinful, the refusal of both is an undoubted duty.

[2.] Secondly, We must look upon things under the consideration of the suspiciousness which they carry with them of a further evil. Some circumstances, or postures of an opportunity and occasion offered, are of such a threatening aspect, that they fairly warn us to hold off. To keep company with a friend may be admitted, when yet that society in a suspicious place, as tavern or whore-house, is to be avoided.

[3.] Thirdly, We must further consider things as we are free or engaged to them, and accordingly where there is appearance of danger or the fear of it, we must keep at a distance, if we are engaged to such things, either by the obligation of the law of nature, or lawful calling, or command of God, or unavoidable providence, or relation. Where these ties are upon us, we cannot avoid the thing or action, but are the more concerned to take heed of being overreached or overtaken by them.

CHAPTER XI.

Of the temptation to distrust upon the failure of ordinary means.—Of the power of that temptation, and the reasons of its prevalency.—Of unwarrantable attempts for relief, with the causes thereof.—Of waiting on God, and keeping his way.—In what cases a particular mercy is to be expected.

I have particularly insisted upon the aims of Satan in this temptation in their variety, and also the cunning connexion and coherences of them. I have also singled out his chief design. I am now in the last place to present you with the suitableness and respects that the subordinate means carry to the principal, and that proportion which may be found in all these to the end designed by them.

The chief means in reference to the end designed, was a distrust of providence, and the subordinate means to bring on that distrust, was the failure of ordinary means of supply: for so he endeavoured to improve his hunger and want in the wilderness, as a manifest neglect of providence towards him, for which, as he tacitly suggests, there was no ground to wait or rely upon it any further, but to betake himself to another course. Hence note,

Obs. 13. *That the failure of ordinary means of help is by Satan improved as his special engine to bring men to a distrust of providence, and from thence to an unwarrantable attempt for their relief in an extraordinary way.*

That the failure of ordinary and usual supplies hath by the devil's subtlety brought a distrust of providence, and run men beyond all hopes of help, is a thing commonly and notoriously known. When men are afflicted, and brought unto unusual straits, and the ordinary ways of relief are out of sight, they are soon tempted to distrust God and man; and to conclude they are cut off, and that their 'hope is perished,' and that 'their eye shall no more see good.' David distressed, proclaims 'all men liars:' concludes that he should at last 'be cut off,' Ps. cxvi. 11, xxxi. 22. Jonah, in the whale's belly, thought that all hope was gone, and that he was cast out of God's sight, chap. ii. 4. The church of Israel in captivity, 'forgot prosperity,' notwithstanding the promise of deliverance after seventy years, and thought no less than that 'her hope and strength was perished,' Lam. iii. 18. And from the scriptures mentioned, we may also see the strength and prevalency of the temptation, especially when it is reduced to particulars. As,

(1.) First, *It is not a thing altogether of no weight that such a temptation should prevail against such persons;* as David and Jonah, and the whole church of Israel, that the manifold experiences that some of them have had of God's faithfulness in delivering, and the seasonableness of help at times of greatest hazard, the particular promises that all of them have had—how dismal and black soever things have seemed—have given the fullest assurances imaginable, that what he had spoken should certainly be performed; the gracious qualifications of such persons as eminently holy and skilled in the duties of trust, and in the ways of providence, and the special advantage which some of them, as prophets, have had above others, to enable them to improve that skill, experience, knowledge, and grace, to a firm adherence to such special promises : that all these things should not be sufficient to keep them off distrust, though at present the ways of deliverence were hid from them, seems strange.

(2.) Secondly, It is wonderful *to what a height such a prevailing temptation hath carried some of them.* David seems to be a little outrageous, and did upon the matter call God ' a liar,' when he said, ' All men are liars ;' which however that some interpret[1] as if it had been David's trust in God, and his confident avouchment of his enemies' prognostications of his ruin, to be but lies, and that this he spake from his firm belief of the promise, ' I believed, therefore have I spoken ;' yet the acknowledgment of his ' haste,' which, compared with Ps. xxxi. 22, is declared as his weakness, will force us to conclude it an ingenuous confession of his distrust at the first, when he was greatly afflicted, though he recovered himself afterwards to a belief of the promise; and that in that distemper he plainly reflected upon Samuel, and calls the promises of God given by him ' a very lie.'

(3.) Thirdly, It is strange also *that present instances of God's providences working out unexpected deliverances should not relieve the hearts of his saints from the power of such distrust;* that when they see God is not unmindful of them, but doth hear them in what they feared, they should still retain in their minds the impression of an unbelieving apprehension ; and not rather free themselves from their expectations of future ruin by concluding, that he that hath and doth deliver will also yet deliver. David had this thought in his heart, that he should ' one day perish by the hand of Saul,' 1 Sam. xxvii. 1, even then when God had so remarkably rescued him from Saul, and forced Saul not only to acknowledge his sin in prosecuting him, but also to declare his belief of the promise concerning David. See chap. xxvi. One would have expected that this should have been such a demonstration of the truth of what had been promised, that he should cast out all fear; and yet, contrariwise, this pledge of God's purpose to him is received by a heart strongly prepossessed with misgiving thoughts, and he continues to think that for all this Saul would one day destroy him.

(4.) Fourthly, *The pangs of this distrust are also so remarkable, that after they have been delivered, and have found that the event hath not answered their fears, they have in the review of their carriage under such fears, recounted this their weakness among other remarkable things*, thereby shewing the unreasonableness of their unbelief, and their wonder that God should pass by so great a provocation, and notwithstanding so unexpectedly deliver them. David in the places before cited was upon a thankful acknowledgment of God's love and wonderful kindness, which be thought he could not perform without leaving a record of his strange and unworthy distrust ; as if he had said, ' So greatly did I sin, and so unsuitably did I behave myself, that I then gave off, and concluded all was lost.'

[1] Ps. cxvi. 11. Pool, Synopsis, *in loc.*

To open this a little further, I shall add the reasons why Satan strikes in with such an occasion as the want of means to tempt to distrust, which are these:—

[1.] First, *Such a condition doth usually transport men beside themselves;* puts them, as it were, into an ecstacy, and by a sudden rapture of astonishment and fear, forceth them beyond their settled thoughts and purposes. This David notes as the ground of his inconsiderate rash speaking: 'It was my haste,' I was transported, &c. Now as passion does not only make men speak what otherwise they would not, but also to put bad interpretations upon actions and things beyond what they will bear, and hasten men to resolves exceedingly unreasonable; so doth this state of the heart, under an amazement and surprise of fear, give opportunity to Satan to put men to injurious and unrighteous thoughts of the providence of God, and by such ways to alienate their minds from the trust which they owe him.

[2.] Secondly, *Sense is a great help to faith.* Faith then must needs be much hazarded when sense is at a loss or contradicted, as usually it is in straits.

That faith doth receive an advantage by sense, cannot be denied. To believe what we see, is easier than to believe what we see not; and that in our state of weakness and infirmity God doth so far indulge us, that by his allowance we may take the help of our senses, is evident by his appointment of the two sacraments, where by outward visible signs our faith may be quickened to apprehend the spiritual benefits offered. Thomas, resolving to suspend his belief till he were satisfied that Christ was risen, by the utmost trial that sense could give, determining not to credit the testimony of the rest of the disciples till by putting his finger into his side he had made himself more certain, Christ not only condescended to him, but also pronounceth his approbation of his belief, accepting it, that he had believed because he had seen. But when outward usual helps fail us, our sense, being not able to see afar off, is wholly puzzled and overthrown. The very disappearing of probabilities gives so great a shake to our faith that it commonly staggers at it; and therefore was it given as the great commendation of Abraham's faith, that he, notwithstanding the unlikelihood of the thing, 'staggered not at the promise;' noting thereby how extraordinary it was in him at that time to keep up against the contradiction of sense, and how usual it is with others to be beaten off all trust by it. It is no wonder to see that faith, which usually called sense for a supporter, to fail when it is deprived of its crutch. And he that would a little understand what disadvantage this might prove to a good man when sense altogether fails his expectation, he may consider with himself in what a case Thomas might have been if Christ had refused to let him see his side, and to thrust his finger into the print of the nails. In all appearance, had it been so, he had gone away confirmed in his unbelief.

[3.] Thirdly, *Though faith can act above sense, and is employed about things not seen, yet every saint at all times doth not act his faith so high.* Christ tells us that to believe where a man hath not had the help of sight and sense, is noble and blessed, John xx. 29; yet withal, he hints it to be rare and difficult: 'he that hath not seen, and yet hath believed,' implies that it is but one amongst many that doth so, and that it is the conquest of a more than ordinary difficulty. Hence it is, that to love God when he kills, to believe when means fail, are reckoned among the high actings of Christianity.

[4.] Fourthly, *When sense is nonplussed, and faith fails, the soul of man is at a great loss.* Having nothing to bear it up, it must needs sink; but having something to throw it down, besides its own propensity downward to distrust, it hath the force of so great a disappointment to push it forward; and such bitterness of spirit, heightened by the malignant influence of Satan, that with a violence like the angel's throwing a millstone into the sea, it is cast into the bottom of such depths of unbelief, that the knowledge of former power and extraordinary providences cannot keep it from an absolute denial of the like for the future. Israel in the wilderness, when they came to the want of bread, though they acknowledged he 'clave the rock,' and gave them water in the like strait, yet so far did their hearts fail of that due trust in the power and mercy of God, which might have been expected, that though they confessed the one, they as distrustfully question and deny the other. 'He clave the rock, but can he provide flesh? can he give bread?' [Ps. lxxviii. 20.] Strange unbelief, that sees and acknowledgeth omnipotency in one thing, and yet denies it in another!

[5.] Fifthly, *Providence hath been an old question.* It is an atheism that some have been guilty of, to deny that God ordereth all affairs relating to his children here below, who yet have not so fully extinguished their natural impressions as to dare to deny the being of God. That God is, they confess, but withal they think that he 'walketh in the circuit of heaven,' and as to the smaller concerns of men, neither doth good nor evil. This being an old error, to which most are but too inclinable; and the more because such things are permitted—as the punishment of his children, and their trials, while others have all their heart can wish—as seem scarce consistent with that love and care which men look for from him to his servants, they are apt enough to renew the thoughts of that persuasion upon their minds—for which the failure of ordinary ways of help seems to be a high probability—that he keeps himself unconcerned, and therefore there seems to be no such cause of reliance upon him. The psalmist so expresseth that truth, 'Men shall say, Verily there is a God that judgeth in the earth,' [Ps. lviii. 11;] that it is discovered to be a special retrievement of it, by many and signal convincing evidences, from that distrust of God and his providences that men usually slide into upon their observation of the many seeming failures of outward means of help.

Secondly, The other branch of the observation, *that from a distrust of providence he endeavours to draw them to an unwarrantable attempt for their relief,* is as clear as the former. Sarah being under a distrust of the promise for a son, because of her age, gave her handmaid to Abraham, that in that way, the promise seeming to fail, she might obtain children by her, Gen. xvi. 2. David, because of the many and violent pursuits of Saul, not only distrusted the promise, thinking he might 'one day perish' by him, but resolves to provide for his own safety by a speedy escape into the land of the Philistines, 1 Sam. xxvii 1 ; a course which, as appears by the temptations and evils he met with there, was altogether unwarrantable. That from a distrust men are next put upon unwarrantable attempts, is clear from the following reasons :—

[1.] First, *The affrightment which is bred by such distrusts of providences will not suffer men to be idle.* Fear is active, and strongly prompts that something is to be done.

[2.] Secondly, Yet such is *the confusion of men's minds in such a case, that though many things are propounded, in that hurry of thoughts they are deprived usually of a true judgment and deliberation,* so that they are oppressed with a multitude of thoughts, as David on the like occasion takes notice, ' In the multitude of my thoughts within me,' &c., [Ps. xciv. 19 ;] and, as he expresseth the case of seamen in a storm, ' they are at their wits' end.'

[3.] Thirdly, *The despairing grievance of spirit* makes them take that which comes next to hand, as a drowning man that grasps a twig or straw, though to no purpose.

[4.] Fourthly, Being once turned off their rock, and the true stay of the promise of God for help, *whatever other course they take must needs be unwarrantable.* If they once be out of the right way, they must needs wander, and every step they take must of necessity be wrong.

[5.] Fifthly, *Satan is so officious in an evil thing,* that seeing any in this condition, he will not fail to proffer his help ; and in place of God's providence, to set some unlawful shift before them.

[6.] Sixthly, And so much the rather do men close in with such overtures, because a *sudden fit of passionate fury doth drive them, and out of a bitter kind of despite and crossness*—as if they meditated a revenge against God for their disappointment—*they take up a hasty wilful resolve to go that way that seems most agreeable to their passion,* saying with king Joram, ' What wait we upon the Lord any longer for ?' [2 Kings vi. 33.] We will take such a course, let come on us what will.

Applic. The service which the observation, well digested, may perform for us, is very fully contained in an advice which David gives on the like occasion, Ps. xxxvii. 34, which is this, ' Wait on the Lord, and keep his way.' Failures of ordinary means should not fill us with distrust, neither then should we run out of God's way for help. He that would practise this must have these three things which are comprehended in it :—

[1.] First, *He must have full persuasions of the power and promise of God.* I do not mean the bare hearsay that God hath promised to help, and that he is able to deliver, but these truths must be wrought upon the heart to a full assurance of them, and then we must keep our eye upon them ; for if ever we lose the sight of this, when troubles beset us, our heart will fail us, and we shall do no otherwise than Hagar, who, when her bottle of water was spent, and she saw no way of supply, sat down, gave up her son and self for lost, and so falls a-weeping over her helpless condition. This was that sight of God, in regard of his power, goodness, faithfulness, and truth, which are things invisible, Heb. xi. 27, which kept up the heart of Moses, that it sunk not under the pressure of his fears, when all things threatened his ruin.

[2.] Secondly, He that would thus wait upon God *had need to have an equal balance of spirit in reference to second causes.* Despise or neglect them he may not, when he may have them, for that were intolerable presumption; and so to centre our hopes and expectations upon them, as if our welfare did certainly depend upon them, is a high affront to God's omnipotency, and no less than a sinful idolizing of the creature; but the engagements of our duty must keep carefully to the first, and the consideration of an independency of an almighty power, as to any subordinate means or causes, must help us against the other miscarriage. When all means visible fail us, we must look to live upon omnipotent faithfulness and goodness, which is not tied to anything, but that without all means, and contrary to the powers of second causes, can do what he hath promised or sees fit.

[3.] Thirdly, There is no waiting upon God, and keeping his way, without *a particular trust in God.* To this we are not only warranted by frequent commands, ' Trust in the Lord, I say, trust in the Lord,' but highly encouraged to it under the greatest assurances of help: Ps. xxxvii. 5, ' Trust in him, and he shall bring it to pass.' ' Trust in the Lord and do good, and verily thou shalt be fed,' ver. 3. The Lord shall help and deliver them, because they trust in him. And this we are to do at ' all times,' and in the greatest hazards, and with the highest security: ' I laid me down and slept; I will not be afraid of ten thousands of people that have set themselves against me round about,' Ps. iii. 5, 6.

Quest. But some, possibly, may say, Is it our duty to sit still in such a case? When all the usual ways of supply fail us, must nothing be attempted?

Ans. (1.) I answer, first, *At such times greater care and diligence is necessary in outward things.* That what one lawful course cannot help, another lawful course may; and as to spiritual diligence, it should be extraordinary. We should be more earnest and frequent in prayer, fastings, meditations, and the exercise of graces.

(2.) Secondly, While we are in the pursuit of duty, and where the substance of it may be preserved entire, if our straits and wants unavoidably put us out of the way, *we may be satisfied to go on, though some circumstances be necessarily waived and hindered.* Phinehas might kill Zimri and Cosbi upon the command of Moses, Num. xxv. 5; and consequently in prosecution of duty, though, other circumstances considered, it was in some respects extraordinary.

(3.) Thirdly, But let the strait be what it will, *we must not forsake duty;* for so we go out of God's way, and do contradict that trust and hope which we are to keep up to God-ward.

Quest. But, it may be further urged, must we, when all means fail, positively trust in God for those very things which we might expect in an ordinary way?

Ans. In some cases our duty is *submission to his will,* and the particular mercy neither positively to be expected not yet distrusted.

Thus did David behave himself when he fled from Jerusalem upon Absalom's rebellion; 'Let him do what seemeth him good.'

But there are other cases wherein it is our duty to fix our trust upon the particular mercy or help. I shall name four; and possibly a great many more may be added. As,

[1.] First, *When mercies are expressly and particularly promised:* as when the kingdom was promised to David; when a son was promised to Abraham. Whatever had been the improbabilities of their obtaining the thing promised, it was their duty positively to believe. This is indeed not a general case.

[2.] Secondly, *When God leads us into straits by engaging us in his service:* as when Israel followed the Lord into the wilderness, in order to an enjoyment of a further mercy, which was the possession of the land of Canaan. When they had no water to drink, nor food to eat, and saw no natural possibility of supply in that wilderness, they ought positively to have expected supplies from God in an extraordinary way; and it is reckoned up against them as their sin that they did not believe. This was the very case of Christ under this temptation; the Spirit led him into the wilderness upon the prosecution of a further design. When there was no bread there to satisfy his hunger, he refuseth to work a miracle for his supply, but leans upon an extraordinary providence.

[3.] Thirdly, *When the things we want are common universal blessings, and such as we cannot subsist without.* If we have nothing to eat, and nothing to put on, yet seeing the body cannot live without both, we must positively expect such supplies from providence, though we see not the way whence they should arise to us. This kind of distrust, which reflects upon the general necessary providence of God, by which he is engaged to preserve his creatures in their stations, 'to clothe the grass of the field, to feed the birds of the air,' &c., Christ doth severely challenge, 'Shall he not much more clothe you, O ye of little faith?' Mat. vi. 30. He hath little or no faith, and in that regard a very prodigy of distrust, that will not believe for necessaries. Hence, Hab. iii. 17, the prophet resolves upon a rejoicing confidence in God, when neither tree, nor field, nor flock would yield any hope in an ordinary way.

[4.] Fourthly, *When God is eminently engaged for our help, and his honour lies at stake in that very matter;* so that whether God will help or no, or whether he is able, is become the controversy, upon which religion in its truth or the honour of God is to be tried; then are we engaged to a certain belief of help. The three children upon this ground did not only assert that 'God was able to deliver them,' or that their death and martyrdom they could bear, which is all that most martyrs are able to arise up to, but they asserted positively that 'God would deliver them,' and that the fire should not burn them. They saw evidently that the contest, whether the Lord was God, was managed at so high a rate, that God was more concerned to vindicate his honour by their preservation, than to vindicate their grace and patience by their constancy and suffering, [Dan. iii.] Another instance we have in Mat. viii. 26, where Christ rebukes his disciples for unbelief, in their fears of shipwreck in a great storm—not that every seaman ordinarily lies under that charge, that gives himself up to the apprehensions of danger—the ground of which charge was this, that Christ was with them, and consequently it had unavoidably contradicted his design, and reflected upon his honour, if he had suffered his disciples at that time to be drowned. Their not minding how far Christ was engaged with them, and not supporting themselves against their fears by that consideration, made Christ tax them for their little faith.

CHAPTER XII.

Of Satan's proceeding to infer distrust of sonship from distrust of providences.—Instances of the probability of such a design.—The reasons of this undertaking.—Of Satan's endeavour to weaken the assurance and hopes of God's children.—His general method to that purpose.

Lastly, we are to consider the suitableness of the means to the end. He had, as we have seen, fitly proportioned the subordinate means to the chief and principal. The failure of ordinary means of help was shrewdly proper to infer a distrust of providence. Now let it be noted how fitly he improves this distrust of providence to bring about the end he aimed at, which was a distrust of his filial interest in God, as if he should have thus reasoned: 'He that in straits is forsaken, as to all the usual supplies that may be expected in an ordinary way, hath no reason to rely on providence; and he that hath no reason to rely on providence for the body, hath less cause to expect spiritual blessings and favours for the soul.' Hence note,

Obs. 14. *That it is Satan's endeavour to make men proceed from a distrust of providence to a distrust of their spiritual sonship, or filial interest in God.* First, I shall evidence that this is Satan's design, and next I shall give the reasons of it. The former I shall make good by these several considerations :—

(1.) First, *We see it is a usual inference that others make of men whose heart fails them, under an absence or disappearance of all means of help in their distresses.* If providence doth not appear for them, they conclude God hath forsaken them. Bildad thus concludes against Job, chap. iv. 6, ' Is not this thy fear, thy confidence, thy hope, and the uprightness of thy ways ?' Which must not only be understood as an ironical scoff at the weakness of his confidence and hope, as not being able to support him against fainting in his trouble, but as a direct accusation of the falseness and hypocrisy of his supposed integrity, and all the hopes and confidence which was built upon it; and ver. 7 doth evidence, where he plainly declares himself to mean that Job could not be innocent or righteous, it being, in his apprehension, a thing never heard of, that so great calamities should overtake an upright man, ' Who ever perished, being innocent ?' The ground of which assertion was from ver. 5, ' It is now come upon thee, and thou faintest.' That is, distresses are upon thee, and thou hast no visible means of help, but despairest ever to see a providence that will bring thee out; therefore surely thou hast had no real interest in God, as his child. Eliphaz also seconds his friend in this uncharitable censure, 'If thou wert pure and upright, he would awake for thee,' Job viii. 6; that is, because he doth thus overlook thee, therefore thou art not pure and upright.

If men do thus assault the comforts of God's children, we have reason enough to think that Satan will; for besides that we may conclude they are set on work by the devil, and what he speaks by them, he will also by other ways promote, as being a design that is upon his heart; we may be confident, that this being a surmise so natural to the heart of man, he will not let slip so fair an advantage, for the forming of it in our own hearts against ourselves.

(2.) Secondly, *The best of God's children, in such cases, escape it very hardly, if at all;* which declares not only the depth and power of that policy, but also how usual it is with Satan to urge the servants of God with it. Job, chap. xix. 25, recovered himself to a firm persuasion of sonship, 'I know that my Redeemer liveth,' &c.; but by the way his foot had well-nigh slipped, when, ver. 10, 11, he cries out, 'He hath destroyed me on every side, and I am gone; he hath also kindled his wrath against me, and he counteth me unto him as one of his enemies.' His earnest resolve not to give up his trust in God, and the confidence of his integrity, is sufficient to discover Satan's eager endeavours to have him bereaved of it.

(3.) Thirdly, *Satan's success in this temptation over the saints of God, who sometime have actually failed,* shews how much it is his work to cast down their hopes of interest in God, by overthrowing their trust in his providences. If he attempts this, and that successfully, on such whose frequent experiences might discourage the tempter, and in probability frustrate his undertaking; we have little cause to think that he will be more sparing and gentle in this assault upon those that are more weak, and less acquainted with those clouds and darknesses that overshadow the ways of providence. David, for all the promises that he had received, and notwithstanding the manifold trials that he had of seasonable and unexpected deliverances, yet when he was distressed, he once and again falls into a fear of his soul, and a questioning of God's favour. He complains as one utterly forsaken, 'Why hast thou forsaken me?' Ps. xxii. 1. In Ps. lxix., he expresseth himself, ver. 1, 'sinking in the deep mire,' as a man that had no firm ground to stand upon, and that his troubles had brought him to fear the state of his soul, not only as deprived of God's favour—and therefore, ver. 17, begs that his face may be no longer hid—but also as suspecting the loss of it; ver. 18, 'draw nigh unto my soul, and redeem it.' Ps. lxxvii., upon the occasion of outward troubles, Asaph falls into such a fit of fear about his spiritual condition, that no consideration of former mercies could relieve him, 'He remembered God,' ver. 3, 'but was troubled;' he 'considered the days of old,' called to remembrance his 'songs in the night;' but none of these were effectual to keep him from that sad outcry of distrust, ver. 7, 'Will the Lord cast off for ever? is his mercy clean gone for ever? hath God forgotten to be gracious?' &c. Which upon the review, in the composing of the psalm, he acknowledgeth an unbelieving miscarriage; I said, 'This is mine infirmity.'

(4.) Fourthly, It is also a common and ordinary thing with most, *to entertain misapprehensions of their spiritual condition, when they meet with disappointments of providence.* Hence the apostle, Heb. xii. 5, 6, when he would quiet the hearts of men under the Lord's chastening, doth of purpose make use of this encouragement, that God speaks to them in the rod as to children, and such as are under his care and love, ' My son, despise not the chastening of the Lord;' ' whom the Lord loveth, he chasteneth,' &c. Which certainly tells us thus much, that it is ordinary for men to doubt their sonship because of their afflictions. We may conjecture what the malady is, when we know what is prepared as a medicine. This would not have been a common remedy, ' that we may be children, though we be scourged,' if the disbelief of this had not been the usual interpretation of afflictions, and a common distemper.

(5.) Fifthly, We may further take notice, *that those disquiets of mind, that were only occasioned by outward things, and seem to have no affinity, either in the nature of the occasion, or present inclination of the party, with a spiritual trouble; yet if they continue long, do wholly change their nature.* They that at first only troubled themselves for losses or crosses, forget these troubles and take up fears for their souls.

Sometime this ariseth from a natural softness and timorousness of spirit. Such are apt to misgive upon any occasion, and to say, Surely if I were his child, he would not thus forsake me; his fatherly compassions would some way or other work towards me.

Sometime this ariseth from melancholy, contracted or heightened by outward troubles. These, when they continue long, and pierce deep, put men into 'a spirit of heaviness,' which makes them refuse to be comforted. Here the devil takes his advantage. Unlawful sorrows are as delightfully improved by him as unlawful pleasures; they are *Diaboli balneum,* his bath in which he sports himself, as the leviathan in the waters. When for temporal losses or troubles men fall into melancholy, if they be not relieved soon, then their grief changeth its object, and presently they disquiet themselves, as being out of God's favour, as being estranged from God, as being of the number of the damned; such against whom the door of mercy is shut, and so cry out of themselves as hopeless and miserable. The observations of physicians afford store of instances of this kind. Felix Platerus gives one, of a woman at Basle who first grieved for the death of her son, and when by this means she grew melancholy, that changed into a higher trouble; she mourns that her sins would not be pardoned, that God would not have mercy for her soul. Another, for some loss of wheat, first vexeth himself for that, and then at last despairs of the happiness of his soul; with a great many more of that kind.[1]

Sometimes a desperate humour doth, from the same occasion, distract men into a fury; of which Mercerus gives one instance from his own knowledge, of a person who, upon the distresses which he met

---

[1] Alii damnatos se putant, et quod Deo curæ non sunt.—*Platerus Tract. Melan.,* cap. 3.

with, fell into a rage against God, uttering speeches full of horror and blasphemy, not fit to be related.[1]

If there be such an affinity betwixt distrust of providence and distrust of sonship, that the one slides into the other naturally; if this be common to all men under troubles, to suspect their souls; if the best do here actually miscarry; if those that do not, yet hardly escape; and if bystanders commonly give this judgment of men in straits, that there is no help for them in their God; we cannot but collect from all this, that it is an advantage which Satan will not neglect, and that he doth very much employ himself to bring it about.

The reasons of it are these:—

(1.) First, *Distrust of providence hath in it the very formal nature of distrust of sonship.* If the object of distrust were but changed, it would without any further addition work that way. He that trusts providence acknowledgeth that God knoweth his wants, that he is of a merciful inclination to give what he sees he hath need of; that he hath manifested this by promise, that he is so faithful that this promise cannot be neglected, and that he hath power to do what he hath promised.[2] He that distrusts providence disbelieves all these, consequentially at least; and he that will not believe that God takes any care of the body, or that he is of a merciful disposition toward him, or thinks either he hath made no such promise, or will not keep it, if any such were made; cannot believe, if that doubt were but once started, that God is his Father, or that he hath interest in the privilege of a son, seeing it is impossible to believe a sonship, while his care, mercy, promises, and power are distrusted. In this then Satan's work is very easy. It is but his moving the question about the Lord's mercy to the soul, and presently, as when new matter is ministered to a raging flame, it takes hold upon it, and with equal, nay greater, force it carries the soul to distrust spiritual mercies, as before it disbelieved temporal kindnesses.

(2.) Secondly, *The same reasons, which any man doth gather from the seeming neglect or opposition of providence, upon which he grounds his distrust of the Lord's kindness in reference to outward things, will also serve as arguments for a distrust of spiritual favours.* The distresses of men seem to argue—[1.] That there is sin and provocation on their part; [2.] And that there is a manifestation of anger on God's part; [3.] And from these apprehensions ariseth bitterness, anxiety, fear, and dejection of spirit, which intercepts all the help and consolation which might arise from other considerations of the Lord's promise or mercy, for the quieting of the heart and fortifying it against such apprehensions. These same grounds, with the prevailing fears and perplexities arising from them, are enough to make us suspect that we are not yet under any such peculiar favours as may bespeak us his children by adoption; so that from the same premises Satan will conclude, that as he hath no care for our bodies, so no love to our souls; that we neither love God nor are beloved of him. Betwixt

---

[1] Quis est ille Deus, ut serviam illi? quid proderit si oraverim? si præsens est, cur non succurrit? cur non me carcere, inedia, squalore confectum liberat? &c. Absit a me hujusmodi Deus.—*Mercerus ad Gen.* cap. xi. fol. 230. [Misprinted in text and note 'Mercennus.' M.'s 'Commentary' on Genesis was a posthumous work, edited by Beza, 1598, folio.—G.]   [2] Dr Reynolds, Serm. on Hosea xiv., ser. 4.

the one conclusion and the other there is but a step, and with a small labour he can cut the channel, and let in that very distrust to run with all its force against our spiritual interest in God.

(3.) Thirdly, *To trust God for the soul is a higher act than to trust him for the body.* The soul being of greater excellency than the body, and the mercy necessary for the happiness of it being more precious and less visible, it must require a higher confidence in God to assure of this than satisfy us in the other. It is more easy to believe a lesser kindness from a friend than a singular or extraordinary favour. He, then, that cannot trust God for temporal mercies, shall be more unable to believe eternal blessings. 'If we run with footmen, and they have wearied us, shall we be able to contend with horsemen? If the shallow brooks be too strong for us, what shall we do in the swellings of Jordan?' [Jer. xii. 5.]

(4.) Fourthly, *When faith is weakened as to one object, it is so tainted and discouraged that it is generally weakened as to all other.* If the hand be so weakened that it cannot hold a ring, it will be less able to grasp a crown. When we are baffled in our trust for temporal mercies, if Satan then put us to it not to believe for spiritual blessings, how can we expect but to be much more at a loss in them? So that he is sure of the victory before he fights, and he that is so sedulous to take advantage against us will not lose so considerable a conquest for want of pursuit. There is indeed one thing that may seem fit to be objected against this, which is, that men may retain their faith in one thing when yet they distrust in another, as the Israelites distrusted the power and goodness of God for bread and flesh in the wilderness, when yet they believed that as he had given water out of the rock, so he could do it again if there were need: Ps. lxxviii. 20, 'He smote the rock, and the waters gushed out; but can he give bread?' as if they had said, We believe he can give water, but it is impossible he should provide bread. But they that would thus object may consider that the reason of men's confidence in one thing, while distrust is in other things prevailing, is not from any real strength of their faith, but a present want of a temptation. If such a confidence were put to it, it would quickly be seen that it were truly nothing. As confident as the Israelites were that they could believe for a supply of water, we find that neither that experience, nor the other of supplying them with manna and quails, were sufficient to keep up their trust in God, but that at the next strait all was to seek: ver. 32, 'For all this they sinned still, and believed not for his wondrous works.'

(5.) Fifthly, Besides all the forementioned advantages that Satan hath in raising this temptation, of distrusting sonship out of a distrust of providence, we may suppose him the more earnest in this matter, *because it is so provoking to God to distrust his providence, that he often, as a just chastisement of that evil, punisheth it by giving them up to distrust him for their souls.* The height of the provocation may be measured by this, that it is not only a denial of God that is above, but usually a vesting some mean and contemptible thing with those attributes which only suit a God infinite and eternal. As Israel did not only forsake the Almighty by their distrust, but place their hopes upon Ashur, upon their own horses and warlike preparations, and at last upon the works of their hands, which they called their gods, Hosea xiv. 2, 3. How offensive this is to the Lord, we may observe by that notable check which the prophet gave Ahaz, Isa. vii. 8, 13, notwithstanding his compliment of refusing a sign, which God offered him for the strengthening of his hope, upon a pretence that he would trust without it,—though indeed he absolutely distrusted him, as appears by 2 Chron. xxviii. 20,—that it was a weaning[1] and tiring out the patience of a long-suffering God: 'Is it a small thing for you to weary men, but will you weary my God also?' God is so active and jealous of all encroachments of this kind, that they may expect he will give up such offenders to be punished by the terrors of a higher distrust. He that is not owned as a God in his providences, will not be owned as a Father for spiritual mercies; they that will not own him for the body, shall not be able to lay hold upon him or his strength to be at peace with him for their souls; and by this piece of just discipline he often cures the distrust of providence in his children, who when they see themselves plunged into terrors and fears about their everlasting welfare, do not only call God just, and accept of the punishment of their iniquity in distrusting him for smaller matters, but now wish with all their hearts that they might have no greater thing to trouble them than what relates to the body or this life.

To sum up all these reasons in one word: Satan hath from the forementioned considerations *a certain expectation of prevalency.* For not only in this case doth God, as it were, fight for him, by giving them up to distrust their filial interest that have provoked him by a distrust of providence, and our faith is also so weakened by the former overthrow that it is not able to maintain its ground in a higher matter; but also this distrust carries that in the nature and grounds of it that will of itself work up to a disbelief of spiritual mercies. He knows, then, that this piece of the victory is an easy consequence of the former; and we may say of it as the prophet Nahum, chap. iii. 12, of the strongholds of Nineveh, It is like 'a fig-tree with the first ripe figs, if they be shaken, they shall even fall into the mouth of the eater.' This temptation of distrusting our sonship falls into Satan's mouth with a little labour, when once he hath prevailed so far as to make us distrust the providence of God in outward matters.

Applic. This must warn and caution us against any unbeseeming unbelieving entertainment of jealousy against the Lord's providence. We are but too apt in our straits to take a greater liberty to question his mercy and power, not foreseeing how closely this borders upon a greater evil. We may say of it, as the apostle speaks of 'babbling in controversies,' that they 'lead to more ungodliness,' and that such words 'eat as a canker,' [2 Tim. ii. 17;] so doth this distrust usually carry us further, and when we fall out with God for small matters, he will be angry in earnest, and withdraw from us our consolations in greater. In the depth of your distresses, when your fears are round about you, and God seems to compass you about with his net,—when lover and friend forsakes, and when there is no appearance of help, endeavour, for the keeping hold of your interest in God, to behave yourselves according to the following directions:—

[1] Query, 'Wearying'?—G.

[1.] First, *Look upon the providences of God to be as a great deep, the bottom of whose ways and designs you cannot reach.* Think of them as of a mystery, which indeed you must study, but not throw away, because you cannot at first understand it. Providences are not to be dealt with as Alexander did by Gordius his knot, who when he could not loose it he cut it. If you see not the end of the Lord, or cannot meet with a door of hope in it, yet 'lay your hand upon your mouth,' speak not, think not evil of things you know not, but wait till the time of their 'bringing forth.'

[2.] Secondly, *You must keep up in your hearts high and honourable thoughts of God,* yea, of his mercy and goodness, and where you cannot see your way, or God's way, before you, yet, as it were by a kind of implicit faith, must you believe that he is holy and good in all his ways.

[3.] Thirdly, Though you may read your sins or God's displeasure in them, and accordingly endeavour to humble yourselves and call yourselves vile, yet must it be always remembered that *eternal love or eternal hatred is not to be measured by them.*

[4.] Fourthly, *Restrain complainings.* It is indeed an ease to complain; 'I will speak,' saith Job, 'that I may be refreshed,' chap. xxxii. 20; notwithstanding a vent being given, it is difficult to keep within bounds. Our complainings entice us to distrust, as may appear in Job, who took a boldness this way more than was fit, as chap. x. 3, 'Is it good unto thee that thou shouldest oppress, and that thou shouldest despise the work of thine hands?'

All this hath been said in the opening of the temptation itself. Now must I consider the motive that Satan used to bring on the temptation by, 'If thou be the Son of God,' &c.

The question that is here moved by some is, whether Satan really knew or truly doubted Christ to be the Son of God. Several learned men think that he was in doubt,[1] and the reasons are variously conjectured. Cyprian conceives that the unity of the two natures in one person did blind him; he knew it to be impossible that the divine nature should hunger, and might think it strange that the human nature should fast so long.[2] Cornelius a-Lapide thinks that Satan knew that there should be two natures united in one person, and that this occasioned Satan's fall, while he proudly stomached the exaltation of the human nature; but he imagines Satan's doubt arose from a doubtful sense of that phrase, 'This is my beloved Son,' as not knowing whether Christ were the natural or an adopted son of God.

But notwithstanding these apprehensions, others conceive that Satan knew very well who Christ was, and that being privy to so many things relating to him, as the promises which went before and directly pointed out the time, the angel's salutation of Mary at his conception, the star that conducted the wise men to him, the testimony from heaven concerning him, with a great many things more, he could not possibly be ignorant that he was the Messias and the Son of God by nature. Neither doth that expression, 'If thou be the Son of God,' imply any doubting, seeing that that is usually expressive of the

[1] Beza, Chemnitius.
[2] Serm. de jejunio et tempt. Christi. Unitas naturarum excæcavit Satanam.

greatest certainty and assurance, as in the speech of Lamech, 'If Cain shall be avenged sevenfold,' that is, as certainly he shall be avenged; so Satan might use it to this sense, 'If, or seeing thou art the Son of God.' Now, whereas it may seem strange that he should set upon Christ, if he knew who he was, I have answered that before, and shall here only add that though Satan did believe Christ to be the Son of God, yet so strongly did the power of malice work in him, that he would have had him to have doubted that he was not so. From all this we have this observation,

Obs. 15. *That the great design of Satan is to weaken the assurance and hopes of the children of God in their adoption.*

This is the masterpiece of his design, the very centre in which most of his devices meet. We may say of him as Esau said of Jacob, 'Is he not rightly called Jacob, a supplanter?' [Genesis xxvii. 36;] he first stole away our birthright at the creation, and now he seeks to take away our blessing in Christ the Redeemer.

The reasons of this undertaking I shall not here insist on. It is sufficiently obvious that the greatest perplexity and sorrow ariseth to the children of God from hence, and that a troop of other spiritual evils, as impatience, fury, blasphemy, and many more, doth follow it at the heels, besides all that inability for service, and at last plain neglect of all duty. All I shall further do at this time shall be to shew in a few particulars, from Satan's carriage to Christ in this temptation, how and after what manner he doth manage that design, in which note:—

(1.) First, *That it is his design to sever us from the promise, and to weaken our faith in that.* When Eve was tempted, this was that he aimed at, that she should question the good earnest of the prohibition, 'Hath God said so?' Was he real in that command, that you should not eat at all? &c. The like he doth to Christ, 'Is it true? or can it be so as that voice declared, that thou art the Son of God?'

(2.) Secondly, *Though this be his design, yet his way to come to it is not at first to deny it, but to question and inquire;* yet after such a manner as may imply and withal suggest a doubting or suspicion that it is not so. He doth not come to Christ thus, 'Thou art not the Son of God; or that voice that gave thee that testimony was but a lie or a delusion;' but he rather proceeds by questioning, which might seem to grant that he was so, yet withal might possibly beget a doubt in his mind.

(3.) Thirdly, *Next he more plainly suggests something that may seem to argue the contrary;* for thus he aggravates Christ's present condition of want, 'Can it be that God would leave thee to these oppressing straits, if thou wert his Son?' At this rate he deals with us, improving the failure of outward means of help, the permission of temptation, the want of comfort, the continuance of affliction, notwithstanding prayers, &c., as probabilities that we belong not to God.

(4.) Fourthly, *After this he urgeth Christ to a sinful miscarriage, to distrust providence, and to rely no longer on the care of his Father.* If Christ had been prevailed with in this, he would have made use of it as an argument to prove that he was not the Son of God indeed. It is usual in his disputings with us about adoption, to put us upon something which may be as an argument out of our own mouths against us. Christ might have answered him in this as the man answered Joab, 'If I should do so, then thou thyself wouldst set thyself against me.'

(5.) Fifthly, When at last he hath gradually ascended to that confidence as to deny our adoption, *then, at a very great disadvantage, he puts us upon the proof, in which he puts by the ordinary evidences, and insists on extraordinary proofs as necessary.* The servants of the Lord that are under this exercise, do find that in this case the ordinary evidences of repentance, mortification, love to the brethren, &c., do nothing for them. Satan puts their spirit upon clamouring for higher evidences. Nothing will serve except they may view the records of eternity, and read their names enrolled in the everlasting decrees, or except God will speak from heaven in an extraordinary way, to testify of them, as Thomas resolved that no less should satisfy his doubt than the feeling and seeing of the print of the nails. To this purpose some stand upon no less than a miracle for proof of sonship. Of which we have two instances of later years, the one Mrs Honywood, the other Mrs Sarah Wight,[1] who in their distresses for their souls were tempted by Satan to make a hasty experiment, the one by throwing a Venice glass, the other by throwing a cup against the wall, with this or the like expression, 'If I must be saved, then let not this glass break'—a desperate temptation! Their manner of desiring satisfaction is so provoking, that it cannot be expected God will give an answer by it, but rather the contrary; and if he should not condescend, as he is not bound—though he strangely preserved the cup and glass fore-mentioned from breaking—what a dangerous conclusion would Satan draw from it! Of this nature and design was that proposal of Satan's to Christ, 'Command that these stones be made bread,' that is, do it as a proof of thy sonship.

Applic. By this we must learn this skill, *not too easily to give up our hopes, or to be prodigal of our interest in Christ, so as to part with it slenderly.* If Satan would chiefly rob us of this, we may learn thence to put a price upon these jewels, and to account that precious, and of singular concernment, which he useth so much cunning to bereave us of. Many of the Lord's servants may justly blame themselves for their lavish unthriftiness in this matter, who, as if it were a necessary piece of humility or modesty, will readily conclude against themselves that they are not God's children, that they are not yet converted, &c. Thus, at unawares, they give up to Satan without a stroke all that he seeks for.

Quest. But you will say, Must all men be confident of adoption?

Ans. No, I mean not so; yet all men must be wary how they cast away their hopes. Particularly,

[1.] First, Though it be a dangerous arrogancy for a sinful, wicked creature to bear himself up in a belief that he is converted and actually instated into the adoption of sons; yet it is as dangerous, on the other hand, for that man to cast off all hope, and to say he is reprobated, and such a one as cannot expect pardon and grace.

[2.] Secondly, Those that are converted, though they may and

---

[1] See their relations in print. [Brooks, *s. n.*—G.]

ought to humble themselves deeply for their sinful miscarriage, and sincerely acknowledge that they deserve not to be called his children, yet must they be careful not to renounce their filial interest. They may say they are prodigal, yet keep to this, that they are sons; though they are wandering sheep, yet must they stick here, that they are sheep still, and that God is still a Father, though a provoked Father, otherwise their folly will give more than all his fury could get, at least so quickly and easily.

CHAPTER XIII.

Then the devil taketh him up into the holy city, and setteth him on the pinnacle of the temple.—Mat. iv. 5.

The preparation to the second temptation.—Of his nimbleness to catch advantages from our answers to temptation.—That Satan carried Christ in the air.—Of his power to molest the bodies of God's children.—How little the supposed holiness of places privilegeth us from Satan.—Of Satan's policy in seeming to countenance imaginary defences.—Of his pretended flight in such cases, with the reasons of that policy.—Of his improving a temptation to serve several ends.

I omit Christ's answer to the first temptation at present, purposing to handle his answers to all the temptations together. And now the second temptation is before us, in which, first, I shall observe a few things in Satan's preparation to the temptation, which takes in [1.] The time; [2.] The manner of his carrying him; [3.] The place where he acted it.

(1.) First, For the time. That is noted in the word 'then,' which [1.] Points at the immediate succession of this to the former assault. The evangelist Luke puts this temptation last, but he only had respect to the substance of the temptation in his narration; not regarding the order of them, which Matthew hath punctually observed, as appears by his close connecting of them with the particles 'then' and 'again,' ver. 5, 8. Besides, whosoever shall consider that in the first, Satan tempted Christ to distrust, which he repelled by telling him that it was his duty, in the failure of outward means, to rely upon divine providence, seeing man lives not by bread alone, &c., he will see so much of connexion in the matter of the temptations that he will easily persuade himself that the second place belongs to this, for this is but, as it were, a fit and pertinent reply to Christ's refusal; as if Satan had said, 'Since thou wilt rely upon the help and providence of God in an extraordinary way of working, give an experiment of that by casting thyself down, which thou mayest with greater confidence do, because he hath promised an extraordinary help, and hath given his angels charge concerning thee,' &c. Hence observe,

Obs. 1. *That Satan is not discouraged easily, nor doth he always desist upon the first repulse, but frequently renews the assault when he is strongly and resolutely resisted.*

This word, 'then,' doth also [2.] Tell us of Satan's nimbleness in catching a present advantage for a new temptation from Christ's answer. He declared his trust in providence; this he presently lays hold on as a fit opportunity to tempt him to presumption. Here note,

Obs. 2. *That when Satan is upon any design, if an occasional advantage occur from our way of refusal, he will not let it slip, but improves it to what it may lead to, though it be contrary to that which he was first labouring for.*

This was the policy which Benhadad's servants used in their address to Ahab, 1 Kings xx. 33; the men did diligently observe whether anything would come from him, and did hastily catch it. If anything come from us we are under his temptation, he is diligent to observe it, and prosecutes it accordingly; which may serve to satisfy the wonder that some have concerning the contrariety in the temptations to which they are urged. They admire how it comes to pass that their temptations should so suddenly alter, that when Satan seems to be so intent upon one design, he should so quickly change, and urge them presently to a different or contrary thing; but they may know that the devil watcheth the wind, and spreads his sail according to the advantage which ariseth from our answer or repulse. So that if we would but plough with our own heifer, and observe our frame of spirit, we should easily find out this riddle. For as it is in disputings and arguings of men, replies beget new matter for answer, and so do they multiply one another; thus are temptations altered and multiplied, and out of the ashes of one assault repelled, another doth quickly spring up.

The second circumstance of preparation is, *Satan's taking him up and setting him on the temple.* That this was not a visionary or an imaginary thing, hath been proved before. Yet granting it to have been real, as in truth it seems to have been, it is disputed what was the *modus*, the way and manner of it. Some think this was no more than Christ's voluntary following of Satan, who guided and conducted the way;[1] partly because the words παραλαμβάνειν and ἄγειν are in Scripture accommodated to a man's taking of any as a companion under his guide and conduct of the way, and to a disposal of them in any kind of station. Thus, where it is said, 'Joseph took Mary and the young child to go to Egypt,' Mat. ii. 13, the same word is used; and when Christ tells his disciples that they shall bring the ass and the colt which they should find tied, the same word which expresseth Christ being set on the temple is there used, Mat. xxii. 2. Partly also, they think it below the dignity of Christ to be thus violently hurried.

Others think that Satan was permitted to take up the body of Christ, and by his power to have conveyed him in the air; and indeed the whole series of the narration, with all the circumstances thereof, are evident for it. The distances of places, the quickness and speediness of the removals, the more proper applications of the words, 'taking' and 'setting,' to Satan as the actor, and the declaration of his power therein, as able to do great things; these make the matter so

[1] Spanheim, Dub. Evan. *in loc.*

clear, that it seems to be an unnatural forcing of the text to give it any other interpretation. Besides, the former opinion of Satan's taking of Christ, as a manuductor or guide, seems every way unreasonable; for if Christ only followed Satan, then it must have been either by a land journey on foot or in the air. This latter it could not be; for if Christ had supported himself in the air by his own power, he had anticipated the temptation, and it would have been folly and madness for Satan to have urged him to fly in the air, after such an evidence of his power; and who can imagine that Christ followed Satan on foot from the wilderness to the temple, or that his access to the roof of the temple was so easy, in such a way when the temple was always so strictly guarded? Note, hence,

Obs. 3. *That Satan is sometime permitted to exercise his power upon the bodies of those that are dear to God.* That he hath power to carry the bodies of men in the air, is sufficiently confirmed by what he doth frequently to witches, who are usually carried, if we can give any credit to the stories that are writ of them, in the air, to places far remote from their dwellings, *equitatio cum Diana aut Herodiade.* And that this power is permitted him upon others, than such as are in compact with him, is as evident from what is testified of those whose forward curiosity hath led to imitate witches in their anointings, who have thereupon been conveyed after them to their assemblies, and when the company hath been suddenly dismissed, they have been found many miles distant from their dwellings; such instances we have in Bodin, and among other things that of Domina Rossa mentioned by him, whom Satan would sometime bind to a tree, sometime to a table, or to a bed's-foot, or to a manger, sometime one hand bound to another; the devil thus molested her from eight years old, a long time.[1] This power of conveying persons in the air is not usual, yet there are some in this place—Newcastle—that have known one frequently molested by Satan at this rate. However, if we take notice of his power to abuse the bodies of holy persons more generally, we shall find it frequent. Mary Magdelene was possessed; Christ mentions a daughter of Abraham bowed down by him many years; Job was filled with botches and sores; and there are many diseases wherein Satan hath a greater hand than is commonly imagined. Physicians frequently conclude so much, while they observe some distempers to elude such remedies as are usually successful upon other persons under the same diseases.

Applic. From this we may infer, [1.] The great power of Satan; who can tell the extent of it? doubtless, if he were permitted, we should see sad instances hereof daily. [2.] This discovers the wonderful care and providence of God over us in our preservation from his fury. [3.] We may further note that the abuse of the bodies of men by Satan, will be no evidence that therefore God doth disregard them, or that they are not precious to him. Christ did undergo this abuse, to give such as shall be so molested, some comfort in his example.

The third circumstance, which is that *of place*, is set down first in general, 'the holy city,' that is Jerusalem, for so Luke speaks expressly,

[1] Bodin, p. 147.

Luke iv. 9. Jerusalem was so called, because of God's worship there established, and his peculiar presence there; but that it should be called so at this time may seem strange, seeing it might now be lamented as of old, ' How is the faithful city become an harlot! Righteousness lodged in it, but now murderers,' [Isa. i. 21.] In answer to this, we must know that God having not yet given her a bill of divorce, he is pleased to continue her title and privilege. This might be profitably improved; but I will not suffer myself to be diverted from the matter of temptation, which is the only thing I propound to prosecute from hence. I shall here only observe,

Obs. 4. *That the holiness or sanctity of a place will be no privilege against temptations.* He is not so fearful, as many imagine, as that he dares not approach a churchyard or a church; neither place nor duty can keep him off. I do not believe the popish fiction of their St Bennet's vision, wherein they tell of his seeing but one devil in a market, and ten in a monastery; yet I question not the truth of this, that the devil is as busy at a sermon or prayer as at any other employment.

But to search a little further into this matter, it seems undeniable that Satan had a design in reference to the place, of which afterward; and I see no reason to exclude our suspicion of a design from the name and title which the evangelist here gives to Jerusalem. It is an expression which, to my remembrance, we meet not with oft in the New Testament. At the suffering of Christ, when the bodies of the saints arose out of their graves, it is said 'they went into the holy city,' Mat. xxvii. 53; but it is evident that it is there so styled upon special design, as if the evangelist would by that point at the staining of their glory, and that in a little time their boast of the temple and holy city should cease, and that all should be polluted with the carcases of the slain. And by the same reason may we suppose that Satan, intending for Christ a temptation of presumption, and backing it with the promise of a guard of angels, had in his eye the usual confidence that the Jews had of that city, as a place where the presence of angels might be more expected than elsewhere. So that it seems Satan intended to impose upon Christ a confidence in order to presumption. From the privilege of the place, here observe,

Obs. 5. *That Satan is willing to gratify us with nominal and imaginary privileges and defences against himself.* He will willingly allow us such defences as are altogether insignificant and delusive, and his policy here is centred upon these two things:—

(1.) First, *He doth industriously prompt us to self-devised inventions*, such as were never appointed or blessed of God to any such use; but only found out by the bold superstitions of men. Of this we have an instance in Balak, who carried Baalam from place to place in his prosecution of his design of cursing Israel; neither can we imagine that a commodious prospect of Israel was all he aimed at, seeing he discovers his mind in this variation of places, ' Peradventure it will please God that thou mayest curse them from thence,' Num. xxiii. 27; clearly implying that he had a confidence that the place might contribute something to his design, and that there was some inherent virtue in those consecrated places; and therefore did he begin with the high-places of Baal, and then to the field of Zophim, and then to the top of Peor, Num. xxii. 27, xxiii. 14, 28. Among the papists we find too much of this. What power they attribute to holy water, blessed salt, sign of the cross, hallowed earth, consecrated places, relics, baptized bells, exorcisms, and abundance of such stuff, may be seen in many of their writings, too tedious to be related.[1]

(2.) Secondly, He is also willing *that men use those real defences and helps which God hath commanded, so that they use them in a formal manner*, which indeed deprives them of all the life and efficacy that might be expected from an instituted means. Thus he readily permits ignorant persons, without any disturbance or molestation, to use the repetition of the Lord's prayer, ten commandments, and creed, or any other prayer, while they persuade themselves that the very saying of the words is a sufficient defence against the devil all that day.

The reasons of Satan's policy in such gratifications are these:—

[1.] First, *While we are kept doing with these, we are diverted from that which might be really helpful.* He puts a broken reed into our hand, that we might be deprived of a staff. Experience confirms this. Those that, with greatest devotion, use these empty inventions, are usually careless in the use of God's own appointments.

[2.] Secondly, *Besides that he thus betrays them by these lying helps, he doth by this means cast them on a further iniquity of idolising these foolish calves of their own invention.* In this case men have a presumptuous expectation from such usages of that which God never promised to do by them, neither ever entered into his heart so to do, seeing he answers them all with this, 'Who hath required these things at your hands?' [Isa. i. 12.] And accordingly their consciences are more concerned for the omission of one of these fooleries, than for the neglect of the greater things of the law. Such are more troubled for the neglect of the sign of the cross or holy water, than for their constant carelessness and want of faith, by which their hearts should be guarded against their enemy.

[3.] Thirdly, *In the meantime he makes work for his own triumph over them that dote upon these sottish inventions.* If we can suppose Satan to have pleasure or mirth at anything, we may be sure he will laugh at such preparations for a spiritual welfare,[2] it being as truly ridiculous for any man to go out with these weapons against Satan, as for a combatant to assail a giant with a paper helmet, a wicker shield, and a wooden dagger. And indeed when Satan counterfeits a flight or fear of such matters, as for his advantage he sometimes doth, it is but in design to beget or confirm in men a confidence of a virtue or strength in these usages against his power, that so they may fix upon them to the neglect of God's own institutions, which he most dreads. Thus we read that he cunningly ceased his oracle at Daphne upon a pretence of

---

[1] Plurimum sunt præservativa locorum, hominum, et jumentorum, verba tituli triumphalis nostri salvatoris, dum scilicet per quatuor partes loci, in modum crucis inscribuntur, Jesus † Nazarenus † Rex † Judeorum †, ritibus ecclesiæ servatis et veneratis, ut per aquæ benedictæ aspersionem, salis consecrati sumptionem, et candelarum in die purificationis et frondium in die palmarum consecratorum, usum licitum vires dæmonis imminuunt, se muniunt.—*Sprenger, Malleus Maleficarum*, part 2, quest. 1. Licitum est aqua benedicta, quæcunque honesta loca, hominum et jumentorum, in salvationem hominum et jumentorum aspergere.—*Id. ibid.*   [2] Query, 'warfare'?—ED.

the silencing power of the bones of the martyr Babilas, which were buried near the place, on purpose to lead unwary Christians to the adoration of saints and their relics.[1] Many such instances we have in Sprenger, of the devil's feigned flight at the sign of the cross, the sprinkling of holy water, the angelical salutation, St Bernard's staff, or certain words and verses hung about the neck.[2] And a great deal of such stuff we may meet with in most of their writers, all which are but cunning contrivances of Satan, to advance a belief of the virtue of these things; and so to stop men there, to the neglect of those spiritual weapons which the Scripture recommends.

These we have observed from the place in general, 'the holy city.' Let us go on to the place in particular where Satan acted all this, 'the pinnacle of the temple.' Various are the conjectures of men about this, whether it were some fane, or the top of some spire, or the place whence the apostle James was thrown down, or the top of the king's porch, which was erected to a great height over a deep valley, or some battlement, &c. But we are not concerned in such inquiries; only here shall I take notice of Scultetus, who, supposing the place to be the top of a fane or spire, and reading in Josephus that the points of such broaches were so sharp that a bird could not rest upon them without piercing its foot, was therefore willing to conclude that these temptations were not really and historically acted, but in vision only.[3] All this ariseth from a wrong interpretation of πτερύγιον, which our English renders *pinnacle*, whereas it properly signifies any battlement or angular prominency, jutting out over the rest like a wing, which would afford a sufficient footing and support.[4]

It is more profitable to inquire after Satan's reason for the choice of such a place. No question but it was upon design, for else he might with equal convenience have tempted Christ to cast himself down from some tree or precipice in the wilderness; but then what that design was, is not so easy to determine. It seems plain that he might suppose that Christ might be the rather animated to the undertaking of flying in the air by the hopes of glory which might be expected from such a performance before so many spectators. But some think that he had a design also upon the men of Jerusalem, and intended some delusion to the Jews,[5] which I am not unwilling to close with, partly because the experiences that we have of his devices assure us that in one temptation his ends are oft manifold; and I cannot but think that Satan would make all things sure, and provide, in his projecting mind, against all events. For if Christ should have yielded and evidenced so great a power in the sight of all the people, it might have been a conviction general that he was the Messiah, about that time universally expected; and partly I am ready to think so, because, in case Christ had done so, it lay so fair to confirm the Jews in a misapprehension of the personal coming of Elias, of whom they understood the prophecy of Mal. iii. 1, 'Behold, I will send my messenger; and he shall prepare the way before me; and the Lord whom ye seek shall suddenly come to his temple, even the messenger of the covenant.'[6] If the Jews ex-

---

[1] Sozomen, Eccles. Hist., lib. v. cap. 18.
[2] Mal. Malefic., part 2, quest. 11, cap. 1, 3.
[3] In Delic. Evang.
[4] Spanheim, Dub. Evan. *in loc.*
[5] Lightfoot, Harm. *in loc.*
[6] Dr Kimchi, *in loc.*

pected Elias to come from heaven to the temple, how strongly would they have been confirmed in this opinion if they had seen a man fly from the temple in the air; and by this means John the Baptist, who was the Elias that was to come, should have been neglected, and Christ himself, though honoured as Elias, not owned for the Messiah.

Obs. 6. Observe then, *That Satan's designs are large, and that he projects the ensnaring or deluding of others by such temptations as seem only to concern those that are under the immediate trouble of them.* He tempts Christ to cast himself down, and also by it, at least, intends a delusion to the Jews. He tempts one man upon the back of another. One is tempted to error; another by that man's temptation is tempted to atheism and rejecting of all religion. One man is tempted to profaneness, another is tempted by that to an uncharitable disrespect of him. It is easy to multiply instance of this.

CHAPTER XIV.

That presumption was the chief design of this temptation.—Of tempting to extremes.—What presumption is.—The several ways of presuming.—The frequency of this temptation, in the generality of professors, in hypocrites, despairing persons, and in the children of God.—The reasons of Satan's industry in this design.—His deceitful contrivance in bringing about this sin.—Preservatives against it.

Next to the preparation which Satan made for the second conflict, already explained, the temptation intended offers itself to our view, which is this, ' Cast thyself down.' What Satan chiefly intended by it, we may collect from Christ's answer, as well as from the thing itself; for he thus replies, ' It is written, Thou shalt not tempt the Lord thy God.' Christ doth not use this scripture to any such sense as this, that he should hereby prohibit Satan to tempt him because he was Satan's Lord and God; but he mentioned this scripture as a rule of obedience: as if he should say, ' I may not cast myself down, and so rely on extraordinary help, seeing I can go down another way;' for the neglect of ordinary means, when we have them, is a tempting of God, which may not be done. So that it appears by this, that Satan here tempted Christ to presumption. There is only this objection in our way, that Deut. vi. 16, the place by Christ cited, refers to the temptation of the Israelites in Massah, mentioned Exod. xvii. 2, where they chide with Moses for water; and there it would seem their tempting the Lord was rather in despairing of his power and help than presuming in the neglect of the ordinary means. I answer, though the occasion and matter of that temptation be different from this of Christ's, yet the presumptuous experiment that they there made of God's presence and power was the same with this which Satan designed; for ver. 7, where the account of that tempting is given, it is said, ' because they tempted the Lord, saying, Is the Lord among us or not?' they put it to this issue, that the being and power of God should be tried by the giving or not giving of water. The manner, then, of that temptation being so agreeable to this, Christ very pertinently applies that command to it, presumption being the thing which Christ was tempted to. It might occasion some wonder in us to see Satan take such strange steps. He was before tempting him to despair, now to presumption; but it is no argument of his lightness or uncertain roving in his way of tempting, but rather of his depth and subtlety. Note then,

Obs. 7. *That it is Satan's policy in tempting, to run from one extreme to another.* The Corinthians were first tempted to a sinful compliance with the adulterous person, and were averse to his excommunication; afterwards they were tempted to the contrary severity, and were as backward to receive him again. The same men that have been overcome by prodigality and excess, when they begin to see the evil of that, are oft tempted to worldliness or covetousness, the contrary disposition. Reasons of this policy are:—

(1.) First, *The avoiding of one extreme gives the soul such a swing, if care be not used to prevent it, that they are cast more than half way upon the other.* Peter, in an extreme of modesty, refused the washing of his feet by Christ; but when he understood the danger, then he runs as far wrong another way—'Not my feet only, but my hands and my head,' John xiii. 9. Thus some are so for purity of churches, that they exclude the weak; others so for unity, that they admit the open scandalous and profane.

(2.) Secondly, *While men avoid one extreme by running into another, they carry with them such strong impressions of the evil they would avoid, and such fierce prejudices, that it is not an ordinary conviction will bring them right, but they are apt to be confident of the goodness of the way they take, and so are the more bold and fixed in their miscarriage.*

Presumption being the great design of Satan in this temptation, we may further observe:—

Obs. 8. *That as distrust on the one hand, so presumption on the other, is one of his grand designs.* Of these two, we may say as it was said of the sword of Hazael and Jehu, that of all those that are slain by the devil, whosoever hath escaped the sword of distrust and despair, the sword of presumption hath slain. To explain this I shall,

1. First, *Shew what presumption is.* It is in the general *a confidence without a ground.* [1.] *First,* It is made up of *audacity*—which is a bold and daring undertaking of a thing—and *security*. [2.] *Secondly,* The ground of it is *an error of judgment.* A blind or a misled judgment doth always nourish it; and this is either a mistake of the nature of such means on which we rely for assistance, as when a man lays as much stress upon a thread as upon a cable, or expects as much nourishment from a stone as from bread;[1] or a mistake of the will of others, from whom we expect aid and help, without a warrant for such a confidence. [3.] *Thirdly,* In its way of working *it is directly opposite to distrust, and is a kind of excessive though irregular hope;* not that in this case a man believes or hopes overmuch, for there can be no excess properly in the exercise of divine graces, but that he hopes too rashly or lightly, without a solid foundation or rea-

[1] Reynolds on Passions, chap. 23, p. 238.

son.[1] Hope hath for its object that which is good under the considerations of futurity, possibility, and difficulty. On the one side, desperation looks upon that good as future, but under so great a difficulty that it forgets the possibility of it, and thereupon surceaseth all endeavours. Presumption, on the other hand, is so keenly apprehensive of the possibility, that it never regards the difficulty, and so thrusts forward into irregular endeavours or expectations. The nature of this will be better understood when the particular instances of presumption are before us.

(1.) First, Then it is presumption, *when from external or subordinate means men expect that for which they were never designed nor appointed of God.* To expect 'grapes of thorns or figs of thistles,' would be a presumption, because God never designed them for such fruits; and no less is it when in any other case men look for high and extraordinary things from any created good above what God hath put into it by the law of creation.

(2.) Secondly, *When men do expect those fruits and effects from anything unto which it is appointed, in neglect or opposition to the supreme cause, without whose concurrent influence they cannot reach their proper ends*—that is, our hopes are wholly centred upon means, when in the meantime our eye is not upon God. Thus 'to make gold our hope,' Job xxxi. 24, 'to make flesh our arm,' Jer. xvii. 5, 'to make Ashur a saviour,' Hosea xiv. 3, or to trust to any creatures whatsoever, is in Scripture condemned as a presumptuous reliance, and, in regard of the necessary disappointment, 'a trusting in a lie;' in which sense it is said that 'every man is a liar,' Ps. lxii. 9. The like presumption it is when we boast great things of ourselves, and, as Peter, make confident engagements, in our own strength, that we will avoid such a sin or perform such a duty; for we are but frail, and all our sufficiency is from the Lord, so that it can be no less than intolerable arrogance to promise anything of ourselves without him; neither can men promise to themselves the continuance of that good or advantage which they have already received from second causes, if their confidence builds itself upon that sole consideration, without a just blame. Job had said he should 'die in his nest,' [chap. xxix. 18,] and David that 'he should never be moved,' [Ps. xvi. 8,] but both of them afterward noted these confidences to have been no other than deceitful presumptions.

(3.) Thirdly, It is a presumption *to expect things above the reach of our present state and condition;* as for a mean man to beg of God authority and rule, or to expect to be set with princes; or for ordinary Christians to look for miracles, signs from heaven, visions, revelations, extraordinary answers to prayers, and the like, all which expectations are groundless, and the issue of a presumptuous pride: *sperare non speranda.*

(4.) Fourthly, *When men expect things contrary to the rules that God hath set for his dispensations of mercy, they boldly presume upon his will.* God hath promised preservation to his children while they are in God's way, but if any shall go out of that way, and sinfully put

---

[1] Non ideo peccatur, quia nimis sperat in Deum; sed quia nimis leviter ac temere, sine ullo fundamento.—*Ames, Medul.,* lib. ii. cap. 6, sec. 33.

himself into dangers and hazards, it would be presumption in him to expect a preservation. It is the same in spiritual things. God promiseth eternal life and the blessings of his covenant to such as give up themselves to him and his laws; will it not be intolerable presumption for men 'to bless themselves in their heart' with expectations of reigning with him in glory, while in the meantime they contradict his own rule and neglect his order, walking in profaneness and living to themselves? This is a high presumption of mercy against his express will. Hence are such courses called 'presumptuous sins,' Ps. xix. 13, and such sinners transgress 'with a high hand.'

(5.) Fifthly, It is also a presumption *to expect any mercy, though common and usual, without the ordinary means by which God in providence hath settled the usual dispensations of such favours;* as when men look for his aid and help for supply of corporal wants, while they throw off all care, and refuse their own endeavours, which are the ways of God's appointment, in the conscientious use whereof such mercies are to be expected. The heathen, upon the consideration of the necessary connexion of means and the end, have usually judged such sluggish expectations to be no better than solemn mockings of a deity: *admotâ manu invocanda est Minerva.* In spiritual things it is no less presumptuous to expect conversion, and an interest in Christ and heaven, while they refuse the careful use of his ordinances; and therefore we are commanded to pray for such blessings, ' to cry after knowledge, and to lift up the voice for understanding,' Prov. ii. 3-5, and to second these prayers with our own utmost endeavours 'to seek for it as for silver, and to search for it as for hid treasures,' and in so doing to expect the finding of the knowledge of God.

(6.) Sixthly, *When ordinary or extraordinary mercies are expected for an unlawful end;* as when the Israelites at Massah called for water, —which they ought to believe God would supply them withal, their condition considered,—but for a test and proof of the being of God; for they said, ' Is God among us, or not?' Exod. xvii. 7. It is by James made a piece of spiritual unfaithfulness and adultery to ask anything of God with a design 'to spend it upon a lust,' [chap. iv. 3.] Ahaz his refusing a sign when God offered it, however he made a show of modesty and believing, argued no other thing but that he was conscious to himself that, in case he had accepted it, he should have abused that favour to an unlawful end, and have tempted God by it, as putting it upon this experiment whether there was a God or not. This is also another act of presumption. When a man becomes guilty of any of these miscarriages, he is presumptuous.

2. Secondly, I further add to this discovery of the nature and kinds of presumption, that this is one of Satan's grand engines; which I prove by two demonstrations:—

(1.) First, *By Satan's common practice in this kind upon all sorts of men, in most occasions.* That which is his frequent practice upon most men, and on most occasions, must of necessity be understood to be chiefly designed. Some men may possibly be free from the trouble of some particular temptations, as Hieronimus Wallerus saith of Luther his master, that he heard him often report of himself that he had been assaulted and vexed with all kind of temptations, saving only that of covetousness; but none can say they have not been assaulted with this. I shall make it out by an induction of particulars:—

[1.] First, *The generality of men that live in the profession of religion are presumptuous, nay, the greatest part of the blind world are so.* They presume of mercy and salvation. The devil preacheth nothing else but all hope, no fear, and in these golden dreams they slide down to hell. If we look into their way of sinning, and then into their hopes, we can judge no less of them. They stick not at the most grievous abominations, the works of the flesh, and in these they continue. It is their trade, their life; they make provisions for them, they cannot sleep except they do wickedly; he that reproveth is derided by them; they make but a mock and sport of those things which, as the shame and reproach of mankind, should rather fly the light and hide themselves as things of darkness. These things they practise without regret or sorrow of heart, without smiting upon the thigh, and in all this they have the confidence to say, 'Is not the Lord among us?' They can call themselves Christians, and have as bold expectations of eternal happiness, as if the committing of these evils were made by God the necessary qualifications to everlasting happiness. What is more common, and yet what more presumptuous? For (1.) These men audaciously hope and expect mercy, expressly contrary to the peremptory threatenings of God. God saith, 'There is no peace to the wicked;' they say, 'We shall have peace.' (2.) These run upon the greatest hazards of ruin and woe, with the least fear, in the contempt of all danger, 'as the horse rusheth into the battle, who mocketh at fear, and is not affrighted, neither turneth his back from the sword,' Job xxxix. 22. (3.) They dare God to do his worst, they provoke God to jealousy, and that to his face; hence was it that Nimrod was said to be a mighty hunter before the Lord, [Gen. x. 9;] and Er, the son of Judah, that he was wicked 'before the Lord,' [Gen. xxxviii. 7,] because such audacious sinners will not, as we may say, go behind his back to sin.

[2.] Secondly, *Hypocrites whose carriage is more smooth, they also are presumptuous;* for while they hide their sin, they do against dictates of conscience presume 'that he that made the eye doth not see,' and that there is a possibility to cheat God as well as men: besides, their boastings and hopes have a special mark set upon them in Scripture as audaciously false; 'the hope of the hypocrite shall be cut off,' [Job viii. 13;] their confidence of the temple of the Lord is but a lie, and so termed expressly by the prophet.

[3.] Thirdly, *Even despairing persons are not always free of presumption.* The act of self-murder is a terrible presuming upon infinite justice. Spira's desire to know the worst was of the same kind. These are indeed extraordinary; but there are some other kinds of despair that come nearer to presumption, as that sensual despair which ariseth out of an excessive love of carnal delights, and a secure contempt of spiritual things; for when sensuality prompts them to eat and drink while they may, despairing and hopeless of a future happiness, 'for to-morrow they shall die,' [Isa. xxii. 13,] and their pleasure cease, they highly presume against the patience and goodness of God.

[4.] Fourthly, *The best of men are too frequently overcome by it.*

(1.) Not only while they are overtaken with sins more grievous, and above the rate of sins of infirmity, to which how liable the holiest saint may be upon temptation, may be gathered from David's prayer, 'Keep thy servant from presumptuous sins, that they have not dominion over me,' [Ps. xix. 13.]   (2.) But by their earnest prosecutions of their own wills when contradicted by providence. It is by the prophet, Isaiah ix. 9, called 'a pride and stoutness of heart,' to contend with providence, to attempt to build with 'hewn stone when the bricks are fallen,' or to 'strive for cedars when divine wrath hath cut down the sycamores.' (3.) How frequently are they guilty of presuming upon their privileges, their strength, their graces, and upon that score venture themselves upon occasions of sin, or bear high above others upon a conceit of their higher attainments, or when they boldly put themselves upon suffering, or upon doing, while they want that due humility and care that should balance them. (4.) There is also a presumptuous rashness, upon which the zeal and good intentions of holy men may sometimes precipitate them. Such was Uzziah's putting forth his hand to hold the ark, for which the Lord smote him. All these instances put together will sufficiently demonstrate that presumption is one of Satan's master designs.

The second demonstration of this truth is from the general subserviency of other things to this. Most of Satan's endeavours and temptations aim at this point, and this is the result and consequence of most sins. That must needs be chief, to which so many things do but serve and minister. In this centre do most of the lines of his policy meet,—pride, vainglory, conceited privileges, supposed advantages, and many things more were but under-agents to this temptation which the devil attempted upon Christ, as hath in part, and presently shall be further, evidenced.

3. Thirdly, Having thus proved that presumption is one of the great things he aims at, I shall next *discover the reasons of his earnestness and industry in his design*, which are these:—

(1.) First, *It is a sin very natural, in which he hath the advantage of our own readiness and inclination.* However that some from a melancholy temper are inclinable to fears and distrust at some time, when these black apprehensions are exalted, yet, these excepted, hopes are more predominant than fears; and self-love, which provides fuel to these hopes, is a natural principle in all. When so many things give him such advantages and promise him a success, we may well suppose he will not miss such an opportunity.

(2.) Secondly, *As it is easy for Satan's attempt, so it is remote from conviction, and not rooted out without great difficulty.* It is a sin that is covered with a pretext of a higher degree of hope. Men in many ways of this iniquity are under persuasions of duty, and by reason of that confidence, fear, which is the soul's sentinel, is asleep. Hence do they not lie so fairly open to counsel or reproof. The Israelites, Deut. i. 27, 28, being under discouragement, refuse to go up to Canaan, when they were upon the border of the land; but being convinced of their sin in distrusting the arm of the Lord, by God's declared wrath and threatening against them, they fall upon the contrary extreme of presumption, and then, ver. 41, 'they would go up and fight;' and the conviction of their former sin made them so confident that this was their present duty—for thus they argue, ' We have sinned against the Lord, we will go up and fight, according to all that the Lord our God commanded us'—that though they were expressly forbidden from God, ver. 42, ' Go not up, neither fight, for I am not among you;' yet were they so strangely carried by their former persuasion, that they refused to be convinced, ' and went presumptuously into the hill.' By which instance we see what great pretences lead on presumption, and how difficultly they are removed, which two things do no less than tempt Satan to lay out himself to the uttermost in that design.

(3.) Thirdly, *The greatness of the sin when it is committed, is another reason of his diligence in the pursuit of it.* It is not only from a simple error or mistake, but that error ariseth from intolerable pride; they say and do such things from the pride and stoutness of their heart, Isa. ix. 9. He that is presumptuous is self-willed, 2 Pet. ii. 10. Hence these sins, which we translate presumptuous, are in the original called prides or arrogancies, Ps. xix. 13; Deut. xvii. 12. Besides, they are contradictions to God's order, separating those things that God hath joined together, as the means from the end, or the end from the means, as if the ' earth should be turned out of its place' for us. And in some cases it is no less than the open affronting of God by abusing his own favours against himself; for thus they deal with him, who are opinionated in sin because of his mercy, concluding, by an irrational consequence, that they ought to be wicked because God is good, or that they may freely offend because he doth not punish.

(4.) Fourthly, *The dangerous issues and consequences of this way of sinning, do not a little animate Satan to tempt to it.* In some cases it was to be punished by death: Deut. xvii. 12, ' The man that doth presumptuously, even that man shall die;' and most usually it is plagued with sad disappointments, by a severe engagement of God's displeasure against it. ' The hypocrite's hope shall perish, it shall be as the giving up of the ghost,' Job viii. 13, and xi. 20. And generally, ' He that thus blesseth himself in his heart, when he heareth the words of the curse,' Deut. xxix. 19, 20, ' the Lord will not spare him, but then the anger of the Lord and his jealousy shall smoke against that man, and all the curses that are written in this book shall lie upon him, and the Lord shall blot out his name from under heaven.'

4. Fourthly and lastly, I shall lay before you *the deceitful contrivance of Satan in bringing this sin about*, by shewing the particulars of his craft against Christ herein. As,

(1.) First, *He takes advantage from his resolve to rely upon providence, contrary to the former temptation of turning stones to bread.* Christ had refused that, telling him it was duty to trust him, who not only by the ordinary means of bread could feed him, but also by any other appointment. To this Satan rejoins, by offering an irregular opportunity of such a trust, in casting himself from the pinnacle of the temple: as if he should say, ' If thou wilt thus rely upon providence, do it in this.' Wherein we may note, that from an obediential dependence, he would draw Christ to an irregular presumption. He retorts Christ's argument back again upon him thus, ' If God is to be relied upon by a certain trust for food, by the like trust he is to be relied upon for preservation; if the belief of supply of bread can consist with a neglect or refusal of ordinary means for the procurement thereof, then may the belief of preservation in casting thyself from the pinnacle of the temple consist also with a neglect of the ordinary means.' Thus, like a cunning sophister, he endeavours to conclude sin from duty, from a seeming parity betwixt them, though indeed the cases were vastly different. For, though it be duty to depend upon providence, when God, in the pursuit of service and duty, brings us out of the sight and hopes of outward means, yet it can be no less than sinful presumption for us to make such experiments of providences, when we need not, and when ordinary means are at hand. After the same manner doth he endeavour to put fallacies upon us, and to cheat us into presumptuous undertakings, by arguing from a necessary trust, in some cases, a necessity of presuming in others, upon a seeming likeness and proportion.

(2.) Secondly, *It was no small piece of Satan's craft to take this advantage, while the impression of trust in the want of outward means was warm upon the heart of Christ.* He hoped thereby the more easily to draw him to an excess. For he knows that a zealous earnestness to avoid a sin, and to keep to a duty, doth often too much incline us to an extreme, and he well hoped that when Christ had declared himself so positively to depend upon God, he might have prevailed to have stretched that dependence beyond its due bounds, taking the opportunity of his sway that way, which, as a ship before wind and tide, might soon be overdriven. And this was the design of his haste in this second temptation, because he would strike while the iron was hot, and closely pursue his advantage, while the strength and forwardness of these resolves were upon him.

(3.) Thirdly, *He endeavours to animate him to this presumption by popular applause, and to tickle him into a humour of affecting the glory and admiration, which by such a strange undertaking might be raised in the minds of the spectators ;* and therefore did he bring him to the most conspicuous place of a great and populous city, not thinking the matter so feasible if he had tempted him to it in a solitary desert.

(4.) Fourthly, *He propounds to him a plausible end, and a seeming advantage,* viz., the clear and undoubted discovery of his divine nature and near interest in God; urging this as a necessary duty, for his own satisfaction, and the manifestation of his sonship to others.

(5.) Fifthly, To drive out of his mind those fears of miscarrying in his attempt, which otherwise might have been a block in his way, *he is officious in strengthening his confidence by propounding treacherous helps and preservatives,* suggesting a safety to him from the privilege of the place where this was to be acted, a holy city and temple, producing more of a divine presence for his safety than other places.

(6.) Sixthly, To make all sure, *he backs all this with a promise of preservation,* that nothing might be wanting to his security.

By this method applied to other things and cases, he endeavours to bring us to presumption.

Applic. The consideration of this should *put us upon a special care and watchfulness against presumption.* It is more designed, and hath a greater prevalency than men are aware of. Two things I shall only at present propound for our preservation, out of Ps. xix. 12, 13.

[1.] First, *He that would be kept from presumptuous sins must make conscience of secret sins, to search for them, to mortify them, to beg pardon for them.* With what face or hope can we expect from God help against these, when we provoke him to leave us to ourselves, by indulging ourselves in the other?

[2.] Secondly, He that would avoid them *must be under the awe and fear of being overcome by them.* He that slights and contemns such visible hazards shall not long be innocent. David here first shews his conscience to be concerned with secret sins, and then begs to be kept from presumptuous sins, and by such earnest begging he next shews how much he dreaded such miscarriages. [Dickson, *in loc.*]

CHAPTER XV.

Self-murder another of his designs in this temptation.—How he tempts to self-murder directly, and upon what advantage he urgeth it.—How he tempts to it indirectly, and the ways thereof.—Of necessary preservatives against this temptation.

We have seen and considered the main end of Satan in this temptation. Let us further consider whether this was the sole end that he propounded to himself. We have little reason to think that he would confine himself to one, when the thing itself doth so clearly suggest another, which might possibly have followed. In most cases, the ends of the devil are manifold. We may therefore easily suppose—and several have noted it [1]—that the devil, that great murderer, had herein a secret design against the life of Christ, and that he tempted him here indirectly to self-murder. And indeed, supposing that Christ had attempted to fly in the air, and had failed in the enterprise, what else could have followed but death and ruin? Hence let us note,

Obs. 9. *That Satan seeks the ruin of our bodies as well as of our souls, and tempts men often to self-murder.* That the devil goes about seeking how he may destroy men, by putting them upon attempts against their own lives, is evident, not only from the experience and confessions of such as have suffered under Satan's suggestions to that end—and it is a temptation more common than we think of, because most men are unwilling to lay open themselves to others in this matter—but also from those many sad instances of men over whom Satan so far prevails, that they execute upon themselves this design by destroying themselves. Yet by the way we may note, that such thoughts are often in the minds of men where Satan is not industriously designing their destruction; for he often casts in such thoughts, not only to try how men take with them, but to affright and disquiet them; and it is usual with men of sad and melancholy tempers to mistake their own fears of such a temptation, for Satan's endeavours against them, when indeed their fear and trouble lest they should be so tempted, makes them think they are tempted indeed.

[1] Dickson, *in loc;* Capel, Tempt., part 2, cap. 9.

Satan drives on the design of self-murder two ways:—

1. First, *Directly, when in plain terms he urgeth men to destroy themselves.* This because it is directly repugnant to the law of nature, which vehemently urgeth them to self-preservation, he cannot effect but by the help of some advantages; yet some ways and methods by experience he hath found to be so available to such an unnatural resolve, that he frequently puts them in practice. As, (1.) first, He works upon *the discontents of men,* and improves the disquiet of their minds, upon the occasion of any loss, vexation, disappointment, or disgrace, to as great a height as he can, and when their lives are made bitter to them, and they are sufficiently prepared by the uneasiness of their condition, then he propounds death as the only remedy to set them at quiet; wherein, besides his officiousness to provide them with instruments of cruelty and opportunity for their use, he follows them with arguments drawn from the sense of their present condition ; the great intendment whereof is to aggravate their smart, and to make their burden seem intolerable, and then self-ruin is but a natural consequence. We may see enough of this in the discontents of good men, and that they naturally work this way. Job speaks the general apprehensions of men in trouble, chap. iii. 20, 21, ' The bitter in soul value not life ; they long for death, and dig for it more than for hid treasures; they rejoice exceedingly, and are glad when they can find the grave.' Jonah in his discontent prefers death before life : ' It is better for me to die than to live,' [chap. iv. 3.] Elias doth the like; and Job seems impatient for it. All this is from the power and working of this temptation, though God held their hand that it did not fully prevail. In Ahithophel the ground of discontent was more a fancied than a real disgrace; his counsel was rejected—which was in itself no great dishonour—and this works up such a perplexing resentment in his mind, that Satan prevails with him to hang himself very deliberately.

(2.) Secondly, *He most frequently draws on men to destroy themselves by terrors and despairing troubles of conscience.* These, as they afford greater disquiet and distress of mind than other kind of discontentments, so doth he more prevail by them ; for a wounded spirit is above ordinary strength, and hard to bear ; only it may seem strange that those who so experimentally feel how ' fearful a thing it is to fall into the hands of the living God,' [Heb. x. 31,] should entertain such a temptation as, to their apprehensions and knowledge, will certainly plunge them into the very ocean of everlasting vengeance. This no doubt Satan finds to be no small obstruction to his design ; but here he useth his skill to open a way for them that would outrun their lives on the one hand, as he labours to pursue them with sense of wrath and indignation on the other hand. To this purpose he tells them, [1.] That all the hell they are to meet with is in their consciences, and that death will free them from all, or at least that death will give a present ease, and that till the resurrection they shall be in quiet. Those that are willing to receive these apprehensions may easily be prevailed with to hasten their own death, seeing they have already fixed this conclusion with themselves, that there is no hope nor pardon for them, that they are reprobates and cut off; for their thoughts can meditate nothing but the terrors of such conclusions. [2.] He sometimes endeavours to persuade them, that by executing this revenge upon themselves, they may make some kind of satisfaction and amends for the sins they have committed; which though most false, yet it is a wonder how far such ungrounded surmises may possess the minds of the desperate. That Judas might have some such thought when he destroyed himself, is conjectured by some;[1] but that must be but a conjecture, seeing none can pretend to know his thoughts; but we may speak with greater freedom of those who have declared the working of such apprehensions upon their minds. [3.] A more plausible pretext he useth when he endeavours to persuade them that they may kill themselves, and yet go to heaven for all that. To this purpose the subtle adversary is not backward to tell them what have been the charitable expressions of some men who have supposed a possibility of repentance *inter pontem et fontem*, as we say, betwixt the stroke or halter and the death. Capel is so apprehensive of the mischievous improvement of this charity, for an encouragement to self-murder, that he with great earnestness cautions all ministers against such liberal expressions.[2] I have known some, and heard of others, that have been so possessed with this imagination of being saved, notwithstanding that having purposed to destroy themselves—though God prevented them that they did it not—they have first by prayer recommended themselves to God, and so prepared themselves to die. [4.] Sometime, though such afflicted ones have no such persuasion but that from death they go immediately to hell, yet are they pushed forward by a certain fearful curiosity of knowing the worst. At that rate did Spira express himself, when he desired to be freed of his life that he might know the utmost of those torments which he feared; as if the affrightments of his fearful expectations were worse than the real feeling of them. [5.] But most of all doth he prevail against that objection of greater misery after death, by running men up to a desperate distraction in their terrors. Their present anguish is made insupportable, so that they hasten out of life, without care or consideration of what shall follow.

(3.) Thirdly, *He tempts men directly to destroy themselves from a principle of heroic boldness and seeming fortitude of mind*—a thing very common among the Romans, who impatient of injuries, and from pride of heart, not willing to subject themselves to affronts, choosed rather to tear their own bowels than to live to see themselves abused. Lucretia being forced by Tarquinius, and not willing to outlive her disgrace, stabbed herself. Cato, not being able to endure the victory of Cæsar, puts an end to his days. Innumerable instances of this kind histories do everywhere afford. These, though they consulted their own passions, and knew of nothing that prompted them but their own generosity or magnanimity, yet were they not without a tempter to such cruel actions. Satan undoubtedly pleased himself by exercising his cruelty upon them so easily, by the help of such a humour, which passed among these blind heathens for the highest proof of virtue and fortitude. To this height it came, insomuch that

---

[1] Capel, Tempt., part 9, cap. 9, citing Augustine for it.
[2] Capel, Tempt., *ibid.*

we find Seneca highly applauding Cato[1] for procuring his liberty by his own death; and setting forth that fact as the most delightful spectacle to the gods. Though indeed, as Augustine notes,[2] it is not fortitude but weakness, and a clear evidence of impatience, which cannot bear other men's insolencies or their own hardships. And if we examine the matter to the bottom, though there be audacity in it to undertake their own death, yet is this led on by no better principles than pride, impatience, and despair: which may the better be discovered if we consider such kind of attempts as they arise from more ignoble and base occasions. Paterculus tells us of a Tuscan soothsayer, who being carried to prison with his friend Fulvius Flaccus, and despairing of pardon, desperately runs his head against the prison door and dashed out his brains; and yet this man was moved to attempt his destruction upon the same general principles by which Cato destroyed himself.

(4.) Fourthly, It is also sufficiently known that Satan *by the force of custom in several countries, doth as it were necessitate men to cut off their own lives.* In some barbarous places, at the death of the husband, the wife, in a brutal affection of the praise of love and loyalty, casts herself to be devoured by the same flame in which the dead body of her husband is consumed.[3] And there are found in other places customs of self-destruction for the avoiding the tedious inconveniences of old age, where it is usual for old persons with joy to prepare their own funeral pile, and to make a quick despatch of their lives, and rather to die at once than by piecemeal, as Seneca expresseth it.[4] Calanus, an Indian philosopher, being dysenterical, obtained leave of Alexander to burn himself for more quick despatch.

(5.) Fifthly, There is yet another way by which men are tempted sometime, though rarely, to hasten themselves out of the world, and that is by *a pretence of an earnest and impatient desire of happiness to come.* That longings for such enjoyments do become the best of saints, and is indeed their excellency, cannot be denied; but to make such a preposterous haste must be a cheat of Satan. That there is a possibility of this, may appear in the story of Cleombrotus, mentioned also by Augustine, who reading Plato's 'Phædo, of the Immortality of the Soul,' that he might hasten thither, threw himself headlong from a wall, and died.[5] Now, though it be hard to find such an instance among Christians, yet we have reason to believe that where Satan perceives such a temptation may take place, he will not be wanting in the prosecution. And if we may conjecture Augustine's thoughts by that question which he propounds—viz., Whether it be lawful for a man to kill himself for the avoiding of sin, which he solidly con-

[1] Seneca, De Providen. cap. 2. Liquet mihi cum magno spectasse gaudio deos—dum gladium sacro pectore infigit. Non fuit diis immortalibus satis spectare Catonem semel.
[2] Aug., De Civit. Dei, P. 1, cap. 22. Major animus merito dicendus est, qui vitam ærumnosam magis potest ferre quam fugere. Et humanum judicium præ conscientiæ luce ac puritate contemnere.
[3] As in the kingdoms of Biznagar—*Purchas, Pilgr.* lib. v. cap. 11—and in the Philippian islands.—*Ibid.*, cap. 16.
[4] Perire membratim et toties per stillicidia amittere animam.—*Sen.*, epist. 101.
[5] Cicero, 1 Tus. quest. Nihil urgebat aut calamitatis aut criminis—sed ad capessendam mortem—Sola affuit animi magnitudo.—*De Civ. Dei*, lib. i. cap. 22.

futes,[1] we may conclude that such thoughts were the usual temptations of good men in his time, and the rather because in the close of that chapter he applies that discourse particularly to the servants of Christ, that they should not think their lives a burden. *Non itaque vobis, O fideles Christi, sit tædio vita vestra.*

2. Secondly, Satan promotes the design of self-murder, not only directly, as we have heard, but also *by some indirect ways he undermines the life of man.* That is, when he doth not formally say to them, Destroy yourselves, but tempts them to such things as he knows will let in upon death. This way of subtle malice I shall explain under these heads:—

(1.) First, *Upon highest pretexts of zeal for God's glory, he sometimes lays a snare for our lives.* I cannot believe but Satan had a hand in that forwardness of ancient Christians, who by an open profession of their faith before persecuting judicatures, did as it were court a martyrdom; and I have the same persuasion of the painful earnestness of many holy preachers, who lavish out their strength in a prodigality of pains for the good of souls, which, like a thief in the candle, wastes them immediately; whereas a better husbanded strength might be truly more advantageous, as continuing the light the longer; and yet so sincere are their ends, so pleasant is their work, that they seldom observe, as they ought, that Satan, when he can do no better, is glad of the opportunity to destroy them with their own weapon; and therefore in this case they may expect he will do all he can to heighten and forward their zeal, not only by adding all the fuel he can to their inward propensity of laboriousness, but also by outward encouragement of the declared acceptations and expectations of their hearers.[2]

(2.) Secondly, *Upon baser pretences of the full enjoyment of sensual pleasures and carnal delights, he doth unawares push men forward to death and dangers.* Thus the voluptuous, the glutton, the drunkard, dig their own graves, and invite death to cut them off before they have lived out half their time. While Satan tempts men to such excesses of riot, he labours not only the destruction of the soul, but also of the body; not only that they be miserable, but that they may be so with all expedition.

(3.) Thirdly, Besides all these, *he hath other subtle ways of contriving the death of men, by putting them upon ways and actions that are attended with hazard.* Thus he sought the death of Christ, not directly but indirectly, by urging him to an action which he thought would unavoidably bring him to death, for a fall from so great a precipice would easily have bereaved any man of life. And sometimes when men are besotted with enthusiastical delusions, he can more easily beguile them with such stratagems. That instance of Stuker[3] is famous, who cut off his brother's head upon a foolish persuasion that God would magnify his great power in giving him life again. If Satan can befool such bewitched slaves into such absurd and unreasonable apprehensions in regard of others, what hinders but that he may so far impose upon them, that they may be willing to practise upon themselves? I remember something to this purpose, of one whom

---

[1] De Civit. Dei, lib. i. cap. 27.   [2] *Vide* Boyle's Reflections, sec. 2, med. 10.
[3] Query, 'Stukeley'?—G.

the devil had well-nigh prevailed with to make a hole in his breast, which of necessity must have let out his life, upon a pretended promise of giving him eternal life, and was accordingly forced to take up a knife and to carry it to his throat.[1] In *anno* 1647, in Yorkshire, a company of people were seduced to sacrifice certain creatures to God, among the rest they sacrificed their aged mother, persuading her she should rise the third day, and for this they were executed at York.

Applic. This may awaken all to be aware of this temptation. Some are sadly concerned in it. Many are the complaints which some of us have met withal about it in private, and the apprehensions of such hazards are sadly disquieting. Through such fears thousands of God's dear children have passed, and many, too many, have been overcome by this weapon. Those of us that have not yet known temptations of this nature, do not know how soon we may be assaulted in this kind. It is necessary for all to stand upon their guard, and for that end it behoves us to have at hand these defences against it :—

[1.] First, It is useful to consider *that this is one of Satan's great plots;* and when we meet with it clothed with never so many pretexts, enforced with never so many seeming necessities, yet must we look upon it as the counsel of an enemy, who certainly intends us no kindness, let him pretend what he will ; and therefore may we be sure it will be our sad inconvenience and disadvantage.

[2.] Secondly, It must be fixed in our minds *that the thing in itself is a high iniquity, a most grievous provocation.* No instance of self-murder, properly such, can be met withal in Scripture, as practised by any holy person. The command is directly against it, ' Thou shalt not kill.' If we may not murder another, as Austin argues, we may not murder ourselves; for he that kills himself kills no other than a man; nay, we may much less lay hand upon our own life.[2] It is a greater violation of the law of nature and of love. Every man is nearest to himself; and his love to himself is the pattern of his love to another. Self-murder must then be a sin of higher aggravations by far than the murder of another person. And the wiser heathens were far from countenancing any such cruelty. If Plato had thought it best, for an immediate enjoyment of immortality, which is the highest pretence of self-murder imaginable, to make an end of life violently, he would certainly have practised it himself, or recommended it to others, but he is so far from this, that he speaks against it as a great wickedness.

[3.] Thirdly, It is necessary that men keep in mind *the danger that follows such an act.* Death brings God's unalterable *mittimus,* and seals up the condition of every man, so that in the same posture he comes to judgment, it puts an end to all hopes and endeavours. Suppose then such tempted creatures to have fears and terrors as great as you can imagine them to be, yet there is a possibility that they may be deceived in them, that their case is not so bad as they fear, or if it be bad enough at present, that it may be better afterwards ; for many

---

[1] See the Narrative of Jo. Gilpin, called ' The Quakers Shaken.'
[2] De Civit. Dei, lib. i. cap. 20. Non occides, non alterum, ergo nec te ; neque enim qui se occidit, aliud quam hominem occidit.—*Aug. De Civit. Dei,* lib. i. cap. 22. Et Comment. Lod. Viv. Ibid.

that have in their anguish resolved against themselves, have been prevented of the execution of their resolves, and have lived to see the Lord and his salvation. And who is able to determine that secret, that their name is not in the book of life? Who can say he is certainly excluded out of God's decree? What madness is it then to rush into certain ruin, when our fears that distress us may be but mistakes! It is not so certain that men shall be damned, because of what they feel or fear at present, as it may be if they destroy themselves.

[4.] Fourthly, To prevent occasions to this temptation, *it must be our care not to give way to discontents for outward things, nor to distressing fears, such as are despairing and hopeless, for our spiritual estate;* or if we have a burden either way upon our mind, we must avoid as much as may be impatient fretfulness, 'lest Satan get advantage of us.' Discontented moods and casting away hope are sad occasions for this temptation. If we find ourselves thus burdened, we must look to it betimes, and not suffer it to go too far. And if this temptation come, we must take heed we keep not the devil's counsel, but discover the matter to some that are wise and faithful, able to advise and pray for us; remembering still that if only outward things trouble us, we have a better way of ease and remedy, by submitting to a chastising providence. If spiritual troubles move this way, we should not run from him, but rather resolve to perish at his foot as humble suppliants for mercy and pardon.

[5.] Fifthly, The temptation must also be opposed with *fasting and prayer*. If this be sincerely practised, it will go away at last.

[6.] Sixthly, Something may also be said for caution against *unnecessary thrusting ourselves, while under such temptations, into places of danger, or into a converse with instruments of death.* This may be too great a daring of the temptation, and in the consequence a mischief. Yet on the other hand, we must not be so cowardly as to be afraid of such places and things, unto which our callings and lawful employments do engage us; not to dare to go over a bridge, or to walk by a river or a pit, if it be our necessary way, is but to give an advantage to Satan to keep us under continual affrightments; and therefore I subscribe to Capel's advice, 'We must abide by it, and fight it out by faith; we must not fly the way, the place, the employment, but go on and look to God, and at last we shall make Satan fly.'[1]

Obj. But if some object to this, that their weakness is great, and their fears are strong, and Satan never idle, and that therefore they have little ground to expect an escape, I shall desire they would consider seriously the instance of Christ in this particular. When he was upon the pinnacle of the temple, a small push might have overthrown him, and yet it was not in Satan's power to do it himself, though he tempted Christ to cast himself down: which may sufficiently satisfy us, that there is a sure hedge of providence about us, and that Satan cannot do us the least hurt by pushing us into a pit or river, or any such danger.

[1] Tempt., part 2, cap. 9.

CHAPTER XVI.

Of pride, Satan's chief engine to bring on presumption.—What pride is, and how it prepares men for sinning presumptuously.—Considerations against pride.—The remedies for its cure.—Pride kindled by a confidence of privileges and popular applause.

The aims of Satan in this temptation being thus explained, I must now offer to your consideration the means by which he sought to bring his end about, which we have noted already, was pride: this he endeavoured to raise up in him two ways:—

(1.) First, By urging to him the privileges of his condition, as taking himself to be the Son of God.

(2.) Secondly, By offering him the occasion of popular applause; to which purpose he brought him into the holy city, where he might be sure of many spectators. I shall hence note,

Obs. 10. *That pride is Satan's proper engine to bring men on to presumption.*

If we should trace the history of presumptuous sins, we shall ever find it to have been so. Adam's first sin was a high presumption against God's express command, but pride was the stair by which he knew they must ascend to it; and therefore he used this argument to corrupt the hearts of our first parents, 'Ye shall be as gods.' The presumption of Uzziah in burning incense upon the altar, was from his pride, 2 Chron. xxvi. 16, 'His heart was lifted up, because he was become strong.' David's presumption in numbering the people was from hence. Thus might we run through many instances. But Satan's own case may be instead of all. His first sin, though we have but conjecture what it was particularly, is concluded by all to have been highly presumptuous, and the Scripture expressly asserts that it was his pride that brought him to it. 1 Tim. iii. 6, 'He that is lifted up with pride, falls into the condemnation of the devil.' And in the general we are told by the prophet, Hab. ii. 4, 'that the soul that is lifted up,' cannot be so upright as patiently to wait upon God in a way of believing, but it will be presuming to evade a trouble by indirect contrivances.

To explain the observation, I shall do no more but shew what pride is, and how fit it is to beget presumption.

Pride is a self-idolising, an over-valuation or admiration of ourselves, upon a real or supposed excellency, inward or outward, appertaining to us. It is in Scripture frequently expressed by the lifting up or exaltation of the soul. And this is done, upon the consideration of any kind of thing, which we apprehend makes us excel others; so that inward gifts of mind, as knowledge, humility, courage, &c., or outward gifts of the body, as beauty, strength, activity, &c., or additional advantages of riches, honour, authority, &c., or anything well done by us, &c., may all be abused to beget and nourish pride, and to fill us with high and lofty thoughts concerning ourselves; and being thus blown up, we are fitted for any presumptuous undertaking. For,

(1.) First, *The mind thus corrupted begets to itself apprehensions of a self-sufficiency:* and therefore, as it is not apt to remember from what fountain all those excellencies come, and to what ends they are to serve; so it brings them to a contempt of others, and to a confidence of themselves. Thus are men by degrees so intoxicated by their own humour, that they mount up to irrational and absurd conceits, fancying that they are more than they are, and that they can do far more than is possible for them to accomplish, till at last they become apparently foolish in the pursuit of their imaginations. I need not instance in the follies of Alexander, who being elated in mind, would be Jupiter's son, and go like Hercules in a lion's skin. Or in the mad frenzies of Caius, who as he would need fancy himself a god, so would he change his godship when he pleased: to-day he would wear a lion's skin and club, and then he must be Hercules; to-morrow in another garb he conceits himself Apollo; a caduceus made him Mercury, a sword and helmet made him Mars, &c. Or in Xerxes, who would whip the seas, and fetter Neptune. The Scripture affords enough of this nature, as the boast of Nebuchadnezzar; 'Is not this great Babel that I have built?' In the insolency of Nineveh, Zeph. ii. 15, 'I am, and there is none besides me.' The blasphemy of Tyre, Ezek. xxviii. 2, who set her heart 'as the heart of God, saying, I am a god, I sit in the seat of God.' The arrogancy of Sennacherib, Isa. xxxvi. 19, 20, 'Where are the gods of Hamath .... that the Lord should deliver Jerusalem out of my hand?' Though all pride in all men ariseth not to so great a height of madness, yet it is the nature of it, and none have any of it without this humour of conceiting themselves above themselves, which strangely prepares them for any presumption.

(2.) Secondly, He that is proud, *as he looks upon himself in a flattering glass, and measures himself by the length of his shadow; so doth he contemn and undervalue things that lie before his attempts as easy and small.* Hence doth he put himself upon things that are far beyond him. David notes the working of a proud heart, Ps. cxxxi. 1, in this particular, 'Neither do I exercise myself in great matters, or in things too high for me,' shewing that it is the guise of pride to outbid itself in its attempts.

(3.) Thirdly, *It is not only forward to attempt, but also desperate to execute without consideration of hazard.* Difficulty and danger, when they stand in the way, should usually deter men from their enterprise; but pride hardens the heart, and, in a blind rage, engageth it to contemn all inconveniencies. If sin and the breach of God's law be set before a person, whose pride engageth him to an unlawful undertaking, he overlooks it as a thing of nought: 'Through the pride of his countenance he will not seek after God: God is not in all his thoughts,' Ps. x. 4.

(4.) Fourthly, Pride ariseth up *to a scornful competition with anything that opposeth it;* and the more it is opposed, the more it rageth, for the contest is for having its will. This was the voice of pride in Pharaoh, 'Who is the Lord, that I should serve him?' [Exod. v. 2.] Hence men are said to 'despise the commandments of God,' [Lev. xxvi. 15,] when in the strength of their pride they are carried on to an open contest for their own ways and desires against peremptory commands and threatenings.

(5.) Fifthly, All this is done by *a pleasing allurement*. It is a witchcraft that strongly holds men, *Amabilis insania mentis gratissimus error;* and they think they are sufficiently rewarded if they be but gratified. Though other things go to wreck, yet they apprehend, if credit and honour be kept up, it is enough. Saul, when Samuel had declared that God would forsake him, yet sought to please himself by keeping up his esteem and authority; 'Honour me,' saith he, 'before the people,' [1 Sam. xv. 30.]

If all these particulars be weighed, what presumptuous act can be propounded by Satan which pride may not lead to? He that swells himself to a conceit of absoluteness, that will needs be attempting things too high, that contemneth all hazards, and is made more forward by opposition, and yet pleaseth himself in all, as in a golden dream, he is as much prepared for any figure or shape that Satan is ready to impress upon him, as melted metals for their mould or stamp.

Applic. Hence must we be warned against pride, as we would avoid *presumption*. If we admit this, we cannot well escape the other. And we are the more concerned to resist pride,

[1.] First, *Because it is a natural sin*. It was the first sin, and our natures are so deeply tainted with it, that it is a sin that first shews itself in our infancy; for children will express a pride in their clothes very early, and it is a general infection, from which none are exempted in some degree or other. The apostle's phrase, 1 John ii. 16, shews that our whole life, and all the concerns thereof, is but the sphere in which pride acts; and therefore, whereas he restrains other lusts to some particular ends or peculiar instruments, he calls this iniquity the 'pride of life,' implying how impossible it is to confine it in a narrow compass.

[2.] Secondly, *It is a subtle sin, and often lies where it is least suspected*. Every man sees it, as it is expressed in 'haughty looks,' in 'boasting speeches,' in 'gorgeous apparel,' in 'insolent behaviour;' but often men are insensibly possessed with this sin and know not of it. Under an affected contempt of honours and fine clothes they secretly hug themselves in their private conceits, and raise up in their own thoughts imaginary trophies of honour and victory, for despising what others so much dote upon. It was observed of Diogenes that he did *intus gloriari*, inwardly boast, and with greater pride contemned honour, riches, plenty, &c., than they were troubled with that enjoyed them. Some decry pride in others, vehemently declare against it as a sin, recommend humility as an ornament of great price in the sight of God, and yet are proud that they are above others in a fancied humility; and, in the management of themselves in their reproofs and exhortations, express such sad symptoms of an insulting humour, that the latent pride of their heart doth appear by it. It is possible for men to give thanks to the Almighty for all they have, and yet to be proud of what is in them. The Pharisee was proud, for so Christ calls him, that 'he was not as other men,' and yet he could 'thank God,' as ascribing all to him; nay, he that is truly sensible of the working of this pride in himself, and dares not approve it, yet he shall find in his heart such a delight when he is stroked or praised; and when some actions, praiseworthy, are not taken notice of, the best shall find that, without great watchfulness, they shall not be able to hold from giving some hints to others, as a memorial to them, of observing their excellency, or from some insinuations of their own commendation.

[3.] Thirdly, Pride is a sin *no less dangerous than subtle.* There are no attempts so strange, unreasonable, monstrous, or absurd, but it may prompt to them. It was a strange arrogancy in Herod to deify himself in his own thoughts, and yet the acclamations of the people swelled him into such a blasphemous imagination, that God thought fit to chastise him, and instruct others by so dreadful a judgment, as clearly baffled his insolency, and made him and his flatterers confess he was but a poor, frail man. Ordinarily pride is attended with a judgment, it is the very prognostic of ruin: 'Pride goeth before destruction, and a haughty spirit before a fall,' Prov. xvi. 18. But these judgments have something in them peculiar, which other judgments for other sins do not always express, to a manifestation of a special abhorrency in God against pride; as, (1.) He commonly smites the thing for which they are proud. Staupitius boasted of his memory, and God smote it; Hezekiah boasted of his treasure, and for that God designed them for captivity; David glorified [himself] in the multitude of his people, but God lessened them by pestilence; Nebuchadnezzar is proud of his Babel, and God drove him from the enjoyment of it. Men are proud of children or relations, and God oft removes them, or makes them a shame and sorrow. (2.) He doth not only this, but also orders the judgment so that it shall bring a shame and contempt upon men in that thing wherein they prided themselves. He will not only punish, but also stain their pride. The haughty daughters of Zion were not only plagued by removing their ornaments, bracelets, and the rest of their bravery, but over and above he 'smites with a scab the crown of their head, and discovers their secret parts, and brings a stink and baldness upon them instead of a sweet smell and well-set hair, and burning instead of beauty,' Isa. iii. 17, 24.

So sad a distemper stands in need of a special care; and for that end we should,

[1.] First, *In all things we have or do, not so much consider what is excellent, or wherein we excel, as what we have not, and wherein we come short.* We should be strange to ourselves, and design that the 'right hand should not know what the left hand doth,' which must be by having our eye upon the imperfections that attend us at the best.

[2.] Secondly, *It must be our care to be suspicious of the working of pride in us;* and also by an industrious watchfulness to give a stop or check to thoughts of this nature when they arise.

[3.] Thirdly, *The conquest of this cannot be expected without a serious and constant labour herein.* A humble soul is compared by David to a weaned child, Ps. cxxxi. 2. But a child is not weaned easily. Wormwood must be laid on the breast, and time allowed, before the child will forget it. He only that is content to exercise a discipline upon himself, and by frequent practices to habituate himself to low and careful thoughts, is likely to overcome it.

Pride, we have seen, was Satan's great engine to bring on presumption. The means by which he endeavoureth to beget pride, as was before noted, were,

[1.] First, *The consideration of privileges*, as being 'the Son of God.' For this expression, 'If thou art the Son of God,' is now urged in a sense different from that which it had in the first temptation. There he propounded it as unlikely that he should be the Son of God, and yet be under such a disregard of providence. In this sense it notably suited his design of drawing him to a distrust of God's care, and consequently of his sonship. Here he is upon a contrary temptation, and therefore propounds this as a thing of which Christ was assured, and from that assurance he thus disputes: 'Thou believest thou art the Son of God, and dost well depend on his care; therefore needest thou not to distrust thy preservation, if thou castest thyself down.'

[2.] Secondly, To help his confidence forward to the undertaking, he suggests *what credit and honour it would be to him, in the sight of all the people, to be so miraculously kept from hurt.* Hence note,

Obs. 11. *That Satan doth usually kindle and nourish pride, by a perverse confidence of our privileges.*

It is very hard for Christians to carry their assurance *even:* not but that grace in its proper working begets humility, and a watchful care against sin and folly; but such is our infirmity that we are easily drawn to be proud of our mercies, and to persuade ourselves that we may make bold with God because we are his children. Hence was that paradox of Mr Foxe, ' That his sins did him most good, and his graces most hurt;' he means, sins occasioned his humility, whereas his graces were apt, through his weakness, to make him proud. And to hide this pride from man, God is forced to keep them sometime from the sight of their assurance, or to discipline them by other temptations, as he did with Paul, lest they should be ' exalted above measure.'

Note further, *Obs.* 12. *That popular applause Satan finds, and useth accordingly, to be a great instigator to pride.*

The great thing that moved the Pharisees in their often fastings and large charity, was that they might have praise of men, and therefore took they care to be seen of men.[1] The heathens noted this to be the great feeder of that humour which animated them, as a drum or trumpet animates soldiers to adventurous acts.[2] And some good men have found no small difficulty to carry steadily, when they have been hoisted up by the breath of men's praise; which hath also occasioned those serious cautions against the danger of flattery and high commendations, ' A flattering mouth worketh ruin,' Prov. xxvi. 28.

---

[1] Digito monstrari, et dicier, Hic est.—[*Horace.*—G.]
[2] Quis vero tam bene modulo suo metiri se novit, ut eum assiduæ et immodicæ laudationes non moveant?—*H. Stephens.*

CHAPTER XVII.

Of Satan's subtlety in urging that of Ps. xci. 11, 12, to Christ.—Of his imitating the Spirit of God in various ways of teaching.—Of his pretending Scripture to further temptation.—The reasons of such pretendings, and the ends to which he doth abuse it.—Of Satan's unfaithfulness in managing of scriptures.—Cautions against that deceit.—The ways by which it may be discovered.

The ways of Satan, hitherto insisted on, to engage Christ in this act of presumption, were secret insinuations and underhand contrivances: but that which he openly and expressly urged to this purpose, was an argument drawn from the promise of God, though sadly abused and misrepresented, 'He shall give his angels charge concerning thee,' &c. This we are next to consider, in which, as cited by him, we may easily see, (1.) That Satan affected an imitation of Christ, in the way of his resistance. Christ had urged Scripture before, and now Satan endeavours to manage the same weapon against him. (2.) It is observable that Scripture is the weapon that Satan doth desire to wield against him. In his other ways of dealing he was shy, and did but lay them in Christ's way, offering only the occasion, and leaving him to take them up; but in this he is more confident, and industriously pleads it, as a thing which he could better stand to and more confidently avouch. (3.) The care of his subtlety herein, lay in the misrepresentation and abuse of it, as may be seen in these particulars: [1.] In that he urged this promise to promote a sinful thing, contrary to the general end of all Scripture, which was therefore written 'that we sin not.' [2.] But more especially in his clipping and mutilating of it. He industriously leaves out that part of it which doth limit and confine the promise of protection to lawful undertakings, such as this was not, and renders it as a general promise of absolute safety, be the action what it will. It is a citation from Ps. xci. 11, 12, which there runs thus, 'He shall give his angels charge over thee, to keep thee in all thy ways.' These last words, 'in all thy ways,' which doth direct to a true understanding of God's intention in that promise, he deceitfully leaves out, as if they were needless and unnecessary parts of the promise, when indeed they were on purpose put there by the Spirit of God, to give a description of those persons and actions, unto whom, in such cases, the accomplishment of the promise might be expected; for albeit the word in the original, which is translated 'ways'—דרכים—doth signify any kind of way or action in the general, yet in this place it doth not; for then God were engaged to an absolute protection of men, not only when they unnecessarily thrust themselves into dangers, but in the most abominably sinful actions whatsoever; which would have been a direct contradiction to those many scriptures wherein God threatens to withdraw his hand and leave sinners to the danger of their iniquities; but it is evident that the sense of it is no more than this, 'God is with you, while you are with him.' We have a paraphrase of this text, to this purpose, in Prov. iii. 23, 'Then shalt thou walk in thy way safely, and thy foot shall not stumble:'

where the condition of this safety, pointed to in the word 'then,' which leads the promise, is expressly mentioned in the foregoing verses, 'My son, let them'—that is, the precepts of wisdom—'not depart from thine eyes. . . . . Then'—not upon other terms—'shalt thou walk in thy way safely.' The ways then in this promise, cited by Satan, are the ways of duty, or the ways of our lawful callings. The fallacy of Satan in this dealing with Scripture is obvious, and Christ might have given this answer, as Bernard hath it, That God promiseth to keep him in his ways, but not in self-created dangers, for that was not his way, but his ruin; or if a way, it was Satan's way, but not his.[1] (3.) To these two, some add another abuse, in a subtle concealment of the following verse in Ps. xci., 'Thou shalt tread upon the lion and adder.' This concerned Satan, whose cruelty and poisonous deceits were fitly represented by the lion and the adder, and there the promise is also explained to have a respect to Satan's temptations—that is, God would so manage his protection, that his children should not be led into a snare.

Hence observe, Obs. 13. *That Satan sometimes imitates the Spirit of God by an officious pretence of teaching the mind of God to men.*

This our adversary doth not always appear in one shape. Sometime he acts as a lion or dragon, in ways of cruelty and fierceness; sometimes as a filthy swine, in temptations to bestial uncleanness and sensual lusts; sometime he puts on the garb of holiness, and makes as if he were not a spiritual adversary, but a spiritual friend and counsellor. That this is frequent with him, the apostle tells us: 2 Cor. xi. 14, 'Satan himself is transformed into an angel of light.' Angels of light are those blessed spirits sent forth to minister for the good of the elect, whose ministry God useth not only for our preservation from bodily hurts, but also for prevention of sin and furtherance of duty. Satan, as wicked as he is, doth counterfeit that employment, and takes upon him to give advice for our good, pretending to teach us in the truth, or to direct and further us in our endeavours.[2]

That he designs an imitation of God and his Spirit, may be discovered by expressing a great many particulars of God's ways and appointments, wherein Satan, as God's ape, partly out of mockery and scorn, partly upon other grounds of advantage to his intendments, doth counterfeit the current coin of the Lord's establishments by a very close imitation. But I shall here confine myself to the point of teaching and instruction, wherein how he proceeds, we shall the better understand by considering how many ways God hath of old, and now still doth use in declaring his mind to his people. The sum of all we have, Heb. i. 12. Heretofore he signified his mind in 'divers manners' by the prophets, and 'in these last days by his Son,' in all which we shall trace the steps of Satan.

(1.) First, *God revealed himself sometime by voice;* as to Abraham, Moses, and others. The devil hath dared to imitate this. There

[1] In Ps. xiv., In viis, nunquid in præcipitiis? Non est via hæc sed ruina, et si via, tua est, non illius.—*Bernard.*

[2] Anthores se vitæ scelestæ immundæque testantur, perhibentur tamen in adytis suis secretisque penetralibus dare quædam bona præcepta de moribus, quibusdam velut electis sacratis suis; quod si ita est, hoc ipso callidior aduertenda est et convincenda malitia spirituum noxiorum.—*Aug. Civit. Dei*, lib. ii. cap. 26.

want not instances of it; in the temptation, which is now under explanation, he did so; and his confessing Christ, 'I know thee who thou art,' [Mat. i. 24,] &c., doth shew that he is ready enough to do it at any time for advantage. Sprenger tells us a story of the devil's preaching to a congregation in the habit and likeness of a priest, wherein he reproved sin, and urged truth, and seemed no way culpable for false doctrine; but I suspect this for a fabulous tale. However, it is undeniable that he sometime hath appeared to men with godly exhortations in his mouth, of living justly, and doing no man wrong, &c.,[1] except we resolve to discredit all history, and the narrations of persons, and some such are known to some in this auditory, who solemnly affirm they have met with such dealing from him.

(2.) Secondly, *God hath sometime revealed himself to men in ecstasies and trances;* such as was that of Paul: Acts xxii. 17, 'I was in an ecstasy or trance,' γενέσθαι με ἐν ἐκστάσει. This also hath the devil imitated. Mohammed made this advantage of his disease, the epilepsy or falling-sickness, pretending that at such times he was in an ecstasy, and had converse with the angel Gabriel. But what he only in knavery pretended, others have really felt. The stories of Familists and deluded Quakers are full of such things. They frequently have fallen down and have lain as in a swoon, and when they have awaked, told wonderful stories of what they have heard and seen.

(3.) Thirdly, *Visions and dreams were usual things in the Old Testament, and famous ways of divine revelation;* but Satan was not behind in this matter. His instruments had their visions too. In Ezek. xiii. 7 we have mention of vain visions and lying divinations; and such satanical dreams are also noted, Deut. xiii. 1, 'If there arise among you a dreamer of dreams.' Those days of confusion, that are not yet out of memory, afforded store of these. While unstable, giddy-headed people began to dote on novelties and questions in religion, they gave opportunity to Satan to beguile them; for he taking advantage of their nauseating of old truths, and their expectation of sublime discoveries, which had sufficiently prepared them for any impression, did so overwork their fancies that they easily conceited themselves to have had divine revelations, and nothing was more ordinary than to hear stories of visions and dreams. And this spread further by a kind of infection, for it grew into a religious fashion; and he was not esteemed that had not something of this nature to experience. And though the folly and impertinences of such things generally, and sometime the apparent wickedness of them, as contradicting truth and the divine rules of holiness, were sufficient discoveries that Satan's hand was in them, yet until time, experience, and the power of God had cooled the intemperate heat of this raving humour, it continued in the good liking and admiration of the more inconsiderate vulgar. And sometime those from whom more seriousness and consideration might have been expected fell into a reverence for these pretences in others, and helped forward this spiritual witchcraft by their countenance and arguings, often abusing that text in Acts ii. 17, 'Your young men shall see visions, and your old men shall dream dreams,' by applying it to a justification of these apparently foolish

[1] Mal. Malefic., part 2, Q. 1, cap. 9.

dotages. And indeed the effect hath discovered they were no better, for many of those things which with great confidence were avouched as certain, were by time proved to be false. Many things were useless, vain, ridiculous, and some were brought to lament and confess their folly after they proceeded far in these ways; and at last, when the former opportunities were worn out, Satan grew weary of that design as being no longer proper to be insisted on. There is now a great calm, so that it is but seldom that we hear of such things talked of. It were needless to give particular instances, when you may at your leisure fetch them from hundreds of pamphlets commonly known.

(4.) Fourthly, One of the most noted ways by which God discovered his mind was that of *inspiration,* by which some eminent persons, called therefore prophets, spake the will of God 'as they were moved or acted by the Spirit of God,' [2 Peter i. 21.] The devil had also his false prophets. Such are frequently taxed in the Old Testament, and foretold in the New: 'False Christs, and false prophets shall arise,' Mat. xxiv. 24; 'There were false prophets among the people, as there shall be false teachers among you,' 2 Peter ii. 1. Many false teachers are gone out into the world. Such a one was Montanus in Tertullian's time, David George, John of Leyden, Hacket, our countryman, were such, and a great many such there have been in all ages. It is notoriously known that Satan hath thus inspired poor, possessed wretches, who have uttered threatenings against sin and woe to sinners. The sayings of such possessed creatures have not long since been gathered into a volume and published, as containing very persuasive arguments to repentance and amendment of life.[1] Besides these, our own times afford too many examples of this kind. Many have put on the guise of the old prophets in a foolish though adventurous imitation of their actions and prophecies. Some have in our streets resembled Jonah in Nineveh, 'Yet forty days,' &c. Some fancied to walk naked like Isaiah; others have come with their earthen pitchers and broken them, imitating these and other types by which God in his true prophets foresignified his judgments to come; in all which actions and garbs, with much earnestness, and in an affected tone, they have called out for repentance in a confident denunciation of woes and miseries, with a bold limiting of the time of forty days, that the same might carry a parallel to Jonah's prophecy, and sometime giving—which is the surest way—an unlimited, uncertain time. How the devil acts in these matters, and by what ways he seduceth them to believe they are inspired of God, or have real visions and revelations, it is not my business now to inquire; only let those that think such things strange, consider that the devil hath the advantage of deep fanciful apprehensions and a working melancholy in such persons, by which he can easily work them to conceit anything, and confidently believe what they have conceited.

(5.) Fifthly, Sometime God notified his mind *by signs and miracles.* Satan hath also his 'lying signs and wonders;' a power God hath permitted him this way, which is very great, and the delusions wrought thereby are strong, hazarding the deception of the elect. This power of doing wonders the devil usually applies to false

---

[1] Jean D'Espagne, 'Popular Errors,' p. 76. [As before.—G.]

doctrines, to strengthen and countenance errors. The apostle testifies, 2 Thes. ii. 9, that Satan shall employ this power for the advancement of the 'man of sin, whose coming shall be with signs and lying wonders.' The beast arising out of the earth, Rev. xiii. 14, ' he shall deceive by the means of those miracles which he hath power to do.' And accordingly the popish legends are full of stories of miracles, whereof, though most be lies, forgeries, and the false contrivements of those who sought to bring the people to receive their doctrines, the credit and advancement of which they sought by such ways; some notwithstanding, though not true miracles, yet were truly acted, to countenance those errors which are pretended to be established by them.

(6.) Sixthly, God doth teach and lead his people *by impulses*. Christ was thus 'led of the Spirit into the wilderness;' and Paul was 'bound in spirit to go to Jerusalem,' [Acts xx. 22.] It is common for Satan to imitate such impulses. We have clear instances of diabolical impulses to sin in Scripture. A strong impulse was on Ananias, 'Satan filled his heart,' [Acts v. 3;] a strong impulse on Judas, ' Satan entered into his heart,' [Luke xxii. 3;] and what then more easy to apprehend, than that Satan can counterfeit better impulses, and violently stir up the hearts of men to actions seemingly good or indifferent? Some hypocrites are moved strongly to pray or preach,—Satan therein aiming at an increase of pride or presumption in them;—and they know no other, but that it is the Spirit of God. God's children may have impulses from Satan, upon pretences of zeal, as the disciples had, when they called for fire from heaven. In these impulses Satan doth not so act the heart of man as the Spirit of God doth, whose commands in this case are irresistible ; but he only works by altering the disposition of our bodies in a natural way; and then having fitted us all he can for an impression, he endeavours to set it on by strong persuasions. Some memorable instances of these impulses might profitably illustrate this. Math. Parisiensis takes notice of a boy, in *anno* 1213, of whom also Fuller makes mention,[1] who, after some loss which the Christians had received in the war against the Turks, went up and down, singing this rhyme—

> 'Jesus Lord, redeem our loss :
> Restore to us thy holy cross.'

And by this means he gathered a multitude of boys together, who could not by the severest menaces of their parents be hindered from following him to their own ruin. Another instance of a strange impulse we have in Josephus:[2] one Jesus, the son of Ananus, about four years before the destruction of Jerusalem, at the feast of tabernacles, begins to cry out, ' Woe, woe, to the east and west, to men and women,' &c., and could by no means be restrained night or day ; and when his flesh was beaten off his bones, he begged no pity nor ease, but still continued his usual crying.

(7.) Seventhly, God doth also by his Spirit teach his people in *bringing things to their remembrance*, John xiv. 26. Satan also in imitation of this, can put into the minds of men, with great readiness

---

[1] Holy War, lib. iii. cap. 24.   [2] Wars of the Jews, lib. vii. cap. 13.

and dexterity, promises or sentences of Scripture, insomuch that they conclude that all such actings are from the Spirit of God, who, as they conclude, set such a scripture upon their heart. Thus dealt Satan with Christ. He urgeth the promise upon him, wherein upon the matter he doth as much, as when he secretly suggests such things to the heart without an audible voice. In this way of craft Satan doth very much resemble the true work of the Spirit; [1.] In the readiness and quickness of suggesting; [2.] In seeming exact-suiting scripture suggested, with the present occasion; and [3.] In the earnestness of his urging it upon the fancies of men. Yet when all this is done, they that shall seriously consider all ends, matter and circumstances, will easily observe it is but the cunning work of a tempter, and not from the Holy Spirit.

Obs. 14. Observe also, *That whatever be the various ways of Satan's imitation, yet the matter which he works and practiseth upon is still Scripture.* To this he confines himself:—

[1.] First, *Because the Scriptures are generally, among Christians, received as the undoubted oracles of God, the rule of our lives and duties, and the grounds of our hope.* It would be a vain and bootless labour to impose upon those that retain this belief, the sayings of the Turkish Alcoran, the precepts of heathen philosophers, or any other thing that may carry a visible estrangement from or contradiction to Scripture. He could not then possibly pretend to a divine instruction, nor could he so 'transform himself into an angel of light:' but by using this covert of divine command, promise, or discovery, he can more easily beget a belief that God hath said it, and that there is neither sin nor danger in the thing propounded, but duty and advantage to be expected; and this is the very thing that makes way for an easy entertainment of such delusions. Poor creatures believe that is all from God, and that they are acted by his Spirit, and that with such confidence that they contemn and descry those, as ignorant of divine mysteries, and of the power of God, who are not so besotted as themselves.

[2.] Secondly, *The Scriptures have a glorious irresistible majesty in them, peculiar to themselves, which cannot be found in all that art or eloquence can contribute to other authors.* It is not play-book language, nor scraps of romances that Satan can effect these cheats withal; and therefore we may observe that in the highest delusions men have had pretences of Scripture; and their strong persuasions of extraordinary discoveries have stricken men into a reverence of their profession, because of the Scripture words and phrases with which their boldest follies are woven up. For let but men inquire into the reason of the prevalency of Familism of old, upon so vast a number of people as were carried away with it, and they shall find that the great artifice lay in the words they used, a language abstracted from Scripture, to signify such conceits as the Scripture never intended. Hence were their expressions always high, soaring, and relating to a more excellent and mystical interpretation of those divine writings. This may be observed in David George, Hen. Nicholas, and others, who usually talk of being consubstantiated with God, taken up into his love, of the angelical life, and a great deal more of the same kind.

The Ranters at first had the like language, and the Quakers after them affected such a canting expression. And we may be the more certain of the truth of this observation, that such a kind of speaking, which borrows its majesty from the style of the Scripture, is of moment to Satan's design; because we find the Scripture itself gives particular notice of it. The false teachers in 2 Pet. ii. 18, are described, among other things, by their 'swelling words of vanity,' which the Syriac renders to be 'a proud and lofty way of speaking.' The original signifies no less—ὑπέρογκα,—they were words swelled like bladders, though being pricked, they be found to be empty sounds, and no substance. There are indeed swelling words of atheistical contempt of those who, as the psalmist speaks, 'set their mouths against heaven,' Ps. lxxiii. 9, 11; but this passage of Peter, as also the like in Jude 16, signify big swollen words, from high pretensions and fancies of knowing the mind of God more perfectly; for they that use them pretend themselves prophets of God, ver. 1, and as to their height in profession, are compared to clouds highly soaring; and in 2 Cor. xi. 14, they are said to be 'transformed into the apostles of Christ,' and to the garb of the 'ministers of righteousness.' And that which is more, this particular design of Satan is noted as the rise of all; 'No marvel, for Satan himself is transformed into an angel of light.'

Having seen the reasons why Satan chooseth Scripture as his tool to work by, I shall next shew to what base designs he makes it subserve.

[1.] First, He useth this artifice *to beget and propagate erroneous doctrines.* Hence no opinion is so vile, but pretends to Scripture as its patron. The Arians pretend Scripture against the divinity of Christ. The Socinians, Pelagians, Papists, yea, and those that pretend to inspirations for their rule, and disclaim the binding force of those antiquated declarations of the saints' conditions, as they call them, yet conform all their sayings to the Scripture expression, and endeavour to prove their mistakes by its authority.

[2.] Secondly, *He makes abused Scripture to encourage sinful actions.* He can cite passages of God's patience and long-suffering, of his pardoning grace and readiness to forgive, and a thousand more, upon no other design than the 'turning of the grace of God into wantonness,' [Jude 4.] When professors turn loose and negligent, when they adventure too far upon sinful pleasures, they lick themselves whole by an overforward grasping at such passages of Scripture, which Satan will with great readiness set upon their hearts; and then they pretend to themselves that their peace is made up with God, and that they have no less than a sealed pardon in their bosoms; which notwithstanding may be known to have only Satan's hand and seal at it, by their overly and formal sorrow for such miscarriages, and their readiness to return to the same follies again.

[3.] Thirdly, By this imitation of the commands and promises of God, *he doth strangely engage such as he can thus delude unto desperate undertakings.*[1] The Familists of Germany were persuaded by this delusion, to expose themselves unarmed to the greatest hazards,

---

[1] Funcius in his Chronol. tells the like of one in Crete, that called himself Moses, anno 434, who persuaded the Jews to follow him for the repossessing of Canaan. ['Funckius.'—G.]

upon vain pretences of promises set home upon them, as that God would fight for them, that they must 'stand still and see the salvation of God,' [Exod. xiv. 13.] Some of later times have paid their lives for their bold misapplication of that promise, 'One shall chase a thousand,' [Deut. xxxii. 30.] Judas of Galilee and Theudas were prompted by Satan to gather multitudes together, though to their own ruin, upon a vain persuasion that they were raised up of God, and that God would be with them.[1]

[4.] Fourthly, He sometimes *procures groundless peace and assurance in the hearts of careless ones by Scripture misapplied*. Many you may meet with who will roundly tell you a long story how they were cast down and comforted by such a scripture brought to their minds, when, it may be much feared, they are but deceived, and that as yet God hath not spoken peace to them.

Lastly, This way of Satan's setting home scriptures proves sadly effectual to beget or heighten *the inward distresses and fears of the children of God*. It is a wonder to hear some dispute against themselves, so nimble they be to object a scripture against their peace, above their reading or ability, that you would easily conclude there is one at hand that prompts them, and suggests these things to their own prejudice. And sometime a scripture will be set so cross or edgeway to their good and comfort, that many pleadings, much time, prayers, and discourses cannot remove it. I have known some that have seriously professed scriptures have been thrown into their hearts like arrows, and have with such violence fixed a false apprehension upon their minds, as that God had cut them off, that they were reprobate, damned, &c., that they have borne the tedious, restless affrightments of it for many days, and yet the thing itself, as well as the issue of it, doth declare that this was not the fruit of the Spirit of God, which is a spirit of truth, and cannot suggest a falsehood, but of Satan, who hath been a liar from the beginning.

Observe lastly, *Obs.* 15. *Though Satan useth Scripture in these deceitful workings, yet he never doth it faithfully.*

(1.) First, *Because it is against his nature, as it is now corrupted by his fall.* There is no truth in him: 'When he speaketh a lie he speaketh of his own, for he is a liar,' John viii. 44; not that he cannot speak a truth, but that he usually is a liar, and that he never speaks truth but with a purpose to deceive.[2]

(2.) Secondly, *To deal faithfully in urging scriptures upon the consciences of men, is also contrary to his interest.* He hath a kingdom which he endeavours to uphold. This kingdom, being directly contrary to that of Christ's, which is a kingdom of light, is therefore called a kingdom of darkness, being maintained and propagated only by lies and deceits. He cannot then be supposed to use Scripture faithfully, because that is the true sceptre of Christ's kingdom, for then should Satan, as Christ argues, Mat. xii. 26, 'cast out Satan, and be divided against himself.'

This unfaithful dealing with Scripture is threefold.

(1.) First, The unfaithfulness of his *design*. Though he speaks

---

[1] Josephus, Anti. Jud., lib. xx. cap. 2.
[2] Etsi semel videatur verax, millies est mendax, et semper fallax.

what is true, yet he doth it with an evil mind, aiming at one of these three things:—

[1.] First, *To deceive and delude.* If he applies promises, or insists upon the privileges of God's children, it is to make them proud or presumptuous. If he urge threatenings, or stir up the conscience to accuse for sin, it is to bring them to despair; if he object the law, it is to enrage lust; and that 'sin by the commandment might become exceeding sinful,' [Rom. vii. 13.]

[2.] Secondly, His design is sometime *to bring the Scripture under suspicion or contempt.* He puts some weak Christians upon unseasonable or imprudent use of Scripture, and then tempts others to laugh at them, and to despise in their hearts those ways of religion which some zealots with too much weakness do manage. Men are apt enough to scoff at the most serious and weighty duties of holiness, even when performed in a most serious manner. If David put on sackcloth, and afflict himself with fasting, it is presently turned to his reproach, 'and the drunkards make a song of it,' [Ps. lxix. 12;] but much more advantage hath the devil to raise up scorn and loathing in the minds of debauched persons, by the affected and unskilful use of Scripture. Some by a narrow confinement of the words *brother* and *sister* to those of their own fellowship, as if none else were to be owned by them, have occasioned the scoff of holy brethren—a phrase notwithstanding used with a grave seriousness by the apostle—in the usual discourses of those who wait all occasions to harden themselves against the power of religion. The like observations they make of other ways and forms of speaking, which some have accustomed themselves unto, in a conscientious conformity to Scripture phrase: in all which the devil observing the weakness and injudiciousness of some on the one hand, and the scornful pride of others on the other hand, is willing to provide matter for their atheistical jeers, by putting all the obligations he can upon the consciences of the weak, to continue in the use of these expressions. For some proof of this matter we may note the secret deceit of Satan, in that liberal profession of Christ to be 'the Son of God,' Mark i. 24; Luke iv. 34, 'I know thee who thou art; the Holy One of God.' Here was truth spoken by him, and one would have thought with great ingenuity;[1] but yet he cunningly insinuated into the minds of the hearers a ground of suspicion that he was not the Son of God; and for that end calls him Jesus of Nazareth, as if Christ had been born there. He knew well that the Jews expected no Messiah from Nazareth, and therefore on set purpose used he that expression, that he might draw him into contempt. And accordingly we find this very mistake, that Christ was born at Nazareth, became an argument against him: John vii. 41, while some were convinced, and said, 'This is the Christ,' others said, 'Shall Christ come out of Galilee?'

[3.] Thirdly, Another part of his design in the use of scriptures is to *put a varnish upon hypocrisy.* He is ready to serve men by putting Scripture expressions in their mouths, and inuring them to a constant use of the phrases of those divine writings, that they may less suspect themselves of the pride, formality, and secret wickedness of

[1] 'Ingenuousness.'—G.

their hearts; and to help on their mistakes concerning their spiritual condition, he can urge upon their consciences those scriptures that serve to engage them in external observances of religion. It may appear by the Pharisee's boast of fasting 'twice a week,' of 'paying tithes,' of 'giving alms,' Luke xviii. 11, that their consciences were someway concerned in these things, so that though they were left without check of conscience 'to devour widows' houses,' yet were they urged to make 'long prayers.' Suitable to this is that which Solomon speaks of the harlot, who, to colour over her wickedness, had her offerings and vows; and when her conscience is appeased with these performances, she can excuse herself in her way of sinning, 'She eats and wipes her mouth, and saith, I have done no wickedness,' Prov. xxx. 20. Satan doth but hereby help to paint a sepulchre, or gild a potsherd, and to furnish men with excuses and pretexts in their way of sinning. Not unlike to this was that service which the devil with great readiness performed—as I was informed from some of good credit—to a young student who had fallen upon some books of magic in a college library, into which having stolen privately one night in pursuit of that study, was almost surprised by the president, who, seeing a candle there at an unseasonable time, suddenly opens the door to know who was up so late, in which strait the devil—to gratify his pupil with a ready excuse—snatcheth away his book, and in a moment lays Montanus his Bible before him, that he might pretend that for his employment.

(2.) Secondly, Another point of Satan's unfaithful dealing with Scripture is *his false citation of it*. It is nothing with him to alter, change, or leave out such a part as may make against him. If he urge promises upon men, in order to their security and negligence, he conceals the condition of them, and banisheth the threatening far from their minds, representing the mercy of God in a false glass, as if he had promised to save and bring to heaven every man upon the common and easy terms of being called a Christian. If it be his purpose to disquiet the hearts of God's children, to promote their fears, or to lead them to despair, then he sets home the commands and threatenings, but hides the promises that might relieve them, and, which is remarkable, he hath so puzzled some by setting on their hearts a piece of Scripture, that when the next words, or next verse, might have eased them of their fears, and answered the sad objections which they raised against themselves from thence, as if their eyes had been holden, or as if a mist had been cast over them, they have not for a long time been able to consider the relief which they might have had. This hiding of Scripture from their eyes, setting aside what God may do for the just chastisement of his children's folly, is effected by the strong impression which Satan sets upon their hearts, and by holding their minds down to a fixed meditation of the dreadful inferences which he presents to them from thence, not suffering them o divert their thoughts by his incessant clamours against them.

(3.) Thirdly, He unfaithfully handleth scriptures, *by wresting the true import and sense of them*. We read of some, 2 Pet. iii. 16, who 'wrest the Scripture.' The word in the original—$\sigma\tau\rho\epsilon\beta\lambda o\hat{v}\sigma\iota$—signifies a racking or torturing of it, as men upon a rack are stretched beyond their due length, to a dislocation of their joints, and sometimes forced to speak what they never did nor intended; so are the Scriptures used. Those that do so are Satan's scholars, and taught of him, though in regard of the Spirit's true teaching, they are called unlearned, which is sufficient to shew Satan's deceitful dealing. He often lays his dead and corrupt sense—as the harlot did with her dead child in the room of the living infant—in the place of the living meaning of the scripture. This may be seen evidently:—

[1.] First, *In heresies or errors.* These are Satan's brood, and there are none so vile, that pretend to Christian religion, but they claim a kindred to Scripture, and are confident on its authority for them. Now seeing truth is but one, and these errors not only contradictory to truth, but to each other, Satan could never spin out such conclusions from the divine oracles, but by wresting them from their true intendments; and he that would contemplate the great sublety of Satan in this his art, need but consider what different strange and monstrous shapes are put upon the Scripture by the several heresies which march under its colours. The Quakers in their way represent it like an old almanack out of date, and withal, in the use they make of it, they render it as a piece of nonsensical furious raving. The Socinians take down the sublime mysteries of Christ's satisfaction and justification by faith, with external rewards and punishments, to a strain as low as the Turkish Alcoran. The papists make it like a few leaves of an imperfect book, wanting beginning and end, and so not fit to be set up as a sufficient rule. The Ranters make it seem rather like language from hell than the commands of the pure and holy God. Some will have it to countenance most ridiculous inventions in worship; others will have it to discharge all outward observations and ordinances, as childish rudiments. Some raise it all to the pitch of enigmatical unintelligible mysteries; others can find no more in the precepts of it than in Aristotle's ethics. Thus by distorting and wresting, Satan hath learned these unskilful ones to make it serve their vilest lusts and humours.

[2.] Secondly, The same art of wresting Scripture is observable in his *secret suggestings.* If he would encourage any in sin, he can wrest Scripture for that, and tell him that God is merciful, that Christ died for sinners, that there is hope of pardon, that saints have done the like: things very true in themselves, but perverted by him to another sense than ever they were intended to by God, who hath spoken these things that we sin not. If he would discourage a saint, he can tell him when he finds him doubting his estate, that the 'fearful and unbelieving have their part in the lake which burns with fire and brimstone,' Rev. xxi. 8; when he finds him under a known sin, he tells that of the apostle, 'If we sin wilfully after we have received the knowledge of the truth, there remains no more sacrifice for sins,' [Heb. x. 26.] When he observes them discomposed and wandering in duty, then he objects, 'They draw nigh me with their lips, but their heart is far from me,' [Isa. xxix. 13.] If he sees them dull and without consolation at the Lord's supper, then to be sure they hear of him, 'He that eats and drinks unworthily, eateth and drinketh damnation to himself,' 1 Cor. xi. 29. If he find him bemoaning that he is not so apprehensive of mercies or judgments as he would be, then he sets home some such scripture as this, ' This people's heart is waxed gross, and their ears are dull of hearing,' Mat. xiii. 15, &c. These scriptures are frequently perverted by Satan from the true and proper meaning of them. I have had complaints from several dejected Christians of these very scriptures urged upon them to their great trouble, when yet it was evident that none of these were truly applied, by Satan's temptation against them.

Applic. These things give us warning not *to take anything of this nature upon trust.* If Satan can so imitate the Spirit of God in applications of Scripture, and bringing it to our remembrance, we have great reason to beware lest we be imposed upon by Satan's design clothed in Scripture phrase; not that I would have men esteem the secret setting of Scripture upon their minds, to be in all cases a delusion, and to be disregarded as such. Some indeed there are that so severely remark the weaknesses of professors of religion, that they raise up a scorn to that which is of most necessary and serious use. Because the devil prevails with some hypocrites to gild themselves with Scripture phrase, and others through imprudent inadvertency are, unknown to themselves, beguiled by Satan, to misapplications of Scripture to their own estate, or to other things; they therefore decry all the inward workings of the heart, as fancy or affected singularity; these do but the devil's work. But that the Spirit of God, whom Satan treacherously endeavours to imitate, doth set home Scripture commands, threatenings, and promises upon the hearts of his people, is not only attested by the experience of all that are inwardly acquainted with the ways of God, but is one of the great promises which Christ hath given for the comfort of his people in his absence: John xiv. 26, ' But the Comforter, which is the Holy Ghost, whom the Father shall send in my name, he shall teach you all things, and bring all things to your remembrance, whatsoever I have said unto you.' This then being granted as a firm unshaken truth, our care must be in discovering and avoiding Satan's counterfeit using of Scripture, and in this we should be more wary;

[1.] First, *Because we are not so apt to suspect what we meet with in such a way, when it is brought to us in the language of Scripture.*

[2.] Secondly, *And those that are not exercised in the Scripture, will be at a sad loss, as not knowing how to extricate themselves from such difficulties as may arise to them from Satan's sophistry.*

[3.] Thirdly, Wariness is also more necessary, *because we are inclinable to believe what suits our desires, and conscience awakened is averse to the rejecting of that which answers its fears.*

Quest. You may say, What is there of direction for us in this case?

Ans. The answer is ready. Two things are given us in charge. (1.) That we be wisely suspicious. A facile hasty credulity is treacherous. Christ forbids, when he foretells the rising of false Christs, Mat. xxiv. 26, the forwardness of a sudden belief, taxing thereby those that are presently taken with every new appearance. It is childish to be carried with every wind. We are warned also of this: 1 John iv. 1, ' Believe not every spirit.' (2.) We are commanded to bring all pretences whatsoever to trial. Though immediate revelation or vision be pretended, or extraordinary commission, yet must all be brought to the touchstone. ' We must prove all things,' 1 Thes. v. 21, ' and try those that say they are apostles,' Rev. ii. 2; nay, ' the spirits are to be tried whether they be of God,' 1 John iv. 1.

Quest. You will say, How must we try?

Ans. I answer, God hath given a public, sufficient, and certain rule, which is *the Scripture, and all must be tried by that;* so that if there be impulses or discoveries or remembrances of Scripture upon any, it must not be taken for granted that they are of God, because they pretend so high, for so we shall make Satan judge in his own cause; but lay all to the line and plummet of the written word, and if it answer not that, call it confidently a delusion, and reject it as accursed, though it might seem in other regards to have been suggested by an angel from heaven.

Obj. But it will be said, Satan pretends to this rule, and it is Scripture that is urged by him.

Ans. I answer, Though it be so, yet he useth not Scripture in its own intendment and sense. For the discovery of his unfaithful dealing;—

[1.] First, *Compare the inference of the suggestion with other scriptures.* If it be from a dark scripture, compare it with those that are more plain, and in every case see whether the general current of the Scriptures speak the same thing; for if it be from Satan, he either plays with the words and phrases, from doubtful and equivalent terms making his conclusion, or his citation will be found impertinent, or, which is most usual, contrary to truth or holiness. If any of these appear by a true examination of the import of the scripture which he seeks to abuse, or by comparing it with the scope and genius of other scriptures, you may certainly pronounce that it is not of God, but Satan's deceit.[1]

[2.] Secondly, *Consider the tendency of such suggestions.* Let no man say that this will come too late, or that it is an after-game. I do not mean that we should stay so long as to see the effects, though this is also a certain discovery of Satan's knavery in his highest pretences. The fanatic furies of the German enthusiasts do now appear plain to all the world to have been delusions, by their end, fruits, and issue. But that while these conclusions are obtruded upon us, we should observe to what they tend, which we shall the better know if all circumstances round about be considered. Sometimes Satan doth covertly hint his mind, and send it along with the suggestions; sometimes our condition will enough declare it, and there is no case but it will afford something of discovery if seriously pondered. If he either prompt us to pride, vainglory, or presumption, or that our condition sway us that way, it will be sufficient ground of suspicion that it is Satan that then urgeth promises or privileges upon us. If we are of a wounded spirit, inclined to distrust, or if we be put on to despair, it is past denial that it is Satan that urgeth the threatenings, and presseth the accusations of the law against us. He that gathers stones, timber, lime, and such materials together, as are usually employed in building,

---

[1] Though it was Scripture that Satan urged to Christ, yet he rejects his inference as false, because contrary to other plain scriptures prohibiting not to tempt the Lord.

doth discover his intention before he actually build his house, and thus may Satan's end be known by his preparations, compared with the sway and inclination of our present temper.

[3.] Thirdly, *It must be remembered that with these endeavours, we often seek the face of the Lord for help and counsel;* and that we apply ourselves to such of the servants of God, as being more knowing than ourselves, and less prepossessed in their judgments, because not concerned, are better able to see into the nature of our straits, and to help us by their advices.

CHAPTER XVIII.

Again the devil taketh him up into an exceeding high mountain, and sheweth him all the kingdoms of the world, and the glory of them.— MAT. iv. 8.

The manner of Satan's shewing the kingdoms of the world.—Of Satan's preparations before the motion of sin.—Of his confronting the Almighty by presumptuous imitation, and in what cases he doth so. —Of his beautifying the object of a temptation, and how he doth it. —His way of engaging the affections by the senses.—Of his seeming shyness.

This is the preparation to the third temptation; in which we have, (1.) The place where it was acted; (2.) The object set before him there.

1. First, The place was an 'exceeding high mountain.' What mountain it was, Nebo, Pisgah, or any other, it is needless to inquire. It is of more use to ask after the reasons of Satan's choice of such a place. The text doth clearly imply one; that was the commodiousness of prospect. Satan intending to give him a view of the kingdoms of the world, chooseth a mountain as fittest for that end. But that this was not all the reason, is not only intimated by some,[1] but positively affirmed by others,[2] who think that Satan in this imitated the like in God to Moses, who was called up to Mount Nebo to view the land which God promised to Israel. Whether these circumstances of the mountain, and the view of the kingdoms of the world, were of purpose contrived to affront God by such an imitation, I will not be positive in it; but we may with greater evidence affirm that in offering the kingdoms of the world as things altogether in his disposal, he doth directly outbrave God by an insolent comparison of his power with that of the Almighty's, whose is 'the earth and the fulness of it,' [Ps. xxiv. 1,] and to whom the sovereignty of the disposal of it doth belong.

2. Secondly, That which Satan sheweth Christ from the mountain is said to be 'the kingdoms of the world, and the glory of them.' Here some busy themselves to conjecture what kingdoms were thus pointed at. Some keep so strictly to the word 'all,' that they are forced to take up with that opinion, that all these temptations were

[1] Lightfoot, Harm. *in loc.*   [2] Perkins, Com. *in loc.* Deut. xxxii. 49, and xxxiv. 1.

only in vision,[1] for they consider that no one mountain in the world can give a prospect over one whole hemisphere, or if it could, yet no eye would be able to discern at so great a distance. But the inconveniences of this surmise have been pointed at before, and it is enough to shew that the text may admit of an interpretation which shall not be encumbered with this supposed impossibility.

Others restrain this to the land of Canaan, as if Satan only shewed this as a famous instance of the glory of all kingdoms. Some think the Roman empire, which was then most flourishing, and lifted up its head above other kingdoms, was the great bait laid before Christ, as if he had a design to divert Christ from the business of his office, by offering him the seat and power of Antichrist.[2] But the text runs not so favourably for any of these opinions as to constrain us to stay upon them. 'Kingdoms of the world' seem to intend more than Canaan or the Roman empire; the word κόσμος used here, and οἰκουμένη in Luke, which we translate 'the world,' do so apply to one another in a mutual accommodation, that we cannot stretch the 'world' to the largest sense of the whole globe of the earth, because it is expressed in Luke by οἰκουμένη, which signifies such a part of the world which is more cultivated and honoured by inhabitants; nor can we so restrain it to the Roman empire—though when they spake their apprehensions of their own empire, they seem to engross all, Luke ii. 1— because Matthew useth the word κόσμος, a word of greater freedom. It seems then that many kingdoms, or the most considerable kingdoms of the then known world, were here exposed to his sight. But then the difficulty still remains, how the devil could shew them to his eye. That it was not a visionary discovery to his mind, hath been said. Some think he shewed these partly by ocular prospect of those cities, castles, towns, vineyards, and fields that were near, as a compend of the whole, and partly by a discourse of the glory, power, and extent of other kingdoms that were out of the reach of the eye; but because the expression which Luke adds, 'in a moment of time'—ἐν στιγμῇ χρόνου—intimates that the way which Satan took was different from common prospecting or beholding, others are not satisfied with that solution of the difficulty, but fly to this supposition, that Satan used only juggling and delusion, by framing an airy horizon before the eyes of Christ, shewing not the kingdoms themselves, but a phantasm of his own making. But seeing this might have been done in any place, and that a high mountain was chosen for furthering the prospect, I think it is safest to conclude that the prospect was ocular, and not fantastical but real, only helped and assisted by Satan's skill and art, as a great naturalist and as a prince of the power of the air, by which means, in reflections or extraordinary prospectives, he might discover things at vast distances; which we may the rather fix upon, because we know what helps for prospect art hath discovered by glasses and telescopes, by which the bodies of the sun, moon, and planets, at such unspeakable distance from us, have in this latter age been discovered to us beyond ordinary belief.[3] And we have reason to think that Satan's skill this way far exceeds anything that we have come to the

---

[1] Hobbes's Leviath., cap. 45, p. 354.   [2] Lightfoot, Harm. *in loc.*
[3] So also Lucas Brugensis thinks *in loc.*

knowledge of, and so might make real discoveries of countries far remote, more than we can well imagine.

These things thus explained, I shall note several observations.

Obs. 1. First, If we consider this great preparation that Satan makes as introductory to the temptation to follow, we may observe, *that where Satan hath a special design, he projects and makes ready all things relating to the temptation before he plainly utter his mind.* He provides his materials before he builds, and lays his train before he gives fire. What is his method we may learn from the practice of those that are trained up in his service. They, in Rom. xiii. 14, are said to ' make provision for the flesh '—πρόνοια—to fore-contrive their sins, and to project all circumstances of time, place, occasion, and advantage for their accomplishment. This is not to be understood of all sins, for in some that are inward in the mind, as vain thoughts, pride of heart, &c., there needs not such provisions. We may say of them their times are always, and in many cases ' the house is swept and garnished ' [Mat. xii. 44] to his hand; he finds all things ready by the forwardness of those who are free in his service, and the sudden accidental concurrence of things. But where the temptation is solemn, and where the thing designed, in the perfecting of it, relates to exterior acts, there he useth this policy, to have all in readiness, though it cost him the labour of ' compassing sea and land' for it, before he expressly speak his purposes. His reasons are these:—

(1.) First, If things necessary for the encouragement and accomplishment of a temptation *lay out of the way, and were not at hand, his suggestions would perish as soon as they were born, and would be rejected as impossible or inconvenient.* To tempt a man to steal when he knows not where nor how, or to revenge when he hath no enemy nor provocation, seem to be no other than if they should be commanded to remove a mountain or to fly in the air, which would quickly be declined as motions affording no ground of entertainment. And therefore that his temptations may not bring a reason of refusal with them as being unseasonable, he takes care to fit his servants with all things requisite for the work he puts them upon.

(2.) Secondly, As temptations of this kind would be no temptations, because not feasible, *without their preparations, so must we not think that it is the bare suggestion of Satan that makes a temptation to pierce.* The reason of its prevalency is not barely because Satan breaks such a motion to us, but because such a motion comes accomplished with all suitable preparations. When it prevails, it is the sinful motion that wounds; but preparations are as the feathers that wing his arrows, without which they would neither fly nor pierce.

Applic. Let this, (1.) First, *Renew our caution and suspicion in everything and every place that Satan is at work against us, though we see no visible snare.*

Let it put us upon such a watchful carefulness in every of our ways, that we may resolve to undertake nothing for which we have not a good and warrantable reason at hand, that if our conscience say to us, What dost thou here? we may be able to give a good account.

(2.) Secondly, If we mind the behaviour of Satan in these preparations and offers, *we see him act after the pattern of highest sovereignty, disposing of earthly kingdoms at such a rate as if all power were in his hand.* Hence we may observe,

Obs. 2. *That when Satan tempts to sin of highest contempt and insolency against God, he then thinks it concerns him to bear himself out by confronting the Almighty in imitating his authority and power.*

This carriage of Satan is not to be found in all his temptations. For in most cases he acts with greatest secrecy; and as a thief that is afraid of discovery, he useth all ways possible for concealment; but when he sets up himself as 'the god of the world,' and stands in competition with the Lord, claiming an interest in the fear and devotion of men, then he boldly avoucheth himself, and labours to outvie God in point of greatness, that he might possess them with a belief that he only ought to be feared. This arrogancy of Satan against God may be seen in three things:—

[1.] First, *In imitating divine ordinances and institutions.* There is not any part of divine worship, the observation whereof God hath enjoined to men, but Satan hath set up something like it for himself. As God appointed his temple, priests, altars, sacrifices, offerings, tithes, sanctuaries, sacraments, &c., so hath Satan had his temples, priests, altars, sacrifices, offerings, sanctuaries, sacraments, &c. This is sufficiently known to any that read his histories; and I could give a full account of it from heathen authors, but that I have done already when I spoke of Satan's subtlety in promoting idolatry in the world. I shall only add here that which Varro relates[1] of the books of Numa Pompilius, which were casually cast up by the plough of one Terentius coming too near the sepulchre of Numa, where these books had been buried. This Numa was the second king of the Romans, who instituted the rites and ceremonies of pagan worship for his subjects, and in these books, which he thought fit to conceal by burying them with him, he had laid open the bottom of these devilish mysteries, so that when they were brought to the senate, they, judging them unfit to be known, adjudged them to the fire; which is a clear ground of suspicion that he had there discovered so much of the causes of these rites, or of the way whereby he came to be instructed in them, that the public knowledge thereof consisted not with the interest of their heathenish religion. This conjecture Austin hath of the matter,[2] who also notes that Numa pretended familiar converse with the nymph Ægeria as a plausible cover to that devilish art of *Hydromantia*, by which he was instructed in ordering the ceremonies of idolatry which he established.

[2.] Secondly, Satan, with no less arrogancy, takes upon him to imitate God *in his acts of power for the countenancing of his worship in the world.* He had his miracles frequently, of which I have spoken elsewhere; so had he his oracles, as at Delphos and other places. Here it shall suffice to note that, as the sending the Lord Jesus into the world, furnished with such power of doing miracles for the confirmation of that office and authority which he had received from God for the redemption of man, was the highest instance that can be given of the mighty power, wisdom, and goodness of God; so Satan

---

[1] Varro, De Cultu Deorum.   [2] De Civit. Dei, lib. vii. cap. 34, 35.

set himself with greatest industry to imitate that. Christ was almost no sooner ascended to the Father, but we hear of Simon Magus, Acts viii. 9, who was cried up as an instance of 'the great power of God;' and after that at Rome he gave out that he was God, confirming the people in such a belief, by the strange things which he there did among them, that a statue was erected for his honour, with this inscription, 'To Simon, a great god.'[1] Long after this the devil raised up Apollonius Tyanæus, a man of an abstemious and commendable life. Him the devil did design to match Christ in his miracles, which were so many and so strange, that Philostratus doth not only compare him to Christ, but prefer him as the more honourable person. Christ himself foretold this stratagem of Satan, that he should raise up 'false Christs' with 'lying signs and wonders.' And to omit instances of former days, it is not beyond the memory of most of you, that the devil renewed this policy in James Nayler, who, in a blasphemous imitation of Christ's riding to Jerusalem, rode to Bristol with a great company before him, crying, 'Holy, holy,' and 'Hosanna to the son of David,' and strewing the way with branches of trees. The authority that was then, taking notice of this and other blasphemous outrages, sentenced him to exemplary punishment; but here also the devil renewed his mockery, for a certain citizen of London of good note, being overcome with delusion, printed a book of Nayler's sufferings, wherein the devil had opportunity to vent his malice more fully, for he compared all the parts of his punishment to the sufferings of Christ; his whipping, he said, was that it might be fulfilled which was spoken by Matthew, 'And Pilate delivered him to be scourged;' his stigmatizing, he said, was that it might be fulfilled which was spoken by the prophet, 'His visage was marred more than any man's;' the boring of his tongue with a hot iron, he said, was the fulfilling of that, and they 'crucified him;' and after other particulars of comparison, in all which he equalled him to Christ, he at last takes notice that the multitude of spectators held off their hats while his tongue was bored through, a thing common in a crowd to give opportunity of sight to those that are behind, and to this act he applies that of the evangelists, 'The vail of the temple was rent from the top to the bottom.'

[3.] Thirdly, *In acts of empire and sovereignty he imitates God*, that is, as God propounds himself as the only Lord God, and enjoins himself to be worshipped accordingly by promises of advantage in case of obedience, and threatenings of miseries and plagues in case of disobedience; so doth Satan set up himself in the world as god to be adored and worshipped, and him do all idolaters worship, as God testifies: Deut. xxxii. 17, 'They sacrificed unto devils, not to God:' Ps. cvi. 37, 'They sacrificed their sons and daughters unto devils:' 1 Cor. x. 20, 'The things which the Gentiles sacrifice, they sacrifice to devils, and not to God.' And though it be true that many of these blind worshippers did not formally worship the devil, but thought they had worshipped God, yet by such cunning did he engage them to take up with ways of worship of his prescribing, that it was in reality a service done to him. But, besides this, in those places of the world

[1] A long-exposed mistake, from a mis-reading of an inscription.—G.

where he hath greater power, he formally propounds himself to be worshipped, and doth accordingly often appear to them in a visible shape; so that many of these blind heathens acknowledge two gods, one good and another cruel and hurtful, which latter they say they must worship, lest he destroy or harm them. By this Satan contests with God for an empire in the world; and to promote it the more he sometimes deals by fair promises of riches, advancement, pleasure, and such other baits, to allure men to his professed service. Thus are witches drawn to a compact with him. Thus Sylvester the Second gave up himself to the devil for the popedom, and so did several others. When this is not enough to prevail, he adds menacings, and breathes forth cruel threatenings, by which means many heathens are kept in awe by him and worship him, *ne noceat*, for no other reason but to preserve themselves from hurt by him. In this temptation he propounds himself to Christ as the object of divine worship, and boasts of the kingdoms of the world as things of his disposal; by which he seeks to draw him to fall down before him.

This course Satan takes for these reasons:—

First, *As this proud and malicious ostentation of his power is some kind of satisfaction to his revengeful humour against God;* so, Secondly, *He doth hereby raise up himself and his wicked institutions of idolatry into credit and esteem with men.* Thirdly, *As this is a mockery to true religion, and a scorn cast upon the ways of God's service, to bring it into disgrace and discredit;* so, Fourthly, *By this means he hardens the hearts of men against God.* This was the consideration by which Pharaoh hardened his heart. When Moses turned his rod into a serpent, changed waters to blood, and did so many signs before him, his magicians did the like; upon which the king might thus reason with himself, that Moses had no other power but what his magicians had, though he might think him a more skilful magician; and therefore there was no reason to believe his message as being from God, seeing his miracles might be no other than the effect of his art to countenance a pretended command from heaven.

Applic. This insolency of Satan may inform us, First, *Of the great patience of God*, that sees these outrageous mockings, and yet doth not by a strong hand put a stop to them. Secondly, *Of the great power and pride of Satan*, that he both can—though not without permission from God—and dare attempt things of this nature. Thirdly, *The great power of delusion*, that can so blind men, that they not only are drawn to act a part in such designs, but believe confidently a divine impulse and heavenly warrant for their so doing. Fourthly, *The miserable slavery of such vassals of Satan* that are thus led by him, who are therefore sadly to be pitied and lamented, as being under such strong chains of captivity.

Obs. 3. Thirdly, *We cannot pass by the art which the devil here useth to set off the temptation, and to make it plausible.* He sets before him the world in all its glory. Here observe, *That Satan, in his temptations to worldly pleasures, doth usually paint the object with all its utmost beauty.*

When I have sometime observed a mountebank upon a stage, giving excessive commendations of a trivial medicine, asserting it good almost for every disease, and with a great many lies and boastings enforcing it upon the credulous multitude, it hath put me in mind of this spiritual mountebankery* of the devil. How doth he gull and delude the foolish by laying out the pleasures of sin! and no otherwise doth he keep them at a gazing admiration of worldly pomp, delights, and satisfaction, which he promiseth them from iniquity, than the serpent Scytale doth with passengers, whom she stays, by amazing them with her beautiful colours, till she have stung them.[1] The art of Satan in this matter lies in four things :—

[1.] First, *If there be anything that can be called a delight, or may any way conduce to a satisfaction in any sin, he will be sure to speak of it in its highest praises.* He not only stretcheth his rhetoric to the height in giving commendations to the most noted pleasures that men propound to themselves, but he seeks out the hidden things of delight, and raiseth in men an itch of desire after the improvement of delight, by the contrivances of wit or art. Thus he tells them of jollity, ravishing mirth, high satisfaction, and, if they will believe him, of unspeakable delight to be had by giving themselves up to the world and the course of it. Nay, he hides nothing that will bear any praise ; the least advantage, the smallest gratification that any sin can afford to human desire, he will be sure to speak of it.

[2.] Secondly, *He carries on this design by lying.* He promiseth more than ever sin can give, and he sends his proselytes out after sin under the highest expectations, and when they come to enjoy it, they often find the pleasure falls short of his boast. He whispers honours, preferments, and riches, in the ear of their hearts, and often pays them with poverty and disgraces, and gives them *pro thesauro carbones*, stones for bread, a serpent for a fish. Witches give frequent accounts of Satan's lying promises ; he tells them of feasts, of gold, of riches, but they find themselves deluded ; he sends them oft hungry away from those banquets, so that they have no more than when a man dreams he eats. He gives that which seems gold in appearance, but at last they find it to be slates or shells. We find in this temptation he is liberal and large in his offers to Christ, and what he requires he will have in present payment, but the reward for the service is future. It is his business to engage men in sin by his promise of advantage, but being once engaged, he takes not himself concerned in honour or ingenuity for performance. Hence doth the Scripture fitly call the pleasures of sin 'lying vanities,' a 'vain show,' a 'dream ;' thereby warning men from a forward belief of Satan's promises, in that they find by experience they shall be at last but lies and disappointments.

[3.] Thirdly, To make his bait more taking, *he conceals all the inconveniences that may attend these worldly delights.* He offers here the kingdoms of the world to Christ, as if all were made up of pleasure. Those cares, troubles, and vexations that attend greatness and rule, he mentions not ; their burden, hazard, and disquiet, he passeth over. Thus in common temptations he is careful to hide from men the miseries that follow these empty pleasures. So that often men do not consider the mischief, till 'a dart strike through their

[1] Solinus, cap. xxvii. and xl.—G.

liver,' Prov. vii. 23, and till a dear-bought experience doth inform them of their mistakes.

[4.] Fourthly, *His power and work upon the fancies of men, is none of the least of his ways whereby he advanceth the pleasures of sin.* That he hath such a power, hath been discoursed before, and that a fancy raised to a great expectation makes things appear otherwise than what they are, is evident from common experience. The value of most things depends rather upon fancy than the internal worth of them, and men are more engaged to a pursuit of things by the estimation which fancy hath begat in their minds, than by certain principles of knowledge. Children by fancy have a value of their toys, and are so powerfully swayed by it, that things of far greater price cannot stay their designs, nor divert their course. Satan knows that the best of men are sometimes childish, apt to be led about by their conceits, and apt in their conceits to apprehend things far otherwise than what they are in truth. Hence is it, as one observes,[1] that of thousands of men that return from Jerusalem, or from Mount Sion, or from the river Jordan, scarce can we find one which brings back the admiration which he had conceived before he had seen them. Fancy doth pre-occupate the mind with a high opinion of things; and these exorbitant imaginations pass to such an excess, that men think to find a satisfaction beyond the nature of these pleasures they aim at, which hath these two inconveniences: the one, that this affects and draws as powerfully as if they were all as real and high as they are conceited to be; the other, that sight and fruition takes away the estimation, and by a disappointment doth deaden and dull the affections to what may be really found there. Thus Satan by one deceit makes men believe that sin hath pleasure, which indeed it hath not, and by that belief leads them on powerfully to endeavour an embracement of them, and at last urgeth them with a delusion.

Applic. In opposition to this deceit of the devil, we must learn to esteem worldly delights as low as he would value them high. And to this purpose the Scripture speaks of them in undervaluing language, calling worldly pomp an opinion, a fantasy, a fashion or figure, an imagination rather than a reality; and further enjoins us not to admire these things in others, not to envy them that enjoyment of them, nor to fret at our want of them, much less to be transported with any angry passion about them, nor to concern ourselves in any earnest pursuit of them.[2]

Obs. 4. Fourthly, *Satan in this temptation did not bravely speak of these things, nor only make an offer in discourse, but he thought it most conducible to his design to present them to his sight.* He knew full well that the heart is more affected by sensible discoveries than by rational discourses.

Note here, *That Satan in temptations of worldly pleasure, endeavours to engage the affections by the senses.*

That it is Satan's great business to work upon the affections, I have shewed at large. Here he endeavoured to prepare the affections of Christ, that so the motion, when it came, might not die, as a spark

[1] D'Espagne's Popular Errors, sec. 1, cap. 4. [As before.—G.]
[2] Δόξα, φαντασία, σχῆμα, Ps. xxxvii. 1, and xlix. 16; Jer. xlv. 5.

falling upon wet tinder, but that the affections being stirred up might cherish the offer, and that the offer by a mutual warmth might more inflame the affections that were heated before.

To this end he works by the senses, and would have Christ's eye to raise his affections of love, desire, hope, and whatever else might wing his soul to activity. There is a great connexion betwixt the senses and the affections. The senses bring intelligence unavoidably, and are apt to stir up our powers to action. As the jackal is said to hunt the prey for the lion, so do the senses for the affections, and both for Satan.

It is also remarkable that Satan, endeavouring to make the eyes of Christ traitors to his affections, and that he thinking it necessary to give him a view of what he proffered him, should not give him time to take a full survey of these kingdoms, but should huddle it up in such a haste, that all, as Luke tells us, was done in 'a moment of time.' Was Satan in haste? or was he unwilling to part with what he so liberally proffered? Surely no, but this transient view was his subtlety, to entice him the more, and to inflame his heart with greater desires.

Obs. 5. Observe then, *That where Satan is most liberal in his proffers, he there manageth his overtures of advantage with a seeming shyness.* And this he doth, *First,* To heighten the worth of them in our estimation, as if they were jewels not to be gazed at, or curious pieces not fit to be exposed to common view. *Secondly,* By this art he makes men more eager in the pursuit. Our natural curiosity presseth us with great earnestness after things of difficult access, and we have also strange desires kindled in us from a prohibition, so that what we list not to choose if we have a liberty of enjoyment, when we are forbidden, we are troubled with impatient longings for it, and cannot be at quiet till we do enjoy it: *nitimur in vetitum.*

When Satan makes nice with men, offering the pleasures of the world, and yet hedging up the way with difficulties, they should make no other construction of it, but that Satan doth, so far as he is concerned, more strongly entice them. He plays at peep with them, that he may make them more earnest to follow him, and to bid high for the possession of these delights.

> Malo me Galatea petit, ...
> Et fugit ad salices, et se cupit ante videri.

CHAPTER XIX.

Satan's ends in tempting Christ to fall down and worship him.—Of blasphemous injections.—What blasphemy is.—The ways of Satan in that temptation, with the advantages he takes therein, and the reason of urging blasphemies upon men.—Consolations to such as are concerned in such temptations.—Advice to such as are so afflicted.

These observations, which the preparation to the temptation hath afforded us, being despatched, the temptation itself follows, which is this, 'fall down and worship me.'

This motion, from such a one as Satan, to such a one as Christ, who was holy and undefiled, God and man, seems to be an incredible piece of arrogancy, pride, and malice; for to propound himself as the object of divine worship, was certainly a desperate assault. It includes, [1.] the highest blasphemy; [2.] the grossest idolatry imaginable. Both these are frequently noted as the design of this temptation.[1] But [3.] the comprehension of this motion takes in the whole withdrawing of the mind from God and religion, or the care of the soul and eternal life; in which sense Satan doth frequently practise this temptation upon men by the motive of worldly pleasures. I shall consider the temptation first, as blasphemous, and so it will give us this observation:—

Obs. 6. *That the best of God's children may be troubled with most vile and hideous blasphemous injections.*

Blasphemy, in the largest sense, is anything spoken or done, by which the honour and fame of God may be wounded or prejudiced; but the formality of blasphemy lies in the purpose or intendment of reproaching God. Such was the blasphemy of the Israelitish woman's son, recorded in Lev. xxiv. 11, where blaspheming is explained by the addition of the word cursing, which in the original—קלל—comes from a word that signifies to 'set light by one.'[2] So that hence, and from the circumstances of the story, we may safely conjecture that this man having an Egyptian to his father, which probably might in scorn be objected to him by his contending adversary, he more readily might be drawn out to vilify the true God; but, be it what it will, it was certainly more than that blasphemy which the Rabbins fancy to be in the repetition of naming the word Jehovah, which in reverence they either leave out, as when they say, 'the arm of the Almighty,' or change it into some other, as Adonai, or the like; and accordingly we may observe, that reproaching God and blaspheming God are joined together, as Ps. xliv. 16; Isa. xxxvii. 23.

In blasphemy, as the matter, there must be thoughts, words, or actions that may aptly express a contempt or reproach of God; so also, as to the form of it, there must be an intendment of reproaching. Now though this be a sin which the heart of a servant of God would

---

[1] Perkins's 'Combate,' *in loc.* Musculus, *in loc.*

[2] Levis, nullius ponderis; leviter de aliquo sentire.—*Jackson, in loc.* Pool, Synopsis, Crit. *in loc.*

most abhor, yet Satan doth sometimes trouble the best with it. We have an instance in Job. His design was to bring him to curse God, for so he professeth in express terms; chap. i. 11, ii. 5, 'Lay thine hand upon him, and he will curse thee to thy face.' And in prosecution of this his boast, he breaks the matter plainly to him by his wife, chap. ii. 9, 'Curse God and die.' Whatever may be spoken of the word as signifying blessing, though some affirm the word ברד, in the proper idiom of that language, and not by an antiphrasis or euphemismus, as some think,[1] signifies as properly to 'curse' as to 'bless,' and is determinable to its signification either way by the circumstances of the place, or whatever men endeavour to excuse his wife, it is plain, not only by Job's answer, that it was evil counsel, but also by Satan's avowed design, that it was directly for cursing God. Besides this instance, if we consider the expression of 'fiery darts,' Eph. vi. 16, we shall find that this temptation is more common to all sorts of Christians than we would imagine. It is plain that these words allude to the poisoned arrows which Scythians and others used. These not only wounded but poisoned, and the venom inflamed with a fiery heat the part or member pierced. By this similitude, it must be granted that not common temptations are hereby understood, but such as were more than ordinarily hurtful, vexing, and dangerous. It may be persecutions are one of these darts, but all reckon temptations of spiritual terrors, and blasphemy, to be undoubtedly pointed at.[2]

The ways of Satan in this temptation are three:—

(1.) First, He endeavours to bring men to blaspheme, *by secret and subtle ways of ensnaring them;* and this is most-what practised in consequential and covert blasphemies, when, though men do not directly intend an open outrage against God, yet Satan brings them to that which might be so interpreted. This seems to have been the case of Job's sons, according to his jealousy of them; 'It may be my sons have sinned, and cursed God in their heart,' Job i. 5; not that they were open blasphemers, for they were surely better educated, neither doth Job express such a fear of them; but that in their mirth their hearts might have been so loosened from the fear of God, that they might be tempted to undue thoughts of God, slighting his threatenings or goodness. To this purpose Broughton translates, 'They have little blessed God in their hearts.'[3] The same thing we may observe in Job himself. When the devil could not prevail with him to 'charge God foolishly,' chap. i. 22, yet he pressed him so hard by his miseries, that he hoped at last to bring him to utter the anguish of his mind in impatient and reflecting expressions, and so far prevailed, that he bitterly 'Curseth the day wherein he was born,' chap. ii. 3, and wisheth that he had 'given up the ghost when he came out of the belly;' which though it came far short of what Satan had boasted of in his achievement against him, yet it had such an unwarrantable tendency that way, that when his friend Eliphaz took notice of his expressions, as savouring of too much distrust, he is forced to make apology for himself, and to excuse it by the desperateness of his con-

---

[1] Selden and Leigh, 'Critica Sacra.' [As before.—G.]
[2] Bayne, *in loc.* Arrowsmith, Tactica Sacra, lib. ii. cap 8.
[3] Caryl, *in loc.*

dition; chap. vi. 26, 'Do you imagine to reprove words and the speeches of one that is desperate?' In such cases, the devil provokes men beyond their intentions, to speak in their haste so inconsiderately, that they know not or mind not, the just consequence of their speeches. It was a degree of blasphemy in David to say, though in his haste, that 'all men were liars;' it was an unbelieving reflection on the promise given him by Samuel. In Mal. iii. 13, the people did not believe that they had 'spoken so much against God,' when yet their words had been 'stout against him.'

(2.) Secondly, Satan endeavours this *by violent injections of blasphemous thoughts that are directly such.* In this I shall note to you,

[1.] First, *That the vilest thoughts of God, of his ways and providences, of Scripture, and of Christ, are frequently suggested.* Things of greatest outrage against heaven, and contempt of the Almighty, as Bernard expresseth it, *Terribilia de fide, horribilia de divinitate;* as, there is no God, or that he is not just, or not faithful to his promises; or that Christ was but an impostor. He sticks at nothing in this kind, though never so contrary to the hope and persuasion of those whom he thus molests.

[2.] Secondly, *These are frequently reiterated upon them,* and their minds so troubled by them, that they cannot free themselves from such thoughts, but he follows on and clamours in their ears, as Gerson[1] observes, *Nega Deum, maledic Deo*—Deny God, curse God.

[3.] Thirdly, And this with so great *a force and impetuosity, that they are compelled to form these thoughts in their minds, and to speak contrary to what they would,* as if their thoughts and tongues were not under their own government, the devil not satisfying himself to bear in these thoughts upon them, but he endeavours, as it were, to make them say after him, and to cast his suggestions into their own mould, that so they might seem properly to be their own; and this they are forced to whether they will or no, even then when their minds are filled with horror, their heart with grief, and their body with trembling. I have discoursed with some who have bitterly complained that their tongues and their thoughts seemed not to be their own, but that Satan ruled them at his pleasure; and that when in opposition to the temptation they would have formed their tongues to speak blessing of God, they have spoken cursing instead of blessing; and that when a blasphemous thought had been cast into their mind, they could not be at rest till they had thought it again.

[4.] Fourthly, These troublesome temptations are oft of *long continuance.* Joannes Climacus tells us[2] of a monk that was troubled with blasphemous thoughts for twenty years together, and could not quit himself of them, though he had macerated his body with watchings and fastings. Some have them going away and returning again by fits, according as the prevalency and ferment of their melancholy gives Satan the advantage of dealing thus with them. For if we inquire why it is thus, especially with the children of God, we must partly resolve it into the 'unsearchable wisdom of God,' who for holy ends of teaching and disciplining his servants, permits Satan thus to molest them; and partly into those particular advantages which Satan

[1] Tom. iv. col. 973.   [2] Scala Paradisi, gradu 23.

hath against them according to the variety of their conditions, which usually are these:—

First, He takes advantage of such *bodily distempers as do deprive men of the use of their reason*, as fevers, frenzies, madness. In these he oft forms the tongues of men to horrid blasphemous speeches.

Secondly, *A pressure of outward afflictions* gives him his desired opportunity; and this he knows to be generally so successful, that he promised himself by this means a victory over Job. Ordinarily, straits and miseries do produce blaspheming. Isa. viii. 21, the prophet notes that when the people should be ' hardly bestead and hungry,' they should ' fret themselves, and curse their king and their God, and look upward,' as avouching what they had done.

Thirdly, Worldly plenty, fulness, and pleasure lay often foundations of this temptation. When their cups are full, and their hearts high, Satan can easily make them ' set their mouth against heaven.' A proud heart will readily say, ' Our tongue is our own, or, Who is the Lord?' [Ps. xii. 4.] This was the engine which the devil managed, if it were as Job suspected, against the sons and daughters of Job, to make them curse God in their hearts; and by this did he seek to prevail upon Christ in this blasphemous temptation.

Fourthly, A melancholy distemper doth usually invite Satan to give blasphemous suggestions. The disturbed and pliable fancies of such, are the advantages which he improves against them.

Fifthly, Inward terrors and distresses of conscience are also an occasion to Satan to move them, as by a desperate humour, to utter hard things of God and against themselves.

But there is yet a third way by which Satan tempts men to blaspheming, *by sudden glances of blasphemous imaginations*, which like lightnings do astonish the heart and then suddenly vanish. These are very common, and the best of men observe them frequently. Satan seems as it were rather to frolic and sport himself in these suggestions, than to intend a serious temptation. Their danger is not so much, yet are they not to be despised, lest these often visits, carelessly entertained, and not dismissed with just abhorrency, do secretly envenom the soul, and prepare it for stronger assaults.

I shall next inquire into the reasons of this trouble which Satan gives the children of God.

[1.] First, *These temptations are very affrighting; though they prevail not, yet they are full of perplexing annoyance.* Corrupt nature startles at them, and receives them not without dread and horror. It is sadly troublesome to hear others blaspheme God. ' The reproaches of those that reproached thee,' saith David, ' fell upon me.' It was as ' a sword in his bones' to hear the blasphemous scoffs of the wicked, when they said to him, ' Where is thy God?' And if it were confusion and shame to him to hear ' the enemy reproach and blaspheme,' as he professeth it was, Ps. xliv. 15, 16, how sadly afflicting would it be for any child of God to observe such things in his own imaginations! If there were no more in it than this, it is enough to put Satan upon that design, because it is a troublesome kind of martyrdom.[1]

[1] Spiritus blasphemiæ, scaturigo est cogitationum adeo horribilium adeoque molestarum, ut ejus tentatio plerumque quasi martyrium est.—*Guil. Paris*, lib. de tenta. et resist.

[2.] Secondly, *This is also a spiteful revenge against God.* All he can do is to blaspheme and rage, and it is a kind of delight to put this force upon those that carry his own image. He would do all he can to make his own children to vilify and reproach their heavenly Father, and to render cursing for blessing.

[3.] Thirdly, This temptation, *though it have not the consent or compliance of God's children, yet it opens a way to many other sins,* as murmuring, distrust, despair, weariness of God's ways and services. When we find Satan thus to run upon us, it is apt to breed 'strange thoughts of God,' that thus permits Satan to take us by the throat, or to make us judge of ourselves as rejected of God, and given up to Satan's power; and if it do this, his labour is not in vain; we are, as one observes,[1] more to fear his subtlety in bringing us by this into other snares, than the violence of the adversary in this suggestion.

[4.] Fourthly, This is a stratagem *for laying the foundation of direful accusations.* The devil in this doth as the Russians are[2] reported to do. They, when they have a spite against any of their neighbours, hide secretly some of their goods in their houses, and then accuse them of theft. When blasphemous thoughts are injected, and men refuse to consent, then Satan raiseth an accusation against them, as Joseph's mistress did, as if they were guilty of all that blasphemy that he tempted them unto; and it is a difficult task to persuade them that these things should be in their minds, and that they should not be the proper issues of their own heart. And very often doth he from hence accuse them of sinning against the Holy Ghost, because of the hideous blasphemies which he had first suggested to them.

Applic. First, This will give us considerations of *consolation,* and that—(1.) *In regard of others.* We observe often our sick friends speak what we would not willingly hear, and it cannot choose but be sadly afflictive to hear their curses and blasphemous speeches; but when we consider the advantage that Satan takes of their distemper, if their lives heretofore have been pious and religious, we comfort ourselves in this, that it is more his malice than their own inclinations; neither should we suffer our hope or charity to be distressed on their behalf. (2.) It is the like ground of consolation for ourselves or others that are violently afflicted with blasphemous thoughts. For,

[1.] First, *If we call to mind that our Lord and Master suffered such things, we that are of his household need not think we receive a strange or unusual measure in that we are molested as he was.*

[2.] Secondly, If we consider that Christ was tempted *without sin on his part,* then may we fetch this conclusion from it, *that it is possible that such thoughts should be cast upon us, and yet that we may not be chargeable with them as our iniquities.*

Thirdly, We may hence see that such temptations *are more frightful than hurtful.* These, as one observes,[3] seldom take, they carry with them so much horror, to those that believe and love the true God, that it keeps them from a participation with Satan in the

---

[1] Magis a dolo metuendum est quam a violentia adversarii, caveat æger ab impatientia, infidelitate, murmuratione aliisque peccatis quæ clam insinuantur.—*Dickson, Therapeut. Sacra,* lib. ii. cap. 29.   [2] Heylin, 'Cosmogr.'

[3] Capel 'Tempt.,' part 2, cap. 3.

sin itself, nay, it fills them with fear and striving against it; they rather, as bugbears, scare and disquiet them, than produce the real effects of compliance with them.

Applic. Secondly, The consideration of this kind of temptation may *fill the hearts and mouths of those of us as have not hitherto been troubled with it, with praise for so merciful a preservation.* If we have not been under this kind of exercise, it is not from any good will that Satan hath to us, but because our God withholds a commission from him. A poor weak Christian wonders that Satan hath not made him a mark for this arrow, that he hath not broken him with this tempest. To answer that wonder, he may know that the same tenderness in God, that will not put 'new wine into old crazy bottles,' nor a 'new stiff piece of cloth into an old tender garment,' nor that will oppress the weak and infirm with strong exercise or burdens; that same tenderness of a compassionate Father doth keep off such trials, because he will not suffer them 'to be tempted above what they are able.'

Applic. Thirdly, This temptation calls for *advice to those that are under it,* to whom I shall direct a few things.

[1.] First, When any are troubled with blasphemous thoughts, let it be considered *in what state and temper their body is.* If it be distempered with melancholy, as is most usual, then the prescription of an able physician is necessary in the first place, without which he that would spiritually advise or counsel shall but beat the air, and his words be so far from the fastness of nails that they shall be as wind. I have known many under great complaints and fears by reason hereof, that have been cured by physic alone; for when, in this case, the fuel is withdrawn, the fire goes out. Correct the melancholy temper that gives the devil this advantage, and the trouble will cease.

[2.] Secondly, It is of great consequence to understand *the nature of these temptations.* If the tempted could see these to be their sufferings rather than their sins, they would with greater ease bear it as an affliction. And to those that complain, abhor, resist, and pray against them, they are not sins, no more than when a harlot layeth her child at an honest woman's door, that child is to be reckoned as the fruit of her wickedness. A giant may dash the son against his father, but so far will the father be from imputing it as rebellious insolence in his child, that he will pity him the more, as suffering by a double injury; for it is not only against his natural affection and reverence to his parent, but it is a bodily hurt beside. Thus will God much more pity his children under these sufferings.

[3.] Thirdly, We must not suffer such thoughts *to lodge in us,* but before they settle, if possible, we must repel them; as Abraham drove away the fowls that came down upon his sacrifice. I know the tempted will say this advice is not practicable; they find these thoughts swarm about them as bees, and when one is driven back another straight comes in its place. But to them I answer, that blasphemous thoughts are repelled two ways. (1.) By stout and resolute resistance. This, though it do not extinguish them, nor free us of the trouble, yet it keeps them from settling upon us, and us from the guilt of them. (2.) By diversion, which the work of a lawful employment, or good society, and other discourses may do. This may give some ease from the molestation, and the other preserves us innocent.

[4.] Fourthly, In temptations to blasphemy *confident refusals do better than disputings*.[1] Here we are to resist with courage and a holy contempt of Satan. If we be too timorous and fearful, he insults the more upon us; as dogs when they are observed follow the passenger with greater eagerness and noise. Abhorrences and positive discharges, like that of Christ in the same case, 'Get thee hence, Satan,' do more for us than to debate the matter with him.

CHAPTER XX.

The nature of idolatry.—Satan's design to corrupt the worship of God.—The evidences thereof, with the reasons of such endeavours. —His general design of withdrawing the hearts of men from God to his service.—The proof that this is his design.—Upon whom he prevails.—That professions and confidences are no evidences to the contrary.—His deceit of propounding sin as a small matter.—The evidences of that method, and the reason thereof.

Thus have I considered the temptation as blasphemous. I proceed next to consider it as idolatrous. The words ἐὰν πεσὼν προσκυνήσῃς, if thou wilt fall down and worship, do give us the true notion of idolatry. The word which we call *worship* comes from κύω, which signifies to kiss, or from κυὼν, which signifies a dog, both being to the same purpose, and signifying any action of reverence by which we signify the respect of our minds. To kiss the hand, or to fawn as a dog, are gestures which express the honour we would give, and being applied to divine worship before, or with respect unto, an undue object, is idolatry; and as such doth Christ reject it in his answer, 'Thou shalt worship the Lord thy God, and him only shalt thou serve.' We worship God, when in ways and actions commanded or prescribed, we testify our belief and resentment of his incommunicable attributes. It is idolatry when either we use the same actions of prescribed worship to that which is not God, or when we testify our respects to the true God in an undue way of our own devising. Here might I take occasion to shew the vanity of the popish subterfuges; their distinction of *latria* and *dulia* is, as Dr [Henry] More observes, hereby overthrown.[2] Satan doth not here set himself up as the omnipotent God, for he acknowledgeth one superior to himself, in that he confesseth that the power he had of the kingdoms of the world was given to him, Luke iv. 6, and therefore not the *latria* but the *dulia* is required of him; and yet this, Christ denies him as being idolatry, in that no religious worship—for that must needs be the sense of his answer—is due to any but God alone. Their other distinction of worshipping an idol, saint, angel, cross, &c., and before

[1] Fæda tentatio magis vincitur fugiendo quam aggrediendo.—*Gerson*, tom. ix. col. 976.
[2] Mystery of Iniquity, lib. i. cap. 9.

such a creature, is also hereby crushed, as is commonly observed :[1] for what the evangelist Matthew expresseth by προσκυνήσῃς μοι, Luke calls ἐνώπιόν μου, before me; so that the Scripture makes no difference betwixt these two, shewing it to be idolatry to use religious worship to that which is not God, or before it. But these things I shall not prosecute; keeping therefore to my design, I shall observe,

Obs. 7. *That it is one of Satan's great designs to corrupt the worship of God.* That this is so will appear,

(1.) First, *If we consider what varieties of worship hath been in the world.* God gave a fixed and stable law, and yet this so little prevailed, that men were upon new inventions presently. I shall not need to reckon up the almost numberless varieties of this kind among the heathen. The instance is plain enough in those that professed the name of the true God; they were still changing for new fashions in religion, borrowing patterns from their neighbours, so that if there were but a new altar at Damascus, or a new idol in any strange city, they must presently have the like, till, as the prophet tells them, 'according to their cities so were their gods,' [Jer. ii. 28.] He that will call to mind that the husbandman did first 'sow good seed in his field,' and that there is such variety of tares and false worship, notwithstanding the plain and positive command of God, fixing and determining his worship, must needs conclude that an enemy, Satan, hath done it.

(2.) Secondly, *If we call to mind how in all ages there hath been a constancy in this inconstant variety.* We hear of it among the heathens. We read enough of it among the Jews, and when they were out of the humour of more shameful idolatries, they yet corrupted the worship of God by their traditions; and of these they were so fond, that they caused the law of God itself to give place to them, and made it void by them. The times of the gospel were not free. Though Christ came to seek such worshippers as should 'worship him in spirit and in truth,' yet before the apostles' deaths, while yet they were persuading to the contrary, there arose up some that corrupted the worship, by leading the people back again to the Jewish ceremonies, and others laboured to bring in 'worshipping of angels,' and at last to 'eat things offered to idols,' with greater defilements. Since the apostles' days the same design hath been carried on in the churches. Rome hath patched together a great deal of Jewish and heathenish ceremonies; and when the man of sin shall be revealed, yet a higher flood of such abominations is to be expected. Who hath wrought all this, but Satan? This is still the same design, and though the work be not in all parts like itself, yet the whole of it evidenceth the working of the same spirit in all.

(3.) Thirdly, *Let us observe how early this began.* We cannot say but that in the days of Adam, who doubtless had received particular commands from God, in which he would not fail to instruct his children, they were seeking to themselves 'many inventions,' Gen. iv. 26. At the birth of Enos, as some conjecture, there were such defilements brought into use in worship, that Seth had respect to it when he called his son Enos, *Sorrowful,* as lamenting that profanation which

[1] Musculus, *in loc.*, and Perkins, *in loc.*

was then begun in 'calling upon the name of the Lord,' for so do many interpret that passage, which in our English we read thus, 'Then began men to call upon the name of the Lord.' The word in the original is הוחל, which signifieth both to *profane* and to *begin*, and may be as properly translated, then 'profaned they in calling upon the name of the Lord.' And there are several reasons that move learned men[1] to fix upon this translation. As (1.) That it is not probable that men began then to call upon God, or publicly to do so, as some would interpret, and not before, as the present English would imply. (2.) That age was noted as corrupt, and therefore it is noted as a rarity that Enoch walked with God. (3.) The Rabbins generally translate חלל to *profane;* but if we should grant the present English, 'Then began men to call upon the name of the Lord,' it would imply that the worship practised by Adam and Abel had been corrupted, and now it was restored again and reformed; which will make the corruption of worship to be yet more early. And after that we read of corruption crept into the family of Seth, as well as now in the family of Cain, Gen. vi. 2; so that the worship of God stood not long in its honour, though Adam and Seth were alive to instruct them; which shews that it was a rebellious departure from the way, fomented and brought on by the malignant spirit Satan.

(4.) Fourthly, But to make all sure, *the Scripture lays all these kinds of corruption of worship at Satan's door.* The defilements of worship taught in Thyatira, by Jezebel, are called 'the depth of Satan,' Rev. ii. 24; the corruptions introduced by antichrist, are from 'the workings of Satan,' 2 Thes. ii. 9. What was promoted by false apostles to that purpose, they had it from their great teacher Satan, who 'transforms himself for such ends into an angel of light,' 2 Cor. xi. 13, 14; so that nothing can be more plain than that this is an old and constant design of Satan.

The particular ways by which Satan effects this design I shall not now touch, but shall in lieu of that give you the reasons of his endeavours this way.

[1.] First, *He knows that this is a sin of a high provocation.* Worship is the proper tribute that is due to God, and it is peculiarly his prerogative to prescribe the way and manner of it. Neither of these honours will he give to any other, but will express his jealousy when any invasion is made upon these his sole prerogatives. Now his worship cannot be corrupted, but one of these at least will in some degree or other be touched. If we set up another object of worship, we deny him to be God; if we worship him in a way of our own invention, we deny his wisdom, and set up ourselves above him, as if we could order his worship better than he hath done in his word.

[2.] Secondly, *If the worship be corrupted, all the exercise of the affections of the heart, and all the service itself is lost, and become unacceptable.* He knows that such worshippers shall meet with this answer, 'Who hath required this at your hands?' [Isa. i. 12.]

[3.] Thirdly, *Corruption in worship*, Satan by long experience knows to have been the ground of those hatreds, quarrels, persecutions, and troubles under which the church hath groaned in all ages, every

---

[1] Drusius, Lightfoot, Tremellius, &c.

difference imposing their way and persuasion upon all dissenters, to the disturbance of peace, breach and decay of love, hindrance of the growth of piety, to the biting and devouring of one another.

[4.] Fourthly, Besides God is provoked by this to *leave his sanctuary*, to remove his glory and his candlestick, to make his vineyard a desolation, and his churches as Shiloh.

[5.] Fifthly, Satan is the more industrious in this, because *his ways are capable of many advantages to further his design, and many specious pretences to cover it.* In Col. ii. 8, he made use of philosophy to corrupt religion, and by unsound principles of some heathens famous for that learning, introduced ' worshipping of angels.' What that could not effect he laboured to perform by ' the traditions of men,' and where that came short, ' the rudiments of the world'—the Mosaical ceremonies were so called here, and in the Epistle to the Hebrews—were his engine by which he battered the plain worship of the New Testament. And as to pretences, the apostle doth there and elsewhere note that decency and order, humility, wisdom, and self-denial, are things very taking, and yet usually pretended for such bold innovations as may corrupt the pure streams of the sanctuary.

Applic. Hence may I leave with you a few memorials.

[1.] First, *This may make us jealous of any alterations in the way of God's worship.* We have reason under the most plausible pretexts to suspect the hand of Satan, because it is one of his main businesses to corrupt the worship.

[2.] Secondly, *This may justify those that out of a conscientious fear of complying with Satan's design, dare not admit of a pin in the tabernacle beside what God hath prescribed, nor leave behind a shoe-latchet of what he hath enjoined.*

[3.] Thirdly, *This will tell us that that worship is best and safest that hath least of mixture of human invention.* We cannot offend in keeping close to the rule, though the worship thereby become more plain, and not so gorgeous in outward appearance. We may soon overdo it by the least addition, and cannot be so certain of God's acceptation, as we are of pleasing the senses of men, by such introducements.

This motion of Satan, ' Fall down and worship me,' is now in the last place to be considered as a particular instance of Satan's general design *of drawing the hearts of men from God his service and ways, to the pleasures of sin;* as if he should say to him, follow my advice, give up thyself to my service, and thou shalt be gratified with all the delights that the world can give thee. To this doth the bait here offered most fitly agree. Hence observe,

Obs. 8. *That it is Satan's general design to withdraw the hearts of men from God, that they may be enslaved to him in the service of sin.*

That the devil doth level all his endeavours to this, cannot be doubted; for,

(1.) First, *He hath a kingdom in this world,* from which he is denominated ' the prince of this world.' And this is not only a rule of exterior force, such as conquerors have over their captivated slaves, who are compelled to subject their bodies, while yet their minds are full of hatred against him who hath thus forced them to subjection;

but it is a rule over the hearts and affections of men, working in 'the children of disobedience' a love and liking of these ways, and begetting in them the image of Satan; so that what work he imposeth they are pleased withal, and 'love to have it so.' Therefore he is not only called their prince, but their god and their father: 'Ye are of your father the devil,' in that with a kind of inward devotion they will and endeavour to perform the lusts which he propounds to them.

(2.) Secondly, *This kingdom is contrary to God's spiritual kingdom*, that being of darkness, this of light; and it is managed by Satan with an envious competition and co-rivalship to that of God; so that as God invites men to the happiness of his kingdom, and sends his Spirit in his word and ordinances to persuade them, Satan doth the like. He sends out his spirit, which the apostle calls 'the spirit of the world,' 1 Cor. ii. 12, and employs all his agents to engage men for him. He requires the heart as God doth, he promiseth his rewards of pleasure, honour, riches, if they will fall down and worship him. Now it is so natural to prosecute an interest thus espoused in a way of opposition, especially to any other that set up for themselves in a contradictory competitorship, that the very natural laws of Satan's kingdom will engage him to stand up for it, and to enlarge it all he can.

Those upon whom he prevails are of two sorts—

(1.) First, *Some are visibly in his service.* These answer the character which was given of Ahab, 1 Kings xxi. 20, 'who sold himself to work wickedness in the sight of the Lord.' The first expression shews that such are wholly in Satan's power and disposal—as things sold are in the possession and power of the buyer—they are at Satan's will. If he say to them, 'Go, they go,' and if he say, 'Come, they come.' Their bodies and spirits are Satan's, they are not their own; and they are his for the ends of sin, for that employment only, so that they are 'wholly corrupt and abominable.' The latter expression, that he did so 'in the sight of the Lord,' manifests their shameless impudency in sin, that they 'declare their sin as Sodom, and hide it not,' that they do not blush, but openly wear the devil's livery and avouch his service. As the works of the flesh are manifest, so these in their practice of such works are manifestly Satan's subjects. These kind of men are frequently in the Old Testament styled 'sons of Belial,'[1] a name very significant, shewing either their devoting of themselves to the devil's service, in that they reject the yoke of God's law, in that they 'break his bonds, and cast his cords from them,' or their pride that they will have none above them, not considering that there is a God, or that the Most High rules, or their averseness to what is good, being 'wholly unprofitable, and to every good work reprobate.' [Titus i. 16.]

(2.) Secondly, *Some are secretly his servants.* They come to the devil, as Nicodemus did to Christ, by night. They will not openly profess him, but yet their hearts are wholly his. Such are called by the name of hypocrites. The pharisees and scribes seemed to declare for God, called themselves Abraham's seed, fasted, gave alms, made

---

[1] בְּלִיַּעַל vel a בְּלִי *non* et עֹל *jugem*, absque jugo; vel a בְּלִי *non* et עַל *supra*, vel a בְּלִי *non*, et יָעַל *profuit*, homo inutilis.

long prayers, and yet were a 'generation of vipers,' and 'of their father the devil.' The secrecy of this underhand engagement to hell is such, that many who are in a league with the devil, and at an agreement with death, do neither know nor believe it concerning themselves. For,

[1.] First, *This private covenant may be where there are the greatest seeming defilements of Satan and high professions of service to God.* The pharisees, as have been said, were the devil's servants, under all the fair show they made of religion and zeal for the law, and yet when Christ plainly told them that they were not Abraham's seed but the devil's seed, they with high indignation and scorn throw back the accusation to Christ, 'Thou art a Samaritan, and hast a devil; we are Abraham's children,' [John viii. 48,] so little believed they the truth when it was told them.

[2.] Secondly, *This may consist with some designment and intention to give God glory.* The Jews, though they submitted not to the righteousness of God, yet, by the testimony of Paul, they had a zeal to God. The very heathens that sacrifice to devils had not formal intentions so to do, as appears by their inscription on the altar at Athens, Acts xvii. 23, 'To the unknown God.' The true God, though unknown, they propounded as the object of their worship; yet falling into those ways of devotion which the devil had prescribed, these intentions could not hinder but that they became his servants.

[3.] Thirdly, *Men may be servants to Satan under great assurances and confidences of their interest in God.* Many go to hell that have lived with *Lord, Lord* in their mouths. Those mentioned in Isa. xlviii. 2, that had no interest in truth and righteousness when they solemnly sware by the name of the Lord, 'yet they called themselves of the holy city, and stayed themselves upon the God of Israel,' [Isa. xlviii. 2.]

Obj. If it seem strange to any that these professions, intentions, and confidences are not enough to secure men from this charge, but that they may be secretly slaves to hell, I answer,

Ans. 1. First, *That those do not necessarily conclude that the heart of such men is right with God.* Formality, natural conscience, and the power of education may do much of this; for though we grant that such are not conscious to themselves of any real design of serving Satan, yet they may either so far miss it in the way of their service, offering that as well-pleasing to God, which indeed he hates, and that through wilful and affected ignorance, as those of whom Christ speaks, John xvi. 2, that should think the killing of God's children a piece of acceptable service; or they may be so mistaken as to the sincerity of their hearts that they may think they have a design to please God in doing of what he requires in order thereunto, when indeed it may not be singly for God but for themselves that they work, in a self-gratification of their natural zeal for their way; or their esteem, credit, and advantage may privately influence them, rather than a spirit of life and power.

Ans. 2. Secondly, *The work which they do, and the ends they serve, will be evidence against professions and intentions.* It is a sure rule, that the work shews to whom men are related as servants, and it is laid down as a certain standard to measure the hearts of men by, when pretences and persuasions seem to carry all before them: Rom. vi. 16, ' His servants ye are to whom ye obey;' 1 John iii. 8, 10, ' He that committeth sin is of the devil: in this the children of God are manifest, and the children of the devil'—that is, when it becomes a question to whom a man belongs, whose child and servant he is, it must be determined by the works he doth. If he engage in the ways of sin, he is of the devil, let him profess what he will to the contrary. This same balance Christ useth to try the truth of the Jews' pretences to God: John viii. 34, ' Whosoever committeth sin, is the servant of sin;' they boasted high, but he shews them that seeing their designs and works were hatred, envy, murder, &c., which are apparently from Satan, it was evident they had learned these of him; and he concludes by this proof, ver. 44, ' that they were of their father the devil.' Thus may we say of those that pretend they honour God, they deify the devil, they intend well, if yet they give themselves up to the pleasing of the flesh, if worldly-minded, if they live in pride, strife, envy, maliciousness, &c.,—which are works of the devil,—it is not all their pretences that will entitle them to God, but they are, for all this, the devil's servants, as doing his works.

Applic. This may put men upon inquiries, *Who are ye for? whose servants are ye?* There are but two that can lay claim to you, and these two divide the whole world betwixt them. There is no state of neutrality: you are either God's servants or the devil's. Ye cannot serve them both; ' now if the Lord be God, serve him.' Satan's service is base, dishonourable, slavish; the service of God, freedom, honour, life, and peace; there is indeed no comparison betwixt them. Happy, then, is that man that can say the Lord is his lot and portion; that can come into God's presence, and there in his integrity avouch the Lord for his God—that can stand upon it. ' My soul hath said unto the Lord, Thou art my God, and I have none besides thee; other lords have had dominion over us, but we will make mention of thy name only,' [Isa. xxvi. 13.]

This temptation, though it were in itself horrid, and as a brood of vipers knotted together, which at once could send out several stings, and make many wounds,—as hath been noted,—yet in the way of propounding, Satan seems to insinuate the largeness of his proffer, and the smallness and inconsiderableness of the service required, as if he should say, ' See how free I am in my kindness; I will not stick to give thee the kingdoms of the world, and the glory of them, and all this for so small a matter as bowing before me, or doing me a little reverence.' This gives us to observe,

Obs. 9. *That when Satan doth design no less than to enslave men to his service, yet he will propound sin as a small thing, or but one act of sin, as a thing not valuable, to engage them to him.* Not but that he desires to run men to excess in wickedness, and delights to see them with both hands earnestly work iniquity with greediness; yet where he sees the consciences of men squeamish, and that they cannot bear temptations to open and common profaneness without danger of revolt from him, there he seems modest, and requires but some small thing, at least at first, till the ways of sin become more familiar to them, and then when they can better bear it, he doubles the tale of bricks, and with greater confidence can urge them to things of greater shame and enormity. That this is his way appears,

[1.] First, *From the common argument which he useth at first to those whom he would draw off from a more careful conversation*, which is this: Do such a thing, it is but for once, and but little; others do the like, and demur not, or the best do as great matters as this comes to. It is but a small thing, considering the strait, or the advantage that may accrue. This is his usual note to candidate iniquity, as experience of all doth testify.

[2.] Secondly, That this is so is also evident from a consideration of *the several ways and courses of sinners*. Some are tempted and overcome by one kind of sin, and not at all urged to others. Some go to hell in a way of covetousness; others are pretty unblameable in most of their carriages, but are overcome by a proud humour; others are given to drink, and yet will not steal nor deal falsely; others take a more cleanly way to hell, rely upon their own righteousness, or are engaged in error, and their life otherwise smooth and fair. The Jews in Christ's time were only engaged against Christ, and for their traditions, but not molested with temptations to open idolatry as formerly. Those who are ignorant are not troubled with temptations to despair, or inward terrors. The reasons of his dealing thus are these:—

[1.] First, *He sees that one sin heartily prosecuted is enough to signify homage to him, and to give him possession.* As we take possession of land by a turf or a twig, so by one sin admitted with full purpose of mind, Satan is let into the heart. As a penny will be sufficient earnest for a bargain of a thousand pounds, so may one sin be a pledge or earnest for the whole soul in a league with hell.

[2.] Secondly, *He knows that one sin persisted in may be enough to destroy the soul;* as one wound may kill, one leak may sink a ship.

[3.] Thirdly, *He knows that one sin breaks the covenant of God*, and turns the heart from him, if men give up themselves to it.

[4.] Fourthly, *One sin wilfully pursued makes a man guilty of the breach of the whole law.* It destroys love and respect to God, undervalues his authority, contemns his threatenings and promises.

[5.] Fifthly, *One sin is enough to make way for more.* Where Satan would have more, yet at first he is pleased with it as a hopeful beginning. It makes room enough for the serpent's head, and then he will afterwards easily wind in his whole body.

Applic. This may warn us not to be emboldened to any sin by the plea *of diminution*; not to venture because it may seem little, or be but for once. A true Christian should be a perfect universalist; he should be universally against all sin, and universally for all duty.

CHAPTER XXI.

Of worldly pleasure.—Proofs that this is Satan's great engine.—What there is in worldly delights that make them so.—Counsels and cautions against that snare.

I come now to the argument which Satan used for all this, 'All these things will I give thee.' He casts a golden apple before him, and seeks to entangle him by worldly greatness and delight. I shall not examine how true or false Satan spake when he called all these things his, and that he could give them to whom he would. It is enough for our purpose to take notice of his pretence, so far as might make his offer probable; and then observe,

Obs. 10. *That the great engine which Satan useth to draw away the heart from God to his service is worldly pleasures and delights.*

I shall first shew that this is Satan's great engine, and then explain what is in it that fits it so much for his purpose. The first of these is evidenced by these particulars:—

1. First, The Scripture doth particularly note to us *a deceit or guile to be in worldly pleasures.* Christ, in Mat. xiii. 22, speaks of 'the deceitfulness of riches;' and that deceit is expressed by such a word as signifies 'a drawing out of the way,' a misleading;[1] so that he means not the uncertainty of these delights, in which sense it is said 'that riches take themselves wings and fly away,' [Prov. xxiii. 5,] which often disappoint and deceive the expectations of those that do most hug them. Nor can this be understood of riches in an active sense, as we attribute deceit to men, who as rational agents can contrive and devise snares; but it only means that these are so *objective* as things that are abused by Satan to delude and betray the sons of men: and these are so frequently made use of by him for such purposes, and with such advantages of power and provocation, that Christ elsewhere, Mat. xix. 23, speaks of it as a thing almost impossible, to have riches and not to be ensnared by them: 'A rich man shall hardly enter into the kingdom of heaven,' [Mat. xix. 23,] which Mark and Luke express by an affectionate amazement, ' Oh, how hardly can a rich man be saved!' [Mark x. 23-25, and Luke xviii. 24, 25.]

2. Secondly, *These are Satan's great net which encloseth multitudes;* a general bait, by which most are hooked into the service of sin. Most temptations come from this ocean as springs from the sea. 'The lust of the flesh, the lust of the eyes, the pride of life,' have their original from the world, 1 John ii. 16. Christ speaks of this ' mammon of unrighteousness' as the only thing that stands up in competition for the hearts of men against God, Mat. vi. 24; and the apostle, 2 Tim. iii. 4, reckoning up the various ways of particular lusts, as covetousness, boasting, pride, blaspheming, &c., concludes them all under this, that they ' are lovers of pleasures more than lovers of God;' shewing us thereby, that though the lusts of men might run out diverse ways, and be exercised upon diverse particular objects, yet they all borrow their original from worldly pleasures, and their design

---

[1] ἀπάτη, ab ἀ priv. et πάτος, via.

is nothing but that in the general. Hence it is that some make the world the great traitor to God; for though they reckon up three great enemies to God and man, 'the world, the flesh, and the devil,' yet 'these three agree in one;' the pleasing of the flesh is the great end and desire of natural men; the world is the storehouse, from which men draw out several pleasures, according to the several ways they take in gratifying their lusts and humours, and the devil is only officious to help all this forward, by enticing and persuading them to 'make these provisions for the flesh.' And who can think other, but that this must be Satan's great engine, when, as hath been said, *first*, the world, and the pleasures of it, is the sum of all iniquity, containing in it virtually or actually the transgression of the whole law. The root it is of all evil, 1 Tim. vi. 10; all profaneness against God, all neglect of duty, all outrage, wrong, or injustice to man, may, and usually doth, spring from hence, insomuch that some have particularly traced it through every command of the decalogue, and found it guilty, either as principal or accessary, of every iniquity. *Second*, Our thoughts may be the more confirmed in this when we see all men entangled by it; for albeit that some temptations seem directly to carry men from a love or care of the world, as despair, terrors of mind, voluntary humility, neglecting of the body, and others of the same kind; yet if the matter be considered, the truth in hand cannot be prejudiced by such an objection. For, [1.] Those who seem in distress of conscience most to loathe the world were yet first entangled by it, and the consideration of that guilt, whether at present justly or unjustly charged upon them, is the usual occasion of these troubles. And, [2.] Those who seem to undervalue money, riches, plenty, &c., are, it may be, no less slaves to other worldly lusts; for pleasures of the world comprehend whatsoever may arise from anything that is in the world to the delight of life. Honour, pride, ambition, prodigality, are 'worldly lusts,' as well as covetousness and desire of power or rule. And those that seem to deny themselves of 'faring deliciously,' or 'wearing soft raiment,' may be as much distressed with an inward desire of applause and honour, as those that would gratify their senses are by sensual lusts.

3. Thirdly, How much the world stands Satan in stead may be observed from *the force of that temptation upon those that have very much engaged in their profession of the ways of God*. It hath often fetched off those that seemed to have given up themselves to God. Demas was once commended by Paul as his fellow-labourer, Philem. 24; yet at last it so prevailed upon him that he complained, 2 Tim. iv. 10, that 'Demas had forsaken him,' and turned his back upon his profession, and so far, if Dorotheus do him right, that he became an idol-priest in Thessalonica, the cause of which horrid apostasy was his 'love to the present world.' Balaam seemed resolute not to act anything against Israel, yet 'the ways of unrighteousness' so far blinded him, that he taught Balak 'to cast a stumbling-block before the children of Israel.' The highest of nominal professors, noted by the 'thorny ground' in Mat. xiii. 22,—who seemed to differ from the good ground only in this, that their fruit was green and not ripe, as Luke expresseth it, 'They brought not fruit to perfection,'—they

were choked in these fair beginnings and offers for holiness by the 'cares and pleasures of the world.' All ages abound with instances of this kind. Æneas Sylvius preached against the pope, set up the council above him, commended the Germans for opposing him; but preferment made him alter his note, and at last he became pope himself. Bonner, the persecutor, seemed at first a good man, a favourer of Luther's doctrine, but advancement changed him to a bloody wolf, a cruel tiger. Spalato forsook popery, but, missing those dignities which he aimed at in England, was, upon hopes of greater preferment, induced to lick up his vomit, and to own popery again. How many examples have we of those who, the higher they grew in the world, became more careless of religion; as Sixtus Quintus, who went as fast back in religion as he went forward in promotion; so that he that at first entering into orders, had a good hope of his salvation, by that time he came to be pope, he became so wicked that he despaired of happiness.

4. Fourthly, *This temptation is one of Satan's last refuges, and often prevails where persecution cannot.* The thorny-ground hearers were above those of the stony ground in this, that they stood out the storm, and bore the scorching heat of persecution, but then the world choked them. Sad experience tells us that churches that did thrive and grow as the palm-tree under their pressures, were spoiled by ease and plenty, which so cherished the seeds of pride, vanity, and contention, that they grew up amain, and did more to their desolation than the cruelty of all their fiercest enemies. Julian, who, by the greatest art and policy, studied to overthrow the Christian's name, so observed this, that he made it his rule rather to corrupt men by honours than to compel them by torments.[1] We have also found that though the Roman synagogue join force to subtlety in the advancement of their dagon, yet they have still looked upon this temptation of the world as most likely to gain the hearts of their rational opposers. Cruelty could overawe the senseless multitude, and could take out of the way those of whose opposition they were afraid, but it seldom with success wrought upon persons guided by light and conscience, to a compliance that would hold long; for though at first some good men were overawed to make subscription and to recant, as it did with Bilney, Bainham, Cranmer, and several others,[2] yet upon the working of conscience, after the stound and dazzle of the temptation was over, they recoiled so resolutely upon them, that they lost more than they gained that way. But those that were willing to nibble at preferments became theirs wholly. Thus they set upon Luther, Galeaceus, Carracciolus, Dr Taylor, and a great many more, though to no purpose, for they were ready to bid their money 'perish with them,' and to bid defiance to their favour as well as to their frowns. Notwithstanding they have made many real conquests by this weapon, and accordingly this is reckoned among the temptations of greatest force: Heb. xi. 37, 'They were stoned, they were sawn asunder, they were tempted,' that is, by the pleasures and preferments of the world. It seems the Holy Ghost would point at this, how fair and plausible soever it be, as one of the devil's most powerful engines.

[1] Honoribus magis homines provocare quam tormentis cogere studuit.—*Nasianzen.*
[2] Foxe, Acts and Mon. [Sub nominibus.—G.]

Next, I promised to discover what it is in the world which makes it so fit for Satan's designs.

(1.) First, *The world brings or affords fit matter to be made the fuel of lust.* For this reason the apostle in the place afore-cited, 1 John ii. 16, forbids us so earnestly to love the world, or the things of the world, because there is nothing in it which is not improveable, as an occasion or provocation to lust. Whatsoever is in the world is lust of flesh, or eyes, or heart; and there is no lust but it may be furnished with a proper object from hence. The appetite, senses, or affections fetch all their delights from hence.

(2.) Secondly, Besides the common materials of sin that are digged out of this mine, the world hath something *of an aptitude in it to tempt.* Not that it hath properly and formally, *insidiationis animum*, an active subtlety to lay snares for men, but yet it is not so purely passive as to make it altogether innocent. There is something of a curse upon it ever since, by the fall of man. It was loosened from its proper, primitive ends; and as the devil spake by the serpent, so doth he urge, speak, tempt, and insinuate by the world, so that it is still an occasion of danger to us, and hath a special advantage over our affections, upon several accounts. As, [1.] In that it is in itself lawful to be used. [2.] In that it is suitable to our desires and tempers. [3.] In some respects it might be necessary and advantageous for the comfort of life, for the support of families, and to enable us to be helpful to others. [4.] It is near to us, under our eye; we have familiar converse with it, it is still with us. [5.] We have a natural propensity to be in love with it; the flesh would fain be pleased, and nothing is more answerable to it than the pleasures of the world. We need not wonder then, when we see it so highly captivating the affections of men, and leading them bound in chains and fetters. Some make it their god; gain is all their godliness and religion; they seek their 'portion in this life,' Ps. xvii. 14; this is their treasure, and here is their heart; and it would be no less wonder if Satan should be guilty of so much oversight, as to neglect the use of an instrument which is every way so fitted for his purpose.

(3.) Thirdly, Besides this fair prospect which it gives to sin, it hath *an enmity to God and his ways, which is no less advantageous to the devil.* This is positively affirmed, James iv. 4, 'The friendship of this world is enmity with God;' not only is this true in a lower sense, as a hindrance, being backward and averse to it, but it is a direct opposition and contrariety to God and his service. Its drawing back and hindering is charge enough against it: for it [1.] withdraws those thoughts, affections, time, care, and endeavours, which should be laid out upon better things, so that holiness must needs be obstructed, dwindle, and decay by it. [2.] It hinders the influence of heaven; it shuts out the light casually, quencheth and resisteth the Spirit, and, meritoriously also, it provokes God to withdraw, to remove his glory, and to give over his striving with them; but the contrariety that it hath to all the parts of holiness is yet more: Christ notes it, Mat. vi. 24. These two masters, God and the world, are contrary in their designs, in their commands, in their natures, so that it is impossible for any man to serve them both. They both require the heart, and they both require it to contrary and incompatible services and ends. These, then, are such masters as would be *domini in solidum,* masters of the whole.¹ Now there cannot be two masters of one thing in that sense; neither, if there were, could the hearts of men serve these different commands, but their work would necessarily engage their affections to one only; they would either 'love the one and hate the other, or hold to the one and despise the other.' This very consideration, if there were no more, doth render the world a desirable instrument for Satan.

(4.) Fourthly, In all this the world hath so many *cunning disguises, and plausible shifts, that it becomes thereby wonderfully serviceable to Satan.* It is the perfection of wicked policy to manage wicked designs under plausible pretences. These the world hath in readiness when it is accused of rebellion and treachery against God. The pleas of necessity, of prosecution of a lawful calling, of providing for a family, of not neglecting the benefits of God, of cheering the heart, and taking the comforts of the labours of their hands, and a great many more, are ready excuses to ward off the force of the convincing word. These the devil drives home, and fastens them into such strong persuasions, that the deluded sinner cannot see the danger that is before him, nor the spiritual adultery or idolatry of his soul, in his excessive love to worldly pleasures.

(5.) Fifthly, The world hath also *a spiritual fascination and witchcraft,* by which, where it hath once prevailed, men are enchanted to an utter forgetfulness of themselves and God, and being drunk with pleasures, they are easily engaged to a madness and height of folly. Some, like foolish children, are made to keep a great stir in the world for very trifles, for a vain show; they think themselves great, honourable, excellent, and for this make a great bustle, when the world hath not added 'one cubit to their stature' of real worth. Others are by this Circe transformed into savage creatures, and act the part of lions and tigers. Others, like swine, wallow in the lusts of uncleanness. Others are unmanned, putting off all natural affections, care not who they ride over, so they may rule or be made great. Others are taken with ridiculous frenzies, so that a man that stands in the cool shade of a sedate composure would judge them out of their wits. It would make a man admire to read of the frisks of Caius Caligula, Xerxes, Alexander, and many others, who because they were above many men, thought themselves above human nature. They forgot they were born, and must die, and did such things as would have made them, but that their greatness overawed it, a laughing-stock and common scorn to children. Neither must we think that these were but some few or rare instances of worldly intoxication, when the Scripture notes it as a general distemper of all that bow down to worship this idol. They live 'without God in the world,' saith the apostle, [Eph. ii. 12,] that is, they so carry it as if there were no God to take notice of them, to check them for their madness. 'God is not in all his thoughts,' saith David, Ps. x. 4, 5. 'The judgments of God are far above out of their sight;' he puffs at his enemies, and saith in his heart, 'he shall never be moved,' &c. The whole psalm describes the worldling as a man that hath lost all understanding, and were acting the part of

¹ Grotius, *in loc.*

a frantic bedlam. What then can be a more fit engine for the devil to work with than the pleasures of the world?

Applic. I shall briefly apply this to two sorts of men, those that are straitened with want and necessities, and those whose 'cups run over,' having all 'that their heart can wish.'

(1.) First, To those that think their measure of outward comforts little, I would from the doctrine now explained tell them that *they have not so much cause to vex and disquiet themselves for their poverty or troubles as they apprehend.* The world is not so desirable a thing as many dream. Did but men consider how great a snare it is, and what dangers attend the fulness of it, they would not so earnestly covet it, nor so passionately lament when it flies from them. If thou hast so much godliness as can quiet thy heart in a contented enjoyment of thy little, that little which thou hast is better than great riches of the wicked. Thou little knowest from what pride, insolency, contempt of God and men, and many other temptations and lusts, God doth preserve thee, by denying thee earthly things. Thou art now, it may be, often looking up to God, striving to believe his word, often examining thy heart, labouring to live upon God and his all-sufficiency, looking after the bread that endures to eternal life; when if thou hadst the temptations of plenty, it may be feared thou wouldst be another man, and be carried away to forget God, to be careless of holy walking, and so make way for bitterness and sorrow at last.

(2.) Secondly, I would also caution poor men not *to enlarge their desires too much after the world, but to fear the temptations of the world.* It is not only a snare to those that enjoy it, but to those that want it: for while they admire it, and engage their affections for it, it ensnares them in sinful undertakings; they are tempted to lie, cheat, dissemble, to use unlawful shifts, to rob, steal, overreach in bargaining, and to neglect the care of the soul in all. Let such call to mind, [1.] That often the providence of God doth of purpose thwart and cross the designs of such, so that though they toil and sweat, running from market to market, ' rising early and sitting up late,' yet he blows upon their gettings, and they wither to nothing, 'while it is yet in their hand;' or if they seem to keep them longer, yet all the end they make with them is but to put them into a 'bag with holes,' [Haggai i. 6,] they 'perish by evil travail,' Eccles. v. 14. [2.] They often are at a great deal of labour in pursuit, and then when the desired object is within their reach, they are overwhelmed with their disappointment, as if providence designed to mock them for their folly. This is excellently set forth, in the emblem of a man climbing up a rock, with great labour, to reach a crown that hung upon the precipice, who when he had stretched himself to grasp it, falls down and breaks his neck. [3.] And when they do by great toil rake together a heap of riches, they are starved frequently in their plenty, and so cursed that they have no more than ' the beholding of their goods with their eyes,' in that God denies them a ' heart to use them,' Eccles. v. 11. [4.] Their gettings allay not their thirst for more, ' He that loveth silver, shall not be satisfied with silver,' Eccles. v. 10. [5.] Often they are given as a scourge and plague; as the quails given to the Israelites 'came out of their nostrils.' The wise man notes it, Eccles. v. 13, 'Riches are kept for the owners thereof to their hurt.'

(3.) Thirdly, To those that have the delights of the world, plentiful estates, full tables, beautiful houses, rich tradings, honours, and dignities, I would desire to give the greatest caution, that they take heed to themselves, *because they walk in the midst of snares.* They should consider, [1.] That the great God hath laid most serious charges upon them, 'not to love the world,' but to withdraw their affections from it, nay, to be crucified to it, as to any captivating delight, and to use it with such an indifferency of mind, that they should be in their deportments towards it as 'if they used it not.' [2.] They should have their danger in their eye. How careful is he of his steps that knows he walks in the midst of serpents which are ready to sting him; the thoughts of this should blunt the edge of our delights. If you were at a feast where you knew there were poisoned dishes, you would be afraid to eat anything. Do you think that Captain Smith[1] when he was taken by the savages of America, and had plenty of meat set before him, which he knew was given to fatten him that he might be better meat when he was killed, had any stomach to eat or to drink? Was that feast pleasing to him that sat under a sharp sword hung over his head in a horse hair, when he expected every moment it should fall upon him and kill him?[2] Such are great men, rich men. With what fear and care should they use these things, when they know there is hazard of mischief from them upon every occasion! How much doth Christ speak in that one sentence, 'It is easier for a camel to go through the eye of a needle, than for a rich man to enter into the kingdom of heaven'! [Mat. xix. 24.] He means not that it is absolutely impossible, but extremely difficult, and the difficulty lies in the hindrances which their riches casts before them. [3.] They should carefully consider for what ends God gives these, and to what use they are to be put. Rich men are but God's pursers; they do but 'carry the bag,' and what is put therein, for public uses. If accordingly, as faithful stewards, they lay it out upon those that have need, they shall 'make friends of the unrighteous mammon,' and it will turn to a spiritual account: but if they think that all is for themselves, and so shut their bowels and purses from others, then they carry the bag no otherwise than as Judas did, and will be easily persuaded to sell Christ and heaven for a little more of earth.

[1] The famous Captain John Smith, the Founder of Virginia.—G.
[2] Damocles.—G.

CHAPTER XXII.

Of Christ's answer in the general.—That these temptations were upon design for our instruction.—Of the agreement betwixt Eph. vi. and Mat. iv.—The first direction.—Of courageous resolves in resisting temptations.—Its consistency with some kind of fear.—The necessity of this courage.—Wherein it consists; and that there is a courage in mourning spirits.

These answers of Christ to the several temptations, which are now to be explained, are different as to their matter, yet the general purport of them being the same, I shall therefore handle them together. They may be considered two ways:—

1. First, *As they are fit and pertinent answers to particular temptations, of distrust, of presumption, of debauching the heart by worldly delights to the service of Satan;* and thus may they be useful in their consideration, to those who are directly moved by Satan to such sins. And when at any time we are tempted in straits to cast away our reliance upon the careful providence of God, we may look upon Christ's answer, that man's life doth not so depend upon the usual means, but that any other thing blessed by divine appointment may be useful to that end. When we are enticed to presume of extraordinary supports, then by Christ's example the temptation may be resisted, by considering, that however God be to be trusted, yet he is at no time to be tempted by unnecessary expectations in the neglect of the ordinary means. If our hearts be wooed by worldly delights to cast off our care of God and religion, we may then call to mind that this is abominable idolatry, and so may we turn off our hearts from sinful compliance by charging our souls with the opposite duties, upon a true discovery of the vileness and inconvenience of the transgressions urged upon us.

2. But, secondly, They may be considered as they give *instruction for the management of our spiritual armour against all Satan's wiles in the general;* and in this sense I shall endeavour to open them, laying down first these two conclusions:—

(1.) First, *That the whole business of these temptations, as permitted to Satan, and submitted unto by Christ, was certainly upon design.* The same wisdom that contrived the wonderful method of the salvation of men by a Redeemer, did also order these temptations; for else Christ could have prevented them, or by a divine authority commanded silence to the tempter, and by his power might have chased him away. As Christ told Pilate, 'Thou couldst have no power at all against me, except it were given thee from above,' [John xix. 11;] thereby manifesting that his suffering was from a higher design than he was aware of; so might he have said to the devil, 'Except this had been designed by an eternal counsel, thou couldst not have made this attempt.' So that we must look further for the spring and rise of this, than to any supposed occasional outbreaking of satanical malice upon him.

(2.) Secondly, That this design, however it touched upon the person and offices of Christ, as mediator and second Adam, for thus it became him to overcome the enemy at the same weapon by which he overcame our first parents, and by this personal experience, to be fitted with feeling compassions to the tempted, yet was it *wholly for our sakes,* as may appear by two things:—

[1.] First, In that Christ, if his answers had only concerned himself, might have given other fit replies to the first temptation, of turning stones to bread. He could have retorted the argument upon Satan, as Jerome and others observe.[1] If I am not the Son of God, it is in vain to require a miracle of me. If I am, it is in vain to tempt me. Or he might have answered, ' That as the Father hath life in himself, so hath he given to the Son to have life in himself, and that by this divine power he could sustain himself without bread.'[2] To the second it might have been a sufficient answer to have excepted against his unfaithfulness in citing that testimony out of Ps. xci., where, by discovering his wilful omission of the clause, ' in all thy ways;' ' He shall keep thee in all thy ways;' his temptation might have fallen to the ground, as no way encouraged from that promise. To the third might have been returned such answers as these: that Satan's offer was a lie; that it was not in his power to dispose of the kingdoms of the world—that these were Christ's already; that these were vain arguments to draw him from the glory of a heavenly kingdom; and finally, that of all creatures Satan, being God's sworn enemy, had least reason to expect divine honour.

[2.] Secondly, In that all Christ's answers were from Scripture, which is properly a ' light to the steps of men,' and all these scriptures cited shew man's duty. He saith not, ' the Son of God shall not live by bread alone,' but ' man lives not by bread alone;' he saith not, Christ must not tempt, but thou, man, shalt not tempt the Lord thy God, &c. By all which we may discern that Christ answered not by arguments peculiarly agreeable to his person and nature, but by such as suit the general state of God's children. And this certainly was for our advantage. He conquered with such weapons, not for any necessity that he had to take that course, but for the need that we had of such instruction; for hereby we see that Satan is conquerable, and also how we must use our weapons.[3] In this also he left us ' an example, that we should follow his steps;' as Gideon said to his soldiers, 'As you see me do, so do you likewise,' [Judges vii. 17.] Thus, as it were, doth our Lord speak to us: For your sakes suffered I these temptations, that I might teach your hands to war, and your fingers to fight; for your sakes I used these weapons of yours, rather than my own, that I might shew you the use of your sword and shield, and how your adversary may be overcome by them; dealing herein with us as a master at arms,—it is Musculus's comparison,—who, for the better instructing and animating of his tyro, takes rather his disciple's sword than his own, to beat his adversary withal, minding not only the conquest of an enemy, but also the encouragement of a young soldier.[4]

[1] Si ad imperium ejus lapides possunt fieri panes, ergo frustra tentas; si autem non frustra, filium Dei suspicaris.   [2] Musculus, *in loc.*
[3] Vide arma quibus tibi non sibi vicit.—*Ambrose.*
[4] Hæc armatura non tam Christo Filio Dei quam nobis illius tyrunculis convenit, uti tamen ille voluit, ut nos suo doceret exemplo, perinde atque si fortis quidam Gygas hostem non suis, sed tyrunculi sui armis feriat et prosternat.—*Musculus.*

If any carry a suspicion in their mind that Christ had not our instruction so much in his eye as hath been said, because he gives not such particular instructions for our spiritual welfare[1] as the apostle in Eph. vi., expecting that our Saviour should have been more punctual in making particular applications from every part of his carriage to our use, and drawing out from thence some positive conclusions or draughts of the way and manner of resistance, they may know that there is no other difference betwixt Eph. vi. and Mat. iv. than there is betwixt precept and example. What the apostle there prescribed in the theory, here Christ teacheth in the practice; here we have in their use the girdle of truth, the shield of faith, the sword of the Spirit, the helmet of salvation, and all the other parts of that armour; and withal we may know that this is a far more advantageous way of teaching young beginners, to let them see things in a plain example, than only to give general precepts. But besides, we are to consider that Christ did many things, the meaning whereof the disciples then present with him did not know as yet, neither was it expected from them that they should; like to what he said to Peter, John xiii. 7, 'What I do thou knowest not now, but thou shalt know hereafter;' but were intended to be laid up in store to be more fully made use of, as after-directions should come in to give them information. He therefore that had purposed to give further light in this matter by his apostle and servant, was now doing that which his design led him to in his personal actings, with a secret respect also to those instructions which he intended after to communicate. We have then no reason to be jealous that these temptations were not intended for our use, but the more to assure ourselves that it was even so, because we find that those very weapons which here Christ in his own person wielded against Satan, are afterwards recommended to us.

Having thus laid the foundation, we must then, if we will imitate our captain, carefully observe his deportment from point to point, that we may draw out those instructions which he intended for us.

And the first thing that I shall take notice of, shall be the courage and magnanimity of our leader. He had endured temptations forty days and nights before, and yet he keeps the field without any appearance of shrinking or running away. Satan no sooner tempts than he is repelled. From this consideration we have this instruction:—

Direct. 1. *That he that would successfully resist temptations, must not fly, but with a courageous resolve set himself to oppose.*

Christians are apt to fear, when Satan comes up against them, and ready to turn their backs: as the Israelites were dismayed at the appearance of Goliath, and fled before him. But if we would conquer, we must, as David, go out against him in 'the name of the Lord.' To this we are called, 1 Cor. xvi. 13, 'Stand fast in the faith, quit yourselves like men, be strong;' and Eph. vi. 14, 'Stand, having your loins girt with truth,' &c. This courage recommended is not a contempt and negligent slighting of danger, nor is it a bold adventurousness upon occasions of sin; it is a holy, humble courage, and doth admit of a threefold fear.

(1.) First, *Of a fear of sin*, that is, a hatred of it. We must fear

[1] Query, 'warfare'?—ED.

sin as the greatest evil. This is no cowardice, but tends to the strongest resolution and highest endeavours against it. From this principle is it that men oppose sin as their mortal enemy, and excite their utmost courage to fight against it. As the Philistines being afraid of Israel, and yet hating to serve the Hebrews, mutually encouraged one another, 'Be strong, and quit yourselves like men, O ye Philistines.' A fear of hatred begets boldness.

(2.) Secondly, Courage admits *of a preventing fear and a provident avoidance.* Occasions of sin are to be fled. We are not with greater earnestness called upon to stand, than we are warned in this case 'to fly.' So the apostle often, 'fly fornication,' 'fly idolatry,' 'fly youthful lusts.' Occasions are best opposed by flying, where calling and duty doth not engage: Prov. iv. 14, 'Enter not into the path of the wicked, and go not in the way of evil men.' He fights best that flies most, where necessity doth not bid him stay, 1 Cor. vi. 18, x. 14, and 2 Tim. ii. 22.

(3.) Thirdly, It also admits of the fear *of a holy jealousy;* such a distrust of ourselves, as puts us to seek to 'the rock which is higher than we' for shelter. God calls us to 'turn into our stronghold,' Nahum i. 7, and to 'lay hold upon his strength,' [Isa. xxvii. 5.] It is rashness or desperateness, and not true courage, to adventure ourselves without our guard or shield. But however we must fear sin, suspect our strength, and fly occasions, yet Satan we must not fly. Here we are bid to stand, for these reasons:—

[1.] First, *It is impossible to fly from him.* He can follow us wherever we go. If we go to holy assemblies, he can come thither. If we shut up ourselves in our closets, he can meet us there. If we betake ourselves to a wilderness or to a crowd, to be sure he will find us out.

[2.] Secondly, *We are expressly charged to make resistance:* James iv. 7, 'Resist the devil;' 1 Peter v. 9, 'whom resist.' This plainly speaks positive endeavours and opposition on our part.

[3.] Thirdly, *A fainting fear is an unbelieving distrust of God's power,* as if he were not 'able to save to the uttermost,' [Heb. vii. 25,] and of Christ's compassionate tenderness, as if he would not 'succour those that are tempted,' [Heb. ii. 18.]

[4.] Fourthly, *Our fainting makes Satan insult.* He triumphs when we turn our backs, and besides hath the greater advantage to wound us or to tread us down at pleasure. It is observed that God provides armour for head and breast, and all the fore parts, by a shield in case of resistance; but if we fly, so little encouragement is there for cowardice, there is no armour for the back.

[5.] Fifthly, *It is most suitable to Christian courage to die in the place, and to put it to the utmost hazard rather than to yield.* According to Vespasian's motto, *Oportet imperatorem stantem mori.* Every Christian should say, 'Shall such a one as I fly?' [Neh. vi. 11;] one that hath given up my name to God; one that hath professed holiness afore men; one that hath so many advantages for resistance, and such sweet encouragements from a victorious general!

Quest. But the great question is, What is this fear that is forbidden, and the courage which is enjoined?

CHAP. 22.] SATAN'S TEMPTATIONS. 449

Ans. The fear forbidden is an unbelieving weakness and pusillanimity, through which, as hopeless of success, men throw down their weapons and yield themselves up to Satan, when the hearts of men fail them to the giving up of the victory.

Spiritual courage, on the contrary, is a serious resolve of fighting it out in the strength of the Lord, and it consists of these two parts:—

First, A sincere resolution to be on Christ's side against all iniquity, a deliberate unfeigned determination to stand for God and his holy ways, against Satan and sin. [1.] The ground of this determination is a conviction of the evil of sin, even to a hatred of it. He that hath not thoroughly weighed the misery of living in sin, and fully purposed within himself to forsake it, can have no true Christian courage when it comes to a pinch. [2.] From this ground he lays himself under solemn engagements to Christ his general, as soldiers list themselves under their captains, that he will follow him and observe his commands; he gives up himself to God by covenant. So that now he is no longer his own, but Christ's servant, bound for his work. [3.] And this with such or so much belief of his promises for aid and victory, that he hath some hopes or expectations at least, that God may at last so assist him that he may attain to some real degree of the mortification of the 'flesh, with the affections and lusts thereof,' [Gal. v. 24.]

Secondly, The second part of this courage consists in *a suitable management of this undertaking.* Courage is not only seen in the first onset, but in the prosecution of the warfare; and this lies in two things. [1.] When there are real endeavours against sin, answerable to this undertaking, in all ways of striving to oppose it. When men do not engage against sin with big words only; or as the children of Ephraim—who, arming themselves and carrying bows, seemed to have stout resolves, but then 'turned back in the day of battle;' but with real and conscientious wrestlings, setting themselves with all their might and care against every temptation, and studying to pursue the victory, where in any degree it is obtained, to a greater height. [2.] When these endeavours are sincerely persisted in, without being quite wearied out or utter fainting, so that it never comes to this, though they may be sometime under Satan's feet, that they relinquish their first solemn engagement, or repent of their undertaking, and then turn their backs upon God, listing themselves under Satan's colours. Such a fainting as this would bereave men of their crown; 'Ye shall reap in due time if ye faint not,' Gal. vi. 9. Upon this hazard are the children of God cautioned, Heb. xii. 3, 'Lest ye be wearied and faint in your mind.' [3.] There is also a particular kind of courage expressed in a holy and humble contempt of Satan's suggestions, when after all means used they cease not to be troublesome. This is not to slight sin but to slight Satan, who, though he is resisted, ceaseth not to molest.[1]

Applic. I shall particularly apply this first direction, [1.] To those that propound ease to themselves in their race or warfare, which is a thing impossible to one that doth the work of a soldier, not considering that work and courageous endeavours do abide them. [2.]

[1] Capel, Tempt., part 2, cap. 9; Ames, Cas. Consc., lib. ii. cap. 18, sec. 14.

2 F

To those that pretend themselves Christ's soldiers, courage and Christian magnanimity is your cognizance. By this must you be known. How do ye stand? what are your resolutions and undertakings? Those Christians that have 'joy and peace in believing' can more easily satisfy themselves in this; but those that fight in tears and grief, in disquiets and troubled thoughts, are apt to conclude themselves unbelieving, because they are fearful; or to think that they look not up to Jesus, the 'author and finisher of their faith,' because they apprehend themselves weary and 'faint in their minds.' For the ease and help of such, I shall shew in a few things that there is as real a Christian courage in such mourners as in some that sing songs of triumph.

[1.] First, It is a real courage and undertaking against sin for any to resolve his utmost, *out of detestation of it, before he can satisfy himself that God will accept of it.* To oppose sin under such a discouragement, or at such a venture, is a courageous hatred; and yet so do these mourners.

[2.] Secondly, *To be under continual grievings because of miscarriages, so that other things of outward enjoyment cease to be pleasing,* is a courageous hatred; but this is their case.

[3.] Thirdly, *To wrestle against sin under high discouragements,* when afflicted and tossed, when Satan runs upon them and shakes them by the neck, and yet they continue their wrestling and withstanding as they are able; this is faithful resistance, 'a resistance unto blood, striving against sin,' Heb. xii. 4; that is, if that expression be proverbial, like that, *ad sanguinem usque,* they resist sin faithfully, under great hazards and inconveniencies, even to wounds and blood, till they have broken heads and broken faces; and can say to God, though we have been 'broken in the place of dragons,' and have these wounds to shew, yet 'have we not departed from thee,' [Ps. xliv. 19,] nor quitted our desires after thee and holiness, for all these buffetings of Satan; but this is the character of these dejected ones.

[4.] Fourthly, It is a courageous hatred that cannot *suffer a sinful motion to fall upon the soul, but it puts all into a combustion within, and raiseth disquiet;* for it is an argument that there is a contrariety betwixt the heart and sin; but this is their case also.

[5.] Fifthly, It is courage and constancy *to hold on in gracious endeavours and strivings;* so that when they fall, as soon as they can re-collect their strength they set on where they left, and renew the battle, never changing their first resolve for holiness against sin. This is implied in the apostle's phrase of 'standing,'—Eph. vi., 'That ye may withstand, and when ye have done all, to stand.' He is accounted to stand that runs not out of the field, but stands to his holy resolve to the last, though the battle go sore against him by fits; but such are these mourners.

There is true courage under mourning and disquiet of heart, so that we may say to such, 'O thou afflicted and tossed,' fear not, 'the glory of the Lord shall shine upon thee,' [Isa. lx. 1.] They that are weak in this sense shall be strong as David.

CHAPTER XXIII.

The second direction, that temptations are not to be disputed.—The several ways of disputing a temptation.—In what cases it is convenient and necessary to dispute with Satan.—In what cases inconvenient, and the reasons of it.

The next thing observable in Christ's carriage to Satan is this, that Christ, though he rejected every temptation by giving a reason of his refusal from the command of God, did not suffer Satan to dispute his temptations further than the first proposal, and in his answers he takes no notice of the reasons or motives by which he laboured to make his temptations prevailing. In the two first temptations he gives no reply to what Satan insinuated by his supposition, 'If thou be the Son of God,' neither by affirming that he was so, nor discovering to him his knowledge of the secret subtlety which he had wrapped up under these plausible pretences. In the third he answers not a word to the vanity and falsehood of his deceitful offer of 'the kingdoms of the world,' though, as hath been observed, he might have opposed strong reasons against them all; and besides, when Satan became insolent and impudent in tempting Christ 'to fall down and worship him,' he chaseth him away with a severe abomination, 'Get thee hence, Satan;' from which we have a second direction, which is this:—

Direct. 2. *That temptations to sin are to be opposed by peremptory denials rather than by disputings.*

This is a note which most commentators have on this place; but it stands in need of a distinct application, because it is not a rule so general but that the practice of God's children have made exception against it. For the clearer explanation of it, I shall,

1. First, *Give you the several kinds of disputings, by which we may see that all are not alike;* for,

(1.) First, *The serious working of the thoughts in a quick denial of a temptation with a reason implied or expressed, though it admit not Satan to any further dispute or argument, may in some sense be called a disputing;* for the Scripture useth διαλογισμὸς for any inward, serious thought. Such a kind of disputing as this is necessary. It cannot be wanting to any that refuse a sinful motion, this being, as we shall see afterward, one of those directions which Christ intended us by his example, and the very thing which Christ practised in every temptation; for he contented not himself to give a naked denial, but still adds a reason of such refusal. Those who in general terms urge that temptations are not to be disputed, do not reckon this as any disputing; and others that do, taking disputing for the refusal of a thing with a reason assigned, think that his procedure in the two first temptations is not imitable by us, but only that of the third, wherein he chased away the devil with angry denial; but the mistake is obvious.

(2.) Secondly, *There is a disputing of unnecessary curiosity and conference.* This is when a sinful motion injected into our hearts is not directly consented to, but then instead of a full denial men begin to raise questions and make objections of lesser moment, or some impertinent queries which strike not at the root; as one observed of himself, that instead of denying a sinful motion, he began to dispute whether it came from Satan or his own inclination; and so, instead of quenching the fire, he busied himself to inquire whence it came. Men deal with temptations in this case as they who being asked whether they will buy such a commodity, hastily answer no, but yet call back the party again and ask whence it came, or what it must cost, and by such entanglements of curiosity engage themselves at last to buy it. Eve failed by such an inconsiderate conference with Satan, for the abrupt beginning of the serpent's speech, ' Yea, hath God said ye shall not eat,' &c., and the summing up of the arguments which prevailed with her to eat, ' When the woman saw that the tree was good for food, and pleasant to the eyes,' &c., [Gen. iii. 6,] do clearly evidence that there was more discourse than is there expressed, and that also tending to ascertain the goodness, pleasantness, and profit of the fruit. This kind of disputing is always unlawful and dangerous, for it is but a wanton dalliance with a temptation, a playing upon the hole of the asp, and commonly ends in a sinful compliance.

(3.) Thirdly, *There is a disputing of a deliberating and parleying indifferency.* This is when the devil puts a thought of sin into their minds, and, while they seem not to be forward to embrace it, leaves it to further consideration, and then they float betwixt resolved and unresolved, betwixt *pro* and *con*, being at a great dispute within themselves what is best to be done, whether the conveniences on the one hand will weigh down the inconveniences on the other. This, in cases of apparent sin, is a wicked halting betwixt two, always unlawful.

(4.) Fourthly, *There are also treacherous partial arguings, wherein the heart takes part with Satan.* These are those debates that are to be found in natural men, about the doing or not doing of sinful things. This looks so like the combat betwixt the flesh and the Spirit, that it hath occasioned an inquiry how they may be distinguished each from other. It is generally concluded that in that strife of the natural man, the light of the understanding and conscience gives opposition to the bent of the affections, and the same faculties, though sanctified in part in the regenerate, are the parties that give opposition each to other; but with this principal difference, that in this strife of the flesh and Spirit the man takes part with God, whereas in the other the affections take the devil's part, and in a malignant averseness to the light, strive to put it out and to get over the conviction of conscience, so that the man strives to sin, and to stop the mouth of such objections as come in to the contrary; this kind of disputing is always sinful.

(5.) Fifthly, *There is yet a disputing in a strict sense, which is a full and solemn debating of a satanical injection, by giving it the full hearing, and admitting Satan to be a respondent to our objections.* Of this it is queried how far it may be convenient and how far inconvenient, because we see Christ in this place did not thus dispute with Satan, and yet we find instances in Scripture of some holy men that have been unavoidably engaged to dispute a temptation to the utmost.

[CHAP. 23.] SATAN'S TEMPTATIONS. 453

To answer this query, I shall, secondly, shew in what cases it may be necessary or convenient to enter the lists with Satan in a holy arguing, and in what cases it is inconvenient and dangerous. There are four cases in which we may dispute a temptation:—

[1.] First, When the motion is of things *doubtful and disputable, whether they be lawful or not.* Here it cannot be avoided; for albeit, as the apostle adviseth, Rom. xiv. 1, 'doubtful disputations' are not to be imposed upon others, so as to tie them up to our persuasions, yet in these things every man, before he can act clearly, is to endeavour his own satisfaction in the lawfulness or unlawfulness of the thing, that so he may be 'fully persuaded in his own mind,' ver. 5. And he gives two strong reasons of this, ver. 22, 23: (1.) From the rack and trouble which otherwise the man may be put upon, while his conscience, unsatisfied, 'condemneth him in that which,' by a contrary practice, 'he alloweth.' (2.) In that this condemnation of conscience, while he doth that, the lawfulness whereof he believeth not, is an evidence of his sin, as well as an occasion of his trouble.

[2.] Secondly, Disputings have place, when *a temptation hath taken hold upon the thoughts, and so far possessed itself, that our corruption riseth up in the defence of the suggestion.* Satan will not quit that hold, though he be an intruder without our leave, till he be beat out of his quarters. The apostle, Eph. vi. 16, implies so much by that expression, of 'quenching the fiery darts' of Satan. It is not proper to understand it of a refusal of the first motion of sin—though interpreters do usually make it comprehensive both of the keeping out of the dart, and the plucking it out—because this evidently supposeth that the dart hath pierced the soul, and now begins to burn and inflame, which will require more labour for the quenching of it, than a refusal of the first motion would put us to. As when fire hath taken hold upon our houses, we shall be forced to bring water for the extinguishing of the flame, which before it had broke out upon the building, an ordinary care might have prevented. And this we [are] further taught by a distinction which the same apostle useth in the same place, of στῆναι and ἀντιστῆναι, standing and withstanding. We must keep off the temptation, that it enter not, by standing against the assault in a peremptory refusal; but if it do enter, then we must be put to it, by a force of holy arguing, to pull out the arrow, and to withstand it.

[3.] Thirdly, Much more need have we of disputing, when the present temptation is *a motion of such a sin which we are habituated unto, and have long practised;* for these kind of sinful motions are not cast out easily. In this case, David adviseth his enemies, Ps. iv. 2-4, who had for a long time, 'loved vanity, and sought after leasing,' that by 'communing with their own heart,' and by disputing against their sinful practices, they should bring themselves under a holy awe, and by that means stop the course of their sinning, ver. 4. This, indeed, is the great thing that sinners are called to by God, to ponder their estate, to consider their ways, to study the evil and danger of sin, to examine themselves, and to reason together with God about the wickedness and ingratitude of their actions, and about the contrary loveliness, blessedness, and happiness of the ways of God, that so they may be brought to repentance; all which are done only by a serious arguing of their case and hazard.

[4.] Fourthly, It is convenient, and in some cases necessary, to dispute a temptation which Satan offers to us, *by the mouths of men, who entice us to share with them in their wickedness;* for here, by arguing, we may not only discourage their further solicitation, and so free ourselves from the like temptation for the future, but we also, by the exercise of a holy charity, endeavour to 'pull them out of the fire,' Jude 23. When Joseph's mistress tempted him, he considered that he had to deal both with the devil and his mistress, Gen. xxxix. 7, 8, and therefore that he might 'resist the devil,' he peremptorily refused the temptation; but that he might take off his mistress from her unlawful prosecution, he argues with her about the ingratitude, danger, and unlawfulness of such an act, ' My master wotteth not what is with me in the house, and he hath committed all that he hath to my hand: there is none greater in this house than I, neither hath he kept anything back from me but thee, because thou art his wife: how then can I do this great wickedness, and sin against God?' When sinners do entice us to cast in our lot amongst them, pity to them, and care of ourselves, will engage us to argue the folly and danger of their ways with them, except they behave themselves as dogs and swine; their carriage giving us just ground to conclude, that they are so set on wickedness, that it may endanger us, rather than profit them, to debate with them. And so was it likely—and the text seems to hint so much—that when Joseph perceived his mistress was resolved upon the pursuit, and that his reasonings were not minded, he persisted in his denial, but forbore his arguings.

But however it may be convenient to dispute, in the last mentioned sense, in these four cases—and others may probably be added—yet there are cases in which it will be inconvenient and hazardous to dispute or argue, and of this order I shall reckon four.

[1.] First, It is not safe to dispute the matter in *vile, infectious temptations, such as are either suitable to our inclinations, or may receive a favourable aspect and countenance from the posture of our affairs and condition.* These temptations, even in our debating against them, are like the opening of a sepulchre, which sends forth a poisonous stream[1] which may infect those that loathe and resist it. It is dangerous to admit fire into the same room where there is gunpowder, though there be no intention to kindle it. It hath been an old observation, that the very confession of infectious sins, though designed to beget shame, and resolution against them for the future, have kindled a new flame, by the unnecessary declaration of the manner and circumstances, so that they have returned from the confessor more infected than when they went; and those very persons whose care it should have been to have put the highest disgrace upon sins so confessed, to the begetting of loathing and abhorrency in the parties and themselves, have by too curious an inquiry received such poison at the ear, that the heart hath been forthwith infected. The like hazard remains to those that are willing to debate such sins with Satan; for though they begin upon the score of resistance, yet the very dwelling

[1] Query, 'steam'?—ED.

on such a subject, when admitted to lay itself open, doth convey such amorous looks unto the treacherous affections, that the heart is in danger of a secret poison. There is no better way in such cases than to command all such thoughts and considerations out of our coasts, and, as we do when the city or town we live in is infected, to withdraw ourselves from the air of such a temptation. We may observe the like care in Joseph, though he thought himself concerned at first, as hath been said, to oppose the unlawful suit of his mistress, yet seeing her desperately set upon her folly, he declined all communication with her, and would not be with her, Gen. xxxix. 10; and at last, when she caught him by his garment, 'he left it in her hand and fled,' ver. 12. He might easily have rescued his garment from her, had he not been aware that his contesting against her might have been an occasion of ensnarement to himself. Christ himself, when he was tempted by Peter to spare himself, [Mat. xvi. 22,]—which was a temptation very taking to human nature, especially when suffering and death is in view,—is more short and sparing in his reasoning against it, than he was when the devil tempted him. He gives no positive reasons against it, as he did when he was tempted to 'fall down and worship the devil,' but dischargeth himself from any further consideration of the matter by a declared abhorrency of the thing, 'Get thee behind me, Satan, for thou savourest not the things that be of God, but the things which be of men.' Which is as if he had plainly said, This is so apparently from the devil, and so much abhorred by me, because so suitable to my condition, that I will not so much as discourse of it or consider it.

[2.] Secondly, Generally in all temptations, though they have not the advantage of our present special estate or inclination, as hath been noted, *of an apparent withdrawment from obedience, or of things unquestionably sinful, it is not convenient to dispute them, but to dismiss them by a denial, except some of the forementioned considerations do alter the case.* In known cases we need not parley, but stoutly deny. Our resolutions for duty, and against sin, should not be to seek. We are certain that sin is to be avoided, and duty to be practised; here we should be peremptory. Abraham being certain of duty, when God called him to 'a place which he should afterward receive for an inheritance,' he disputed not the uncertainty, the danger or inconvenience that possibly might attend his removal, but went out, 'not knowing whither he went,' Heb. xi. 8. Paul being called by God to preach among the heathen, though 'flesh and blood' were ready with arguments against it, yet he would not so much as confer with them, but immediately obeyed, Gal. i. 16. Like instances I might fetch from other holy men. Cyprian, when the president gave it to his own choice whether he would obey or be put to death, commanding him to take it into consideration, he readily replied, *In re tam sancta non est deliberandum*, that it was not to deliberate in so plain a case. Mrs Ann Askew, when at the stake ready to be burnt, a pardon was offered by the Lord Chancellor; she would not so much as look on it, but returned this answer, that she came not thither 'to deny her Lord and Master.' Bishop Hooker,[1] in the same condition, had a box laid

---

[1] Hooper ?—G.

before him with a pardon in it, which when he understood—he was so afraid of tampering with a temptation—he cried out, 'If ye love my soul, away with it; if ye love my soul, away with it.' And many others there were in all ages, so far from accepting such 'unlawful deliverances,' that they would not take into consideration the unrighteous terms upon which they might have escaped.

[3.] Thirdly, *When a temptation, after all means used, continues to be troublesome, and is rather an annoyance than an infection, then must we not dispute it, but by a holy contempt despise it.* Temptations to blasphemy are oft of this nature, as hath been noted in its place, and there are other things by which Satan creates to God's children great disquiet, while they in the meantime abhor the sin, and cry out of the trial. Here when the 'messenger of Satan' will not depart, it is an advice that hath the general approbation of holy experienced men,[1] that we should despise the temptation, as an approved way to our quiet and ease; for while we think to repel such assaults by struggling with arguments, we do but increase the force of them; as he that thinks to shelter himself against the wind, by holding up his cloak before him, doth but derive upon himself a stronger blast.

[4.] Fourthly, *In temptations of inward trouble and terror, it is not convenient to dispute the matter with Satan.* David in Ps. xlii. 11, seems to correct himself for his mistake; his soul was 'cast down within him,' and for the cure of that temptation, he had prepared himself by arguments for a dispute; but perceiving himself in a wrong course, he calls off his soul from disquiet to an immediate application to God and the promises, 'Trust still in God, for I shall yet praise him;' but in Ps. xi. 1, he is more aforehand with his work, for while his enemies were acted by Satan to discourage him, he rejects the temptation at first, before it settled upon his thoughts, and chaseth it away as a thing that he would not give ear to: 'In thee, Lord, do I put my trust; how say ye then to my soul, Flee as a bird to your mountain?' And there are weighty reasons that should dissuade us from entering the lists with Satan in temptations of inward trouble. As,

[1.] First, *The determination of the sincerity of the soul and its converted state is a question of no small difficulty*—a knotty controversy, more intricate and abstruse than those controversies that in the schools are of greatest name for difficulty; for this is liable to more weighty objections, and stands in need of nicer distinction. As Dr Goodwin observes,[2] 'They that converse with dejected spirits, find so much quickness and nimbleness of reasoning, turning every way to ward off the force of an argument brought for their consolation, that even wise and able heads are oft put to a stand, and know not what to answer.' Would it then be fit to give Satan this advantage? or to admit him so far into our reasoning? He that will invite Satan to such a contest, shall be sure to have his hands full.

---

[1] Tentatus a Satana cum nullum evadendi modum sentis, simpliciter claude oculos, et nihil responde, et commenda causam Deo.—*Luther*, tom. iii. f. 396. Sicut tutissimum est canem latrantem contemnere, et præterire, ita una vincendi ratio est contemnere rationes Satanæ, neque cum iis disputare. Satan nihil minus ferre potest quam sui contemptum.—*Id.*, f. 376; *Ames, Cases of Consc.*, lib. i. cap. 6.

[2] Child of Light, cap. 7, p. 41. [As before.—G.]

[2.] Secondly, This kind of temptation doth usually *disable men for arguing;* it oftentimes confounds the brain, stupifies the understanding, and weakens the memory. Heman complains of himself as 'distracted by terrors,' [Ps. lxxxviii. 15.] Job calls himself desperate, [chap. vi. 26.] Such persons are not surely in a fit case to manage a temptation with so cunning a sophister as Satan.

[3.] Thirdly, If they descend into the battle, he is not only *too strong for them, but commonly after a while they take Satan's part against themselves, and comply with him, concluding against their own peace.*

[4.] Fourthly, *There is also a better way at hand than to enter into a dispute;* and that is, by going to God by a present faith, love or repentance, when the truth of any of these is questioned. It is a difficult task to prove sometime that former acts of faith, love, or other graces were sincere. This may admit of such objections from a wounded spirit, that it will be hard to answer them; but in this case it is a nearer way to see if there be not in all these complainings some present acts of these graces; whether such complainants are not willing to embrace Christ upon any terms, whether they do not hate sin, whether they would not unfeignedly be reconciled to God, &c. It oft falls out that this doth stay the trouble when examinations of former acts do nothing for them. Some men are at more pains, as one saith, to repair and fit an old building, than would serve to rear a new one. Yet must it be remembered that though it were the best course to resist temptations of this nature at first, by avoiding unnecessary disputings, notwithstanding when this—as I noted before of other temptations—hath seized upon the heart and taken possession, then shall we be forced to 'fill our mouths with arguments,' and whether we will or no, must we undergo a contest. As we see in David, who when his troubles had prevailed upon him, was forced to plead with God, with himself, with the temptation, and to have recourse to former experience, 'the days of old, and the years of the right hand of the Most High,' [Ps. lxxvii. 10,] and all little enough.

All that I shall further say concerning the inconveniences of disputing with Satan, shall be to give you *the reasons manifesting these unnecessary communings with him to be every way hazardous and unsuitable.* As,

(1.) First, *It is an honour to Satan, and a disgrace to ourselves.* Men are loath to be seen contesting with persons of a far inferior rank, especially in such things which have procured to such a noted infamy. It is a usual piece of generosity in men of spirit that they scorn to strive with a scold, or contend with a beggar, or be found in company of those that are under an evil name deservedly; and in matters that are vile and base, it is highly disgraceful to admit them to a debate. Such things will either get more credit than they deserve, while they seem to be countenanced by a dispute, or else shall communicate their discredit to those that shall shew such familiarity with them.

(2.) Secondly, *By refusing to dispute temptations, we raise up in our hearts an active abhorrency of them, and by that abhorrency we are cautioned and strengthened against them.* It must needs awaken our hatred into a present activity against that sin, which our consideration at first view presents to us so abominable, that it deserves no other answer but to be whipped out of our sight. And when our heart is thus alarmed, it cannot but stand upon its guard. It is a course that holy men have taken to keep men at a greater distance from sin, to present it as a thing of greatest abhorrency; and that is the intendment of that expression, Rom. vi. 1, 'Shall we sin, that grace may abound? God forbid.' The vileness of that abuse of gospel grace he shews by setting it below the merit of any serious thought; he sharpens their apprehensions against it by an outcry of detestation. The like he doth, Eph. v. 3, where he endeavours to set their hearts against uncleanness and covetousness, by telling them that it was unbecoming saintship that such things should be 'so much as once named by them.'

(3.) Thirdly, *Disputing is a secret invitation to the devil to urge the temptation further.* We do but toy with him, and give him occasion to follow us. Eve found the truth of this by sad experience; she so managed herself, that she plainly intimated she had a mind to hear what the devil could say for the eating of the forbidden fruit; and so urged the prohibition of God, and the threatening, that she sought from Satan a confirmation of her secret unbelief rather than faithfully endeavoured a repulse of the temptation, and mentioned the threatening under such terms of uncertainty and peradventure, as an objection which she desired might be removed, rather than from a firm belief of that death spoken of, fortifying herself in her duty; by all which Satan was so encouraged to proceed, that he presently confirmed her in her distrust.

(4.) Fourthly, *These disputings usually return nothing of advantage to our account, but to Satan's.* We unnecessarily enter the lists with him, and that upon very unequal terms, he being, as Saul said of Goliath and David, a 'man of war from his youth,' and we but weak, unskilful striplings. We go out of our trenches and leave our weapons behind us. We expose our naked breasts to all his darts, and by discoursing with him he gains time wherein the poison may more powerfully work upon our affections. If he was too hard for our first parents at this weapon, we, whose hearts are not so faithful to God as theirs in innocency, but corrupted by Satan, who hath also a party in us, are not likely to come off with triumph.

(5.) Fifthly, *These presage, consequently, an overthrow.* A parleying city holds not long out. It implies in itself an inclination to yield, when armies are willing to treat. Daily examples and experience of those that give up themselves to sin after communication with Satan sadly witness this truth.

The sum of this direction is this, that when a motion of sin is put into our heart, instead of disputing where it may be avoided, we should peremptorily deny it and send it away with an angry rebuke or severe abomination: I may not do it; How can I do this wickedness? Get thee hence; or, 'The Lord rebuke thee, Satan.'

CHAPTER XXIV.

The third direction, of repelling a temptation without delay.—The necessity of so doing.—What a speedy denial doth contain.

The magnanimity of Christ, and the peremptoriness of his denial, we have noted. We must further observe the immediateness of his answer; he suffered not any of these motions to stay long with him; here was not a *Cras tibi respondebo*, Come again to-morrow and I will answer. He would not take time with the devil, but had his answer ready. No sooner was he tempted, but the temptation was repelled; for these expressions—' But he answered and said;' 'Jesus said unto him;' 'Then saith Jesus unto him,'—shew the quickness and speediness of these returns, that he answered presently, forthwith. Hence we have a third direction in our resisting of Satan, which is this:—

Direct. 3. *Temptations are best answered when they are presently denied and forthwith repelled.* The direction is of great importance; it is not for us to pass by a temptation with silence, or to defer an answer. For these reasons:—

(1.) First, The nature of temptations, *as dangerous or infectious, doth sufficiently enforce a necessity of their speedy removal.* Things of danger require a sudden stop. If poison be taken into the body, we speedily labour to cast it up, or to overcome it by antidotes. We labour to stay the spreading of a gangrene presently. Who thinks it fit to delay when fire hath taken hold upon a house? The very opportunity of help is in the speediness of the endeavour. It is too late to bring water when the house is consumed, too late to apply a remedy when the disease hath conquered. They that consider what a temptation is, will see no reason to move slowly in opposing.[1]

(2.) Secondly, *Silence encourageth Satan.* It is not with him as it is with men; it is the policy of some to overlook their petitioners, and by silence to scare them from any further address; but Satan hath more impudence than to be put out of countenance by delay, and more active malice than to be discouraged by silence; nay, it doth on the contrary embolden him. Modest requests are disheartened by silence, but such motions which, by their nature, imply a disgrace, and carry no reason for their acceptance but what they expect to find in the consent of those to whom they are made, if they be not presently refused, they give encouragement to hope for entertainment. An immodest request to a chaste matron, if not forthwith expressly abominated, encourageth to further attempts. Sin being so great an affront to a holy heart, the motion of it cannot be entertained with silence, but Satan is emboldened to expect consent in time, and follows his advantage accordingly. He usually flies at a valiant peremptory resistance; but if the pulse of the soul beat slowly upon the motion, he grounds his hope upon that, and is animated to a further procedure.

[1] Sero medicina paratur,
Cum mala per longas convaluere moras.

(3.) Thirdly, *Our wills are apt to be inclined by delay.* Though grace have made straight our crooked natures, yet we still carry such a sway to our former dispositions, that a small thing, having the advantage of our natural bias and inclination, makes us, like a deceitful bow, turn to our old stand. For the understanding and will of the regenerate are but imperfectly good, the faculties that should obey are unruly. In such a case how dangerous may delays prove! Who will suffer a seditious incendiary in an army, formerly inclined to mutiny? Who will permit leaven to remain in that mass, which he desires may not be leavened, and not quickly remove it? Who will neglect a spark upon dry tinder, that would not have it consumed, and not instantly put it out? If it was so great a mischief to Eve in innocency, as hath been said, to delay her peremptory denial, of how much greater hazard is it to us! Delays are dangerous to a very proverb, and silence may end in consent.

(4.) Fourthly, *Silence is also some degree of consent.* It is strange to find a man delaying an answer to temptation, and yet no way guilty of consenting. In things that are to be opposed with care and hatred, no man can withhold his hand without blame. He that is not against Satan, who is to be perpetually resisted, is so far for him as he is not against him. He that delays justice which is due, denies it. The judge in the parable was called unjust, not because he had devoured the widow's house, but because he deferred to do her right.[1] He that hinders not evil when and as soon as he can, doth command and approve it. These are received axioms amongst men, and have the same truth in them if applied to resistance of temptations. And this may further appear by considering, [1.] The weakness of the will in the regenerate. When our wills are really set upon good and against evil, yet we cannot say they are perfectly for the one and against the other, but that there is still some degree of averseness to good, and of inclination to evil in our wills, or else we should not meet with complainings of imperfections under sincere resistances; as in the apostle, 'The evil that I would not, that do I,' [Rom. vii. 19.] [2.] The acts of the will in consenting may be so sudden, short, and quick, that they may be almost insensible, and as forward and ready as the motion. [3.] The will may be interpretatively voluntary and consenting, when yet it forms not in itself any positive approbation. It may be guilty, in that it doth not more strongly and speedily dissent: for the suspension or negation of the will's act, where it ought to act, cannot avoid the charge of coming short of duty.

(5.) Fifthly, Not to answer presently, *is to lose the best opportunity of answering.* It is less dangerous, more easy, more comfortable to be speedy in denial. The sooner fire is put out, or the disease is stayed, the less hurt is done; and it is far less labour to quench a spark than a flame; to pluck up a young plant than an old standard; to kill the cockatrice in the egg. A temptation opposed speedily, is with greater ease overcome, than after it hath settled though but a little: for it presently makes a party within us; our affections are soon engaged, our understanding soon bribed, and then we have not only Satan but ourselves to oppose; and this self so divided, that

---

[1] Differre justitiam est negare justitiam. Qui non prohibet cum potest, jubet.

Chap. 24.]   SATAN'S TEMPTATIONS.   461

when we come to fight, our wills are against our wills, our affections against our affections, our wishes and prayers clash and contradict each other. As Austin confesseth of himself: 'I prayed,' said he, 'and then feared lest thou shouldst hear me too soon; I desired to satisfy, rather than to extinguish lust.'[1] At the first assault the soul is oft in a better posture, more unanimous and consistent with itself; then is the golden opportunity of resistance. For, as one saith,[2] it is better to do it while reason is on our side, than when both reason and affection conspire against us. And, lastly, it would be more honour and satisfaction to us, rather not to have admitted such a guest, than after such admittance into our thoughts to be forced to cast him out.[3] In the review of our actions we shall have more comfort to have been resolute against any sin than to hold our peace.

The necessity of a quick and speedy rejection of a sinful motion is then beyond dispute, and there needs no more to be said for the explanation of this direction, but an account of what is implied in a speedy denial. It contains these four things:—

[1.] First, *That it must issue from a fixed determination against sin.* Some refuse a temptation with the same mind that carried Lot's wife out of Sodom, and are forced beyond their own inclination, but these go not far till they 'look back;' and no wonder: for if he that is sincerely peremptory against sin at the first motion, may by the solicitation of the flesh be inclined afterward, there is little expectation that he whom the first motion finds indifferent and but coldly denying, should hold out long. But that refusal that must give any encouragement to hopes of success, must be an answer of holy indignation against the offer of temptation, and that confirmed into a serious resolve of heart not to yield.

[2.] Secondly, *This positive denial must be also wisely jealous of Satan, in motions that are unlikely, or that may seem light, little, and not directly intended.* Though it may be but a transient glance, or a thing that is out of our road, yet must nothing be contemned or undervalued. Jealousy will take notice of small actions or circumstances, and no less suspicious must we be of every proffer made to us, lest Satan by any means get an advantage against us.

[3.] Thirdly, *The refusal must be so quick, that it may be ready to take the temptation by the throat.* At the first motion or rising of it in our mind, we must endeavour to stifle it in the birth, that it may be as the 'untimely fruit of a woman that never sees the sun,' [Job iii. 16;] we must not give it time to grow up to a rod of wickedness, but must nip it in the earliest buddings of it. It is the nature of grace, if we do but faithfully pursue the inclinations of it, to be quick in its opposition. So doth the apostle's phrase teach us, Gal. v. 17, 'The flesh lusteth against the spirit, and the spirit against the flesh:' the spirit is as ready to repel, as the flesh to suggest. No sooner doth the one stir, but the other is ready with an opposition, and the reason of it is from the active contrariety that is betwixt them; for so the

---

[1] Ego adolescens petieram a te castitatem, et dixeram; da mihi castitatem, sed noli modo; timebam enim ne me cito exaudires et cito sanares, malebam expleri quam extingui.—*Confes.*, lib. viii. cap. 7.

[2] Greenham on Ps. cxix. 101.   [3] Turpius ejicitur quam non admittitur hospes.

word, ἀντίκειται, there used, would express it; they are sworn enemies, animated by principles of constant opposition, as water and fire are, which cannot meet in peace together, but a present noise and combat is raised from this conjunction.

[4.] Fourthly, When this is done, *we must endeavour to maintain and stick to our first disallowance.* A child of God, I know, in sinful yieldings of infirmity, may say as the apostle, 'What I do, I allow not,'—that is, [1.] What he then consents to, he did not allow at the first, till importunity prevailed. [2.] Though his affections incline to sin, yet his constant settled judgment is against it; and though he do it, he cannot say he approves it. Neither of these are the things I aim at; but this, that as the first motions of sins are disallowed, we should endeavour to keep at that, to stand our ground, to withhold the least after-delight or approbation. Not but that we must be forced sadly to acknowledge the real truth of what the apostle speaks in the place last cited, that these different principles, which of them soever carry the victory, do so impede one another, that when grace carries it, yet it cannot do the utmost it would or aims at; so that in the stoutest oppositions, there may be some secret degrees of allowance unavoidably; notwithstanding we must so manage our denial, that, if it were possible, we should not afford the smallest inclination toward it; the least, the better and nobler conquest.

CHAPTER XXV.

The fourth direction, of repelling a temptation by Scripture arguments.—Of several things implied in the direction.—The necessity of answering by Scripture arguments.—The excellency of the remedy.—How Scripture arguments are to be managed.

The next particular in Christ's answers to be observed by us is his citations of Scripture as an invincible reason against all the devil's temptations; he beats them all back with this weapon, 'It is written.' That this was written for our learning, and that, otherwise than for our instruction, he lay not under any necessity of using this method, hath been evidenced before, and it is a thing which all commentators[1] do take notice of. From this we have another direction for the right way and order of resisting temptations, which is,

Direct. 4. *That temptations are best repelled by arguments drawn from the word of God.*

For the explanation of this, it may be considered what is first *presupposed in this direction;* for when it is affirmed that we must answer by reasons from Scripture, this implies—

(1.) First, *That temptations are not to be opposed by groundless refusals.* It is no way safe to say we will not, because we will not, nor to insist upon our own bare resolve; for this would be wilfulness, rather than an obediential refusal, and unwarrantable self-confidence,

---

[1] Ideo Jesus omnes illas tentationes solis sacris Scripturis vicit, ut doceret nos sic pugnare et vincere.—*Cajetan, in loc; Jansenius,* &c.

rather than a humble wrestling. There are some, of whom it may be said, as the prophet once charged the Jews, Isa. xxii. 11, that when Satan comes up against them, they look in that day ' to the armour of the house of the forest,' they ' repair the wall,' and ' cast ditches for fortification ;' they prepare themselves to the battle ' in their own strength, but they look not unto the maker thereof,' to him who by his mighty power must fashion our hearts to resistance. The vanity of such undertakings is enough manifested in the event, for commonly such men go on in a bravado of resolution, but are so altered at the first appearance of the enemy, that they yield without a stroke. Who could be more confident than Peter that he would not deny his Master, whatever others did ? and yet how soon did his heart fail him. We may warrantably deny a sinful motion, without being explicit in our reason against it, especially in usual temptations, and when they thrust themselves into our minds at such times when our thoughts are charged with an attendance upon other duties, in which nevertheless the heart hath a secret and implicit regard to the command of God ; but in no case must we go down to the battle in the strength of a wilfulness, lest it go against us. And thus do they who, when they are reproved for some miscarriage, as of drinking, will presently with great confidence make engagements not to drink wine or strong drink, not to go into a tavern or alehouse, without any humble respect to duty, or the power of God for the conquest of the sin ; and accordingly we see that usually such promises and obligations do not hold ; either they wilfully break them, or they become sinfully witty to make evasions for the practice of sin, without the breach of the oath or promise.

(2.) Secondly, The direction supposeth that *we must deny the sin with the arguments of greatest strength and authority.* There were occasions and hints of other answers to these temptations that offered themselves in Christ's way, and yet he waives them all, fixing only upon Scripture reasons as the best and strongest. It is no Christian wisdom to urge those inferior considerations of shame, loss, inconvenience, &c. Some have no other reason betwixt them and sin, but *What will men say?* or *What will become of me?* But besides that, these would only be a train to bring on disputings, and that it is no way safe to venture our souls upon such defences, when better may be had ; for who will venture his life upon a staff when he may have a sword ? It is easy for Satan to break these bows, and to cut these spears in sunder. He can balance such reasons with equal reasons, and presently make us believe that we have as good reason to commit the sin as those urged by us for the not committing of it.

(3.) Thirdly, This direction of using Scripture reason doth clearly imply that *the force and power of Scripture is not in the words or characters, but in the mind and reason of it;* not that Scripture used as a charm or spell, as if the devil were afraid of the sound and words of it, can beat back the devil, but it is the authority of its command which works upon the mind the highest impressions of fear and care, and as a strong argument prevails with us to forbear. Notwithstanding the plainness and undeniableness of this inference, not only do ignorant men bless themselves against the devil by repeating some phrases or sentences of Scripture impertinently, and such as have no direct signification of the matter in hand betwixt Satan and them, as if the devil could not endure to hear the *paternoster*, or durst not come within the sound of the name Jehovah, but also papists—and of them such as might be supposed more considerate than to be carried by such conceits—have placed a virtue in the words and sounds of Scripture, and therefore do they command, though under some limitations and restrictions, the hanging of sentences of Scripture about the neck in scrolls, for the driving away of evil spirits, though in a clear contradiction to the reason which they give in the general against this course, which is this, that the ' power of Scripture is not in the figures and characters, but in the mind and understanding of it;' and therefore profits as ' pondered in the heart,' not as ' hung about the neck;' and upon as slender grounds do they place a more than ordinary virtue, in the angelical salutation, in the seven words upon the cross, in the triumphal title, ' Jesus of Nazareth, King of the Jews,' &c.[1] Such kind of oppositions are but a mock to Satan. We cannot think to ' bore the jaw of this leviathan with a thorn,' or to come to him with ' this bridle,' or to ' play with him as with a bird,' [Job xli. 2;] he durst allege scripture himself to Christ, and therefore it is not the phrase or sound that affrights him.

(4.) Fourthly, The direction doth imply *an argumentative, proper, and fit use of Scripture commands or promises.* We see Christ urged not any scripture indifferently, but he used fit words, and chose to himself select smooth stones out of this brook to sling against this spiritual Goliath. Every temptation had an answer that doth most fully and properly confront it. He regarded the main of the temptation, and suffered not himself to be diverted from that prosecution, by engaging himself in that which might have been perplexed and controversial, though he had a fit opportunity to reprove Satan for a dishonest craft of representing scripture in a sense of his own making, and so might have rejected the temptation of casting himself down, as leaning upon a false foundation, in that God did not promise in Ps. xci. to preserve any that should presumptuously expect a protection while they run out of God's ways; yet he waived this answer, and opposed the assault by a plain scripture which chargeth the contrary duty.

Secondly, Having seen what this direction doth imply in these things that are to be removed from the sense and intendment of it, I shall next, for ascertaining of the reality and importance of it, shew that temptations are to be resisted by Scripture arguments, by these two evidences:—

(1.) First, *God's recommending of the commands of Scripture for such a purpose:* Deut. vi. 6, ' These words which I command thee this day, shall be in thine heart: and thou shalt bind them for a sign upon thine hand, and they shall be as frontlets between thine eyes,' &c. Whether the latter part of the command is to be understood literally, as the Jews apprehended and practised, though some think

---

[1] Malleus Mallefic, part 2, quæs. 11, cap. 6. Virtus evangelii est in intellectu et non in figuris, ergo melius in corde posita prosunt, quam circa collum suspensa.—*Barthol., Sibilla Peregr.*, quæs. dec. 3, c. 9, q. 9.

otherwise, is not necessary to be asserted, seeing it is granted by all that they were to have the commands of the law so ready in their minds and memories, as if they had been written on their hands and upon their foreheads. That God designed this precept for the resistance of sin and temptation cannot be doubted, and that the advantage which might hence arise to them was not only the information of their minds, in point of sin and duty, is as unavoidable ; for that and more is intended by that part of the injunction, ' These words which I command thee, shall be in thine heart ;' but when ? Besides this information, which the knowledge of the law would afford them, and their humble compliance with it, as just and good, which would enable them to say, ' Thy law, O Lord, is within my heart ;' he further enjoins them the quick and ready remembrances of these laws, as if they were ' frontlets between their eyes, and signs on their hands.' It can signify no less than this, that in so doing they would be able to resist those motions by which Satan would seek to engage them to the violation of these commands. Neither need we to doubt hereof, when Christ himself hath so fully taught us, by his own example, in resisting temptations, the particular use of the remembrance of the law. In the New Testament the apostle is most express in this matter : Eph. vi. 17, 'Take the sword of the Spirit, which is the word of God,' where not only the use of Scripture commands and promises against Satan's suggestions is taught, but also the high avail and potency of this weapon in reference to its end. It is called a sword, and in that comparison it shews the active resistance which may be made by it ; and it is called, not a sword of flesh, for ' the weapons of our warfare are not carnal,' but ' of the Spirit,' to shew how mighty it is in repelling Satan.

(2.) Secondly, Another evidence of its usefulness is from *the success which the children of God have had in the right management of this weapon.* It is observable that while Christ answered by Scripture, Satan was silenced, and had not what to reply to the answer, but was forced to betake himself to a new temptation. David in many places highly magnifies the power of the command, in the success he had by it ; Ps. xvii. 4, he shews how available it was to preserve him in his common converse from the sinful snares laid before him, ' Concerning the works of men, by the word of thy lips I have kept me from the paths of the destroyer.' In Ps. xviii. 22, 23, he tells us that he was shielded from the sins of his inclination and love, which are hardest to prevent, by the opposition that he gave to the motions of them, in setting up the statutes of God against them ; ' All his judgments were before me, and I did not put away his statutes from me; I was also upright before him, and I kept myself from mine iniquity.' In Ps. cxix. 11, he puts his *probatum est* upon the head of this receipt, and speaks of it as his constant refuge, ' Thy word have I hid in my heart, that I might not sin against thee.' In Ps. xxxvii. 31, he speaks of it as a tried case of common experience to all the children of God, ' The law of God is in his heart, none of his steps shall slide.' I shall add to this the experience of Luther, when, saith he, in Epistle to the Galatians, ' the motions of the flesh do rage, the only remedy is, to take the sword of the Spirit, that is, the word of salvation, and to fight against them; of this I myself have good experience; I have suffered many great passions and vehement, but so soon as I laid hold of any place of Scripture, and stayed myself upon it, as upon an anchor, straightway my temptations did vanish away, which without the word had been impossible for me to endure, though but a little space, much less to overcome.'[1]

(3.) Thirdly, The excellency of this remedy will further appear from these following reasons:—

[1.] First, In that it is *a universal remedy*. There can be no temptation, either of seducement or of affrightment, but the Scripture will afford a suitable promise or command to repel it. So that it, like the flaming sword in the cherubim's hand at paradise, turns every way to guard the soul. I need not give instances of its power against sinful motions, having done that already, and of such temptations which war against the peace of the soul. I need but say this in the general, that as the nature of such temptations is to disguise God, and to render him dreadful to us, in the appearances of wrath and incompassionate implacableness—and this Luther sets down as a certain rule—so have we in Scripture such declarations of the mind and tender inclinations of God, and such full and clear promises to assure us of this, and those so adapted to every case, to every kind of hard thought which we might take up against him, that we may find enough in them to break all those malicious misrepresentations of Satan, and to keep up in our mind 'right thoughts of God;' which if we will adhere to, not suffering such promises to be wrested out of our hands, nor our hearts to give way to malignant impressions of cruelty, revenge, or unmercifulness in God, though we be cast into darkness, into the deeps, we may find some bottom on which to fix such beginnings of hope, as may at last grow up to a spirit of rejoicing in God our Saviour; and in this case, when our heart and Satan dictate to us that God is our enemy, we ought, as it were, to shut our eyes, to refuse to hearken to our own sense and feeling, and to follow the word; but if we once give up the word of promise, it is impossible the wound of conscience should be healed with any other consideration.

[2.] Secondly, *This remedy is comprehensive of most other remedies against Satan's temptations.* In Eph. vi., there are several other pieces of spiritual armour recommended, and yet there is such a manifest mutual respect betwixt this and those, that any may conclude that however they be distinguished in their names, yet they are conjoined in their operation. The girdle, so far as it relates to truth of judgment and opinion, depends on the word of Scripture for information; the shoes, which are defensive resolves to walk with a steady foot in the ways of religion, notwithstanding the hardships that attend holiness, are prepared to us, by the comfortable and peace-bringing promises of the gospel; the righteousness which is our breastplate, is only set

---

[1] Canon est, quod in omnibus tentationibus—alium fingimus Deum esse quàm sit, putamus enim Deum tunc non esse Deum sed horribile spectrum.—Tom. iv. f. 147. Reclamat (Sathan) in corde tuo, te non esse dignum ista promissione—est autem opus ardenti oratione, ne extorqueatur nobis promissio.—*Luther in Gen.*, cap. 21, f. 188. Cor dictat Deum adversum verbum Dei, sequi debeo non sensum meum.—*Idem*, tom. iv. f. 156. Nulla alia re potest sanari hoc vulnus conscientiæ, quam verbo Divinæ promissionis.—*Id.* tom. iv. f. 400.

forth and wrought out to us by the Scripture and its ordinances; faith which is our shield, and hope which is our helmet, they neither of them act without the warrant and encouragement of it; and whereas other parts of the armour are defensive, this of the Scripture is compared to the sword, which not only defends, but also offends and beats back the enemy. If the matter be seriously considered, all these parts of armour are but these two, the graces of the Spirit—faith, hope, patience in their sincere exercise, and the word of Scripture as the instrument by and in which they shew their operations; so that all this armour being put to use, in every particular temptation, it amounts to no more than this we are speaking of, viz., that sinful motions are to be rejected by a believing, sincerely resolute opposing of them, with arguments from the word of God.

[3.] Thirdly, Scripture, as it is the word and command of the great King of heaven, hath *a daunting and commanding authority over the consciences of men.* 'Where the word of a king is, there is power,' Eccles. viii. 4, and such is the majesty of a divine law, that it hath power over the consciences of those that are yet in their sins, and can wound, affright, constrain, and bind even the rebellious; so that so long as they retain any of their natural impressions of a divine power, they have some awe for his commands, which may be seen and argued, where it would be least expected, from the enragement of the hearts of sinners, when 'sin by the commandment,' accidentally, 'becomes exceeding sinful,' Rom. vii. 13, 14. For as that outrageous fierceness doth arise from the contrariety that is betwixt a carnal heart and a spiritual law; so that contrariety would never work if the authority of that law, having a power to restrain, and give check to the corruption of the heart, were not some way owned by the conscience; for where no countermanding law is owned, there can be no irritating, provoking restraint. This it can do to the vilest of men; but of how much more power may we imagine the word to be with good men, whose hearts tremble at the word, when they 'bind the law upon their heart,' and charge their consciences with it? It is surely 'quick and powerful, sharper than a two-edged sword,' [Heb. iv. 12;] nor doth it only, by unlovely affrightments, terrify them from sin, but by commanding duty make the heart in love with it, so that it becomes a delightful satisfaction to be preserved from the snare.[1]

[4.] Fourthly, There is no argument that can be used against temptations that can be more *afflictively discouraging to Satan.* Satan, as bad as he is, cannot but believe those truths which he knows, and he knows that there are many truths in Scripture which respect him, as threatenings of punishment and divine vengeance; he believes these things and trembles, James ii. 19. His unavoidable knowledge or remembrance of these things begets horror in him, he cannot but be under a dread of these truths. What can be supposed so to wound him as the bringing these things to memory, by urging the command of God against him? Dr Arrowsmith [2] gives two instances of this kind, the one of Christopher Haas in Sweedland—from the epistle

---

[1] Quam suave mihi subitò factum est carere suavitatibus nugarum, et quas amittere metus fuerat, jam demittere gaudium erat.—*Aug. Confes.*, lib. ix. cap. 1.

[2] Tact. Sacr., lib. i. cap. 3, sec. 6.

dedicatory to the five tomes of Brentius's works—the other of Daniel Cramer, rector of a school at Stettin in Germany; on both which the devil made a bold attempt in a personal appearance; from the first, demanding a catalogue of his sins in writing; from the other, demanding a paper in which one of the students had obliged himself to Satan's service; they both referred him to that text of Gen. iii. 15, 'The seed of the woman shall bruise the head of the serpent.' And this was retorted upon him with such a strong exercise of faith, that he presently desisted the suit and vanished.

[5.] Fifthly, *This weapon cannot easily be wrested out of our hands.* When we urge a divine prohibition against a temptation, what can he say in answer? he cannot deny it to be the word of God, or to be true, or that we are not obliged to it. He made none of these returns to Christ, but, by his silence, owned that it was God's holy command obliging us to duty. Neither dares he stand upon these exceptions to us, except he find our faith inclined to waver, or our minds weak and wounded by inward troubles of spirit; and when he puts on a boldness to deny Scripture to be the word of God, or that it signifies God's real intendments in his threatening—for by begetting unbelief of the truth of Scripture, and by suggesting hopes of escape and pardon, notwithstanding the violation of the commands of it, he wrests, when he doth prevail, this weapon out of our hands—yet he is forced to fetch a compass, and by many previous insinuations to make his way to these atheistical assertions. Thus he did with Eve, first, finding her a little inclinable, he dropped in privily something that might argue the improbability of the threatened penalty, and then at last positively denied it. But now if we hold to this, that 'the command is true and holy, and just and good,' he cannot wrest our plea from us.

[6.] Sixthly, *Nothing doth more undermine temptations, by rendering the reasons and motives thereof vain and empty, than doth the contrary commands of Scripture.* Temptation hath always some enticement of pleasure or profit, and these only seem to be taking or reasonable, while we consider not the word of God, as rotten wood or fish shine only in the dark; but when we are urged with sinful pleasures, how mean, base, dangerous, and unlovely be they, when the command to the contrary gives information that they are snares and lead to death, or the provocation of the Almighty.

[7.] Seventhly, *While we resist with Scripture arguments, we engage God, whose command we would stand by, to go down to the battle with us.* We 'lay hold upon his strength,' and put obligations upon him to take us out of the snare, and to deliver us from him who is 'too strong' for us.

(4.) Fourthly, It remains that, in a word, I shew *how the commands or arguments of Scripture are to be used in resisting Satan,* which is thus, When you have any sinful thought cast into your mind, presently reject the offer, by charging your heart with duty, from some opposite command; as if you be urged to acts of uncleanness, presently refuse, thus; No, I must not, God hath commanded the contrary, he hath said, 'Thou shalt not commit adultery.' If a covetous thought arise, reject it with this, God hath said, 'Thou shalt not covet.' If you be tempted to please the flesh, and follow vain delights, answer it with this, 'If ye live after the flesh, ye shall die;' and the like must be done in other temptations.

Obj. Some may perhaps think that this is easy work and quickly done, and that it seems to attribute a virtue and power to the words of Scripture, as if Satan were charmed by the language or phrase.

Ans. However at the first view this may seem easy, yet he that shall consider how much exercise of grace goes necessarily to the right use of Scripture opposition, shall not see cause to slight it as common, nor yet to think that any virtue is attributed to the words. For,

[1.] First, The Scripture here is only recommended *as a fit instrument, and no further or higher praise is given.* Though therefore we may attribute the whole of the conquest to the instrument alone, yet this hinders not, but that as an instrument peculiarly fitted for these ends, we may commend it above all other instruments, as we may justly commend bread for nourishing above a stone, and expect more from it than from a chip; so have we reason to expect more by the use of Scripture against Satan, than from other means of defence which God hath not set up for that service.

[2.] Secondly, *It is a concomitancy of divine power and aid that conquers for us.* The instrument is Scripture, but the power by which it works is from God.

[3.] Thirdly, *Neither is it any careless formal use of Scripture expressions that will give encouragement for expectation of a divine concurrence;* but the use of Scripture in this business implies an exercise of all graces, for it is an urging of Scripture under a fourfold consideration.

First, As being certainly persuaded of their truth, and fully keeping to that belief.

Secondly, As being thankfully apprehensive of the holiness, goodness, and profitableness of the commands, and cheerfully adhering to them as the only way and means to bring us to union with Christ, and to preserve us in it.

Thirdly, As being highly and indispensably obliged by them to perform the duty commanded therein, and to avoid the sins forbidden.

Fourthly, All this in a humble expectation of a divine help, according to the promise of God. Now he that can plead the command or promise against a temptation in this manner, doth not do an ordinary work, neither will he ascribe the success to the words and phrase of Scripture.

Some may, peradventure, wonder why Christ, by his example, had not recommended prayer, seeing it is of such unquestionable use in our undertakings against Satan. But that inquiry may be fully satisfied, if it be considered that Christ did peculiarly prepare himself to this encounter by 'solemn fasting,' ver. 2, which doth include praying; for such complicated duties are often denominated by that part which is extraordinary, and usually in Scripture a fast is only mentioned where prayer is chiefly intended. That this fast of Christ related to the temptation, and that also as a means of preservation, hath been spoken of in its place; it remains only that from hence I add a fifth direction.

CHAPTER XXVI.

The fifth direction, of prayer, and of the seriousness required of those that expect the advantage of prayer.—Of God's hearing prayer while the temptation is continued.—Of some that are troubled more, while they pray more.

Direct. 5. *That in all our endeavours of resistance, frequent and earnest prayers are not to be neglected.*

This is so frequently recommended, and so fully handled by most authors, that I shall refer you to such authors as particularly treat of it; noting only that the apostle, in Eph. vi. 18, when he recommends it to us in these words, 'Praying always with all prayer and supplication in the Spirit, and watching thereunto with all perseverance, and supplication for all saints,' he doth mind us that he that expects the advantage of that duty must be peculiarly fitted, and seriously diligent in that work. For,

(1.) First, *He must have a praying frame of heart;* he must 'pray always,' or, as the apostle elsewhere, he must 'pray continually.' Not as if this duty must swallow up all the rest, and that a Christian had no other services to attend than prayer, but that he must be on a design to wrestle with God by prayer; and this must be constantly carried on, though the acts of prayer be intermitted; and besides that, in such cases, he may keep his usual stated times for that duty, he must have his heart so much upon his design, that every occasion or offer of temptation will presently put him upon the duty; nay, he must, in respect of the frequent intercourse of his heart with God in frequent ejaculations and breathings of soul, be as a man wholly resolved into that duty, as Paul was at his first conversion, who, as that expression 'behold he prays' [Acts ix. 11] doth intimate, seems to have been all prayer, and wholly taken up with that duty.

(2.) Secondly, *He must pray in the spirit,* his soul must be truly in the duty. A more than ordinary earnestness is necessary at solemn times, he must put out all his strength, he must cry mightily, and with his whole heart.

(3.) Thirdly, When his spirit grows dull, *he must reinforce it,* watch his heart he must; and if it be needful to quicken it up, he must add fasting or meditation, or whatever other means may be helpful.

(4.) Fourthly, In this course *he must continue without giving off the duty.* Though God behave himself as if he minded not his cry, or took no notice of his hazard, yet without weariness must our supplications follow him. It must be continued with 'all perseverance.'

(5.) Fifthly, *The heart that undertakes this must not be so narrow as to be centred upon his own concern only.* When he is melted into a spirit of meekness and compassion for others, and is not so solicitous for peace or ease, that he could hug himself in his private enjoyment without concerning himself to tender and help those that are in the same dangers, when his supplications are for 'all saints' as well as for himself, then may he expect to receive an olive branch of peace from heaven in the return of his prayer.

Obj. It is often objected by such, that they pray but are not heard; and that temptations continue, notwithstanding many cries and wrestlings.

Ans. [1.] First, *It is a great mistake to think that prayers are not heard or do not prevail, because the temptation is not quite removed.* Prayers may be acceptable to God, and recorded among his remembrances, where the temptation, for exercise and other holy ends, may be continued.

[2.] Secondly, *What God hath promised to such prayer, he fails not to make good.* He hath not promised to exempt us from temptation, but from the power and prevalency of it. If 'his grace be sufficient for us,' 2 Cor. xii. 9, in the meantime, it is an answer as good as Paul got when he was importunate; 'If together with the temptation he gives an issue, that we may be able to bear it,' 1 Cor. x. 13, there is his faithfulness in keeping promise. He nowhere promised that Satan should not tempt, but that he should not prevail. While we can hold up our hands in the mount to God, and our praying frame will ascertain us of this; 'for a man is never overcome by a temptation so long as he can pray against it;' for so long he delights not in it so long he consents not, and till he do consent Satan cannot prevail. Prayer will either make the temptation give way, or the temptation will make prayer give way; but so long as we hold out with earnestness, the temptation cannot prevail.

Obj. Some further object, that the more they pray they are the worse, and more infested by Satan than they were before they undertook that course.

Ans. 1. *It may be they may have more trouble from Satan.* David 'thought on God, and his trouble was increased,' [Ps. xxxix. 3,] and no wonder. Satan's spite and fury puts him upon giving greatest molestations to those of whom he despairs to subdue.

Ans. 2. Secondly, But though they may be more troubled, *yet they may be furthest from conquest.*[1] These disquiets are like the trouble of the working of physic, which at first taking may make a man more sick, and yet bring him nearer to a state of health and strength; fear not then, faint not, resist faithfully, and to the utmost, and ' God shall bruise Satan under thy feet shortly,' [Rom. xvi. 20.]

[1] That is, from being conquered.—G.

FINIS.

INDEXES, &c.

I.—TEXTS ILLUSTRATED.

	CHAP.	VER.	PAGE		CHAP.	VER.	PAGE		CHAP.	VER.	PAGE
Genesis	2.	23	21	Mat.	4.	6	382, seq	Ephes.	4.	27	12
,,	3.	1	22	,,	4.	7	402. seq	,,	6.	12	20
,,	4.	11-16	288	,,	4.	8	415, seq	Philip.	4.	7	210
,,	4.	26	431, 432	,,	4.	9	430, seq	Col.	1.	16	15, 16
,,	10.	4	102	,,	6.	24	441	,,	2.	8	203
,,	49.	17	14	Luke	11.	24	91, seq. 97	1 Thes.	4.	16	20
Exodus	22.	18	27	John	2.	24. 25	24	2 Thes.	2.	9-11	142
Deut.	6.	16	382	,,	8.	54	14	1 Tim.	1.	20	17
,,	8.	3	356	,,	12.	24	17	,,	6.	20	162
,,	18.	10	27, 28	,,	16.		17	2 Tim.	2.	16	17
,,	23.	18	137	Romans	1.	28	143	,,	2.	26	56
Judges	21.	18, 20	78	,,	3.	7, 8	116	Heb.	3.	13	53
1 Kings	20.	33	377	,,	14.	23	296	,,	6.	4	301
Job	11.	12	3	,,	15.	19	142	,,	10.	2	255
Psalms	37.	34	364	,,	16.	18	162	,,	10.	26	301
,,	91.	11, 12	402, seq	1 Cor.	4.	13	40	,,	11.	37	440
Proverbs	3.	23	402	,,	11.	29	297	James	1.	14	54
Isaiah	41.	23	25	2 Cor.	2.	11	55	,,	1.	22, 29	55
Jerem.	18.	9	23	,,	4.	4	62	,,	4.	4	441
Ezekiel	33.	11	293	,,	11.	3	112	1 Peter	5.	8	8, seq
Daniel	10.	13	20	,,	12.	7	238	2 Peter	3.	16	411, 412
Malachi	3.	1	381	,,	13.	5	256	1 John	3.	8	13
Matthew	4.	1-11	313, seq	Gal.	1.	16	111	,,	3.	12	12
,,	4.	1	313-328	,,	5.	1, 2	200	,,	5.	16	299
,,	4.	2	328-336	,,	5.	20, 21	28	Jude		9	19, 55
,,	4.	3	337-341	,,	6.	1	320	Rev.	2.	24	162
,,	4.	4	341, seq	Ephes.	3.	10	23	,,	11.	15	17
,,	4.	5	376-382	,,	4.	17	144	,,	12.	12	11

II.—GENERAL MATTERS.

Abhorrency, 457, 458.
Absconded, 163.
Accusations by Satan, 231, 232; direful, 428.
Acontius, 169, 193, 207.
Acosta, 198.
Acquirements, 152.
Actions, of wonder and astonishment, by Satan, 30; unreasonableness of some, 68; mistake of, 188, 189; Satan uses Scripture to promote sinful, 408.
Activity in duty, 212.
Adam, Melchior, 135, 147.
Additions, 124.
Admiration, 43.
Adonis, 180.
Adoption, Satan seeks to weaken, 374; are all to maintain their? 375.
Adrianus, 178.
Advantage pursued by Satan, 45, 46, 251, 258, 259, 345, 346.
Adventurousness, rash, 320.
Adversary, Satan an—malice, enmity, power, cruelty, diligence. 10.
Æsop, 181.
Ætius Spartianus, 178.
Ætna, 173.
Affections, Satan uses, 67.

Afflicted, reasons for Satan's tempting the, 335, 336.
Afflictions, 222. 223, 273, 274, 335, 336, 427.
Affright, Satan seeks not to, 86, 87.
Affrightments, 238, 240; grievous, 249, 427.
Afraid, be not of, Goliath, 311.
Agatocles, 40.
Aggravations, of sin, 83, 278, 279; unjust, of sins of God's children, 299, 300.
Aims, Satan, various, in a single temptation, 353.
Alacrity, in duty, 212.
Alexander, 26, 68.
Alexander, (heretic,) 204.
Allegorical reflections, 163.
Allurement, 399.
Alterations, be jealous of, in worship, 433.
Alvarez, 174.
Alypius, 65.
Amazement, 303.
Ambrose, 446.
Americans, 17, 44.
Ames, or Amesius, 10, 57, 255, 288, 293, 384, 449, 456.
Androgeus. 39.
Anger of Satan, 12, 206; angry disposition, 220.

Angel, Satan an, power of, 14, 15; angels, strength of, *ib.*; Sadducees, opinions on, 49, 50.
Anguish and horror of Satan, 13.
Annoyance, temptation an, 456.
Answers, of Christ to Satan, 445, *seq.*; fit and pertinent, 445; best from Scripture, 462, *seq.*
Antichrist, 38.
Antiochus, 109.
Antony, M., 70.
Antony of Padua, 180.
Apion, 109, 110.
Apish imitation of divine things, 198.
Apochryphal adjections, 179.
Apollonius, 173.
Apollonius Tyanæus, 419.
Apostasy of Satan, 12.
Apostolici, 170.
Apparitions, 33.
Appearances, remarkable, of God, 279
Applause, popular, 401.
Apprehensions, against God, 303.
Aptitude in the world to tempt, 441.
Aquinas, 31.
Arguings, fallacious, 113, 114; partial, 452.
Arguments, deny sin with strongest, 463; of Satan, 295, 296.
Arianism, 131.
Aristotle, 27, 179.
Arius, 204.
Armour, management of spiritual, 415.
Arrowsmith, 19, 102, 240, 327, 425, 467.
Arrogancy, 375; of Satan against God, how shewn, 418, *seq.*
Art, of Satan in setting forth temptations, lies in four things, 421, 422.
Arthington, 146.
Askew, Ann, 455.
Assaults, of saints, by Satan, 18.
Assays, 247.
Assertions, bold, 167.
Aspersions, slanderous, 188.
Atheists, 48; principles of, put out light, 82; thoughts, 242; persons troubled with atheistical thoughts, 243.
Authority of Satan, 17; nature of, explained, 17, 18; over persons and things, *ib.*; efficacy of, 18, 19.
Augustine, 15, 19, 22, 32, 38, 48, 52, 65, 117, 129, 147, 177, 179, 180, 201, 202, 324, 328, 393, 394, 395, 403, 418, 461, 468.
Averrhoes, 48.
Avicenna, 30.
Awe of sin, 93, 94.

Baal-zebub, 36.
Bad end, evident, 357.
Barlow, 53.
'Barricades' of Satan, 98.
Baxter, 29, 146, 178, 181.
Bayne, 20, 220, 425.
Belief, facile, 154.
Bellona, 39.
Benedict, St, 174.
Bernard, 328, 403.
'Beside,' 195.
Best, of God's children hardly escape under temptation of distrust, 368.
Beza, 22, 56, 373.
Bias, 151; to error rather than truth, 151, 152; by bodily temper, 152.
Bisnagar, 39.
Blasphemous thoughts congenial to Satan; (1.) from his nature, 244; (2.) practice, 245; (3.) professed design, *ib.*; (4.) sad experience, *ib.*; injections, 304, 424, 425; how Satan works to get man to, 425; violent injections of, 426; sudden glances of, imagination, 427; reasons of this temptation, 427, *seq.*; advice to those tempted by, 429, 430.
Blessings, universal, 366.
Blinds, Satan, 62, 63; by stirring up lust, proved, 68, *seq.*; how lust, 70, 71.
Bochart, 21.
Bodies, 66; afflicted by mind, 218; in co-partnership of sorrow, 309, 310; Satan permitted to have power over, 378.
Bodin, 43.
Bœhmen, 166, 167.
Boldness heroic, a snare to self-murder, 392.
Bolsecus, 187.
Boniface, Pope, 57, 58, 175.
Boyle, 394.
Bretterge, Mrs, 305, 309.
Bribes, of Satan, 205.
Bridget, St, 173.
Broughton, 59.
Bucholcer, 191.
Burden of injections by Satan, 241.
Burton, 66.
Business, Satan's, to tempt, ours to resist, 339; and how, 339, 340.

Cain, 288, 289.
Cajetan, 33, 462.
Calisthenes, 68.
Calovius, 132.
Calumnies, 186.
Calvin, 16, 20, 32, 50, 58, 65, 142, 167, 187, 210, 337.
Campian, 164.
Camus, 181.
Capel, 57, 58, 82, 326, 390, 392, 396, 428, 429, 449.
Cappellus, 165.
Cardan, 38.
Care, distressed, cease all, 310.
Carthaginians, 39.
Caryl, 57, 59, 425.
'Catching away' the word, 87, 88; Satan lies at 'catch,' 243.
Cathari, 170.
Cato, 393.
'Catoche,' 212.
Causes, Satan knows, of things, 25; second, 365.
Caution, great against Satan, 417.
Cedrenus, 178.
Celestine, v.. 175.
Chambers, 294.
Chamier, 19, 20, 181.
Change, Satan blinds by, a temptation, 77, 95, 96; of nature of temptation, 369.
Cheats, 29.
Chemnitius, 203, 373.
Children, 151.
Chokes, Satan, the word, 88.
Cicero, 393.
Clarke, 35, 121.
Cleombrotus, 393.
Climacus, 426.
Coccius, 189.
Collinges, 215.
Comforts, inward, extinguished, 228, 229; disturbances, scatter thoughts of, 229; stock of, wastes, 229; outward, little, 443.
Company, evil, 67.
'Composition,' Satan gives a, in religious duty, 95.

GENERAL INDEX.

Complainings, 373.
Complies, Satan, 78; compliance with parties, 199, 200; though not yet, opens way to sins, 428.
Confederacies and contrivances, 179.
Consent, 'threaped,' 80.
'Concealing,' 70; concealment of wounds, 307; Satan tempts by, 421, 422.
Conclusions, direful, 334.
Condition, Satan takes advantage of our, in temptation, 346, 347.
Confident, warning from temptations, to the over, 325.
Confronting of Almighty by Satan, 418.
Conscience, wounded, 61; in man, 62; scared, 94; molested, 231, 232; scrupulosity of, 253; doubting, 255; evil, 255, 256; denying, 257; how distinguish between terrors of, and melancholy, 292; total distress of, 292, 293; terrors of, 391.
Consent, by silence, 460.
Consolation, for those troubled by blasphemy, 428.
Contrary commands of Scripture to temptations, 468.
Contrasts, between Christ and Satan, 209.
Coveting, 221.
Contempt, 221; of religion, 334; Satan seeks to bring Scripture under, 410.
'Contemplative' heads, 243.
Contentions and disputes, 149.
Continuance, troubles of long, 295; temptations of long, 426.
Contrivances, 87; curious, 183.
'Conversation,' careful, 437.
Conversion, time of, temptation, 47; easy, 260; conscience wounded, before and after, by God, 261, 262; false notions concerning, 270, 271; not always with terror, 270; nor able to tell exact time, ib.; nor always accompanied with gifts of prayer, ib.
Coppinger, 139.
Corinthian, church, 128.
Corrupted, duties worst of all, 103; doctrines lead to corrupt practices, 137; ingenuous, society of those who are, 190; Satan seeks to corrupt God's worship, 431, 432; reasons, 432, seq.
Corruption stirred, 453.
Cortez, 41.
Courage, commanded, 448; what spiritual, is, 449.
'Courses' of sinners, 437.
'Crack,' 169.
Craft, (see Subtlety.)
Cramer, 467.
Credulous, 286.
Cross, Satan tempts by things, to our temper, why, 60.
Croy, de, 202.
Cruelty of Satan, 36-44.
Curiosity, adventurous, 156, 157, 451, 452.
Curse, of Satan, 12.
Curtius, Q., 68.
Custom, power of, 193, 194; force of, 393.
Cyprian, 373.

Dædalus, 179.
'Damnation' misapplied, 296.
Damocles, 444.
Darkness, Satan ruler of, 17.
Daunting, power of Scripture, 467.
David, temptations of, 56, 84.
Debauchery, atheistical, 157.
Deceits, 58; in use of Scripture, 410.

Deceptions, 31; all the devil's qualifications for 'deceit,' 52, 53.
Degrees, of misery, 310.
Delay, 459.
'Deliberate' determinations, 81, 82.
Deliberating, 452.
Deluded, 144.
Demons, 201.
Demoniacs, diseases, 50; Mede on, 51.
Demonstrated, things, 153.
Demurs and delays, 89.
Denials, not disputing, in temptation, 451, seq.; best, and why, 459, seq.
Departure, feigning, 91.
Dervises, 171.
Descartes, 64.
Designs, large, of Satan, 582; unfaithful, of Satan in use of Scripture, 409; Christ's temptations permitted by design, 445.
Desires, 54; enlarge not, 443.
Despague, 42, 148, 151, 405, 422.
Despair, 217; is presumptuous, 386.
Devices, 23.
Devil, though a 'spirit,' a proper subject of sin, 10, 11; wickedness of, capable of increase, 11; has great occasions for malice, ib.; fall of, 11, 12; power of, as a, 16, 17; meaning of, as a word, 22; denial of existence of, 48.
Devils, large number of, 19; order among, 19, 20; reality of existence of, argued, 51, 52 believed in by the heathen, 52.
'Devotional,' 168.
Diana, 39.
Diascorides, 28.
Dickson, 141, 219, 242, 255, 390, 428.
Differences, in God's children, 114.
Dignity of God's children, a snare by Satan, 114.
Diligence, of Satan, 45; instances of, 45, seq.
Diodati, 50.
Dionysius, 19.
Directly and indirectly, Satan blinds, 73, seq.
Disadvantage, fall of saints special, 315.
Disappointment of Satan certain, 14.
Discomposures of soul, 219; effects of, 229 devil works on, 230; much sin in, ib.; obstruct duties, 230, 231; devil accuses by, 231.
Discontents, 391.
Discouragements, 106; Satan not easily discouraged, 376, 377; Scripture, afflicting discouragement to Satan, 467, 468.
Discovery, Satan's contrivances to hinder, 87; full of notions, and ways of, 165.
Disguises, the world's, 442.
Dispensation, divine, of spiritual sadness, 259, 260.
Disputes, 206, 207.
Disputings, kinds of, 451, seq.; actual, 452; when we may, a temptation, 453; when not, 454, seq.; a better way than, 457; reasons why not, with Satan, 457, seq.
Disquiet, Satan sometimes seeks only to, 61; disquiets, 184; advantages to Satan by, 211.
Distance between God and man by sin, Satan uses, 98.
Distempers, bodily, 427.
Distinctions, 78; of the learned, show ignorance, 150.
Dismission of thought, 78.
Distractions in holy seasons, 46, 47, 79, 120; before religious services, 123; Satan raises, 211; unfits for duty, 212.

GENERAL INDEX. 475

Distresses, spiritual, 287; complicated, *ib.*; have a further end, *ib.*; consent of the party, 287, 288; higher degree, 288; not all from melancholy, shewn, 290, 291; God's deserting, *ib.*; weight of, 307.
Distrust, 335, 361; of providence, passes to, of Sonship, 367.
Disturbances, outward, 121, 122, 224; in Satan's power, 233.
Diverting of reason, 77.
Divisions, 134, 135.
Doctrine, false, in gorgeous attire, 195; erroneous, 408.
Dominicus, 179.
Domineer, Satan doth tyrannically, 249.
Dominis de, 158.
Dreams, 404.
Dury, John, 164.
Duty, burden of, 106, 107; want of success in, 107, 108; dislike of, 109; unnecessariness of, 115; suspending, 116, 117; vitiated, 123, 124; hindered, 212; difficult, 214; unfruitful, *ib.*; sinful, *ib.*
Dyke, 75.

Earnestness, take off, 117.'
Ease, wrongly sought, 217.
Ecstasies, 404.
Effects, ascribed to wrong causes, 180.
Effeminacy, 221.
Egyptians, 162, 163.
Election, terrors about, 246, 247; suspicions of non-election, 250.
Ellis, 164.
Empedocles, 173.
End, and means, 116.
Endeavours, constant course of Satan's, 129.
Endeavours, 303.
Endor, witch of, 34.
Ends, of things, used to blind, 74; base, 119.
Enemies and rebels, Satan pursues men as, 100.
Enemy, ' sword of an,' 305.
Engines by which Satan works : sophistry, 266; Scripture abused, 267, 268; false marks a sign of unregeneracy, 269-271; misrepresentation of God, 271, *seq.*; comparisons with holy lives of others, 280; lessens graces of saints, *ib.*; fear, 285, *seq.*
England, New, appearances of Satan in, 44; errors in, 160.
Enigmatical speaking of Satan, 26.
Enmity to God, 441, 442.
Enmity of Satan, 12, 13.
Ensnaring, ways of Satan, 425.
Entanglements, 71, 72.
Entice, 62.
Enticing to temptation, 454.
Entrance on special service, a time of temptation, 313, 314.
Envious disposition, 220.
Epiphanius, 129, 135.
Equality and inequality of privilege and duty, 115.
Error, 127; Satan, great contriver of, *ib.*; reasons of Satan in, 130; is sinful, 130, 131; of an increasing nature, 131; a plague, *ib.*; errorists, 131, 132; leads to schisms, &c., 132, 133; hinders reformation, 133, 134; fixes atheism, 135, 136; obstructs graces, 139; punishment it brings, 140; vileness of some, 144, 145; unusual actions for, 145, 146; blind even the wise, 146; suddenness of prevalency, *ib.*; fury in spreading, *ib.*; from learned men, 149; approbation given to, 154; arguments for, 158; countenance of Scripture for, 158, 159; foundation of, laid near truth, 160; promoted by excellence of those holding, 168; captain and ringleader in, 169; the ease and peace it brings, 183; proffers of peace from, 184; insensible procedure of, 190; gradual fixing, 191; garb of, 195; avoidance of one for another, 204; puts on truth's clothes, 207; Satan uses Scripture to promote, 408.
Escape, possibility of, from penalty, 76.
Eusebius, 129, 145, 198, 202, 203.
Eve, temptation of, 56, 57, 82.
Evil company, 67.
Example, evil, 67.
Excess, 124, 125.
Exchange, a temptation, 95, 96; secret, 96.
Execrations, against self, 216, 217.
Experience of Satan, 24.
Extenuations of sin, 76.
External things, 152.
Extreme, Satan runs from the, and why, 383.
Extremes, 73.

Fables, lying, 181; instances, *ib.*; traditionary, 197.
Failure of God's children under temptation of distrust, 368.
Faith, false notions of nature of, 270; weakened, 371.
False citation of Scripture, 411.
Familists, 160.
Fancy, fancies, 31, 123; Satan works on, 422.
Fascination, 140, 141, 442.
Fashion, sins out of, 96.
Fast of Christ, 328, *seq.*; why, 329, *seq.*
Favour, special, a time of temptation, 314.
Favourable, too, opinion of self, 285.
Fears, suspicious, 246; impressions of, 251, 252; come by fits, 252, 253; return, 253; add to the weight of other troubles, *ib.*; not always accompanying conversion, 270; an engine of temptation, 285; increase of, 304; prepare for Satan's most dismal suggestions, 365; make all seem the sword of an enemy, *ib.*; no advice eases, 305, 306; lead to conclusions of misery, 306; threefold, 447, 448; what, forbidden, 448, *seq.*
Februation, 43.
Feigning departure, 91.
Fenner, 67, 73.
' Finishing' of sin, 83, *seq.*
First temptation, Christ's, 346, *seq.*
Fixes, Satan, thoughts, 237.
Follows, Satan, with a high hand, 99.
Food of the soul, Satan robs of, 101.
Foretell, Satan can, 26.
' Formal' use of defences, Satan allows, and why, 380, *seq.*
Forsake, three ways Satan seems to, designs, 91, *seq.*
' Forty days,' 329, 330.
Foxe, 308, 440.
Frances, St, 174.
Fratricelli, 166.
Friends, Satan tempts by—examples, 330.
Fruition of peace, 184.
Fuel, Satan seeks his own, 13; of lust, 441.
Fuller, 28, 406.
Funckius, 408.
Furious fits, 225; Bible examples, 225, 226.
Future, whether Satan knows the, 25

Galen, 48.
Game, after-, 242.
Garnet, 180.
Gellius, 182.
Gerson, 238, 426, 430.
Gilpin, John, 146, 395.
Glances, transient, 251.
Glanvil, 29, 30.
Glauber, 164.
Gnostics, 166.'
God, the source of all happiness, 3, 4; quarrelled, 217 ; misrepresentation of God's nature, 272; providence, 272-274; in the works of his Spirit, 274, 275; misrepresented as a tyrant, 298 ; as designing men's ruin, 299.
Gods, false, 201.
Godwyn, 28, 40, 198.
'Goeth out,' not 'cast out,' 97.
Gomesius, 164.
Good, seeming, 351, 352; hindrance of greater, 352.
Goodwin, (misspelled Godwin,) 24, 57, 61, 62, 261, 456.
'Gospels,' counterfeit, 189.
Grace, restraining, 93; growth of, not always visible, 271 ; mistaken signs of, *ib.* ; Satan lessens, of saints, 280, *seq.* ; tempts in relation to, 281, *seq.* ; extraordinaries of, *ib.* special assistances, *ib.*; eminencies, *ib.*; Satan tempts when, is weakest, 284, 2 5; hinders not temptation, and why, 323, *seq*.
Gradual, Satan in temptations, 341, 342; reasons, 342.
'Great' temptation, what, 342; external, complex, perplexing, *ib.*; proceeded on advantages, greater power of Satan, to abominations, professed benefits, provoking, engagement of all natural powers, some warranted as duty, 343.
Greenham, 95, 97, 115, 116, 461.
Gregory, 338, 440.
Gregory the Great, 202.
Grief fixed, contentment in, 215, 216.
Grievous sins, 295.
Grotius, 442.
Guessing of Satan, 24.

Haas, 467.
Habits, vicious, 152.
'Habituated' sin, 24, 453, 454.
Hacket, 139.
Han, 29.
Hakluyt, 178.
Happiness, impatient desire of, 393.
Harvey, 187.
Haste in sinning, 81.
Hatred against Satan, 122.]
Hatred of Satan, 12.
Hazard, 46 ; to life by some lusts, 69 ; and disadvantage by abuse of services, 103 ; of duties, 110, 111 ; ways of religion said to be of intolerable, 317 ; ways of, 394, 395.
Heart, the stage of all action, 3, 4 ; God and Satan meet in, 4 ; the 'deceits' of, point to Satan, 53; enticed, 62 ; sottish, 78, 79 ; prepared for venomous impressions, 215 ; hard and impenitent, 302, 303 ; Satan seeks to withdraw, from God and to enslave to sin, shewn, 433, 434 ; prevails, 434, 435 ; not right with God, 435.
Heathen, 153.
Heightening of duty, 115 ; of jealousies and fears against Satan, 123 ; of the sins of the tempted, 318, 409.

Heightens, Satan, grace, 280, 283.
Hell, 9.
Helmont, 30.
Hephæstion, 68.
Heresies, 412.
Heylin, 180, 182, 187, 428.
Hiding, necessity of, duty, 113.
Hindrances, external, 104.
Hobbs, 29, 50, 337, 416.
Hobson, Paul, 176.
Honeywood, 375.
Honour, God's, at stake, 366.
Hooper, 455.
Hope, 46 ; give not readily up, 375.
Hopelessness of prevailing, 80.
Horace, 109, 173, 401.
Huffing=hoving, or heaving, or swelling, 77
Humility, excess of, 108, 109.
Humours, 224.
Hunger of Christ, 347.
Hunting of his prey, by Satan, 45.
Hypocrites are presumptuous, 386 ; varnish on, 410, 411.

Ignorance variously shewn, 147, *seq.*; conversion of the ignorant, results, 260.
Ignorant devout, humbled by Satan, 247, 248.
'Imaginary,' 143.
Imagination, Satan's use of, 65, 66, 250.
Imitations of divine services and Bible incidents, 102, 198, 419 ; Satan imitates God by pretence of teaching, 403.
Impetuosity, 426.
Impressions, dismal, of Satan, 305.
Importunity, 79 ; impudent, 243, 244.
Impotent, mind rendered, 229.
Impulses, 406.
Incas, 198.
Incessant, Satan in temptation, 331 ; things relating to such, 331, 332; encouragement under, 332.
Inclinations, 66, 152, 155.
Indicia, 25.
Indignation of Satan, 12.
Indisposition of body, 104, 105 ; of soul, 105.
Indirect courses, 335.
Infectious, temptations, 459.
Infirmity, 75, 76, 188.
'Ingenuousness,' 48 ; submissive, 120 ; feigned, 275.
Injects, Satan's temptations, 61; impetuousness of, 122 ; injections of terror, 238 ; impetuous, 239; incessant, *ib.*; odious, 239, 240 ; abhorrency, 240 ; difference between atheistical injections and temptations, 242 ; of abominable sin, 250, 251.
Injury, 222.
Insight, Satan has deep, 26.
Insolency, 418.
'Inspiration,' false, 172 ; 405.
Insult = triumph, 448.
'Intercepting' of light by Satan, 70.
Interest, Scripture contrary to, 409.
'Interest' shaken by light, 90.
'Internal' work, 114.
Inventions, self-devised, 379, 380 ; human, in divine worship, 434.
Invisible, Satan in temptation usually, 330.
Invitation, secret, to Satan by disputing, 458.
Invocation of saints, 201.
Inward temptations and outward distresses, 333 ; terrors and trouble, 456 ; reasons for not disputing with Satan in, 456, *seq*.
Irenæus, 19.

GENERAL INDEX.

Jackson, 424.
James, 189.
Jenison, 22, 24, 180.
Job and Satan, 13.
Josephus, 27, 40, 49, 110, 179, 198, 406, 409.
Jostle, 105.
Joy not received, 229.
Jugglers' words, 166.
Julian, 164, 194, 208.
Junius, 242.

Karsten, 173.
Kent, maid of, 180.
Kimchi, 381.
Kingdom of Satan, 433, 434.
Kneperdollin, 146.
Knowledge of Satan, 21, seq.; measured by that of Adam in innocency, 21; by names given to him, 22; nature of, 22, 23; natural, experimental, accessory, ib.; imperfection of, 147; nature of, 148; unsuitableness of our capacities, 148, 149.

Lacedæmonians, 39.
Lamech, 289.
Language, strange, 166.
Lapide, a-, 373.
Lathbury, 180.
Law, enmity and opposition of the, 85.
Lawful, seeming, 351, 352; to be seriously weighed, 353.
Leaving, of, sins, 119.
Legion of temptations, 79.
Leigh's *Critica Sacra*, 10, 27, 141, 425.
Leyden, John of, 139.
Libanius, 195.
Light of nature, of Scripture, &c., 55; Satan opposes, and how, 90, 91; prevailing power of, 94.
Lightfoot, 40, 227, 289, 313, 329, 333, 351, 356, 381, 415, 417.
List, 294.
Livy, 178.
Loretto, 172.
Lorinus, 300.
Lucas Brugensis, 416.
Lucian, 48, 179.
Lust, £a'an acts on, 63; how, 64.
Luther, 21, 340, 456, 466.
'Lying' spirits, 87; downright, 189; Satan carries on his designs by, 421.
Lyra, 22.
Lysimachus, 110.

Maccovius, 127.
Machiavel, 110.
Maimonides, 28.
Malice, of the devil explained and evidenced, 10, 11; very great, 12, 13; instances of, 13, 14; of wicked men, 14; against God, 101; against believers, 258.
Manton, 54, 62.
Marks, false, of regenerate and unregenerate, 269-271.
Martin, St, 340.
Martyr, Peter, 106, 132, 143.
'May-be,' 253.
Meanness of religious service, outwardly, 111.
Means, abandoned, 310, 311; to an end, plausible, 357; failure of ordinary, a strong engine of temptation, 360; examples, 360, 361; why Satan uses this, 362.
Mede, 51, 52, 172, 201.
Melancholy, 245, 248, 250, 265, 289, 290, 291, 427.

Mercerus, 370.
Mercies, particularly promised, 366.
Messalians, 170.
Minos, 39.
Miracles, whether Satan can work, 31; counterfeit, 177; testimony to truth, 182; Satan's advantage to feign, ib.; God reveals by, 405.
Misapprehensions, of state, 88, 369.
Miscarriages, 125, 188, 275, 301; used by Satan, and difficult to answer, 275, 276.
Miseries, Satan delights in men's, 218; of others, 223, 224.
Misrepresentation of God by Satan, 298; how, 298, 299.
Mitigation of barbarous rites, 42.
Mohammed, 179.
Mondus, 179.
Montanus, 139, 166.
Montezuma. 39, 41.
More, 29, 30, 50, 430.
Munster, 166.
Murder, self-, 390; Satan aims at two ways, and by various means, 391, seq.; indirectly sought by Satan, and how, 394, 395; be aware of this temptation, 395; defences against, 395, 396; one of Satan's great plots, 395; a high iniquity, ib.; danger of, 395, 396; give no occasion for, by discontent, 396.
Murmuring, 79.
Musculus, 170, 325, 328, 424, 431, 446.

Names given to Satan, 338.
Narsinga, 39.
Nature, (see *Secrets*,) Satan knows operations of, 32, 33.
Nayler, 419.
Necessity, of sinning, 75; plea of, 347; reasons, 347, 348; cheats on this plea, 349; must not be deceived by, ib.
Needful, service presently, 117.
Negligence, 117.
Nicholas, H., 160, 162, 166, 167.
Notions, hidden, 162; and ways, 165.
Novatus, 166.
Nudipedales, 170.

Obedience, temptation to withdrawment from, 455.
Observation and study of Satan, 24.
Obsessions, 35.
Occasions, fit, 45, 65, 81; extraordinary, 92; much in Satan's hands, 235; prepares, 235, 236; awakens old, 236; aggravates, 236, 237; offered, 251; fit, 295.
Opinions, 'corrupt,' 74.
Opportunity, suitable, 92, 93; hindrances of, 116; best, for answering, 460, 461.
Origen, 163, 201
Outbreakings against God, 334.
Outcries, doleful, 309.
Outward distress and inward temptations, 333, 334, 365; comforts those whose are little, 443.
Outward not inward, 123, 124.
Ovid, 27, 197.
Owen, 203.

Particular trust in God, 365.
Passionateness, 67.
Passions, 62; nature of, 67, 68; discompose, 105, 106; stirred up, 206; Satan sets on work, 236, 237.
Paterculus, 393.
Peace, inward, 183; fruition of, 184; Satan's efforts against, 209; fruit of holiness, 210;

GENERAL INDEX.

gives inward strength, *ib.*; to get, a duty, 210, 211; a badge of kindness, 211; disturbed by Satan, 224.
Performance, manner of, of duty, 113.
Peripatetics, 48.
Perkins, 202, 241, 288, 293, 294, 415, 424, 431.
Persecutions, 37, 88.
Petrus, 300.
Philastratus, 178.
Phrases, Scripture, 161.
'Pickeer,' 137.
Pinnacle of temple, 381.
Piscator, 141, 142, 210, 340.
Place, sanctity of, does not hinder Satan, 379.
Places, holy, most dishonoured by Satan, 102,
Plainness, 196.
Platerus, 265, 291, 369.
Plato, 21, 27, 202, 203, 393.
Plausible, 356, 357; how Satan makes an end, 357.
Pleasures, worldly, a great engine of Satan, 438, *seq.*; best overcome by, 386, 387; reason why Satan uses so much, 387, 388; deceitful contrivances for this sin, 388, 389; special watchfulness against, 389, 390; how, 390; how brought about, 398, *seq.*
Plenty, worldly, a temptation, 427; snares of, 444.
Plessis du, 201.
Pliny, 32.
Plutarch, 26, 39, 44, 48, 201.
Poisonings *v.* witchcrafts, 27, 28.
Polanus, 31.
Polybius, 181.
Pomponatius, 48.
Pool, (Matthew,) 13, 28, 34, 42, 61, 356, 361, 424.
Popery and paganism, 200, 202.
Porphyrius, 44, 48.
Porphyry, 164.
Porta, 31.
Possession, how Satan maintains, 83.
Possessions, 34, 35.
Power of Satan very great, 14; though fallen, still great, proved, 16; instances, *ib.*; explained, 142, 143; and promise of God, 364.
Prayer, a spear, 101; included in fasting, 469; in all resistance, is to be added, 470; seeming not heard, 471.
Precipitancy, 80.
Precipitated, 65.
Prejudice, 90, 106.
Pre-occupate, 422.
'Perverse' misrepresentations, 85.
Presumption, 383; what it is, 383, *seq.*; instances of, 384, *seq.*; Satan's engine, 385; proved by his common practice, 385, 386.
Pretences, specious, 162; of friendship, 350; wonder such not seen through, 358.
Prevalency, Satan's expectation of, 372.
Pride, 114, 125, 206, 220, 397; what it is, 397 *seq.*; warning against, and why, 399, 400; how to guard against, 400, 401; Satan's means to excite, 401.
Prideaux, 131, 135, 173, 181, 189, 192.
Privileges, perverse confidence in, 401.
Profane dispositions, 112.
Professions, hollow, 435, 436.
'Professors,' sins of, 112.
Proffers, Satan liberal in, 423.
Promise, Satan seeks to separate us from the, 374; he does not deny, but questions and inquires, *ib.*; next more plainly suggests,

ib.; urgeth the miscarriage, 374, 375; puts on proof, 375.
Proposal of temptation, 61.
Prosperity, outward, 184, 185; of wicked, 222.
Providence, distrust of, the nature of distrust of sonship, 370; leads to distrust of spiritual favours, 370, 371; provoking to God to distrust him, 371, 372; Jealousy against God's, 372, 373; a great deep, 373; eternal displeasure not to be measured by, 373.
Providences, worst interpretation of, 216.
Provocations, given by Satan, 235.
Provokings, 37, 90.
Proxy, 61.
'Publican,' 109.
Purchas, 39, 40, 41, 42, 171, 172, 197, 198, 199, 393.
Purgatory, 208.
Pursuit, Satan sometimes abates, and how, 95.
Pythagoras, 173.

Quakers, 167.
Questions to be determined for peace of the soul, 259.
'Quick,' 44.
Quickness of Satan, 19, 25.
Quiet, Satan keeps all, and how, 85, *seq.*

Reason, overcome by lust, 69, 70; corrupted and perverted by Satan, 72; how this is done, 73, *seq.*
Rebuke, a first, does not drive Satan away, 376, 377.
Recidivation, 277.
Recommended, use of Scripture in resisting temptations, by God, 465.
Refreshment, soul, 260.
Refuge, lies a, 185, 186.
Refusal, Satan seizes any advantage in our way of, 377.
Refusals, groundless, 462, 463.
Regenerate and reprobate, 257.
Reiteration of sins, 83, 426.
Rejection, must contain four things, 461, 462.
Religion, what offers for study, 3; inward and outward of, 5.
'Reluсts,' conscience, 78.
Remedy, excellence of Scripture as a, shewn, 466, *seq.*; includes all others, *ib.*
Remembrance, things brought to, 406, 407.
Representation, wrong, of duties, 113.
Reproaches, 109.
Reprobates, 288.
Reserves, 354; reasons of Satan's policy in this, 354.
Resist not, fly temptations, 447; why, 448.
Resistance, 79, 80; stout, 333; objections answered, *ib.*
Restraint on Satan, 60.
Retreat, Satan hinders, 98.
Revelation, to Satan, 25, 26; credulity, concerning, 174; God gives, 174, 175.
Revenge, spiteful, of Satan, 428.
Reynolds, 66, 143, 370, 383.
Rivetus, 33.
Rossa, Domina, 43.
Ruffinus, 180.
Rules, of Satan, in tempting, 59, 60.
Rutherford, 106.
Ruthwell, 122.

Sacrifices, set on by Satan, 41.
Sadducees, opinions of, 48, 49, *seq.*

GENERAL INDEX. 479

Sadness, spiritual: several degrees thereof, 254, 255; instances of, 258; provision for in Scripture, *ib.*; reasons of, 258, *seq.*; three classes troubled with, 260; times of, from Satan: conversion, 263; repentance for some great sin, 264; discomposure of spirit under affliction, *ib.*; prepared by atheistical thoughts, *ib.*; melancholy, 264, 265; sickness or deathbed, 265, 266.
Saints assaulted by Satan, 18; examples, *ib.*; intercession of, 201, 202.
Sakes, Christ tempted for our, shewn, 445, *seq.*
Satan and God meet in the heart, 4; discovery of intrigues of, *ib.*; devices and deceits of, 4, 5; likely to oppose the acceptance of '*Dæmonologia Sacra*,' 4, 5; subtlety and craft of, 52, *seq.*; business to tempt, 338; proofs, *ib.*, *seq.*
Satisfaction in duty hindered, 213.
Savonarola, 161.
Scaliger, 198.
Scarecrows, theological, 83.
Schoolmen's classification of knowledge, 22.
Sclater, 20, 31, 142, 143, 183, 338.
Scoff not at the judgments of Satan's temptations, 311.
Scot, 27, 28, 34.
Screw, temptations like a, 355.
Scripture, Satan has great understanding of, 26; never faithfully, and why, 40; warrant for error, 159; hidden notions in, 162, 163; abused or perverted, 267–269; uses always, and why, 407, 408; base ends he turns it to, 408, 409; unfaithful in, how, 409, 410; all to be tried by, 414; compare Scripture with, *ib.*; force of, not in mere characters, 463, 464; argumentative use of, 464; shewn to be intended by God, 465, *seq.*; how, thus recommended, 469.
Scultetus, 337.
Second temptation, Christ's, 382, *seq.*
Secrecy of Satan's movings, 33; of Satan, 70, 71; assurances of, 88, 89.
Secrets of nature, searches into, 3; small discoveries of, *ib.*; not to be made our sole business, *ib.*; more weighty matters than, *ib.*; made use of, 32; servants of Satan, 434, 435.
Security, men hushed in, 97; 125, 314.
Seducers, women, 191.
Selden, 425.
Senarclæus, 340.
Senault, 67.
Seneca, 393.
Sennertus, 27, 29.
Senses, 64; Satan tempts through, 422, 423.
Sensual pleasures, 394.
Serenus, 202.
Sermons, *Dæmonologia Sacra* delivered as, 5.
Servants, men of Satan, 434, 435.
Services, religious, opposed by Satan, 100.
Severities, 170, 171, 232, 233.
Sextus, 24.
Shame, gloried in, 69.
Sickness, 223.
Side of Christ, 449.
Signs, 405, 406.
Silence, 459.
Simon Magus, 419.
Sin, deceitfulness of, charged on Satan, 53, 54; all acts of, through Satan, 54; by deception, *ib.*; pleasures of, set forth, 74, 75; finished, 83; leads to more, 84; change of heinous, for as heinous, 69; long con-tinued in, tempted by Satan, 248; Satan heightens, of the regenerate, 276, 277; delight in, heightened by Satan, 421; made small, 436; reasons of this, 437.
Sincerity, determination of, difficult, 456.
Sinful, where it is not Satan's interest to tempt to things sinful, he will to good, 351, 352.
Skill of Satan, 26.
Slaves, 36.
Sluggishness, spiritual, 105.
Small things, Satan pursues, 13, 14, 75; temptations, 343, 344.
Socrates, 205.
Soldiers, Christ's, counsels to, 450.
Solicitation, 62, 79, 84.
Solitude, 321, 322.
Sophisms of Satan, 75.
Sophistry, 266, 267.
Soul 'precious,' 8; vigilance in care of, *ib.*; body, 371.
Sovereignty, acts of, by Satan, and why, 419, 420.
Sozomen, 194, 208, 381.
Spanheim, 49, 321, 329, 330, 337, 351, 377, 381.
Speaking, distresses force to, 307.
Speeches, fair, 165.
Spira, 308.
'Spirit,' Satan regarded as a, 15; takes part in temptation, 317.
Spirits, nature of, 152.
Sprenger, 380.
'Standard,' 461.
Statues, 177.
Stephens, 401.
Stillingfleet, 136, 166, 173.
Sting of Christ's first temptation, 351.
Stock, Richard, 164.
Straits, 366.
'Strange' things, 122; language, 166; encouragements to those who think their temptations, 325, *seq.*
Stratagems of Satan, 158.
Strength, of Satan, 10, 11, *seq.*; services in our own, 118.
Strictness, 170; pretences of religious, 171 holy, think not less of, from Satan's temptations, 311.
Studies, Satan man, 59; why, *ib.*
Stumbling-block, 214, 215.
Submission to God's will, 365, 366.
Subtlety, of Satan, 47, 52, *seq.*, 55, 56; instances of, 56, 57; why Satan uses, 57, 58; and violence, 243.
Success, less or more, of Satan, 103; in use of Scripture, 465, 466.
Sufficiency, self-, 398.
Suggestings, secret, 412.
Suggestions, Satan drops, 70, 71; 237; tendency of, 414.
Suitable temptations, 59.
Superstitions, 39.
Support, secret in temptation, 318, 319; in absence of ordinary means, 329.
Surprisal, sudden, 71, 194; strange, 251.
Suspect kindness of Satan, 350.
Suspicious fears, 246, 248, 249; wisely, 413.
Swinkfieldians, 166.
Sylvius, Æneas, 440.
Sympathy, excess of, 221.

Taautus, 197.
Tacitus, 41, 178.
'Taking,' 122.

Takingness of certain expressions accounted for, 167.
Tauler, 166.
Temper, passionate, 233; cool and calm, tempted by Satan, 234, 235.
Temple, Christ set on, 377; how taken to, 377, 378; pinnacle, 381.
Temptation, time of Christ's, 313; why permitted at special seasons, 315; use of the knowledge of this, 316; how Christ was carried to, *ib.*; place of Christ's, 321, 322; the end of, 322; why Christ submitted to, 322, *seq.;* what expectation of success could Satan have in, 323, *seq.;* manner of, 340; Christ's first, 346; rise of, *ib.*; preparation for second temptation, 376; time, *ib.*; place, 378, 379; third, of Christ, 415; place, *ib.*; object, 415, 416.
Temptations, management of, by Satan, 26; in general, 58; above, 77, 78; violence of, made worse than they are, 318; end of God in permitting, *ib.*; harmlessness of, 278; when the sting is taken out, 319; not to run into, *ib.*; why, *ib.*; nothing will hinder Satan from any, 323, 324; may be without guilt or impurity, 325, *seq.;* how to know when, are of Satan or of ourselves, *ib., seq.;* specially, in extraordinary, 327, *seq.;* the affliction of, 328; Christ's, compared with ours, 344; the first, *ib.;* Satan in, usually follows a beaten path, 345; vile, infectious, not to be disputed with, 454, 455.
Tempted, spiritual state of the, 318.
Tenison, 29, 337.
Tergiversation, 314, 315.
Terror, flashes of, 293, 294.
Terrors of cursed reprobates, 288.
Tertullian, 39, 146, 189, 203.
Texts misapplied by Satan, 402.
Theocritus, 27.
Theodoret, 69, 115, 187, 207.
Theodosius, 68.
Third temptation, 415.
Thoughts, whether Satan knows men's, 23; what in, out of his reach, 23, 24; how far he can pry, 24, 25; distraction of, 120, *seq.;* atheistical, 243; blasphemous, 244; keep up high and honourable, of God, 373.
'Threaping,' 80, 168, 243, 297.
Thrusting into perilous places, 396.
Title-page, original, of *Dæmonologia Sacra,* 2; of Part I., 7; of Part II., 126; of Part III., 312.
Tophet, 40.
Torlachs, 171.
Trances, 404.
Troubles, advantage taken of, 79; cause distraction, 80; further, 226, 227; examples of, 227, 228; doubtful inquiries as to grounds of, 241; God limits, to do good by, 262; according to truth, 262, 263.
Trust, take not things on, 413.
Truth, Satan acknowledges, for evil ends, 102; God's interest in, 127; modified, 155; error near, 160, 161; Satan seeks to corrupt the professors of, 188; corrupting established, 192, 193; despiting of, 199; deprive, of convincing power. *ib.;* bribes in relation to, 205; error clothed in, 207.
Tyrannus, 179.
Tyrus, Maximus, 116.

Unacceptable, services rendered, 118.

Uncalled-for temptations, 319; when, 319, 320.
Unfaithful, Satan in dealing with Scripture three ways, 409, 410.
Universal, Scripture, a, remedy in temptation, 466.
Unpardonable sin, 300.
Unsanctified texts describing, used by Satan, 275.
Unseasonable services, 119.
Unsettle, from foundation, 183.
Unsuitableness of our hearts to services, 108.
Unthankfulness, 216.
Unwarranted, relief, 363; men put to, shewn, 364.
Unworthiness, 108, 109.

Valerius Maximus, 178.
Valesians, 170.
Variety in worship, shews Satan's corruption, 431.
Varnish on a bad end, 357.
Varro, 418.
Vergerius, 308.
Vespasian, 178.
Vexations of spirit, 233, 234.
Vilest thoughts of God, 426.
Virgil, 27, 39, 141, 254.
Virtue, name of, given to what is bad, 73.
Visible, Satan sometimes, 340; reasons, 341.
Vision, Christ's temptation not a, why, 337, *seq.*; God reveals by, 404.
Vitzilliputzli, 198.
Vives, 32, 42, 44, 202, 395.
Voice, God revealed by, so Satan, 403, 404.

Wariness, 413.
Watchfulness, imitate Satan's, 359.
Ways, various, of Satan, 46.
Weapons, Satan deprives us of, 100.
Whitaker, 164, 175.
Wickedness, of Satan capable of increase, 11.
Wieldy = yielding, 79.
Wierus, 44.
Wight, Mrs, 375.
Wilderness, scene of Christ's temptation, 321; why, 321, 322.
Will, 55.
Willis, 237, 265.
Wills and shalls. 82.
Witchcraft, 27, 29.
Wonders, 31.
Working of thought, 451.
Worldly pleasure, great engine of Satan, 438, *seq.*; how so, 441, 442.
Worship, Satan sets himself up for, 101, 102.
'Wounded' spirits. 36; in regenerate and reprobate, 257, 258; conscience by God and Satan, question on, 261.
Wrath, Divine, sense of, 308.
Wresting, import of Scripture, by Satan, 296, 411, 412; seen in results, 412, 413; Scripture, a weapon not easily, out of our hands, 468.

Xavier, 179.

Young persons, troubled by Satan, 247.

Zanchius, 17.
Zeal, pretences of, 394.
Zeilan, 39.
Zembla, Nova, 177, 178.